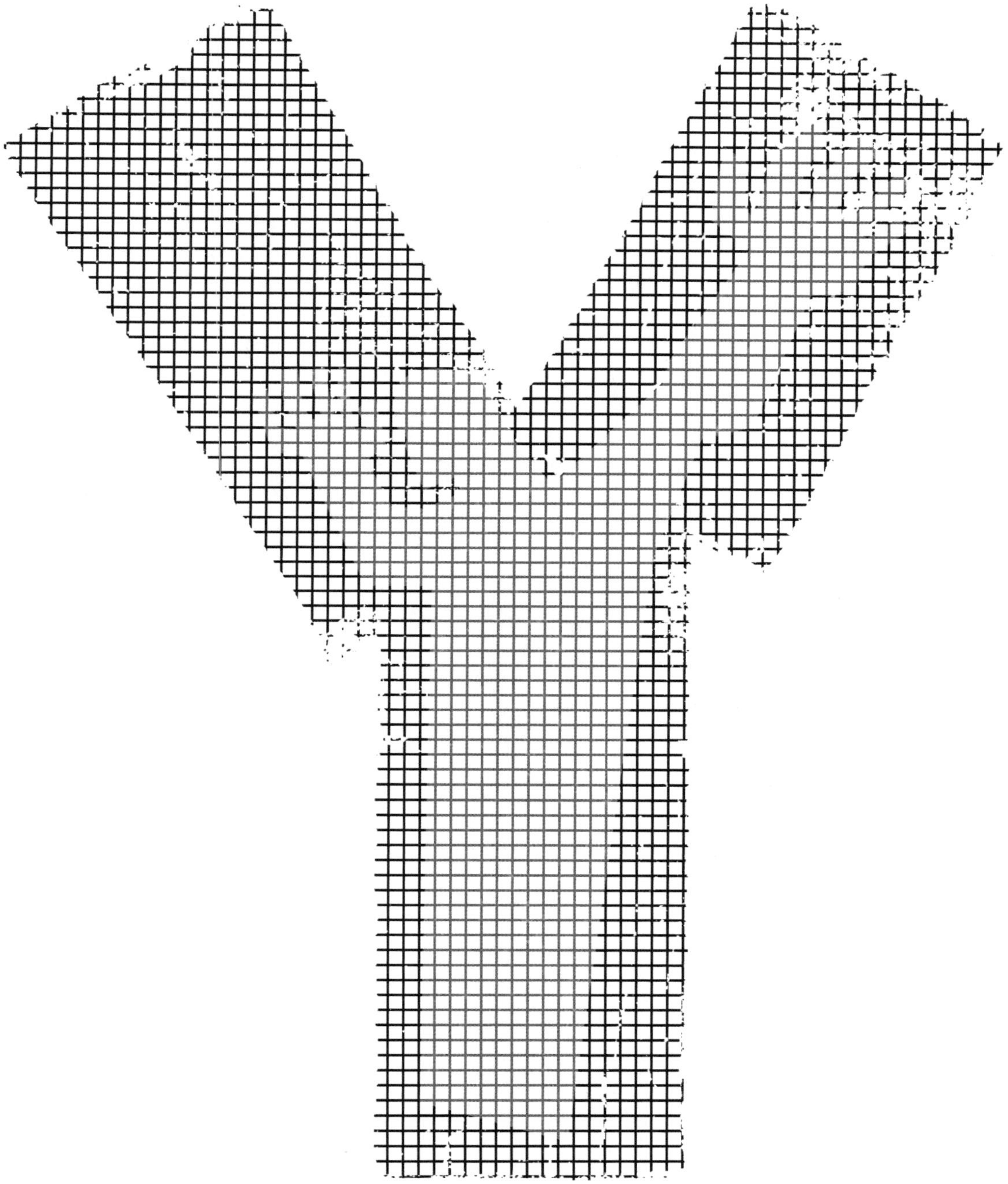
Y

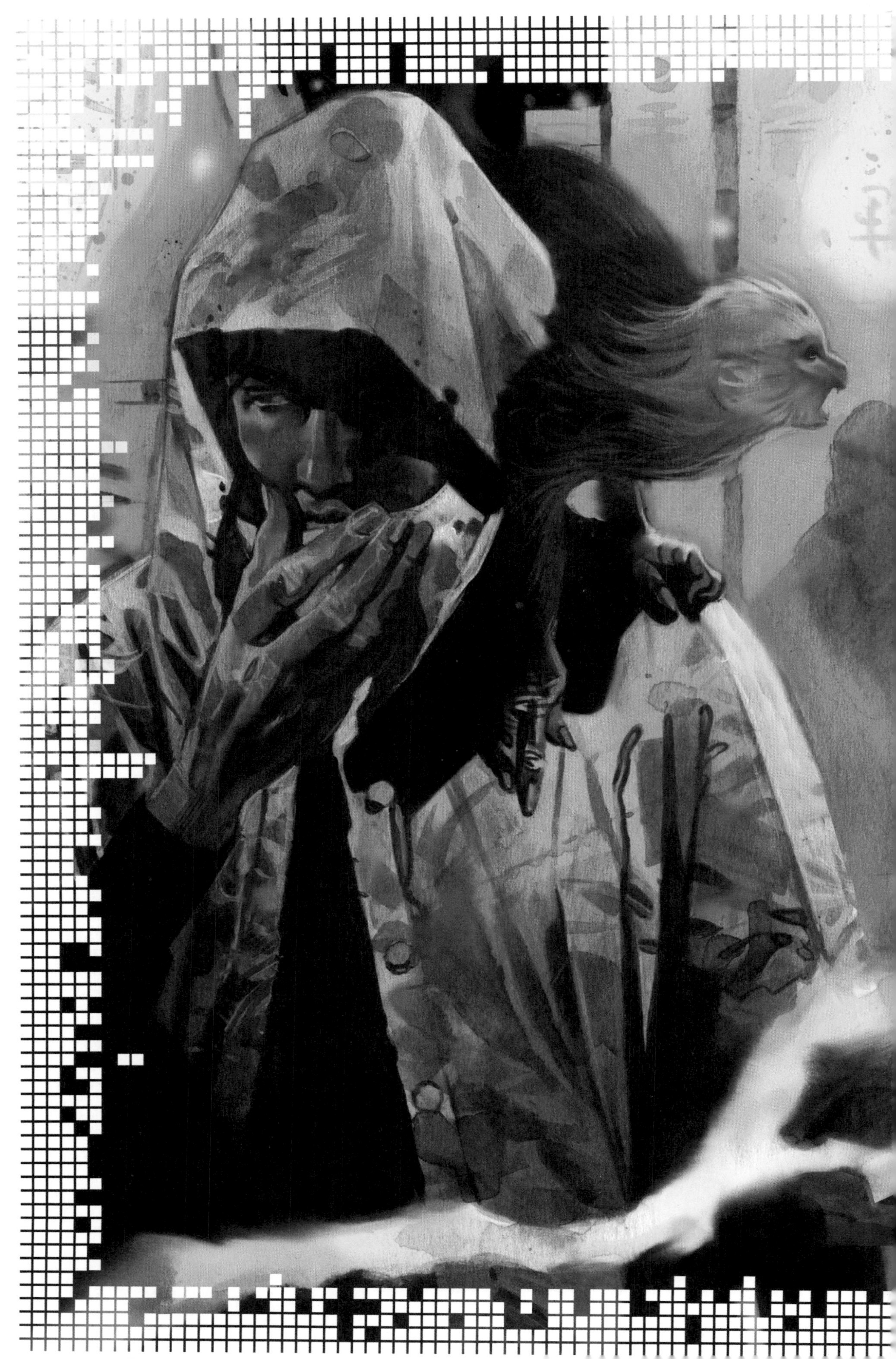

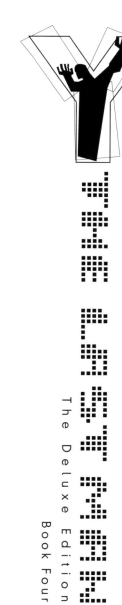

Y THE LAST MAN

The Deluxe Edition

Book Four

Brian K. Vaughan Writer

Pia Guerra, Goran Sudžuka Pencillers

José Marzán, Jr. Inker

Zylonol Colorist

Clem Robins Letterer

Massimo Carnevale Original Series Covers

Y: THE LAST MAN created by Brian K. Vaughan and Pia Guerra

Karen Berger SVP – Executive Editor
Will Dennis Editor – Original Series
Casey Seijas Assistant Editor – Original Series
Bob Harras Group Editor – Collected Editions
Scott Nybakken Editor
Robbin Brosterman Design Director – Books
Louis Prandi Art Director

DC COMICS
Diane Nelson President
Dan DiDio and Jim Lee Co-Publishers
Geoff Johns Chief Creative Officer
Patrick Caldon EVP – Finance and Administration
John Rood EVP – Sales, Marketing and Business Development
Amy Genkins SVP – Business and Legal Affairs
Steve Rotterdam SVP – Sales and Marketing
John Cunningham VP – Marketing
Terri Cunningham VP – Managing Editor
Alison Gill VP – Manufacturing
David Hyde VP – Publicity
Sue Pohja VP – Book Trade Sales
Alysse Soll VP – Advertising and Custom Publishing
Bob Wayne VP – Sales
Mark Chiarello Art Director

Cover illustration by
Massimo Carnevale.

Logo design by
Terry Marks.

Y: THE LAST MAN —
THE DELUXE EDITION
BOOK FOUR

Published by DC Comics.
Cover and compilation
Copyright © 2010 Brian K.
Vaughan and Pia Guerra.
All Rights Reserved. Script
Copyright © 2005 Brian K.
Vaughan and Pia Guerra.
All Rights Reserved.

DC Comics, 1700 Broadway,
New York, NY 10019
A Warner Bros.
Entertainment Company.
Printed and bound in
the USA. First Printing.
ISBN: 978-1-4012-2888-0

SUSTAINABLE
FORESTRY
INITIATIVE

Certified Fiber Sourcing
www.sfiprogram.org

Fiber used in this product line meets the
sourcing requirements of the SFI program.
www.sfiprogram.org NFS-SPIC0C-C0001801

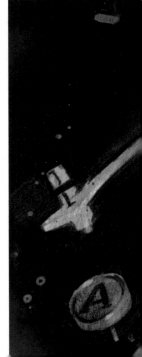

Y: THE LAST MAN — Contents

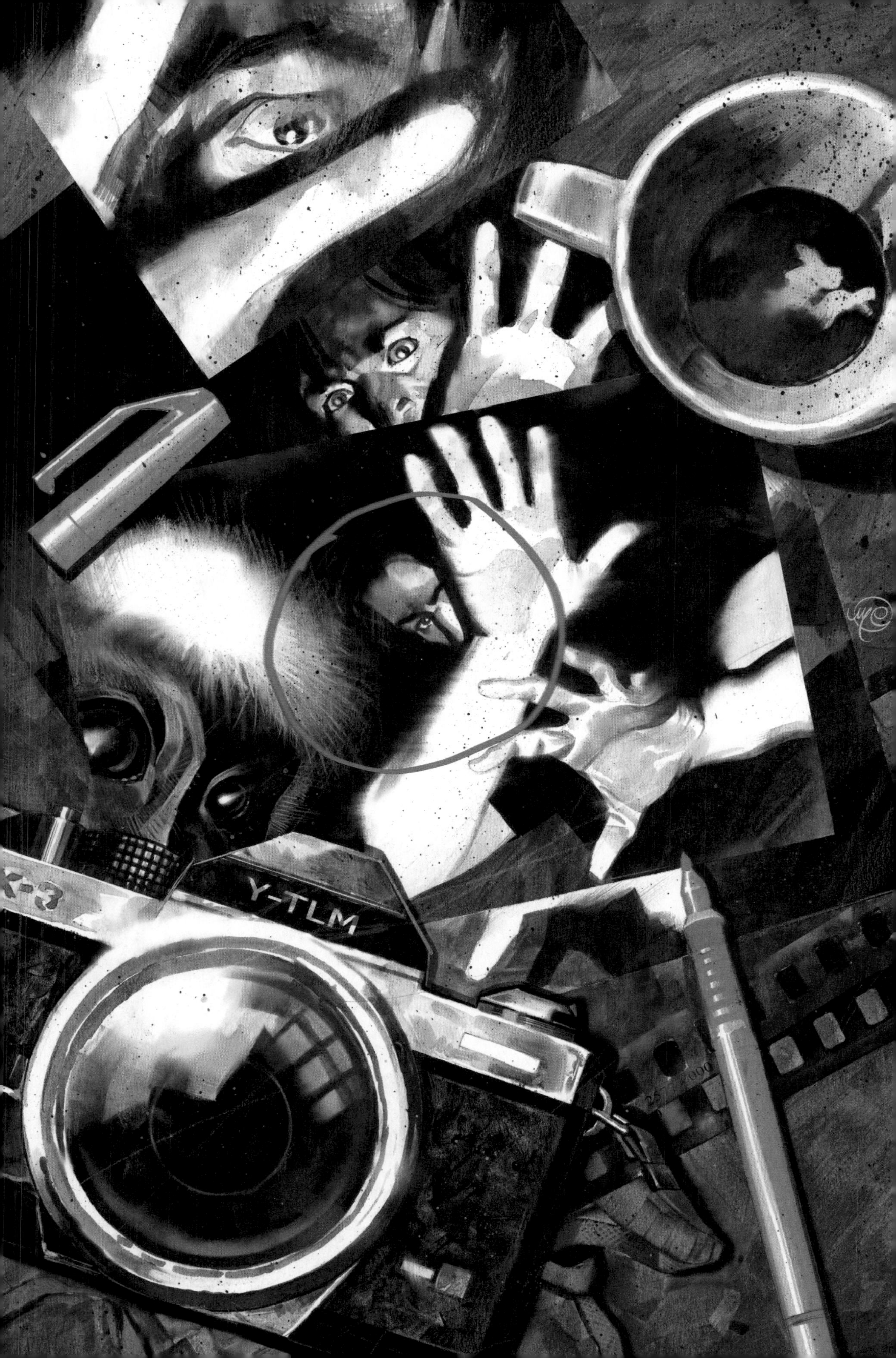
Y-TLM

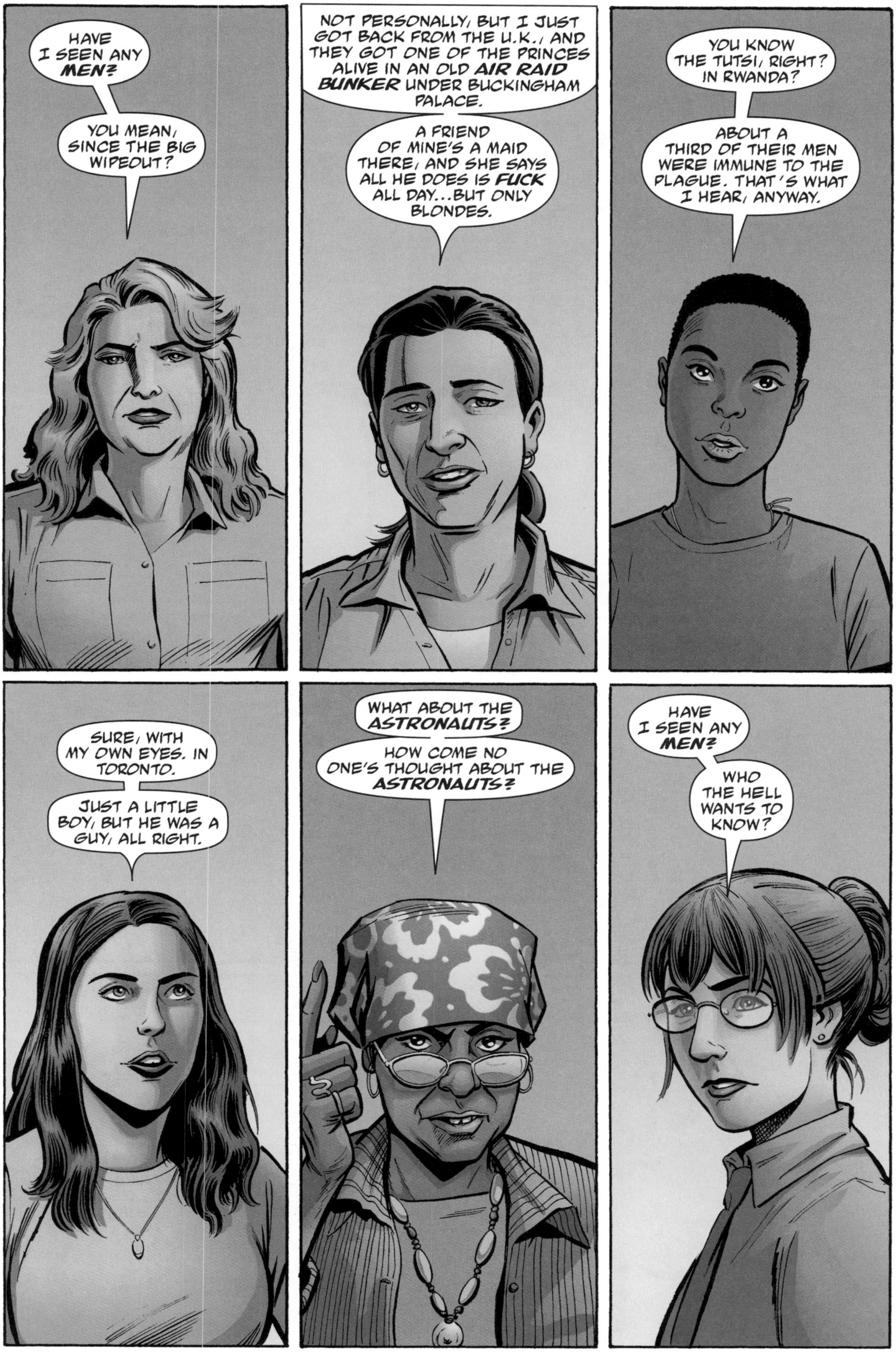
HAVE I SEEN ANY MEN?
YOU MEAN, SINCE THE BIG WIPEOUT?
NOT PERSONALLY, BUT I JUST GOT BACK FROM THE U.K., AND THEY GOT ONE OF THE PRINCES ALIVE IN AN OLD AIR RAID BUNKER UNDER BUCKINGHAM PALACE.
A FRIEND OF MINE'S A MAID THERE, AND SHE SAYS ALL HE DOES IS FUCK ALL DAY...BUT ONLY BLONDES.
YOU KNOW THE TUTSI, RIGHT? IN RWANDA?
ABOUT A THIRD OF THEIR MEN WERE IMMUNE TO THE PLAGUE. THAT'S WHAT I HEAR, ANYWAY.
SURE, WITH MY OWN EYES. IN TORONTO.
JUST A LITTLE BOY, BUT HE WAS A GUY, ALL RIGHT.
WHAT ABOUT THE ASTRONAUTS?
HOW COME NO ONE'S THOUGHT ABOUT THE ASTRONAUTS?
HAVE I SEEN ANY MEN?
WHO THE HELL WANTS TO KNOW?

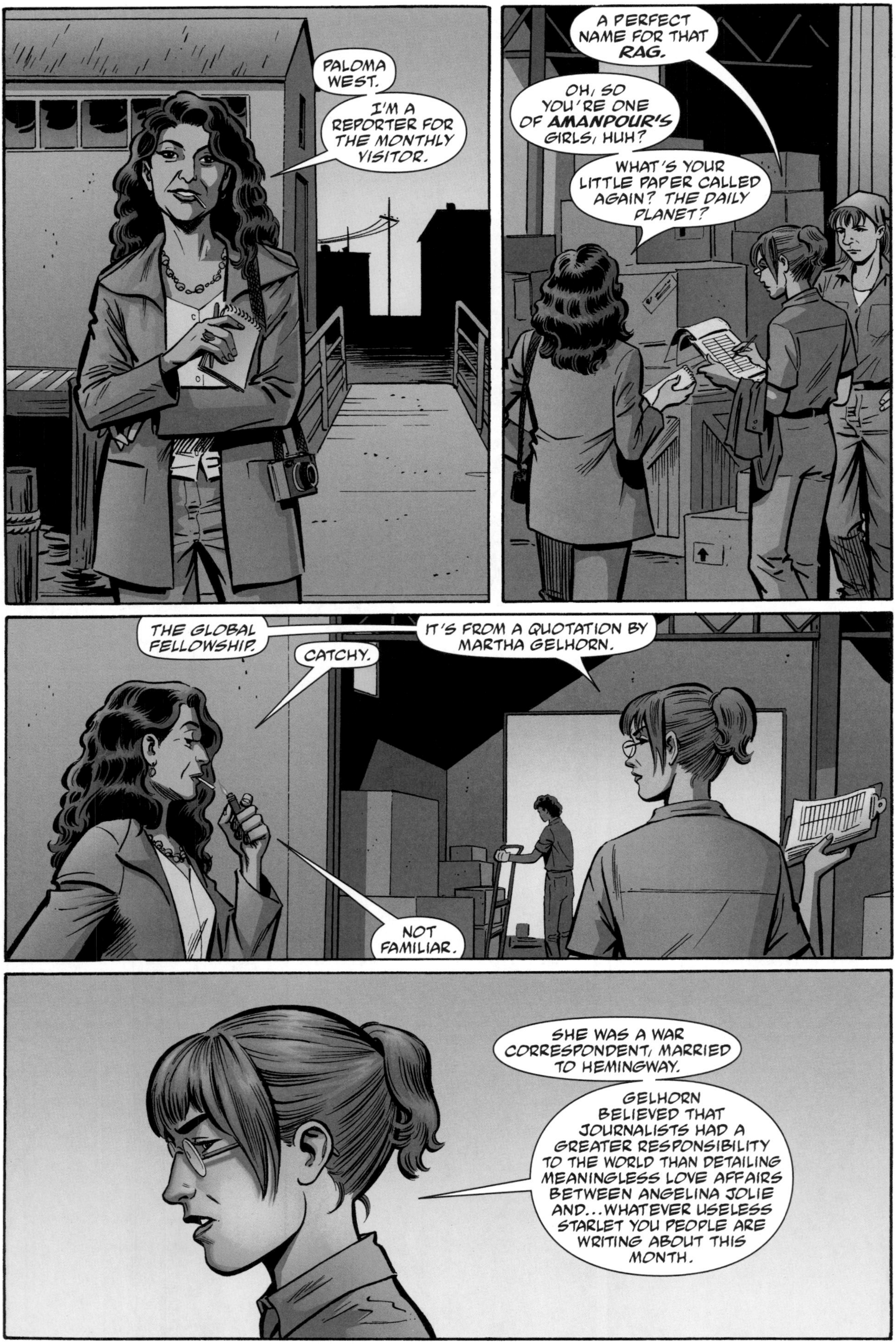
PALOMA WEST.
I'M A REPORTER FOR THE MONTHLY VISITOR.
A PERFECT NAME FOR THAT RAG.
OH, SO YOU'RE ONE OF AMANPOUR'S GIRLS, HUH?
WHAT'S YOUR LITTLE PAPER CALLED AGAIN? THE DAILY PLANET?
THE GLOBAL FELLOWSHIP.
CATCHY.
IT'S FROM A QUOTATION BY MARTHA GELHORN.
NOT FAMILIAR.
SHE WAS A WAR CORRESPONDENT, MARRIED TO HEMINGWAY.
GELHORN BELIEVED THAT JOURNALISTS HAD A GREATER RESPONSIBILITY TO THE WORLD THAN DETAILING MEANINGLESS LOVE AFFAIRS BETWEEN ANGELINA JOLIE AND...WHATEVER USELESS STARLET YOU PEOPLE ARE WRITING ABOUT THIS MONTH.

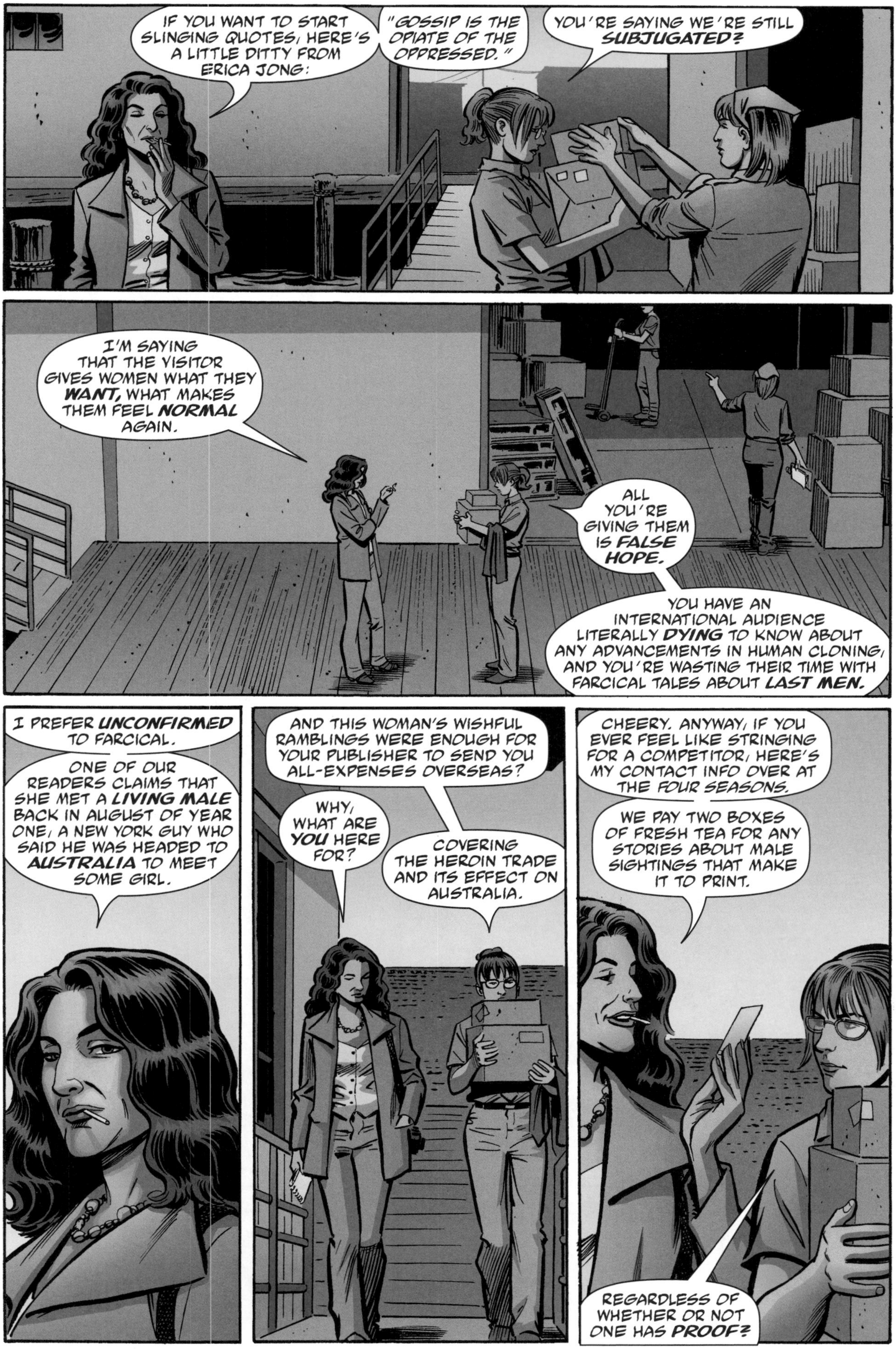
IF YOU WANT TO START SLINGING QUOTES, HERE'S A LITTLE DITTY FROM ERICA JONG:
"GOSSIP IS THE OPIATE OF THE OPPRESSED."
YOU'RE SAYING WE'RE STILL SUBJUGATED?
I'M SAYING THAT THE VISITOR GIVES WOMEN WHAT THEY WANT, WHAT MAKES THEM FEEL NORMAL AGAIN.
ALL YOU'RE GIVING THEM IS FALSE HOPE.
YOU HAVE AN INTERNATIONAL AUDIENCE LITERALLY DYING TO KNOW ABOUT ANY ADVANCEMENTS IN HUMAN CLONING, AND YOU'RE WASTING THEIR TIME WITH FARCICAL TALES ABOUT LAST MEN.
I PREFER UNCONFIRMED TO FARCICAL.
ONE OF OUR READERS CLAIMS THAT SHE MET A LIVING MALE BACK IN AUGUST OF YEAR ONE, A NEW YORK GUY WHO SAID HE WAS HEADED TO AUSTRALIA TO MEET SOME GIRL.
AND THIS WOMAN'S WISHFUL RAMBLINGS WERE ENOUGH FOR YOUR PUBLISHER TO SEND YOU ALL-EXPENSES OVERSEAS?
WHY, WHAT ARE YOU HERE FOR?
COVERING THE HEROIN TRADE AND ITS EFFECT ON AUSTRALIA.
CHEERY. ANYWAY, IF YOU EVER FEEL LIKE STRINGING FOR A COMPETITOR, HERE'S MY CONTACT INFO OVER AT THE FOUR SEASONS.
WE PAY TWO BOXES OF FRESH TEA FOR ANY STORIES ABOUT MALE SIGHTINGS THAT MAKE IT TO PRINT.
REGARDLESS OF WHETHER OR NOT ONE HAS PROOF?

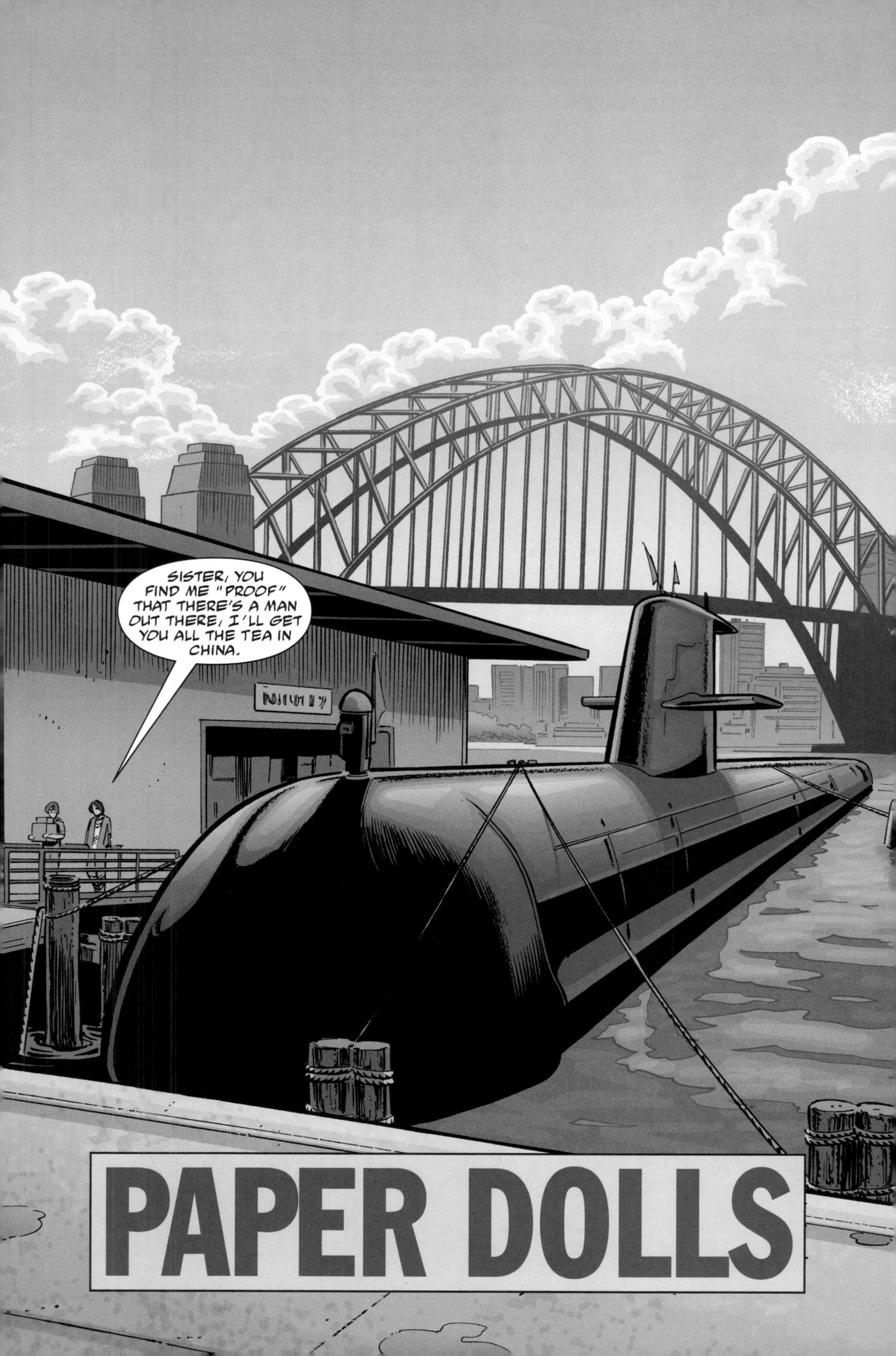
SISTER, YOU FIND ME "PROOF" THAT THERE'S A MAN OUT THERE, I'LL GET YOU ALL THE TEA IN CHINA.
PAPER DOLLS

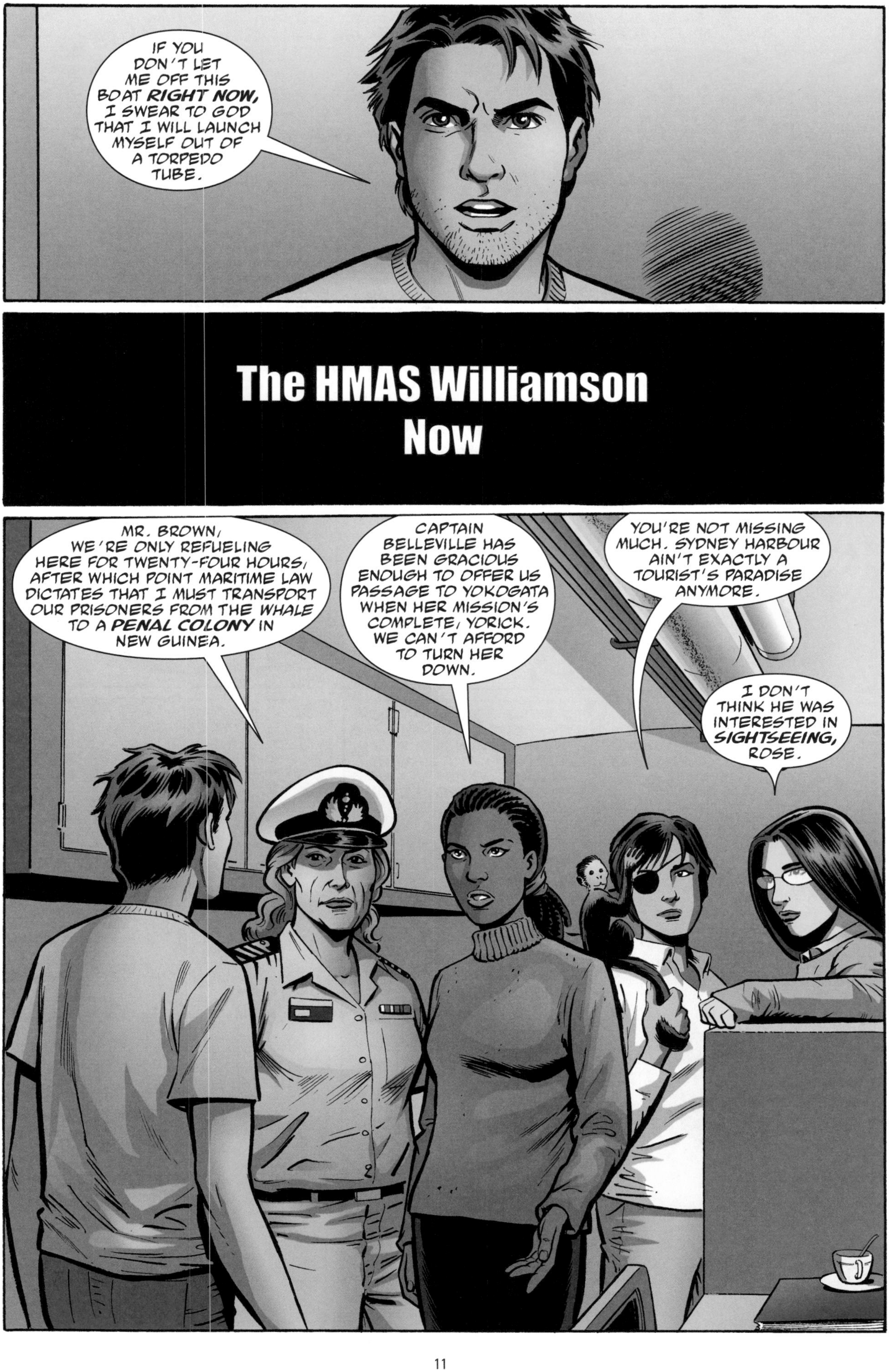
IF YOU DON'T LET ME OFF THIS BOAT RIGHT NOW, I SWEAR TO GOD THAT I WILL LAUNCH MYSELF OUT OF A TORPEDO TUBE.
The HMAS Williamson
Now
MR. BROWN, WE'RE ONLY REFUELING HERE FOR TWENTY-FOUR HOURS, AFTER WHICH POINT MARITIME LAW DICTATES THAT I MUST TRANSPORT OUR PRISONERS FROM THE WHALE TO A PENAL COLONY IN NEW GUINEA.
CAPTAIN BELLEVILLE HAS BEEN GRACIOUS ENOUGH TO OFFER US PASSAGE TO YOKOGATA WHEN HER MISSION'S COMPLETE, YORICK. WE CAN'T AFFORD TO TURN HER DOWN.
YOU'RE NOT MISSING MUCH. SYDNEY HARBOUR AIN'T EXACTLY A TOURIST'S PARADISE ANYMORE.
I DON'T THINK HE WAS INTERESTED IN SIGHTSEEING, ROSE.

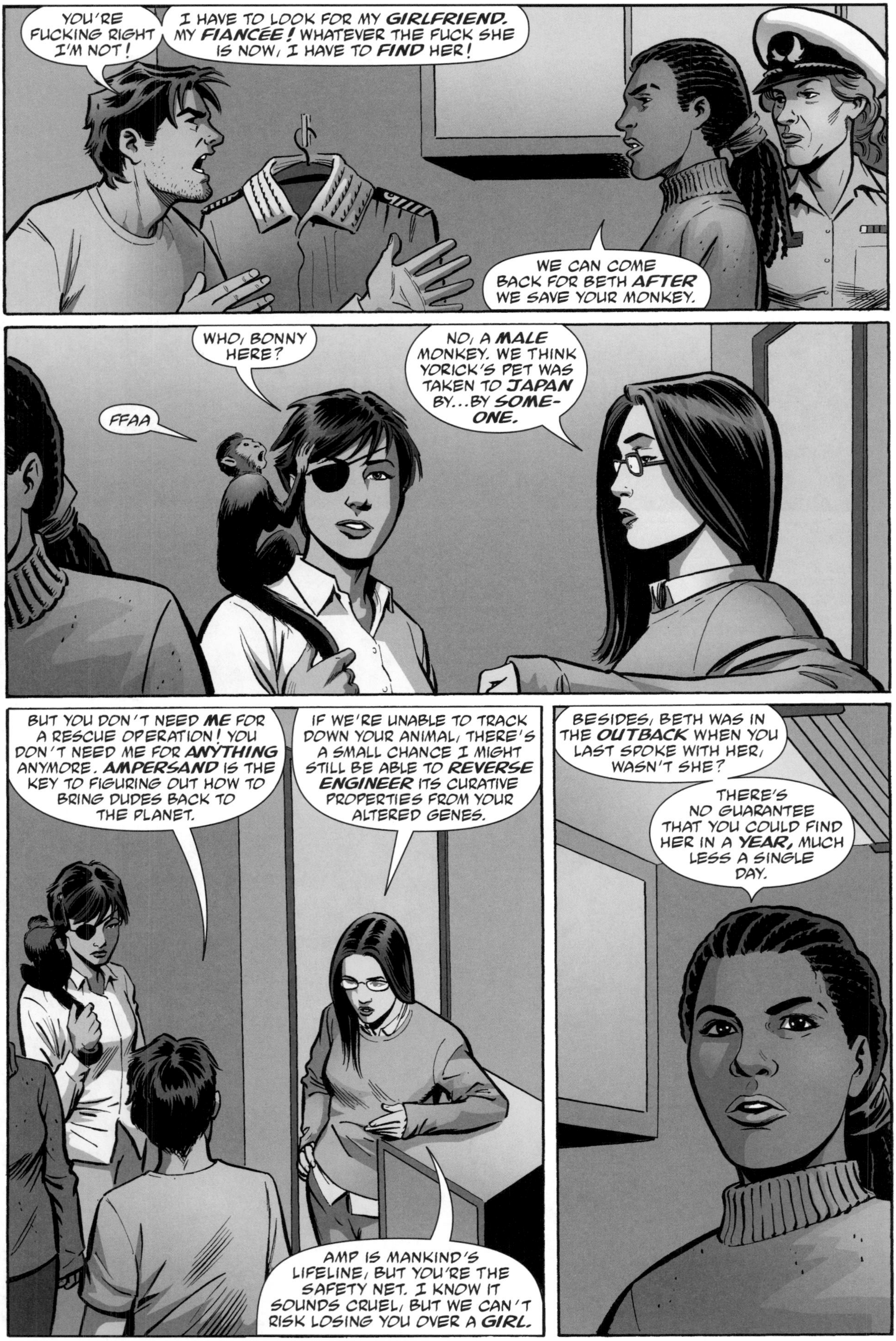

YOU'RE FUCKING RIGHT I'M NOT!
I HAVE TO LOOK FOR MY GIRLFRIEND. MY FIANCÉE! WHATEVER THE FUCK SHE IS NOW, I HAVE TO FIND HER!
WE CAN COME BACK FOR BETH AFTER WE SAVE YOUR MONKEY.
WHO, BONNY HERE?
FFAA
NO, A MALE MONKEY. WE THINK YORICK'S PET WAS TAKEN TO JAPAN BY...BY SOME-ONE.
BUT YOU DON'T NEED ME FOR A RESCUE OPERATION! YOU DON'T NEED ME FOR ANYTHING ANYMORE. AMPERSAND IS THE KEY TO FIGURING OUT HOW TO BRING DUDES BACK TO THE PLANET.
IF WE'RE UNABLE TO TRACK DOWN YOUR ANIMAL, THERE'S A SMALL CHANCE I MIGHT STILL BE ABLE TO REVERSE ENGINEER ITS CURATIVE PROPERTIES FROM YOUR ALTERED GENES.
AMP IS MANKIND'S LIFELINE, BUT YOU'RE THE SAFETY NET. I KNOW IT SOUNDS CRUEL, BUT WE CAN'T RISK LOSING YOU OVER A GIRL.
BESIDES, BETH WAS IN THE OUTBACK WHEN YOU LAST SPOKE WITH HER, WASN'T SHE?
THERE'S NO GUARANTEE THAT YOU COULD FIND HER IN A YEAR, MUCH LESS A SINGLE DAY.

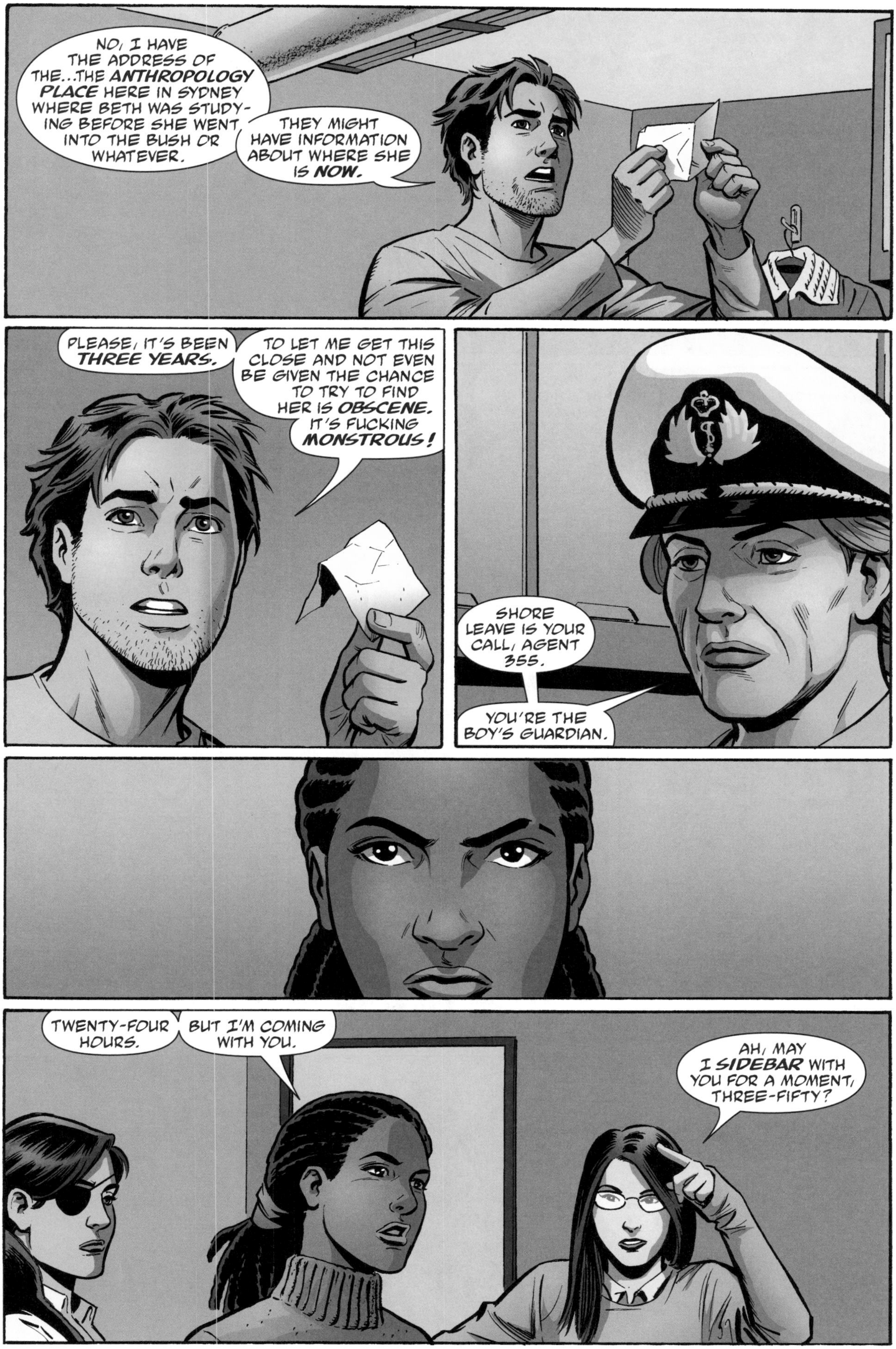
NO, I HAVE THE ADDRESS OF THE...THE ANTHROPOLOGY PLACE HERE IN SYDNEY WHERE BETH WAS STUDYING BEFORE SHE WENT INTO THE BUSH OR WHATEVER.
THEY MIGHT HAVE INFORMATION ABOUT WHERE SHE IS NOW.
PLEASE, IT'S BEEN THREE YEARS.
TO LET ME GET THIS CLOSE AND NOT EVEN BE GIVEN THE CHANCE TO TRY TO FIND HER IS OBSCENE. IT'S FUCKING MONSTROUS!
SHORE LEAVE IS YOUR CALL, AGENT 355.
YOU'RE THE BOY'S GUARDIAN.
TWENTY-FOUR HOURS.
BUT I'M COMING WITH YOU.
AH, MAY I SIDEBAR WITH YOU FOR A MOMENT, THREE-FIFTY?

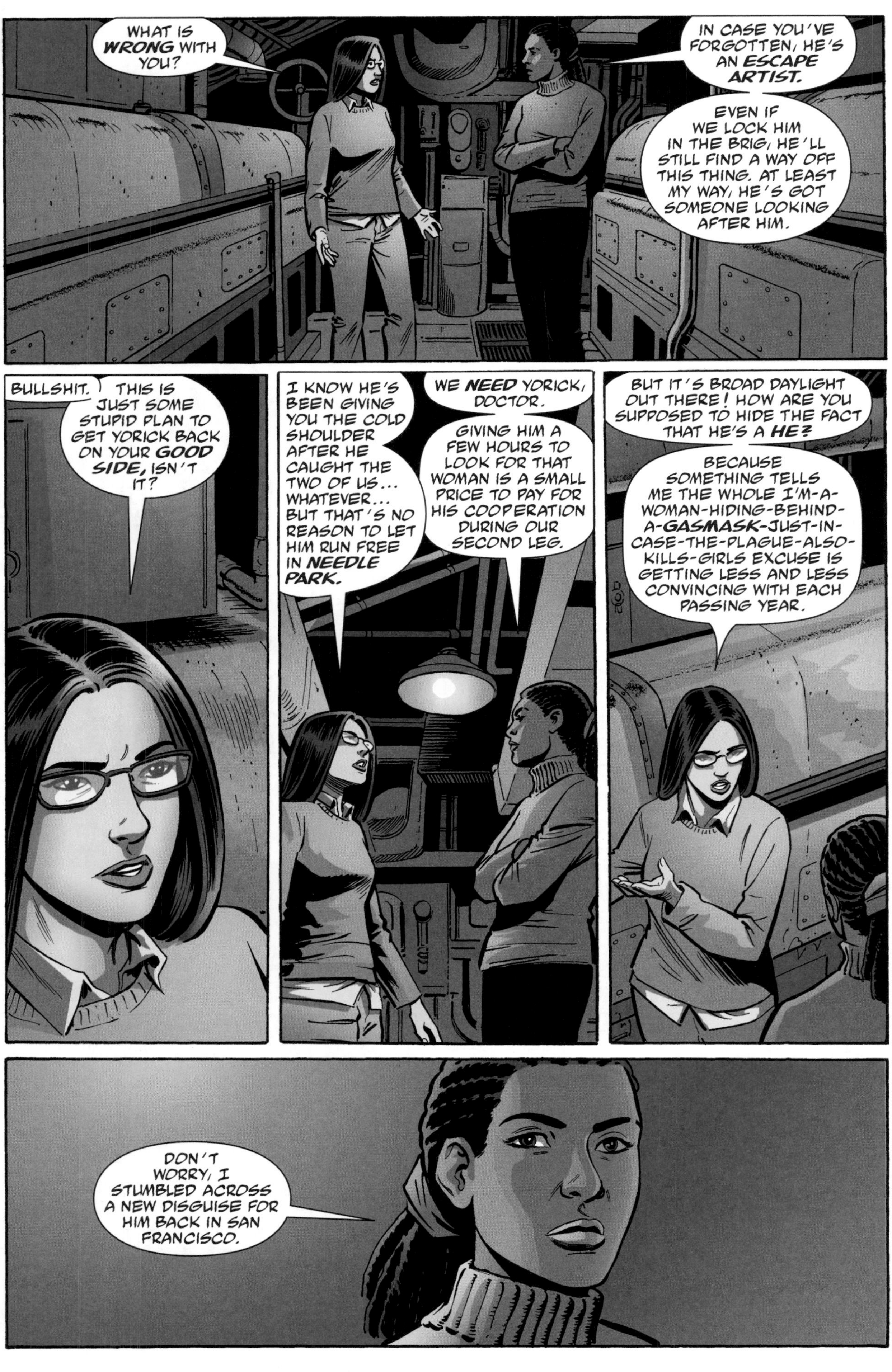
WHAT IS WRONG WITH YOU?
IN CASE YOU'VE FORGOTTEN, HE'S AN ESCAPE ARTIST.
EVEN IF WE LOCK HIM IN THE BRIG, HE'LL STILL FIND A WAY OFF THIS THING. AT LEAST MY WAY, HE'S GOT SOMEONE LOOKING AFTER HIM.
BULLSHIT.
THIS IS JUST SOME STUPID PLAN TO GET YORICK BACK ON YOUR GOOD SIDE, ISN'T IT?
I KNOW HE'S BEEN GIVING YOU THE COLD SHOULDER AFTER HE CAUGHT THE TWO OF US... WHATEVER... BUT THAT'S NO REASON TO LET HIM RUN FREE IN NEEDLE PARK.
WE NEED YORICK, DOCTOR.
GIVING HIM A FEW HOURS TO LOOK FOR THAT WOMAN IS A SMALL PRICE TO PAY FOR HIS COOPERATION DURING OUR SECOND LEG.
BUT IT'S BROAD DAYLIGHT OUT THERE! HOW ARE YOU SUPPOSED TO HIDE THE FACT THAT HE'S A HE?
BECAUSE SOMETHING TELLS ME THE WHOLE I'M-A-WOMAN-HIDING-BEHIND-A-GASMASK-JUST-IN-CASE-THE-PLAGUE-ALSO-KILLS-GIRLS EXCUSE IS GETTING LESS AND LESS CONVINCING WITH EACH PASSING YEAR.
DON'T WORRY, I STUMBLED ACROSS A NEW DISGUISE FOR HIM BACK IN SAN FRANCISCO.

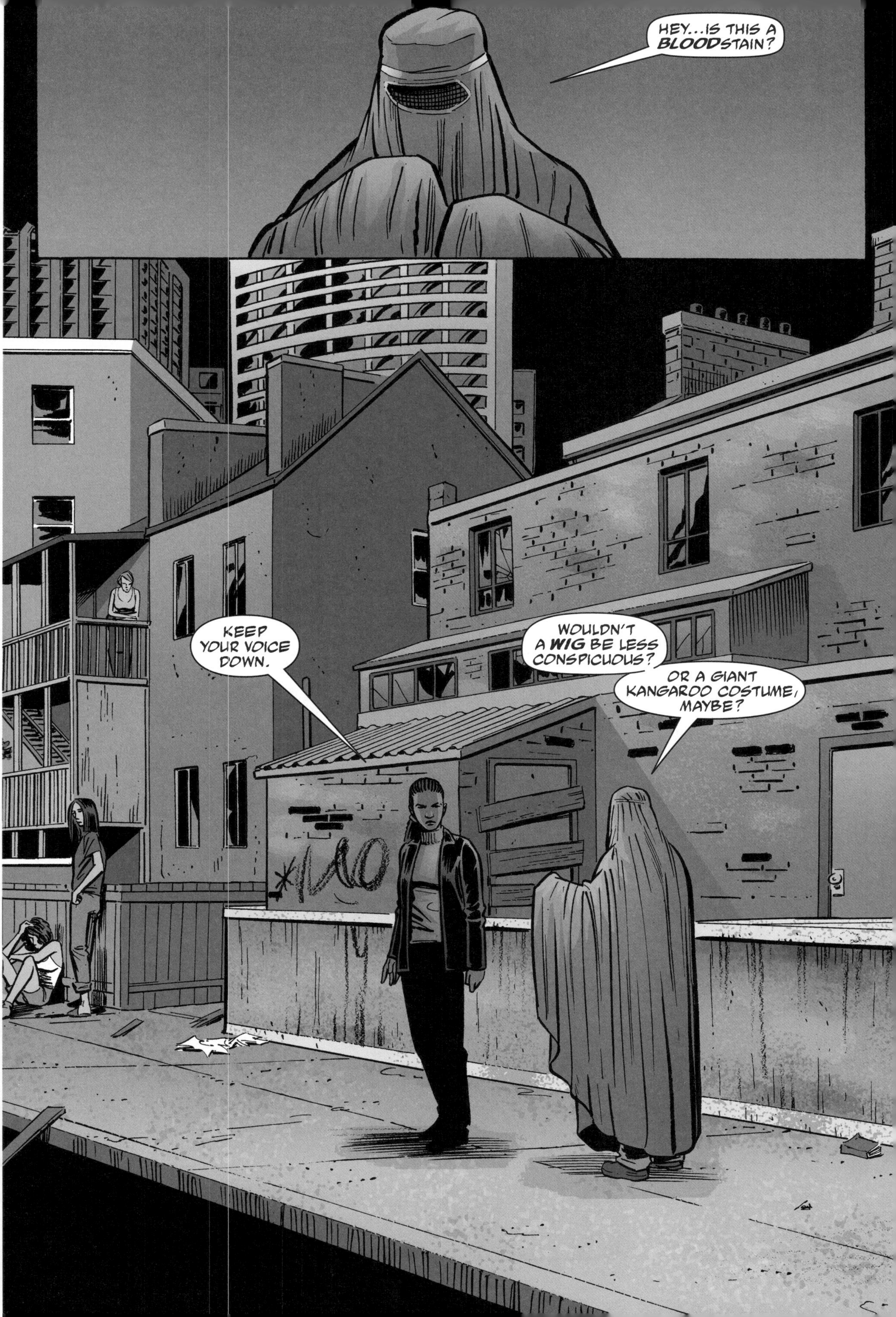
HEY...IS THIS A BLOODSTAIN?
KEEP YOUR VOICE DOWN.
WOULDN'T A WIG BE LESS CONSPICUOUS?
OR A GIANT KANGAROO COSTUME, MAYBE?

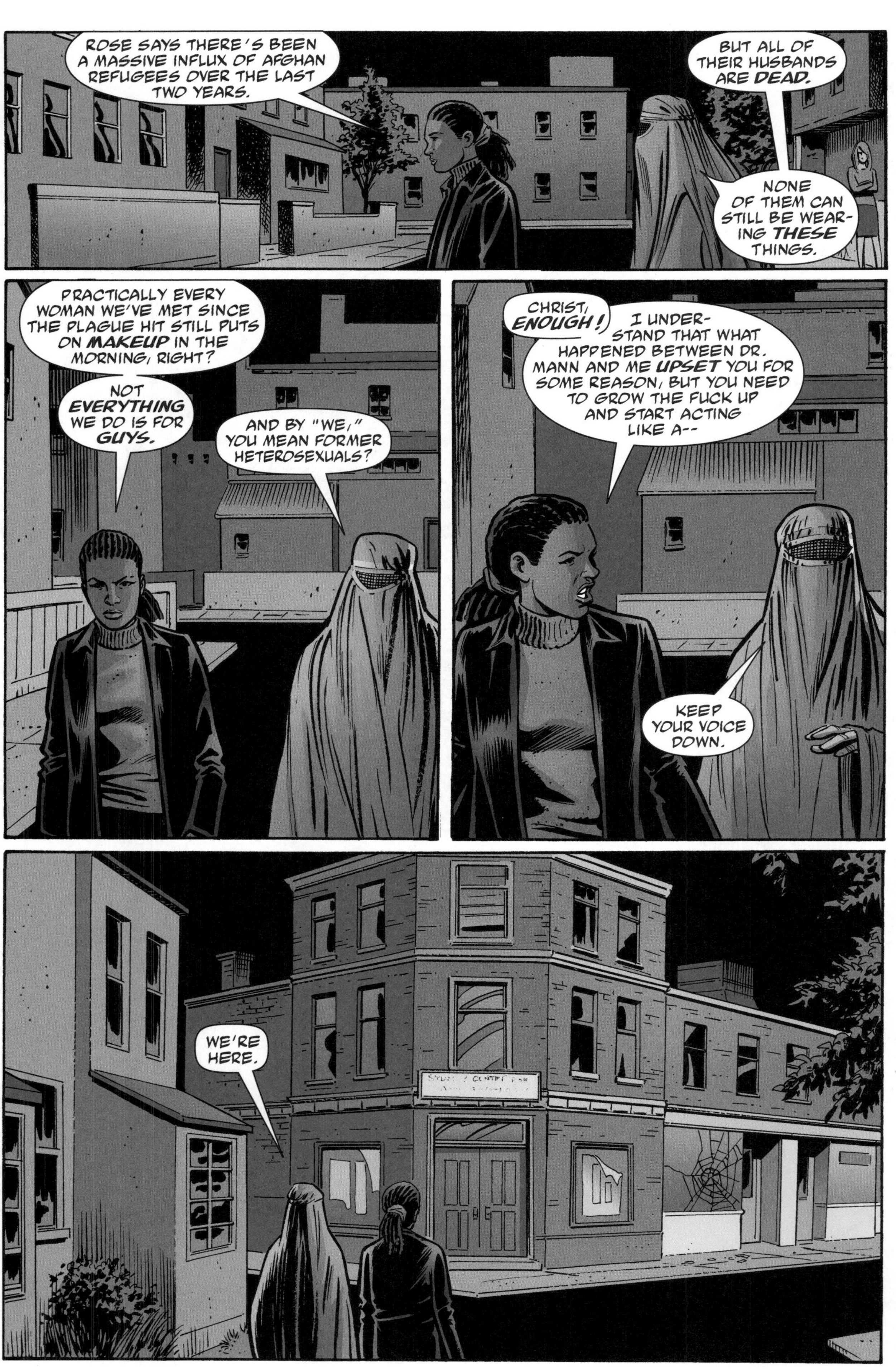
ROSE SAYS THERE'S BEEN A MASSIVE INFLUX OF AFGHAN REFUGEES OVER THE LAST TWO YEARS.
BUT ALL OF THEIR HUSBANDS ARE *DEAD.*
NONE OF THEM CAN STILL BE WEAR-ING *THESE* THINGS.
PRACTICALLY EVERY WOMAN WE'VE MET SINCE THE PLAGUE HIT STILL PUTS ON *MAKEUP* IN THE MORNING, RIGHT?
NOT *EVERYTHING* WE DO IS FOR *GUYS.*
AND BY "WE," YOU MEAN FORMER HETEROSEXUALS?
CHRIST, *ENOUGH!*
I UNDER-STAND THAT WHAT HAPPENED BETWEEN DR. MANN AND ME *UPSET* YOU FOR SOME REASON, BUT YOU NEED TO GROW THE FUCK UP AND START ACTING LIKE A--
KEEP YOUR VOICE DOWN.
WE'RE HERE.

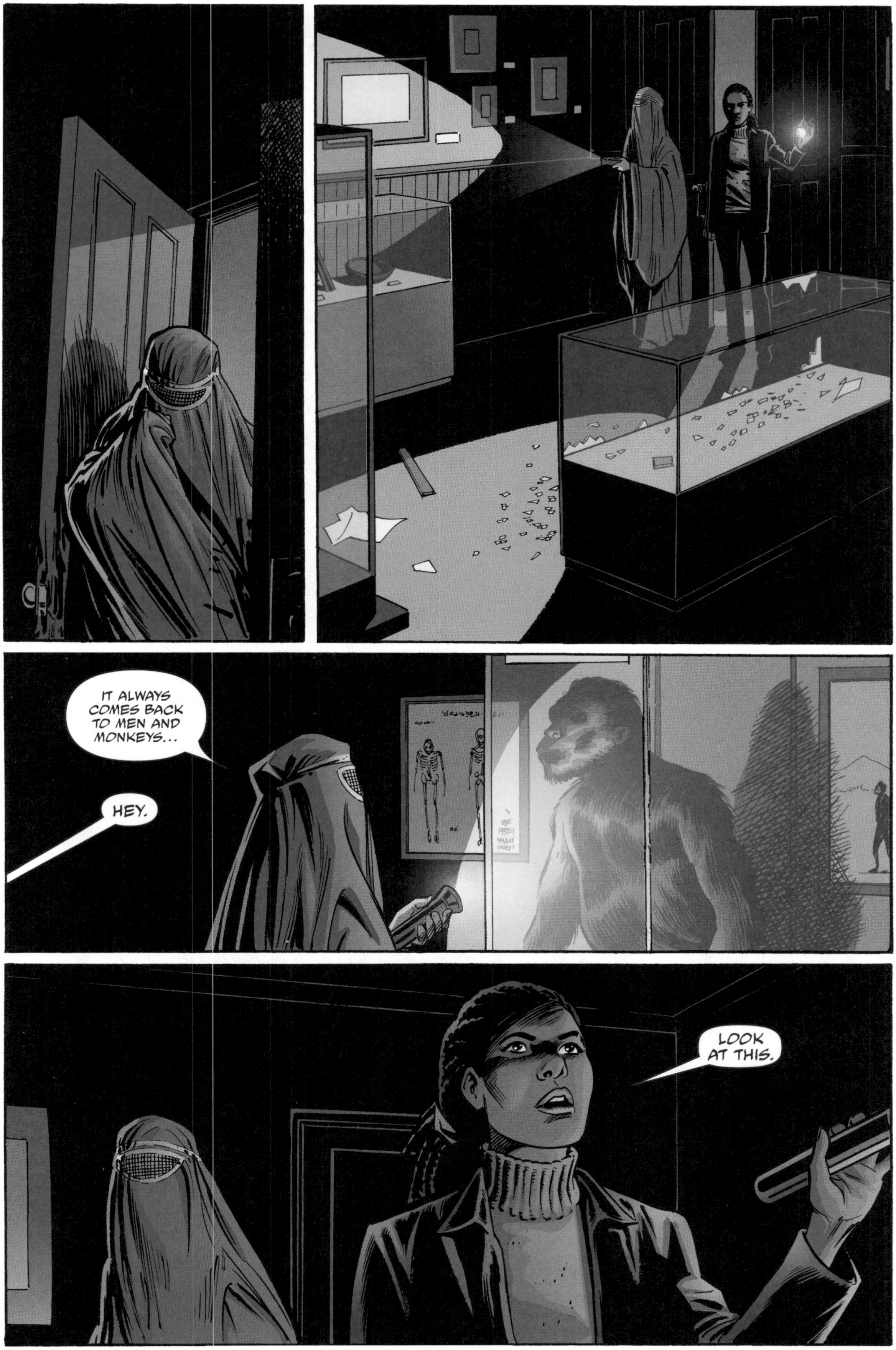

IT ALWAYS COMES BACK TO MEN AND MONKEYS...
HEY.
LOOK AT THIS.

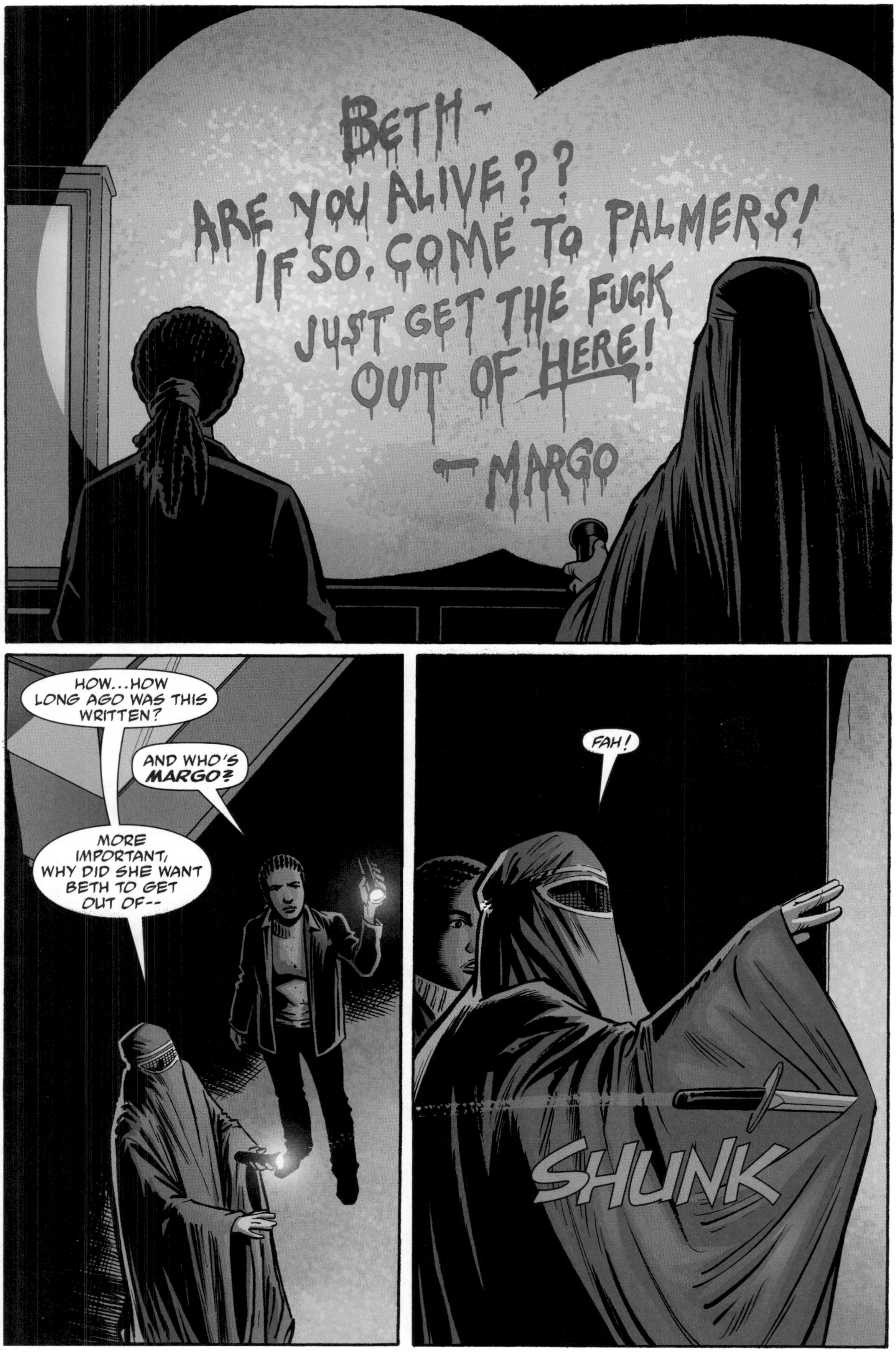
BETH -
ARE YOU ALIVE??
IF SO, COME TO PALMERS!
JUST GET THE FUCK
OUT OF HERE!
- MARGO
HOW...HOW LONG AGO WAS THIS WRITTEN?
AND WHO'S MARGO?
MORE IMPORTANT, WHY DID SHE WANT BETH TO GET OUT OF--
FAH!
SHUNK

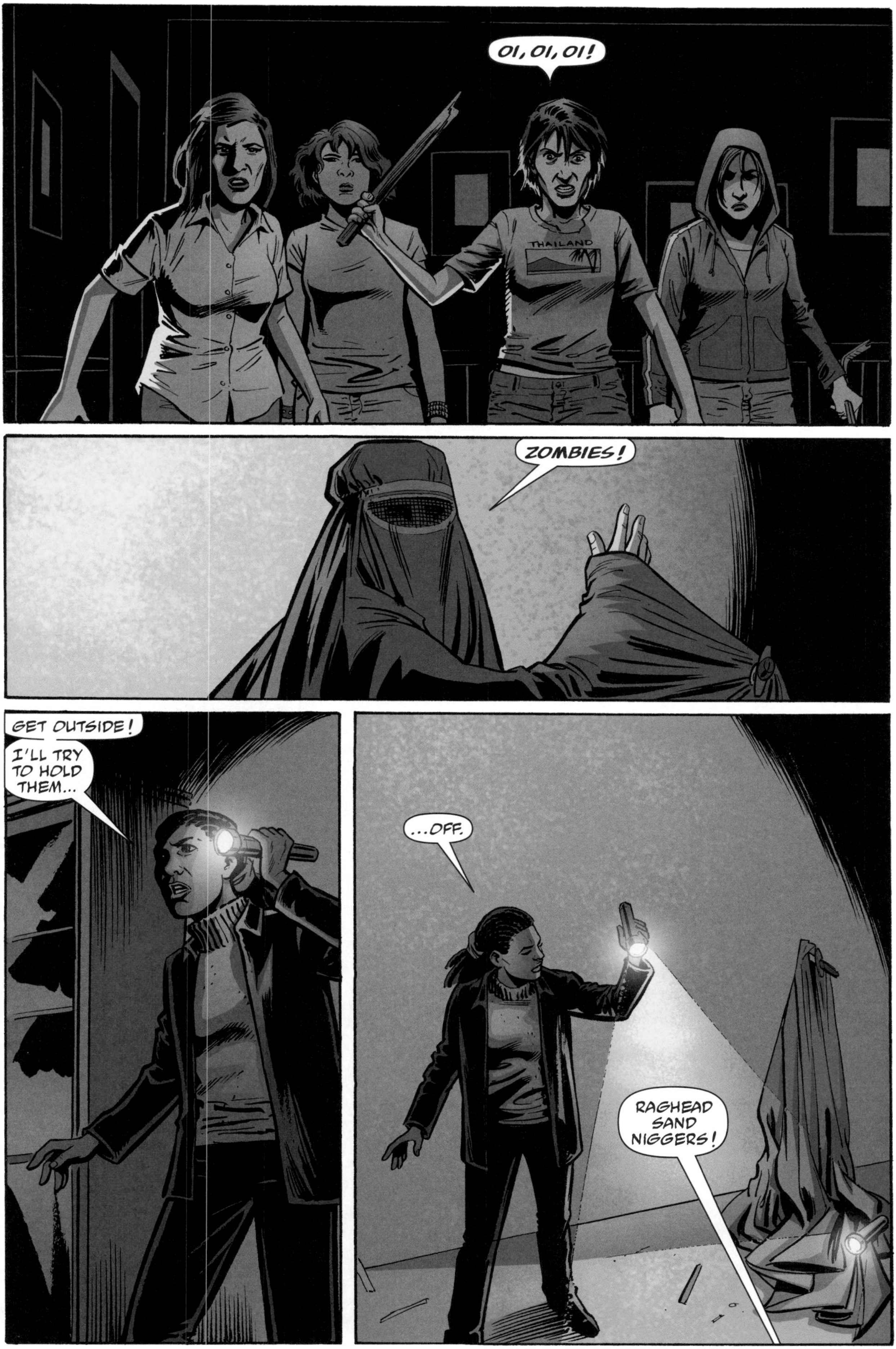
OI, OI, OI!
ZOMBIES!
GET OUTSIDE!
I'LL TRY TO HOLD THEM...
...OFF.
RAGHEAD SAND NIGGERS!

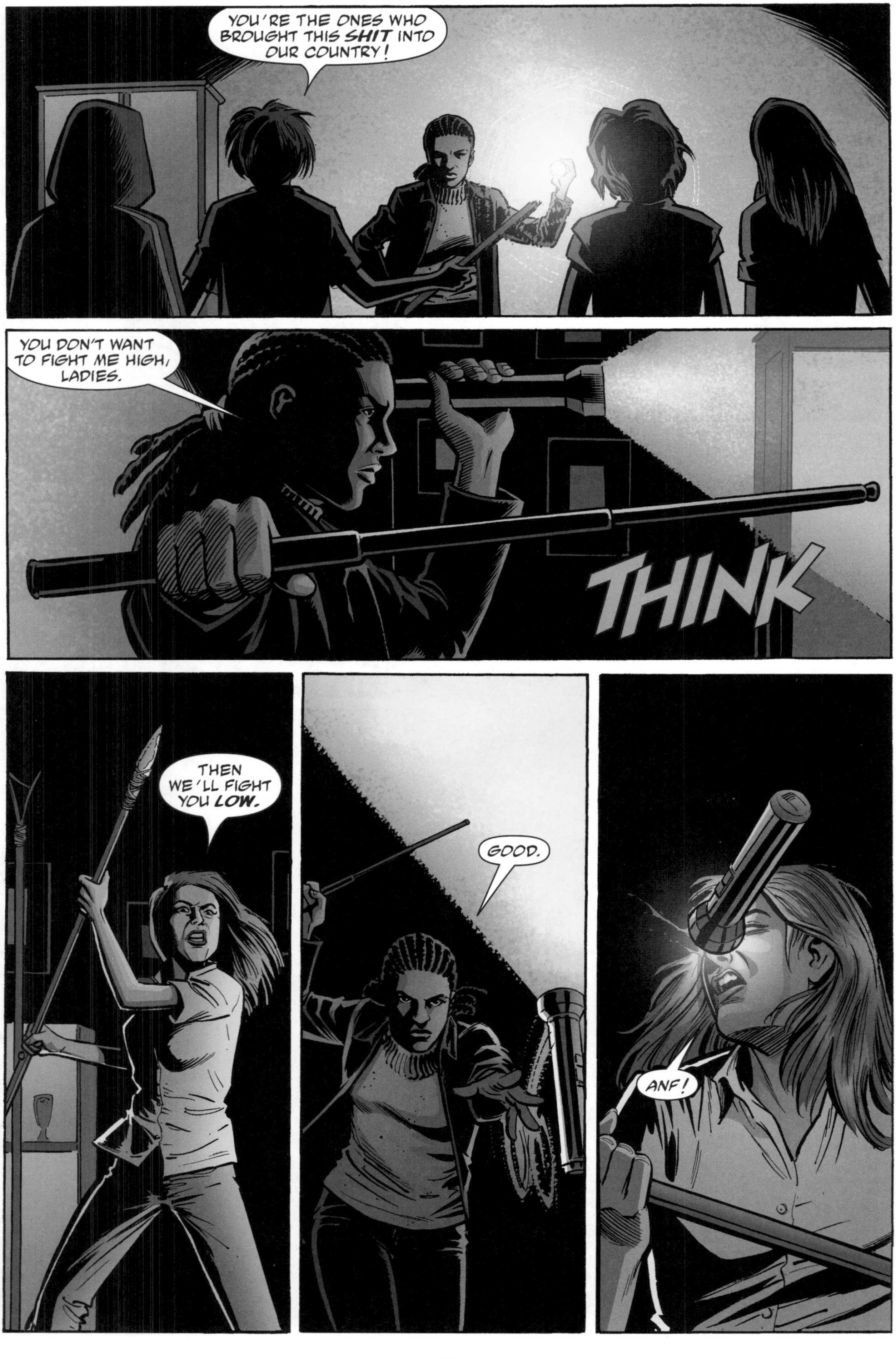
YOU'RE THE ONES WHO BROUGHT THIS SHIT INTO OUR COUNTRY!
YOU DON'T WANT TO FIGHT ME HIGH, LADIES.
THINK
THEN WE'LL FIGHT YOU LOW.
GOOD.
ANF!

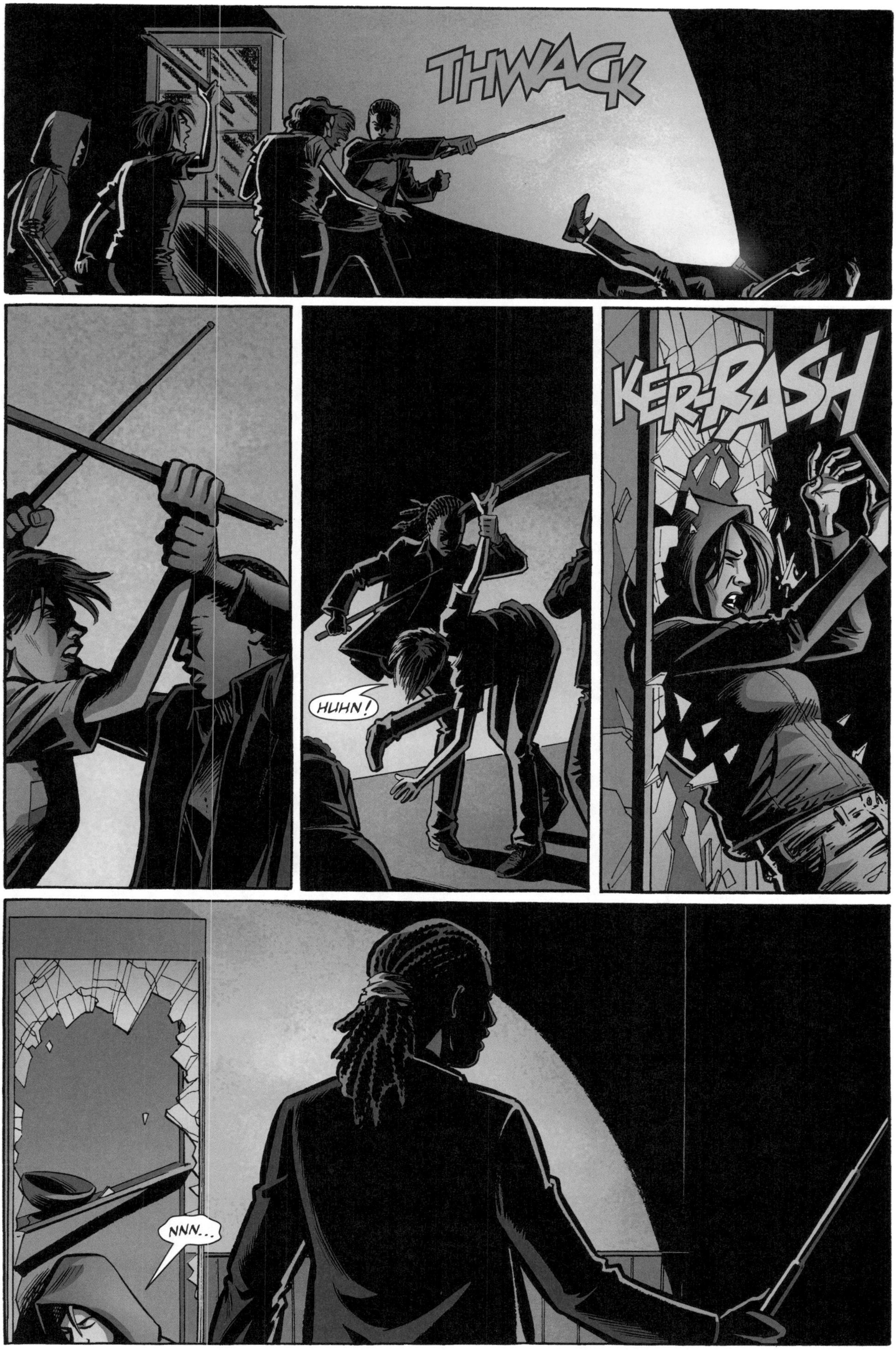
THWACK
KER-RASH
HUHN!
NNN...

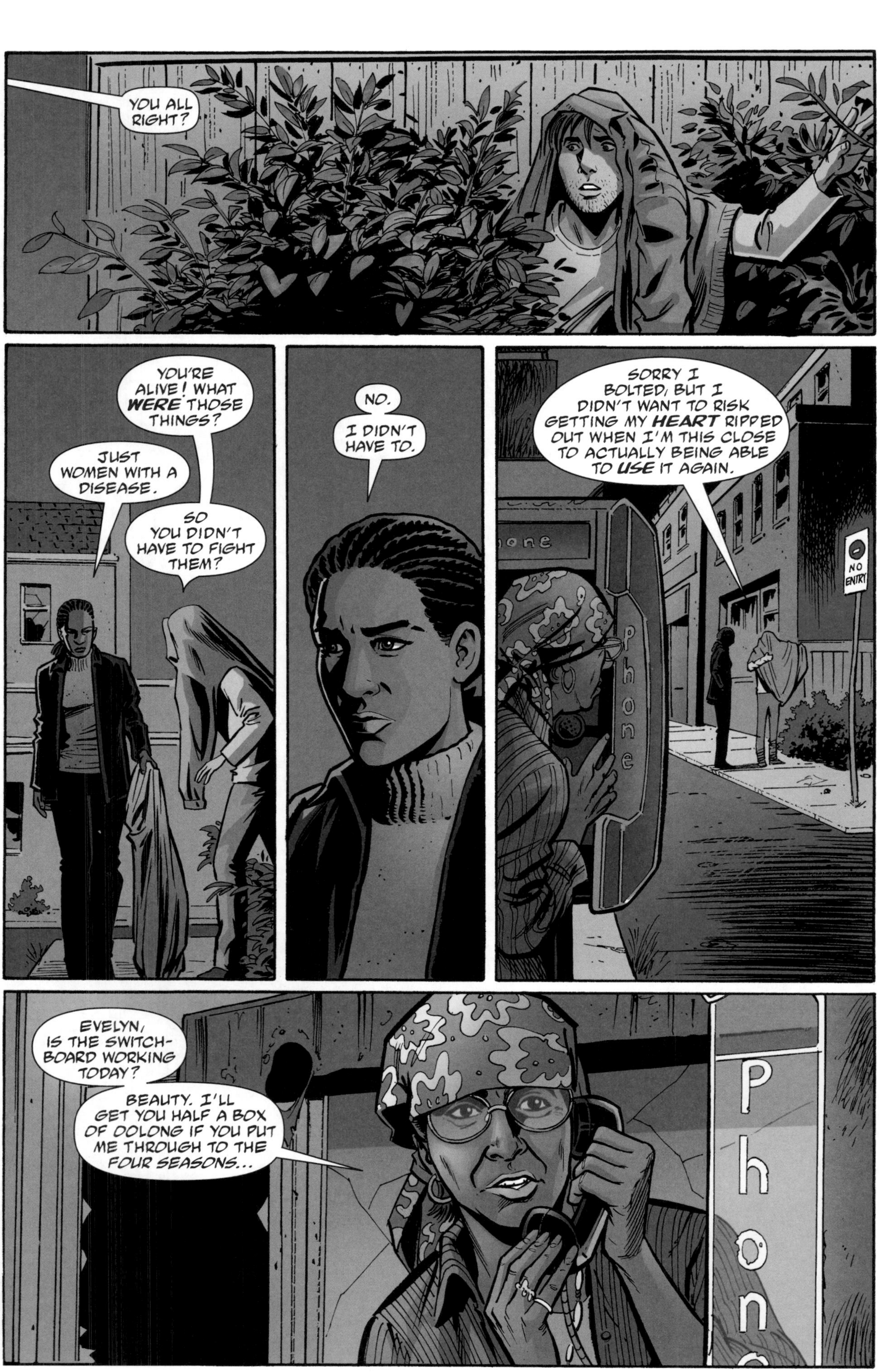
YOU ALL RIGHT?
YOU'RE ALIVE! WHAT WERE THOSE THINGS?
JUST WOMEN WITH A DISEASE.
SO YOU DIDN'T HAVE TO FIGHT THEM?
NO.
I DIDN'T HAVE TO.
SORRY I BOLTED, BUT I DIDN'T WANT TO RISK GETTING MY HEART RIPPED OUT WHEN I'M THIS CLOSE TO ACTUALLY BEING ABLE TO USE IT AGAIN.
phone
phone
NO ENTRY
EVELYN, IS THE SWITCH-BOARD WORKING TODAY?
BEAUTY. I'LL GET YOU HALF A BOX OF OOLONG IF YOU PUT ME THROUGH TO THE FOUR SEASONS...

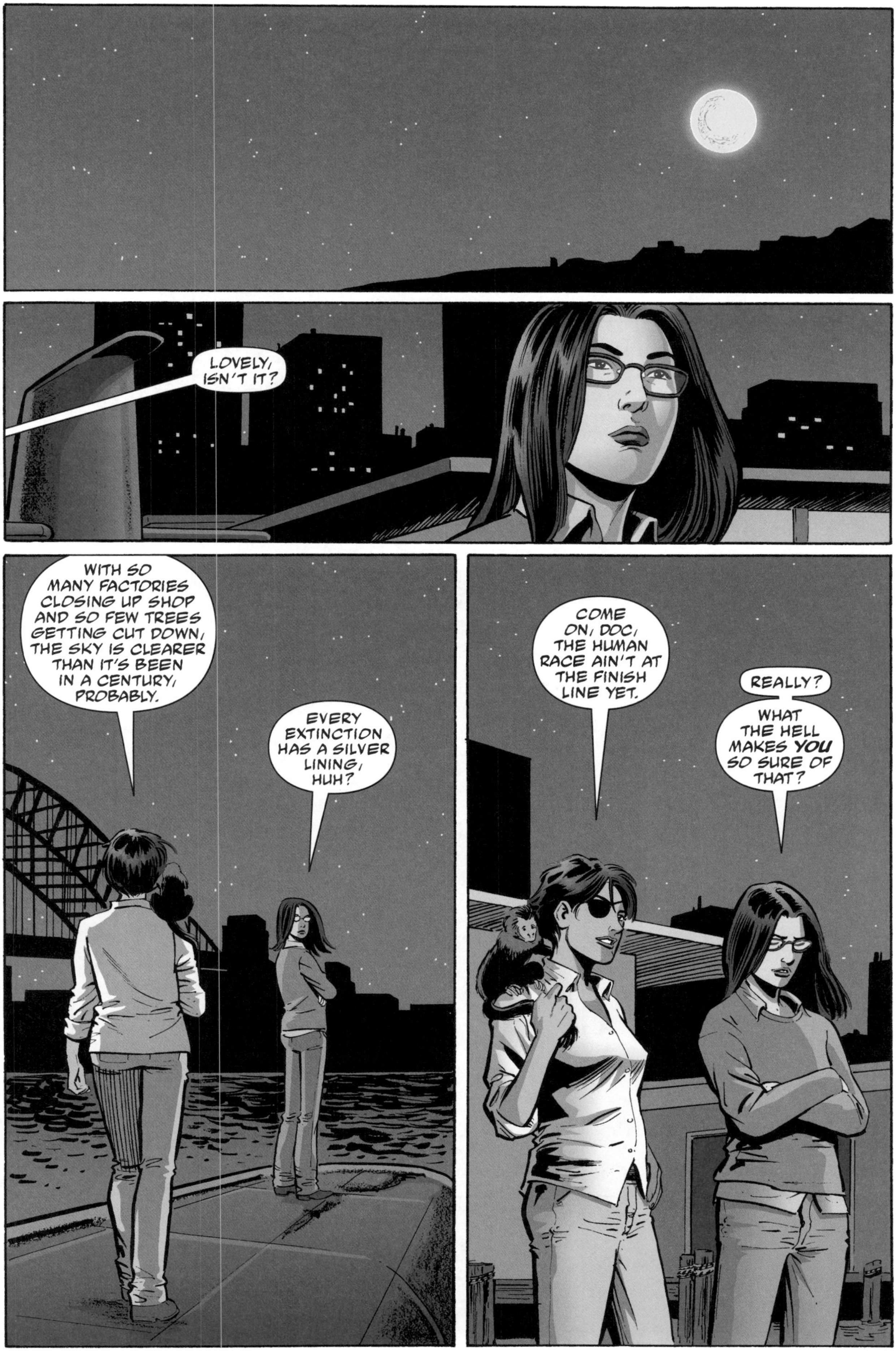
LOVELY, ISN'T IT?
WITH SO MANY FACTORIES CLOSING UP SHOP AND SO FEW TREES GETTING CUT DOWN, THE SKY IS CLEARER THAN IT'S BEEN IN A CENTURY, PROBABLY.
EVERY EXTINCTION HAS A SILVER LINING, HUH?
COME ON, DOC, THE HUMAN RACE AIN'T AT THE FINISH LINE YET.
REALLY?
WHAT THE HELL MAKES **YOU** SO SURE OF THAT?

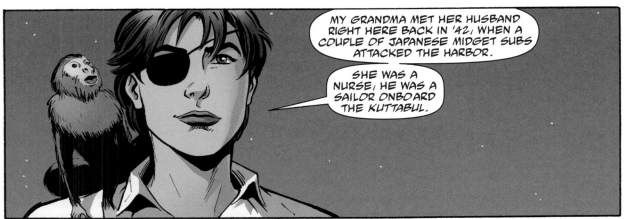

MY GRANDMA MET HER HUSBAND RIGHT HERE BACK IN '42, WHEN A COUPLE OF JAPANESE MIDGET SUBS ATTACKED THE HARBOR.

SHE WAS A NURSE, HE WAS A SAILOR ONBOARD THE *KUTTABUL.*

THEY WERE BOTH *CERTAIN* THE WORLD WAS GONNA END THAT NIGHT... BUT LOOK AT HOW THINGS TURNED OUT. THEIR *GRANDKID'S* GOT A JAPANESE GIRL FOR A *MATE.*

THE FUTURE NEVER SHAPES UP LIKE YOU FIGURE IT WILL, YEAH?

HN.

YOU *ARE* JAPANESE, AREN'T YOU?

HALF.

I JUST WASN'T AWARE THAT I WAS YOUR "MATE."

RELAX, YOU UPTIGHT TWAT.

I'M JUST SAYING YOU'RE A *FRIEND* IS ALL.

I KNOW...

...BUT I'VE GOT TOO MANY FRIENDS ALREADY.

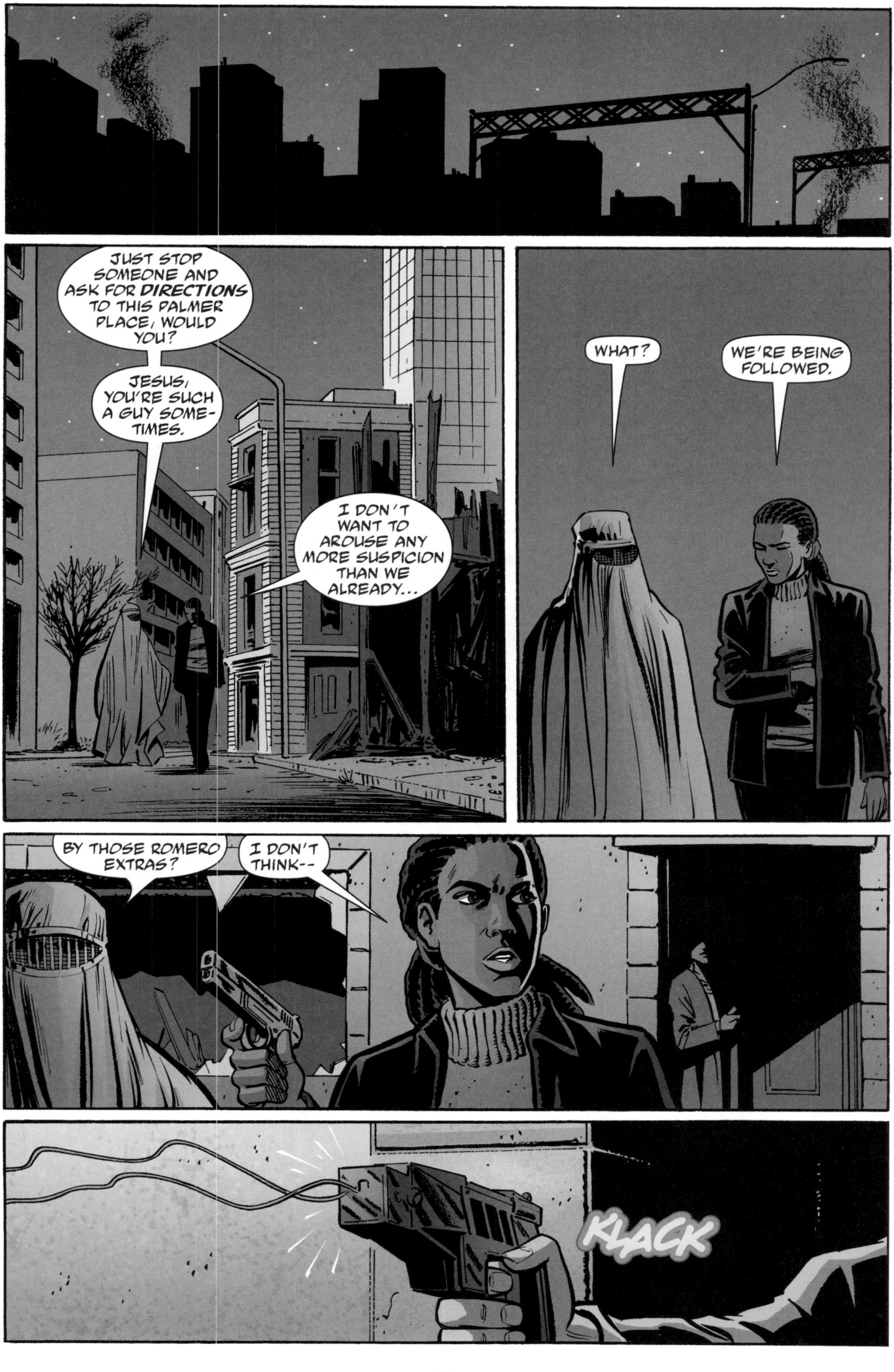
JUST STOP SOMEONE AND ASK FOR DIRECTIONS TO THIS PALMER PLACE, WOULD YOU?
JESUS, YOU'RE SUCH A GUY SOME-TIMES.
I DON'T WANT TO AROUSE ANY MORE SUSPICION THAN WE ALREADY...
WHAT?
WE'RE BEING FOLLOWED.
BY THOSE ROMERO EXTRAS?
I DON'T THINK--
KLACK

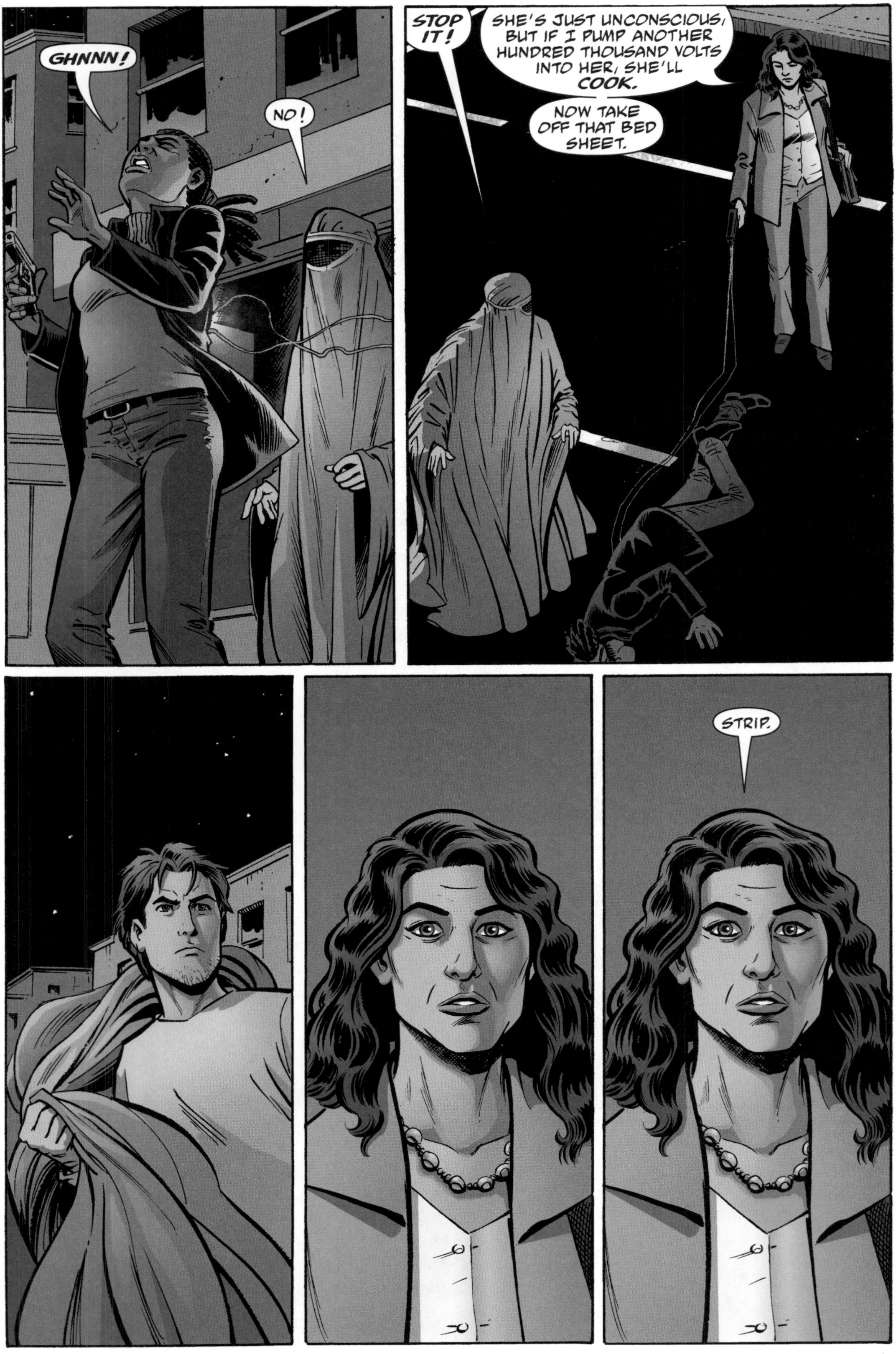
GHNNN!
NO!
STOP IT!
SHE'S JUST UNCONSCIOUS, BUT IF I PUMP ANOTHER HUNDRED THOUSAND VOLTS INTO HER, SHE'LL COOK.
NOW TAKE OFF THAT BED SHEET.
STRIP.

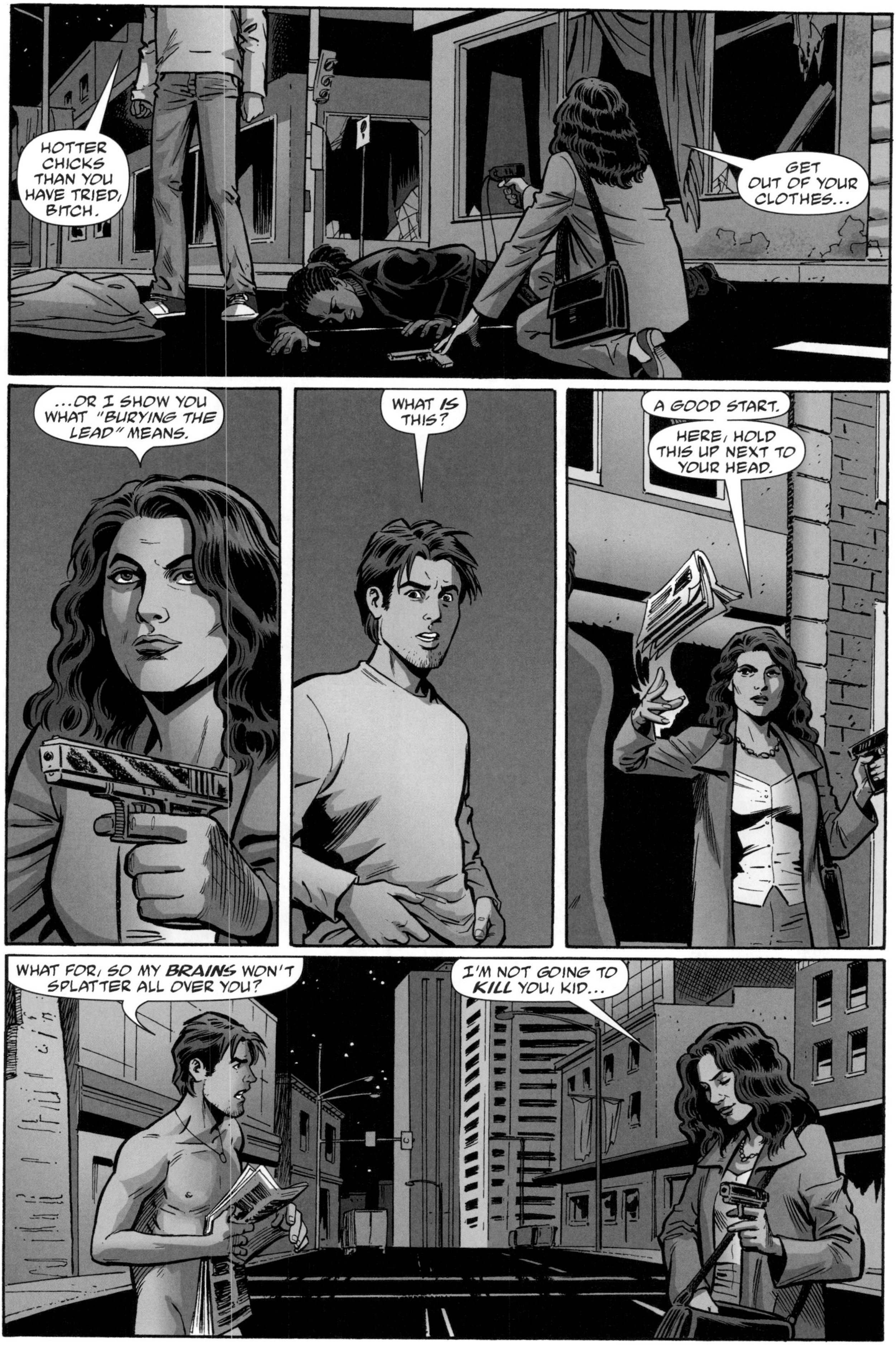
HOTTER CHICKS THAN YOU HAVE TRIED, BITCH.
GET OUT OF YOUR CLOTHES...
...OR I SHOW YOU WHAT "BURYING THE LEAD" MEANS.
WHAT *IS* THIS?
A GOOD START.
HERE, HOLD THIS UP NEXT TO YOUR HEAD.
WHAT FOR, SO MY **BRAINS** WON'T SPLATTER ALL OVER YOU?
I'M NOT GOING TO **KILL** YOU, KID...

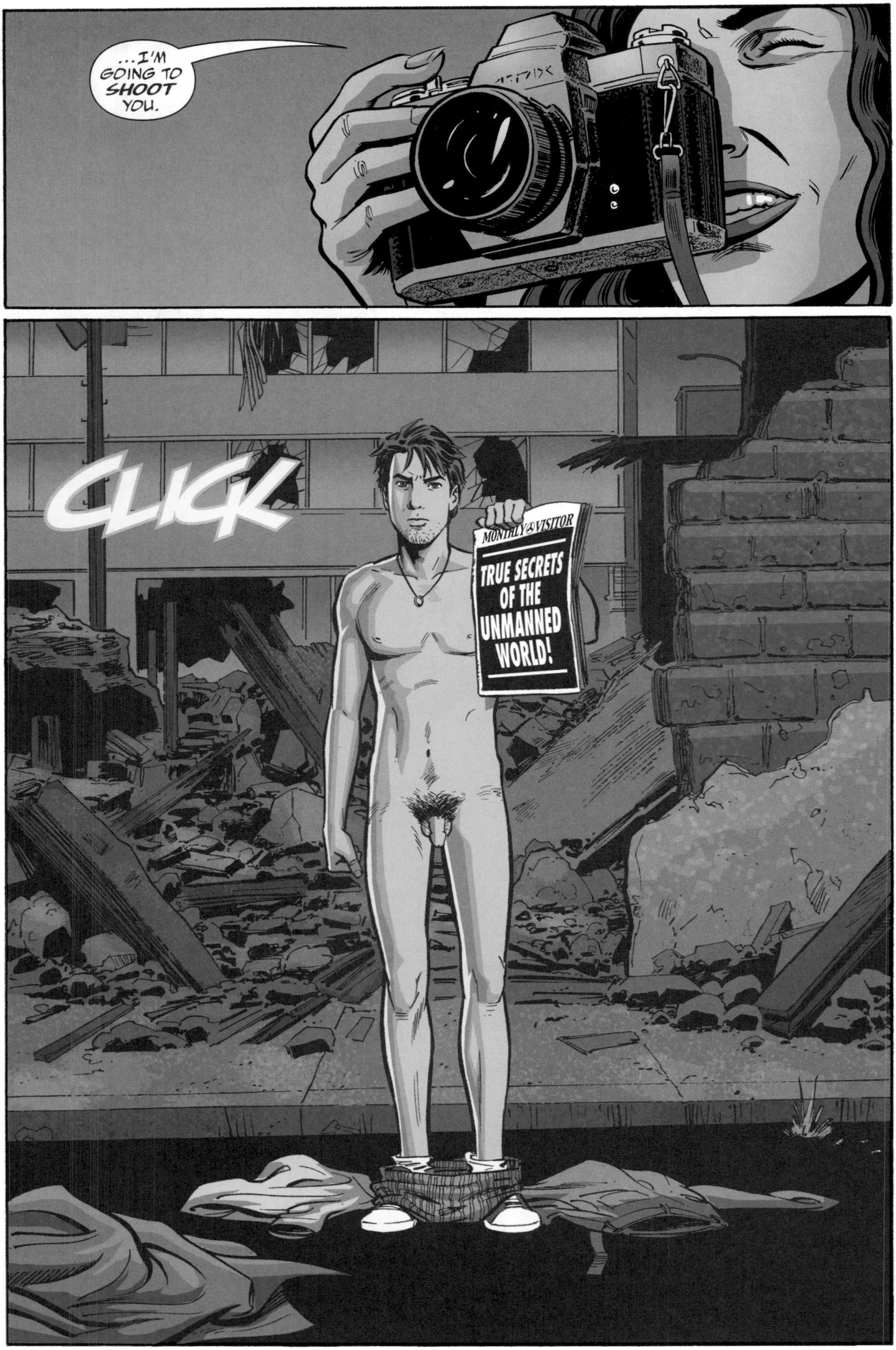
...I'M GOING TO SHOOT YOU.
CLICK
MONTHLY VISITOR
TRUE SECRETS OF THE UNMANNED WORLD!

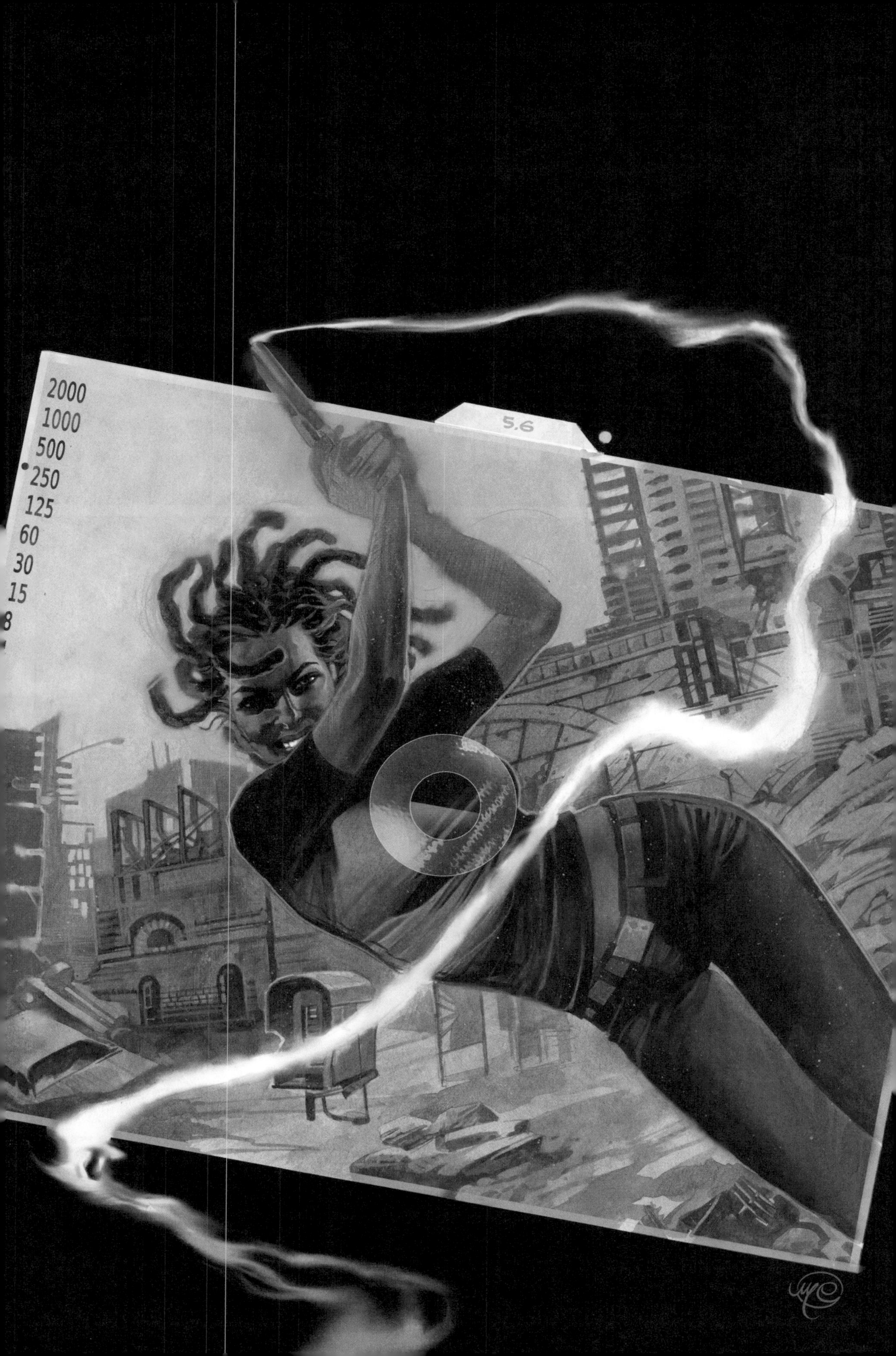
2000
1000
500
250
125
60
30
15
8
5.6

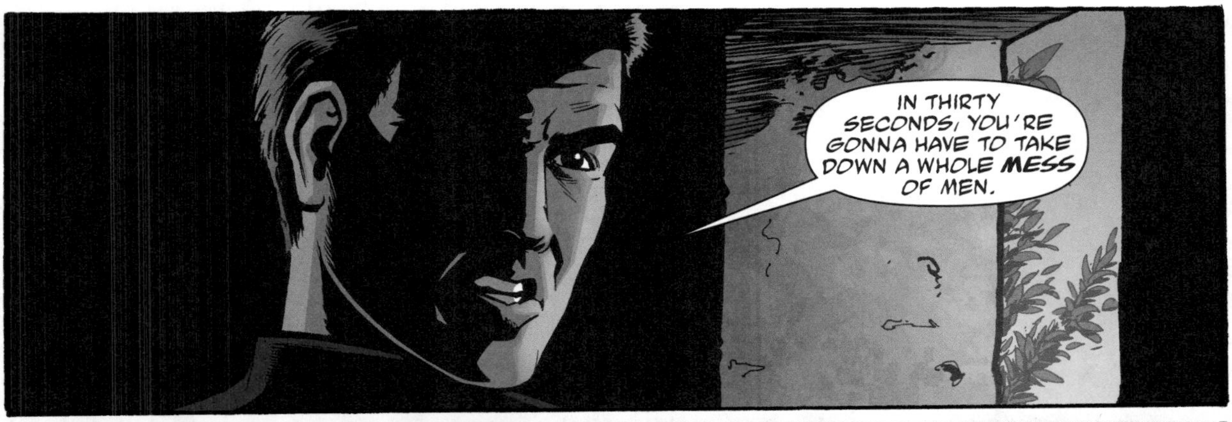
IN THIRTY SECONDS, YOU'RE GONNA HAVE TO TAKE DOWN A WHOLE MESS OF MEN.

Adis Ababa, Ethiopia
Thirteen Years Ago

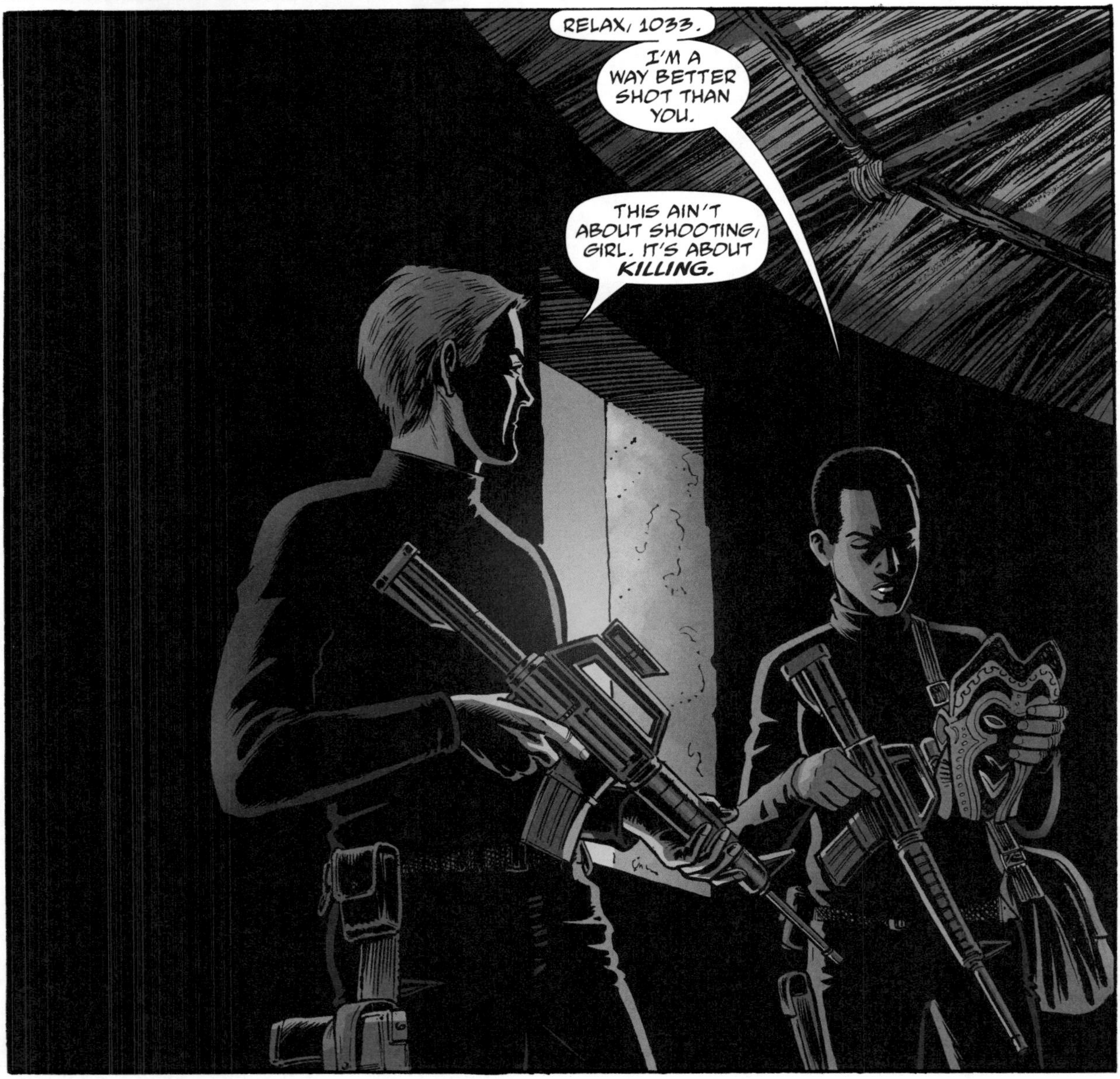
RELAX, 1033.
I'M A WAY BETTER SHOT THAN YOU.
THIS AIN'T ABOUT SHOOTING, GIRL. IT'S ABOUT KILLING.

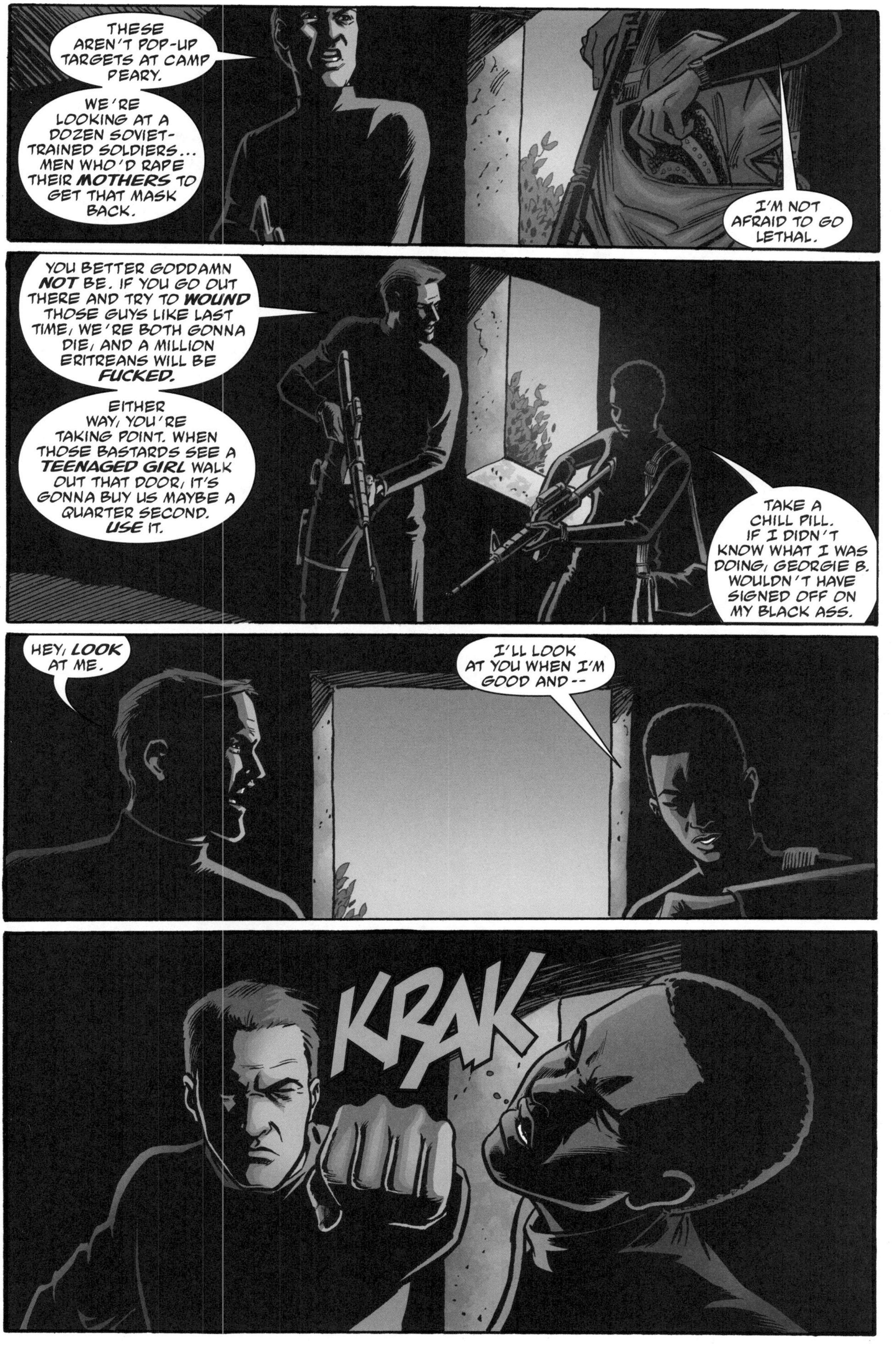
THESE AREN'T POP-UP TARGETS AT CAMP PEARY.
WE'RE LOOKING AT A DOZEN SOVIET-TRAINED SOLDIERS... MEN WHO'D RAPE THEIR **MOTHERS** TO GET THAT MASK BACK.
I'M NOT AFRAID TO GO LETHAL.
YOU BETTER GODDAMN **NOT** BE. IF YOU GO OUT THERE AND TRY TO **WOUND** THOSE GUYS LIKE LAST TIME, WE'RE BOTH GONNA DIE, AND A MILLION ERITREANS WILL BE **FUCKED.**
EITHER WAY, YOU'RE TAKING POINT. WHEN THOSE BASTARDS SEE A **TEENAGED GIRL** WALK OUT THAT DOOR, IT'S GONNA BUY US MAYBE A QUARTER SECOND. **USE** IT.
TAKE A CHILL PILL. IF I DIDN'T KNOW WHAT I WAS DOING, GEORGIE B. WOULDN'T HAVE SIGNED OFF ON MY BLACK ASS.
HEY, **LOOK** AT ME.
I'LL LOOK AT YOU WHEN I'M GOOD AND --
KRAK

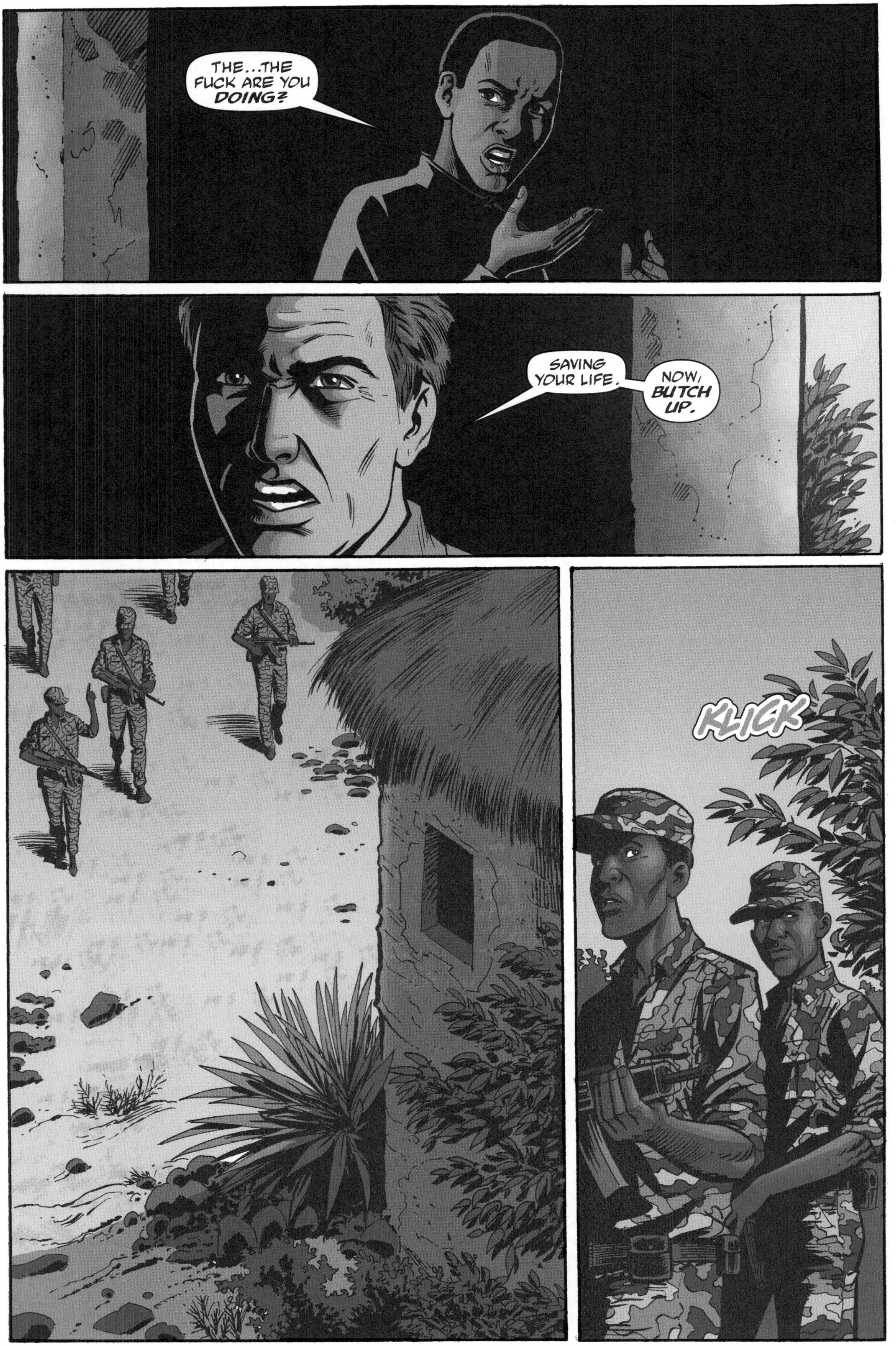
THE...THE FUCK ARE YOU DOING?
SAVING YOUR LIFE.
NOW, BUTCH UP.
KLICK

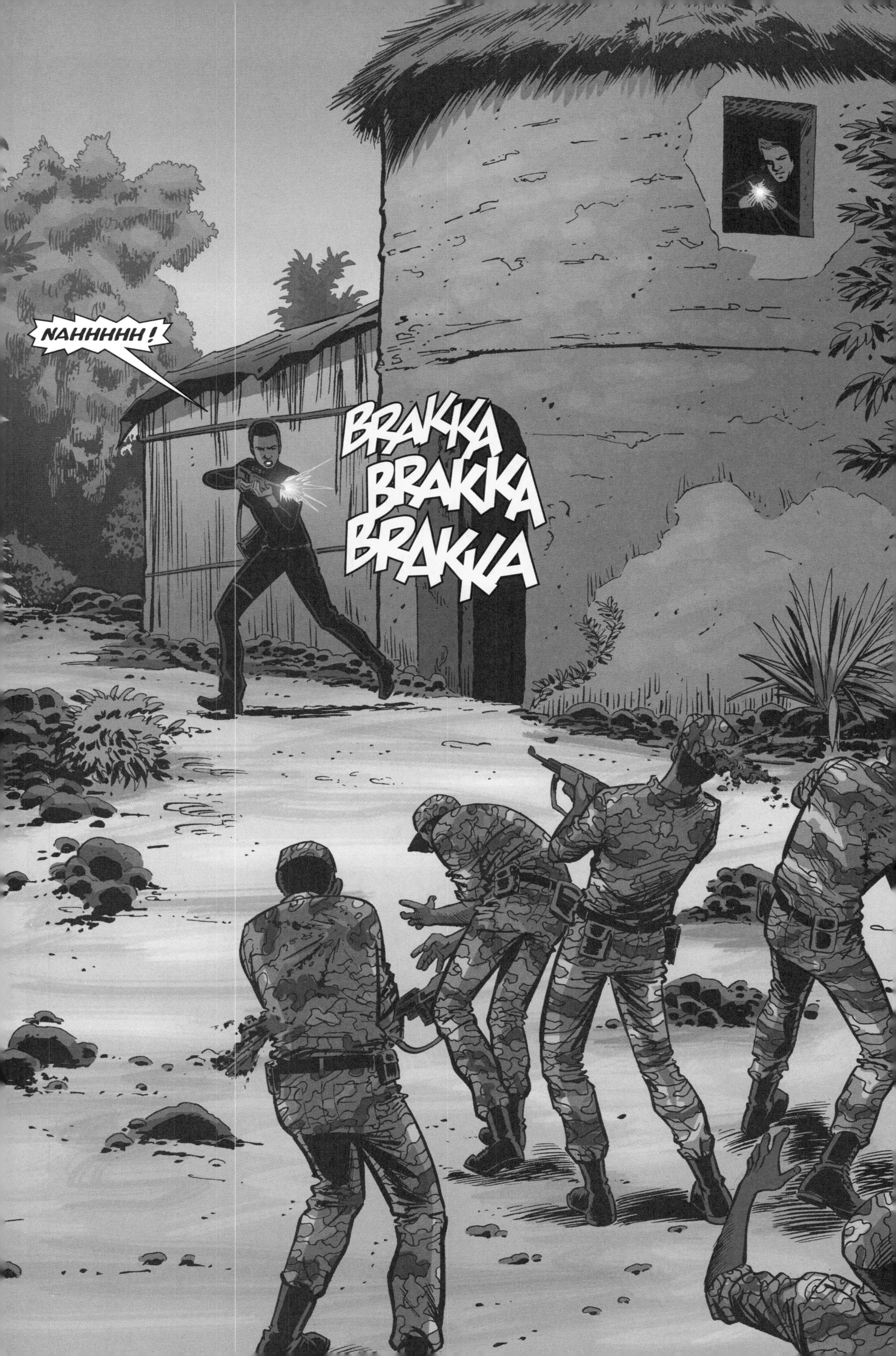
NAHHHHH!
BRAKKA
BRAKKA
BRAKKA

NNN...
Sydney, Australia
Now
OH, SO NOW YOU DECIDE NOT TO BE DEAD?
JESUS, LINCOLN HAD A BETTER BODY-GUARD.

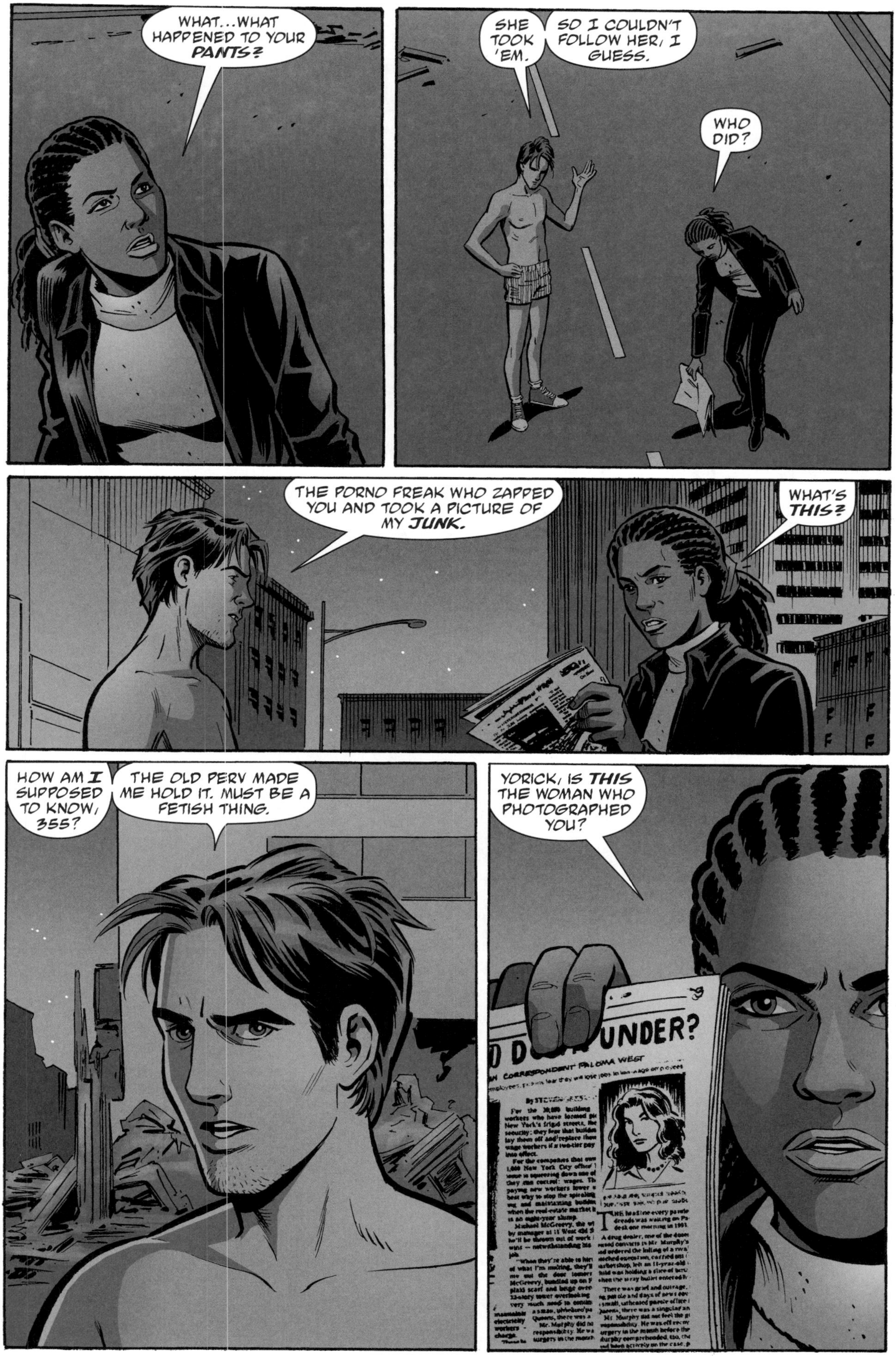
WHAT...WHAT HAPPENED TO YOUR PANTS?
SHE TOOK 'EM.
SO I COULDN'T FOLLOW HER, I GUESS.
WHO DID?
THE PORNO FREAK WHO ZAPPED YOU AND TOOK A PICTURE OF MY JUNK.
WHAT'S THIS?
HOW AM I SUPPOSED TO KNOW, 355?
THE OLD PERV MADE ME HOLD IT. MUST BE A FETISH THING.
YORICK, IS THIS THE WOMAN WHO PHOTOGRAPHED YOU?
UNDER?
CORRESPONDENT PALOMA WEST

WHAT IS THAT, HER MUGSHOT?

SHE'S NOT A SEX OFFENDER, SHE'S A **REPORTER**.

UNLESS WE FIND HER, THAT PICTURE OF YOU IS GOING TO BE ON THE FRONT PAGE OF EVERY NEWSPAPER IN THE WORLD.

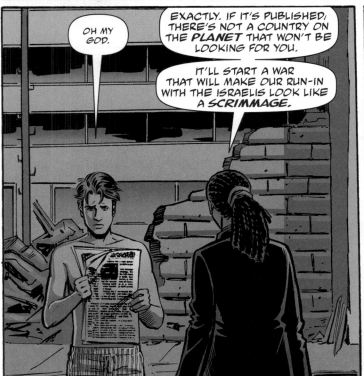

OH MY GOD.

EXACTLY. IF IT'S PUBLISHED, THERE'S NOT A COUNTRY ON THE **PLANET** THAT WON'T BE LOOKING FOR YOU.

IT'LL START A WAR THAT WILL MAKE OUR RUN-IN WITH THE ISRAELIS LOOK LIKE A **SCRIMMAGE**.

I...I DIDN'T EVEN HAVE TIME TO CHUMP UP.

I WAS LIKE, **PRETERNATURALLY** FLACCID. I--

COME ON.

WE HAVE A RUMOR TO KILL.

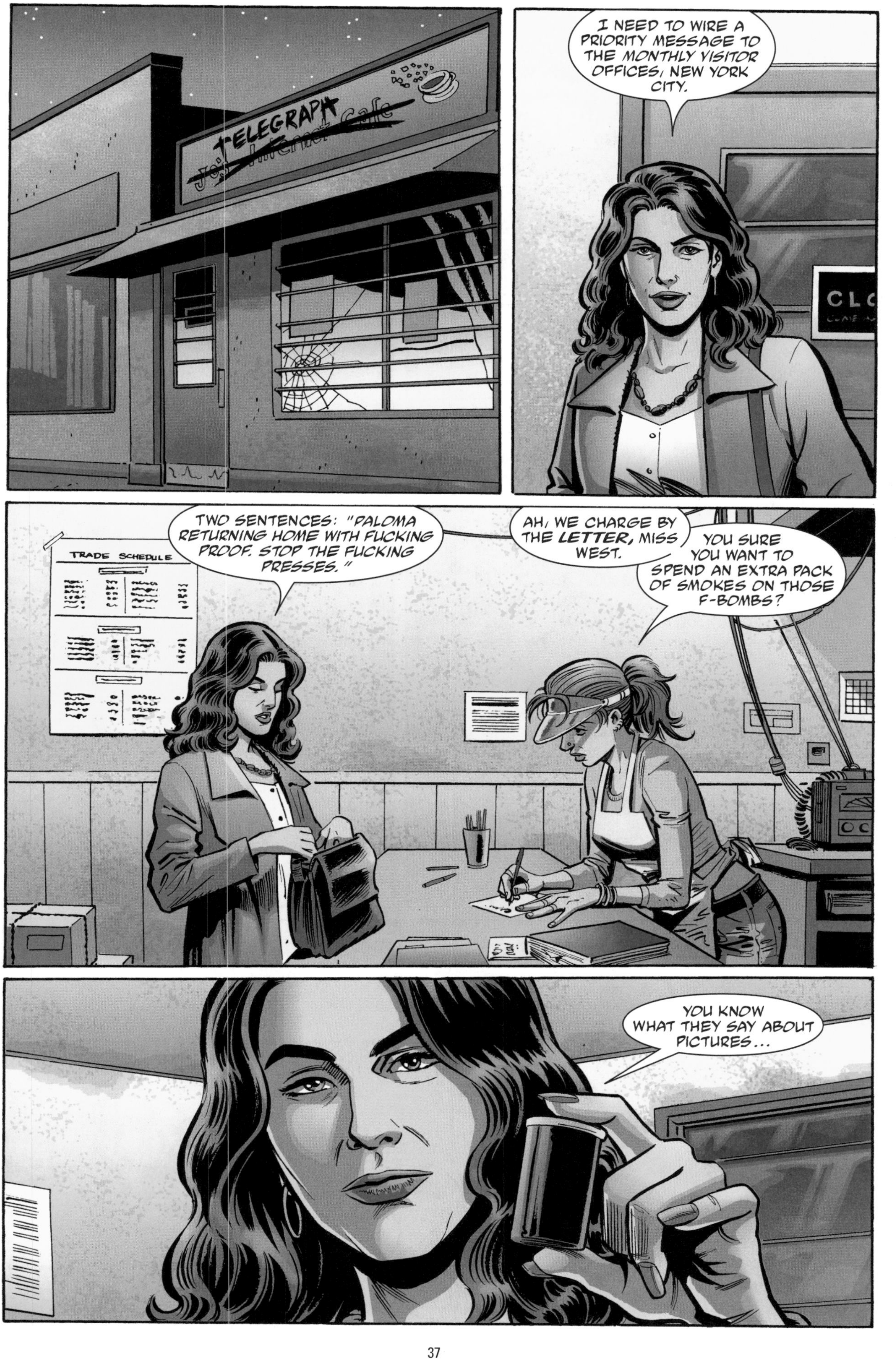
TELEGRAPH
I NEED TO WIRE A PRIORITY MESSAGE TO THE MONTHLY VISITOR OFFICES, NEW YORK CITY.
TRADE SCHEDULE
TWO SENTENCES: "PALOMA RETURNING HOME WITH FUCKING PROOF. STOP THE FUCKING PRESSES."
AH, WE CHARGE BY THE LETTER, MISS WEST.
YOU SURE YOU WANT TO SPEND AN EXTRA PACK OF SMOKES ON THOSE F-BOMBS?
YOU KNOW WHAT THEY SAY ABOUT PICTURES...

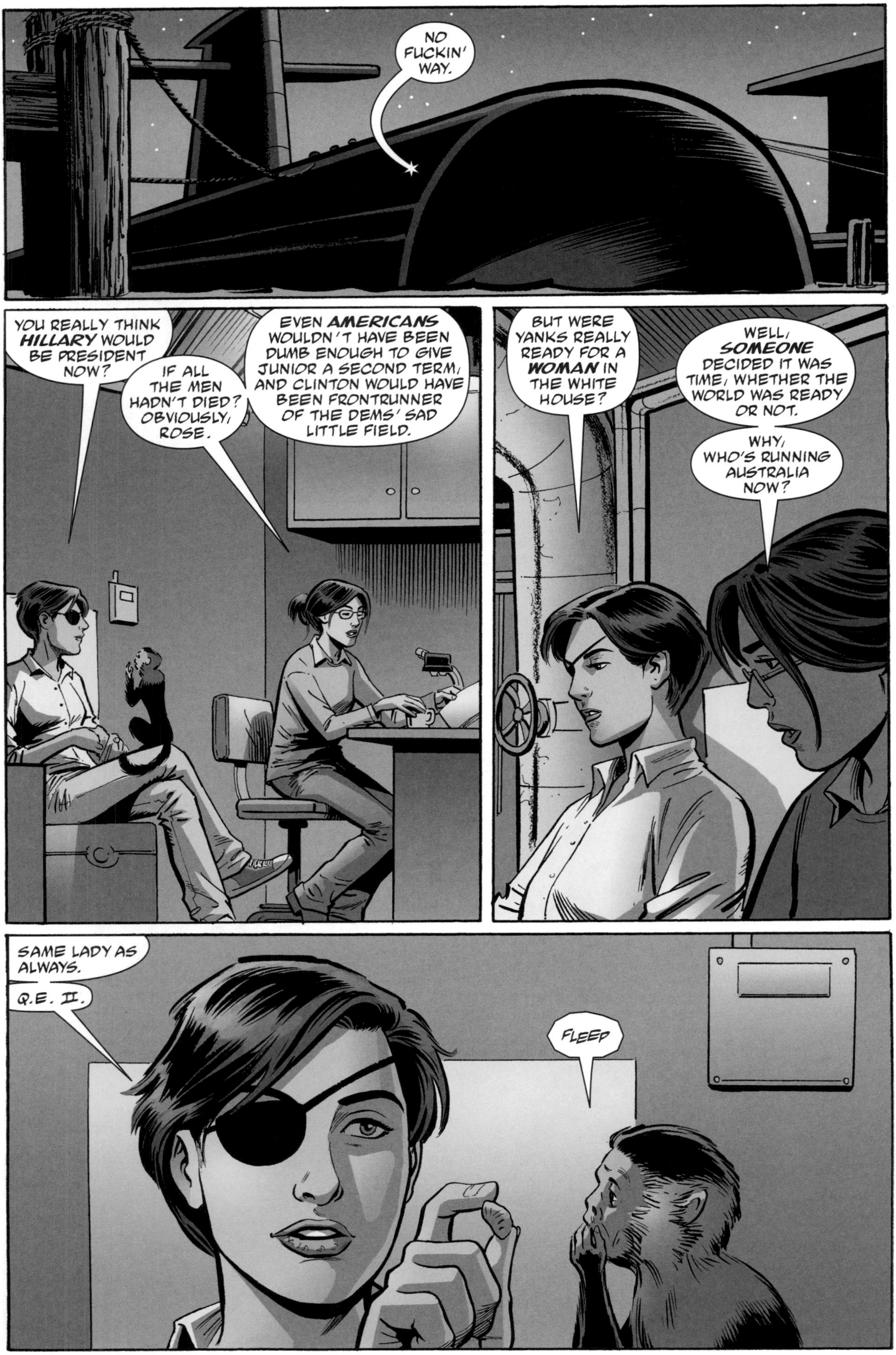
NO FUCKIN' WAY.
YOU REALLY THINK HILLARY WOULD BE PRESIDENT NOW?
IF ALL THE MEN HADN'T DIED? OBVIOUSLY, ROSE.
EVEN AMERICANS WOULDN'T HAVE BEEN DUMB ENOUGH TO GIVE JUNIOR A SECOND TERM, AND CLINTON WOULD HAVE BEEN FRONTRUNNER OF THE DEMS' SAD LITTLE FIELD.
BUT WERE YANKS REALLY READY FOR A WOMAN IN THE WHITE HOUSE?
WELL, SOMEONE DECIDED IT WAS TIME, WHETHER THE WORLD WAS READY OR NOT.
WHY, WHO'S RUNNING AUSTRALIA NOW?
SAME LADY AS ALWAYS.
Q.E. II.
FLEEP

YOU'RE TAKING ORDERS FROM *QUEEN ELIZABETH?*

WELL, MORE LIKELY WHATEVER DOWNING STREET SUITS ARE PULLING HER STRINGS NOW... BUT YEAH.

WE'RE NOT NEW ZEALAND, DR. MANN. THEY HAD *TWO* GALS AS PRIME MINISTER EVEN BEFORE THE BIG WIPEOUT, AND ABOUT A THIRD OF THEIR PARLIAMENT WAS *SHEILAS.*

HERE, ANYTIME A WOMAN TRIED TO GET ELECTED, IF SHE WAS SINGLE, MEN WOULD CALL HER A LESBIAN, AND IF SHE WAS A MUM, THEY'D SAY SHE WASN'T FIT TO SERVE.

SO WHEN ALL THE GUYS KICKED, THERE WEREN'T ENOUGH GOVERNMENT TYPES LEFT TO RESTORE ORDER, AND THE QUEEN ENDED UP APPOINTING HER *OWN* GOVERNOR-GENERAL.

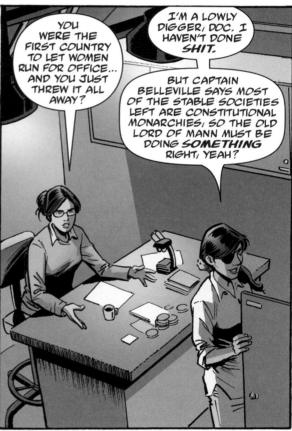

YOU WERE THE FIRST COUNTRY TO LET WOMEN RUN FOR OFFICE... AND YOU JUST THREW IT ALL AWAY?

I'M A LOWLY DIGGER, DOC. I HAVEN'T DONE *SHIT.*

BUT CAPTAIN BELLEVILLE SAYS MOST OF THE STABLE SOCIETIES LEFT ARE CONSTITUTIONAL MONARCHIES, SO THE OLD LORD OF MANN MUST BE DOING *SOMETHING* RIGHT, YEAH?

MOTHER OF CHRIST.

WHY AM I WORKING SO HARD TO *SAVE* THIS BACKWARDS-ASS PLANET?

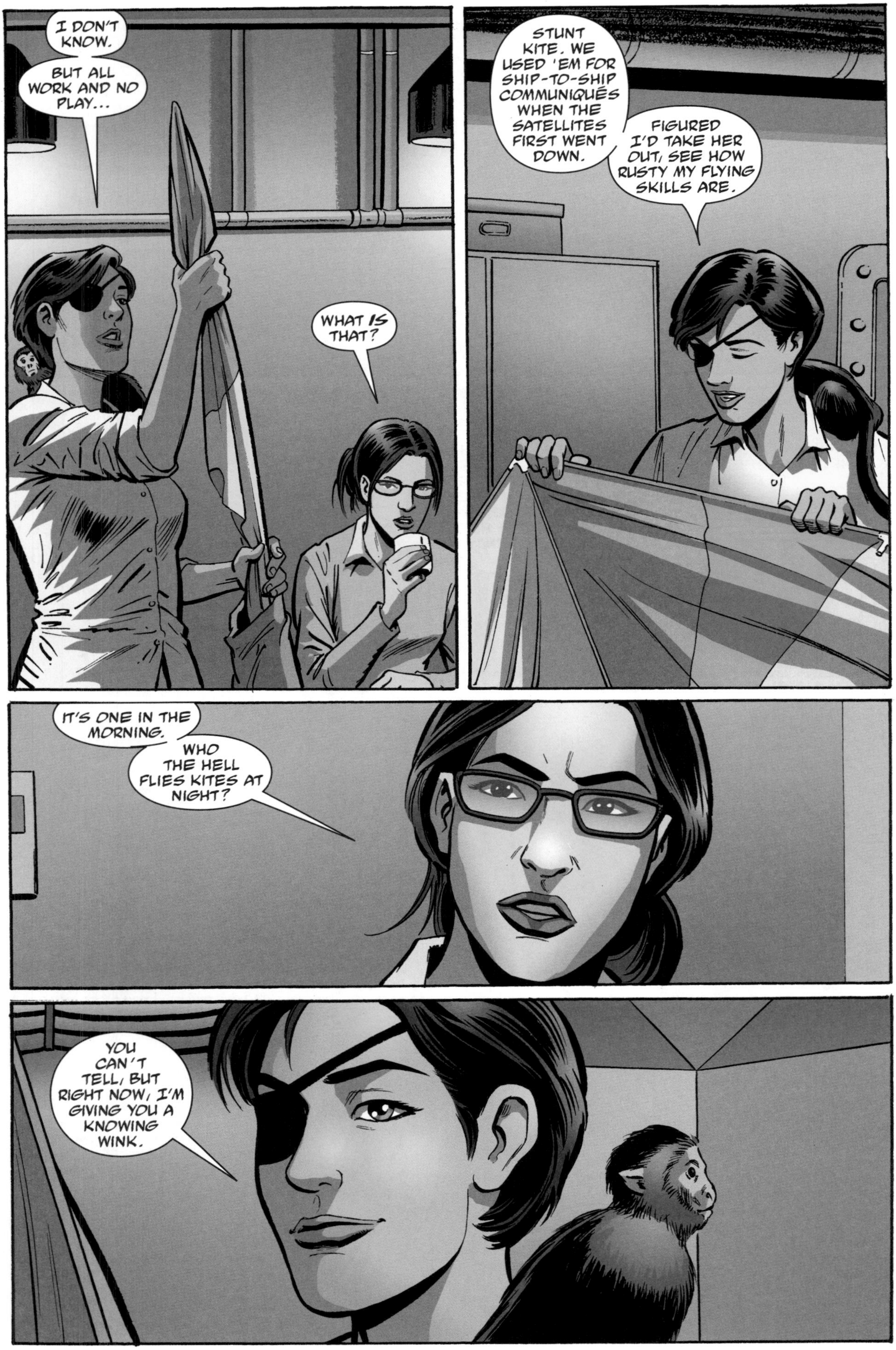
I DON'T KNOW.
BUT ALL WORK AND NO PLAY...
WHAT IS THAT?
STUNT KITE. WE USED 'EM FOR SHIP-TO-SHIP COMMUNIQUÉS WHEN THE SATELLITES FIRST WENT DOWN.
FIGURED I'D TAKE HER OUT, SEE HOW RUSTY MY FLYING SKILLS ARE.
IT'S ONE IN THE MORNING.
WHO THE HELL FLIES KITES AT NIGHT?
YOU CAN'T TELL, BUT RIGHT NOW, I'M GIVING YOU A KNOWING WINK.

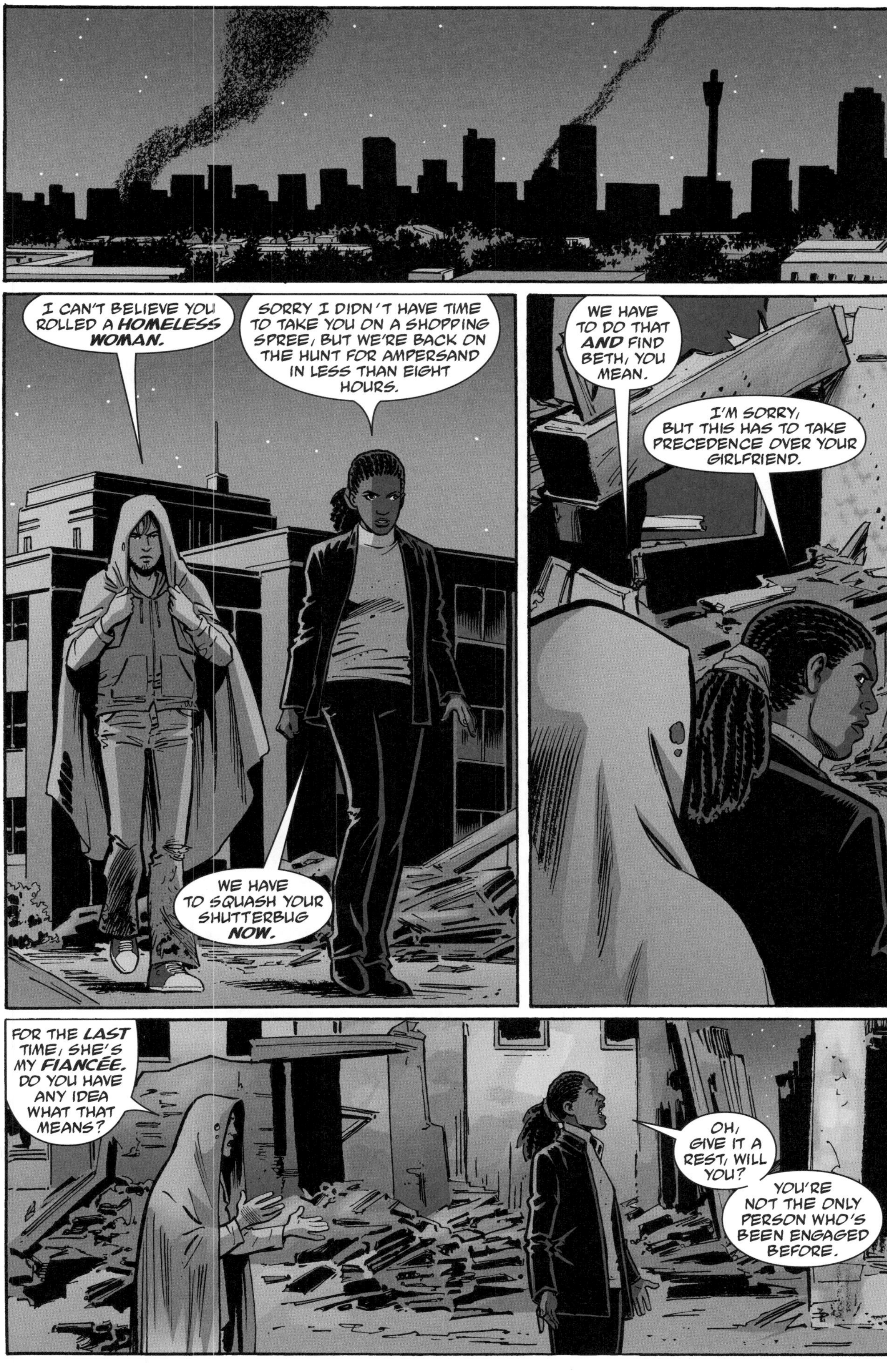
I CAN'T BELIEVE YOU ROLLED A HOMELESS WOMAN.
SORRY I DIDN'T HAVE TIME TO TAKE YOU ON A SHOPPING SPREE, BUT WE'RE BACK ON THE HUNT FOR AMPERSAND IN LESS THAN EIGHT HOURS.
WE HAVE TO SQUASH YOUR SHUTTERBUG NOW.
WE HAVE TO DO THAT AND FIND BETH, YOU MEAN.
I'M SORRY, BUT THIS HAS TO TAKE PRECEDENCE OVER YOUR GIRLFRIEND.
FOR THE LAST TIME, SHE'S MY FIANCÉE. DO YOU HAVE ANY IDEA WHAT THAT MEANS?
OH, GIVE IT A REST, WILL YOU?
YOU'RE NOT THE ONLY PERSON WHO'S BEEN ENGAGED BEFORE.

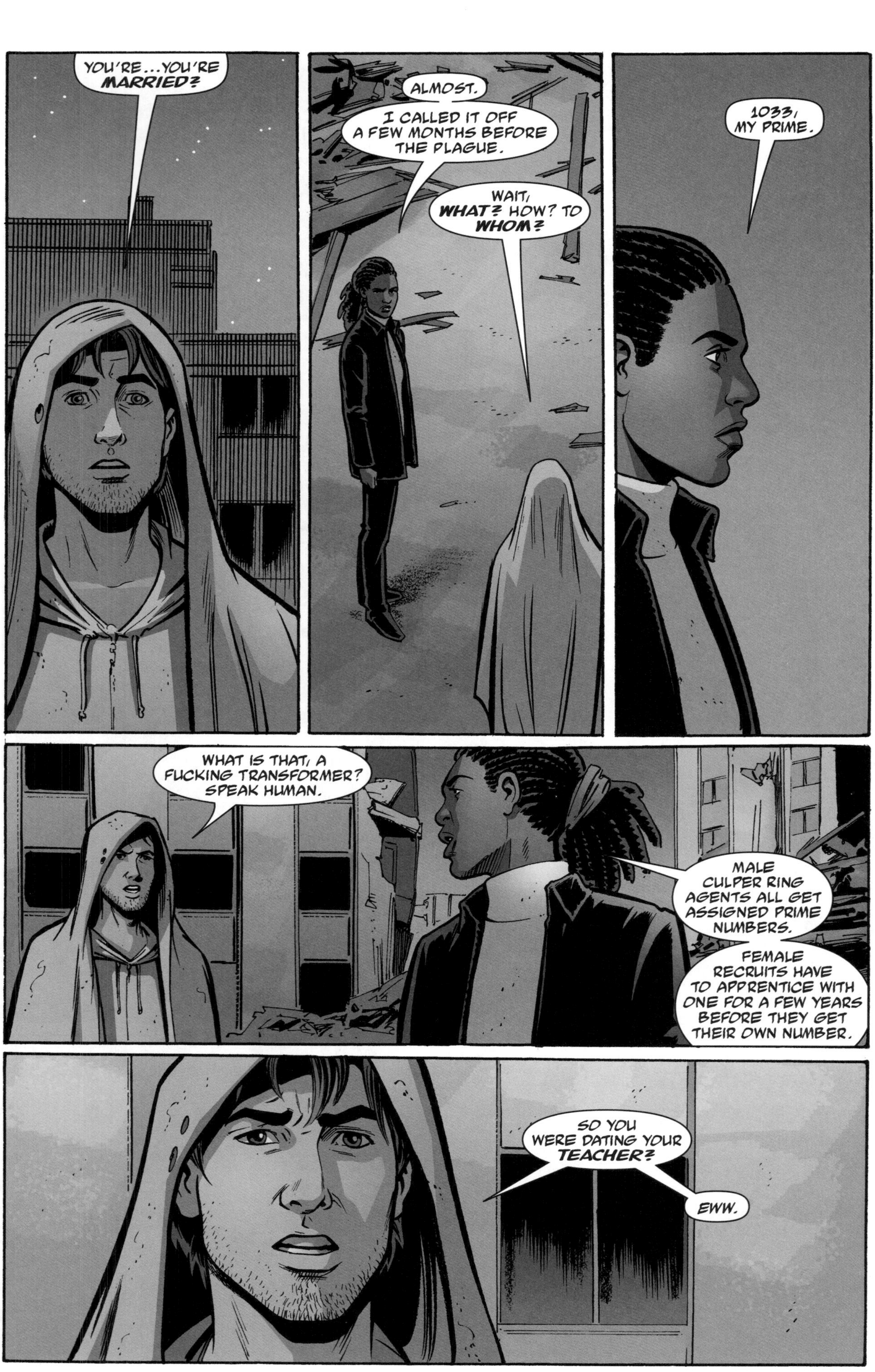
YOU'RE...YOU'RE MARRIED?
ALMOST.
I CALLED IT OFF A FEW MONTHS BEFORE THE PLAGUE.
WAIT, WHAT? HOW? TO WHOM?
1033, MY PRIME.
WHAT IS THAT, A FUCKING TRANSFORMER? SPEAK HUMAN.
MALE CULPER RING AGENTS ALL GET ASSIGNED PRIME NUMBERS.
FEMALE RECRUITS HAVE TO APPRENTICE WITH ONE FOR A FEW YEARS BEFORE THEY GET THEIR OWN NUMBER.
SO YOU WERE DATING YOUR TEACHER?
EWW.

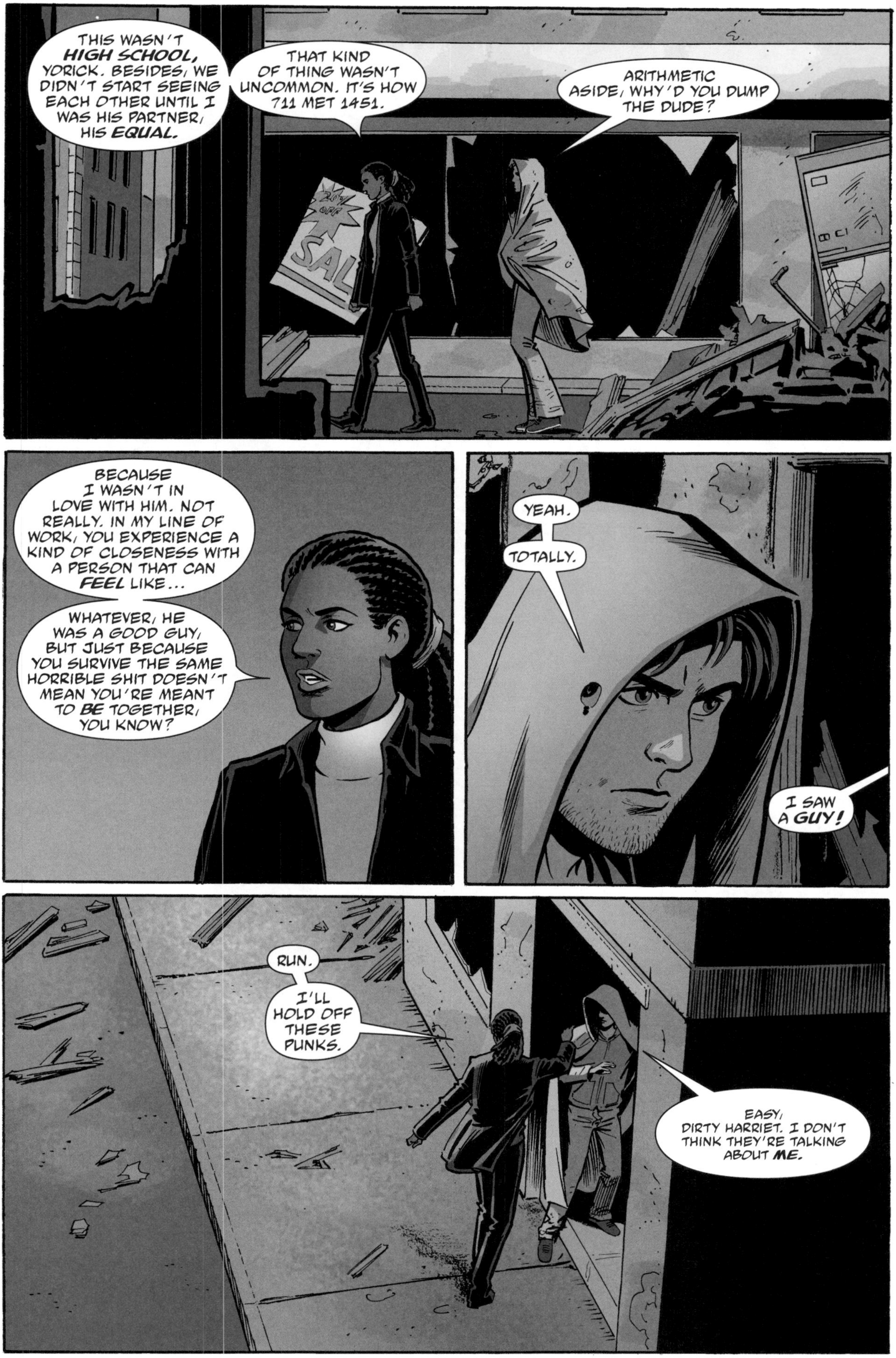
THIS WASN'T **HIGH SCHOOL,** YORICK. BESIDES, WE DIDN'T START SEEING EACH OTHER UNTIL I WAS HIS PARTNER, HIS **EQUAL.**
THAT KIND OF THING WASN'T UNCOMMON. IT'S HOW 711 MET 1451.
ARITHMETIC ASIDE, WHY'D YOU DUMP THE DUDE?
BECAUSE I WASN'T IN LOVE WITH HIM. NOT REALLY. IN MY LINE OF WORK, YOU EXPERIENCE A KIND OF CLOSENESS WITH A PERSON THAT CAN *FEEL* LIKE...
WHATEVER, HE WAS A GOOD GUY, BUT JUST BECAUSE YOU SURVIVE THE SAME HORRIBLE SHIT DOESN'T MEAN YOU'RE MEANT TO *BE* TOGETHER, YOU KNOW?
YEAH.
TOTALLY.
I SAW A **GUY!**
RUN.
I'LL HOLD OFF THESE PUNKS.
EASY, DIRTY HARRIET. I DON'T THINK THEY'RE TALKING ABOUT **ME.**

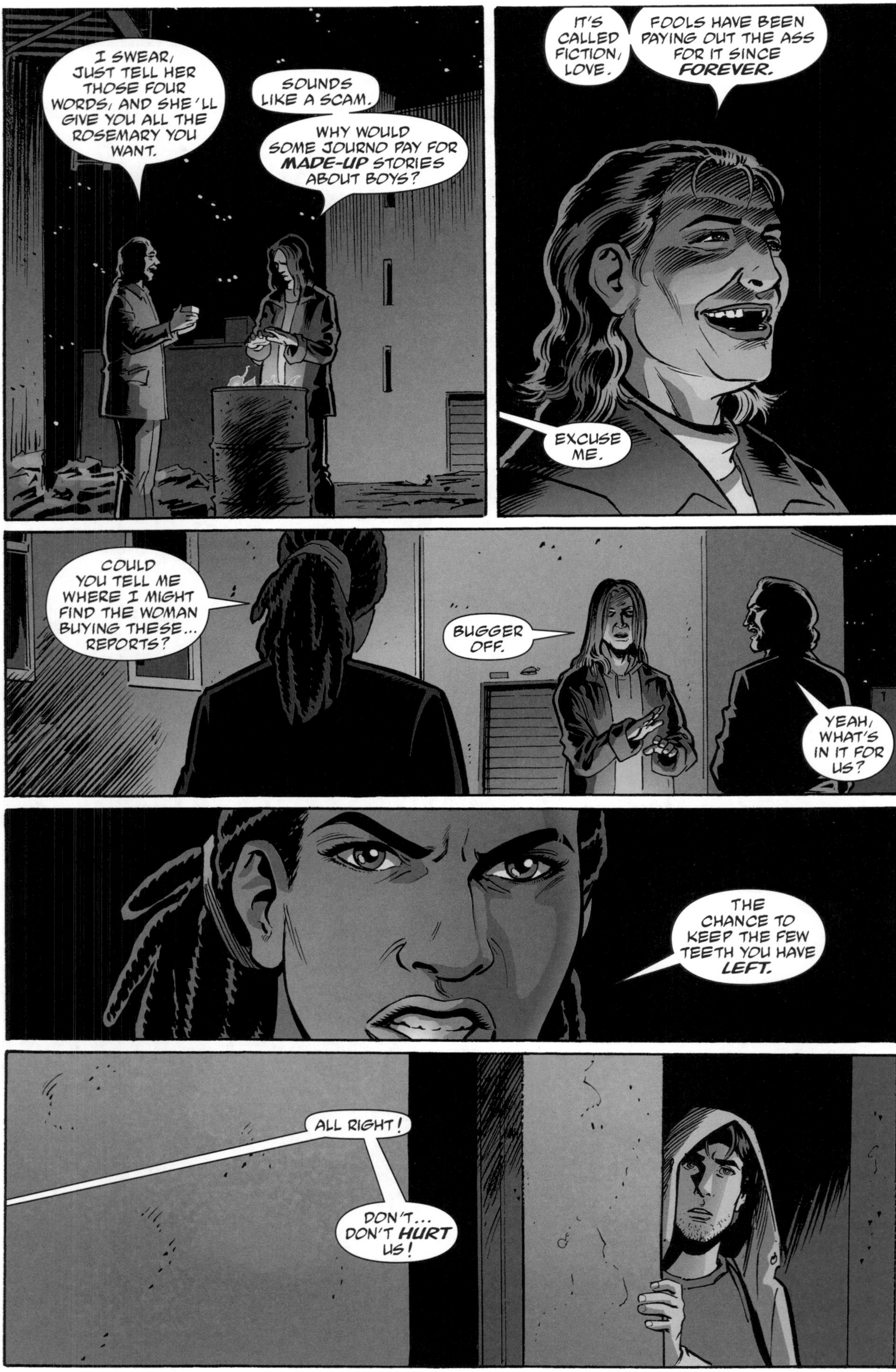
I SWEAR, JUST TELL HER THOSE FOUR WORDS, AND SHE'LL GIVE YOU ALL THE ROSEMARY YOU WANT.
SOUNDS LIKE A SCAM.
WHY WOULD SOME JOURNO PAY FOR MADE-UP STORIES ABOUT BOYS?
IT'S CALLED FICTION, LOVE.
FOOLS HAVE BEEN PAYING OUT THE ASS FOR IT SINCE FOREVER.
EXCUSE ME.
COULD YOU TELL ME WHERE I MIGHT FIND THE WOMAN BUYING THESE... REPORTS?
BUGGER OFF.
YEAH, WHAT'S IN IT FOR US?
THE CHANCE TO KEEP THE FEW TEETH YOU HAVE LEFT.
ALL RIGHT!
DON'T... DON'T HURT US!

HEH.

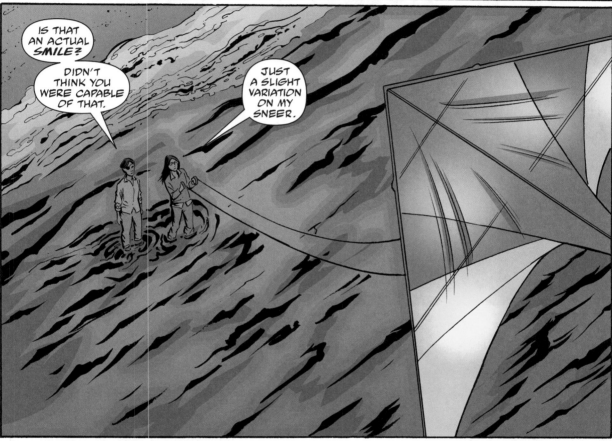

IS THAT AN ACTUAL *SMILE*?

DIDN'T THINK YOU WERE CAPABLE OF THAT.

JUST A SLIGHT VARIATION ON MY SNEER.

YOU'RE NOT HALF-BAD WITH THAT THING.

BEGINNER'S LUCK, BUT MY MOM AND I USED TO FLY OLD ONE-LINERS, WHEN WE'D COME BACK TO CHINA TO VISIT...

CRAP.

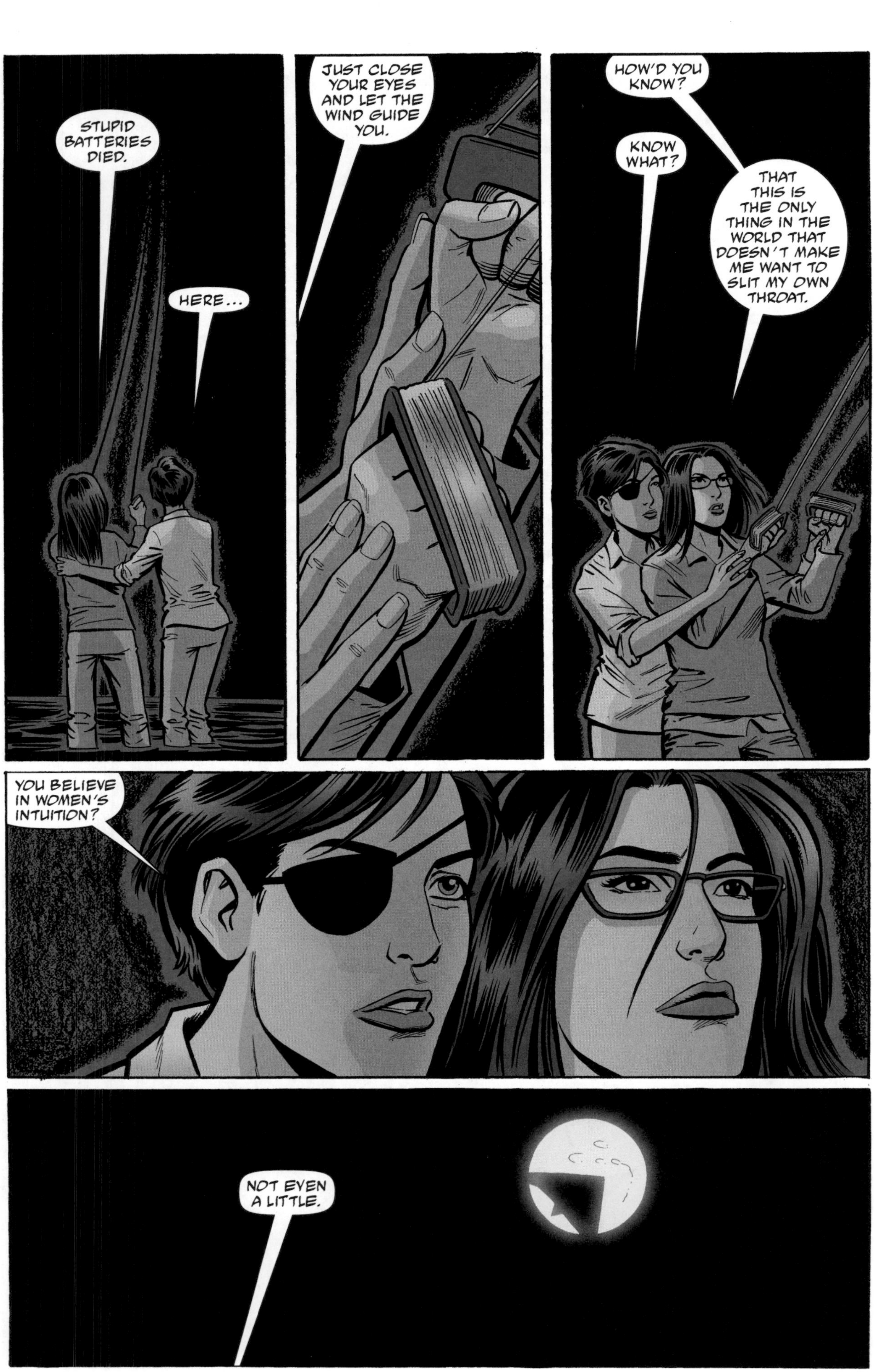

STUPID BATTERIES DIED.
HERE...
JUST CLOSE YOUR EYES AND LET THE WIND GUIDE YOU.
HOW'D YOU KNOW?
KNOW WHAT?
THAT THIS IS THE ONLY THING IN THE WORLD THAT DOESN'T MAKE ME WANT TO SLIT MY OWN THROAT.
YOU BELIEVE IN WOMEN'S INTUITION?
NOT EVEN A LITTLE.

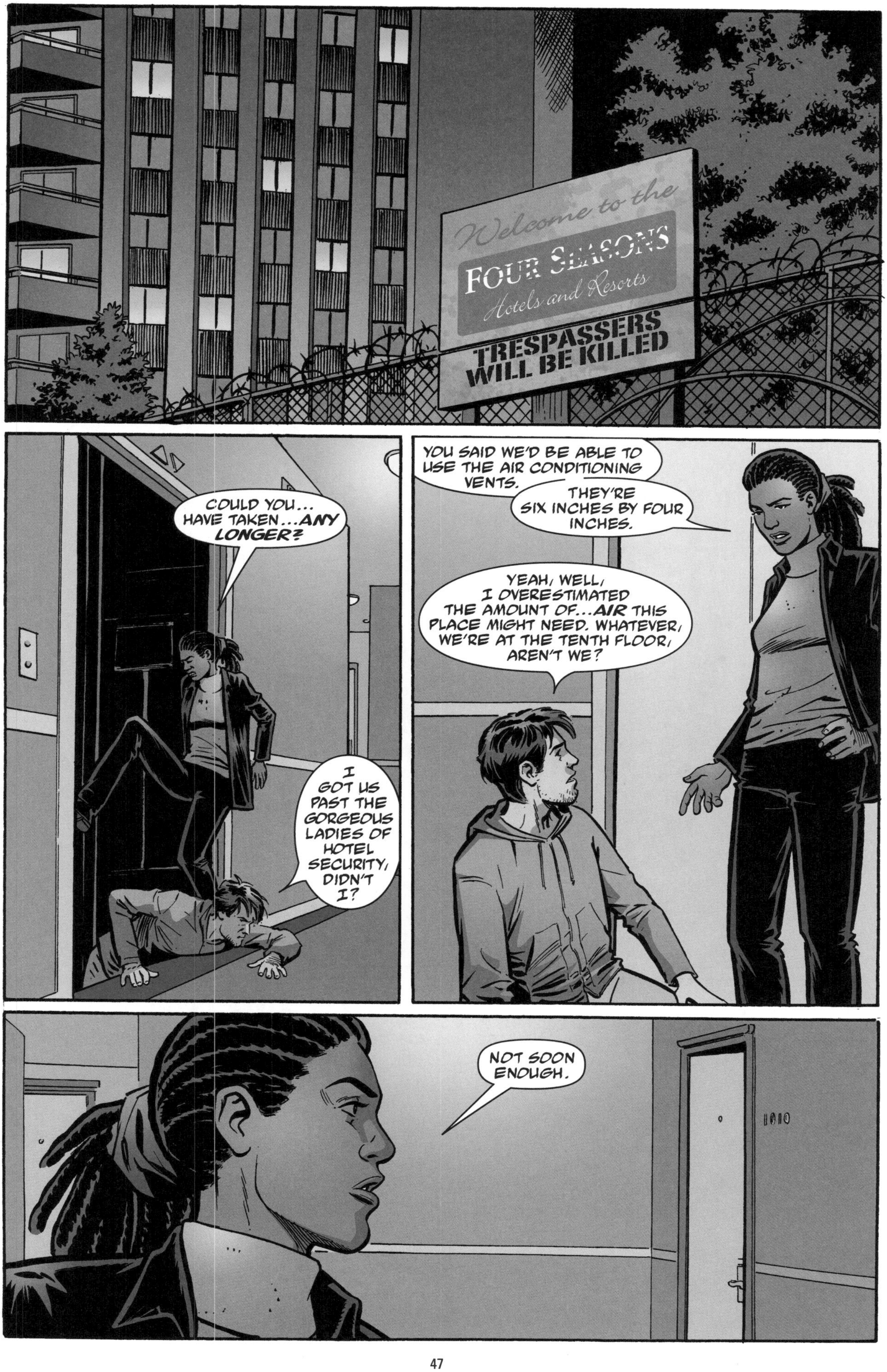
Welcome to the
FOUR SEASONS
Hotels and Resorts
TRESPASSERS WILL BE KILLED
COULD YOU... HAVE TAKEN...ANY LONGER?
I GOT US PAST THE GORGEOUS LADIES OF HOTEL SECURITY, DIDN'T I?
YOU SAID WE'D BE ABLE TO USE THE AIR CONDITIONING VENTS.
THEY'RE SIX INCHES BY FOUR INCHES.
YEAH, WELL, I OVERESTIMATED THE AMOUNT OF...AIR THIS PLACE MIGHT NEED. WHATEVER, WE'RE AT THE TENTH FLOOR, AREN'T WE?
NOT SOON ENOUGH.
1010

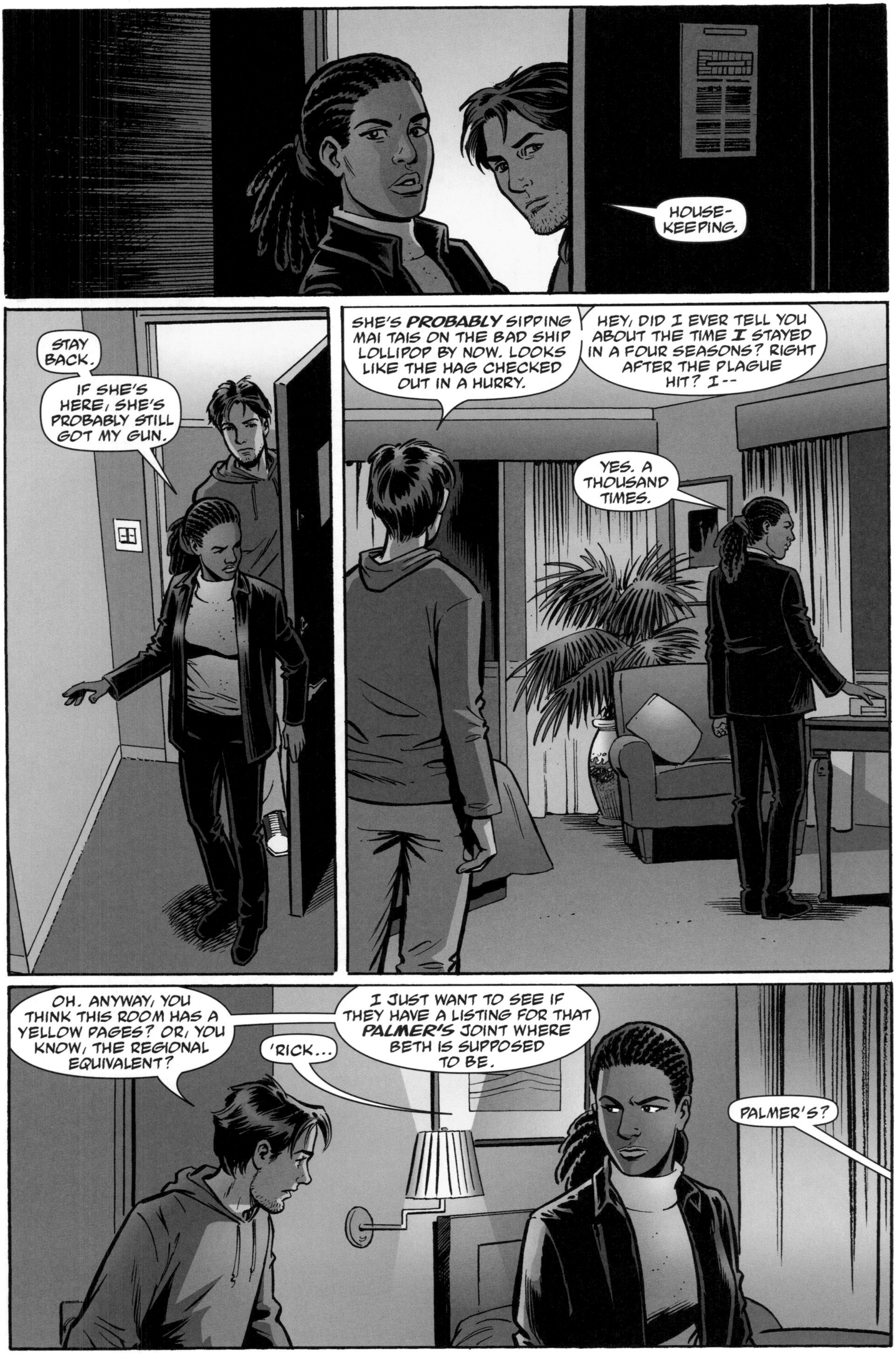
HOUSE-KEEPING.
STAY BACK.
IF SHE'S HERE, SHE'S PROBABLY STILL GOT MY GUN.
SHE'S PROBABLY SIPPING MAI TAIS ON THE BAD SHIP LOLLIPOP BY NOW. LOOKS LIKE THE HAG CHECKED OUT IN A HURRY.
HEY, DID I EVER TELL YOU ABOUT THE TIME I STAYED IN A FOUR SEASONS? RIGHT AFTER THE PLAGUE HIT? I--
YES. A THOUSAND TIMES.
OH. ANYWAY, YOU THINK THIS ROOM HAS A YELLOW PAGES? OR, YOU KNOW, THE REGIONAL EQUIVALENT?
I JUST WANT TO SEE IF THEY HAVE A LISTING FOR THAT PALMER'S JOINT WHERE BETH IS SUPPOSED TO BE.
'RICK...
PALMER'S?

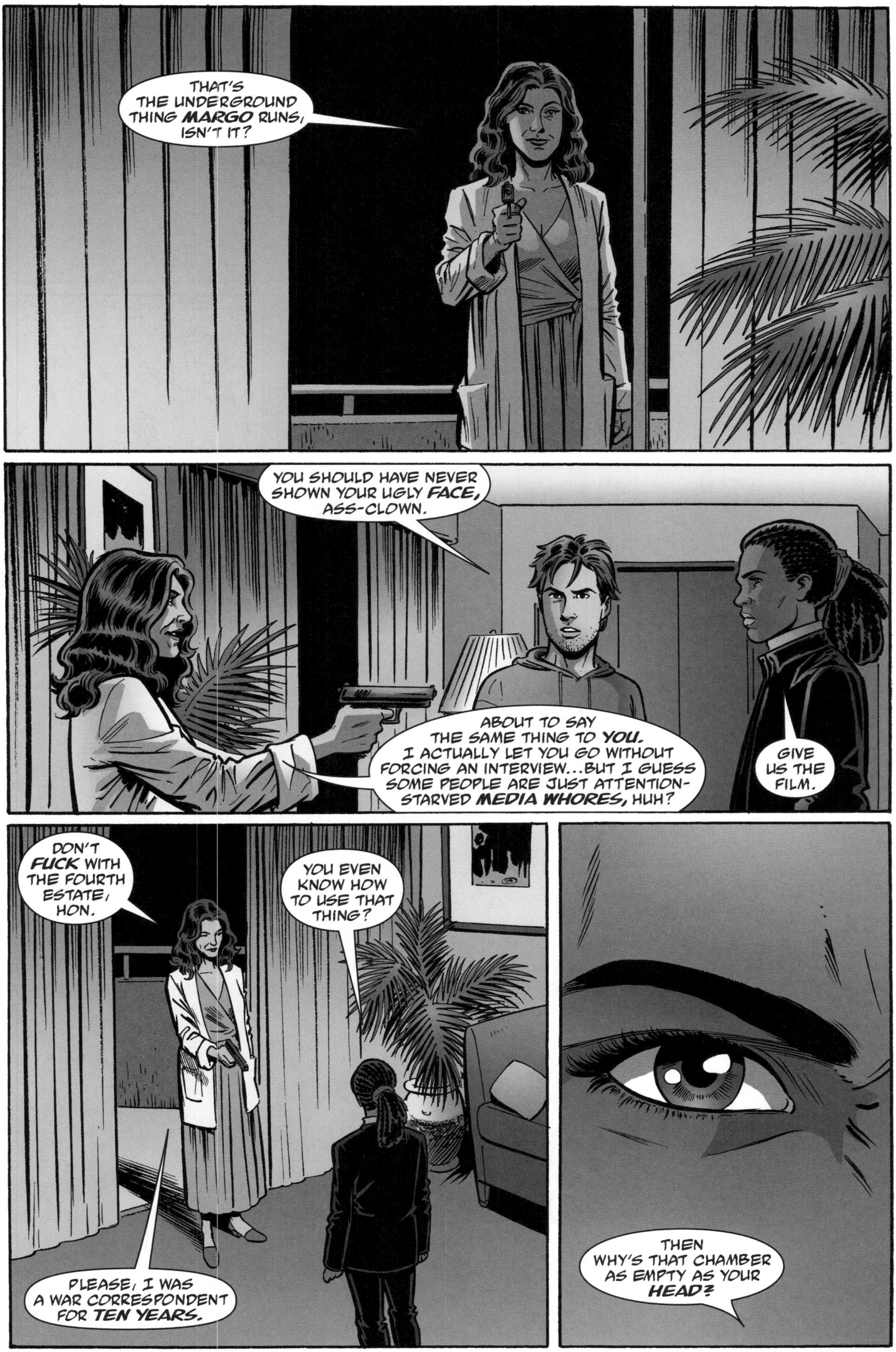
THAT'S THE UNDERGROUND THING MARGO RUNS, ISN'T IT?
YOU SHOULD HAVE NEVER SHOWN YOUR UGLY FACE, ASS-CLOWN.
ABOUT TO SAY THE SAME THING TO YOU. I ACTUALLY LET YOU GO WITHOUT FORCING AN INTERVIEW...BUT I GUESS SOME PEOPLE ARE JUST ATTENTION-STARVED MEDIA WHORES, HUH?
GIVE US THE FILM.
DON'T FUCK WITH THE FOURTH ESTATE, HON.
YOU EVEN KNOW HOW TO USE THAT THING?
PLEASE, I WAS A WAR CORRESPONDENT FOR TEN YEARS.
THEN WHY'S THAT CHAMBER AS EMPTY AS YOUR HEAD?

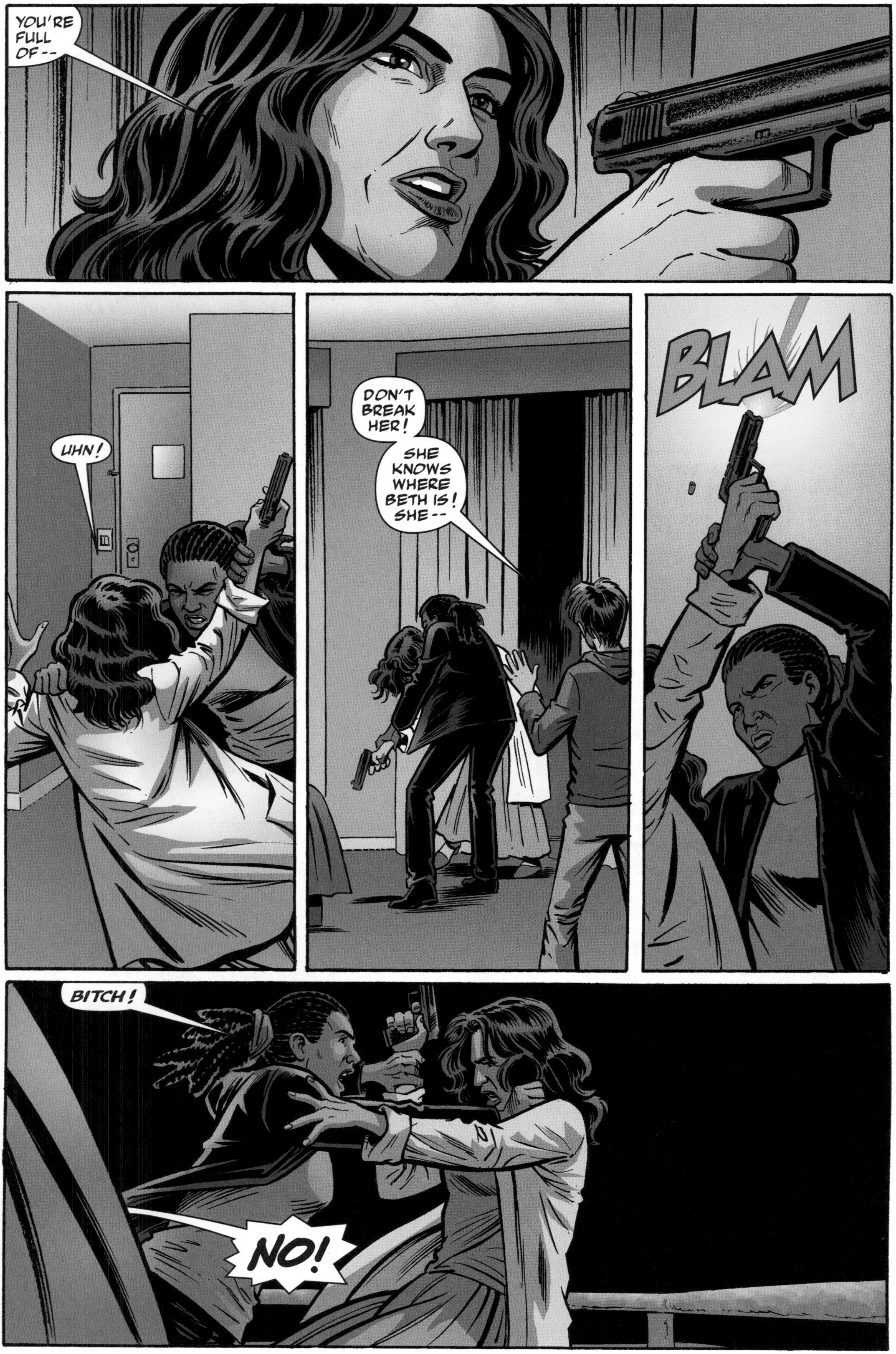
YOU'RE FULL OF --
UHN!
DON'T BREAK HER!
SHE KNOWS WHERE BETH IS! SHE --
BLAM
BITCH!
NO!

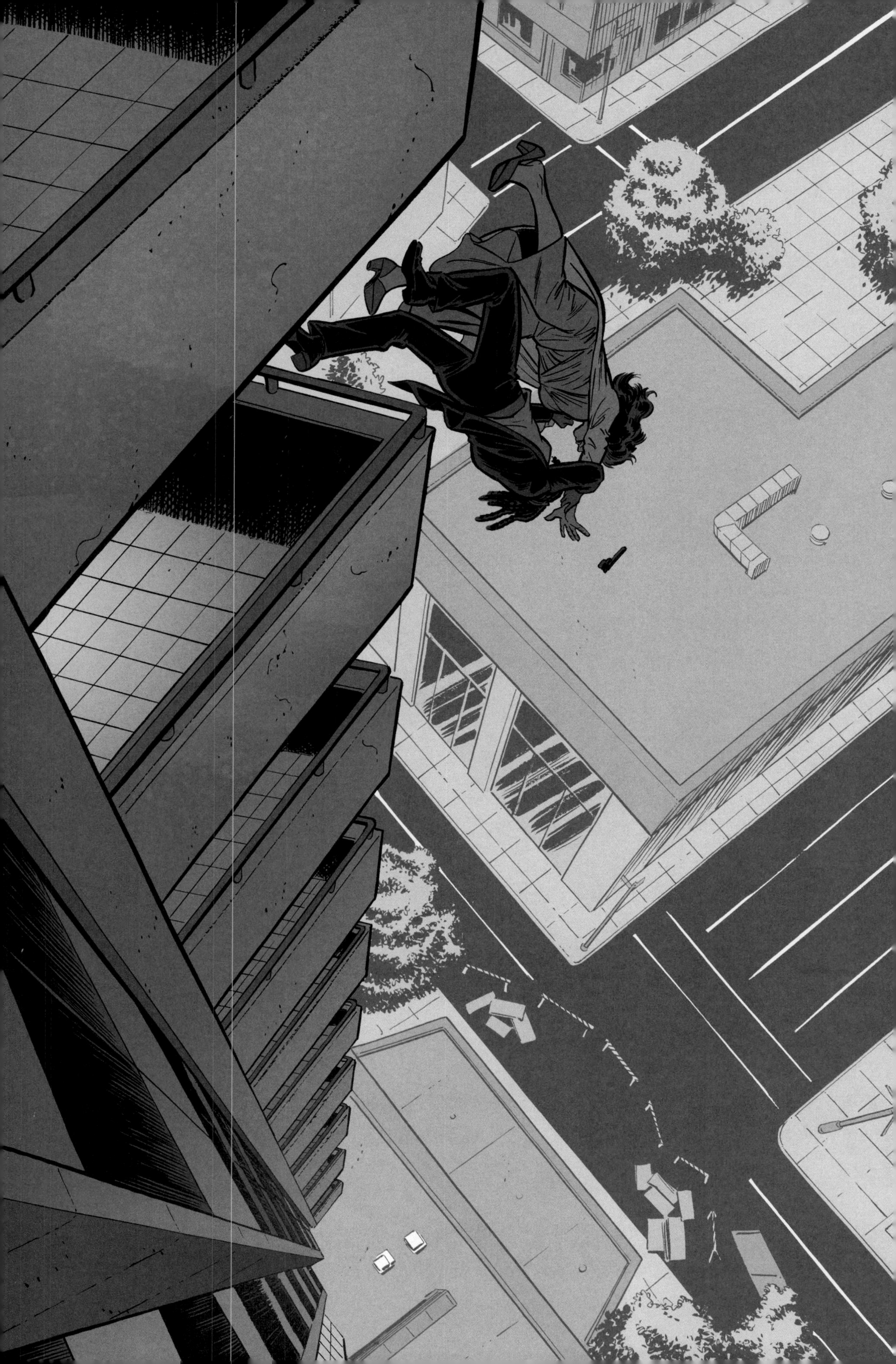

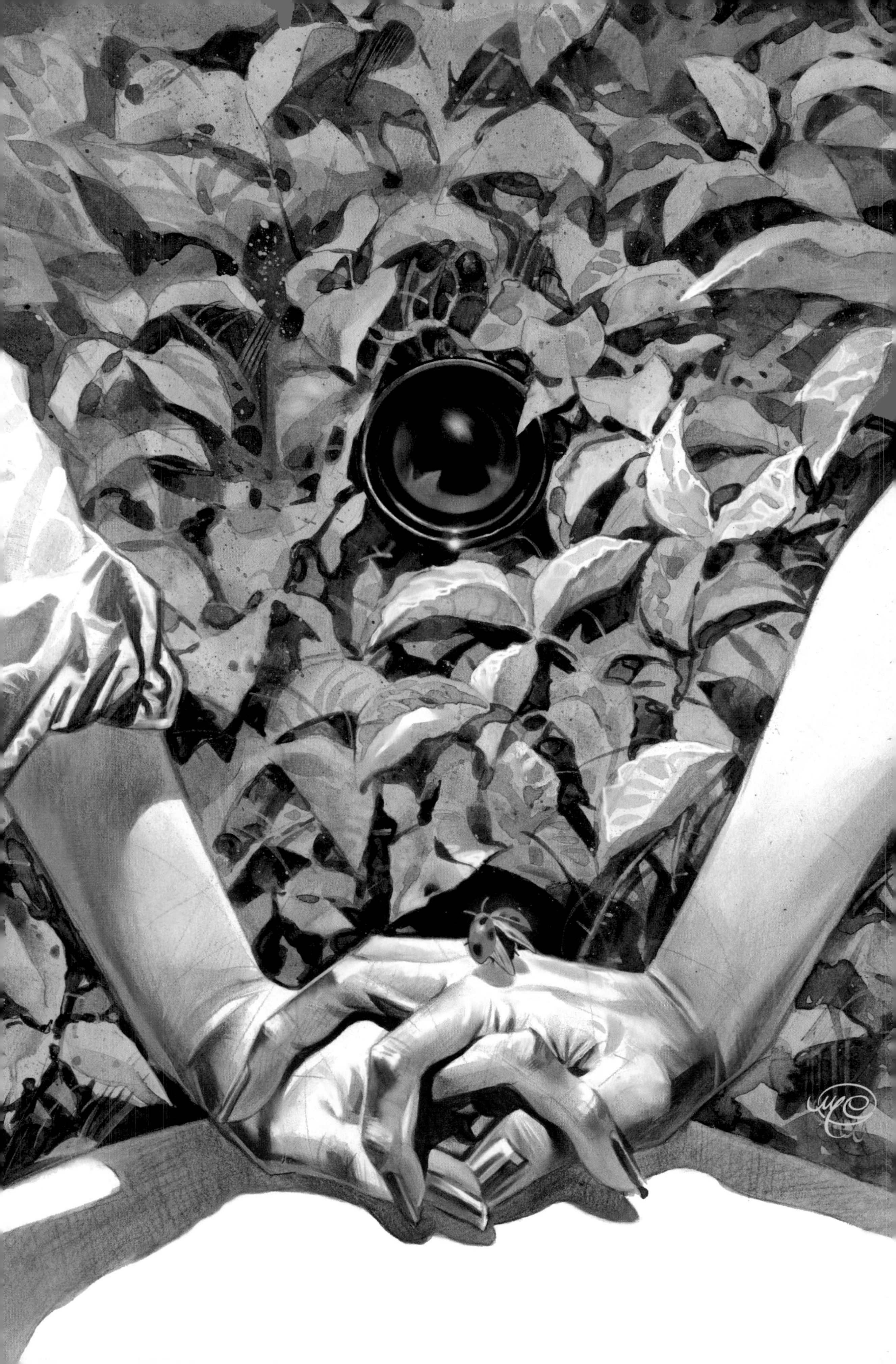

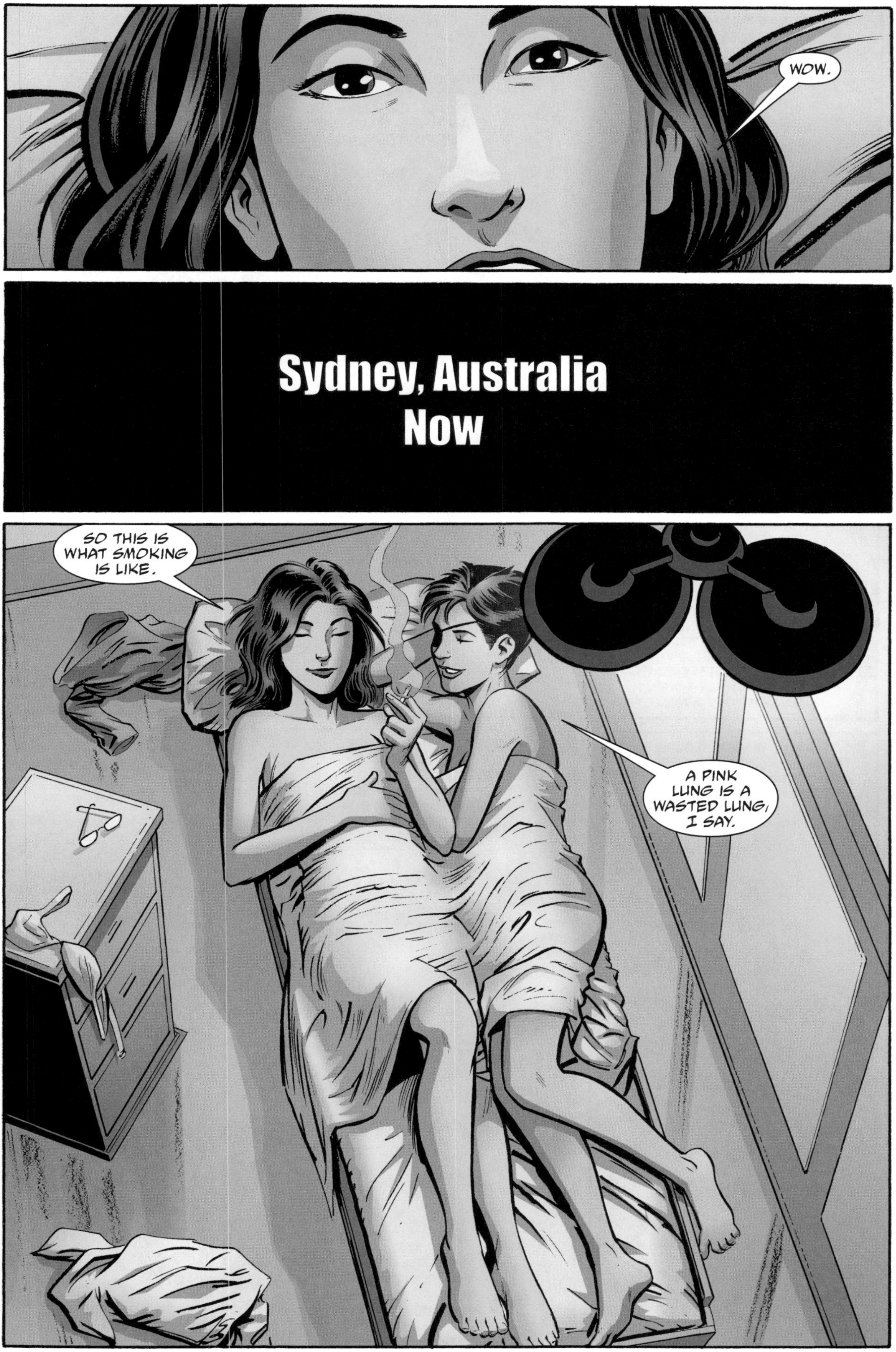
WOW.
Sydney, Australia
Now
SO THIS IS WHAT SMOKING IS LIKE.
A PINK LUNG IS A WASTED LUNG, I SAY.

WAS THAT ALL RIGHT, DOCTOR?

ROSE, ANYONE WHO FINDS MY G-SPOT ON THE FIRST TRY IS ALLOWED TO CALL ME *ALLISON.* AND YES, THAT WAS DEFINITELY "ALL RIGHT."

I'M JUST TRYING TO FIGURE OUT HOW A LIFELONG PACIFIST KEEPS ENDING UP IN BED WITH TRAINED *KILLERS.*

I'M NOT A KILLER, ALLISON. NOT NORMALLY, ANYHOW. SPIES ARE SUPPOSED TO COLLECT INTEL *WITHOUT* BEING NOTICED. BLOODSHED USUALLY GETS IN THE WAY OF THAT.

BUT YOU KNOW HOW TO DEFEND YOUR-SELF? IF YOU HAVE TO?

MY ESPIONAGE DAYS ARE DONE, MATE. IN CASE YOU'VE FORGOTTEN, BELLEVILLE SORTA *DECOMMISSIONED* ME AFTER THINGS WENT FUBAR ON THE WHALE.

I KNOW, BUT I WAS THINKING, WHEN MY FRIENDS AND I DISEMBARK IN JAPAN, MAYBE YOU *SHOULD* COME WITH US.

YOU'RE... YOU'RE SERIOUS?

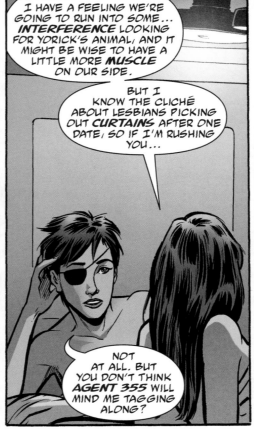

I HAVE A FEELING WE'RE GOING TO RUN INTO SOME... *INTERFERENCE* LOOKING FOR YORICK'S ANIMAL, AND IT MIGHT BE WISE TO HAVE A LITTLE MORE *MUSCLE* ON OUR SIDE.

BUT I KNOW THE CLICHÉ ABOUT LESBIANS PICKING OUT *CURTAINS* AFTER ONE DATE, SO IF I'M RUSHING YOU...

NOT AT ALL. BUT YOU DON'T THINK *AGENT 355* WILL MIND ME TAGGING ALONG?

I'M SURE SHE'D APPRECIATE THE HELP.

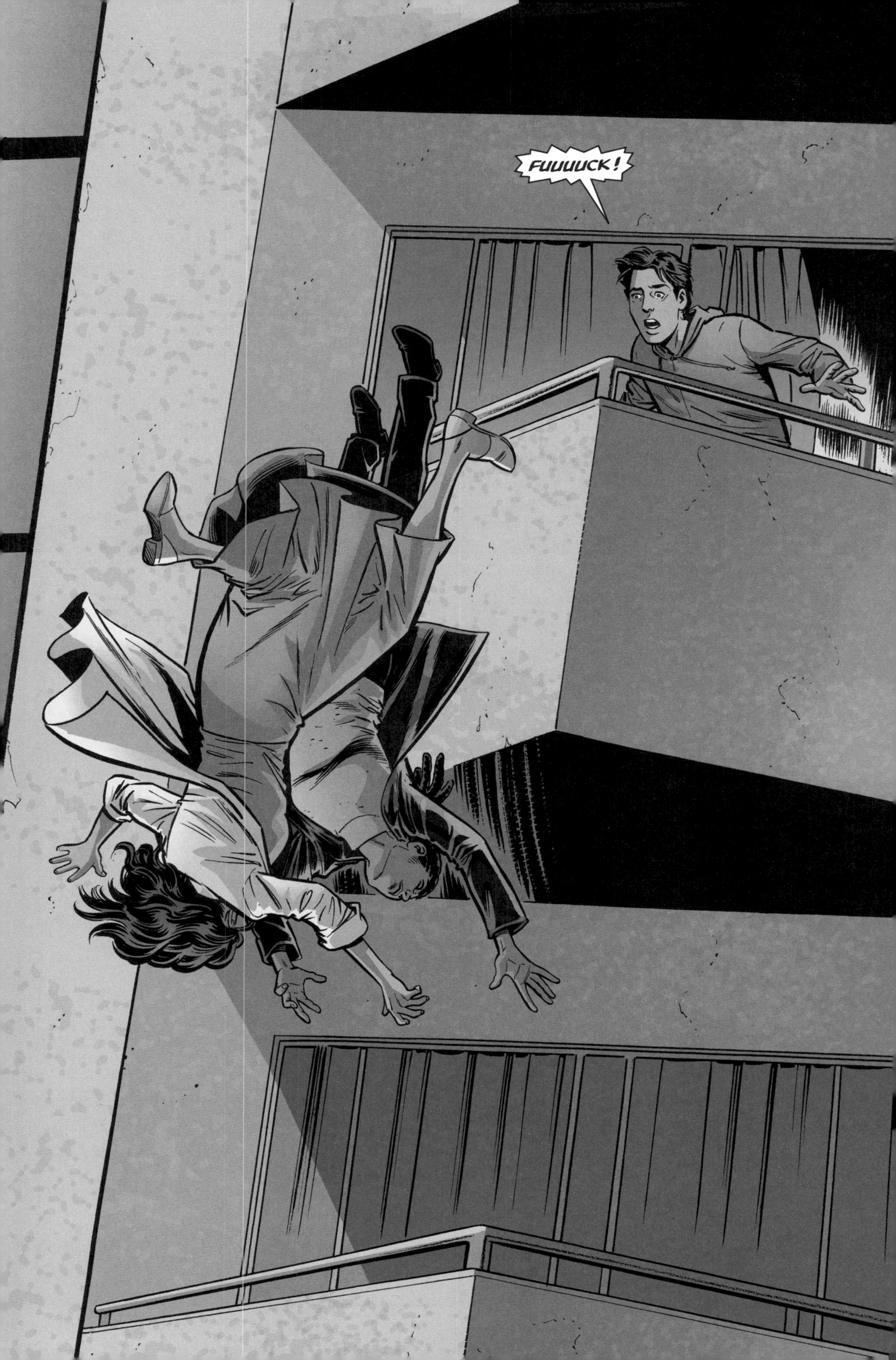
FUUUUCK!

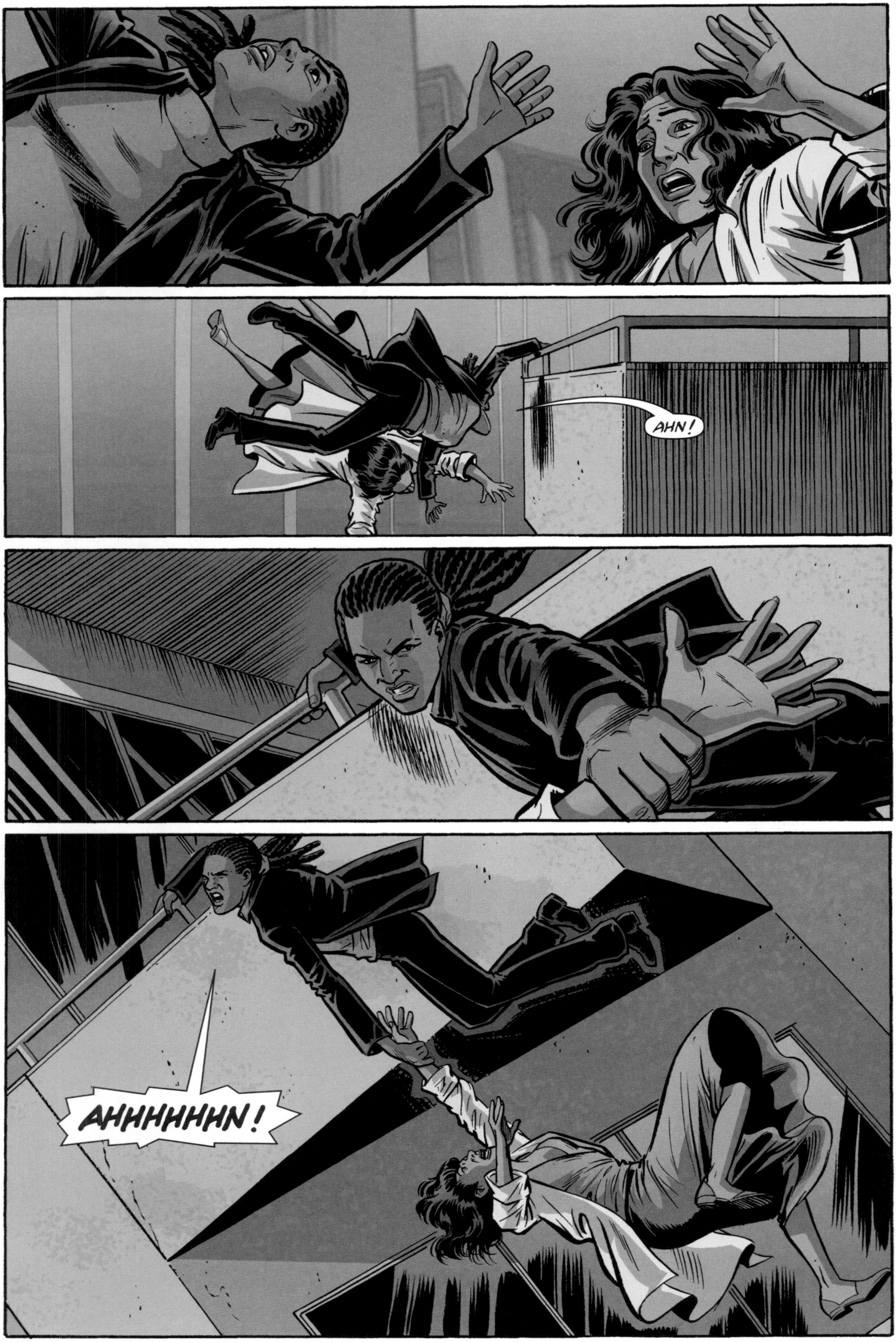
AHN!
AHHHHHHN!

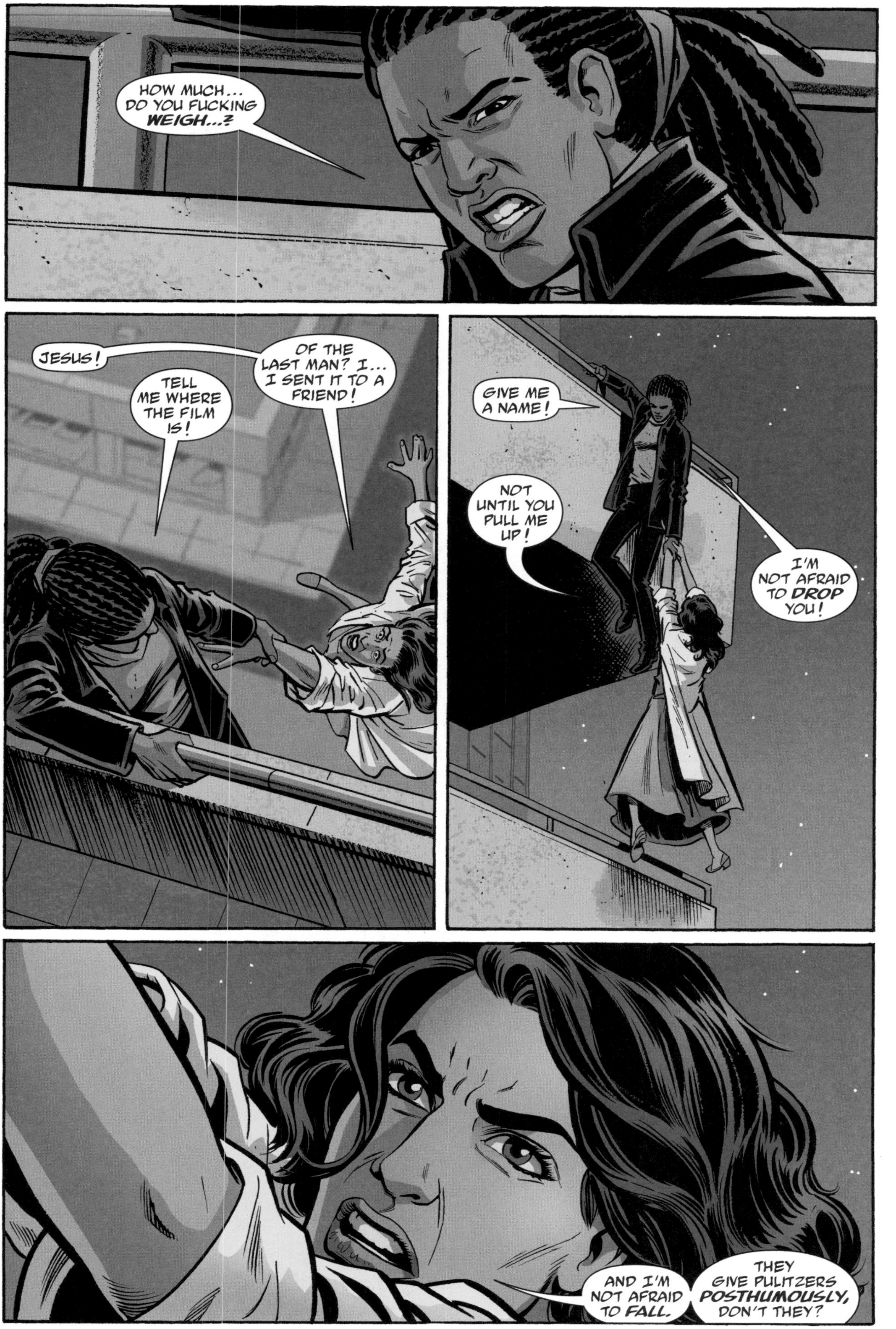
HOW MUCH... DO YOU FUCKING WEIGH...?
JESUS!
TELL ME WHERE THE FILM IS!
OF THE LAST MAN? I... I SENT IT TO A FRIEND!
GIVE ME A NAME!
NOT UNTIL YOU PULL ME UP!
I'M NOT AFRAID TO DROP YOU!
AND I'M NOT AFRAID TO FALL.
THEY GIVE PULITZERS POSTHUMOUSLY, DON'T THEY?

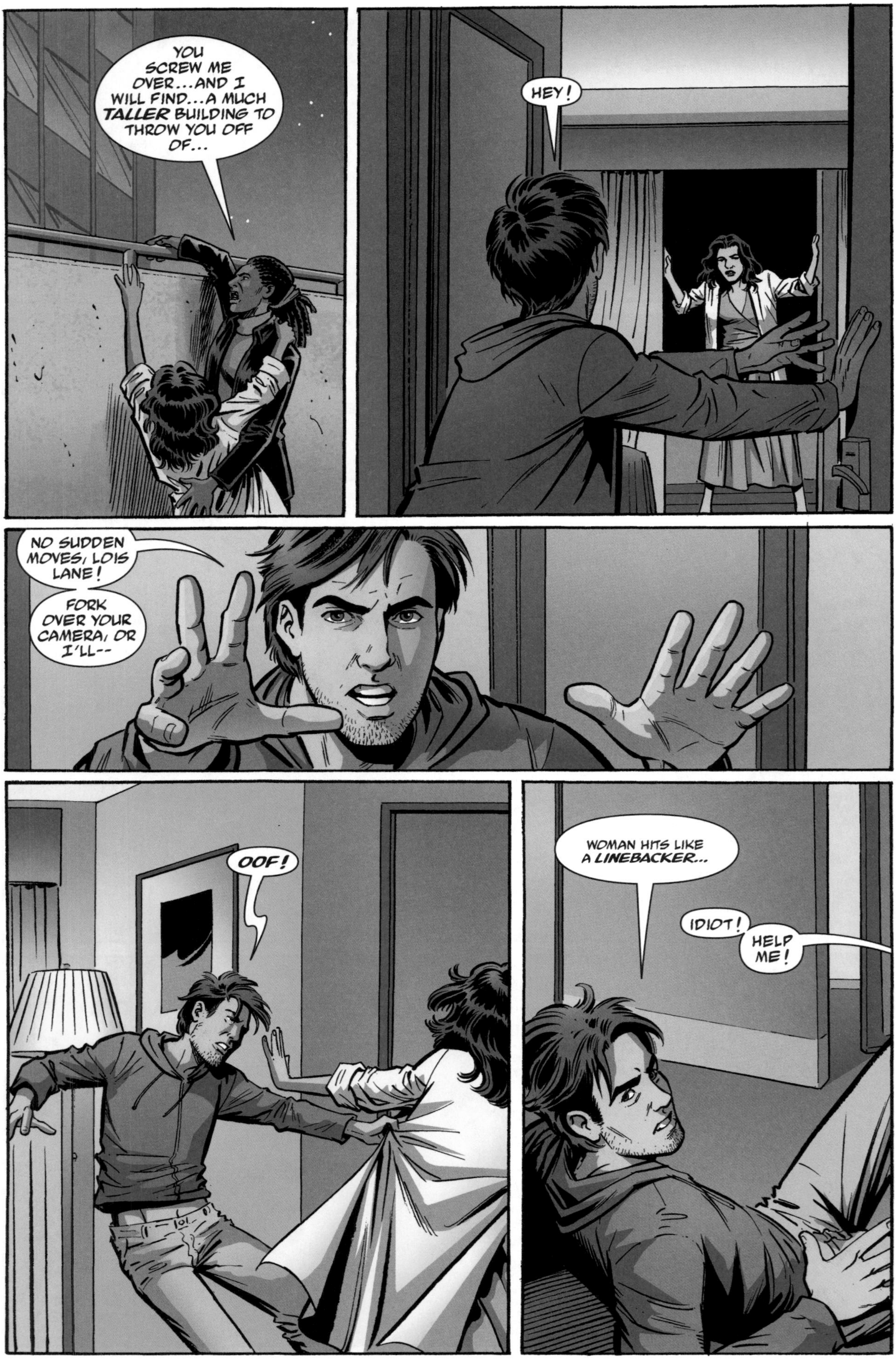
YOU SCREW ME OVER...AND I WILL FIND...A MUCH *TALLER* BUILDING TO THROW YOU OFF OF...
HEY!
NO SUDDEN MOVES, LOIS LANE!
FORK OVER YOUR CAMERA, OR I'LL--
OOF!
WOMAN HITS LIKE A *LINEBACKER*...
IDIOT!
HELP ME!

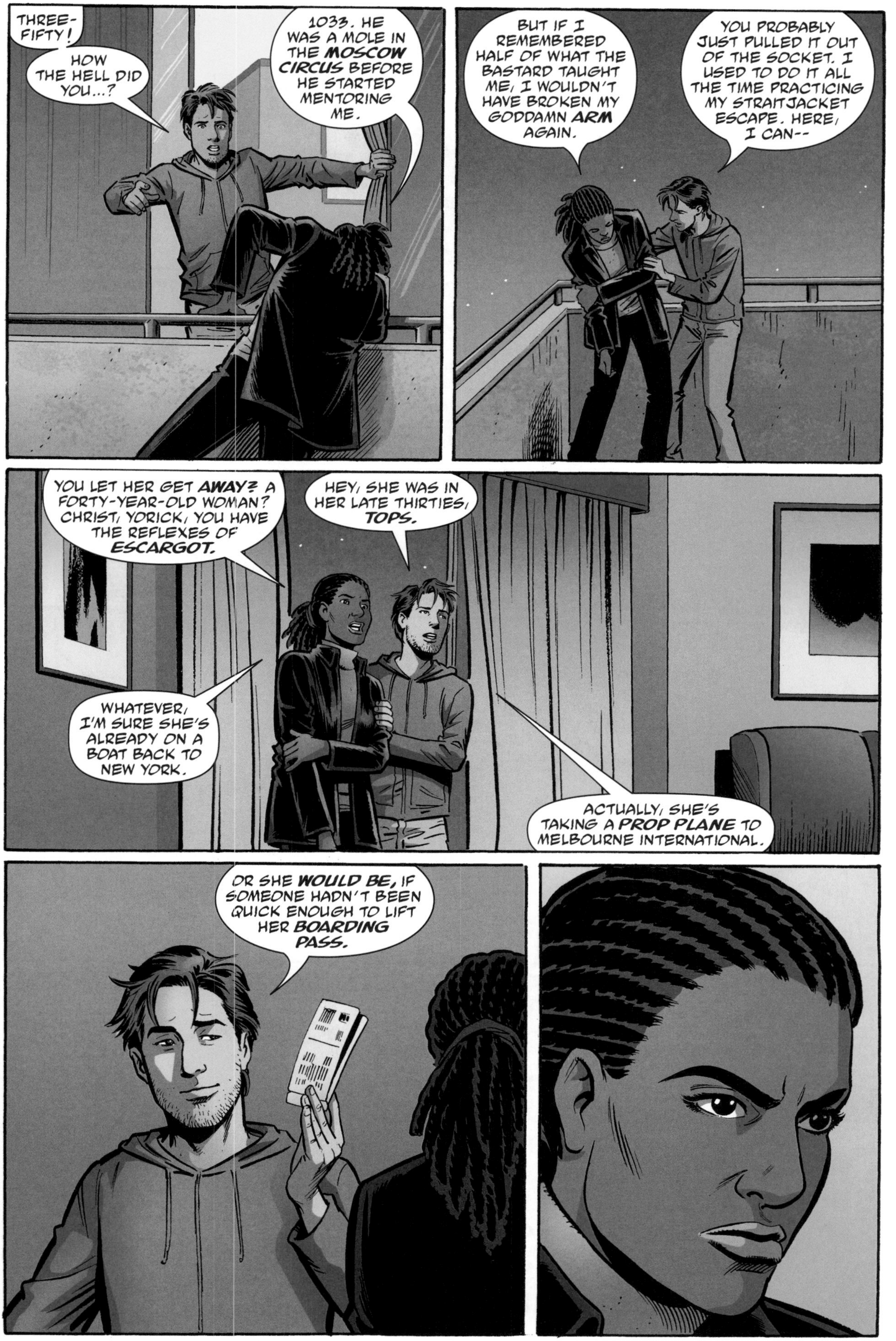
THREE-FIFTY!
HOW THE HELL DID YOU...?
1033. HE WAS A MOLE IN THE MOSCOW CIRCUS BEFORE HE STARTED MENTORING ME.
BUT IF I REMEMBERED HALF OF WHAT THE BASTARD TAUGHT ME, I WOULDN'T HAVE BROKEN MY GODDAMN ARM AGAIN.
YOU PROBABLY JUST PULLED IT OUT OF THE SOCKET. I USED TO DO IT ALL THE TIME PRACTICING MY STRAITJACKET ESCAPE. HERE, I CAN--
YOU LET HER GET AWAY? A FORTY-YEAR-OLD WOMAN? CHRIST, YORICK, YOU HAVE THE REFLEXES OF ESCARGOT.
HEY, SHE WAS IN HER LATE THIRTIES, TOPS.
WHATEVER, I'M SURE SHE'S ALREADY ON A BOAT BACK TO NEW YORK.
ACTUALLY, SHE'S TAKING A PROP PLANE TO MELBOURNE INTERNATIONAL.
OR SHE WOULD BE, IF SOMEONE HADN'T BEEN QUICK ENOUGH TO LIFT HER BOARDING PASS.

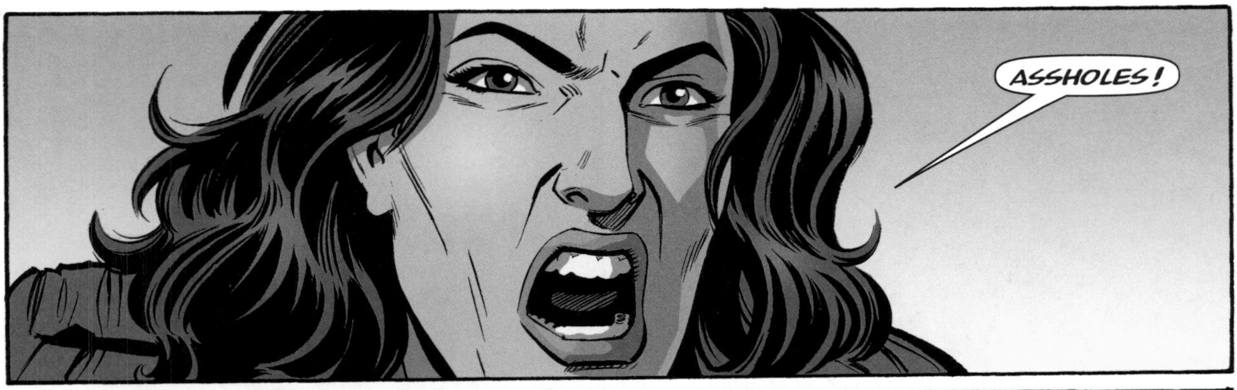
ASSHOLES!

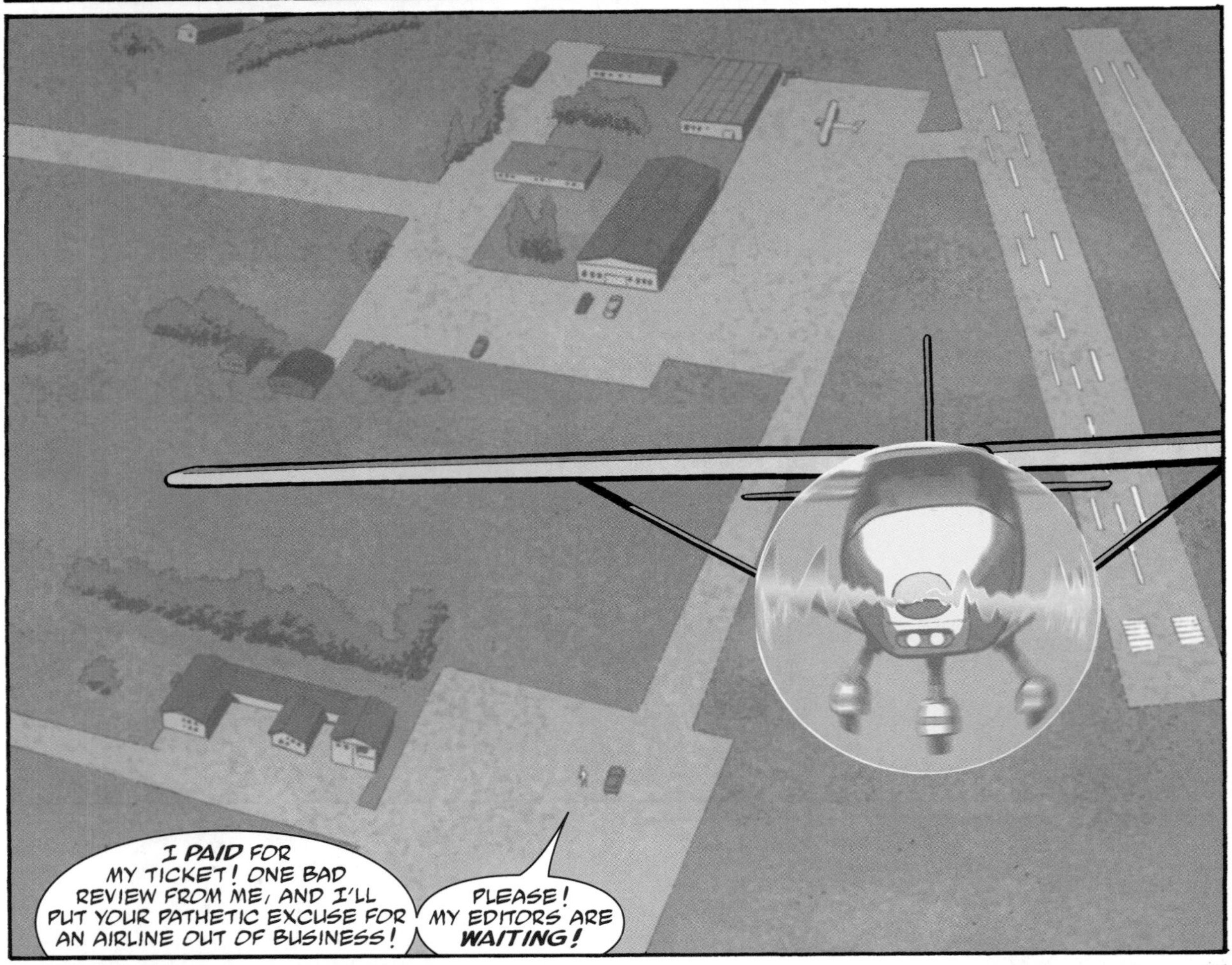
I PAID FOR MY TICKET! ONE BAD REVIEW FROM ME, AND I'LL PUT YOUR PATHETIC EXCUSE FOR AN AIRLINE OUT OF BUSINESS!
PLEASE! MY EDITORS ARE WAITING!

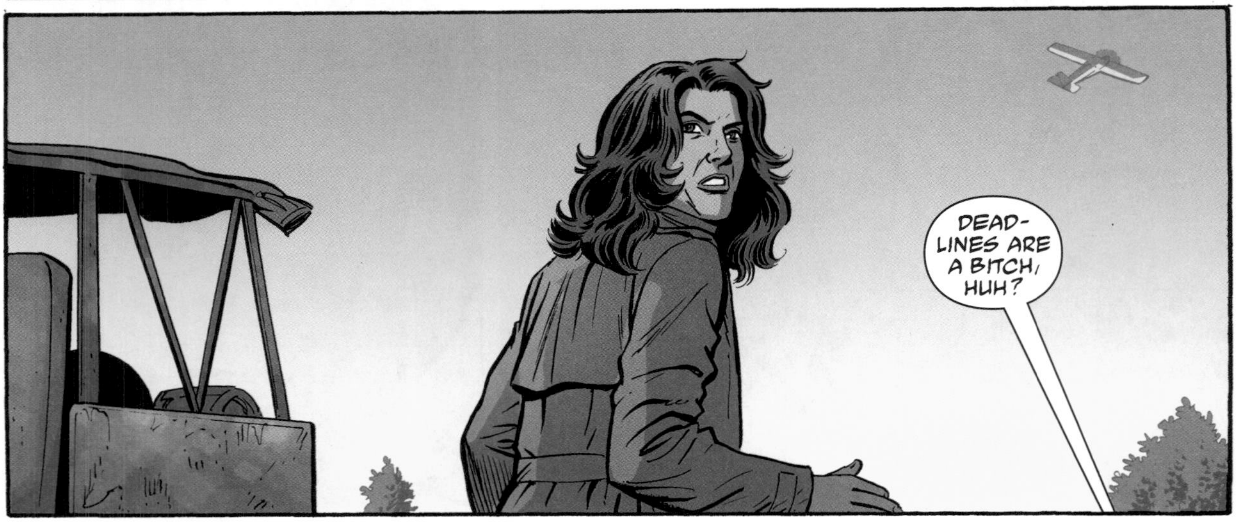
DEAD-LINES ARE A BITCH, HUH?

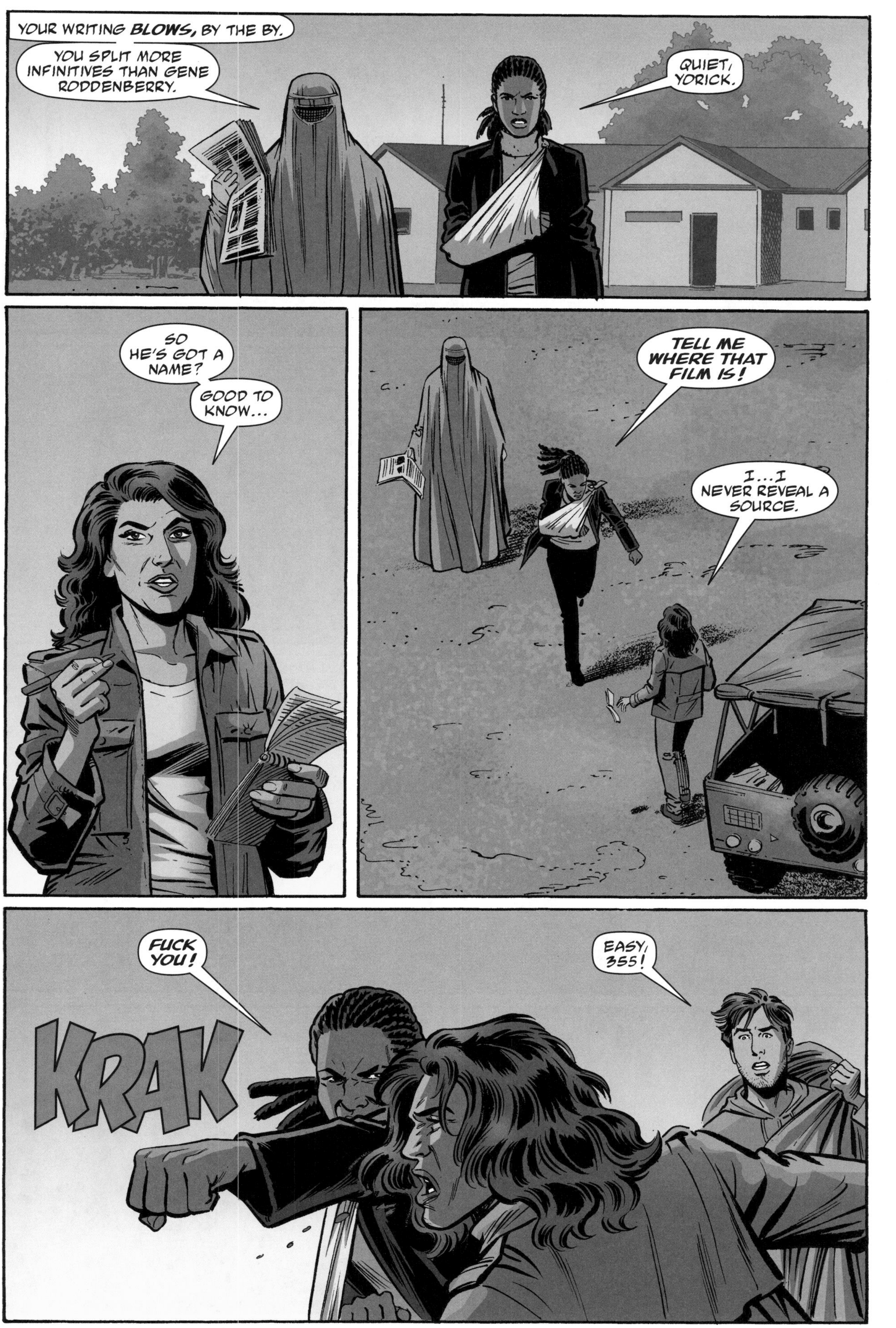
YOUR WRITING BLOWS, BY THE BY.
YOU SPLIT MORE INFINITIVES THAN GENE RODDENBERRY.
QUIET, YORICK.
SO HE'S GOT A NAME?
GOOD TO KNOW...
TELL ME WHERE THAT FILM IS!
I...I NEVER REVEAL A SOURCE.
KRAK
FUCK YOU!
EASY, 355!

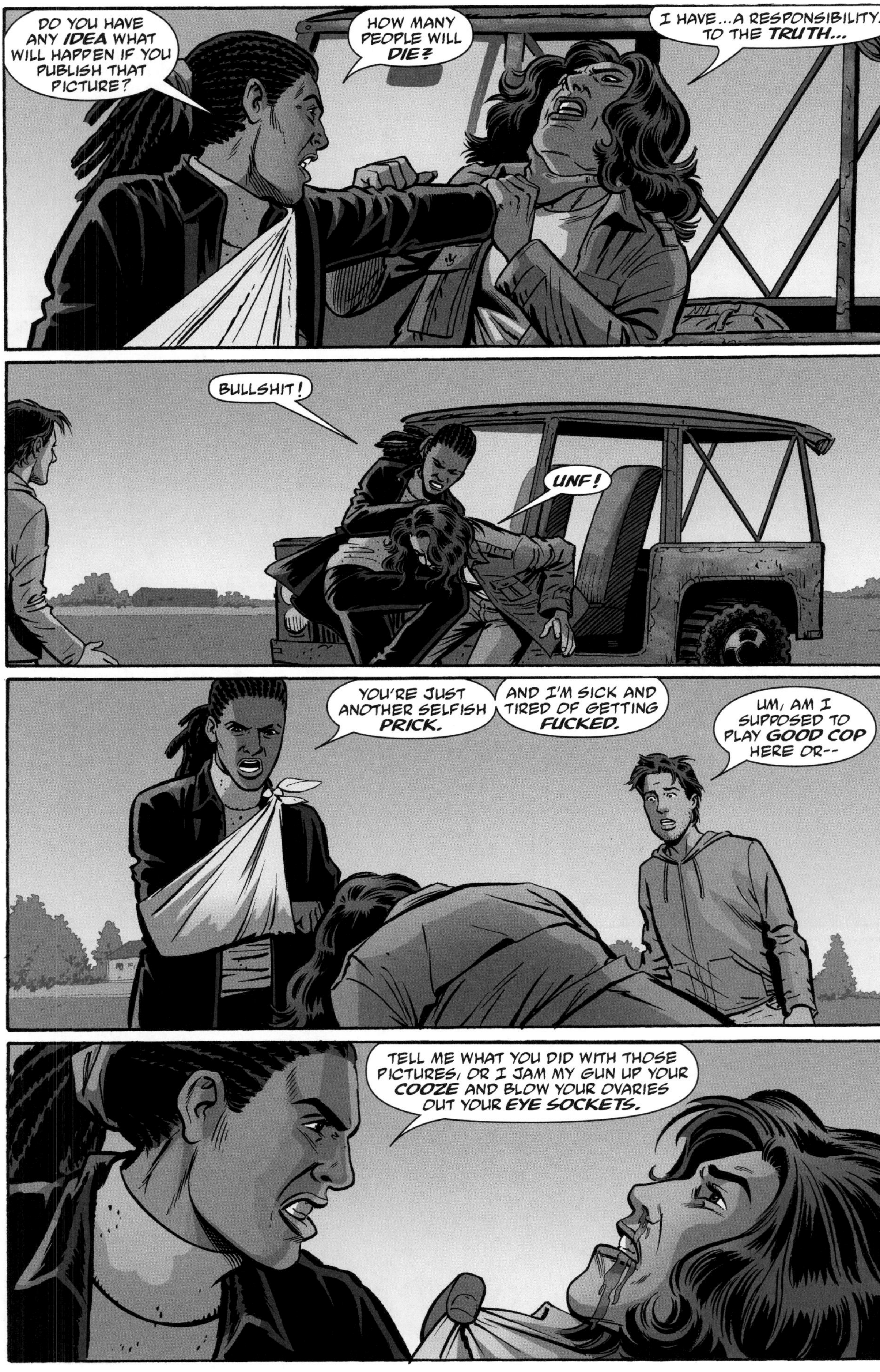
DO YOU HAVE ANY IDEA WHAT WILL HAPPEN IF YOU PUBLISH THAT PICTURE?
HOW MANY PEOPLE WILL DIE?
I HAVE...A RESPONSIBILITY... TO THE TRUTH...
BULLSHIT!
UNF!
YOU'RE JUST ANOTHER SELFISH PRICK.
AND I'M SICK AND TIRED OF GETTING FUCKED.
UM, AM I SUPPOSED TO PLAY GOOD COP HERE OR--
TELL ME WHAT YOU DID WITH THOSE PICTURES, OR I JAM MY GUN UP YOUR COOZE AND BLOW YOUR OVARIES OUT YOUR EYE SOCKETS.

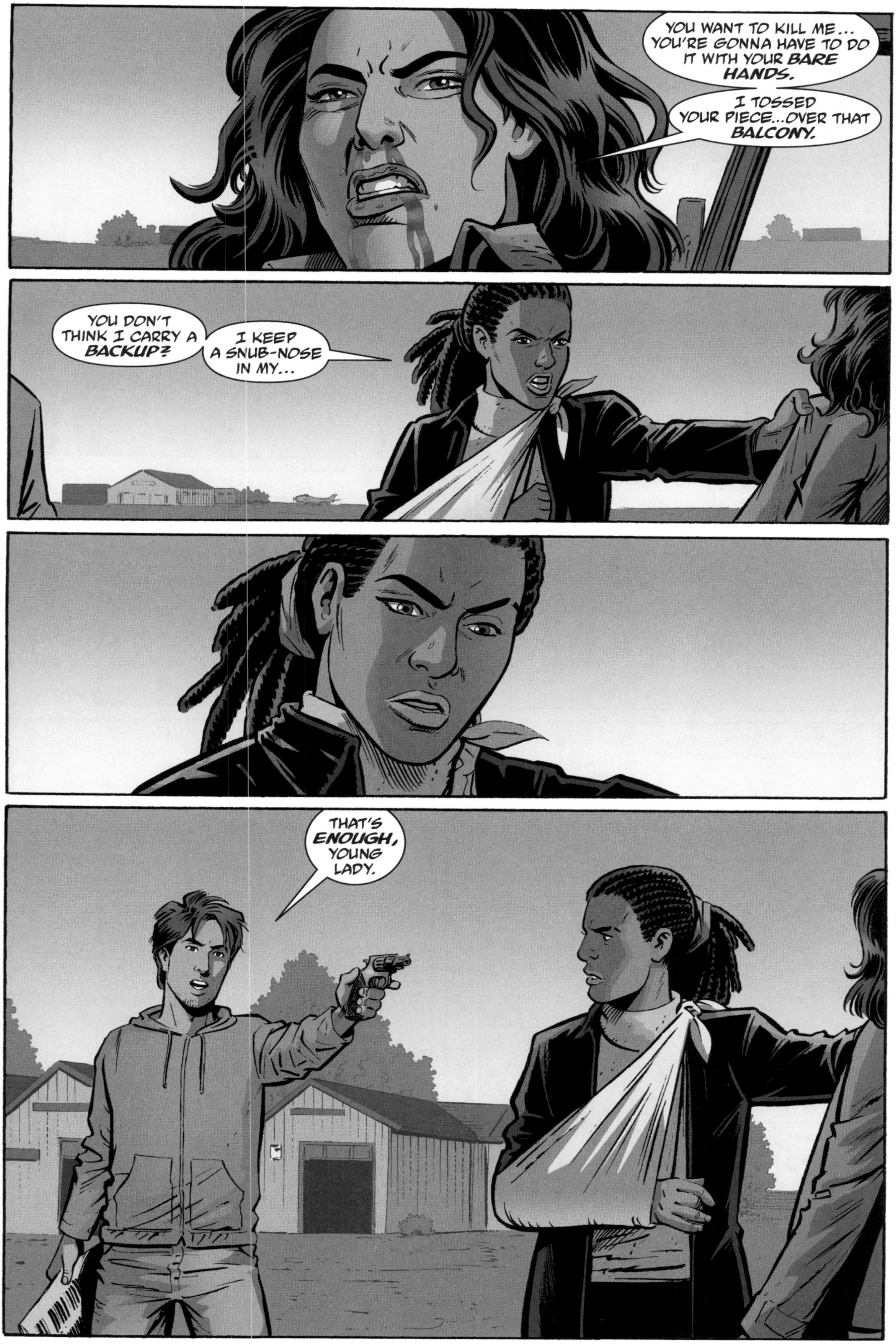
YOU WANT TO KILL ME... YOU'RE GONNA HAVE TO DO IT WITH YOUR BARE HANDS.
I TOSSED YOUR PIECE...OVER THAT BALCONY.
YOU DON'T THINK I CARRY A BACKUP?
I KEEP A SNUB-NOSE IN MY...
THAT'S ENOUGH, YOUNG LADY.

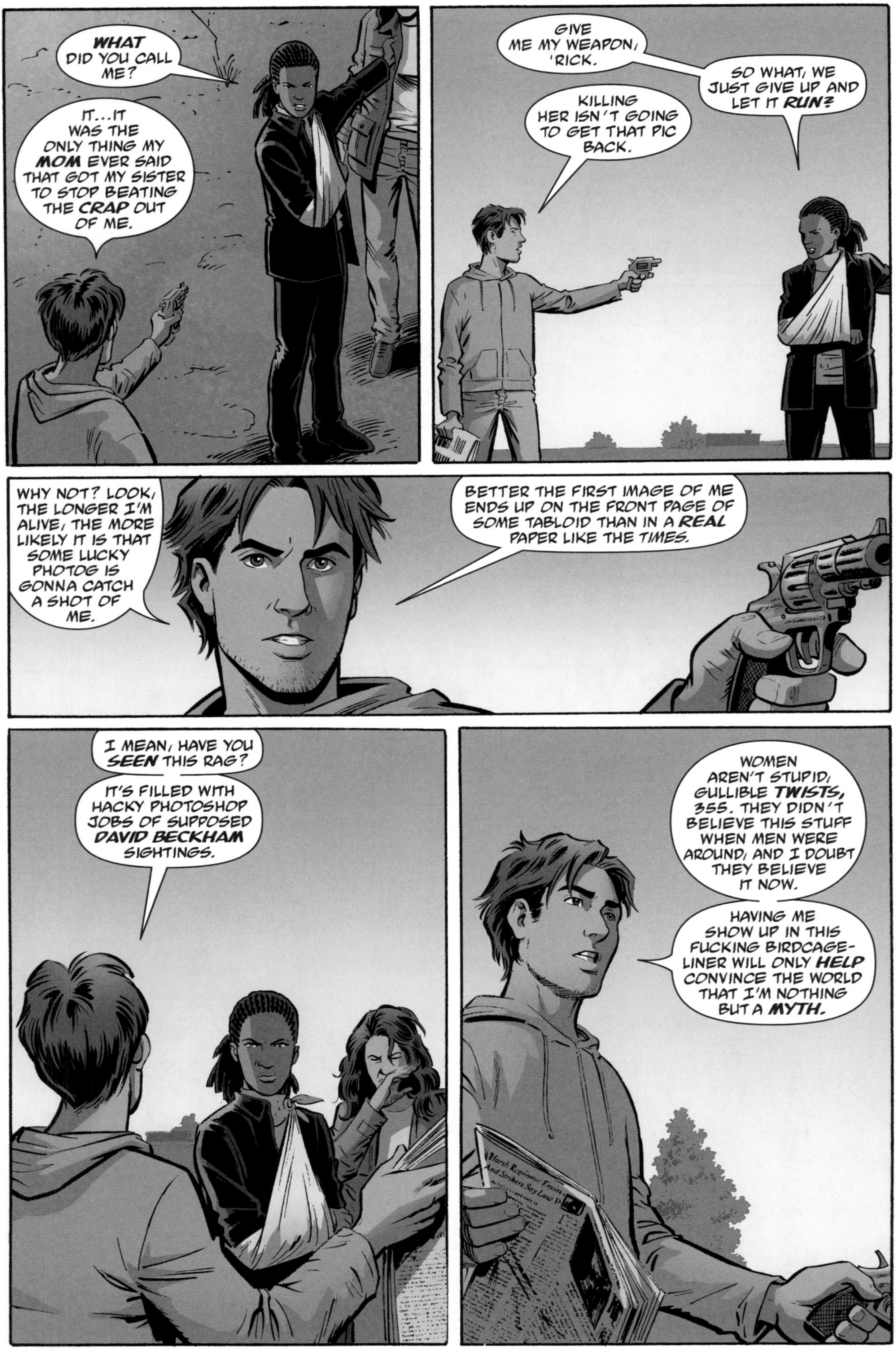
WHAT DID YOU CALL ME?
IT...IT WAS THE ONLY THING MY MOM EVER SAID THAT GOT MY SISTER TO STOP BEATING THE CRAP OUT OF ME.
GIVE ME MY WEAPON, 'RICK.
KILLING HER ISN'T GOING TO GET THAT PIC BACK.
SO WHAT, WE JUST GIVE UP AND LET IT RUN?
WHY NOT? LOOK, THE LONGER I'M ALIVE, THE MORE LIKELY IT IS THAT SOME LUCKY PHOTOG IS GONNA CATCH A SHOT OF ME.
BETTER THE FIRST IMAGE OF ME ENDS UP ON THE FRONT PAGE OF SOME TABLOID THAN IN A REAL PAPER LIKE THE TIMES.
I MEAN, HAVE YOU SEEN THIS RAG?
IT'S FILLED WITH HACKY PHOTOSHOP JOBS OF SUPPOSED DAVID BECKHAM SIGHTINGS.
WOMEN AREN'T STUPID, GULLIBLE TWISTS, 355. THEY DIDN'T BELIEVE THIS STUFF WHEN MEN WERE AROUND, AND I DOUBT THEY BELIEVE IT NOW.
HAVING ME SHOW UP IN THIS FUCKING BIRDCAGE-LINER WILL ONLY HELP CONVINCE THE WORLD THAT I'M NOTHING BUT A MYTH.

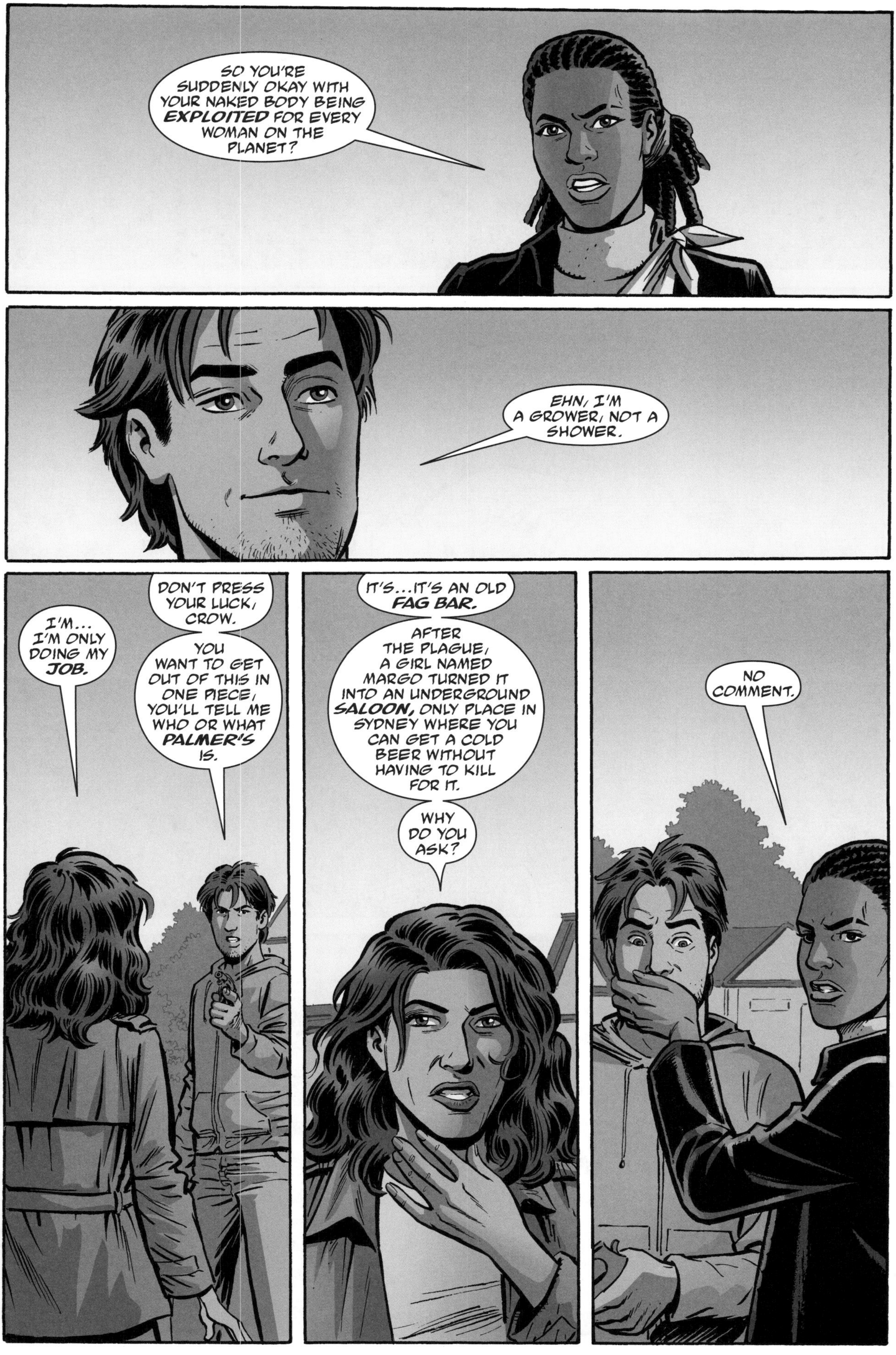
SO YOU'RE SUDDENLY OKAY WITH YOUR NAKED BODY BEING EXPLOITED FOR EVERY WOMAN ON THE PLANET?
EHN, I'M A GROWER, NOT A SHOWER.
I'M... I'M ONLY DOING MY JOB.
DON'T PRESS YOUR LUCK, CROW.
YOU WANT TO GET OUT OF THIS IN ONE PIECE, YOU'LL TELL ME WHO OR WHAT PALMER'S IS.
IT'S...IT'S AN OLD FAG BAR.
AFTER THE PLAGUE, A GIRL NAMED MARGO TURNED IT INTO AN UNDERGROUND SALOON, ONLY PLACE IN SYDNEY WHERE YOU CAN GET A COLD BEER WITHOUT HAVING TO KILL FOR IT.
WHY DO YOU ASK?
NO COMMENT.

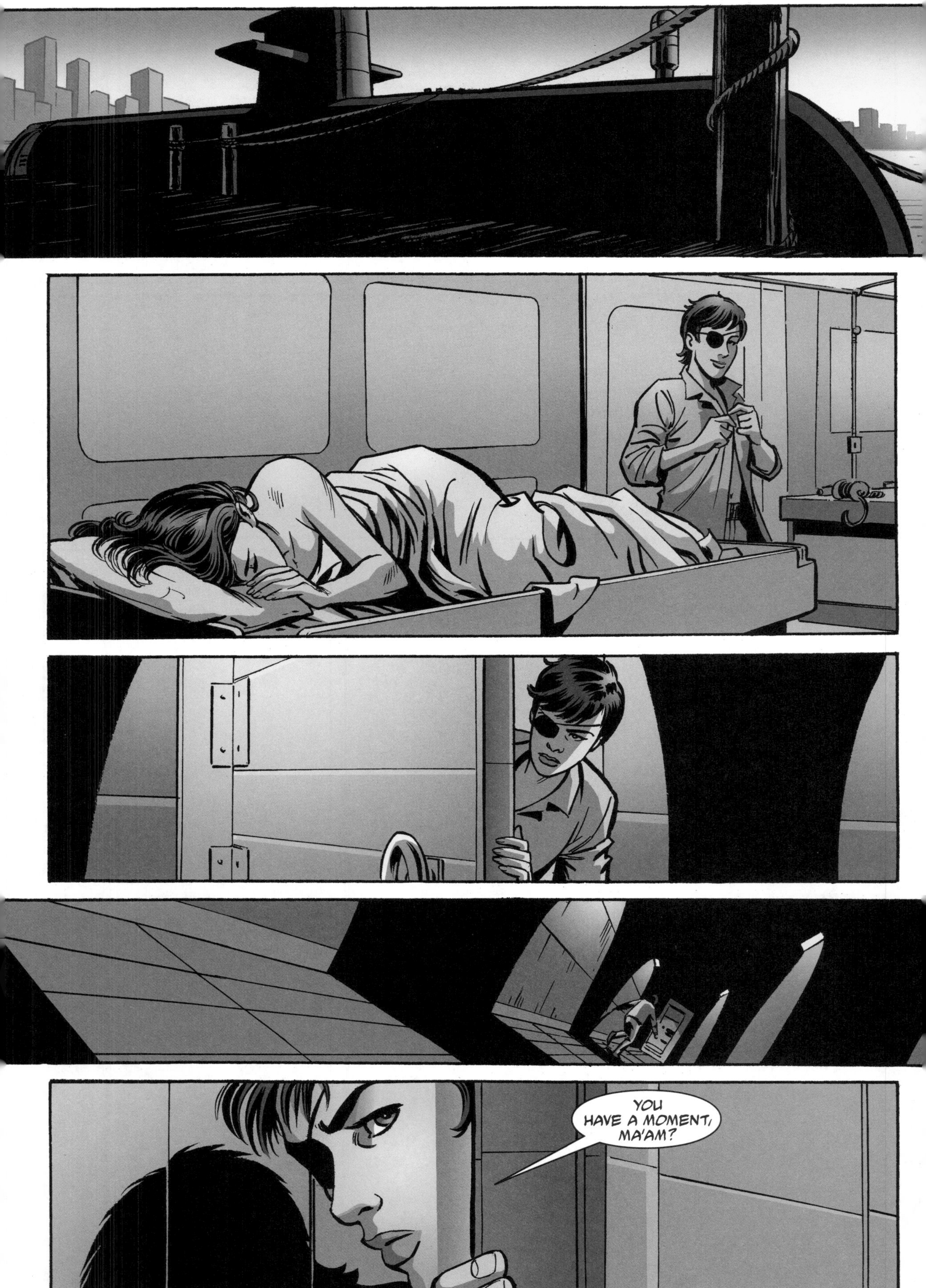
YOU HAVE A MOMENT, MA'AM?

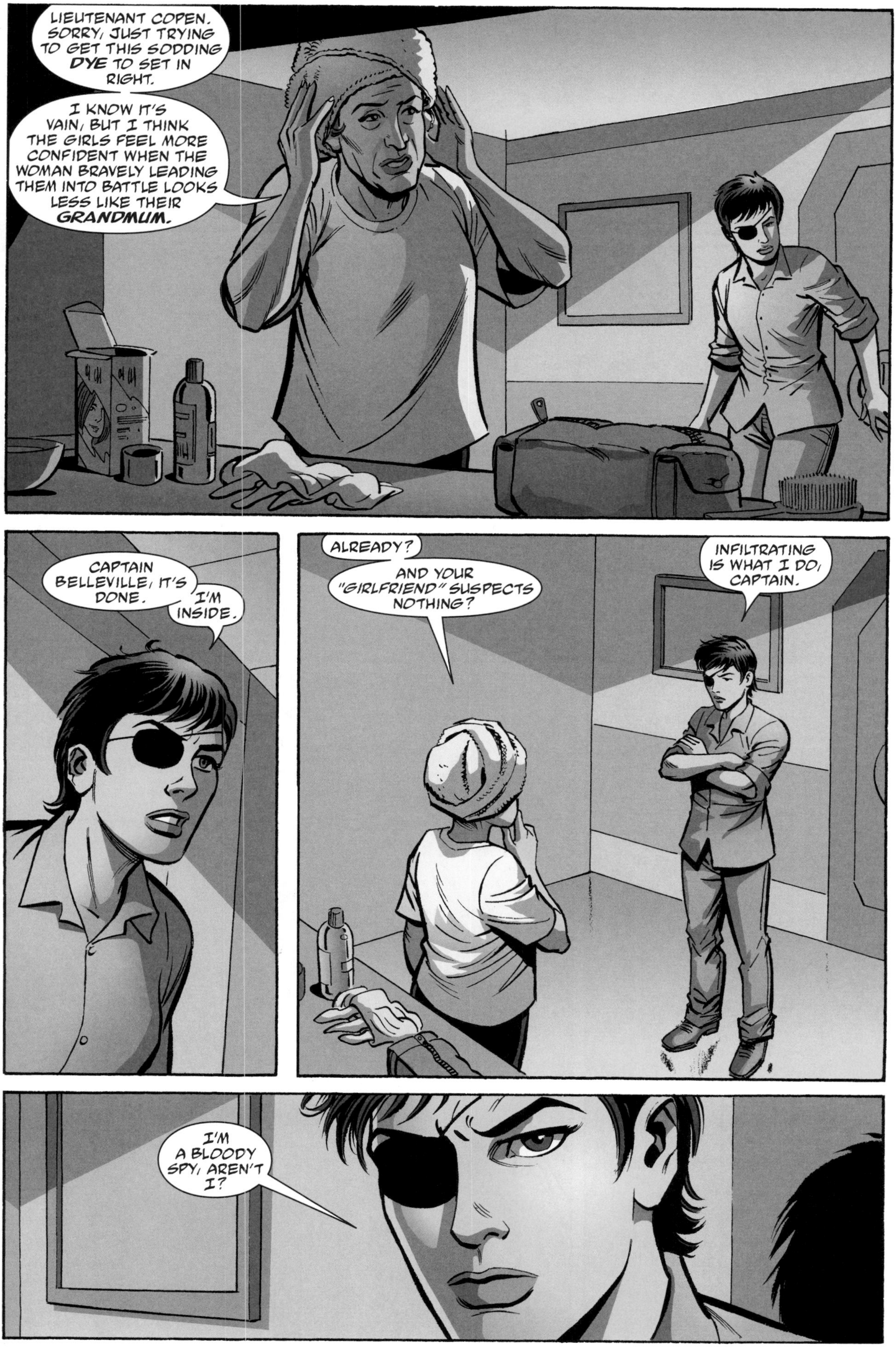
LIEUTENANT COPEN. SORRY, JUST TRYING TO GET THIS SODDING DYE TO SET IN RIGHT.
I KNOW IT'S VAIN, BUT I THINK THE GIRLS FEEL MORE CONFIDENT WHEN THE WOMAN BRAVELY LEADING THEM INTO BATTLE LOOKS LESS LIKE THEIR GRANDMUM.
CAPTAIN BELLEVILLE, IT'S DONE.
I'M INSIDE.
ALREADY?
AND YOUR "GIRLFRIEND" SUSPECTS NOTHING?
INFILTRATING IS WHAT I DO, CAPTAIN.
I'M A BLOODY SPY, AREN'T I?

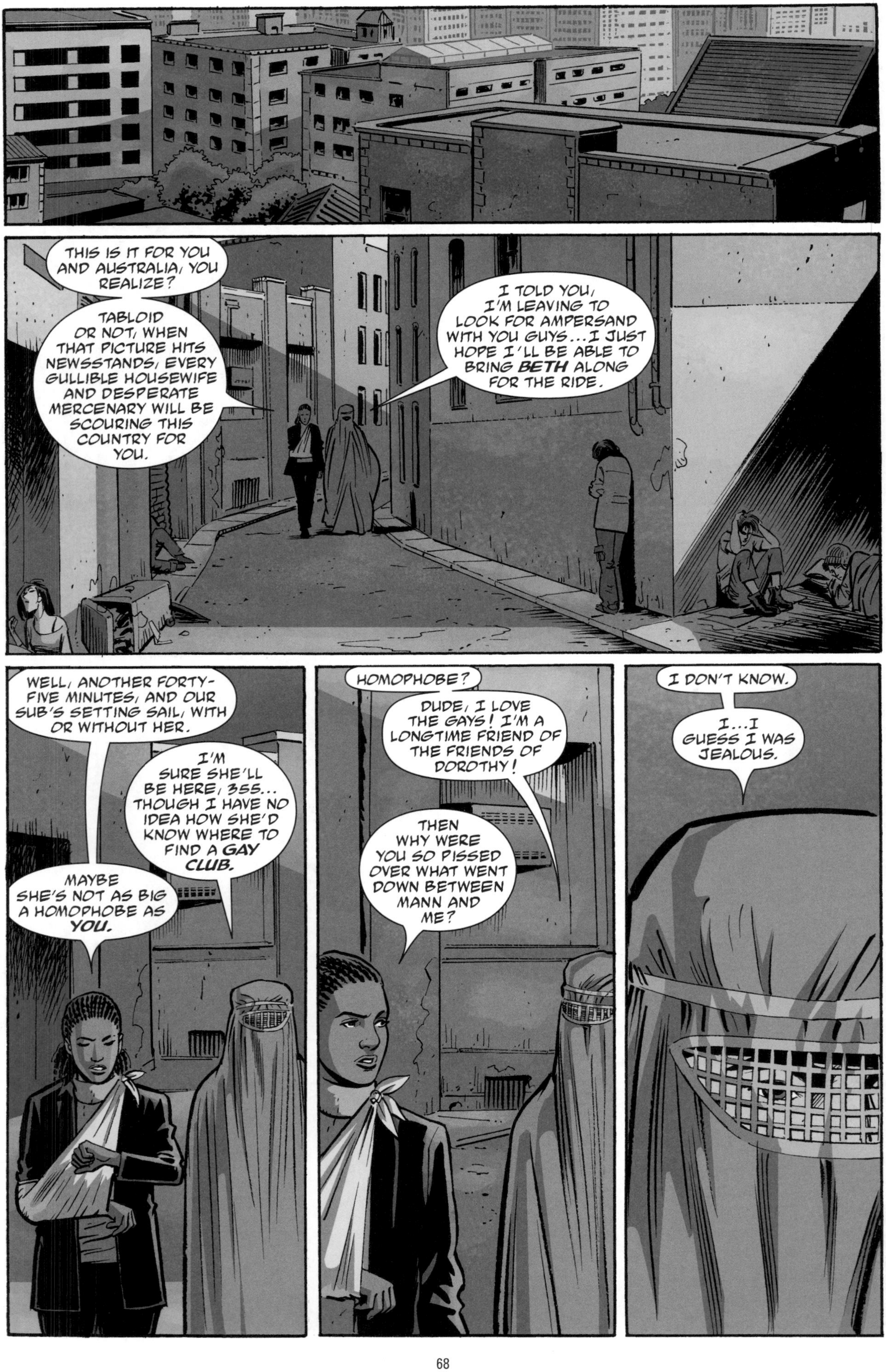
THIS IS IT FOR YOU AND AUSTRALIA, YOU REALIZE?
TABLOID OR NOT, WHEN THAT PICTURE HITS NEWSSTANDS, EVERY GULLIBLE HOUSEWIFE AND DESPERATE MERCENARY WILL BE SCOURING THIS COUNTRY FOR YOU.
I TOLD YOU, I'M LEAVING TO LOOK FOR AMPERSAND WITH YOU GUYS... I JUST HOPE I'LL BE ABLE TO BRING BETH ALONG FOR THE RIDE.
WELL, ANOTHER FORTY-FIVE MINUTES, AND OUR SUB'S SETTING SAIL, WITH OR WITHOUT HER.
I'M SURE SHE'LL BE HERE, 355... THOUGH I HAVE NO IDEA HOW SHE'D KNOW WHERE TO FIND A GAY CLUB.
MAYBE SHE'S NOT AS BIG A HOMOPHOBE AS YOU.
HOMOPHOBE?
DUDE, I LOVE THE GAYS! I'M A LONGTIME FRIEND OF THE FRIENDS OF DOROTHY!
THEN WHY WERE YOU SO PISSED OVER WHAT WENT DOWN BETWEEN MANN AND ME?
I DON'T KNOW.
I... I GUESS I WAS JEALOUS.

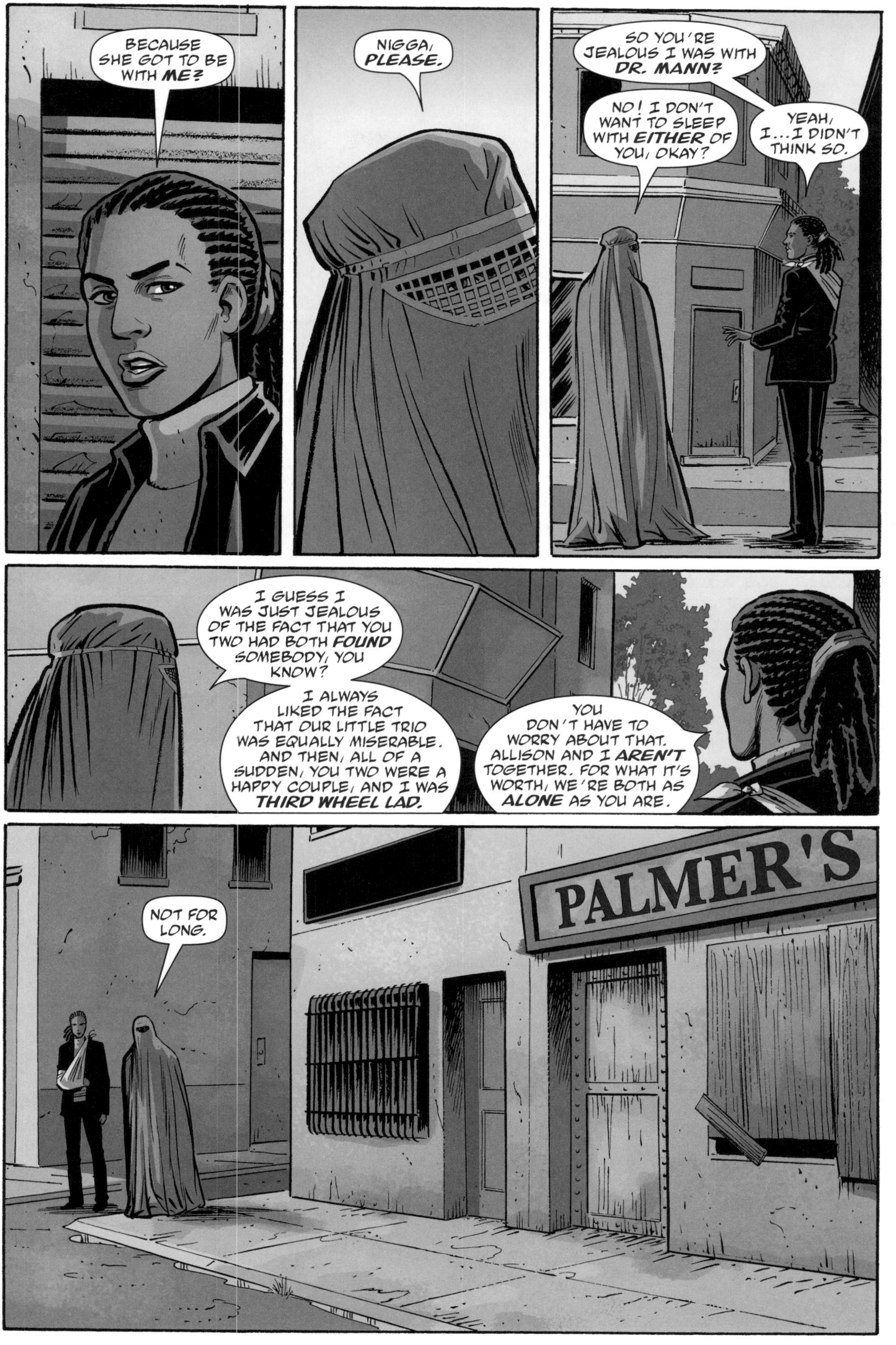
BECAUSE SHE GOT TO BE WITH ME?
NIGGA, PLEASE.
SO YOU'RE JEALOUS I WAS WITH DR. MANN?
NO! I DON'T WANT TO SLEEP WITH EITHER OF YOU, OKAY?
YEAH, I...I DIDN'T THINK SO.
I GUESS I WAS JUST JEALOUS OF THE FACT THAT YOU TWO HAD BOTH FOUND SOMEBODY, YOU KNOW?
I ALWAYS LIKED THE FACT THAT OUR LITTLE TRIO WAS EQUALLY MISERABLE. AND THEN, ALL OF A SUDDEN, YOU TWO WERE A HAPPY COUPLE, AND I WAS THIRD WHEEL LAD.
YOU DON'T HAVE TO WORRY ABOUT THAT. ALLISON AND I AREN'T TOGETHER. FOR WHAT IT'S WORTH, WE'RE BOTH AS ALONE AS YOU ARE.
NOT FOR LONG.
PALMER'S

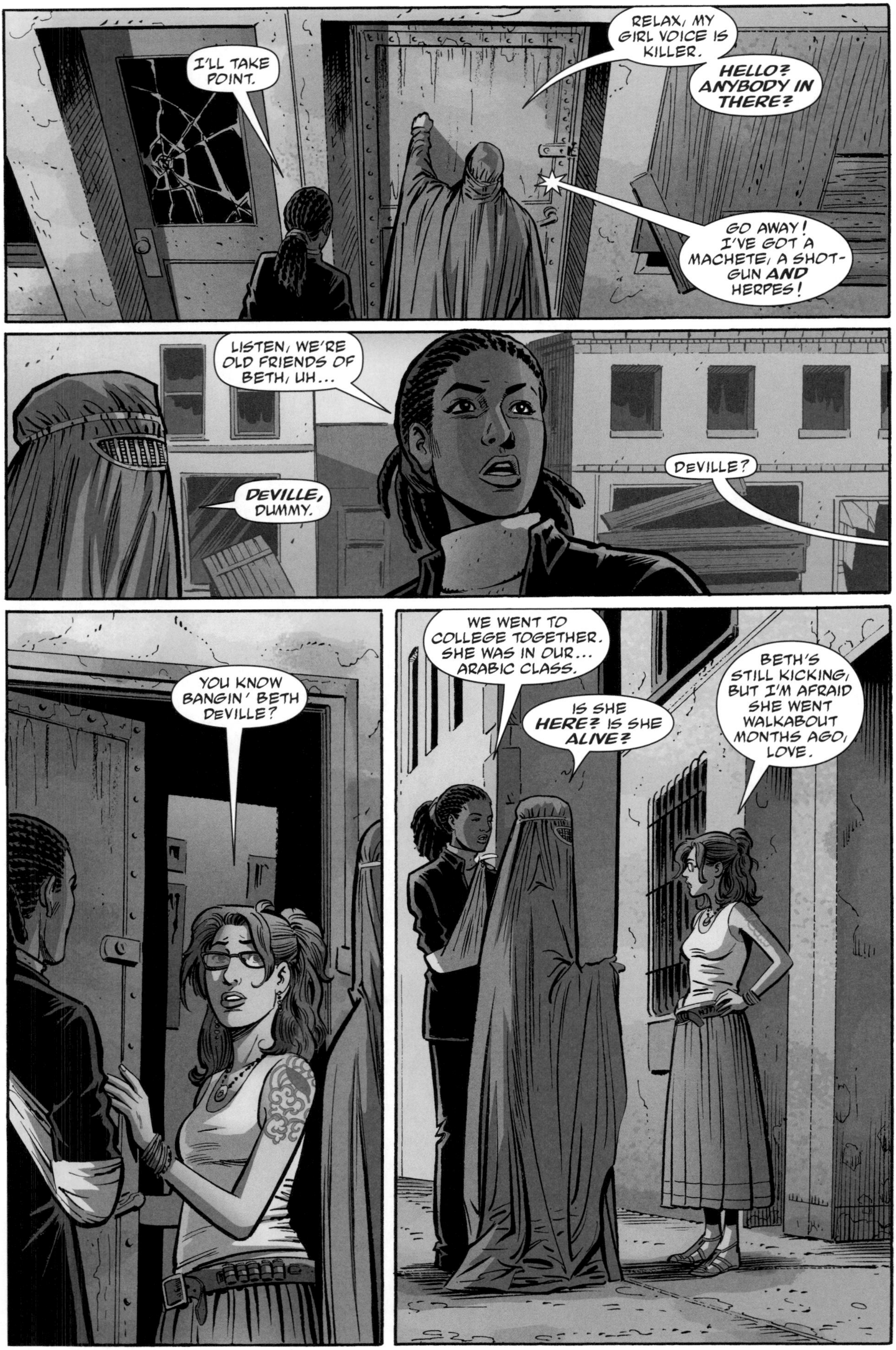
I'LL TAKE POINT.
RELAX, MY GIRL VOICE IS KILLER.
HELLO? ANYBODY IN THERE?
GO AWAY! I'VE GOT A MACHETE, A SHOTGUN **AND** HERPES!
LISTEN, WE'RE OLD FRIENDS OF BETH, UH...
DEVILLE, DUMMY.
DEVILLE?
YOU KNOW BANGIN' BETH DEVILLE?
WE WENT TO COLLEGE TOGETHER. SHE WAS IN OUR... ARABIC CLASS.
IS SHE **HERE?** IS SHE **ALIVE?**
BETH'S STILL KICKING, BUT I'M AFRAID SHE WENT WALKABOUT MONTHS AGO, LOVE.

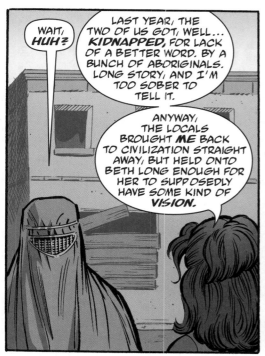

WAIT, **HUH?**

LAST YEAR, THE TWO OF US GOT, WELL... **KIDNAPPED**, FOR LACK OF A BETTER WORD. BY A BUNCH OF **ABORIGINALS.** LONG STORY, AND I'M TOO SOBER TO TELL IT.

ANYWAY, THE LOCALS BROUGHT **ME** BACK TO CIVILIZATION STRAIGHT AWAY, BUT HELD ONTO BETH LONG ENOUGH FOR HER TO SUPPOSEDLY HAVE SOME KIND OF **VISION.**

A VISION OF **WHAT?**

SOME OLD BOYFRIEND OF HERS. **YANNI** OR SOMETHING. OUR LUNATIC GIRL THINKS HE MIGHT BE ALIVE, SO SHE LEFT TO **FIND** HIM.

LEFT TO FIND HIM **WHERE?**

PARIS.

PARIS... **FRANCE?**

SHE SAID IT HAD SOME KIND OF SPECIAL MEANING FOR 'EM.

BUT...BUT I HAVE NO **IDEA** WHAT THAT MEANS!

LIKE I SAID, APPARENTLY ONLY THE TWO OF THEM WOULD UNDERSTAND.

SO SHE'S RISKING HER LIFE TO TRAVEL HALFWAY AROUND THE WORLD FOR SOMETHING SHE SAW IN A **DREAM?**

PRETTY MUCH, YEAH.

THAT STUPID, GULLIBLE **TWIST.**

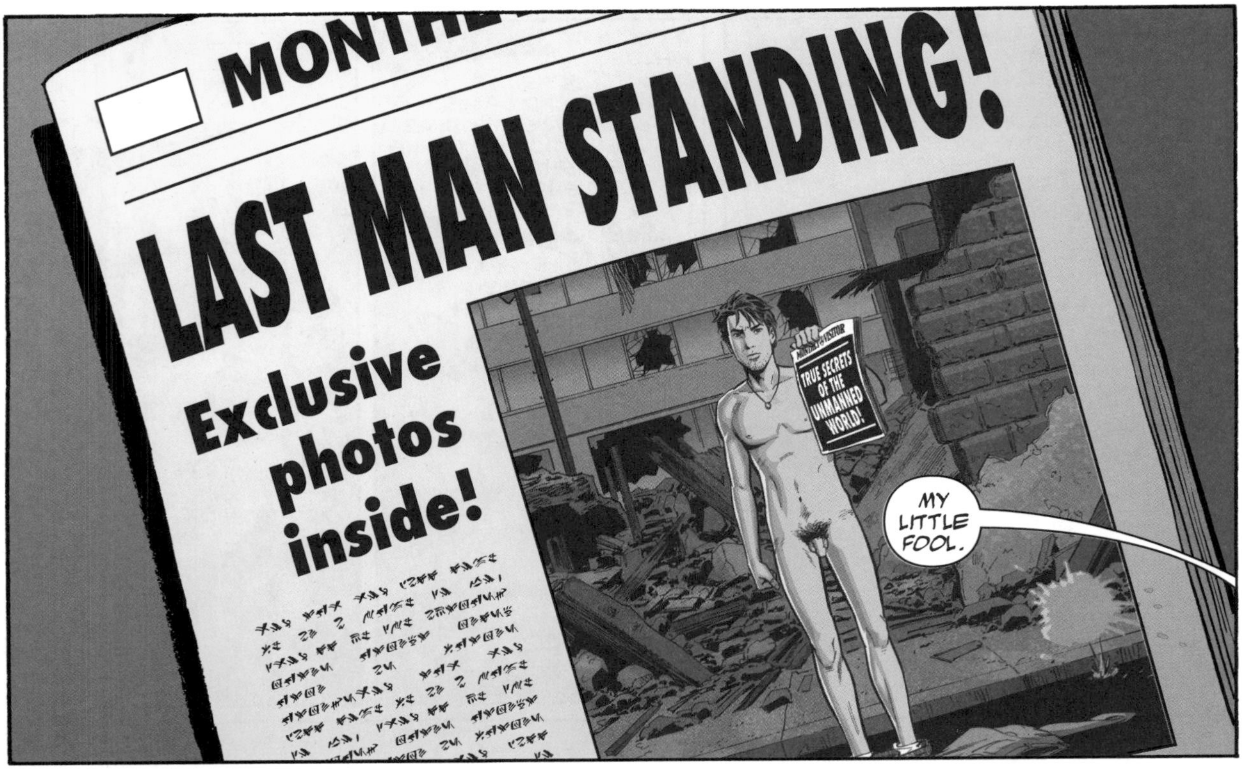
MONTHLY
LAST MAN STANDING!
Exclusive photos inside!
TRUE SECRETS OF THE UNMANNED WORLD!
MY LITTLE FOOL.

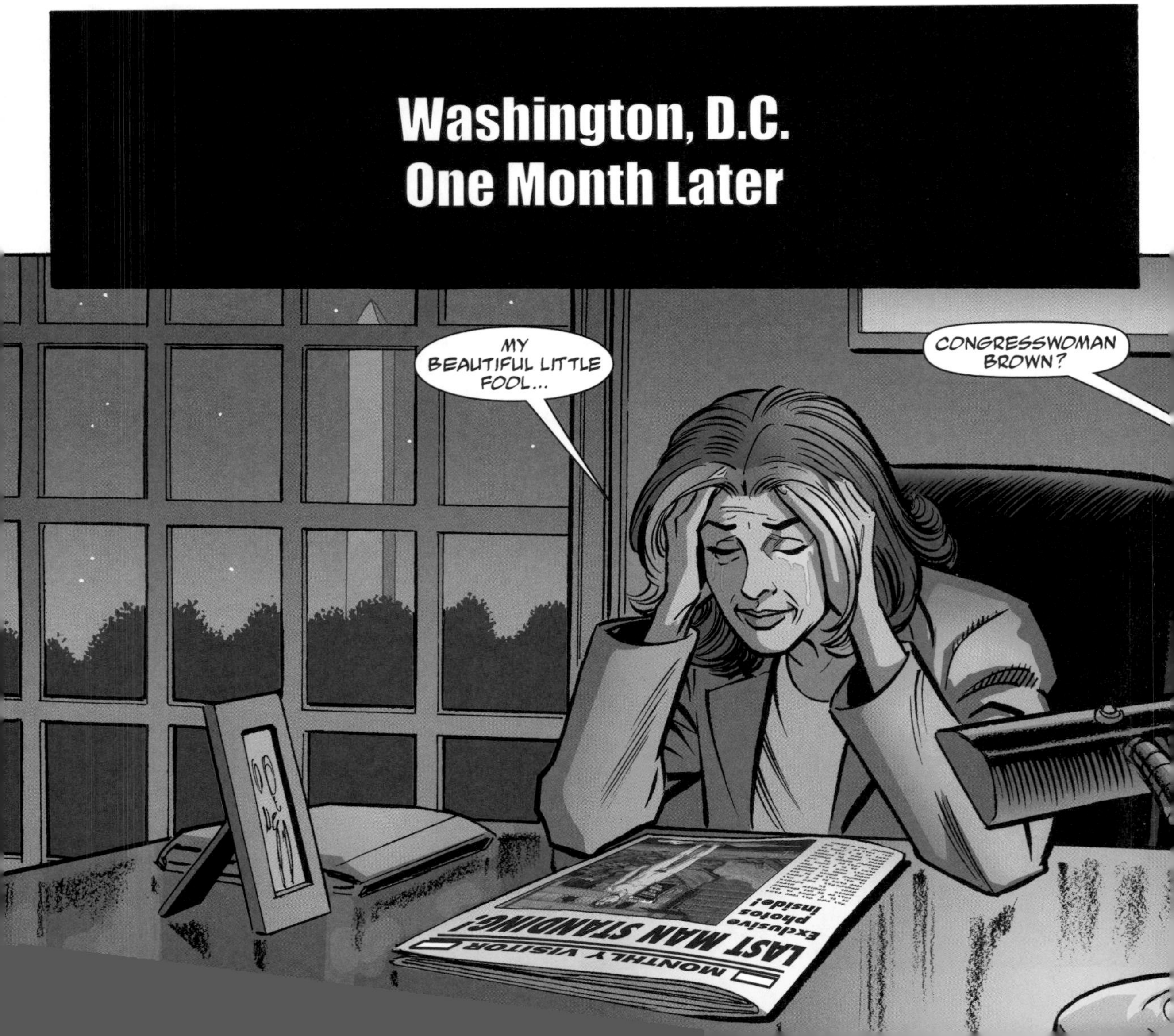
Washington, D.C.
One Month Later
MY BEAUTIFUL LITTLE FOOL...
CONGRESSWOMAN BROWN?
MONTHLY VISITOR
LAST MAN STANDING!
Exclusive photos inside!

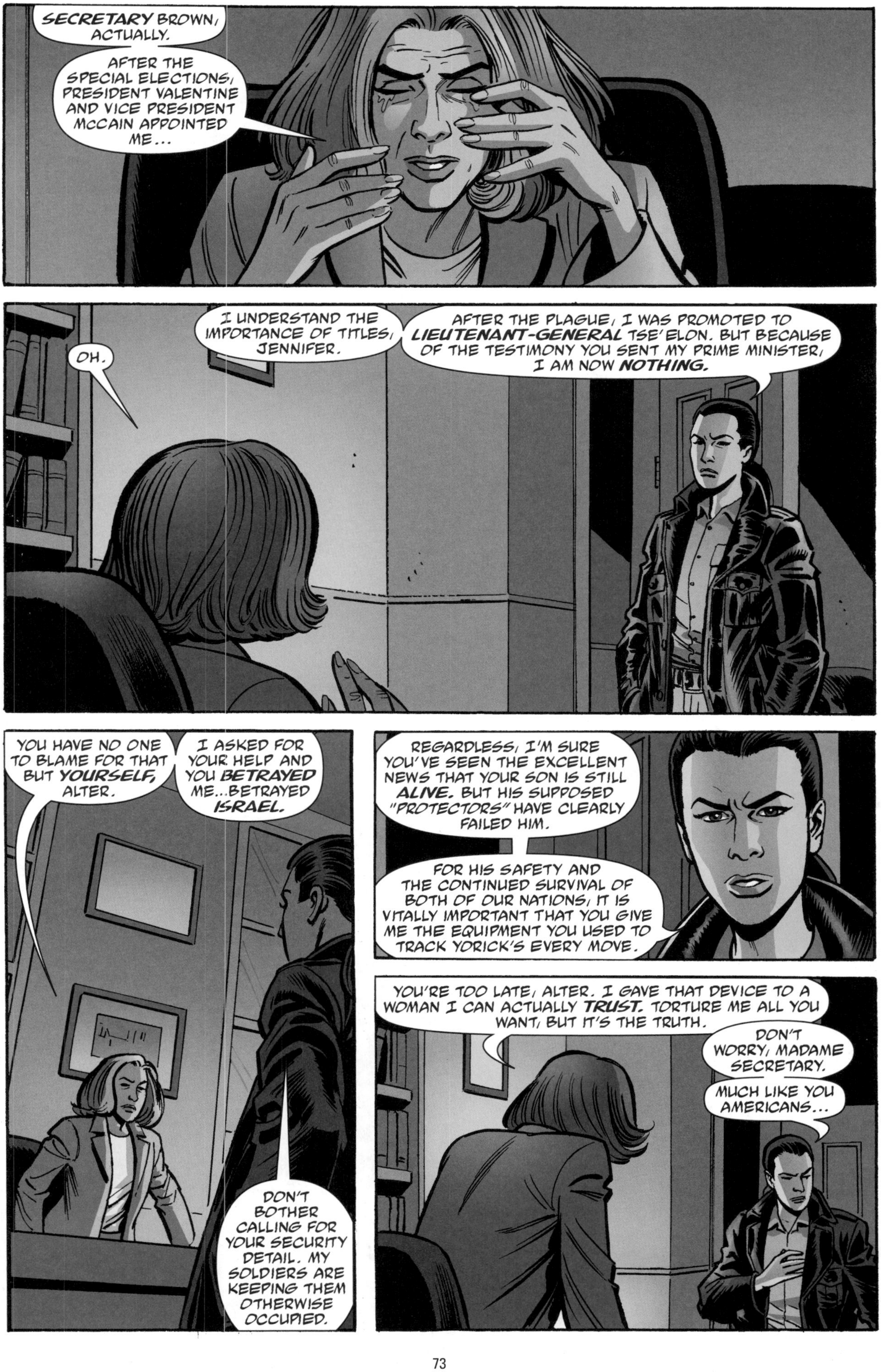
SECRETARY BROWN, ACTUALLY.
AFTER THE SPECIAL ELECTIONS, PRESIDENT VALENTINE AND VICE PRESIDENT McCAIN APPOINTED ME...
OH.
I UNDERSTAND THE IMPORTANCE OF TITLES, JENNIFER.
AFTER THE PLAGUE, I WAS PROMOTED TO LIEUTENANT-GENERAL TSE'ELON. BUT BECAUSE OF THE TESTIMONY YOU SENT MY PRIME MINISTER, I AM NOW NOTHING.
YOU HAVE NO ONE TO BLAME FOR THAT BUT YOURSELF, ALTER.
I ASKED FOR YOUR HELP AND YOU BETRAYED ME...BETRAYED ISRAEL.
DON'T BOTHER CALLING FOR YOUR SECURITY DETAIL. MY SOLDIERS ARE KEEPING THEM OTHERWISE OCCUPIED.
REGARDLESS, I'M SURE YOU'VE SEEN THE EXCELLENT NEWS THAT YOUR SON IS STILL ALIVE. BUT HIS SUPPOSED "PROTECTORS" HAVE CLEARLY FAILED HIM.
FOR HIS SAFETY AND THE CONTINUED SURVIVAL OF BOTH OF OUR NATIONS, IT IS VITALLY IMPORTANT THAT YOU GIVE ME THE EQUIPMENT YOU USED TO TRACK YORICK'S EVERY MOVE.
YOU'RE TOO LATE, ALTER. I GAVE THAT DEVICE TO A WOMAN I CAN ACTUALLY TRUST. TORTURE ME ALL YOU WANT, BUT IT'S THE TRUTH.
DON'T WORRY, MADAME SECRETARY.
MUCH LIKE YOU AMERICANS...

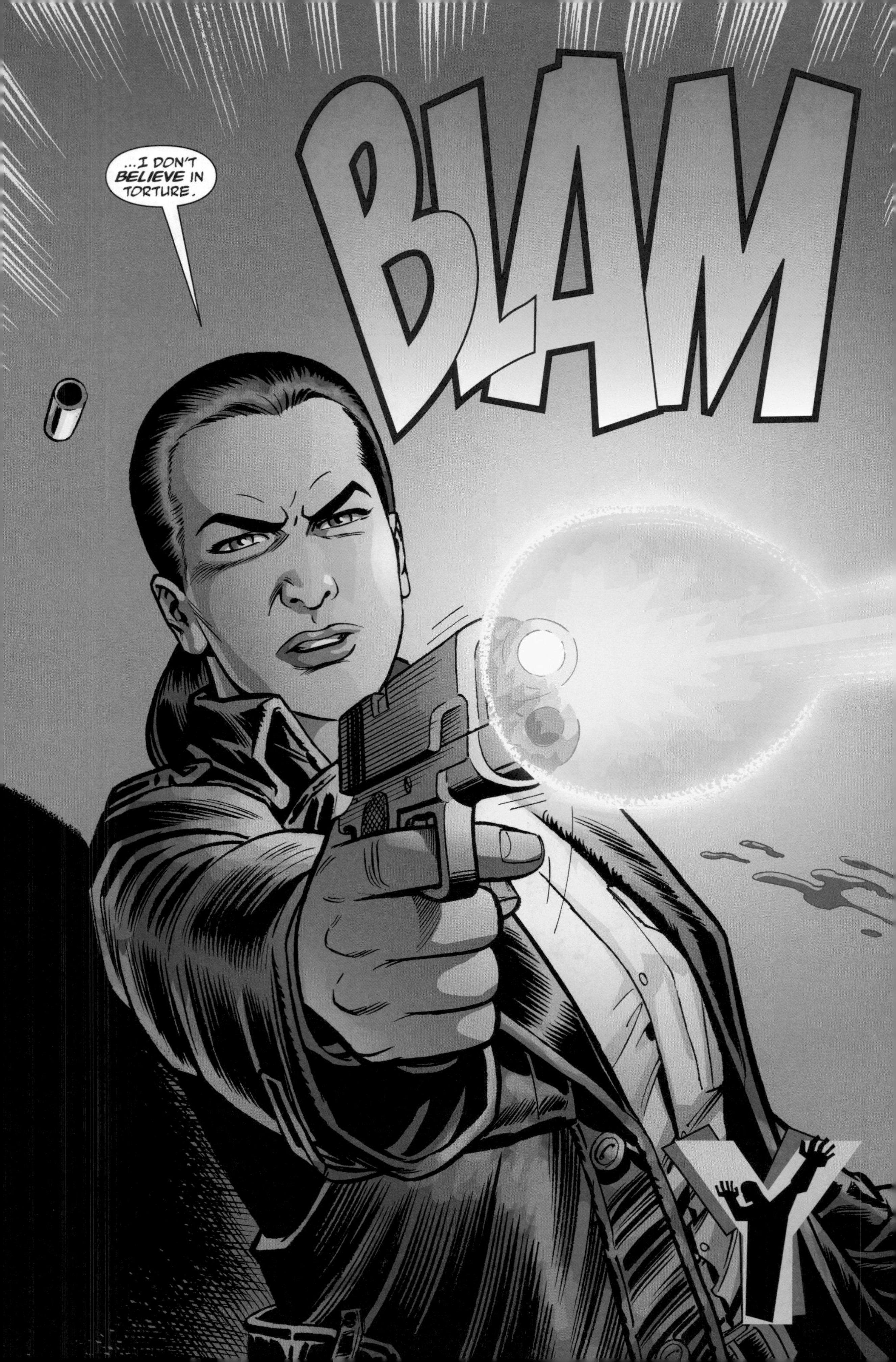
...I DON'T BELIEVE IN TORTURE.
BLAM

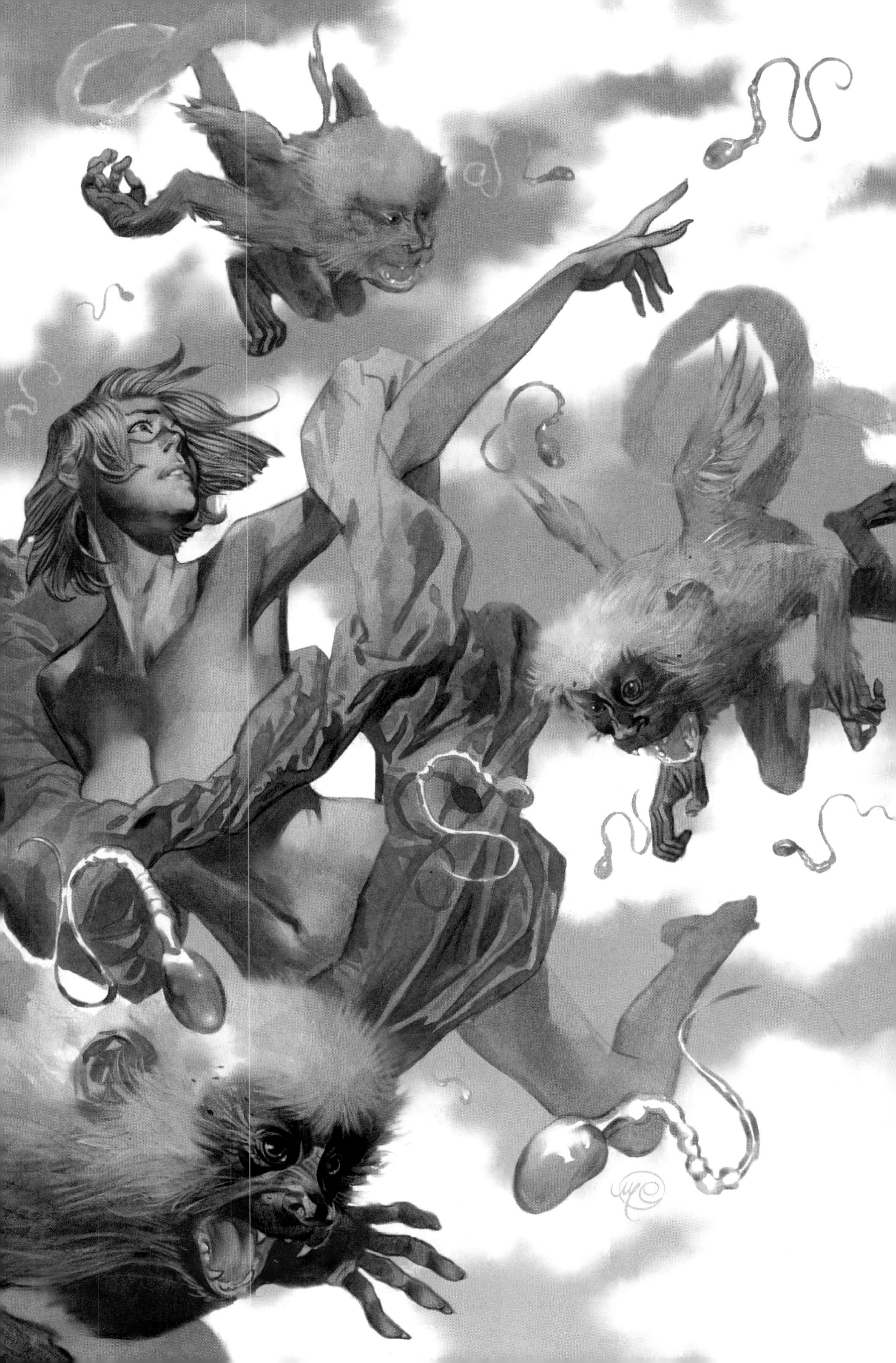

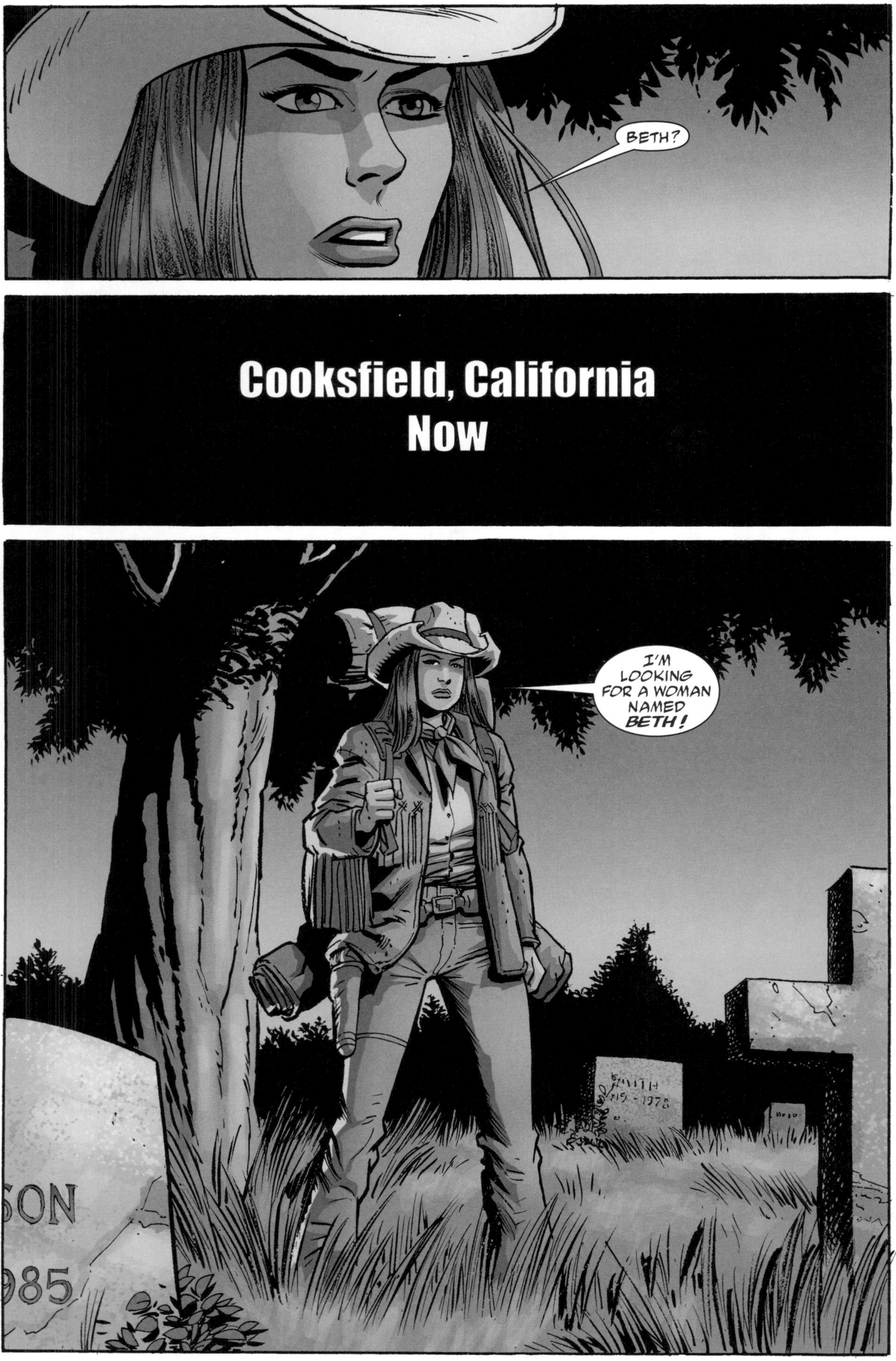
BETH?
Cooksfield, California
Now
I'M LOOKING FOR A WOMAN NAMED BETH!

THE FRONT DOOR OF YOUR **CHURCH** WAS LOCKED, SO I HOPPED THE FENCE BACK HERE AND --

VSSSH

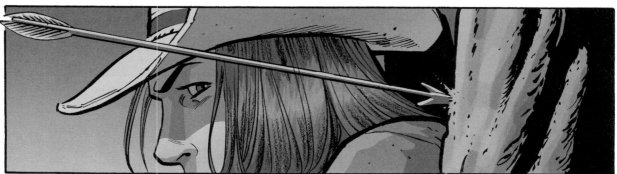

FUN. BEEN LOOKING FORWARD TO KILLING AN **AMAZON.**

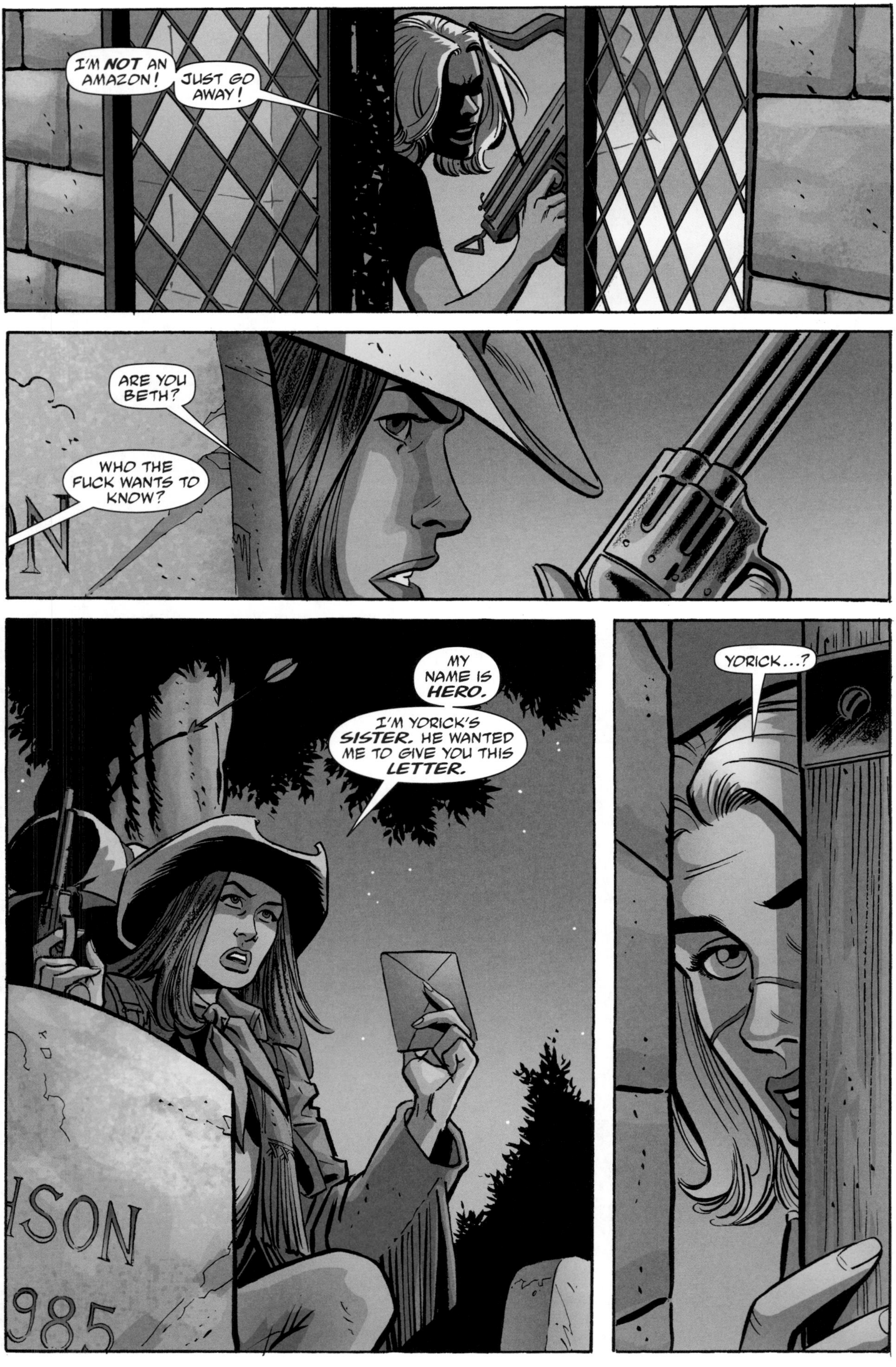
I'M NOT AN AMAZON!
JUST GO AWAY!
ARE YOU BETH?
WHO THE FUCK WANTS TO KNOW?
MY NAME IS HERO.
I'M YORICK'S SISTER. HE WANTED ME TO GIVE YOU THIS LETTER.
YORICK...?

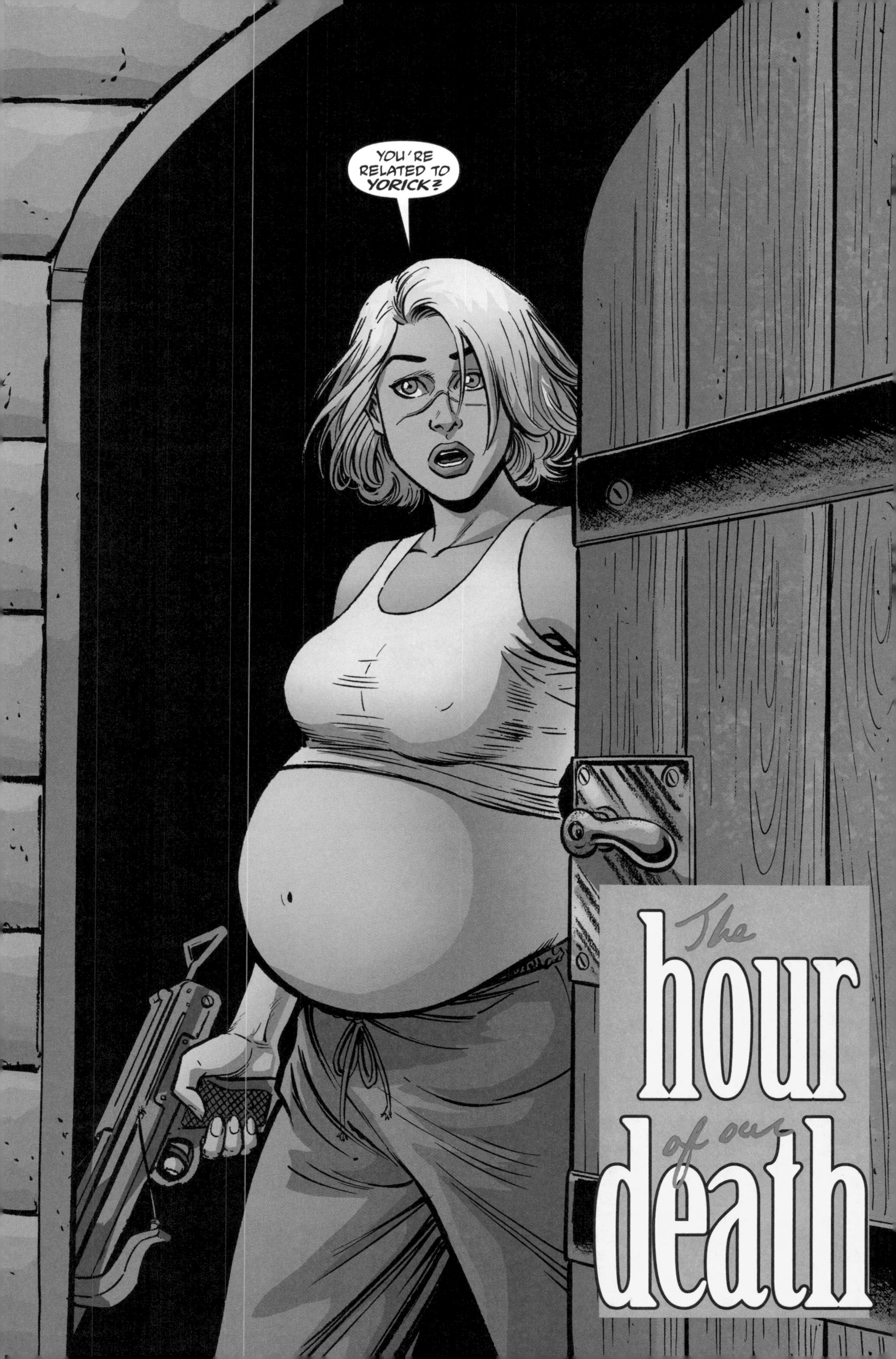
YOU'RE RELATED TO YORICK?
The hour of our death

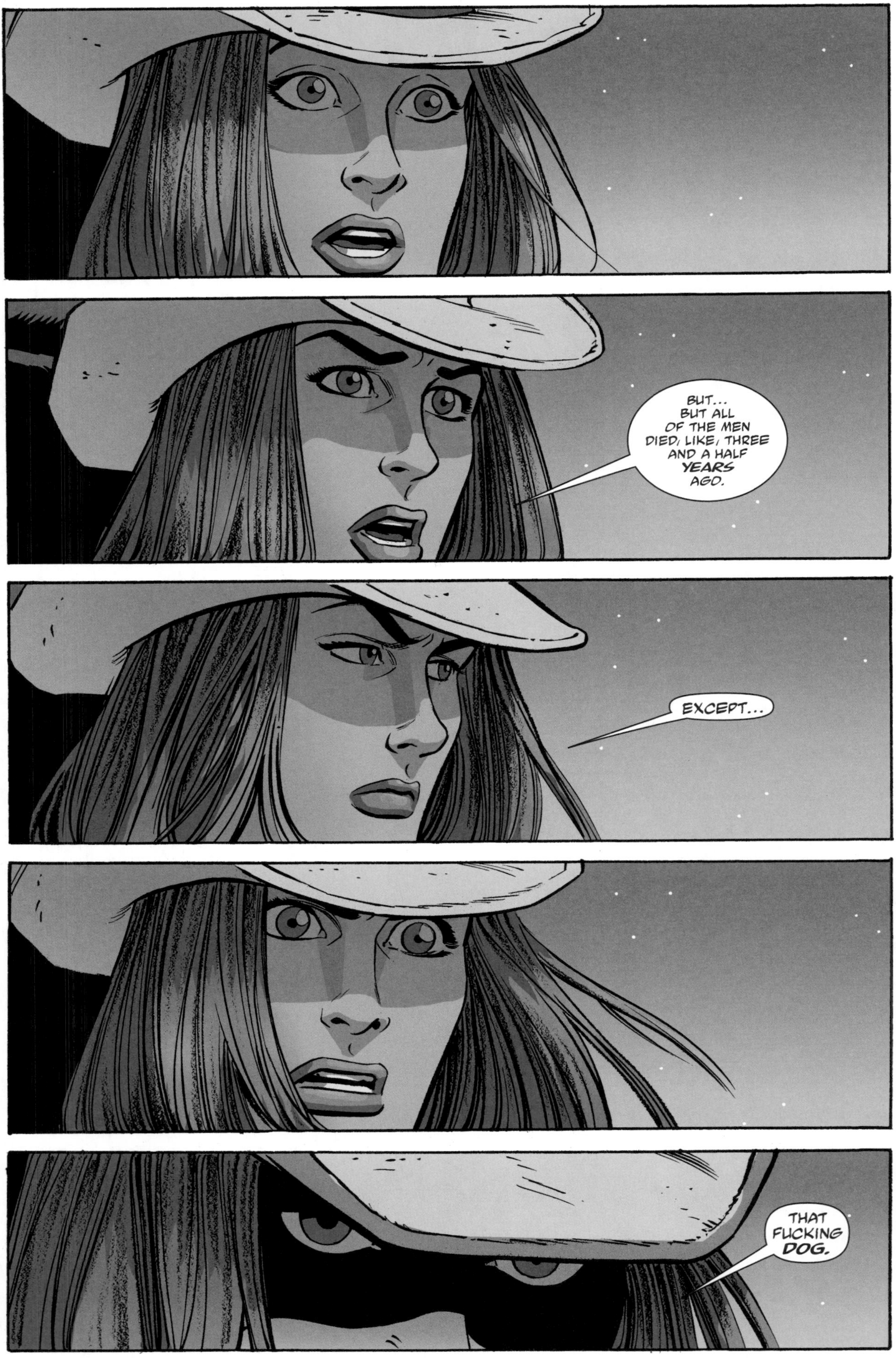
BUT... BUT ALL OF THE MEN DIED, LIKE, THREE AND A HALF YEARS AGO.
EXCEPT...
THAT FUCKING DOG.

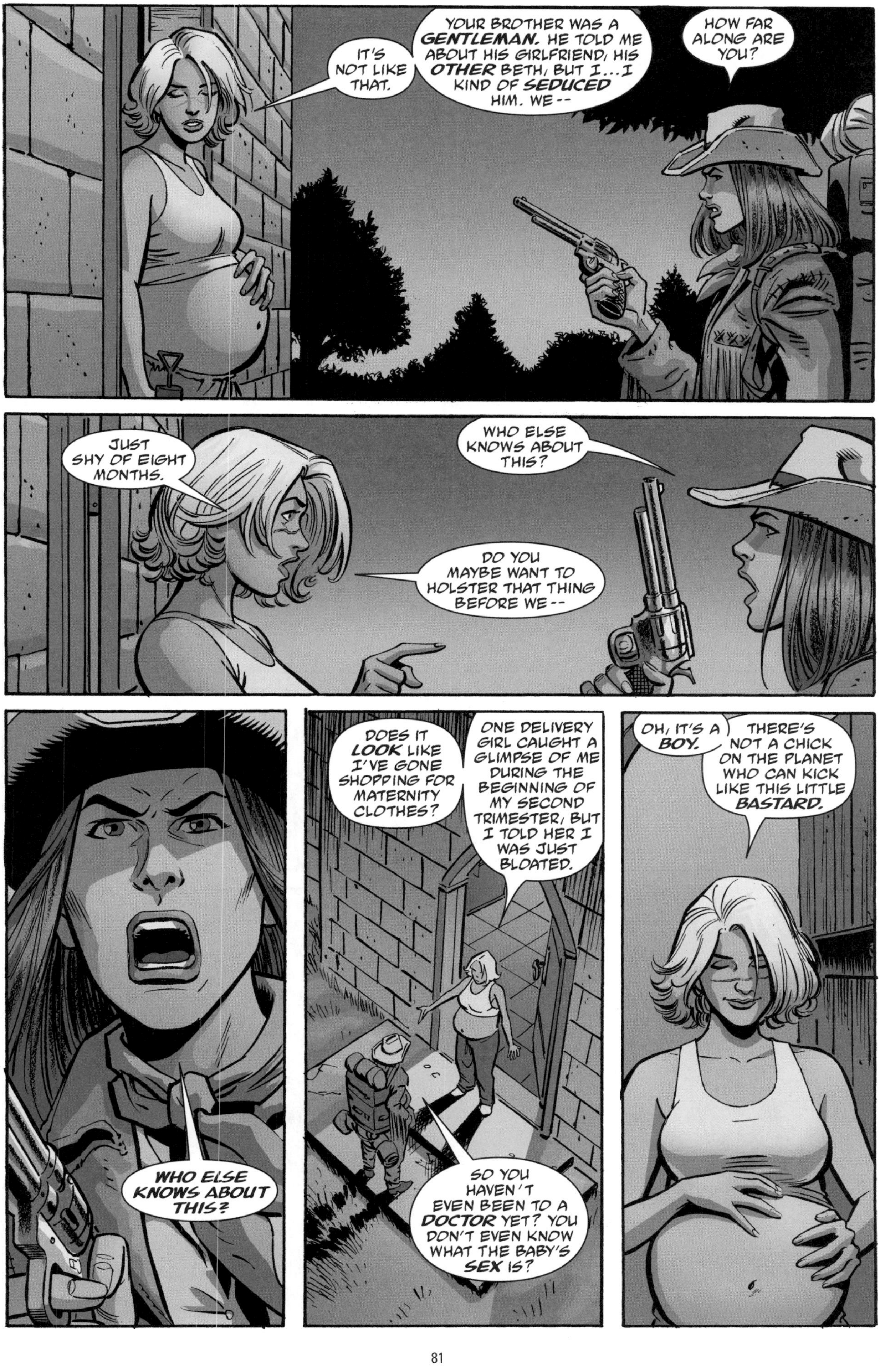

IT'S NOT LIKE THAT.
YOUR BROTHER WAS A **GENTLEMAN.** HE TOLD ME ABOUT HIS GIRLFRIEND, HIS **OTHER** BETH, BUT I... I KIND OF **SEDUCED** HIM. WE--
HOW FAR ALONG ARE YOU?
JUST SHY OF EIGHT MONTHS.
WHO ELSE KNOWS ABOUT THIS?
DO YOU MAYBE WANT TO HOLSTER THAT THING BEFORE WE--
WHO ELSE KNOWS ABOUT THIS?
DOES IT **LOOK** LIKE I'VE GONE SHOPPING FOR MATERNITY CLOTHES?
ONE DELIVERY GIRL CAUGHT A GLIMPSE OF ME DURING THE BEGINNING OF MY SECOND TRIMESTER, BUT I TOLD HER I WAS JUST BLOATED.
SO YOU HAVEN'T EVEN BEEN TO A **DOCTOR** YET? YOU DON'T EVEN KNOW WHAT THE BABY'S **SEX** IS?
OH, IT'S A **BOY.**
THERE'S NOT A CHICK ON THE PLANET WHO CAN KICK LIKE THIS LITTLE **BASTARD.**

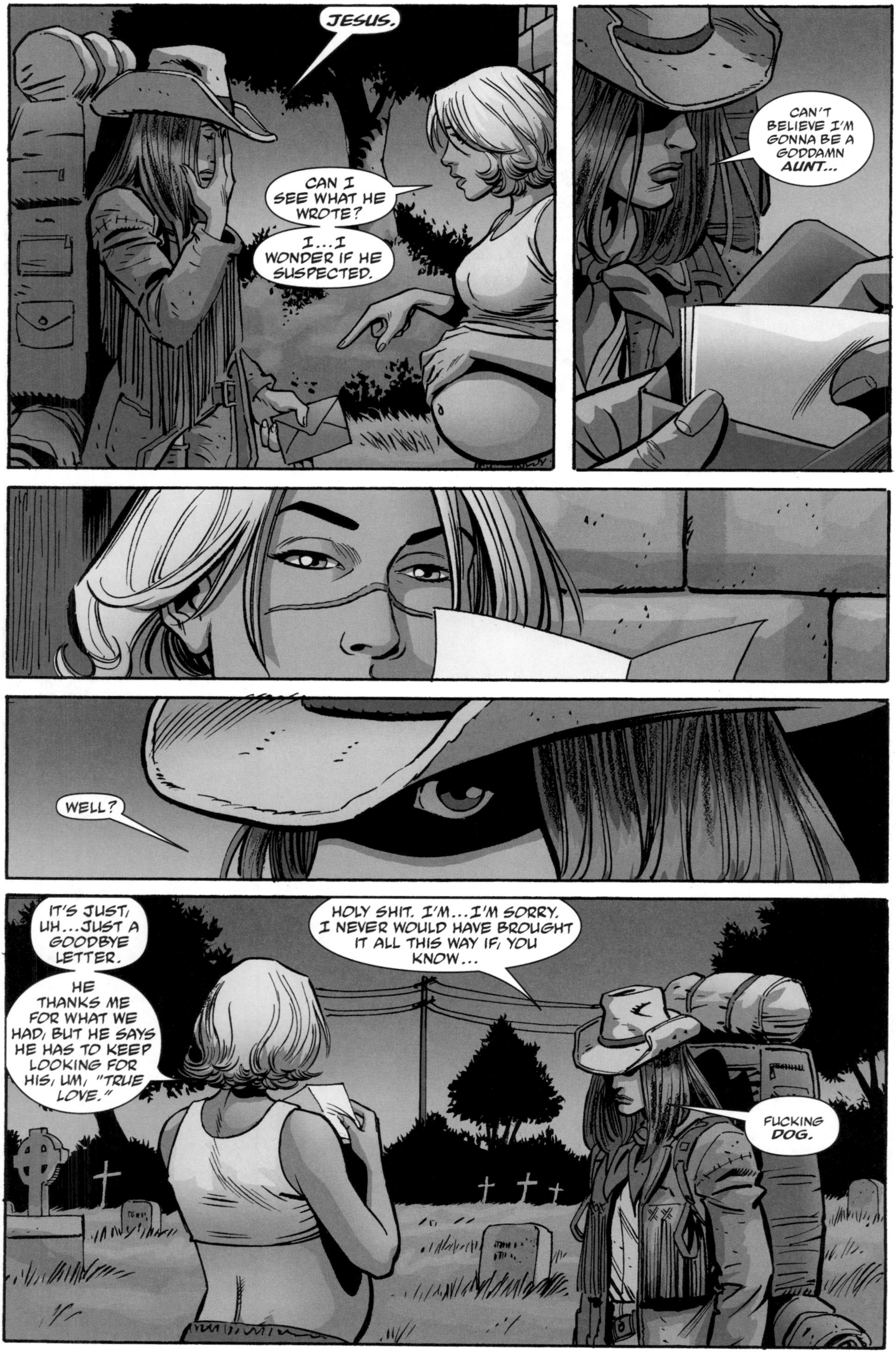
JESUS.
CAN I SEE WHAT HE WROTE?
I...I WONDER IF HE SUSPECTED.
CAN'T BELIEVE I'M GONNA BE A GODDAMN AUNT...
WELL?
IT'S JUST, UH...JUST A GOODBYE LETTER.
HE THANKS ME FOR WHAT WE HAD, BUT HE SAYS HE HAS TO KEEP LOOKING FOR HIS, UM, "TRUE LOVE."
HOLY SHIT. I'M...I'M SORRY. I NEVER WOULD HAVE BROUGHT IT ALL THIS WAY IF, YOU KNOW...
FUCKING DOG.

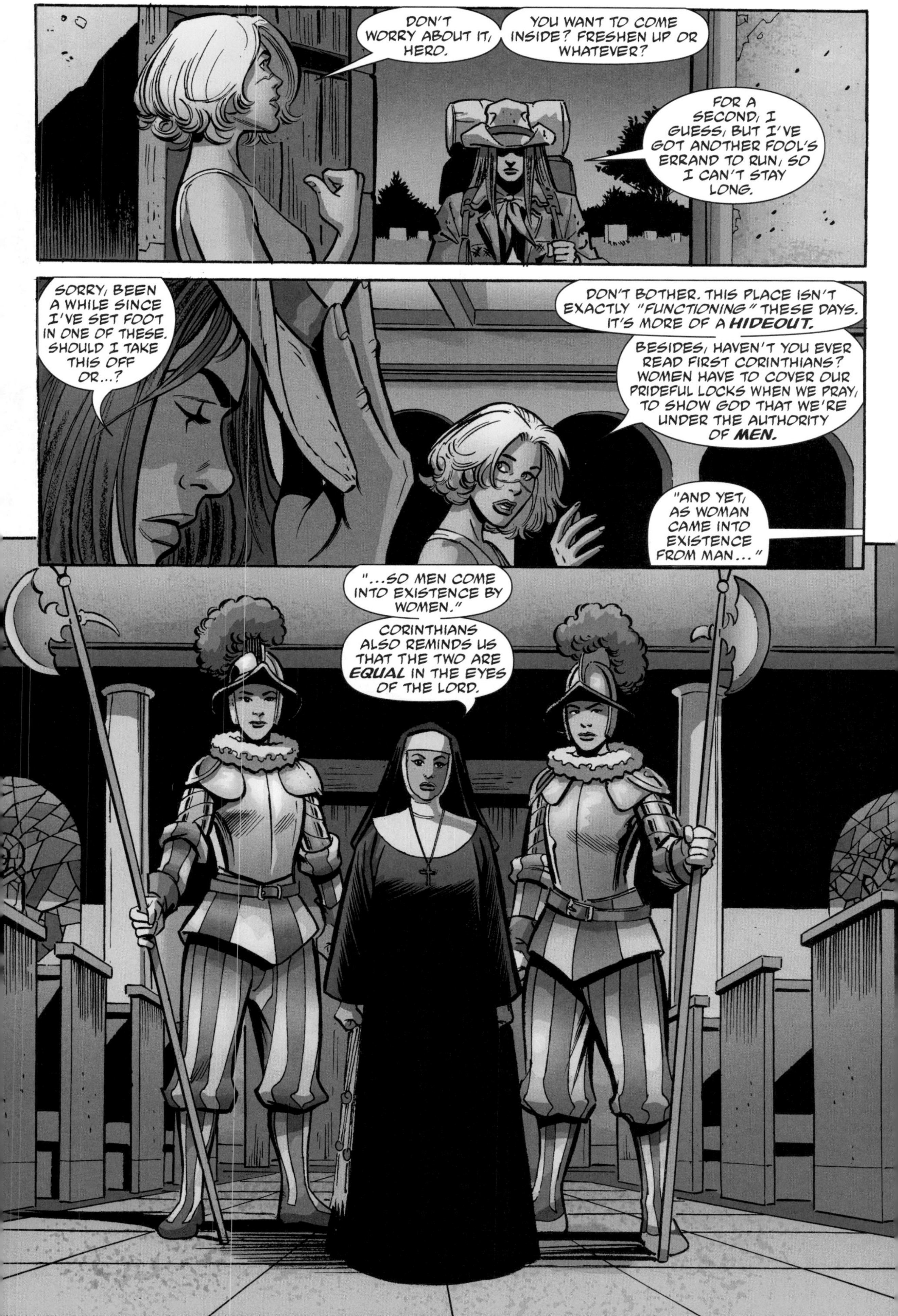
DON'T WORRY ABOUT IT, HERO.
YOU WANT TO COME INSIDE? FRESHEN UP OR WHATEVER?
FOR A SECOND, I GUESS, BUT I'VE GOT ANOTHER FOOL'S ERRAND TO RUN, SO I CAN'T STAY LONG.
SORRY, BEEN A WHILE SINCE I'VE SET FOOT IN ONE OF THESE. SHOULD I TAKE THIS OFF OR...?
DON'T BOTHER. THIS PLACE ISN'T EXACTLY "FUNCTIONING" THESE DAYS. IT'S MORE OF A HIDEOUT.
BESIDES, HAVEN'T YOU EVER READ FIRST CORINTHIANS? WOMEN HAVE TO COVER OUR PRIDEFUL LOCKS WHEN WE PRAY, TO SHOW GOD THAT WE'RE UNDER THE AUTHORITY OF MEN.
"AND YET, AS WOMAN CAME INTO EXISTENCE FROM MAN..."
"...SO MEN COME INTO EXISTENCE BY WOMEN."
CORINTHIANS ALSO REMINDS US THAT THE TWO ARE EQUAL IN THE EYES OF THE LORD.

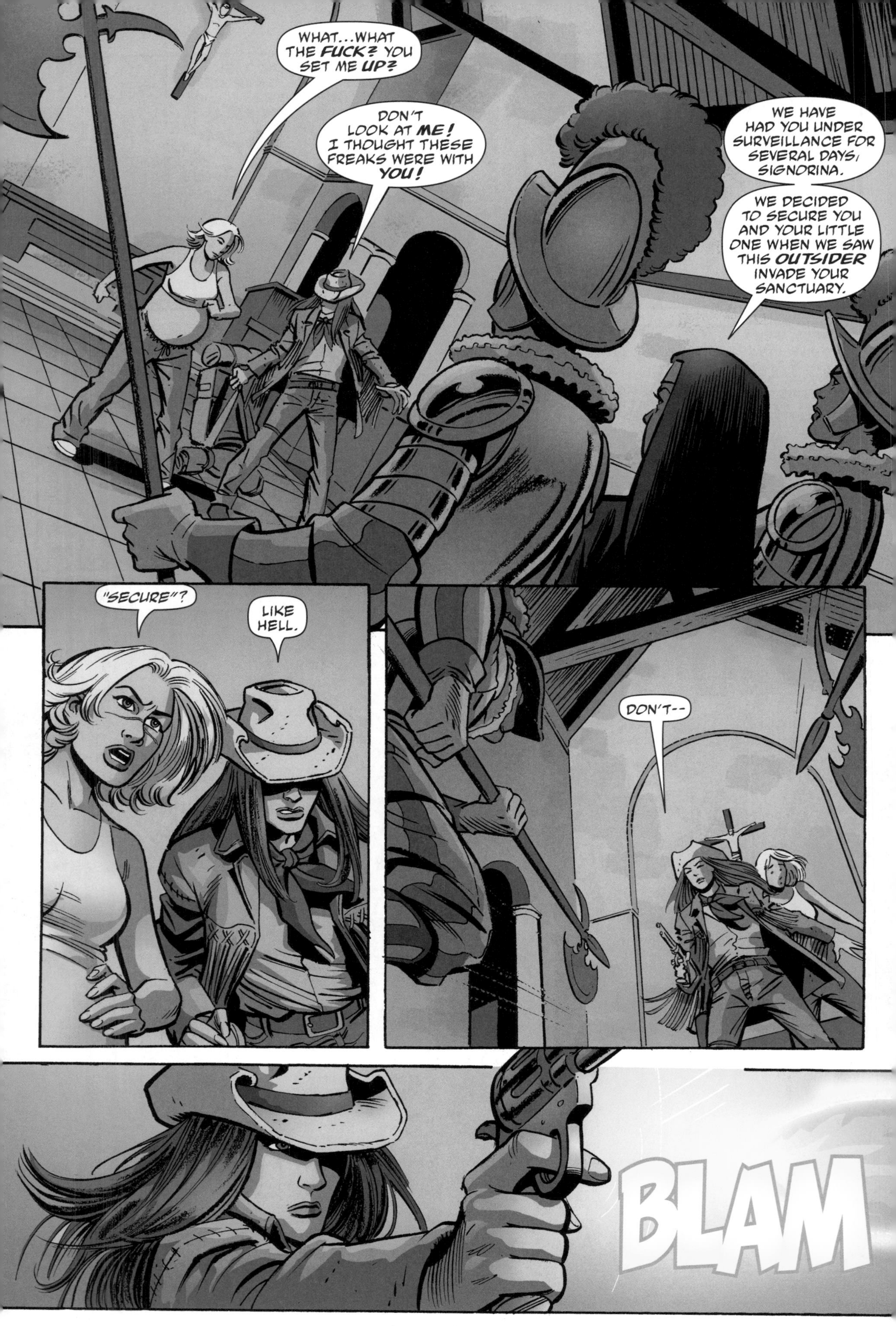
WHAT...WHAT THE FUCK? YOU SET ME UP?
DON'T LOOK AT ME! I THOUGHT THESE FREAKS WERE WITH YOU!
WE HAVE HAD YOU UNDER SURVEILLANCE FOR SEVERAL DAYS, SIGNORINA.
WE DECIDED TO SECURE YOU AND YOUR LITTLE ONE WHEN WE SAW THIS OUTSIDER INVADE YOUR SANCTUARY.
"SECURE"?
LIKE HELL.
DON'T--
BLAM

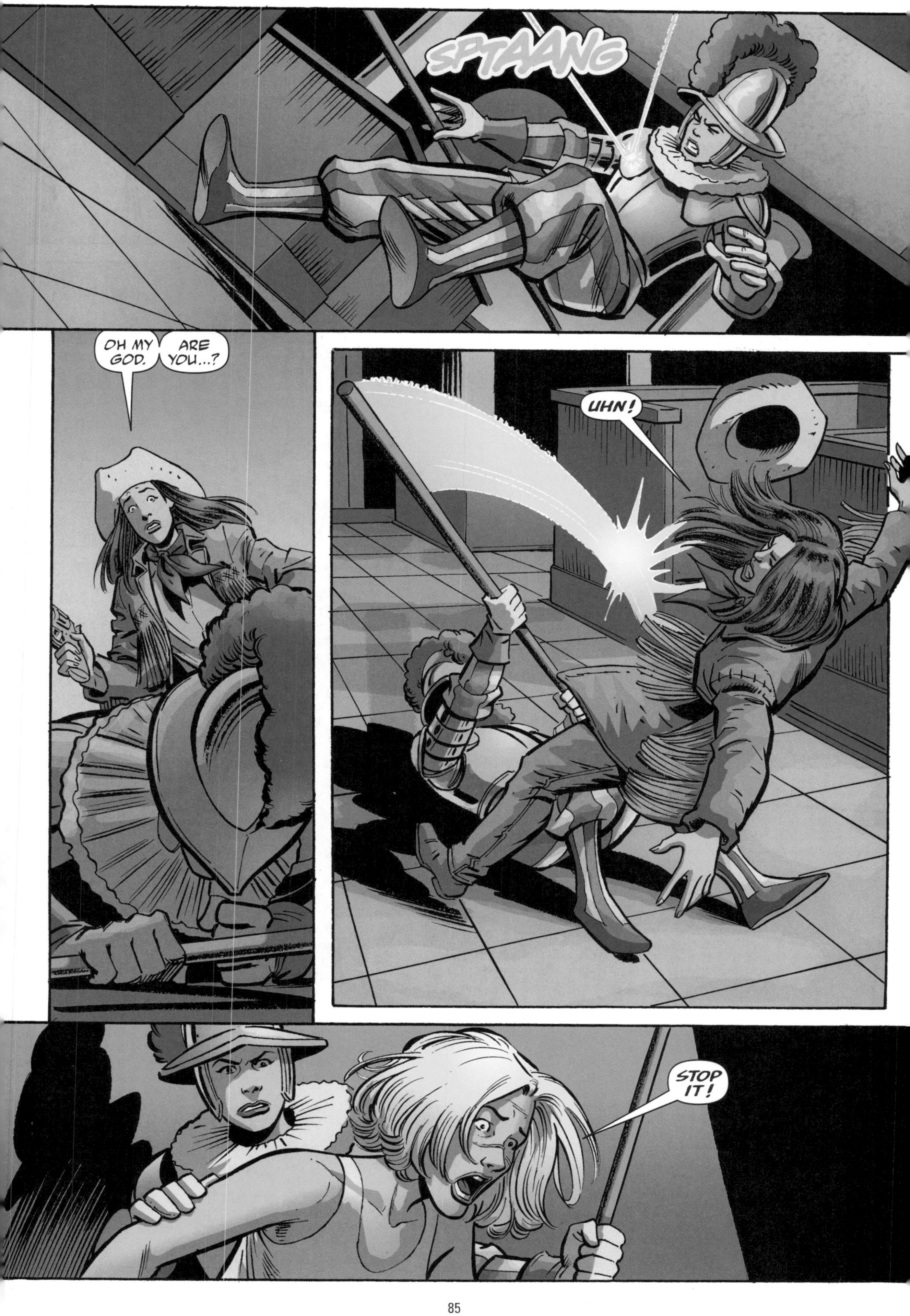
SPTAANG
OH MY GOD.
ARE YOU...?
UHN!
STOP IT!

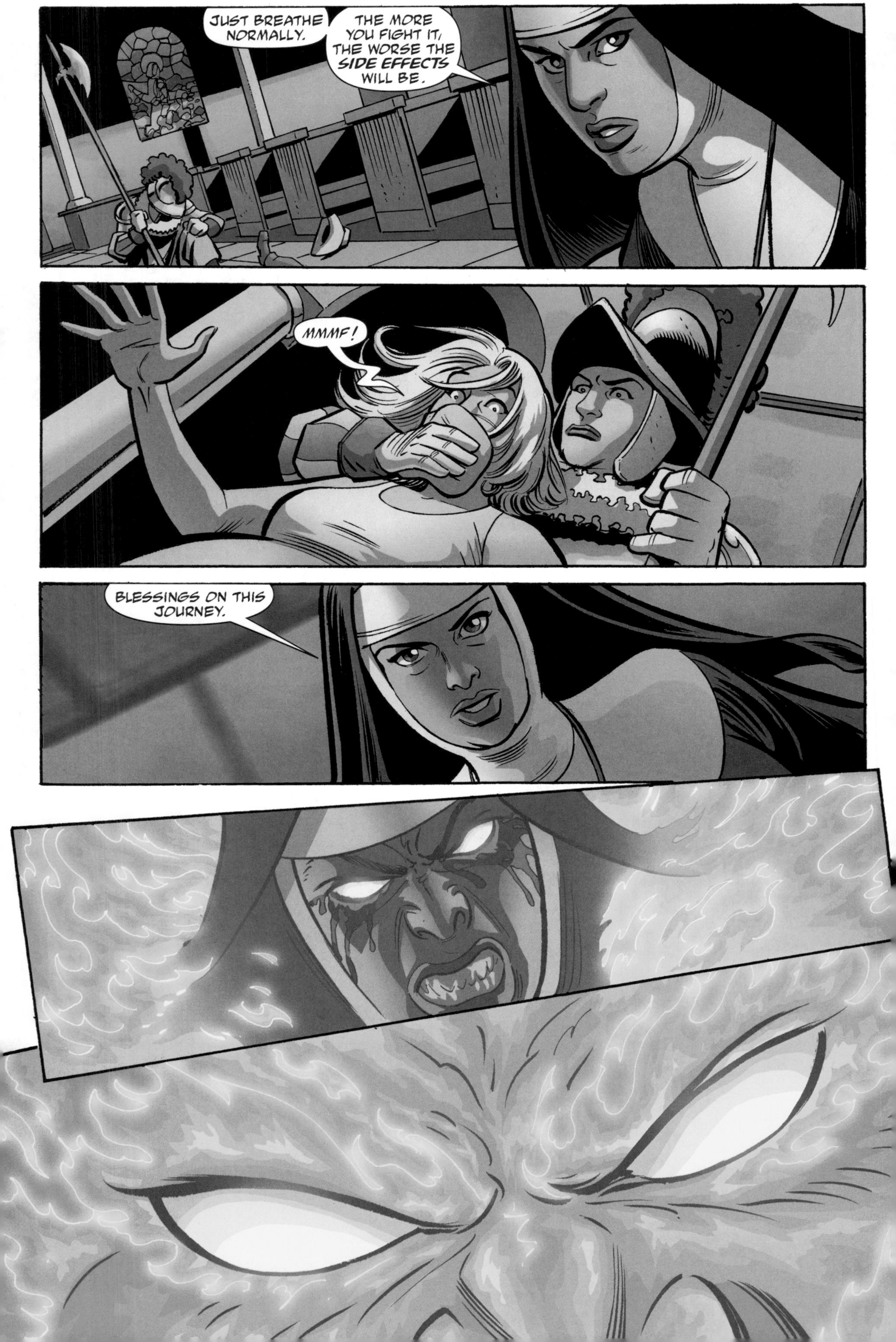
JUST BREATHE NORMALLY.
THE MORE YOU FIGHT IT, THE WORSE THE SIDE EFFECTS WILL BE.
MMMF!
BLESSINGS ON THIS JOURNEY.

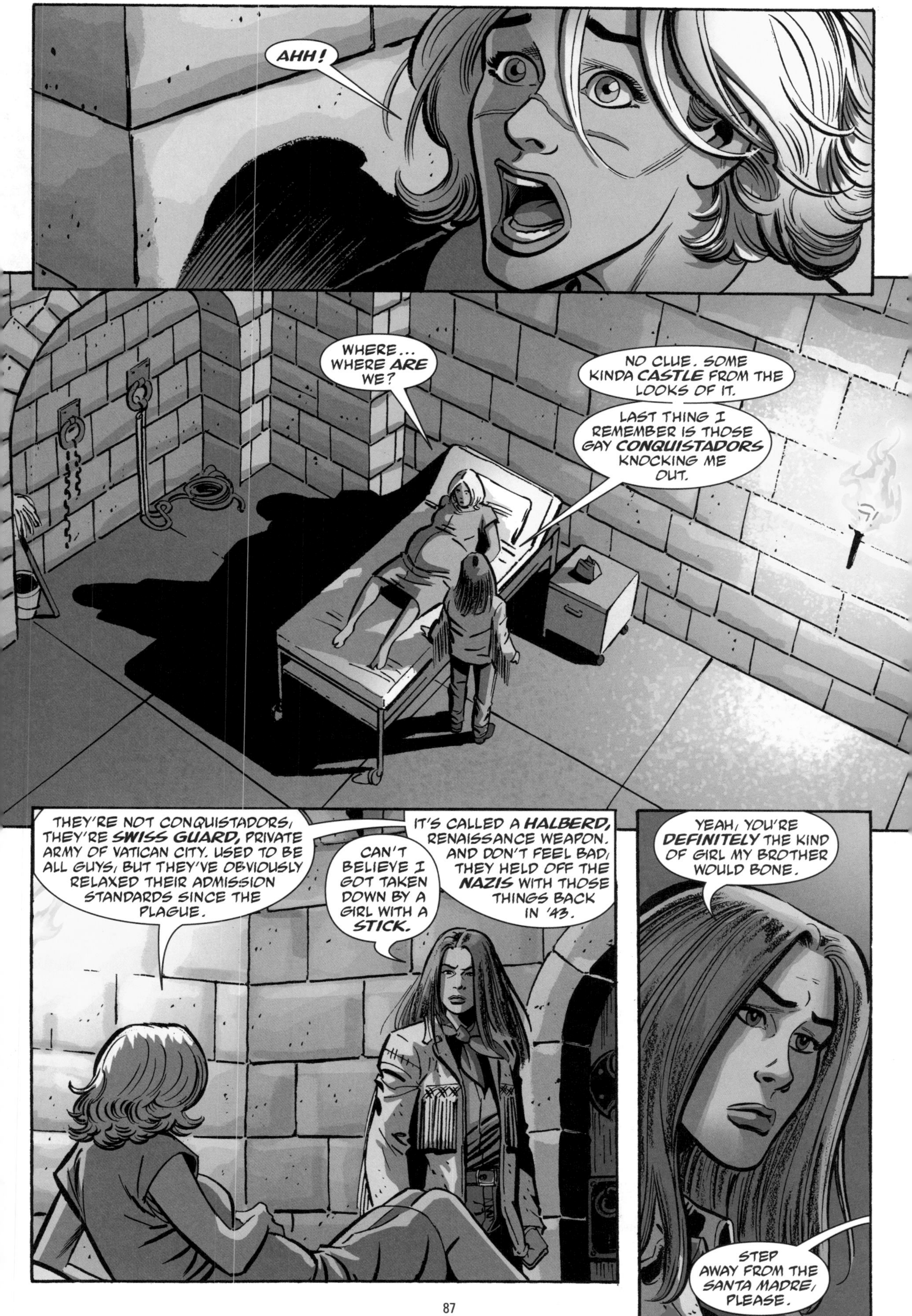
AHH!
WHERE... WHERE ARE WE?
NO CLUE. SOME KINDA CASTLE FROM THE LOOKS OF IT.
LAST THING I REMEMBER IS THOSE GAY CONQUISTADORS KNOCKING ME OUT.
THEY'RE NOT CONQUISTADORS, THEY'RE SWISS GUARD, PRIVATE ARMY OF VATICAN CITY. USED TO BE ALL GUYS, BUT THEY'VE OBVIOUSLY RELAXED THEIR ADMISSION STANDARDS SINCE THE PLAGUE.
CAN'T BELIEVE I GOT TAKEN DOWN BY A GIRL WITH A STICK.
IT'S CALLED A HALBERD, RENAISSANCE WEAPON. AND DON'T FEEL BAD, THEY HELD OFF THE NAZIS WITH THOSE THINGS BACK IN '43.
YEAH, YOU'RE DEFINITELY THE KIND OF GIRL MY BROTHER WOULD BONE.
STEP AWAY FROM THE SANTA MADRE, PLEASE.

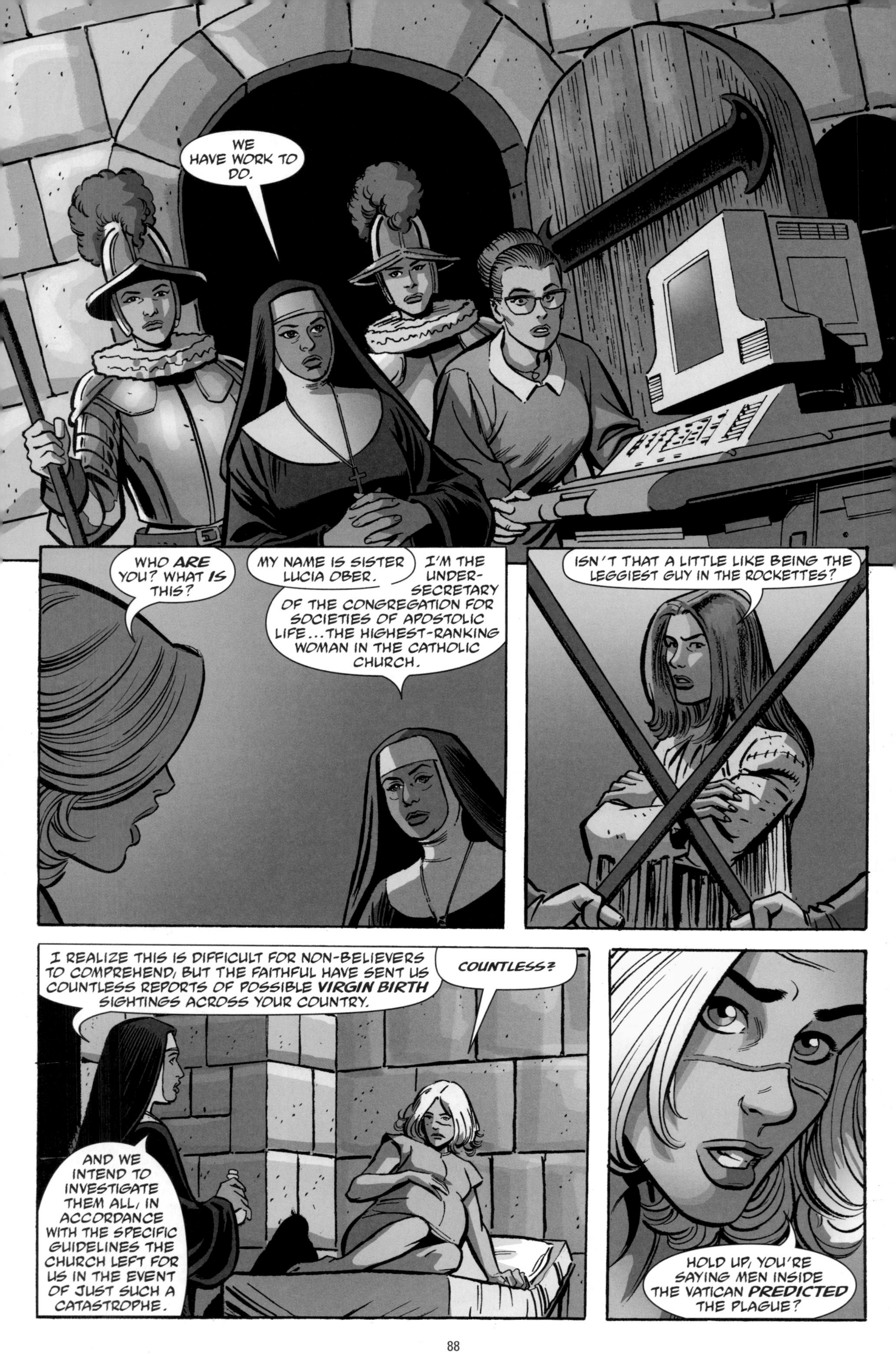
WE HAVE WORK TO DO.
WHO **ARE** YOU? WHAT **IS** THIS?
MY NAME IS SISTER LUCIA OBER.
I'M THE UNDER-SECRETARY OF THE CONGREGATION FOR SOCIETIES OF APOSTOLIC LIFE... THE HIGHEST-RANKING WOMAN IN THE CATHOLIC CHURCH.
ISN'T THAT A LITTLE LIKE BEING THE LEGGIEST GUY IN THE ROCKETTES?
I REALIZE THIS IS DIFFICULT FOR NON-BELIEVERS TO COMPREHEND, BUT THE FAITHFUL HAVE SENT US COUNTLESS REPORTS OF POSSIBLE **VIRGIN BIRTH** SIGHTINGS ACROSS YOUR COUNTRY.
COUNTLESS?
AND WE INTEND TO INVESTIGATE THEM ALL, IN ACCORDANCE WITH THE SPECIFIC GUIDELINES THE CHURCH LEFT FOR US IN THE EVENT OF JUST SUCH A CATASTROPHE.
HOLD UP, YOU'RE SAYING MEN INSIDE THE VATICAN **PREDICTED** THE PLAGUE?

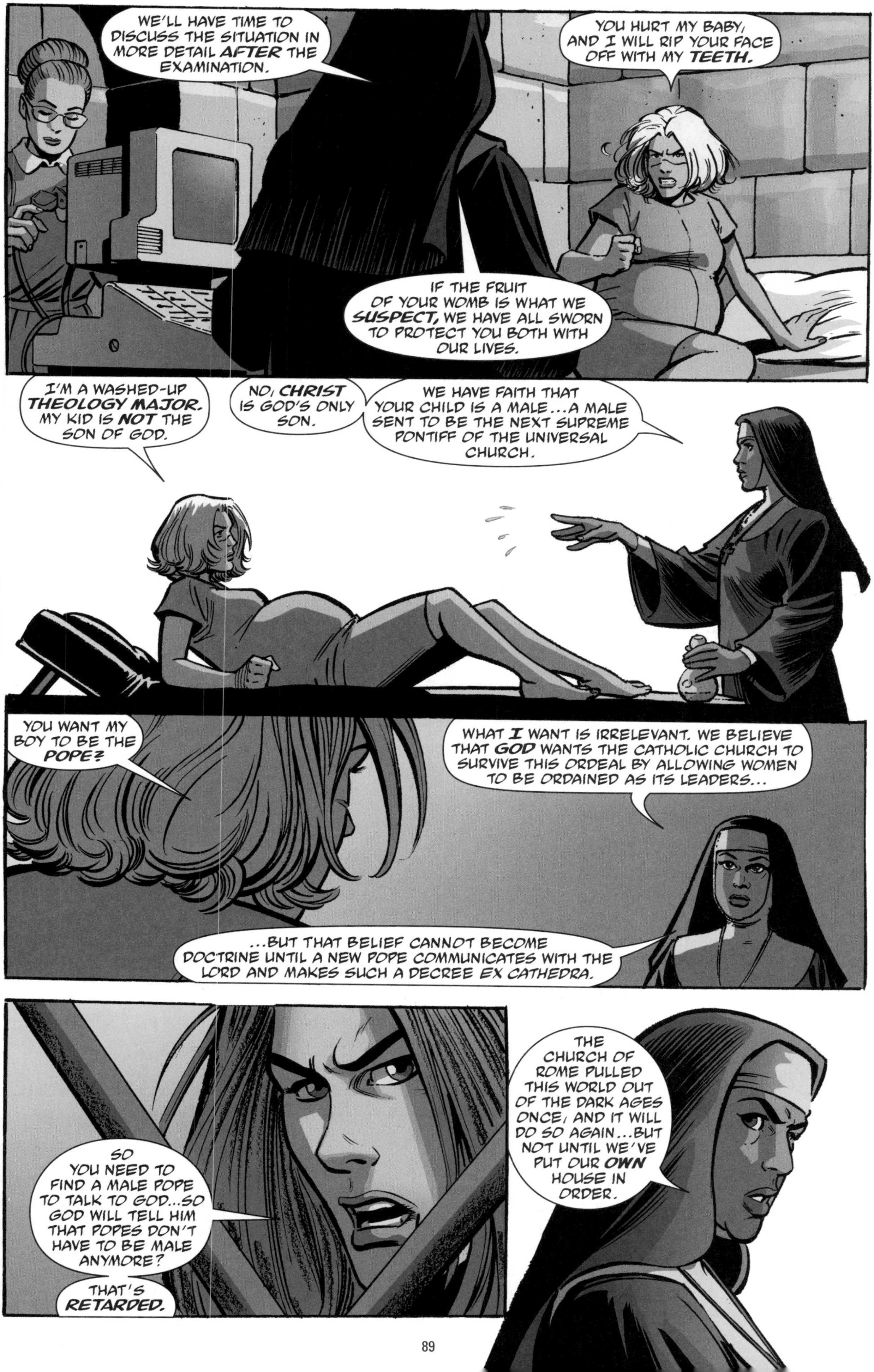
WE'LL HAVE TIME TO DISCUSS THE SITUATION IN MORE DETAIL AFTER THE EXAMINATION.
YOU HURT MY BABY, AND I WILL RIP YOUR FACE OFF WITH MY TEETH.
IF THE FRUIT OF YOUR WOMB IS WHAT WE SUSPECT, WE HAVE ALL SWORN TO PROTECT YOU BOTH WITH OUR LIVES.
I'M A WASHED-UP THEOLOGY MAJOR. MY KID IS NOT THE SON OF GOD.
NO, CHRIST IS GOD'S ONLY SON.
WE HAVE FAITH THAT YOUR CHILD IS A MALE...A MALE SENT TO BE THE NEXT SUPREME PONTIFF OF THE UNIVERSAL CHURCH.
YOU WANT MY BOY TO BE THE POPE?
WHAT I WANT IS IRRELEVANT. WE BELIEVE THAT GOD WANTS THE CATHOLIC CHURCH TO SURVIVE THIS ORDEAL BY ALLOWING WOMEN TO BE ORDAINED AS ITS LEADERS...
...BUT THAT BELIEF CANNOT BECOME DOCTRINE UNTIL A NEW POPE COMMUNICATES WITH THE LORD AND MAKES SUCH A DECREE EX CATHEDRA.
SO YOU NEED TO FIND A MALE POPE TO TALK TO GOD...SO GOD WILL TELL HIM THAT POPES DON'T HAVE TO BE MALE ANYMORE?
THAT'S RETARDED.
THE CHURCH OF ROME PULLED THIS WORLD OUT OF THE DARK AGES ONCE, AND IT WILL DO SO AGAIN...BUT NOT UNTIL WE'VE PUT OUR OWN HOUSE IN ORDER.

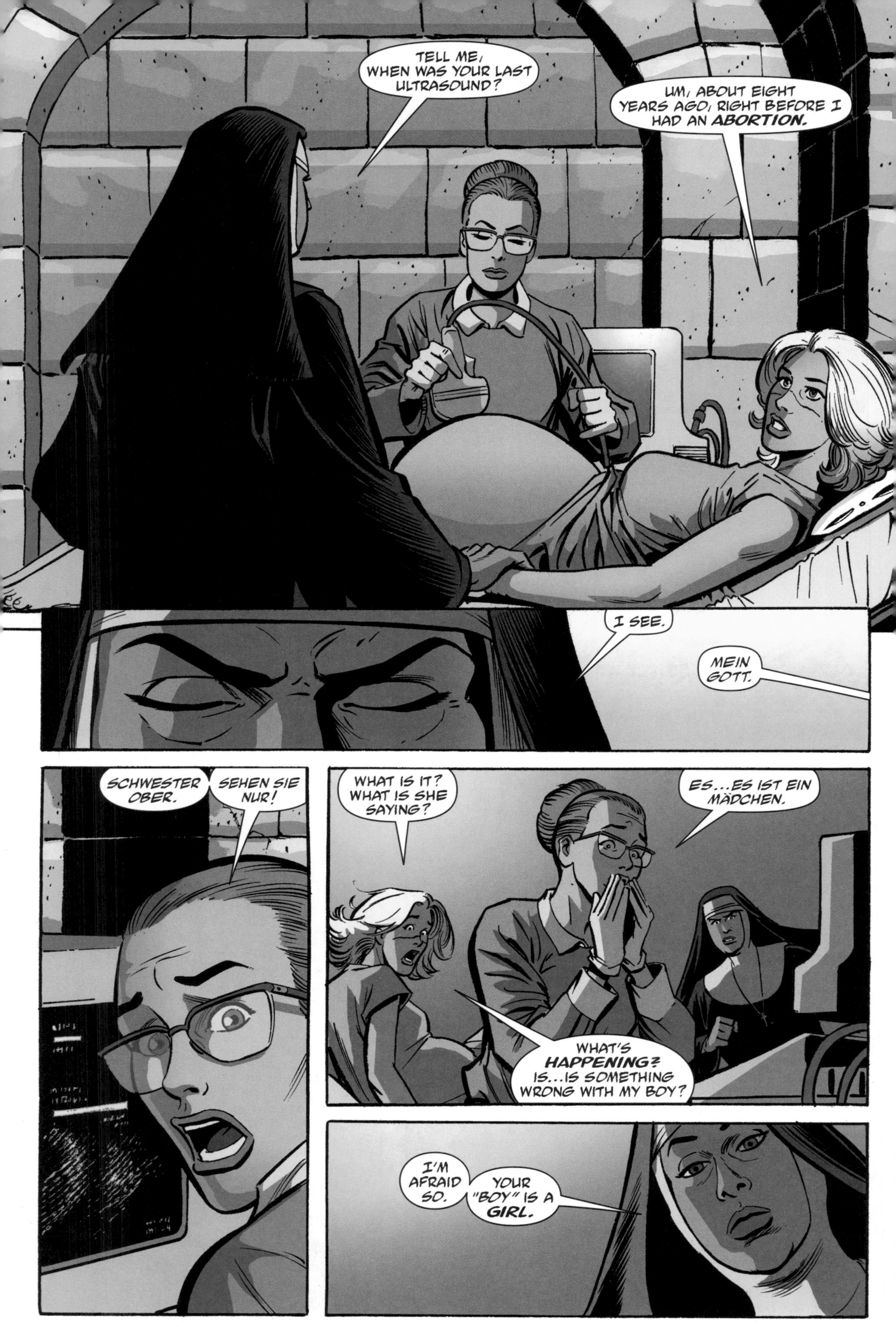
TELL ME, WHEN WAS YOUR LAST ULTRASOUND?
UM, ABOUT EIGHT YEARS AGO, RIGHT BEFORE I HAD AN **ABORTION.**
I SEE.
MEIN GOTT.
SCHWESTER OBER.
SEHEN SIE NUR!
WHAT IS IT? WHAT IS SHE SAYING?
ES...ES IST EIN MÄDCHEN.
WHAT'S **HAPPENING?** IS...IS SOMETHING WRONG WITH MY BOY?
I'M AFRAID SO.
YOUR "BOY" IS A **GIRL.**

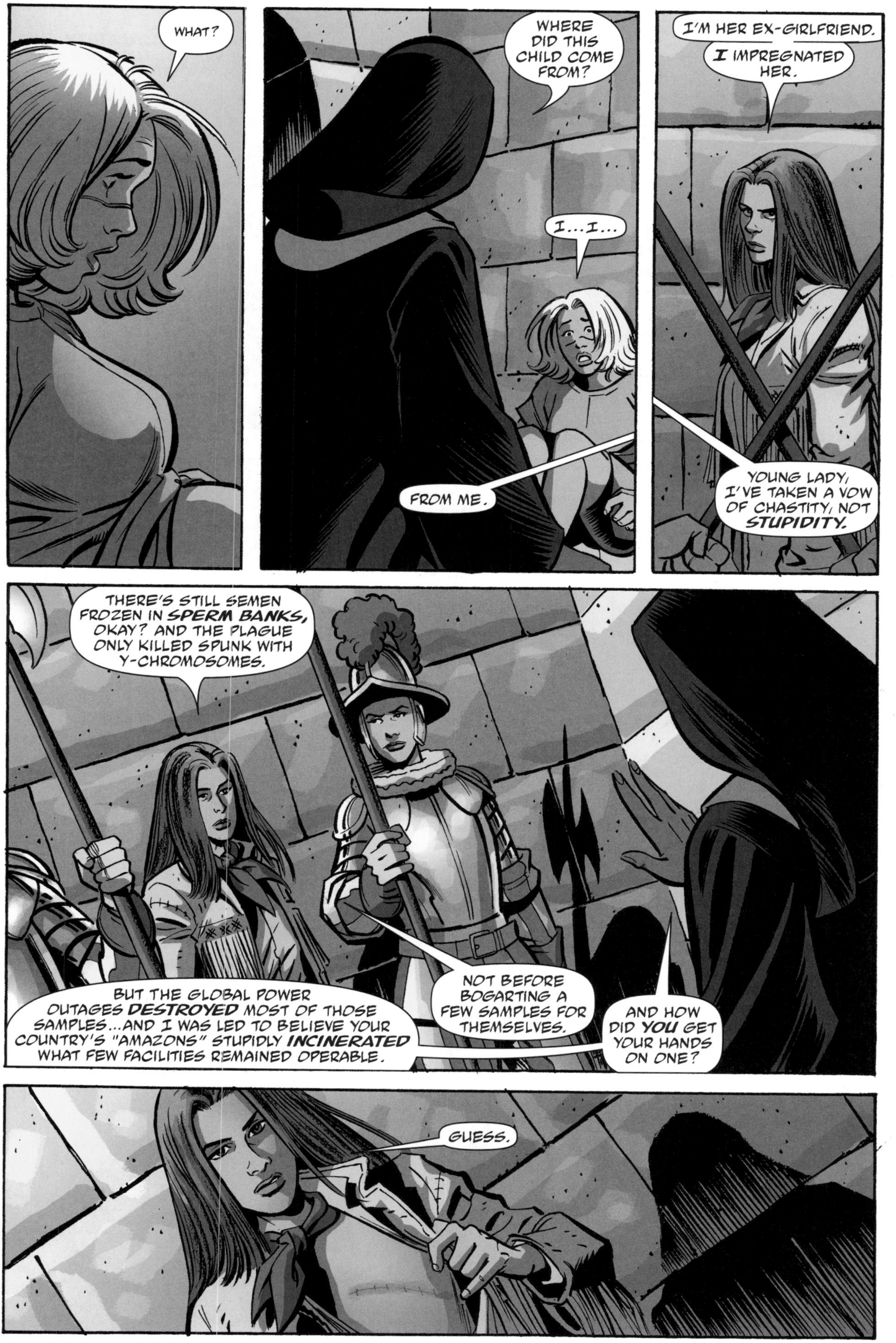
WHAT?
WHERE DID THIS CHILD COME FROM?
I...I...
FROM ME.
I'M HER EX-GIRLFRIEND. I IMPREGNATED HER.
YOUNG LADY, I'VE TAKEN A VOW OF CHASTITY, NOT STUPIDITY.
THERE'S STILL SEMEN FROZEN IN SPERM BANKS, OKAY? AND THE PLAGUE ONLY KILLED SPUNK WITH Y-CHROMOSOMES.
BUT THE GLOBAL POWER OUTAGES DESTROYED MOST OF THOSE SAMPLES...AND I WAS LED TO BELIEVE YOUR COUNTRY'S "AMAZONS" STUPIDLY INCINERATED WHAT FEW FACILITIES REMAINED OPERABLE.
NOT BEFORE BOGARTING A FEW SAMPLES FOR THEMSELVES.
AND HOW DID YOU GET YOUR HANDS ON ONE?
GUESS.

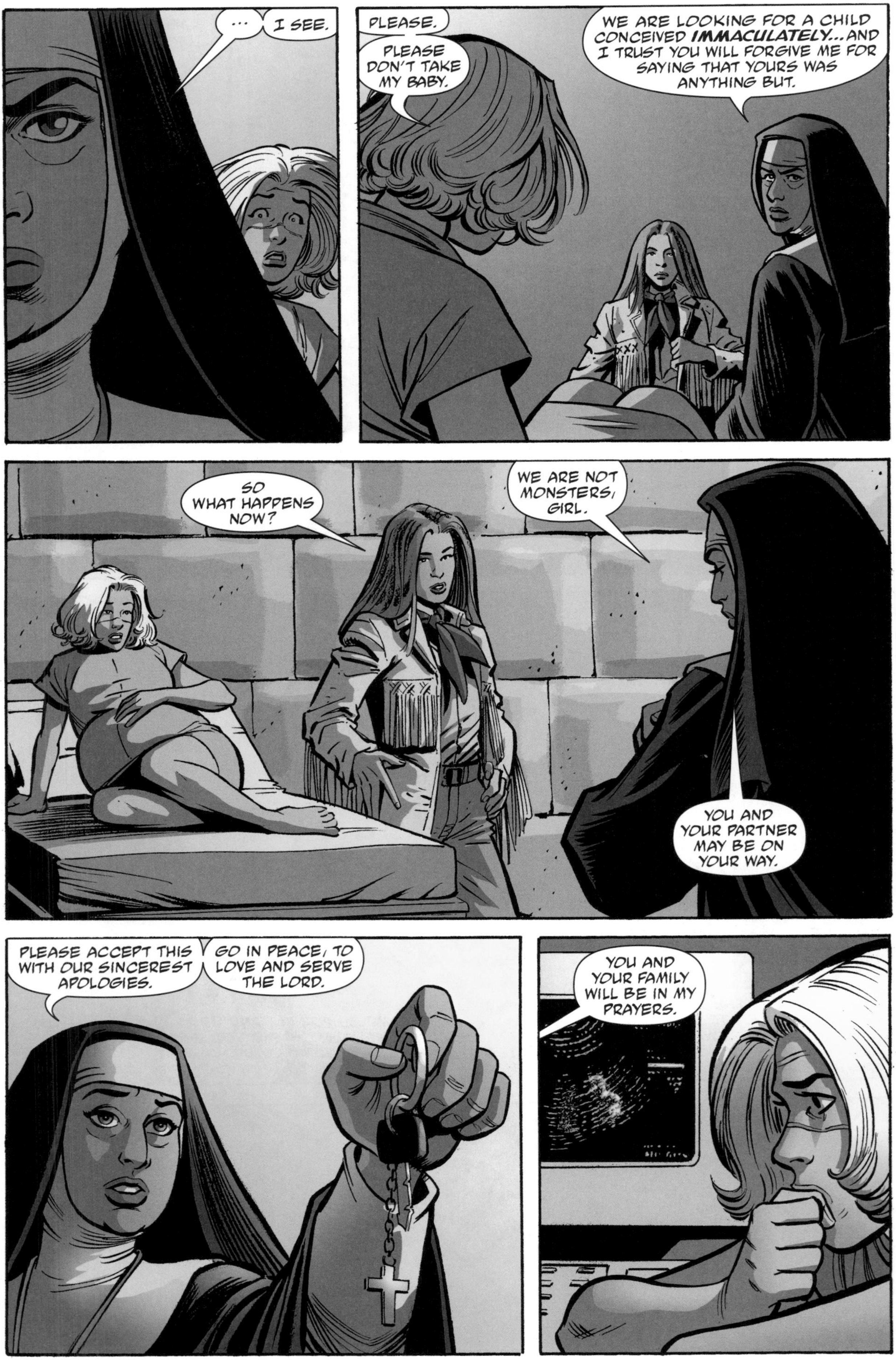
...
I SEE.
PLEASE.
PLEASE DON'T TAKE MY BABY.
WE ARE LOOKING FOR A CHILD CONCEIVED **IMMACULATELY...** AND I TRUST YOU WILL FORGIVE ME FOR SAYING THAT YOURS WAS ANYTHING BUT.
SO WHAT HAPPENS NOW?
WE ARE NOT MONSTERS, GIRL.
YOU AND YOUR PARTNER MAY BE ON YOUR WAY.
PLEASE ACCEPT THIS WITH OUR SINCEREST APOLOGIES.
GO IN PEACE, TO LOVE AND SERVE THE LORD.
YOU AND YOUR FAMILY WILL BE IN MY PRAYERS.

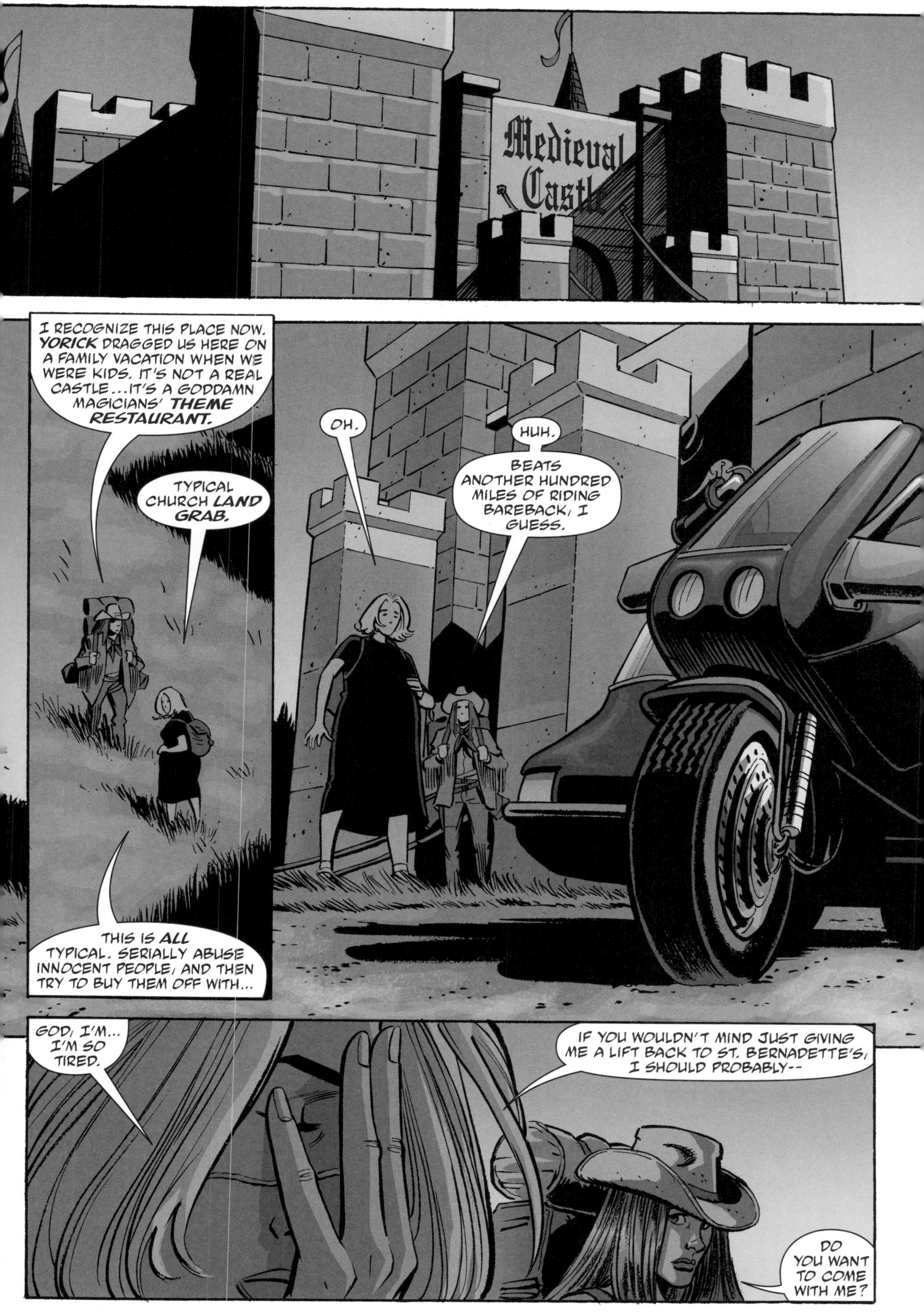
Medieval Castle
I RECOGNIZE THIS PLACE NOW. YORICK DRAGGED US HERE ON A FAMILY VACATION WHEN WE WERE KIDS. IT'S NOT A REAL CASTLE... IT'S A GODDAMN MAGICIANS' THEME RESTAURANT.
TYPICAL CHURCH LAND GRAB.
THIS IS ALL TYPICAL. SERIALLY ABUSE INNOCENT PEOPLE, AND THEN TRY TO BUY THEM OFF WITH...
OH.
HUH.
BEATS ANOTHER HUNDRED MILES OF RIDING BAREBACK, I GUESS.
GOD, I'M... I'M SO TIRED.
IF YOU WOULDN'T MIND JUST GIVING ME A LIFT BACK TO ST. BERNADETTE'S, I SHOULD PROBABLY--
DO YOU WANT TO COME WITH ME?

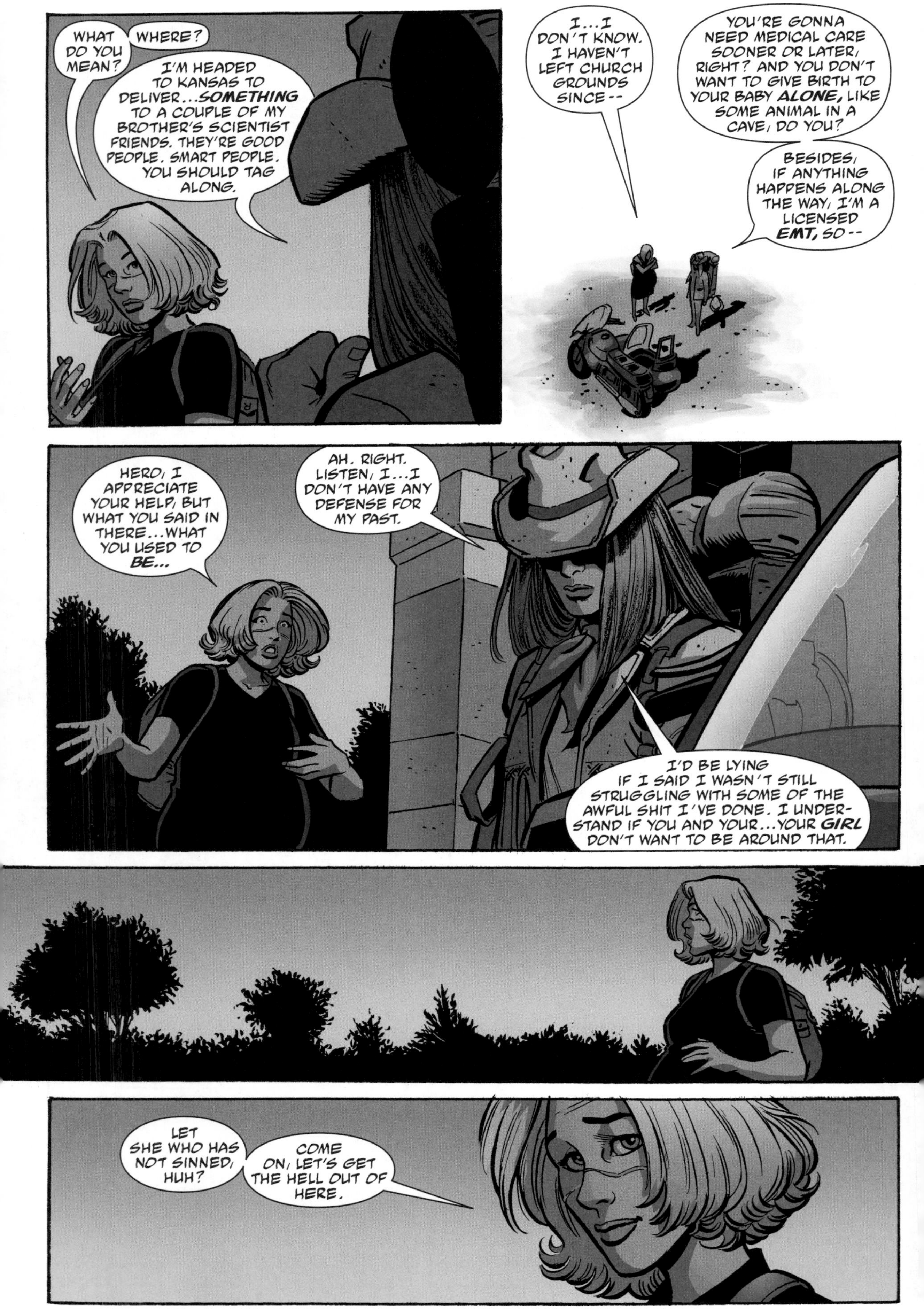
WHAT DO YOU MEAN?
WHERE?
I'M HEADED TO KANSAS TO DELIVER...SOMETHING TO A COUPLE OF MY BROTHER'S SCIENTIST FRIENDS. THEY'RE GOOD PEOPLE. SMART PEOPLE. YOU SHOULD TAG ALONG.
I...I DON'T KNOW. I HAVEN'T LEFT CHURCH GROUNDS SINCE --
YOU'RE GONNA NEED MEDICAL CARE SOONER OR LATER, RIGHT? AND YOU DON'T WANT TO GIVE BIRTH TO YOUR BABY ALONE, LIKE SOME ANIMAL IN A CAVE, DO YOU?
BESIDES, IF ANYTHING HAPPENS ALONG THE WAY, I'M A LICENSED EMT, SO --
HERO, I APPRECIATE YOUR HELP, BUT WHAT YOU SAID IN THERE...WHAT YOU USED TO BE...
AH. RIGHT. LISTEN, I...I DON'T HAVE ANY DEFENSE FOR MY PAST.
I'D BE LYING IF I SAID I WASN'T STILL STRUGGLING WITH SOME OF THE AWFUL SHIT I'VE DONE. I UNDERSTAND IF YOU AND YOUR...YOUR GIRL DON'T WANT TO BE AROUND THAT.
LET SHE WHO HAS NOT SINNED, HUH?
COME ON, LET'S GET THE HELL OUT OF HERE.

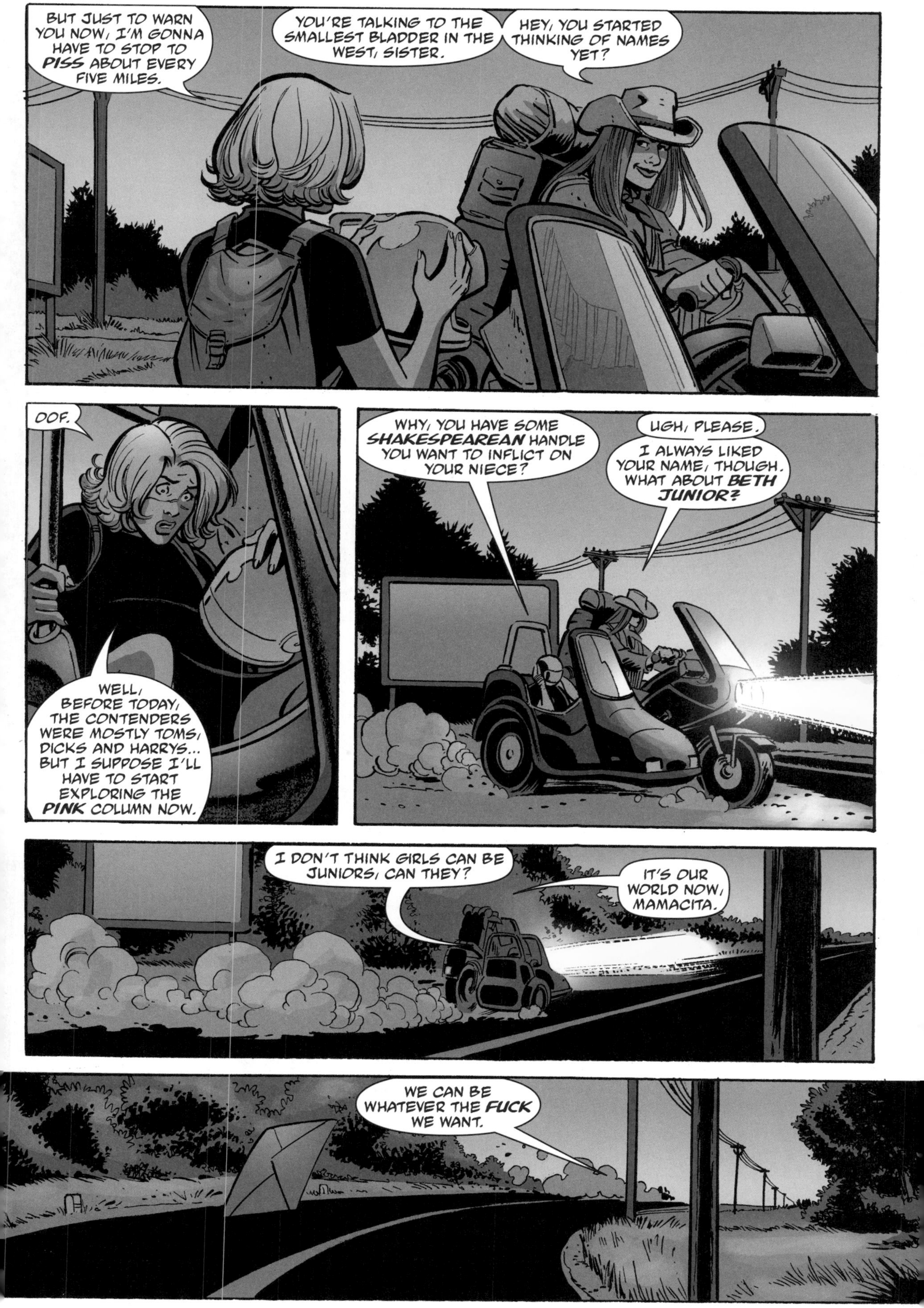
BUT JUST TO WARN YOU NOW, I'M GONNA HAVE TO STOP TO PISS ABOUT EVERY FIVE MILES.
YOU'RE TALKING TO THE SMALLEST BLADDER IN THE WEST, SISTER.
HEY, YOU STARTED THINKING OF NAMES YET?
OOF.
WELL, BEFORE TODAY, THE CONTENDERS WERE MOSTLY TOMS, DICKS AND HARRYS... BUT I SUPPOSE I'LL HAVE TO START EXPLORING THE PINK COLUMN NOW.
WHY, YOU HAVE SOME SHAKESPEAREAN HANDLE YOU WANT TO INFLICT ON YOUR NIECE?
UGH, PLEASE.
I ALWAYS LIKED YOUR NAME, THOUGH. WHAT ABOUT BETH JUNIOR?
I DON'T THINK GIRLS CAN BE JUNIORS, CAN THEY?
IT'S OUR WORLD NOW, MAMACITA.
WE CAN BE WHATEVER THE FUCK WE WANT.

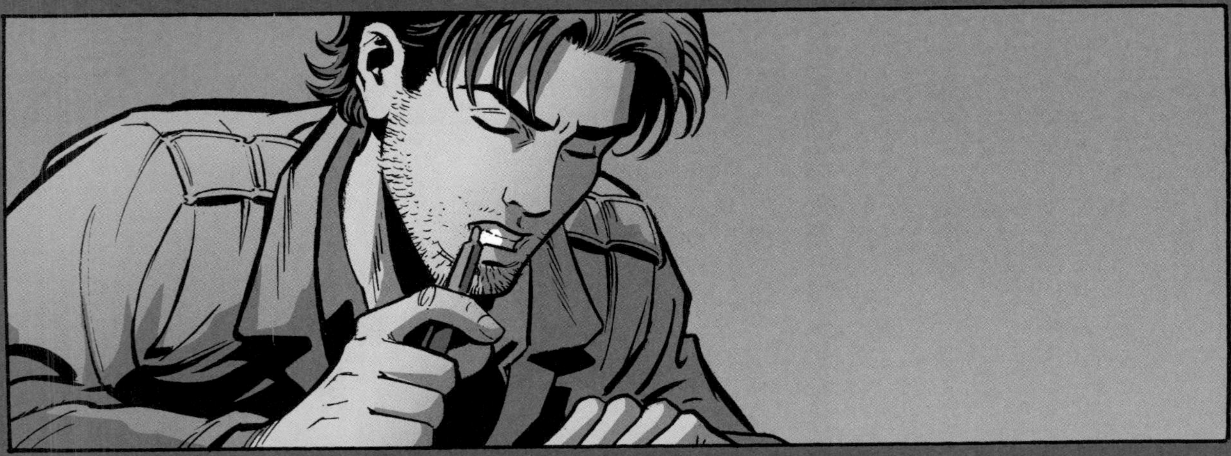

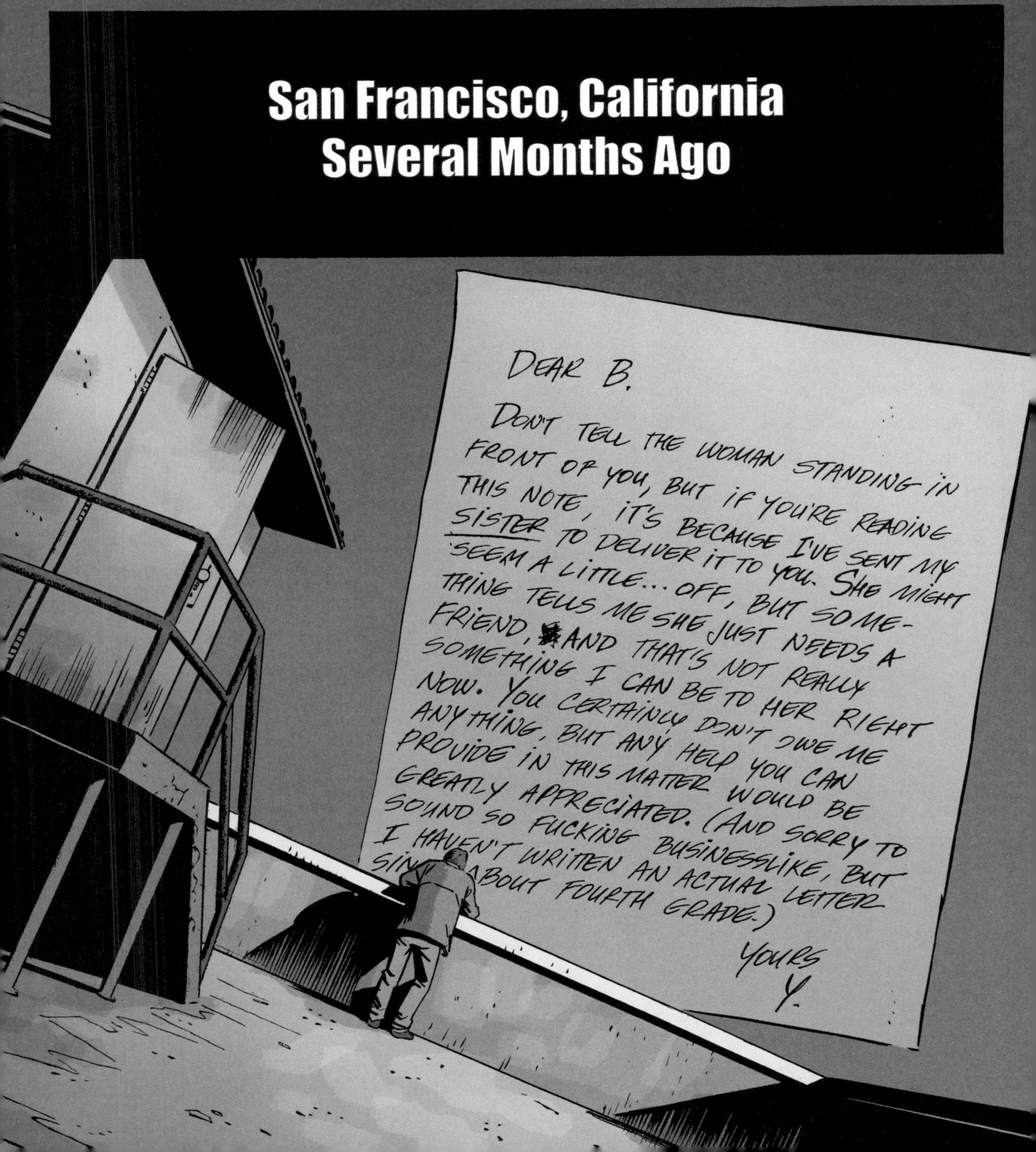
San Francisco, California
Several Months Ago
DEAR B.
DON'T TELL THE WOMAN STANDING IN FRONT OF YOU, BUT IF YOU'RE READING THIS NOTE, IT'S BECAUSE I'VE SENT MY SISTER TO DELIVER IT TO YOU. SHE MIGHT SEEM A LITTLE... OFF, BUT SOMETHING TELLS ME SHE JUST NEEDS A FRIEND, AND THAT'S NOT REALLY SOMETHING I CAN BE TO HER RIGHT NOW. YOU CERTAINLY DON'T OWE ME ANYTHING, BUT ANY HELP YOU CAN PROVIDE IN THIS MATTER WOULD BE GREATLY APPRECIATED. (AND SORRY TO SOUND SO FUCKING BUSINESSLIKE, BUT I HAVEN'T WRITTEN AN ACTUAL LETTER SIN ABOUT FOURTH GRADE.)
YOURS
Y.

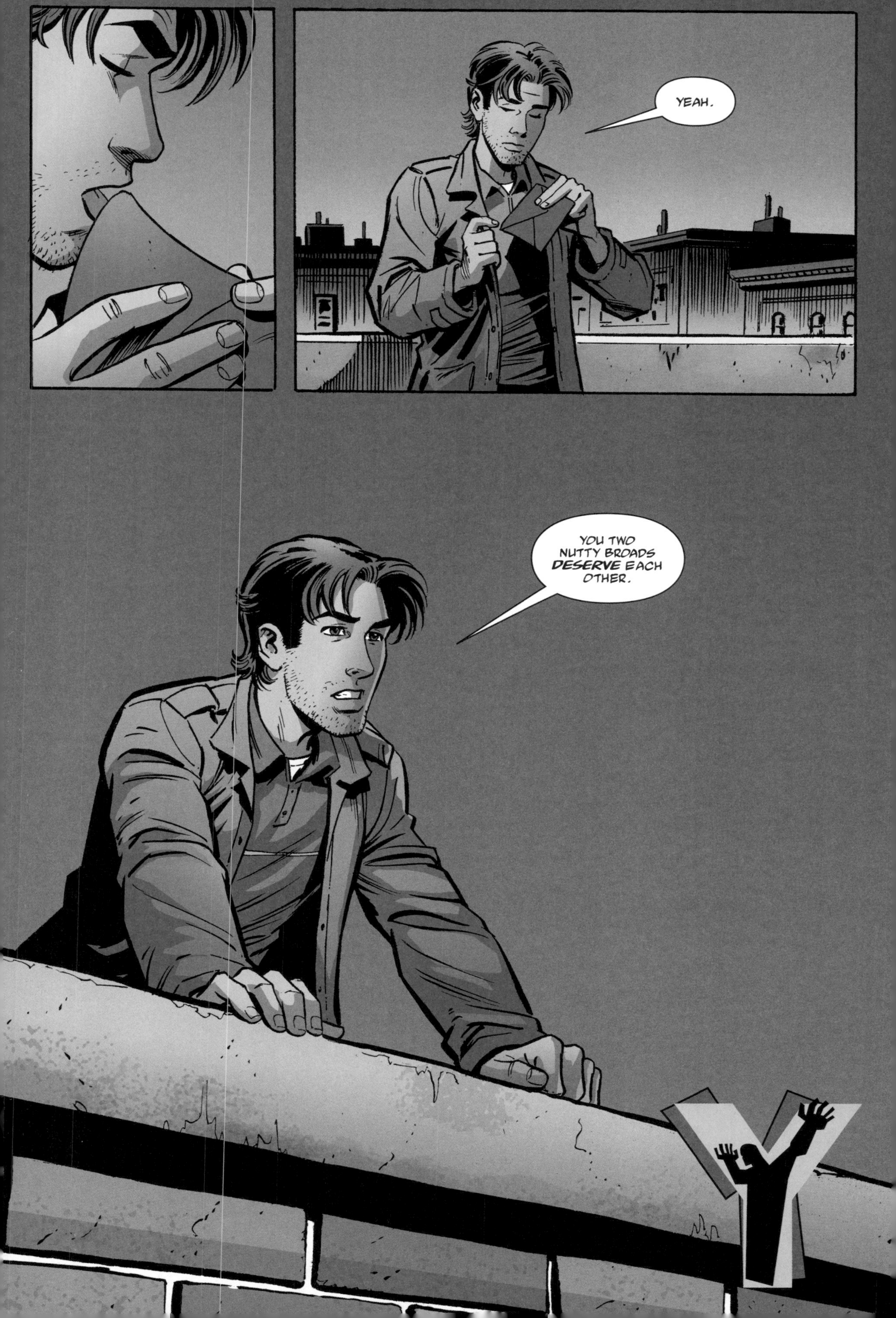
YEAH.
YOU TWO NUTTY BROADS DESERVE EACH OTHER.

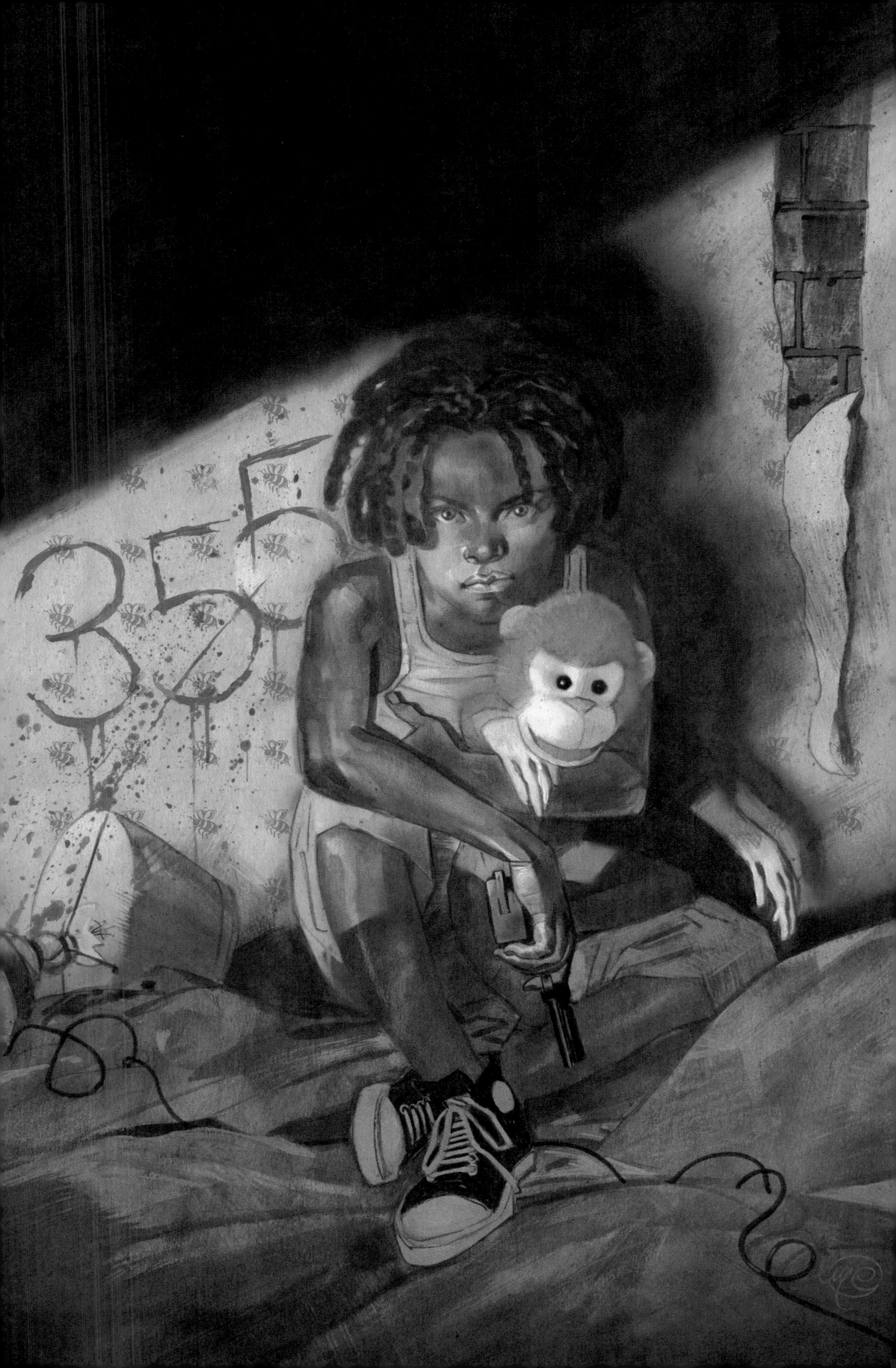

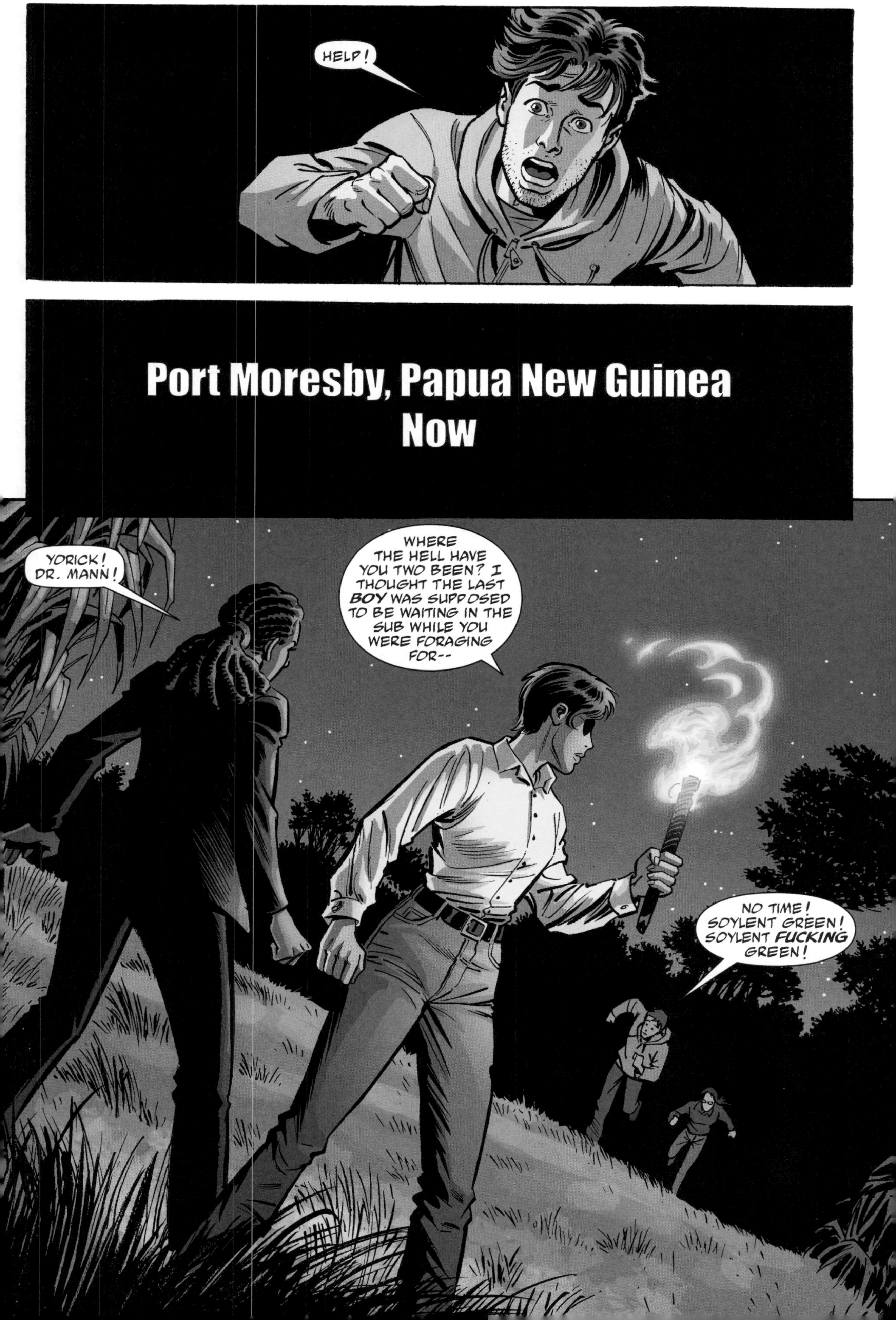
HELP!
Port Moresby, Papua New Guinea
Now
YORICK! DR. MANN!
WHERE THE HELL HAVE YOU TWO BEEN? I THOUGHT THE LAST BOY WAS SUPPOSED TO BE WAITING IN THE SUB WHILE YOU WERE FORAGING FOR--
NO TIME! SOYLENT GREEN! SOYLENT FUCKING GREEN!

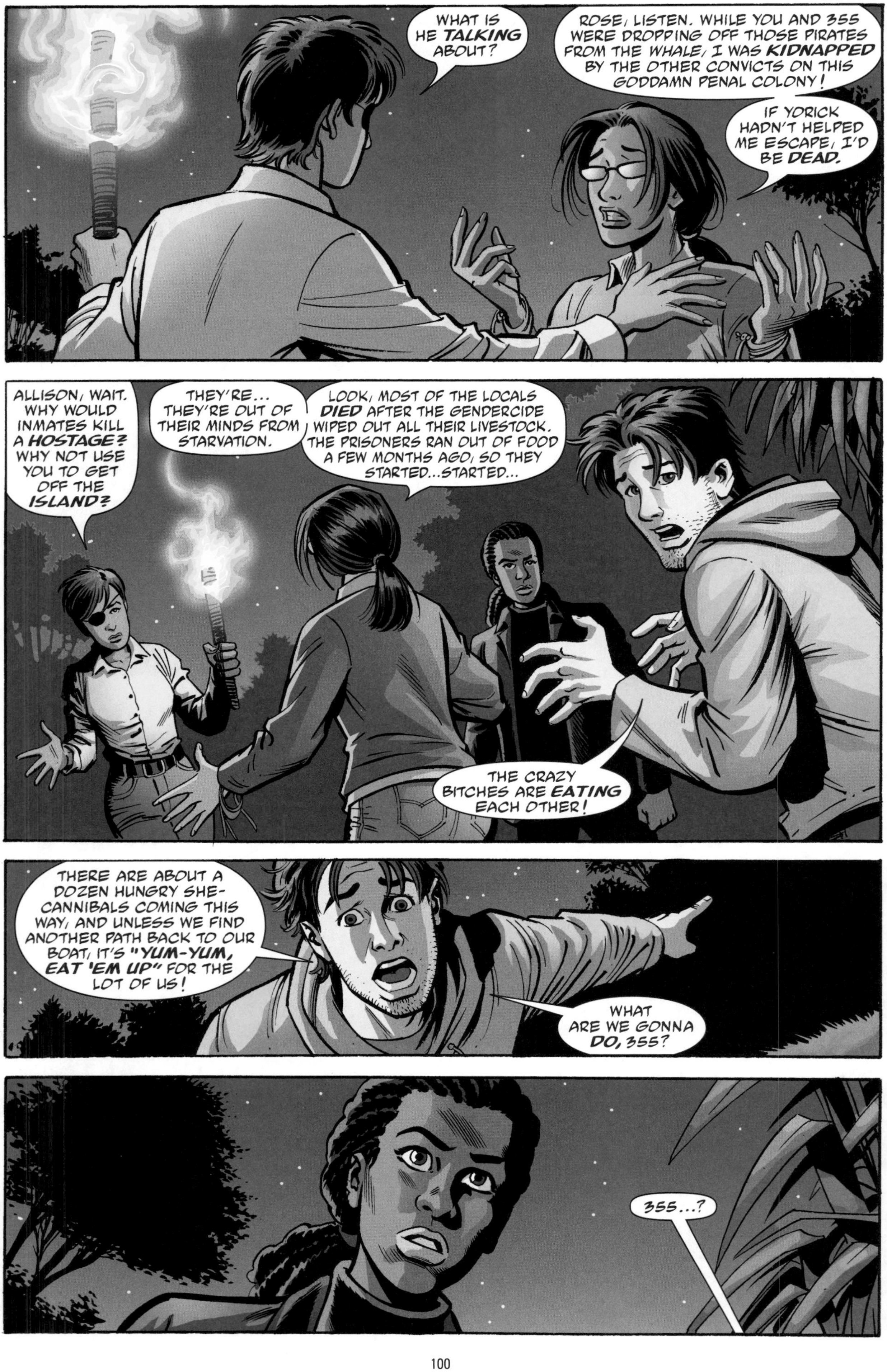
WHAT IS HE TALKING ABOUT?
ROSE, LISTEN. WHILE YOU AND 355 WERE DROPPING OFF THOSE PIRATES FROM THE WHALE, I WAS KIDNAPPED BY THE OTHER CONVICTS ON THIS GODDAMN PENAL COLONY!
IF YORICK HADN'T HELPED ME ESCAPE, I'D BE DEAD.
ALLISON, WAIT. WHY WOULD INMATES KILL A HOSTAGE? WHY NOT USE YOU TO GET OFF THE ISLAND?
THEY'RE... THEY'RE OUT OF THEIR MINDS FROM STARVATION.
LOOK, MOST OF THE LOCALS DIED AFTER THE GENDERCIDE WIPED OUT ALL THEIR LIVESTOCK. THE PRISONERS RAN OUT OF FOOD A FEW MONTHS AGO, SO THEY STARTED...STARTED...
THE CRAZY BITCHES ARE EATING EACH OTHER!
THERE ARE ABOUT A DOZEN HUNGRY SHE-CANNIBALS COMING THIS WAY, AND UNLESS WE FIND ANOTHER PATH BACK TO OUR BOAT, IT'S "YUM-YUM, EAT 'EM UP" FOR THE LOT OF US!
WHAT ARE WE GONNA DO, 355?
355...?

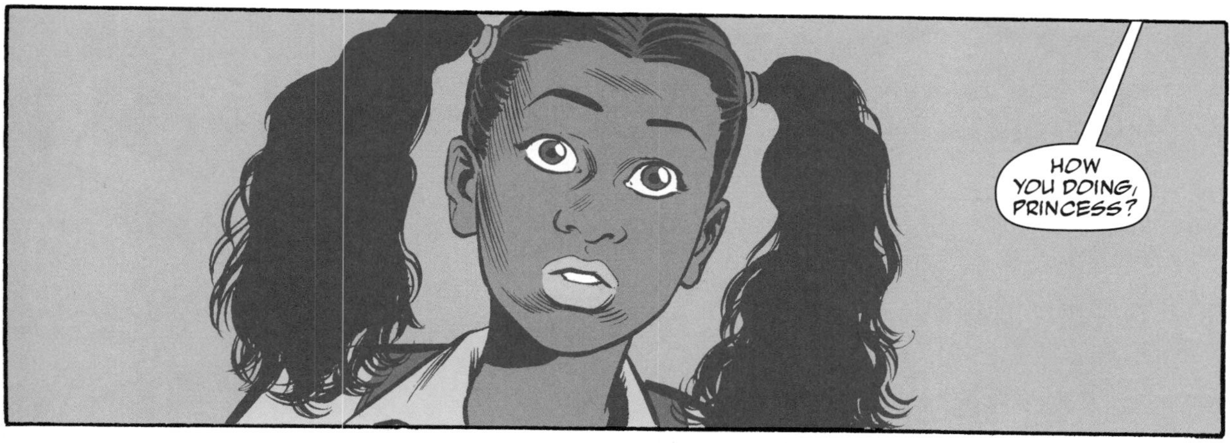
HOW YOU DOING, PRINCESS?

Detroit, Michigan
Twenty-Five Years Ago

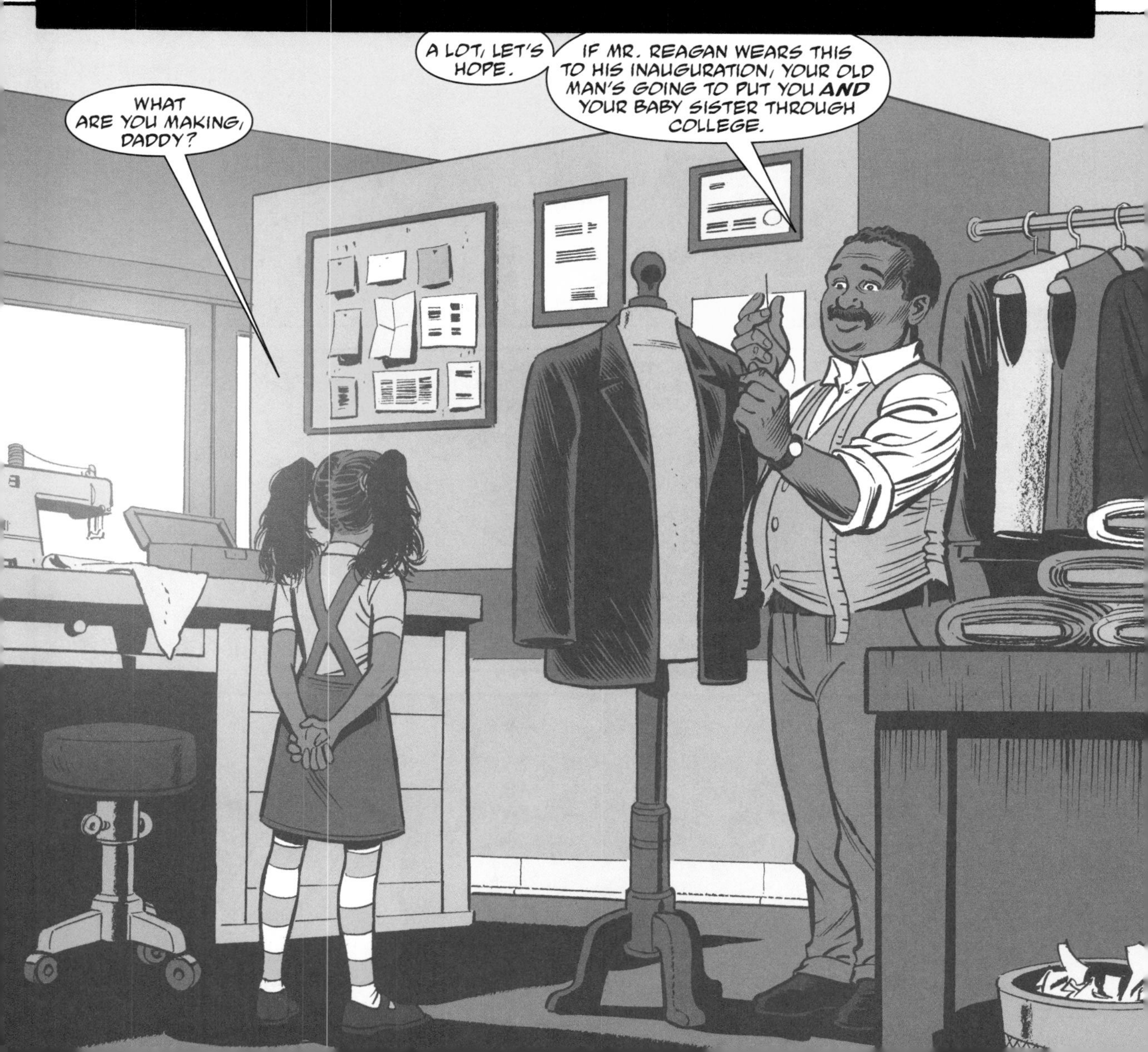
WHAT ARE YOU MAKING, DADDY?
A LOT, LET'S HOPE.
IF MR. REAGAN WEARS THIS TO HIS INAUGURATION, YOUR OLD MAN'S GOING TO PUT YOU ***AND*** YOUR BABY SISTER THROUGH COLLEGE.

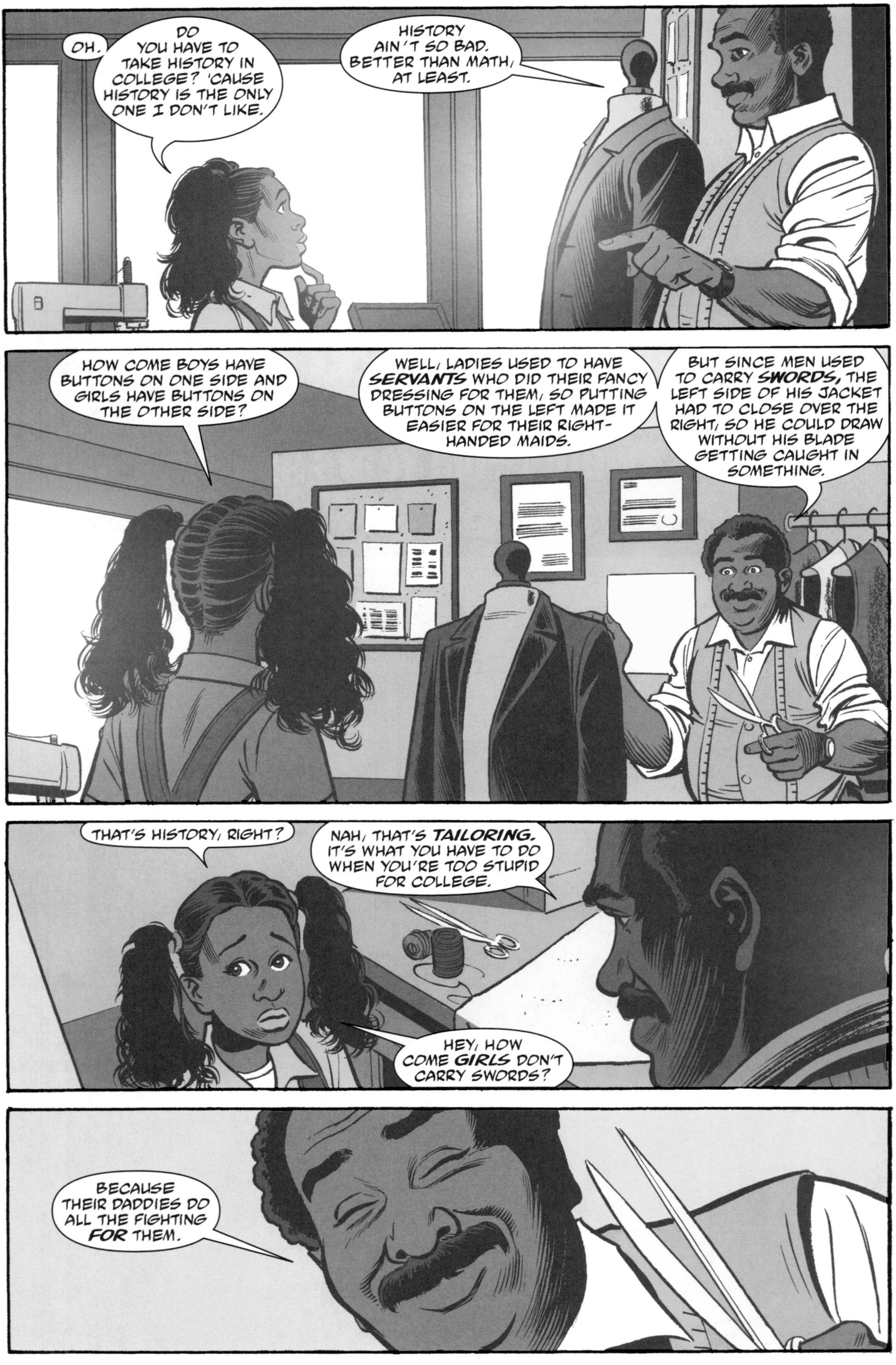
OH.
DO YOU HAVE TO TAKE HISTORY IN COLLEGE? 'CAUSE HISTORY IS THE ONLY ONE I DON'T LIKE.
HISTORY AIN'T SO BAD. BETTER THAN MATH, AT LEAST.
HOW COME BOYS HAVE BUTTONS ON ONE SIDE AND GIRLS HAVE BUTTONS ON THE OTHER SIDE?
WELL, LADIES USED TO HAVE SERVANTS WHO DID THEIR FANCY DRESSING FOR THEM, SO PUTTING BUTTONS ON THE LEFT MADE IT EASIER FOR THEIR RIGHT-HANDED MAIDS.
BUT SINCE MEN USED TO CARRY SWORDS, THE LEFT SIDE OF HIS JACKET HAD TO CLOSE OVER THE RIGHT, SO HE COULD DRAW WITHOUT HIS BLADE GETTING CAUGHT IN SOMETHING.
THAT'S HISTORY, RIGHT?
NAH, THAT'S TAILORING. IT'S WHAT YOU HAVE TO DO WHEN YOU'RE TOO STUPID FOR COLLEGE.
HEY, HOW COME GIRLS DON'T CARRY SWORDS?
BECAUSE THEIR DADDIES DO ALL THE FIGHTING FOR THEM.

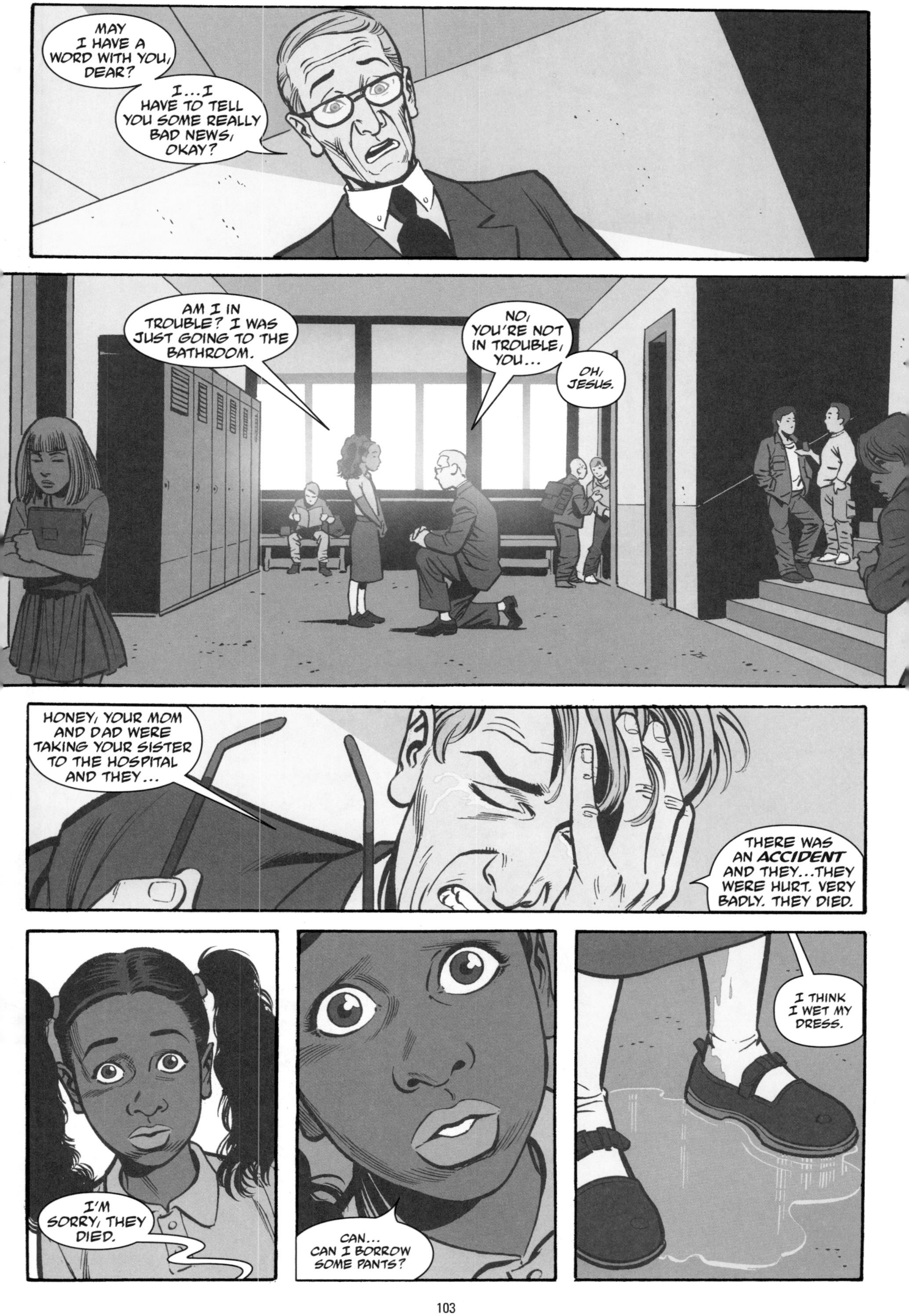
MAY I HAVE A WORD WITH YOU, DEAR?
I...I HAVE TO TELL YOU SOME REALLY BAD NEWS, OKAY?
AM I IN TROUBLE? I WAS JUST GOING TO THE BATHROOM.
NO, YOU'RE NOT IN TROUBLE, YOU...
OH, JESUS.
HONEY, YOUR MOM AND DAD WERE TAKING YOUR SISTER TO THE HOSPITAL AND THEY...
THERE WAS AN ACCIDENT AND THEY...THEY WERE HURT. VERY BADLY. THEY DIED.
I'M SORRY, THEY DIED.
CAN... CAN I BORROW SOME PANTS?
I THINK I WET MY DRESS.

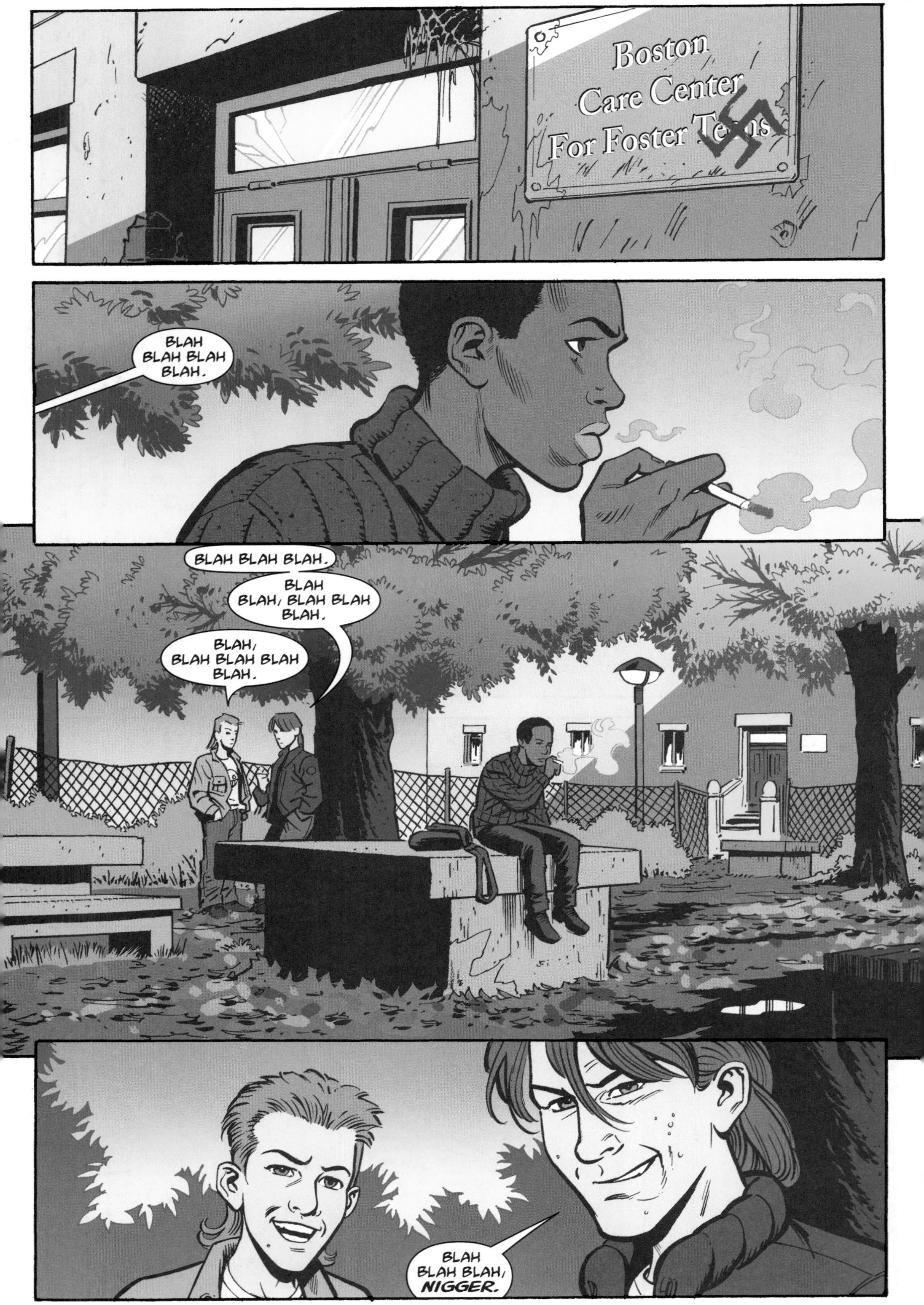
Boston
Care Center
For Foster
BLAH BLAH BLAH BLAH.
BLAH BLAH BLAH.
BLAH BLAH, BLAH BLAH BLAH.
BLAH, BLAH BLAH BLAH BLAH.
BLAH BLAH BLAH, NIGGER.

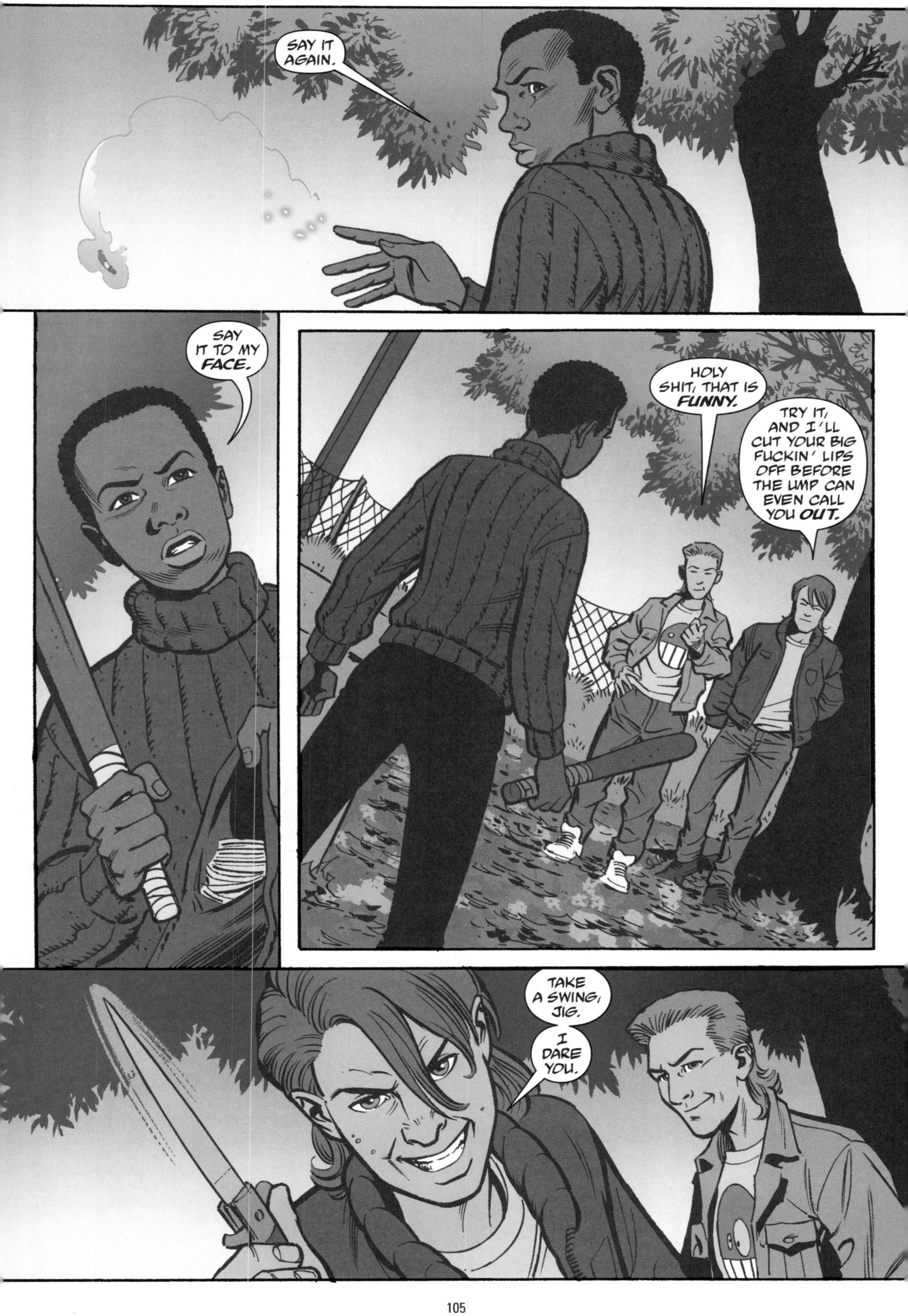
SAY IT AGAIN.
SAY IT TO MY FACE.
HOLY SHIT, THAT IS FUNNY.
TRY IT, AND I'LL CUT YOUR BIG FUCKIN' LIPS OFF BEFORE THE UMP CAN EVEN CALL YOU OUT.
TAKE A SWING, JIG.
I DARE YOU.

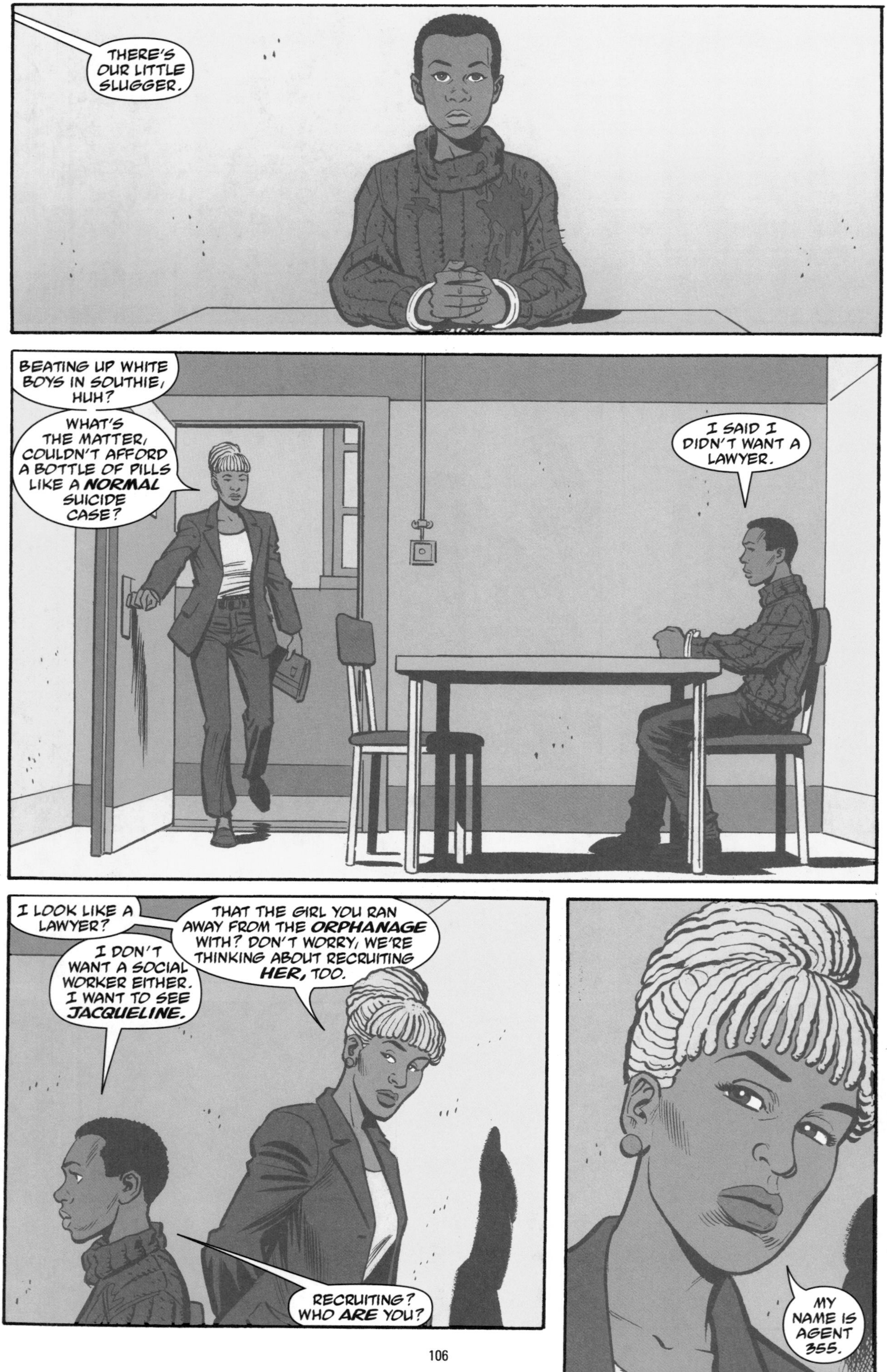
THERE'S OUR LITTLE SLUGGER.
BEATING UP WHITE BOYS IN SOUTHIE, HUH?
WHAT'S THE MATTER, COULDN'T AFFORD A BOTTLE OF PILLS LIKE A NORMAL SUICIDE CASE?
I SAID I DIDN'T WANT A LAWYER.
I LOOK LIKE A LAWYER?
I DON'T WANT A SOCIAL WORKER EITHER. I WANT TO SEE JACQUELINE.
THAT THE GIRL YOU RAN AWAY FROM THE ORPHANAGE WITH? DON'T WORRY, WE'RE THINKING ABOUT RECRUITING HER, TOO.
RECRUITING? WHO ARE YOU?
MY NAME IS AGENT 355.

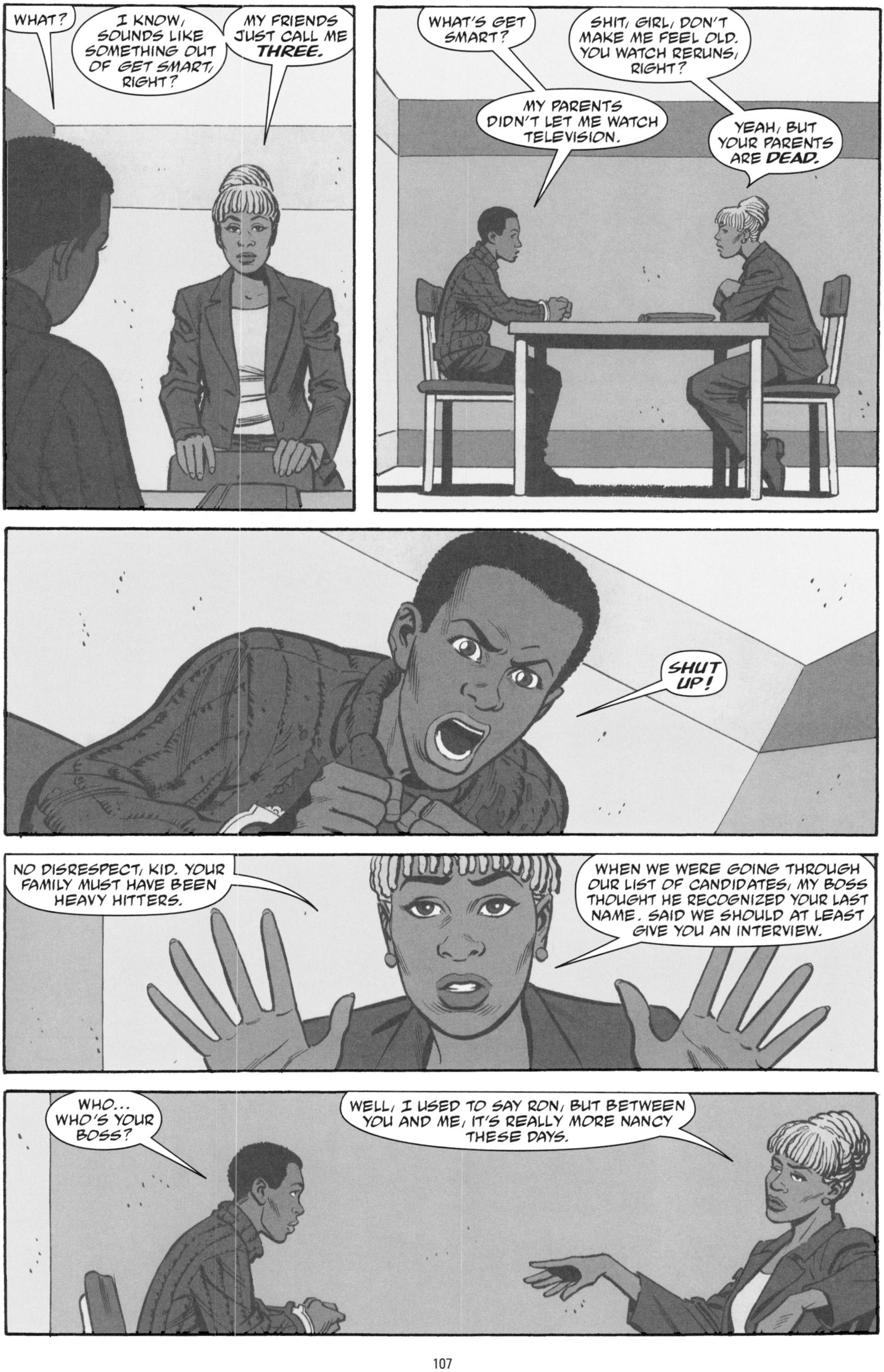
WHAT?
I KNOW, SOUNDS LIKE SOMETHING OUT OF GET SMART, RIGHT?
MY FRIENDS JUST CALL ME THREE.
WHAT'S GET SMART?
MY PARENTS DIDN'T LET ME WATCH TELEVISION.
SHIT, GIRL, DON'T MAKE ME FEEL OLD. YOU WATCH RERUNS, RIGHT?
YEAH, BUT YOUR PARENTS ARE DEAD.
SHUT UP!
NO DISRESPECT, KID. YOUR FAMILY MUST HAVE BEEN HEAVY HITTERS.
WHEN WE WERE GOING THROUGH OUR LIST OF CANDIDATES, MY BOSS THOUGHT HE RECOGNIZED YOUR LAST NAME. SAID WE SHOULD AT LEAST GIVE YOU AN INTERVIEW.
WHO... WHO'S YOUR BOSS?
WELL, I USED TO SAY RON, BUT BETWEEN YOU AND ME, IT'S REALLY MORE NANCY THESE DAYS.

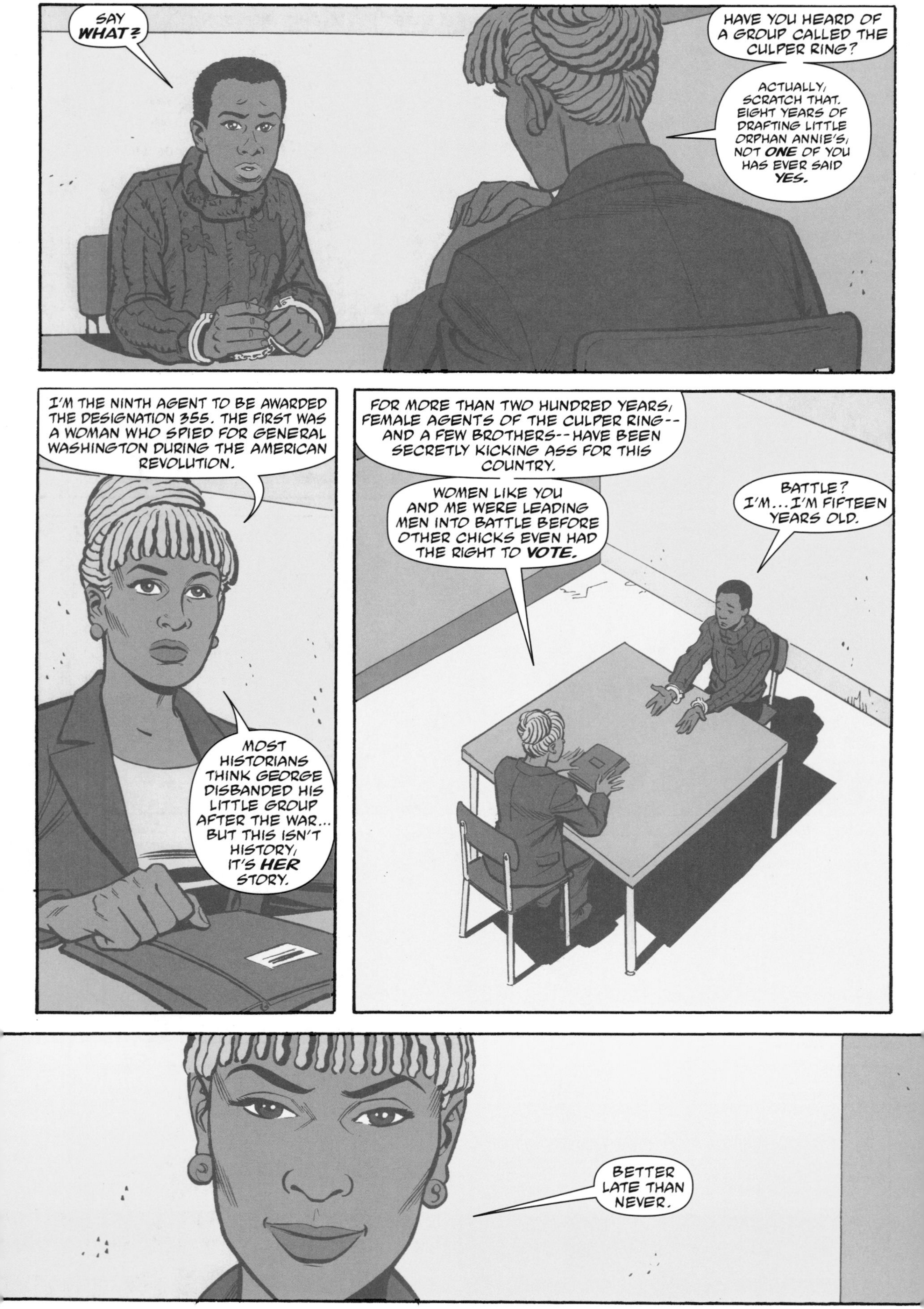
SAY WHAT?
HAVE YOU HEARD OF A GROUP CALLED THE CULPER RING?
ACTUALLY, SCRATCH THAT. EIGHT YEARS OF DRAFTING LITTLE ORPHAN ANNIE'S, NOT ONE OF YOU HAS EVER SAID YES.
I'M THE NINTH AGENT TO BE AWARDED THE DESIGNATION 355. THE FIRST WAS A WOMAN WHO SPIED FOR GENERAL WASHINGTON DURING THE AMERICAN REVOLUTION.
MOST HISTORIANS THINK GEORGE DISBANDED HIS LITTLE GROUP AFTER THE WAR... BUT THIS ISN'T HISTORY, IT'S HER STORY.
FOR MORE THAN TWO HUNDRED YEARS, FEMALE AGENTS OF THE CULPER RING-- AND A FEW BROTHERS--HAVE BEEN SECRETLY KICKING ASS FOR THIS COUNTRY.
WOMEN LIKE YOU AND ME WERE LEADING MEN INTO BATTLE BEFORE OTHER CHICKS EVEN HAD THE RIGHT TO VOTE.
BATTLE? I'M...I'M FIFTEEN YEARS OLD.
BETTER LATE THAN NEVER.

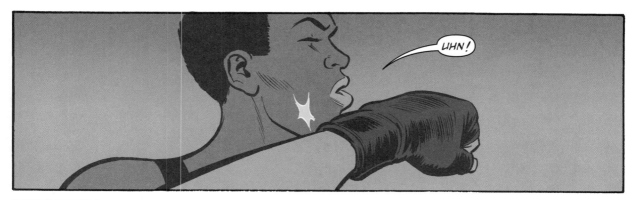

UHN!

NOT SO TOUGH WITHOUT THE **BAT,** ARE YOU?

SCREW YOU, THREE.

NINE TIMES OUT OF TEN, A MAN IS GONNA BE STRONGER THAN YOU. BIOLOGY'S A BITCH, BUT THERE YOU GO.

FORGET WHAT YOU SAW ON *CHARLIE'S ANGELS,* EVEN AN **AVERAGE** GUY IS USUALLY GONNA BE ABLE TO OVER-POWER YOU.

I TOLD YOU...

...I DON'T **WATCH** TV.

UNF!

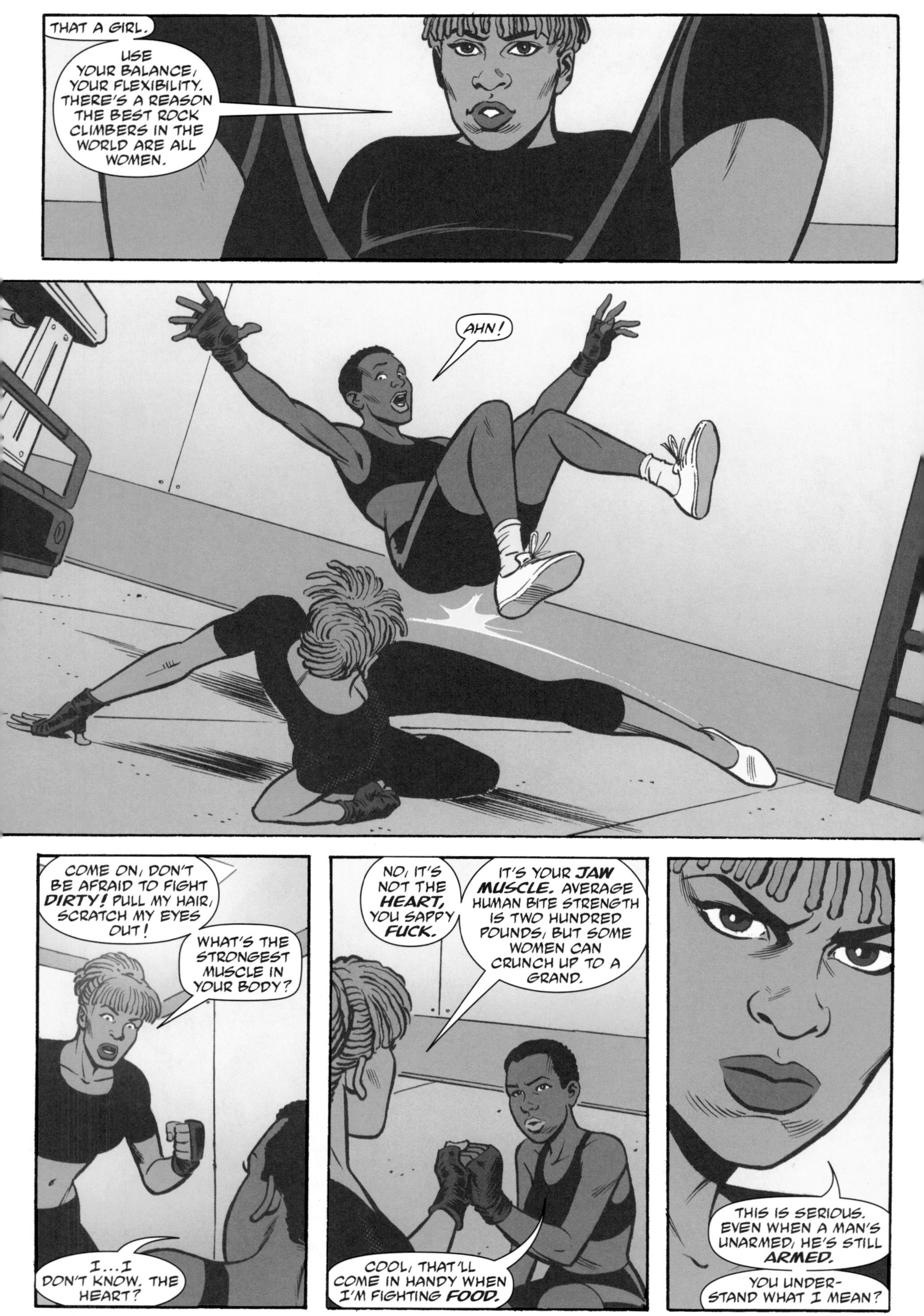
THAT A GIRL.
USE YOUR BALANCE, YOUR FLEXIBILITY. THERE'S A REASON THE BEST ROCK CLIMBERS IN THE WORLD ARE ALL WOMEN.
AHN!
COME ON, DON'T BE AFRAID TO FIGHT DIRTY! PULL MY HAIR, SCRATCH MY EYES OUT!
WHAT'S THE STRONGEST MUSCLE IN YOUR BODY?
I... I DON'T KNOW. THE HEART?
NO, IT'S NOT THE HEART, YOU SAPPY FUCK.
IT'S YOUR JAW MUSCLE. AVERAGE HUMAN BITE STRENGTH IS TWO HUNDRED POUNDS, BUT SOME WOMEN CAN CRUNCH UP TO A GRAND.
COOL, THAT'LL COME IN HANDY WHEN I'M FIGHTING FOOD.
THIS IS SERIOUS. EVEN WHEN A MAN'S UNARMED, HE'S STILL ARMED.
YOU UNDER-STAND WHAT I MEAN?

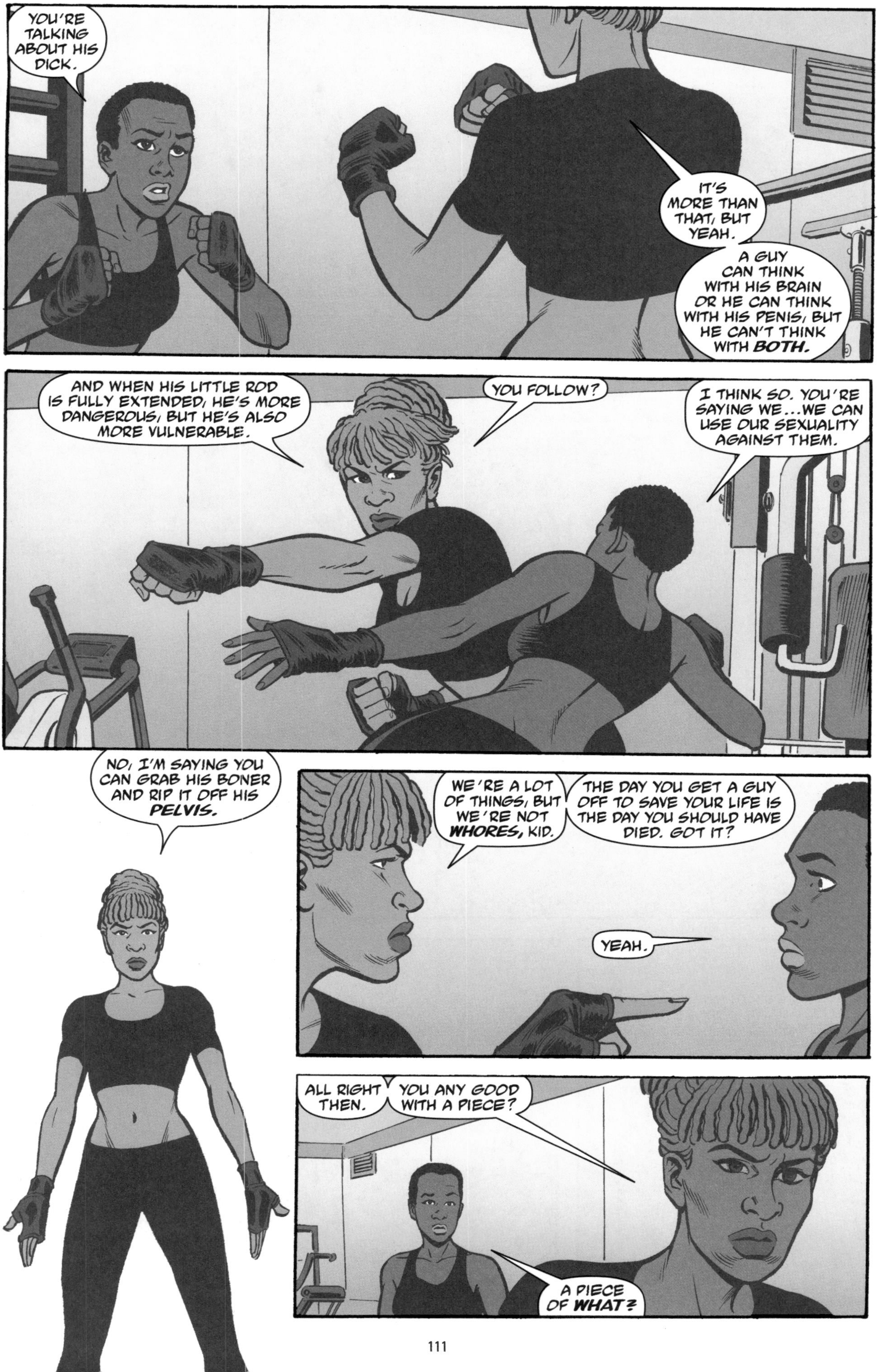

YOU'RE TALKING ABOUT HIS DICK.
IT'S MORE THAN THAT, BUT YEAH.
A GUY CAN THINK WITH HIS BRAIN OR HE CAN THINK WITH HIS PENIS, BUT HE CAN'T THINK WITH *BOTH.*
AND WHEN HIS LITTLE ROD IS FULLY EXTENDED, HE'S MORE DANGEROUS, BUT HE'S ALSO MORE VULNERABLE.
YOU FOLLOW?
I THINK SO. YOU'RE SAYING WE... WE CAN USE OUR SEXUALITY AGAINST THEM.
NO, I'M SAYING YOU CAN GRAB HIS BONER AND RIP IT OFF HIS *PELVIS.*
WE'RE A LOT OF THINGS, BUT WE'RE NOT *WHORES,* KID.
THE DAY YOU GET A GUY OFF TO SAVE YOUR LIFE IS THE DAY YOU SHOULD HAVE DIED. GOT IT?
YEAH.
ALL RIGHT THEN.
YOU ANY GOOD WITH A PIECE?
A PIECE OF *WHAT?*

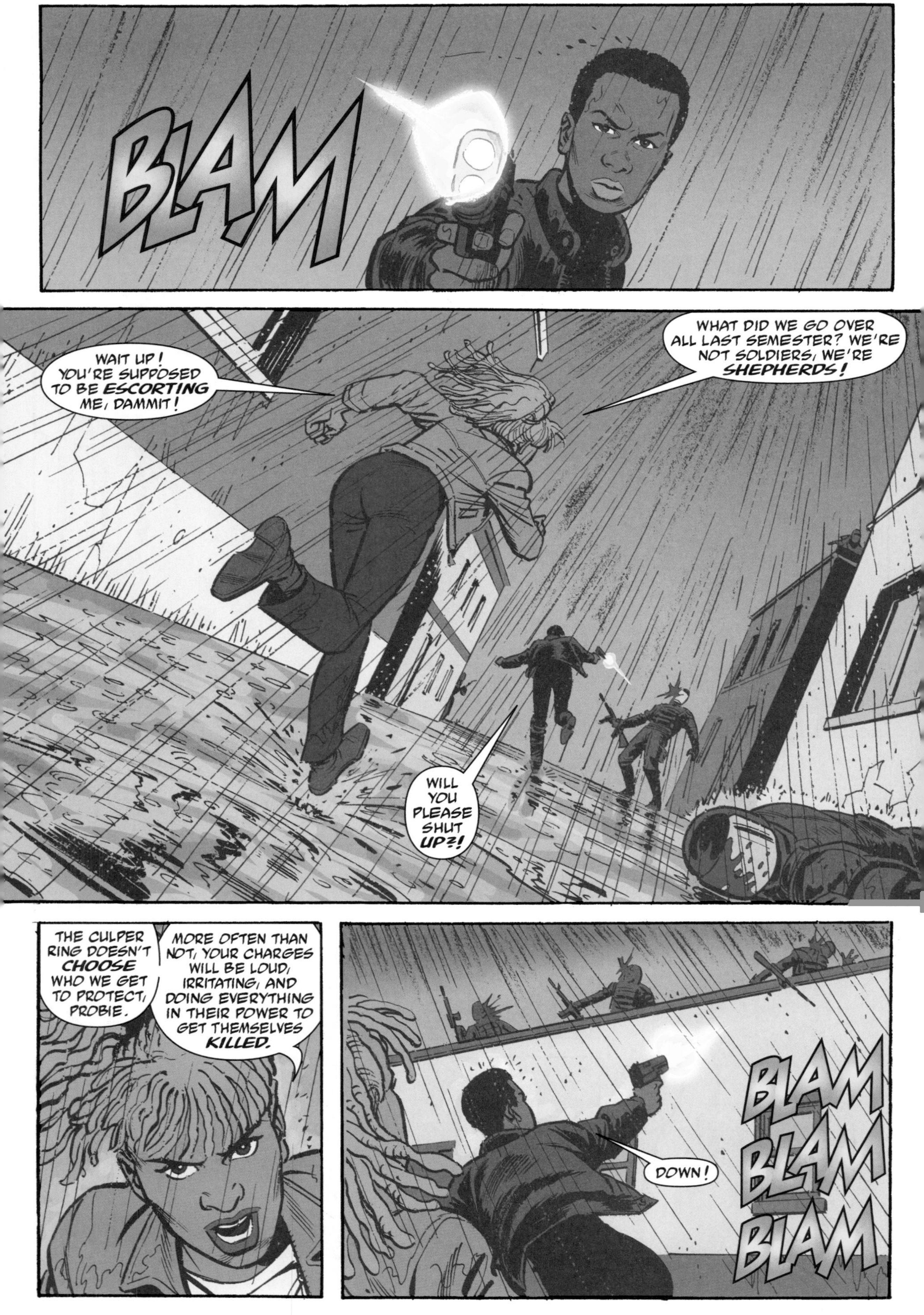
BLAM
WAIT UP! YOU'RE SUPPOSED TO BE ESCORTING ME, DAMMIT!
WHAT DID WE GO OVER ALL LAST SEMESTER? WE'RE NOT SOLDIERS, WE'RE SHEPHERDS!
WILL YOU PLEASE SHUT UP?!
THE CULPER RING DOESN'T CHOOSE WHO WE GET TO PROTECT, PROBIE.
MORE OFTEN THAN NOT, YOUR CHARGES WILL BE LOUD, IRRITATING, AND DOING EVERYTHING IN THEIR POWER TO GET THEMSELVES KILLED.
DOWN!
BLAM
BLAM
BLAM

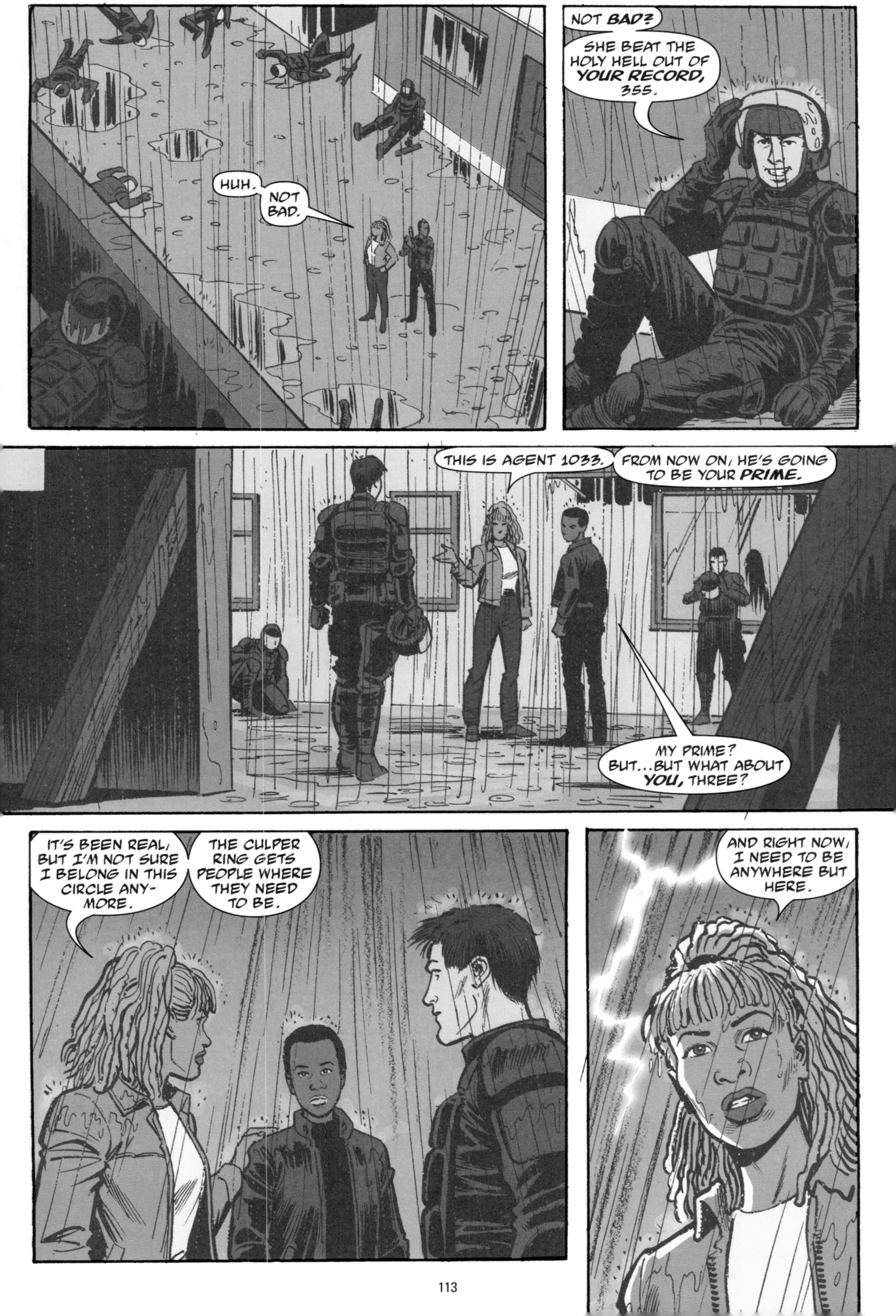
HUH.
NOT BAD.
NOT BAD?
SHE BEAT THE HOLY HELL OUT OF YOUR RECORD, 355.
THIS IS AGENT 1033.
FROM NOW ON, HE'S GOING TO BE YOUR PRIME.
MY PRIME? BUT...BUT WHAT ABOUT YOU, THREE?
IT'S BEEN REAL, BUT I'M NOT SURE I BELONG IN THIS CIRCLE ANY-MORE.
THE CULPER RING GETS PEOPLE WHERE THEY NEED TO BE.
AND RIGHT NOW, I NEED TO BE ANYWHERE BUT HERE.

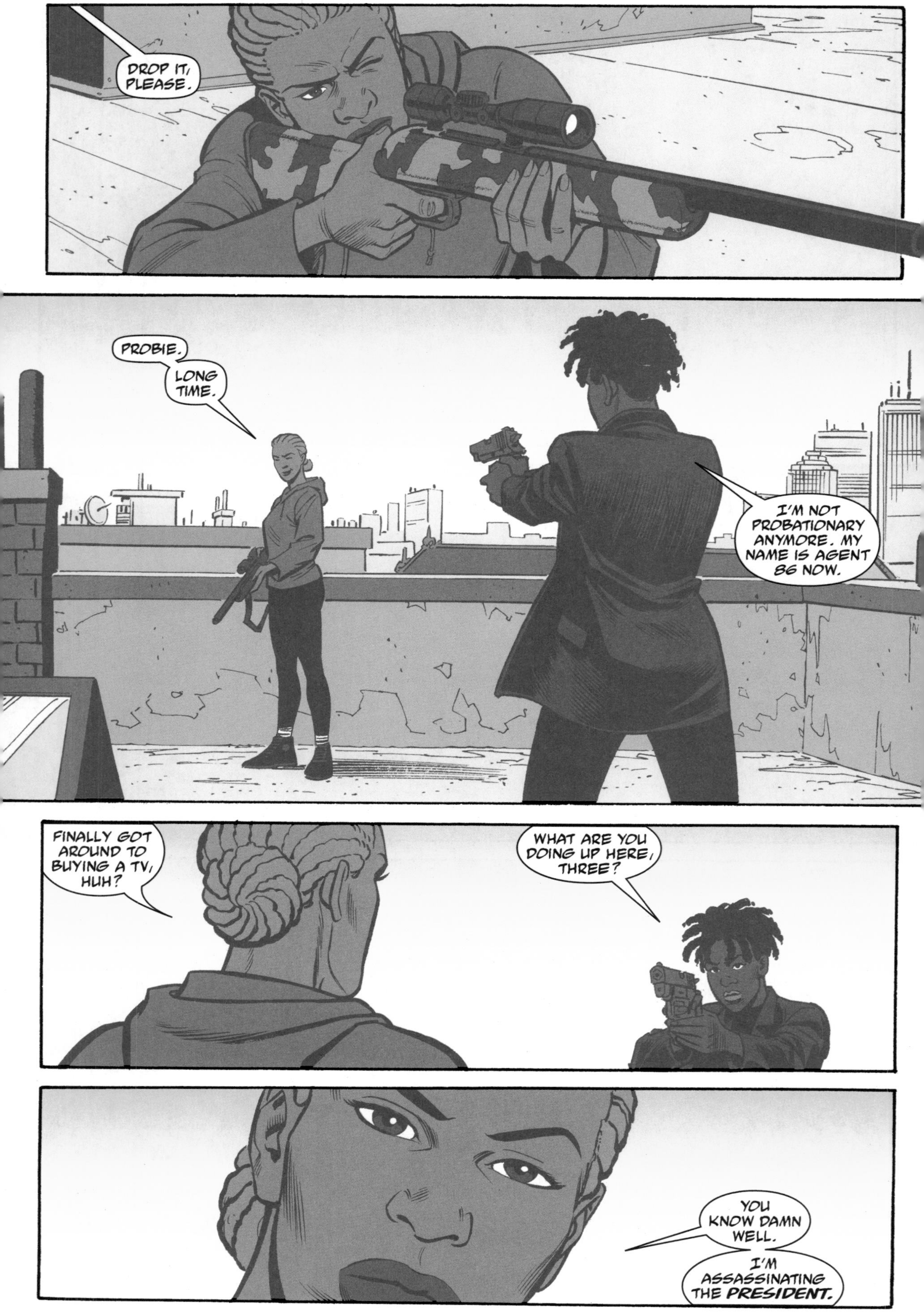
DROP IT, PLEASE.
PROBIE.
LONG TIME.
I'M NOT PROBATIONARY ANYMORE. MY NAME IS AGENT 86 NOW.
FINALLY GOT AROUND TO BUYING A TV, HUH?
WHAT ARE YOU DOING UP HERE, THREE?
YOU KNOW DAMN WELL.
I'M ASSASSINATING THE **PRESIDENT.**

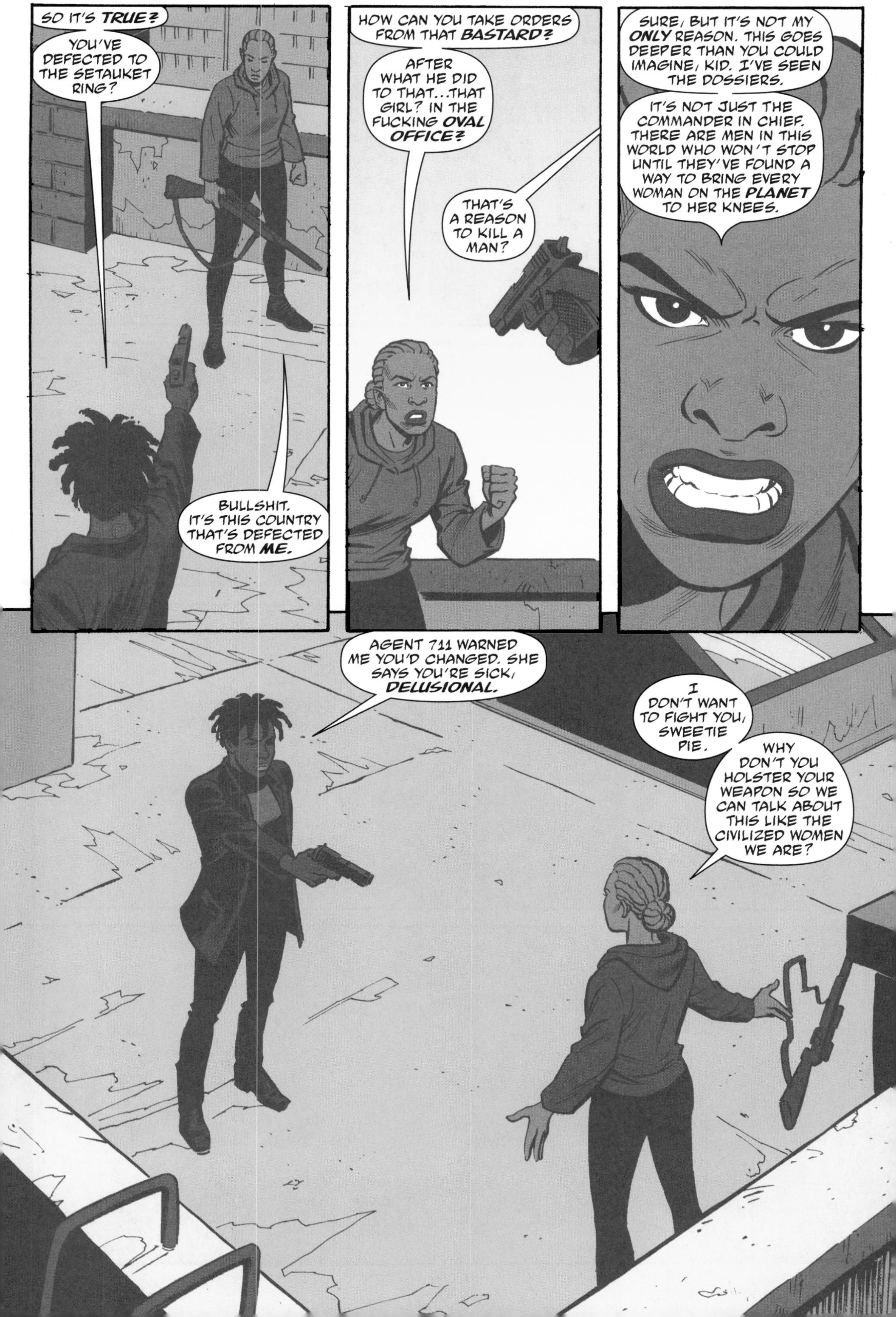

SO IT'S TRUE?
YOU'VE DEFECTED TO THE SETAUKET RING?
BULLSHIT. IT'S THIS COUNTRY THAT'S DEFECTED FROM ME.
HOW CAN YOU TAKE ORDERS FROM THAT BASTARD?
AFTER WHAT HE DID TO THAT...THAT GIRL? IN THE FUCKING OVAL OFFICE?
THAT'S A REASON TO KILL A MAN?
SURE, BUT IT'S NOT MY ONLY REASON. THIS GOES DEEPER THAN YOU COULD IMAGINE, KID. I'VE SEEN THE DOSSIERS.
IT'S NOT JUST THE COMMANDER IN CHIEF. THERE ARE MEN IN THIS WORLD WHO WON'T STOP UNTIL THEY'VE FOUND A WAY TO BRING EVERY WOMAN ON THE PLANET TO HER KNEES.
AGENT 711 WARNED ME YOU'D CHANGED. SHE SAYS YOU'RE SICK, DELUSIONAL.
I DON'T WANT TO FIGHT YOU, SWEETIE PIE.
WHY DON'T YOU HOLSTER YOUR WEAPON SO WE CAN TALK ABOUT THIS LIKE THE CIVILIZED WOMEN WE ARE?

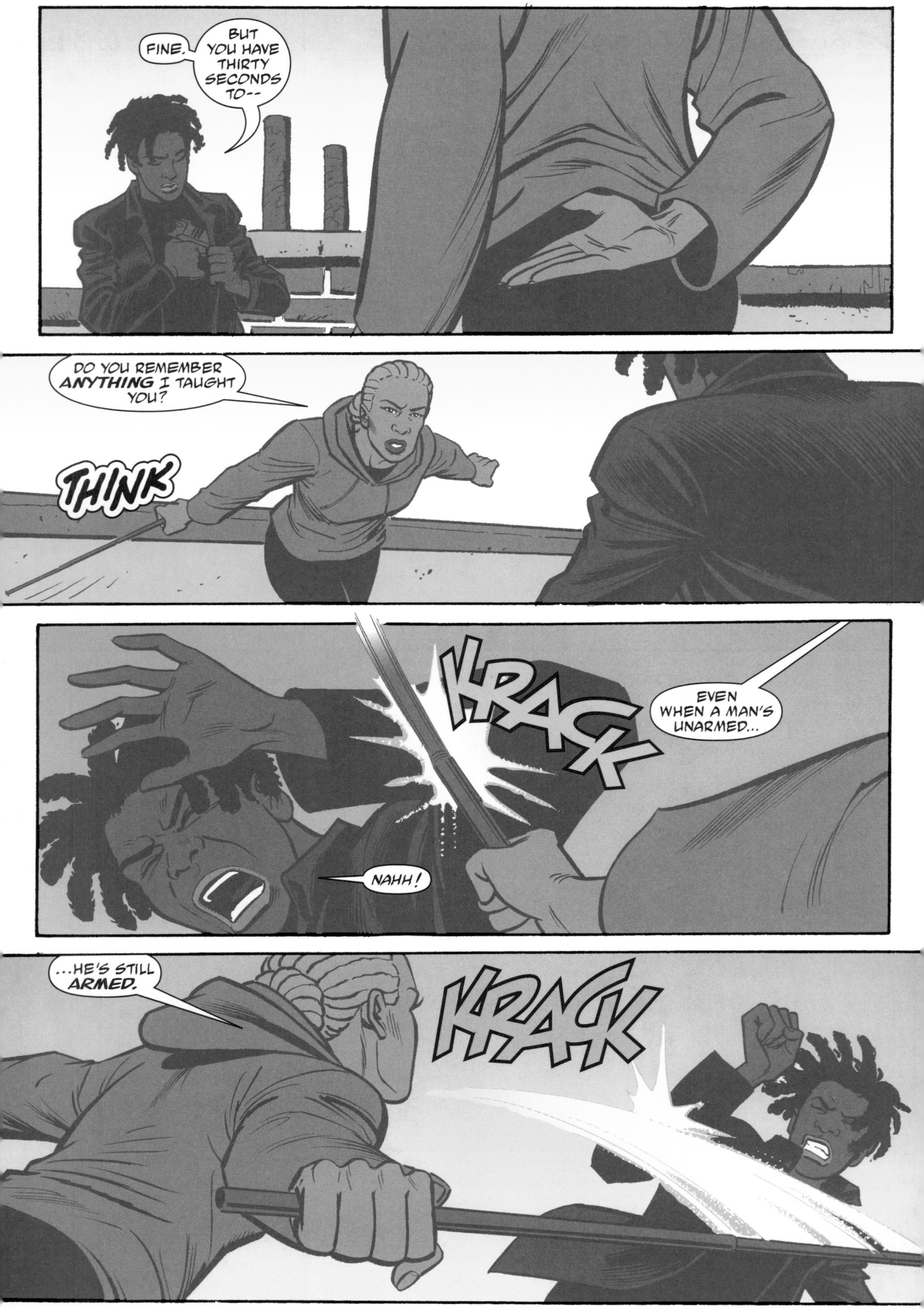
FINE.
BUT YOU HAVE THIRTY SECONDS TO--
DO YOU REMEMBER ANYTHING I TAUGHT YOU?
THINK
KRACK
EVEN WHEN A MAN'S UNARMED...
NAHH!
...HE'S STILL ARMED.
KRACK

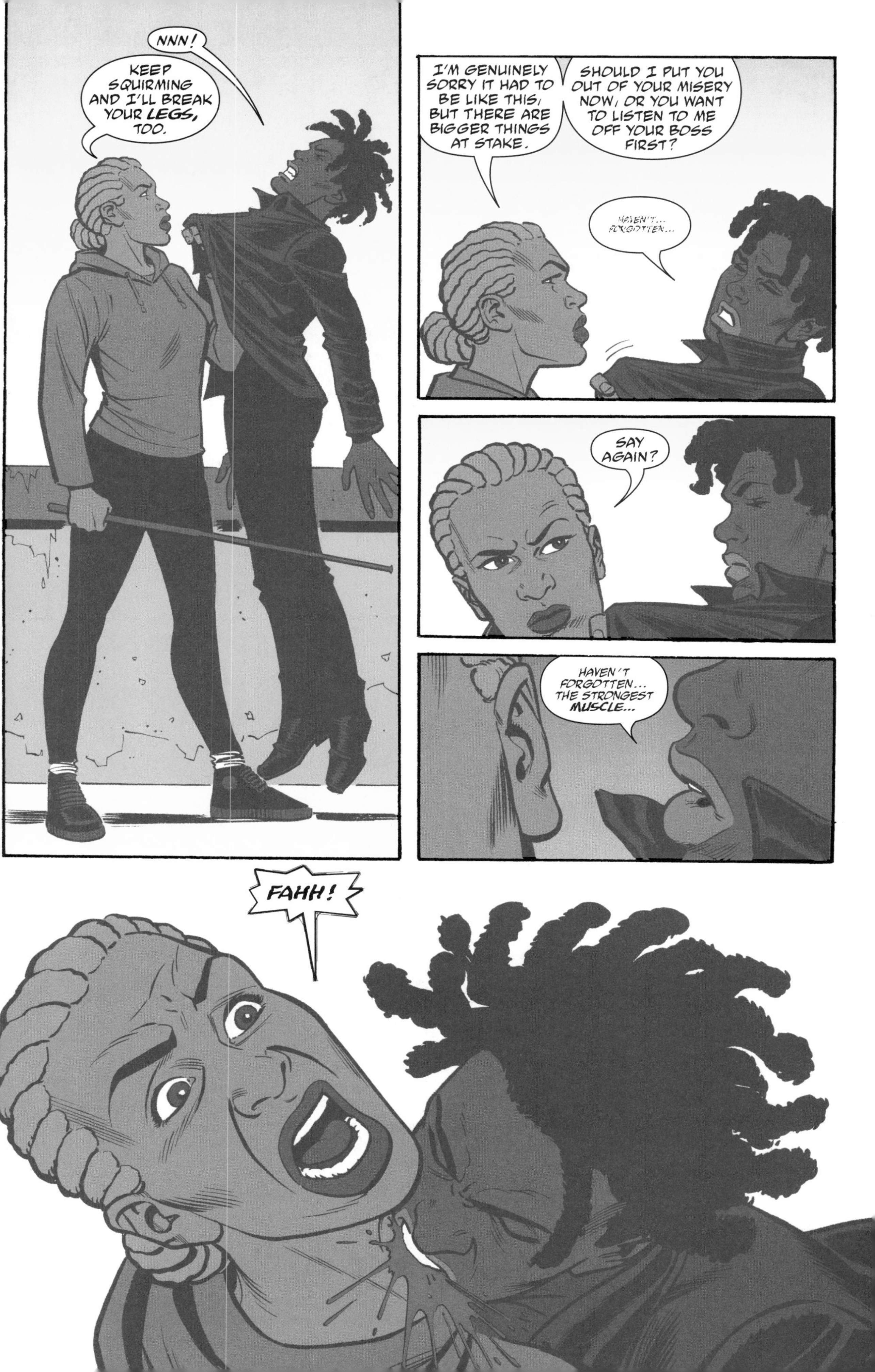
NNN!
KEEP SQUIRMING AND I'LL BREAK YOUR LEGS, TOO.
I'M GENUINELY SORRY IT HAD TO BE LIKE THIS, BUT THERE ARE BIGGER THINGS AT STAKE.
SHOULD I PUT YOU OUT OF YOUR MISERY NOW, OR YOU WANT TO LISTEN TO ME OFF YOUR BOSS FIRST?
HAVEN'T... FORGOTTEN...
SAY AGAIN?
HAVEN'T FORGOTTEN... THE STRONGEST MUSCLE...
FAHH!

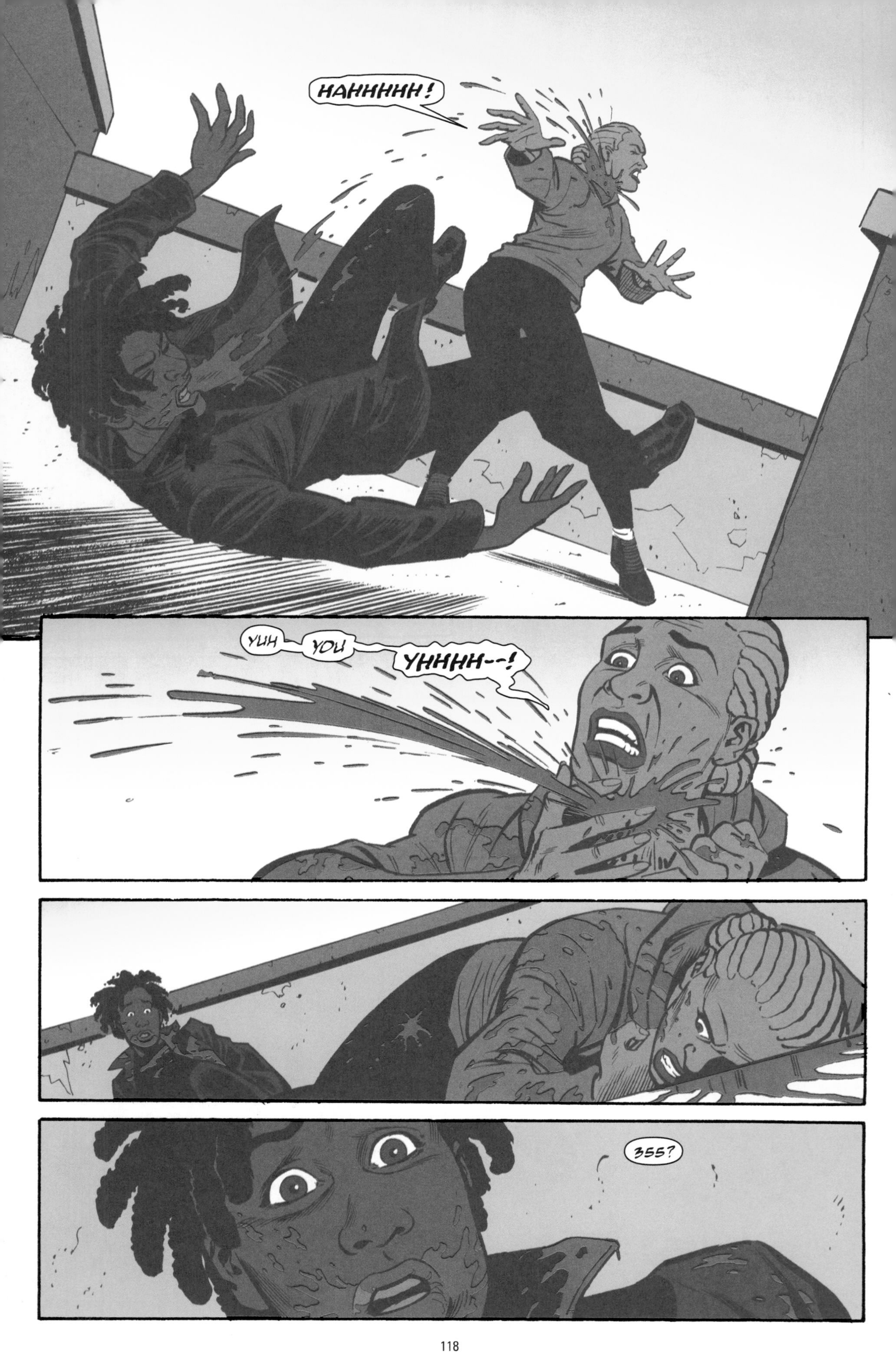
HAHHHHH!
YUH
YOU
YHHHH--!
355?

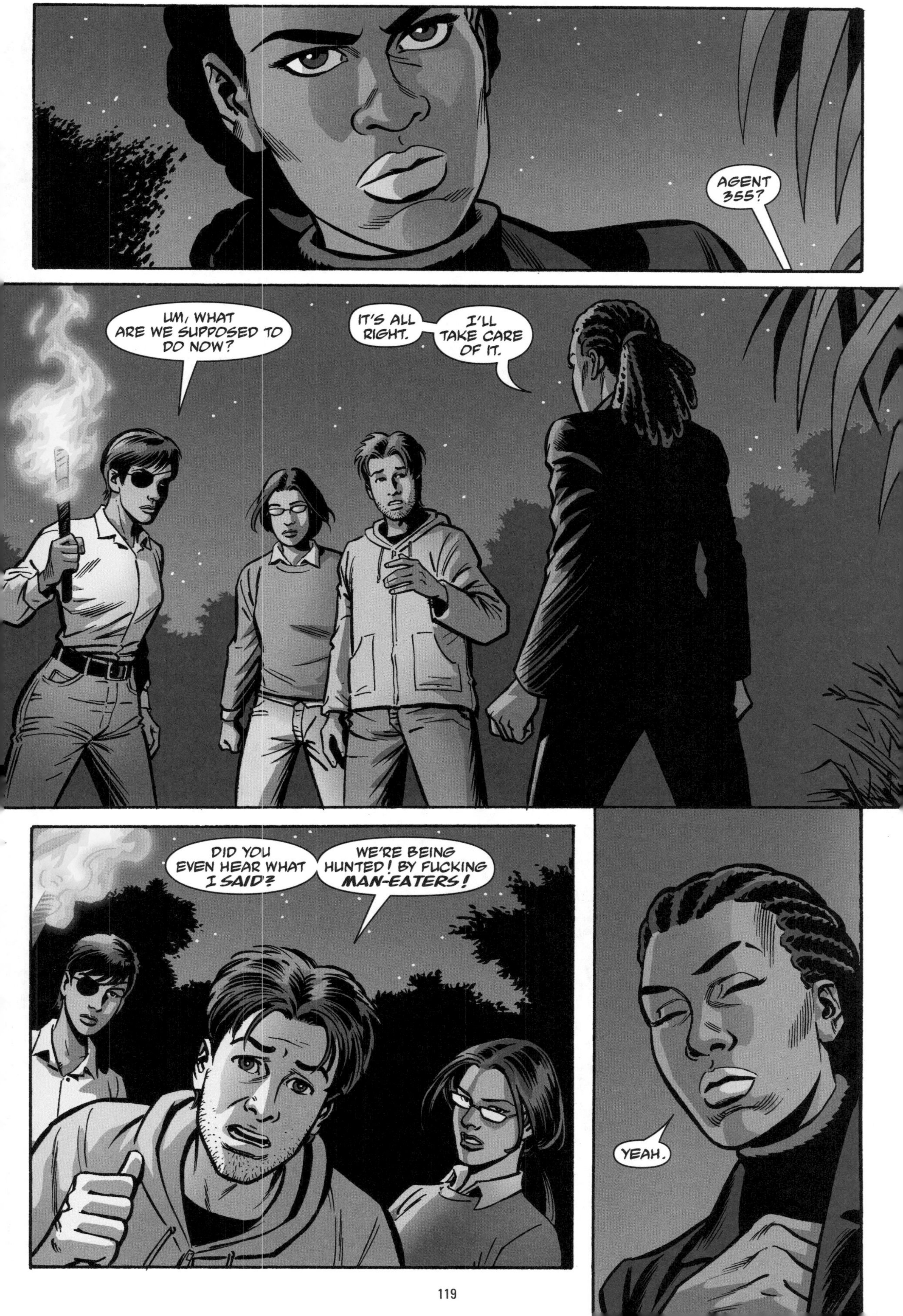
AGENT 355?
UM, WHAT ARE WE SUPPOSED TO DO NOW?
IT'S ALL RIGHT.
I'LL TAKE CARE OF IT.
DID YOU EVEN HEAR WHAT I SAID?
WE'RE BEING HUNTED! BY FUCKING MAN-EATERS!
YEAH.

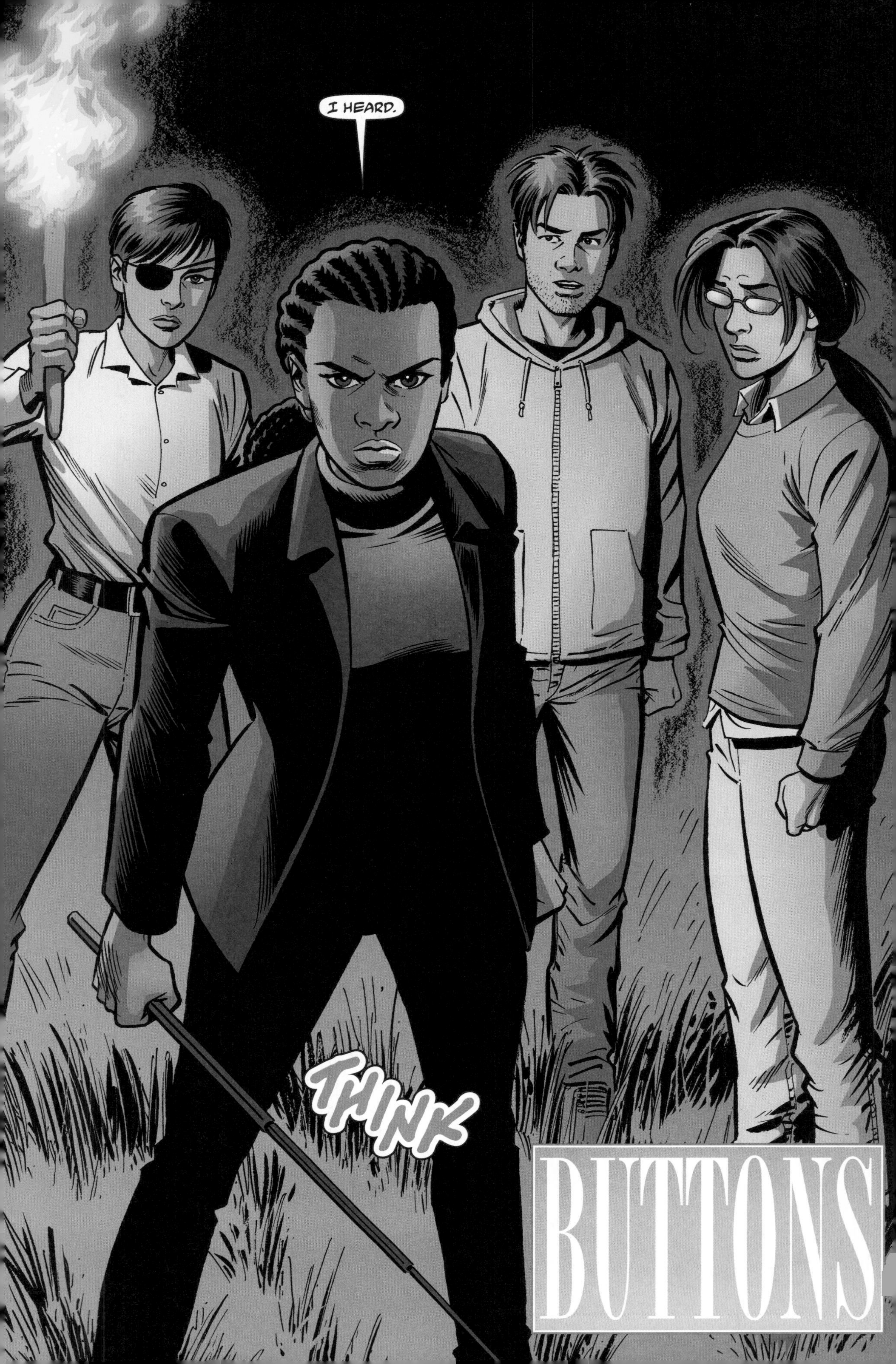
I HEARD.
THINK
BUTTONS

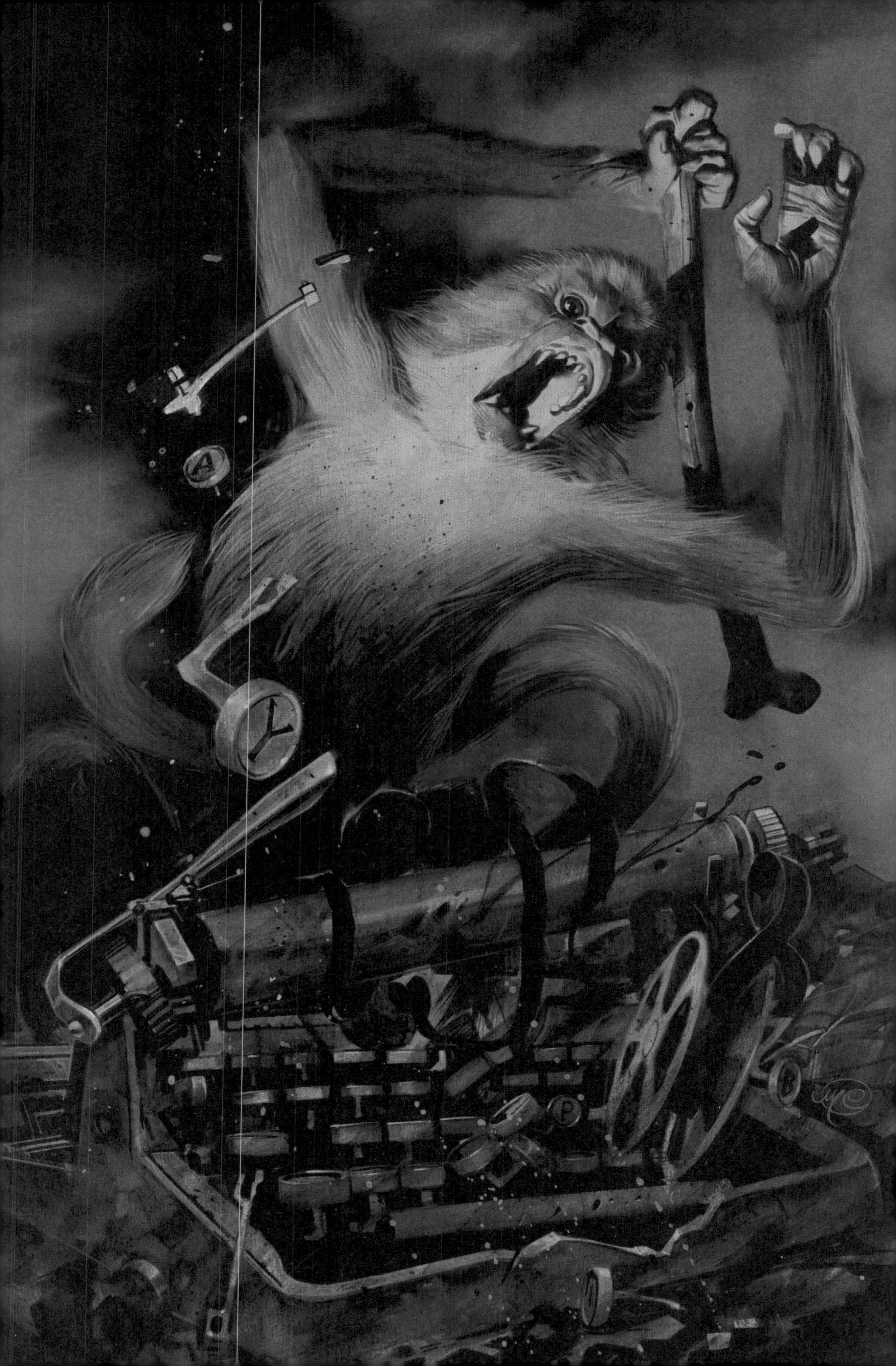

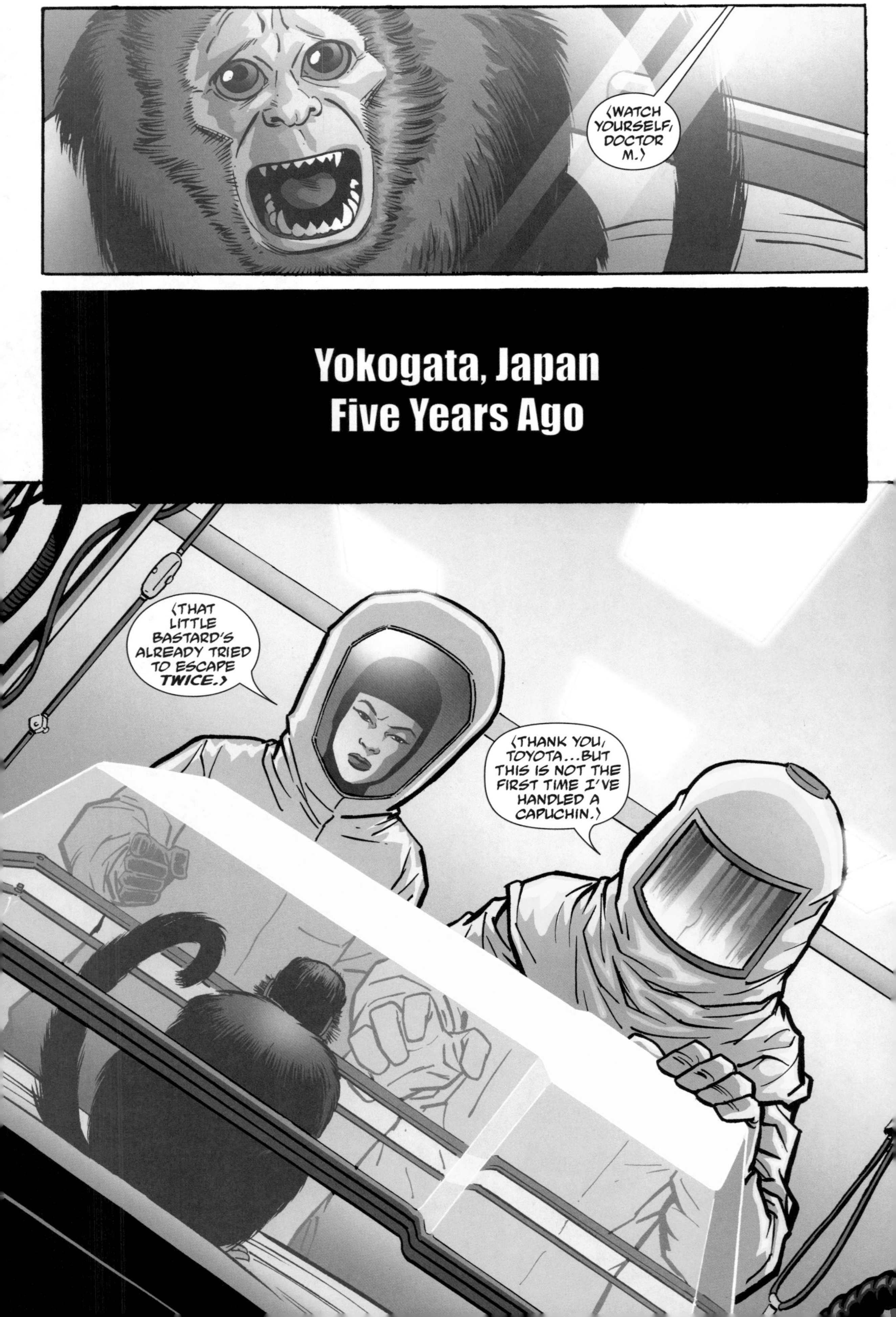
⟨WATCH YOURSELF, DOCTOR M.⟩
Yokogata, Japan
Five Years Ago
⟨THAT LITTLE BASTARD'S ALREADY TRIED TO ESCAPE **TWICE.**⟩
⟨THANK YOU, TOYOTA...BUT THIS IS NOT THE FIRST TIME I'VE HANDLED A CAPUCHIN.⟩

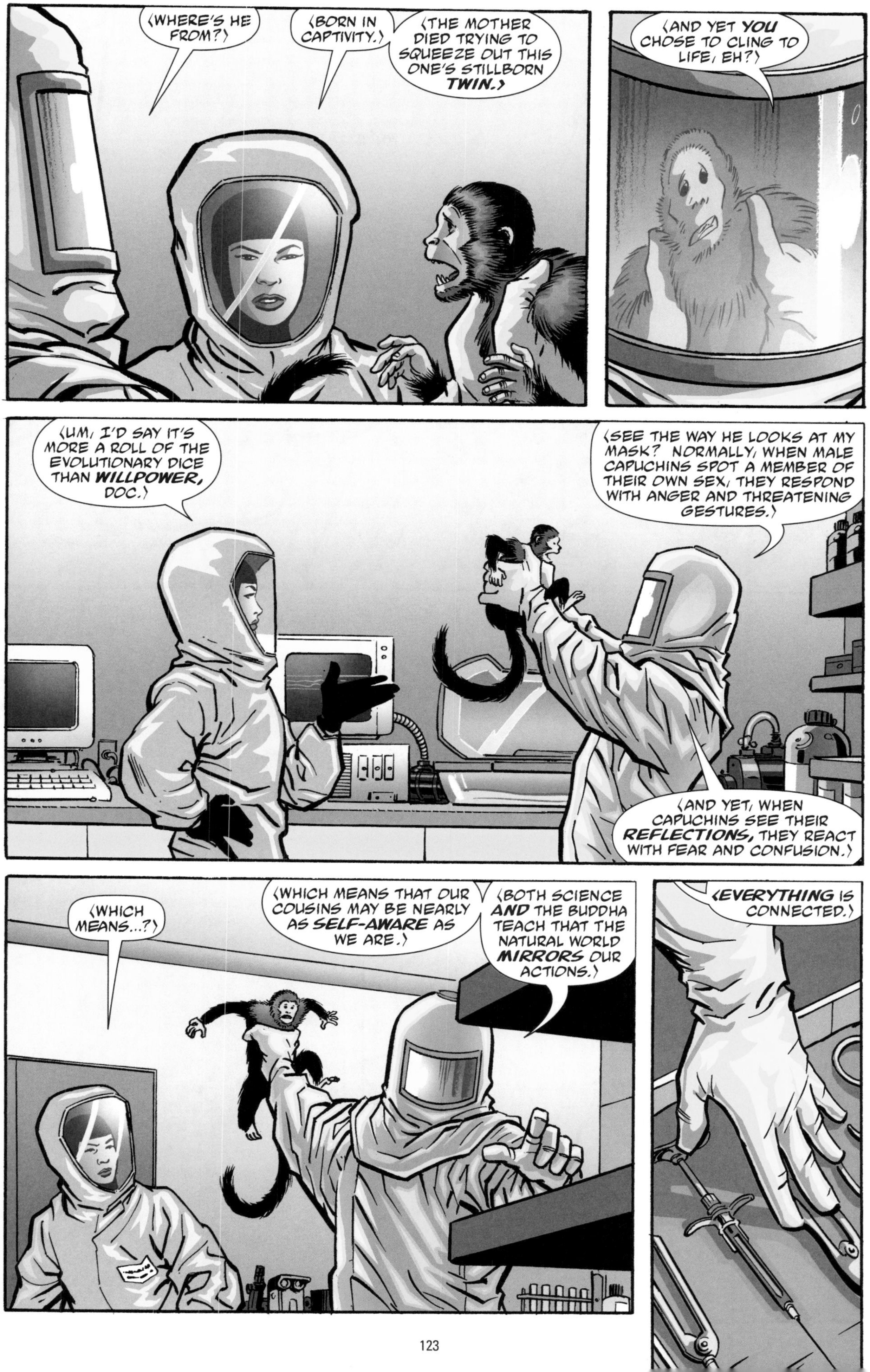
⟨WHERE'S HE FROM?⟩
⟨BORN IN CAPTIVITY.⟩
⟨THE MOTHER DIED TRYING TO SQUEEZE OUT THIS ONE'S STILLBORN TWIN.⟩
⟨AND YET YOU CHOSE TO CLING TO LIFE, EH?⟩
⟨UM, I'D SAY IT'S MORE A ROLL OF THE EVOLUTIONARY DICE THAN WILLPOWER, DOC.⟩
⟨SEE THE WAY HE LOOKS AT MY MASK? NORMALLY, WHEN MALE CAPUCHINS SPOT A MEMBER OF THEIR OWN SEX, THEY RESPOND WITH ANGER AND THREATENING GESTURES.⟩
⟨AND YET, WHEN CAPUCHINS SEE THEIR REFLECTIONS, THEY REACT WITH FEAR AND CONFUSION.⟩
⟨WHICH MEANS...?⟩
⟨WHICH MEANS THAT OUR COUSINS MAY BE NEARLY AS SELF-AWARE AS WE ARE.⟩
⟨BOTH SCIENCE AND THE BUDDHA TEACH THAT THE NATURAL WORLD MIRRORS OUR ACTIONS.⟩
⟨EVERYTHING IS CONNECTED.⟩

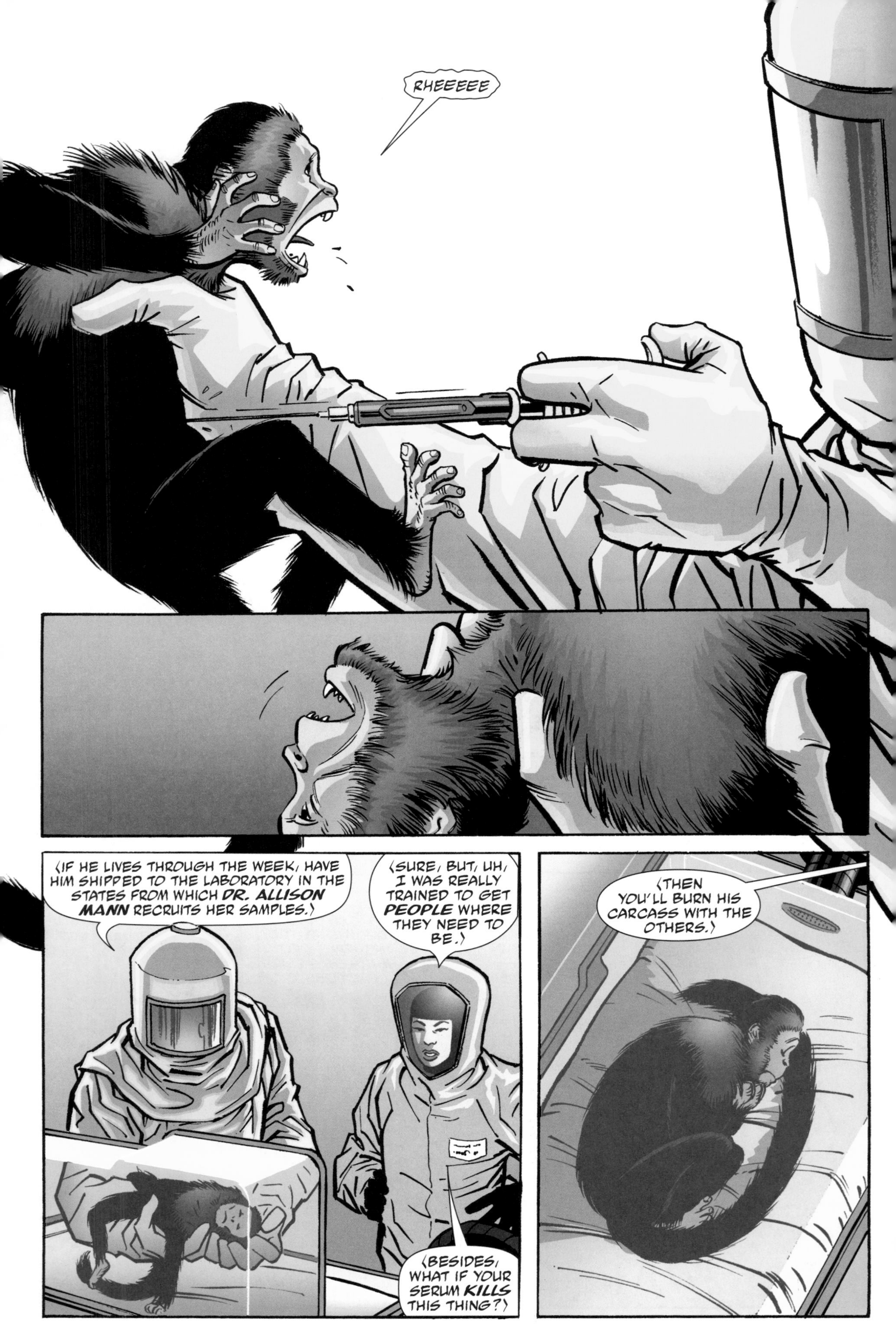
RHEEEEE
(IF HE LIVES THROUGH THE WEEK, HAVE HIM SHIPPED TO THE LABORATORY IN THE STATES FROM WHICH DR. ALLISON MANN RECRUITS HER SAMPLES.)
(SURE, BUT, UH, I WAS REALLY TRAINED TO GET PEOPLE WHERE THEY NEED TO BE.)
(BESIDES, WHAT IF YOUR SERUM KILLS THIS THING?)
(THEN YOU'LL BURN HIS CARCASS WITH THE OTHERS.)

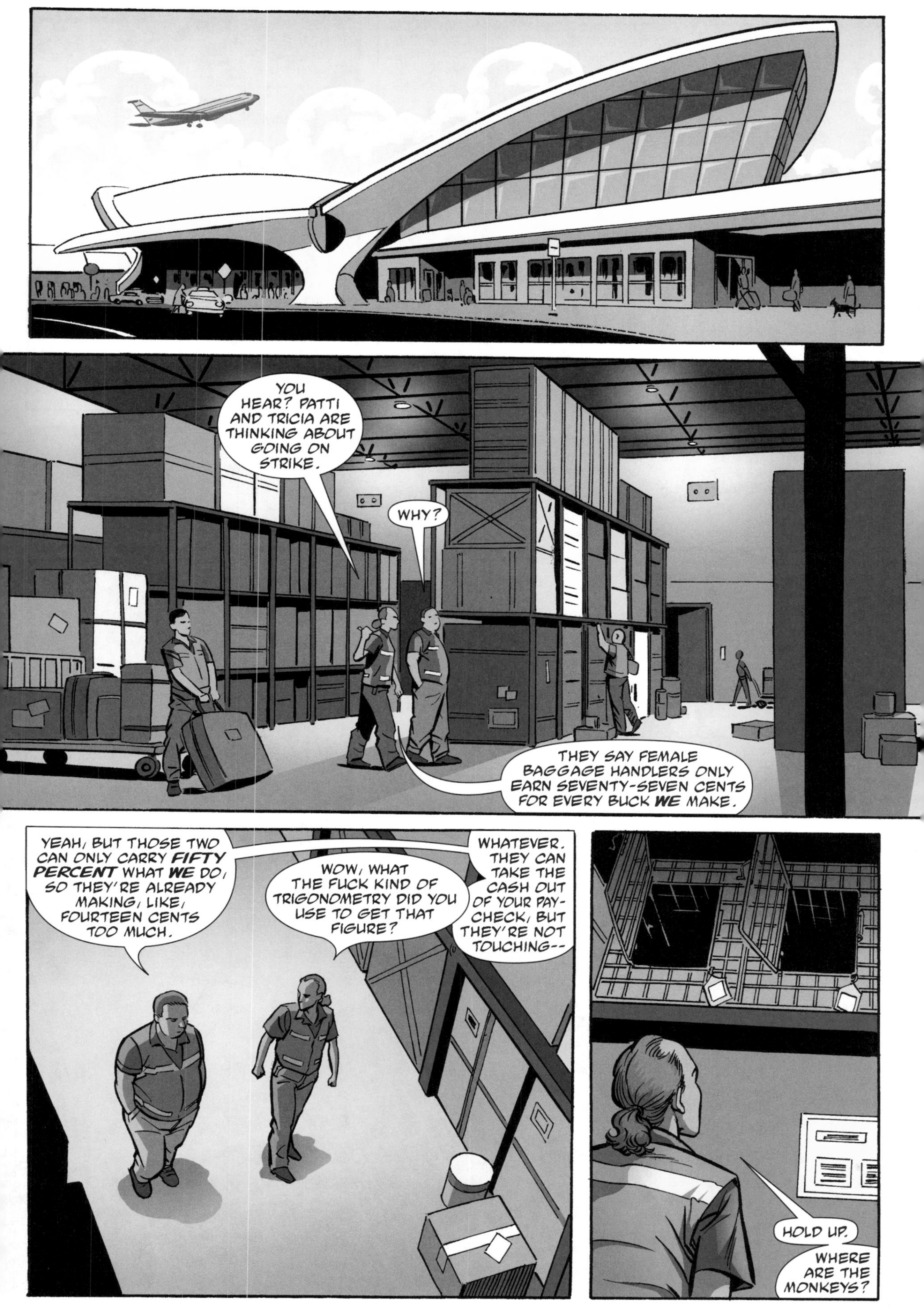
YOU HEAR? PATTI AND TRICIA ARE THINKING ABOUT GOING ON STRIKE.
WHY?
THEY SAY FEMALE BAGGAGE HANDLERS ONLY EARN SEVENTY-SEVEN CENTS FOR EVERY BUCK WE MAKE.
YEAH, BUT THOSE TWO CAN ONLY CARRY FIFTY PERCENT WHAT WE DO, SO THEY'RE ALREADY MAKING, LIKE, FOURTEEN CENTS TOO MUCH.
WOW, WHAT THE FUCK KIND OF TRIGONOMETRY DID YOU USE TO GET THAT FIGURE?
WHATEVER. THEY CAN TAKE THE CASH OUT OF YOUR PAY-CHECK, BUT THEY'RE NOT TOUCHING--
HOLD UP.
WHERE ARE THE MONKEYS?

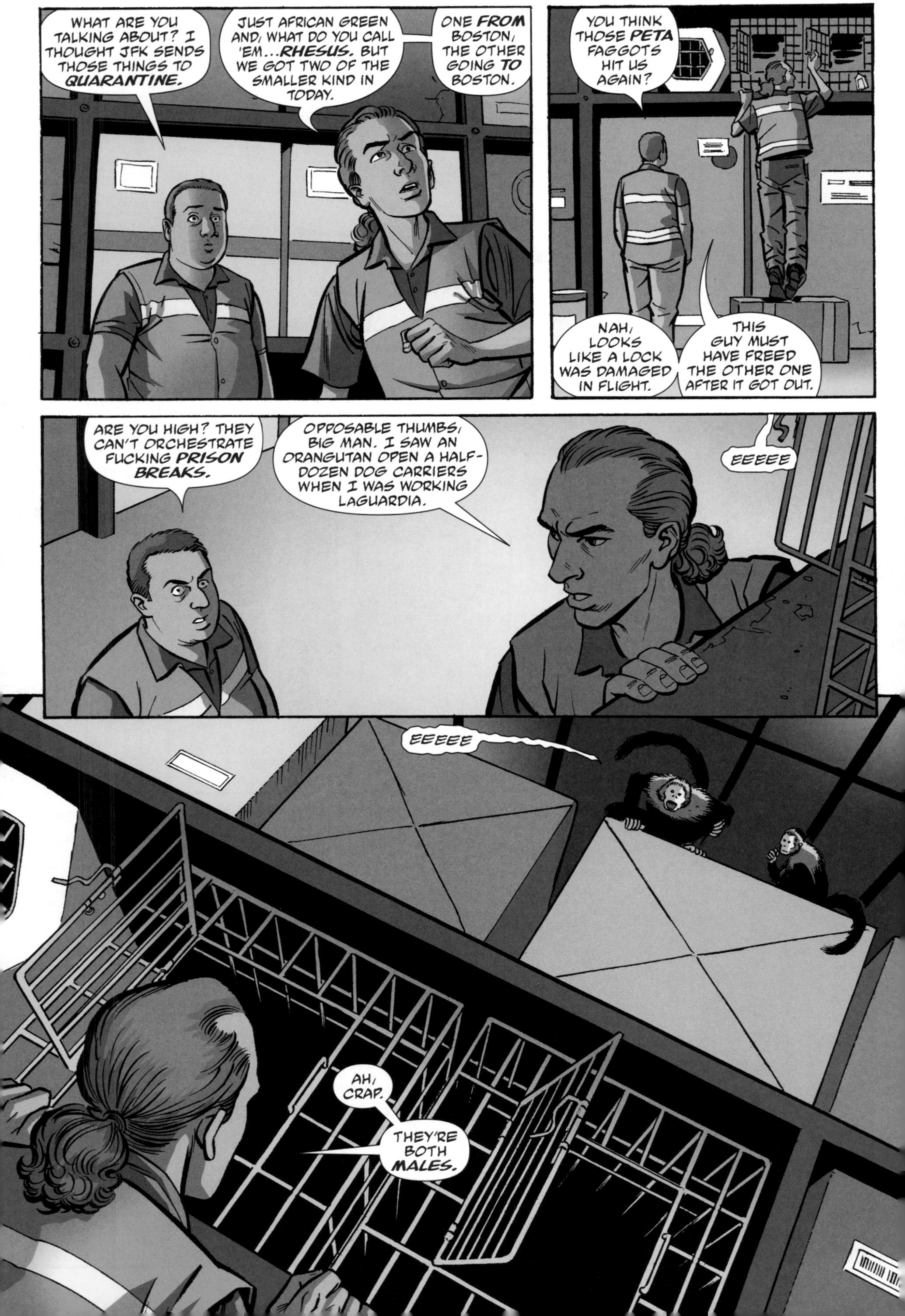
WHAT ARE YOU TALKING ABOUT? I THOUGHT JFK SENDS THOSE THINGS TO QUARANTINE.
JUST AFRICAN GREEN AND, WHAT DO YOU CALL 'EM...RHESUS. BUT WE GOT TWO OF THE SMALLER KIND IN TODAY.
ONE FROM BOSTON, THE OTHER GOING TO BOSTON.
YOU THINK THOSE PETA FAGGOTS HIT US AGAIN?
NAH, LOOKS LIKE A LOCK WAS DAMAGED IN FLIGHT.
THIS GUY MUST HAVE FREED THE OTHER ONE AFTER IT GOT OUT.
ARE YOU HIGH? THEY CAN'T ORCHESTRATE FUCKING PRISON BREAKS.
OPPOSABLE THUMBS, BIG MAN. I SAW AN ORANGUTAN OPEN A HALF-DOZEN DOG CARRIERS WHEN I WAS WORKING LAGUARDIA.
EEEEE
EEEEE
AH, CRAP.
THEY'RE BOTH MALES.

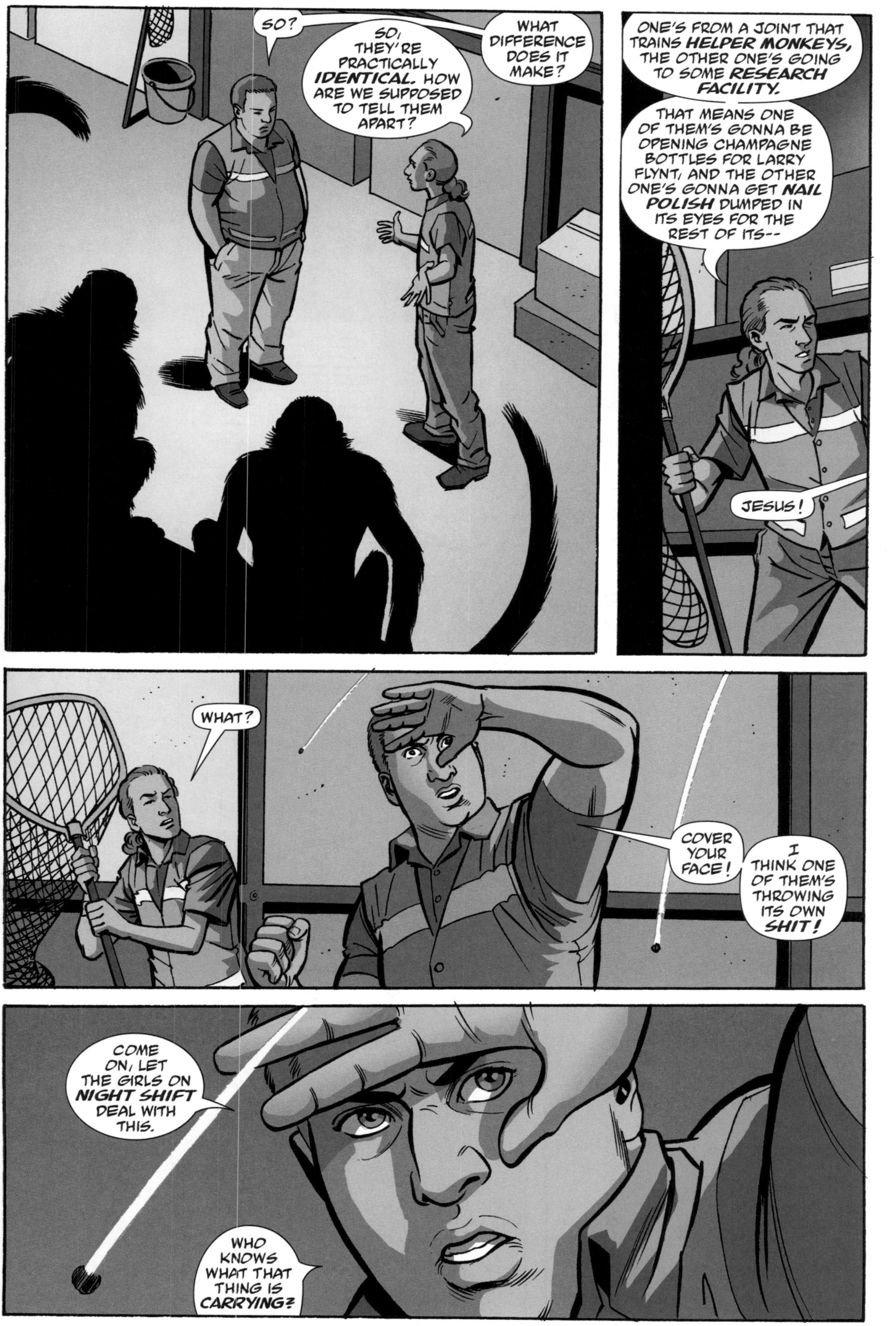

SO?
SO, THEY'RE PRACTICALLY IDENTICAL. HOW ARE WE SUPPOSED TO TELL THEM APART?
WHAT DIFFERENCE DOES IT MAKE?
ONE'S FROM A JOINT THAT TRAINS HELPER MONKEYS, THE OTHER ONE'S GOING TO SOME RESEARCH FACILITY.
THAT MEANS ONE OF THEM'S GONNA BE OPENING CHAMPAGNE BOTTLES FOR LARRY FLYNT, AND THE OTHER ONE'S GONNA GET NAIL POLISH DUMPED IN ITS EYES FOR THE REST OF ITS--
JESUS!
WHAT?
COVER YOUR FACE!
I THINK ONE OF THEM'S THROWING ITS OWN SHIT!
COME ON, LET THE GIRLS ON NIGHT SHIFT DEAL WITH THIS.
WHO KNOWS WHAT THAT THING IS CARRYING?

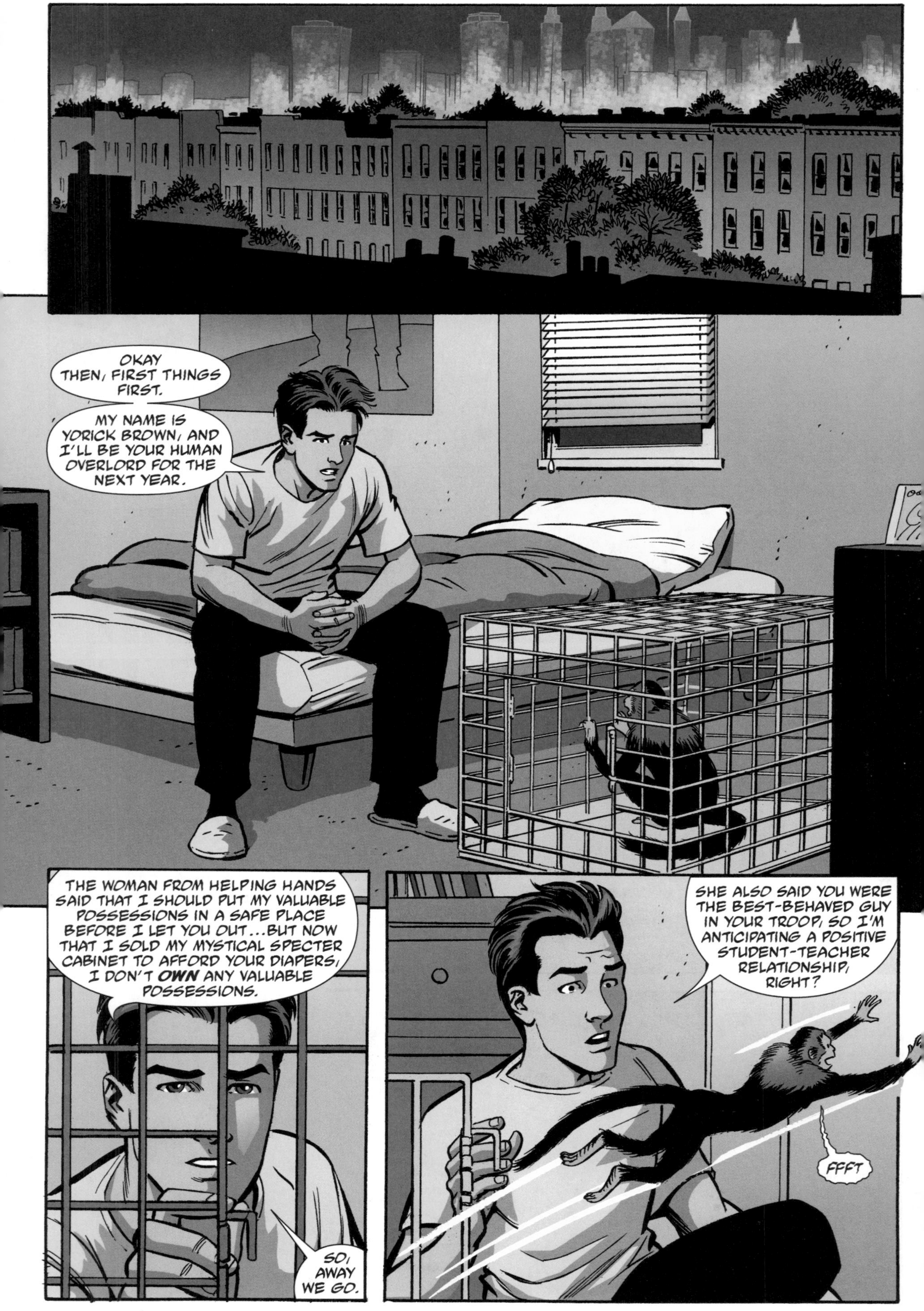
OKAY THEN, FIRST THINGS FIRST.
MY NAME IS YORICK BROWN, AND I'LL BE YOUR HUMAN OVERLORD FOR THE NEXT YEAR.
THE WOMAN FROM HELPING HANDS SAID THAT I SHOULD PUT MY VALUABLE POSSESSIONS IN A SAFE PLACE BEFORE I LET YOU OUT...BUT NOW THAT I SOLD MY MYSTICAL SPECTER CABINET TO AFFORD YOUR DIAPERS, I DON'T OWN ANY VALUABLE POSSESSIONS.
SO, AWAY WE GO.
SHE ALSO SAID YOU WERE THE BEST-BEHAVED GUY IN YOUR TROOP, SO I'M ANTICIPATING A POSITIVE STUDENT-TEACHER RELATIONSHIP, RIGHT?
FFFT

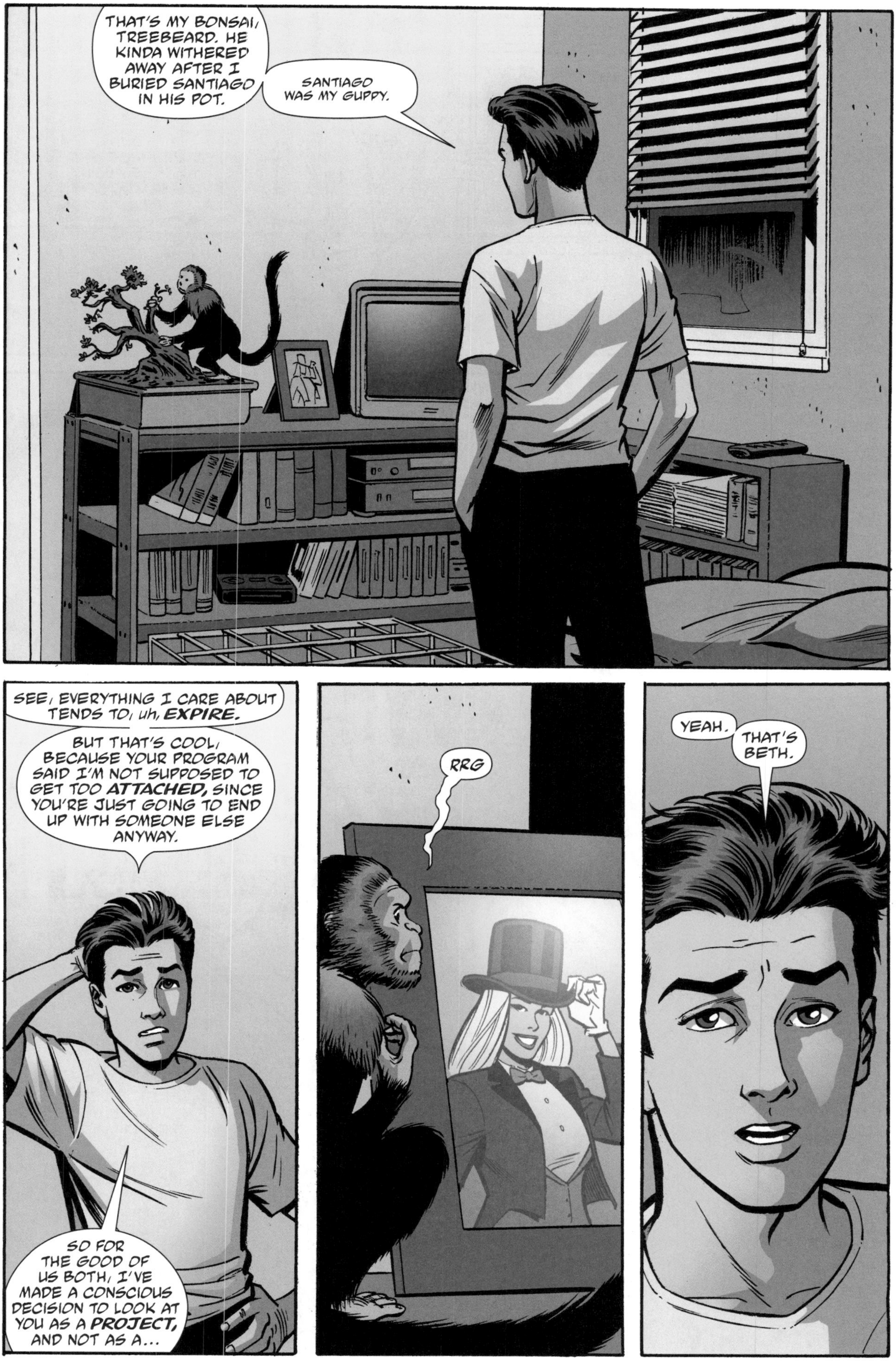
THAT'S MY BONSAI, TREEBEARD. HE KINDA WITHERED AWAY AFTER I BURIED SANTIAGO IN HIS POT.
SANTIAGO WAS MY GUPPY.
SEE, EVERYTHING I CARE ABOUT TENDS TO, uh, EXPIRE.
BUT THAT'S COOL, BECAUSE YOUR PROGRAM SAID I'M NOT SUPPOSED TO GET TOO ATTACHED, SINCE YOU'RE JUST GOING TO END UP WITH SOMEONE ELSE ANYWAY.
SO FOR THE GOOD OF US BOTH, I'VE MADE A CONSCIOUS DECISION TO LOOK AT YOU AS A PROJECT, AND NOT AS A...
RRG
YEAH.
THAT'S BETH.

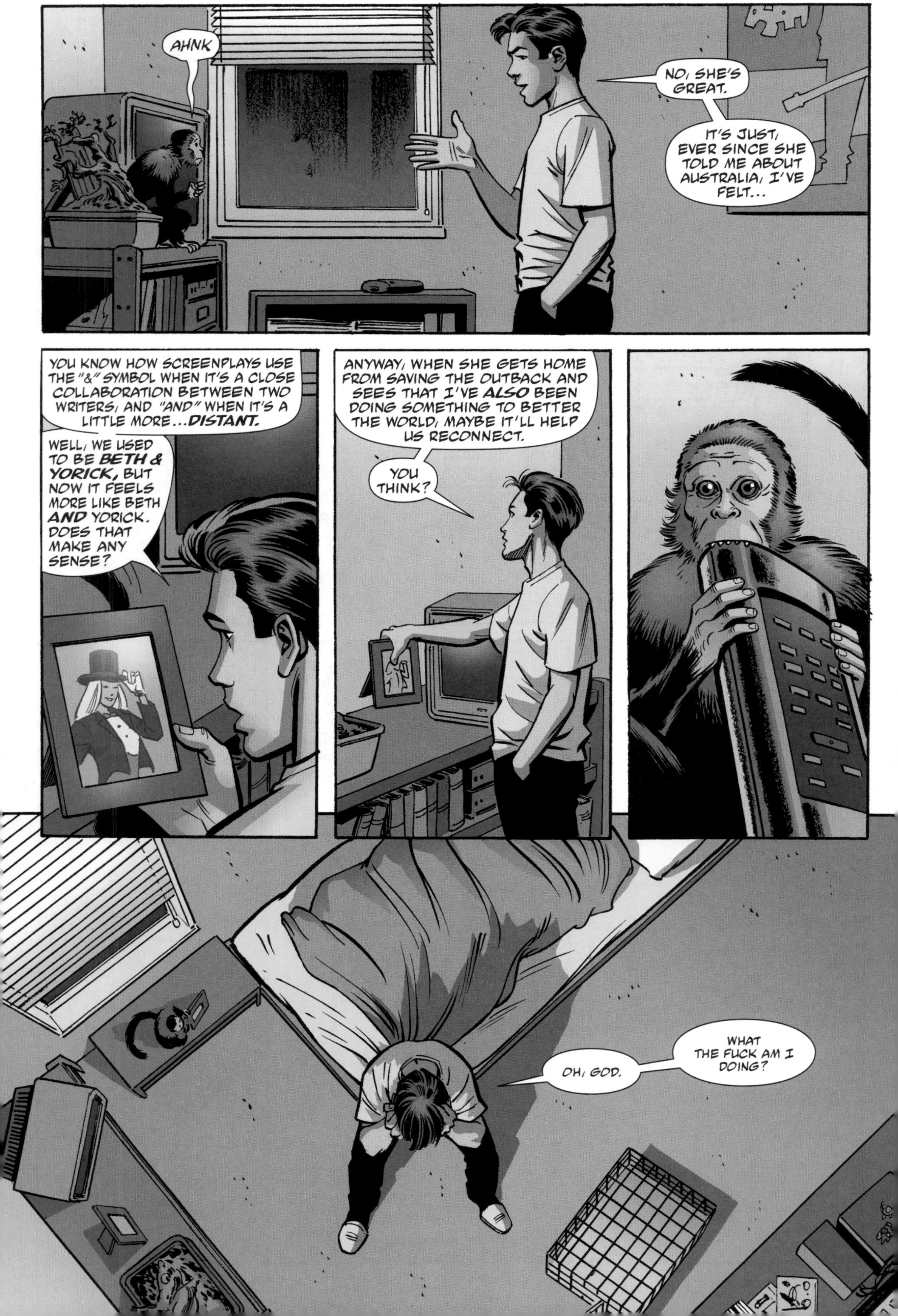
AHNK
NO, SHE'S GREAT.
IT'S JUST, EVER SINCE SHE TOLD ME ABOUT AUSTRALIA, I'VE FELT...
YOU KNOW HOW SCREENPLAYS USE THE "&" SYMBOL WHEN IT'S A CLOSE COLLABORATION BETWEEN TWO WRITERS, AND "AND" WHEN IT'S A LITTLE MORE...DISTANT.
WELL, WE USED TO BE BETH & YORICK, BUT NOW IT FEELS MORE LIKE BETH AND YORICK. DOES THAT MAKE ANY SENSE?
ANYWAY, WHEN SHE GETS HOME FROM SAVING THE OUTBACK AND SEES THAT I'VE ALSO BEEN DOING SOMETHING TO BETTER THE WORLD, MAYBE IT'LL HELP US RECONNECT.
YOU THINK?
OH, GOD.
WHAT THE FUCK AM I DOING?

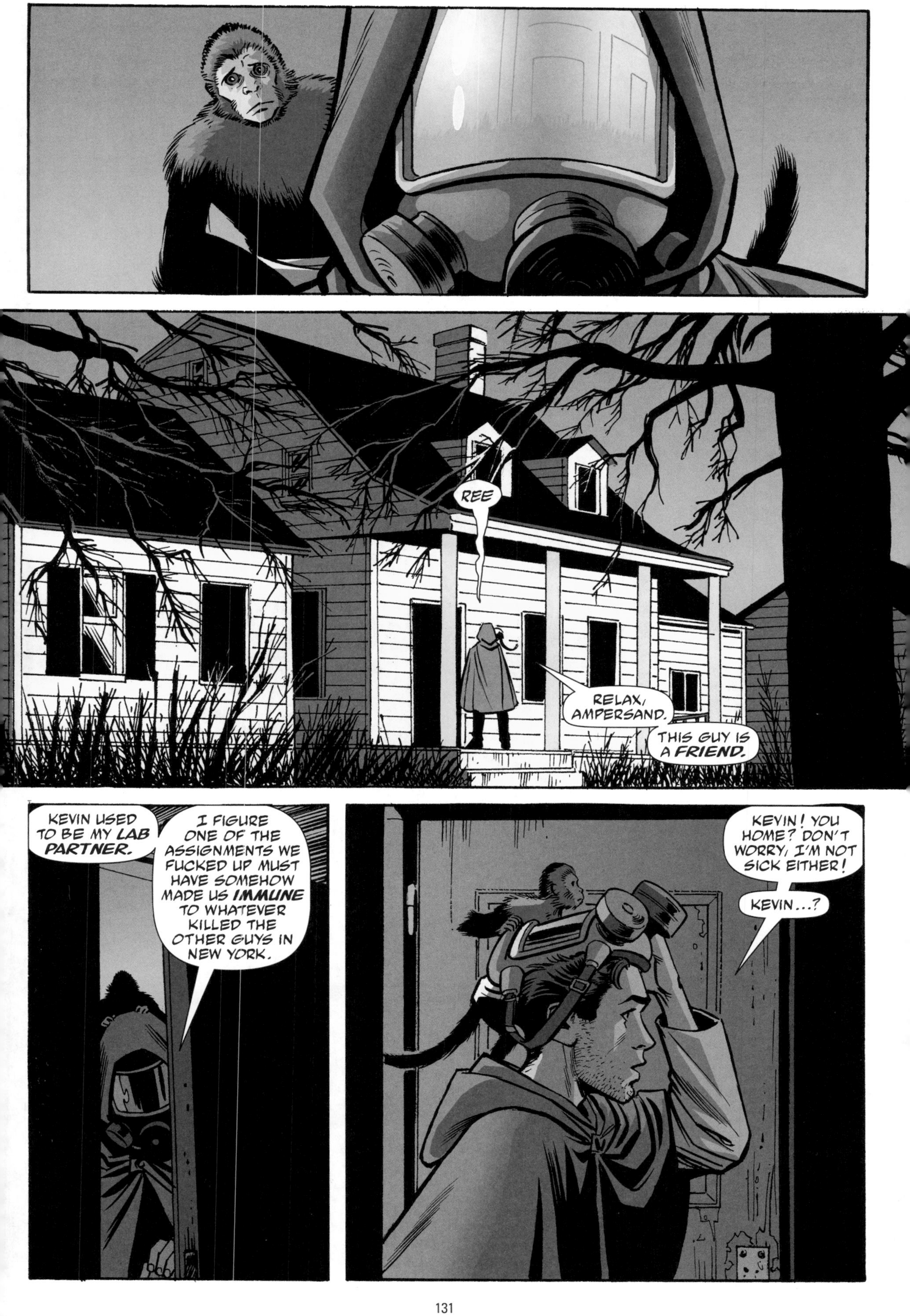
REE
RELAX, AMPERSAND.
THIS GUY IS A FRIEND.
KEVIN USED TO BE MY LAB PARTNER.
I FIGURE ONE OF THE ASSIGNMENTS WE FUCKED UP MUST HAVE SOMEHOW MADE US IMMUNE TO WHATEVER KILLED THE OTHER GUYS IN NEW YORK.
KEVIN! YOU HOME? DON'T WORRY, I'M NOT SICK EITHER!
KEVIN...?

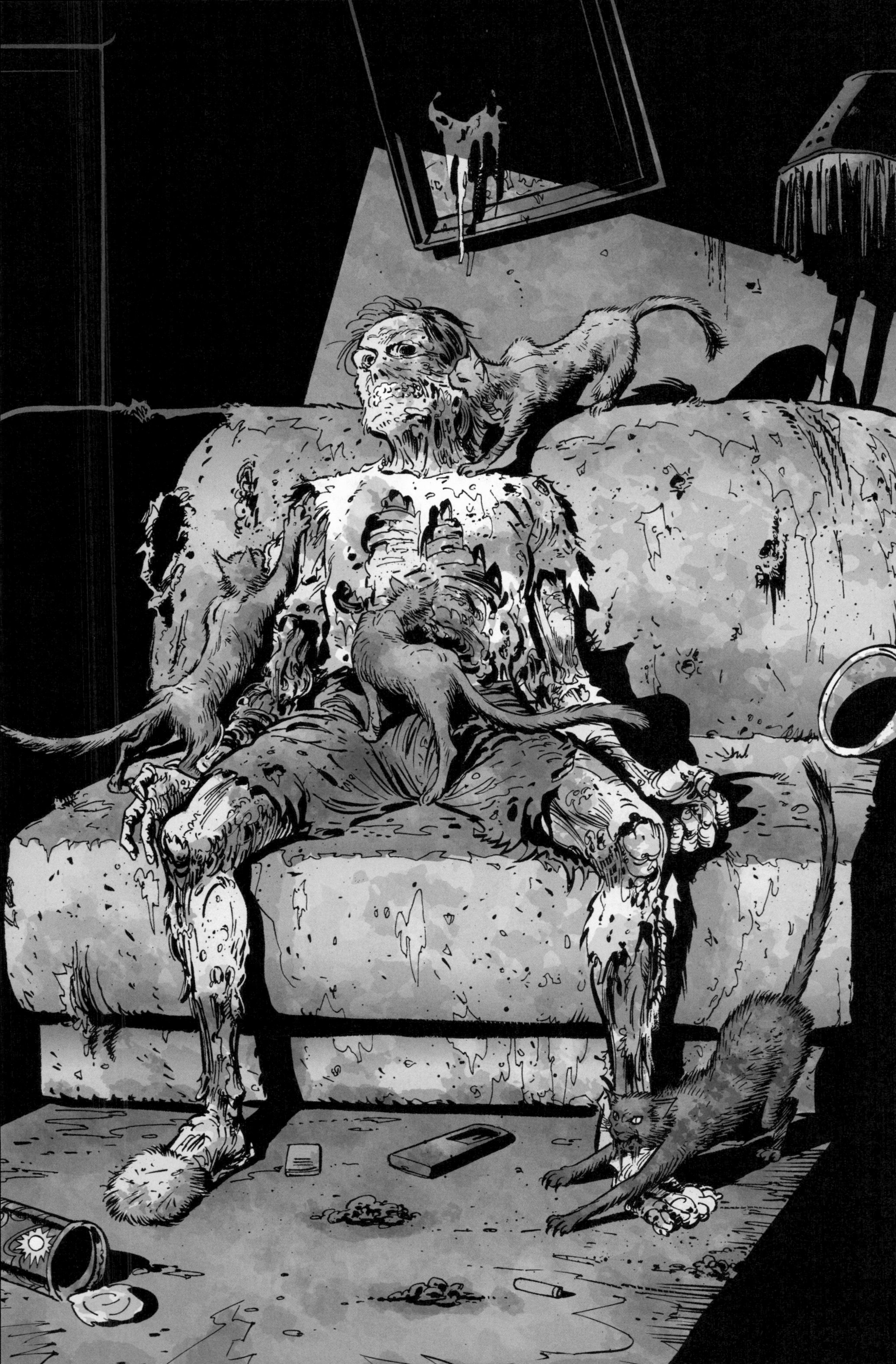

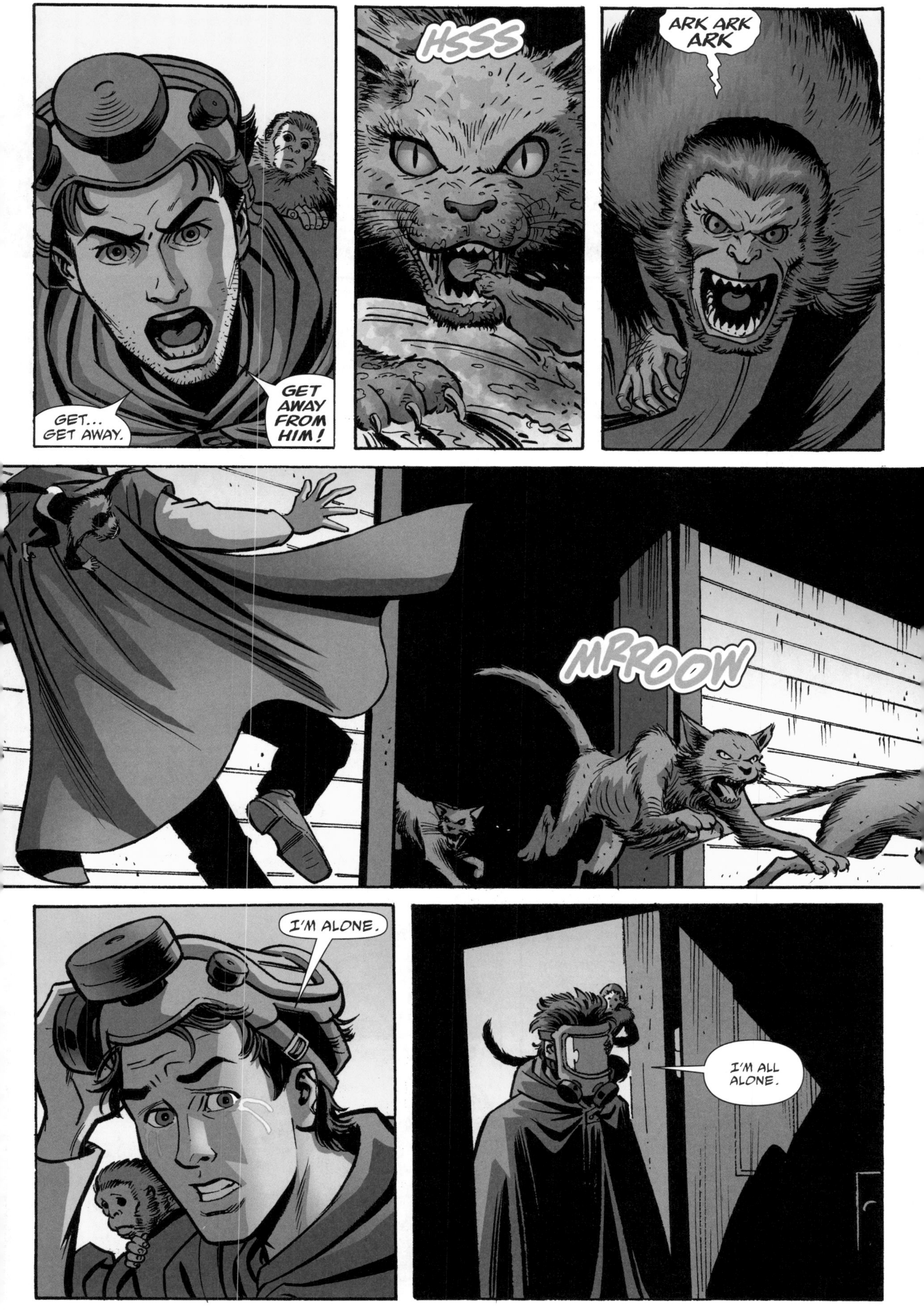
GET... GET AWAY.
GET AWAY FROM HIM!
HSSS
ARK ARK ARK
MRROOW
I'M ALONE.
I'M ALL ALONE.

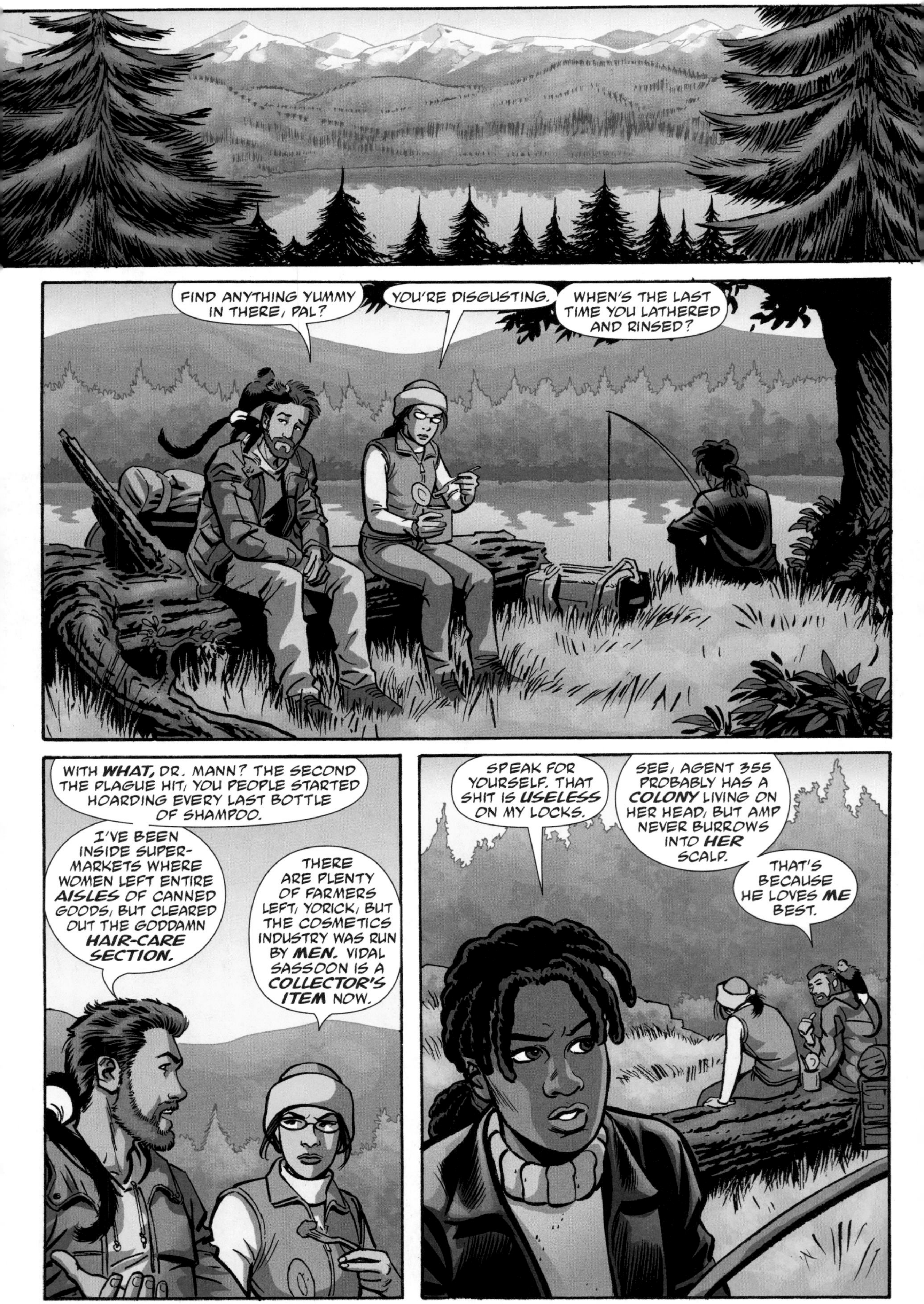
FIND ANYTHING YUMMY IN THERE, PAL?
YOU'RE DISGUSTING.
WHEN'S THE LAST TIME YOU LATHERED AND RINSED?
WITH WHAT, DR. MANN? THE SECOND THE PLAGUE HIT, YOU PEOPLE STARTED HOARDING EVERY LAST BOTTLE OF SHAMPOO.
I'VE BEEN INSIDE SUPER-MARKETS WHERE WOMEN LEFT ENTIRE AISLES OF CANNED GOODS, BUT CLEARED OUT THE GODDAMN HAIR-CARE SECTION.
THERE ARE PLENTY OF FARMERS LEFT, YORICK, BUT THE COSMETICS INDUSTRY WAS RUN BY MEN. VIDAL SASSOON IS A COLLECTOR'S ITEM NOW.
SPEAK FOR YOURSELF. THAT SHIT IS USELESS ON MY LOCKS.
SEE, AGENT 355 PROBABLY HAS A COLONY LIVING ON HER HEAD, BUT AMP NEVER BURROWS INTO HER SCALP.
THAT'S BECAUSE HE LOVES ME BEST.

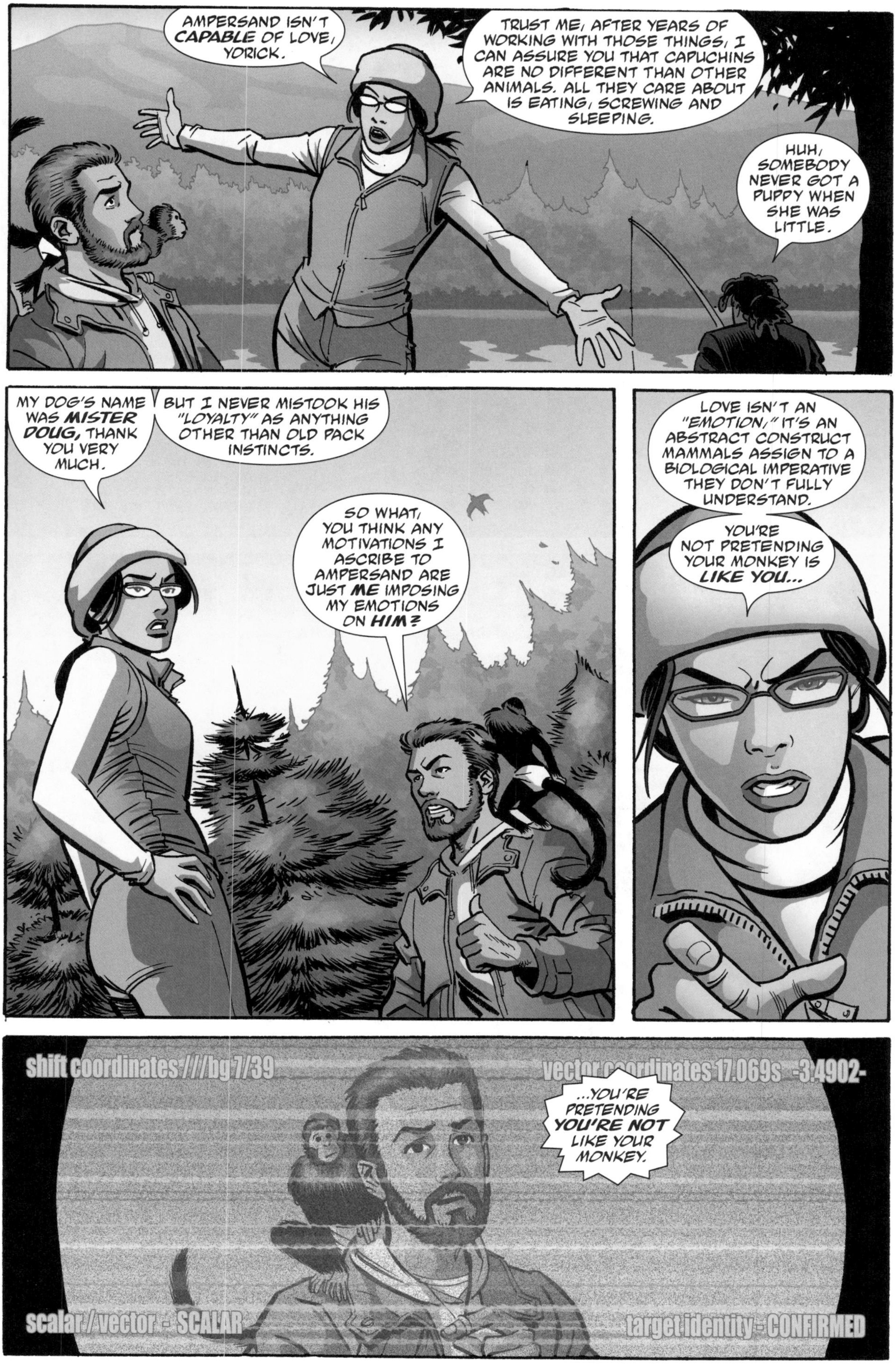
AMPERSAND ISN'T CAPABLE OF LOVE, YORICK.
TRUST ME, AFTER YEARS OF WORKING WITH THOSE THINGS, I CAN ASSURE YOU THAT CAPUCHINS ARE NO DIFFERENT THAN OTHER ANIMALS. ALL THEY CARE ABOUT IS EATING, SCREWING AND SLEEPING.
HUH, SOMEBODY NEVER GOT A PUPPY WHEN SHE WAS LITTLE.
MY DOG'S NAME WAS MISTER DOUG, THANK YOU VERY MUCH.
BUT I NEVER MISTOOK HIS "LOYALTY" AS ANYTHING OTHER THAN OLD PACK INSTINCTS.
SO WHAT, YOU THINK ANY MOTIVATIONS I ASCRIBE TO AMPERSAND ARE JUST ME IMPOSING MY EMOTIONS ON HIM?
LOVE ISN'T AN "EMOTION," IT'S AN ABSTRACT CONSTRUCT MAMMALS ASSIGN TO A BIOLOGICAL IMPERATIVE THEY DON'T FULLY UNDERSTAND.
YOU'RE NOT PRETENDING YOUR MONKEY IS LIKE YOU...
shift coordinates ////bg 7/39
vector coordinates 17.069s -3.4902-
...YOU'RE PRETENDING YOU'RE NOT LIKE YOUR MONKEY.
scalar // vector - SCALAR
target identity - CONFIRMED

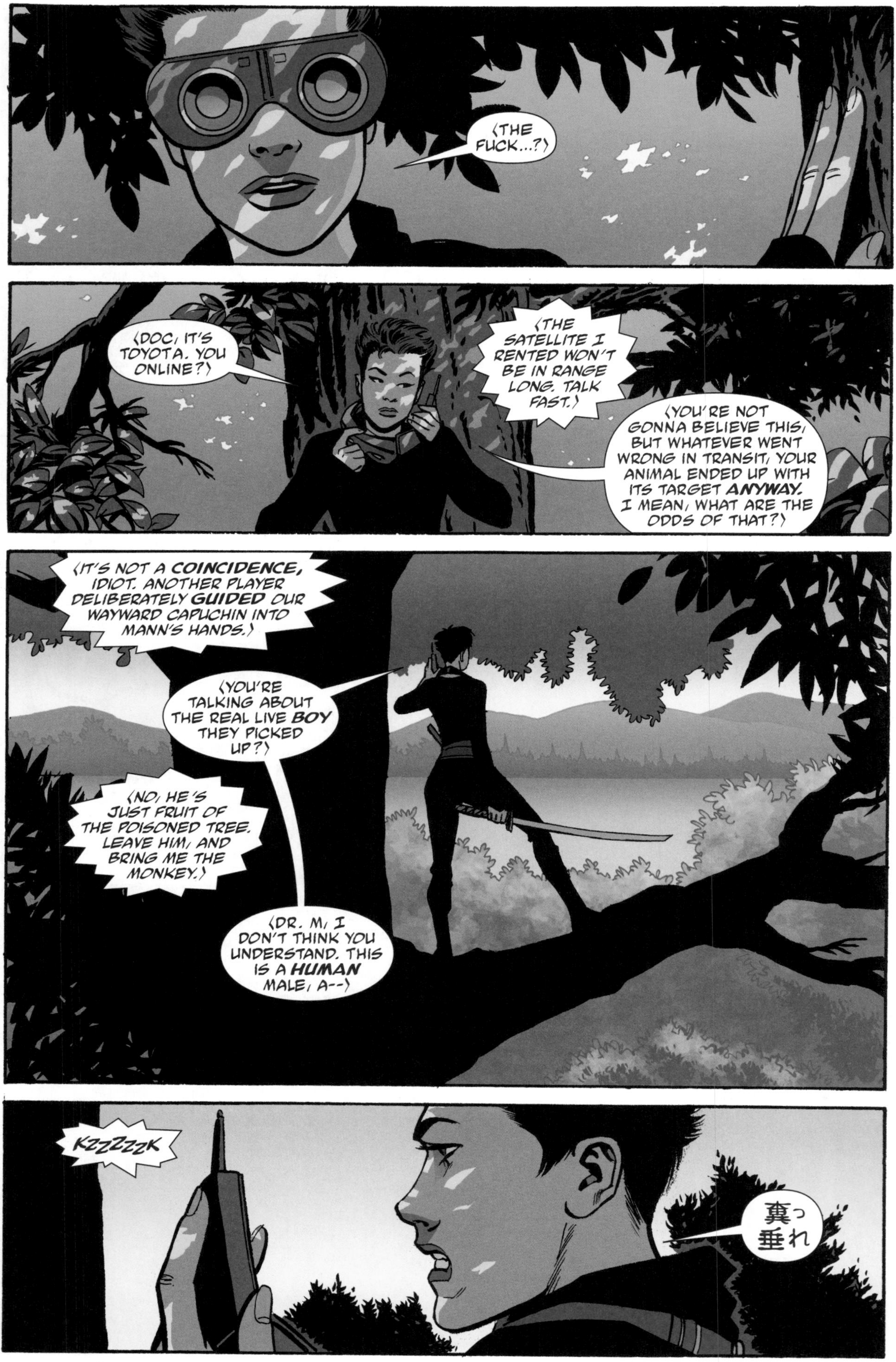
⟨THE FUCK...?⟩
⟨DOC, IT'S TOYOTA. YOU ONLINE?⟩
⟨THE SATELLITE I RENTED WON'T BE IN RANGE LONG. TALK FAST.⟩
⟨YOU'RE NOT GONNA BELIEVE THIS, BUT WHATEVER WENT WRONG IN TRANSIT, YOUR ANIMAL ENDED UP WITH ITS TARGET ANYWAY. I MEAN, WHAT ARE THE ODDS OF THAT?⟩
⟨IT'S NOT A COINCIDENCE, IDIOT. ANOTHER PLAYER DELIBERATELY GUIDED OUR WAYWARD CAPUCHIN INTO MANN'S HANDS.⟩
⟨YOU'RE TALKING ABOUT THE REAL LIVE BOY THEY PICKED UP?⟩
⟨NO, HE'S JUST FRUIT OF THE POISONED TREE. LEAVE HIM, AND BRING ME THE MONKEY.⟩
⟨DR. M, I DON'T THINK YOU UNDERSTAND. THIS IS A HUMAN MALE, A--⟩
KZZZZZK
糞っ垂れ

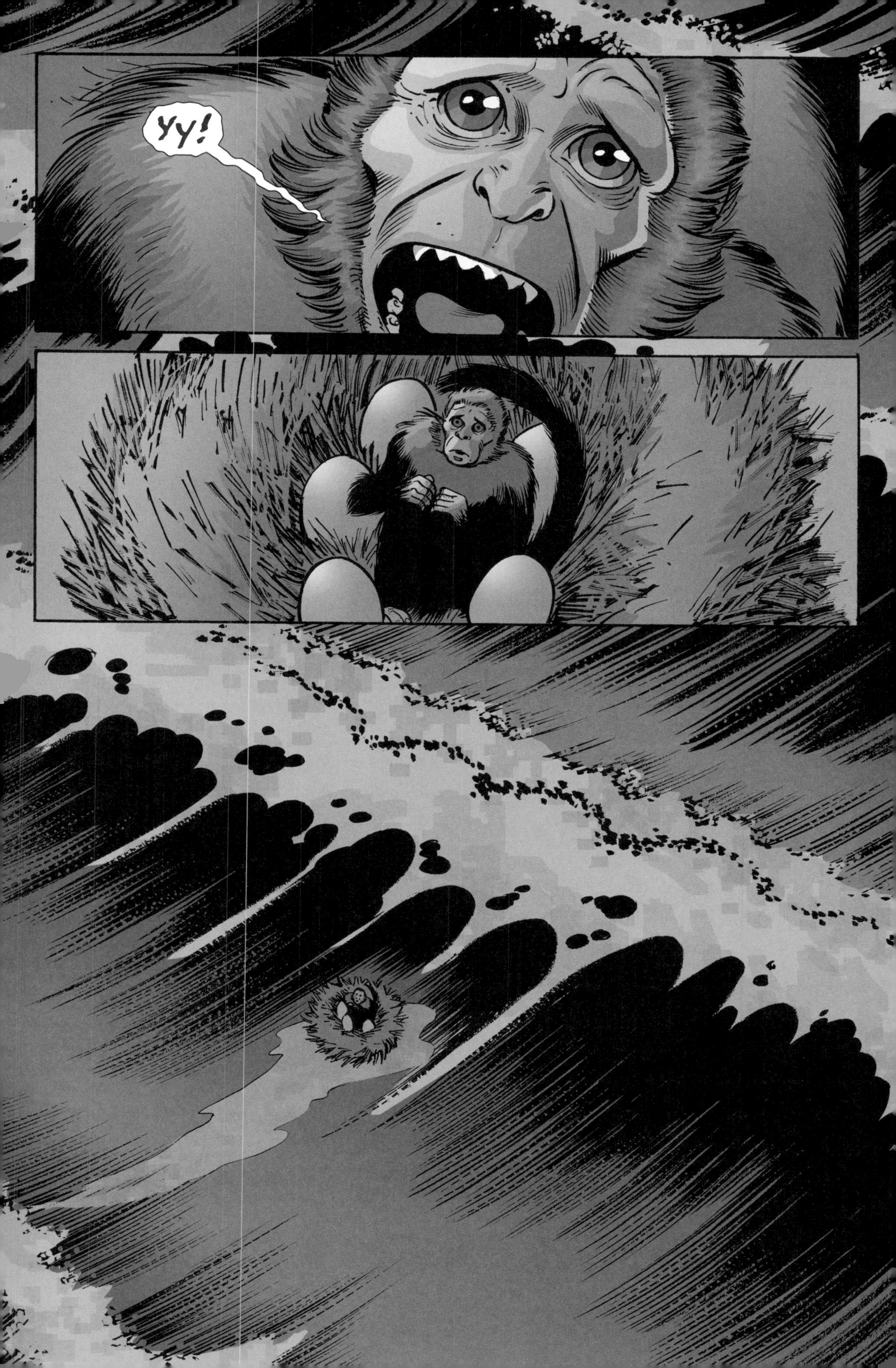
YY!

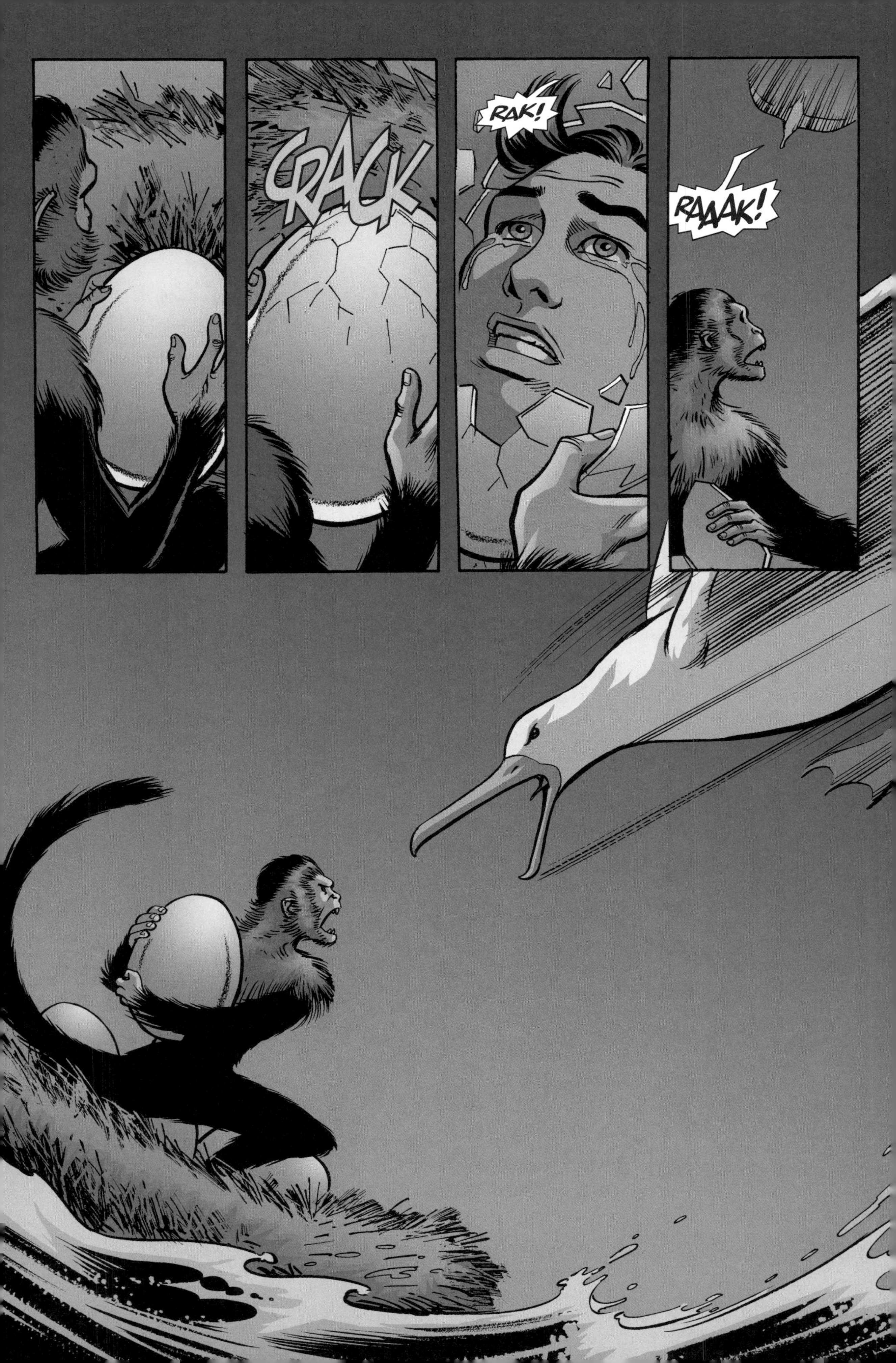
CRACK
RAK!
RAAAK!

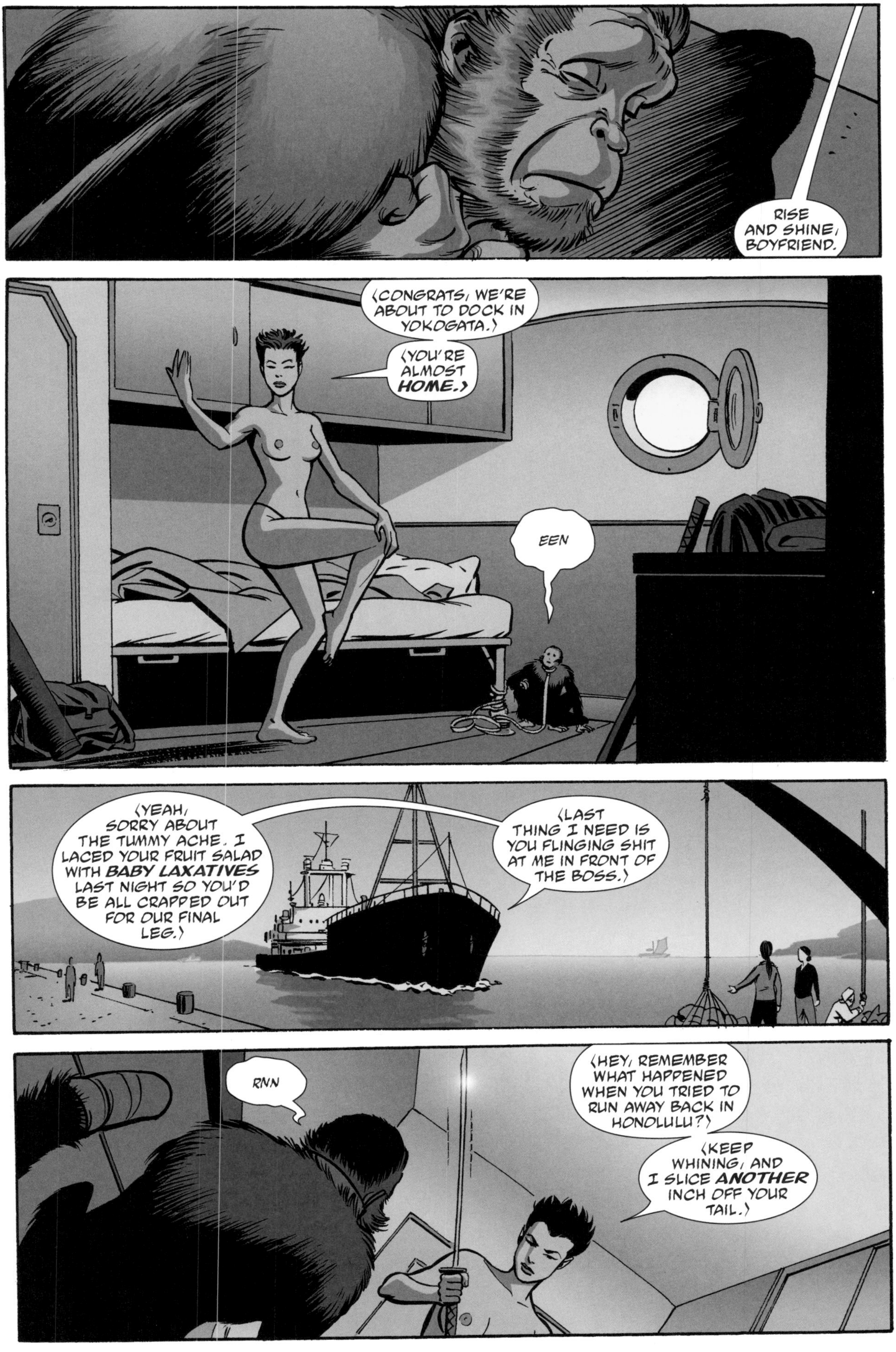
RISE AND SHINE, BOYFRIEND.
⟨CONGRATS, WE'RE ABOUT TO DOCK IN YOKOGATA.⟩
⟨YOU'RE ALMOST HOME.⟩
EEN
⟨YEAH, SORRY ABOUT THE TUMMY ACHE. I LACED YOUR FRUIT SALAD WITH BABY LAXATIVES LAST NIGHT SO YOU'D BE ALL CRAPPED OUT FOR OUR FINAL LEG.⟩
⟨LAST THING I NEED IS YOU FLINGING SHIT AT ME IN FRONT OF THE BOSS.⟩
RNN
⟨HEY, REMEMBER WHAT HAPPENED WHEN YOU TRIED TO RUN AWAY BACK IN HONOLULU?⟩
⟨KEEP WHINING, AND I SLICE ANOTHER INCH OFF YOUR TAIL.⟩

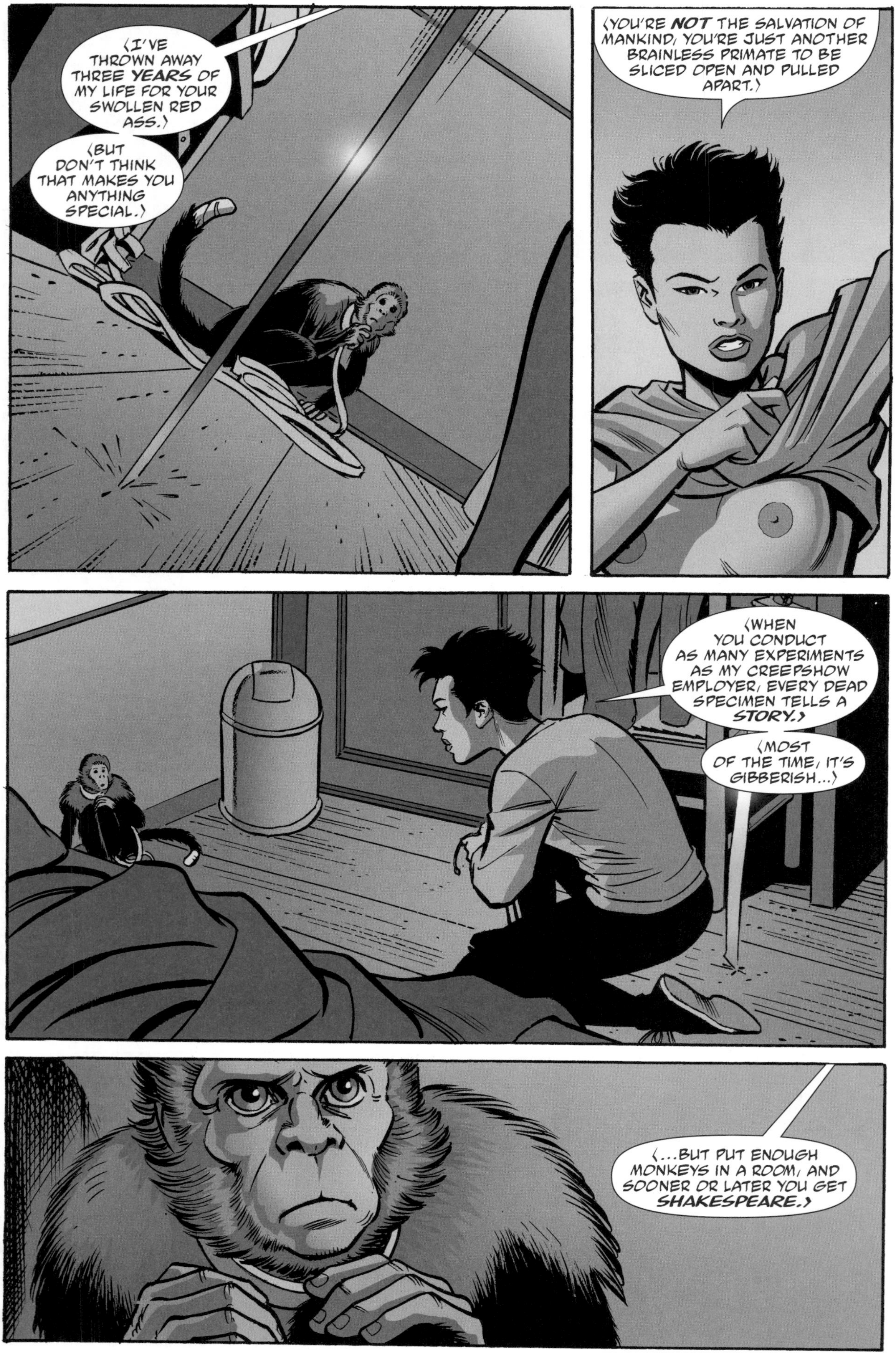
⟨I'VE THROWN AWAY THREE YEARS OF MY LIFE FOR YOUR SWOLLEN RED ASS.⟩
⟨BUT DON'T THINK THAT MAKES YOU ANYTHING SPECIAL.⟩
⟨YOU'RE NOT THE SALVATION OF MANKIND, YOU'RE JUST ANOTHER BRAINLESS PRIMATE TO BE SLICED OPEN AND PULLED APART.⟩
⟨WHEN YOU CONDUCT AS MANY EXPERIMENTS AS MY CREEPSHOW EMPLOYER, EVERY DEAD SPECIMEN TELLS A STORY.⟩
⟨MOST OF THE TIME, IT'S GIBBERISH...⟩
⟨...BUT PUT ENOUGH MONKEYS IN A ROOM, AND SOONER OR LATER YOU GET SHAKESPEARE.⟩

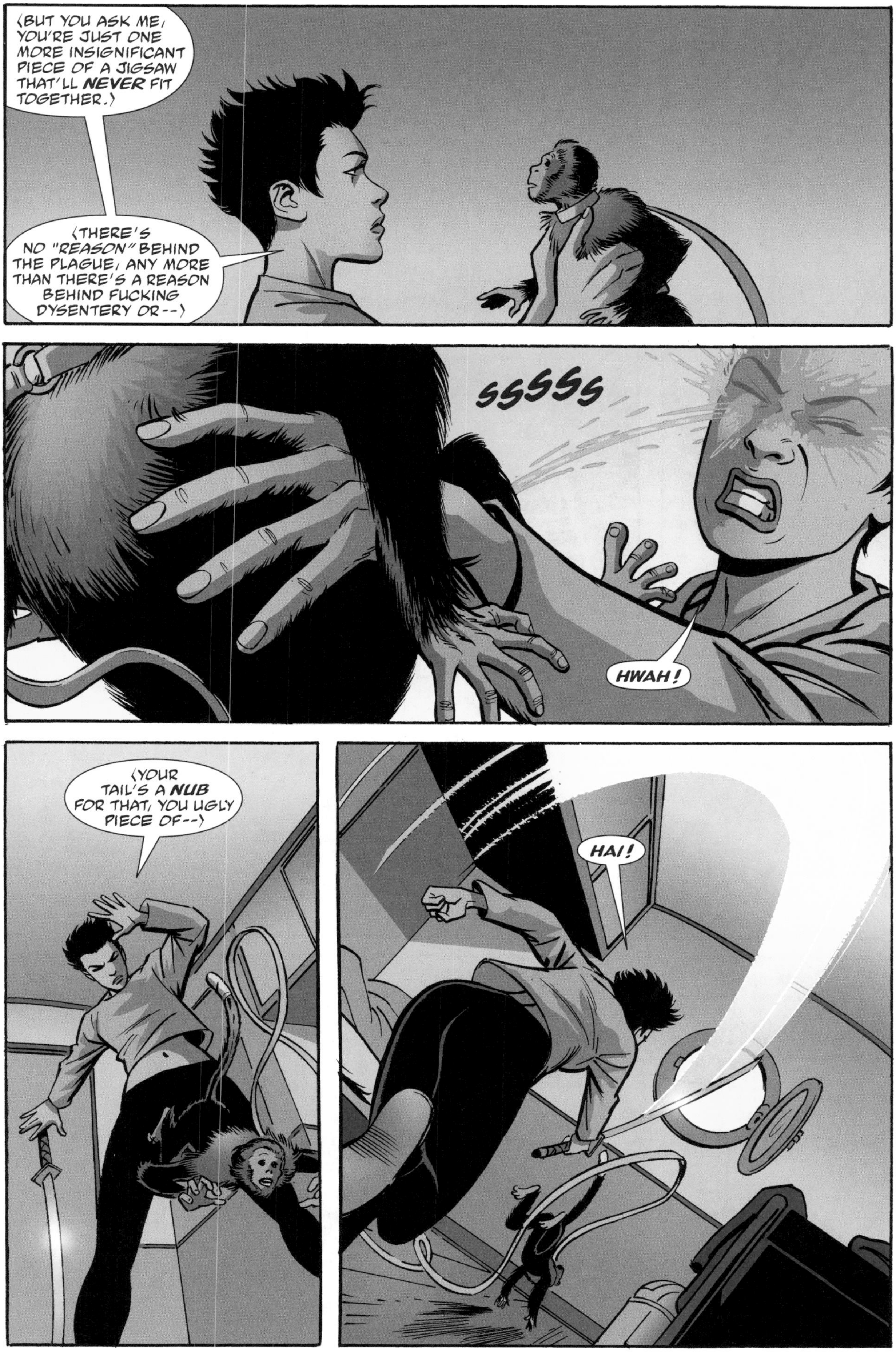
⟨BUT YOU ASK ME, YOU'RE JUST ONE MORE INSIGNIFICANT PIECE OF A JIGSAW THAT'LL ***NEVER*** FIT TOGETHER.⟩
⟨THERE'S NO "REASON" BEHIND THE PLAGUE, ANY MORE THAN THERE'S A REASON BEHIND FUCKING DYSENTERY OR--⟩
SSSSS
HWAH!
⟨YOUR TAIL'S A ***NUB*** FOR THAT, YOU UGLY PIECE OF--⟩
HAI!

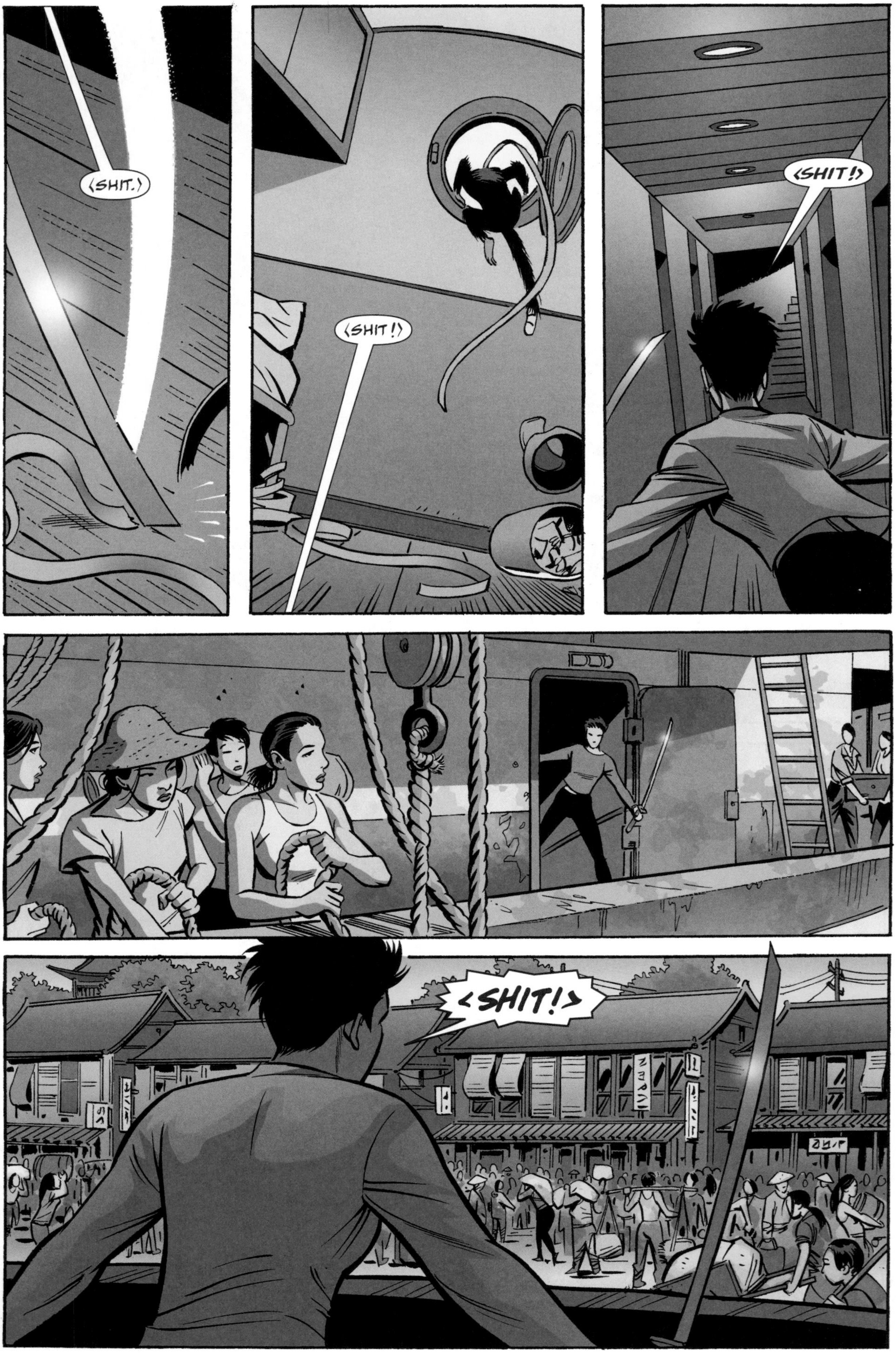
‹SHIT.›
‹SHIT!›
‹SHIT!›
‹SHIT!›

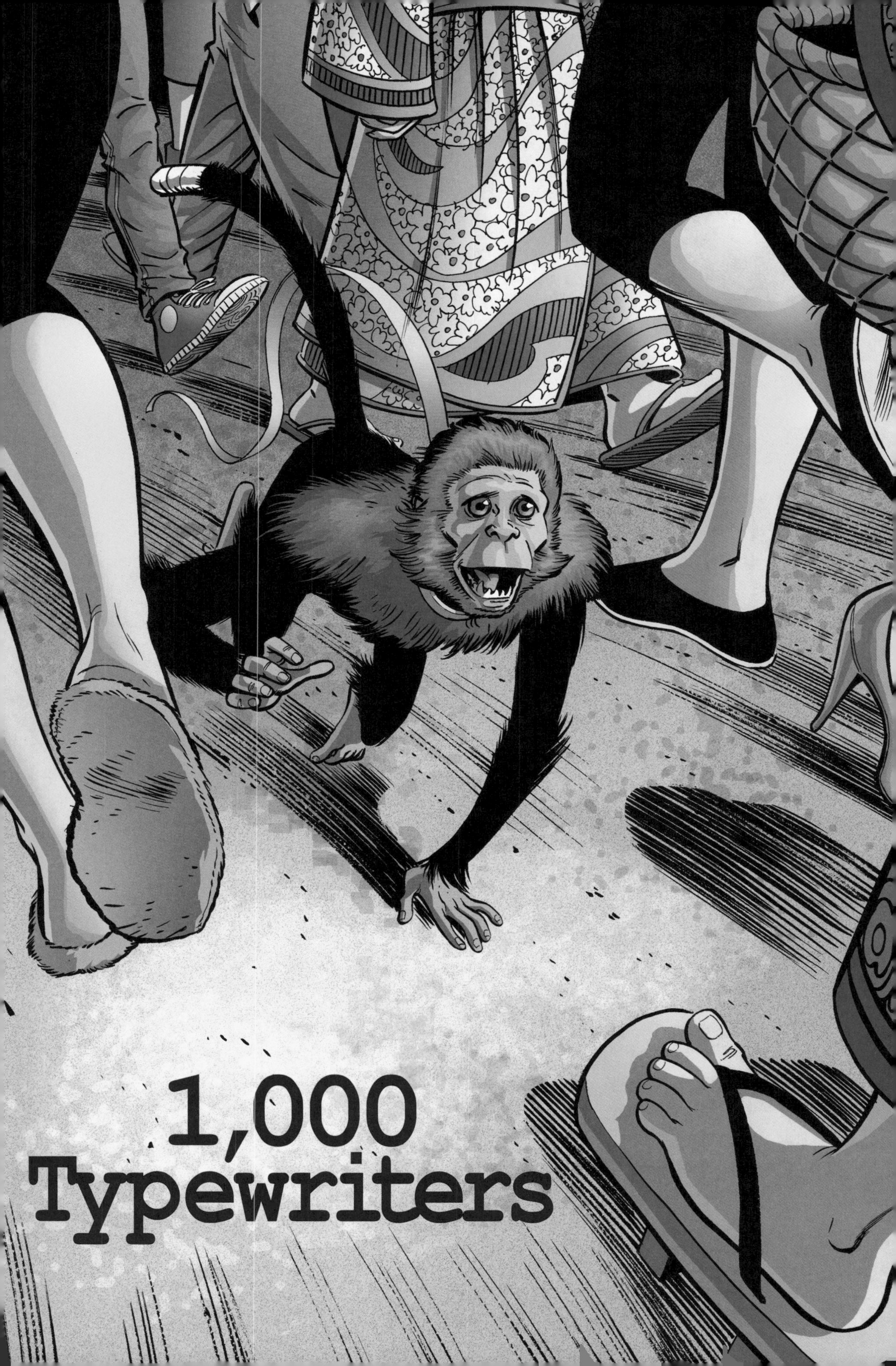
1,000
Typewriters

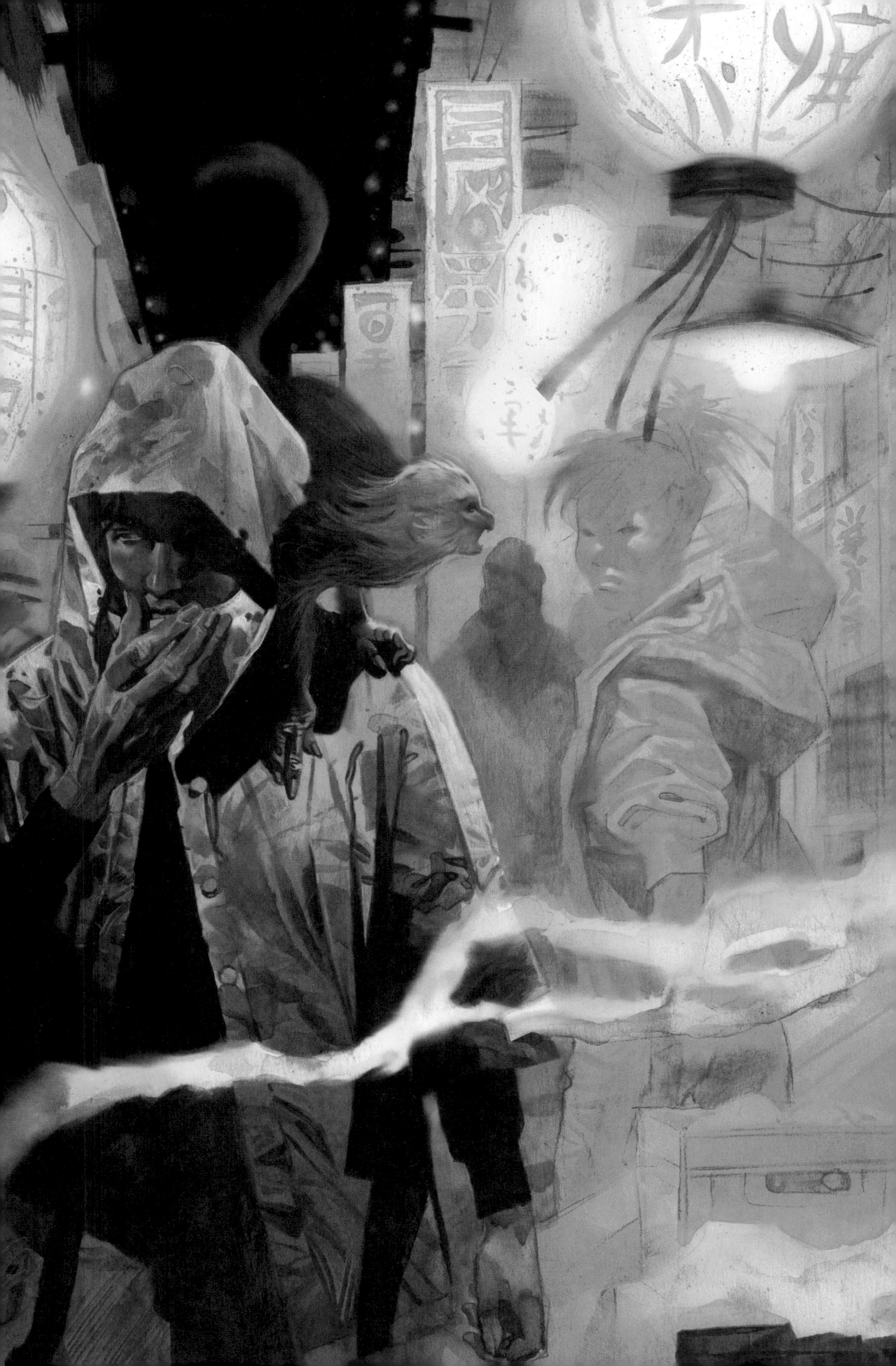

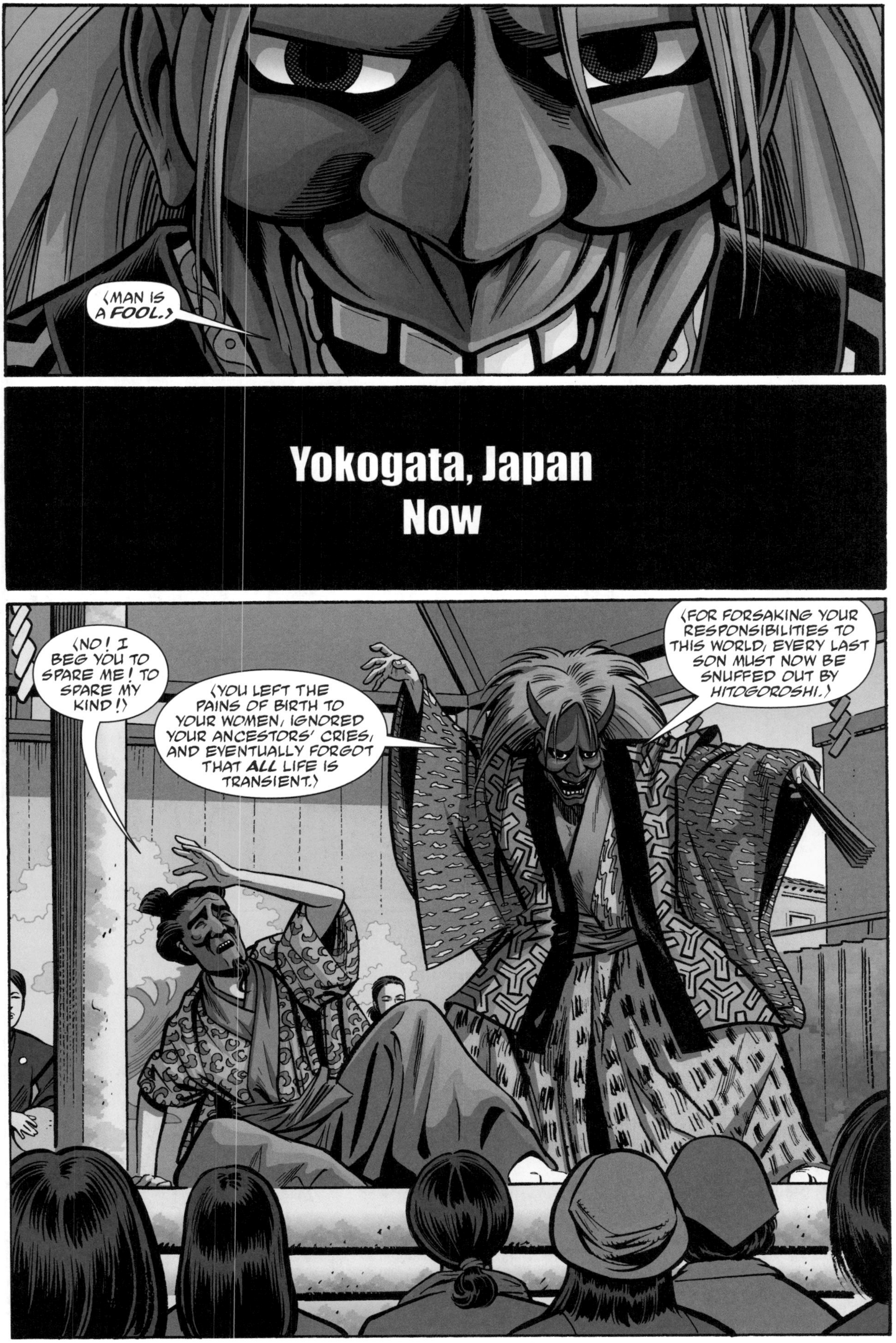
‹MAN IS A FOOL.›
Yokogata, Japan
Now
‹NO! I BEG YOU TO SPARE ME! TO SPARE MY KIND!›
‹YOU LEFT THE PAINS OF BIRTH TO YOUR WOMEN, IGNORED YOUR ANCESTORS' CRIES, AND EVENTUALLY FORGOT THAT ALL LIFE IS TRANSIENT.›
‹FOR FORSAKING YOUR RESPONSIBILITIES TO THIS WORLD, EVERY LAST SON MUST NOW BE SNUFFED OUT BY HITOGOROSHI.›

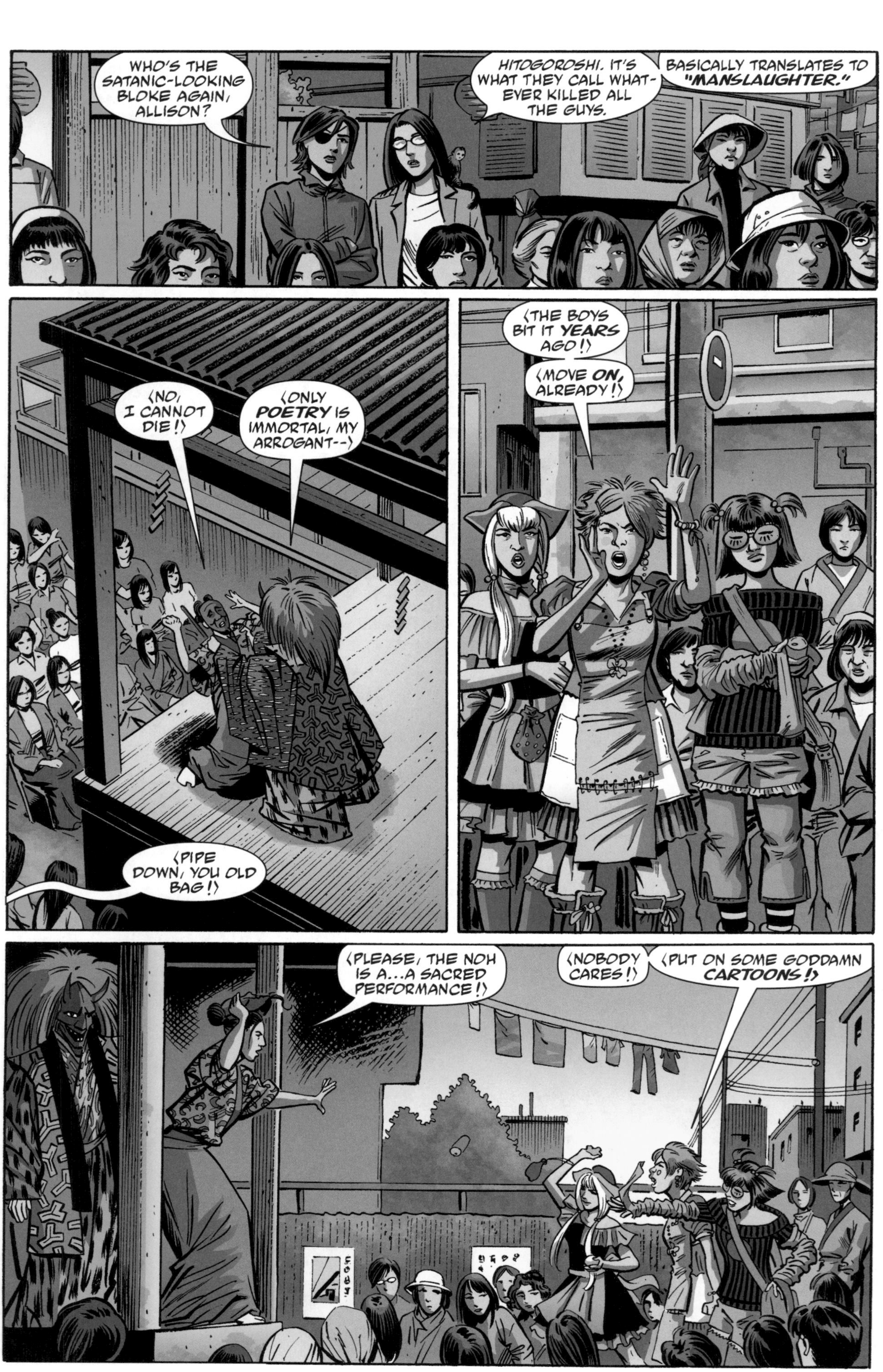
WHO'S THE SATANIC-LOOKING BLOKE AGAIN, ALLISON?
HITOGOROSHI. IT'S WHAT THEY CALL WHAT-EVER KILLED ALL THE GUYS.
BASICALLY TRANSLATES TO "MANSLAUGHTER."
‹NO, I CANNOT DIE!›
‹ONLY POETRY IS IMMORTAL, MY ARROGANT--›
‹PIPE DOWN, YOU OLD BAG!›
‹THE BOYS BIT IT YEARS AGO!›
‹MOVE ON, ALREADY!›
‹PLEASE, THE NOH IS A...A SACRED PERFORMANCE!›
‹NOBODY CARES!›
‹PUT ON SOME GODDAMN CARTOONS!›

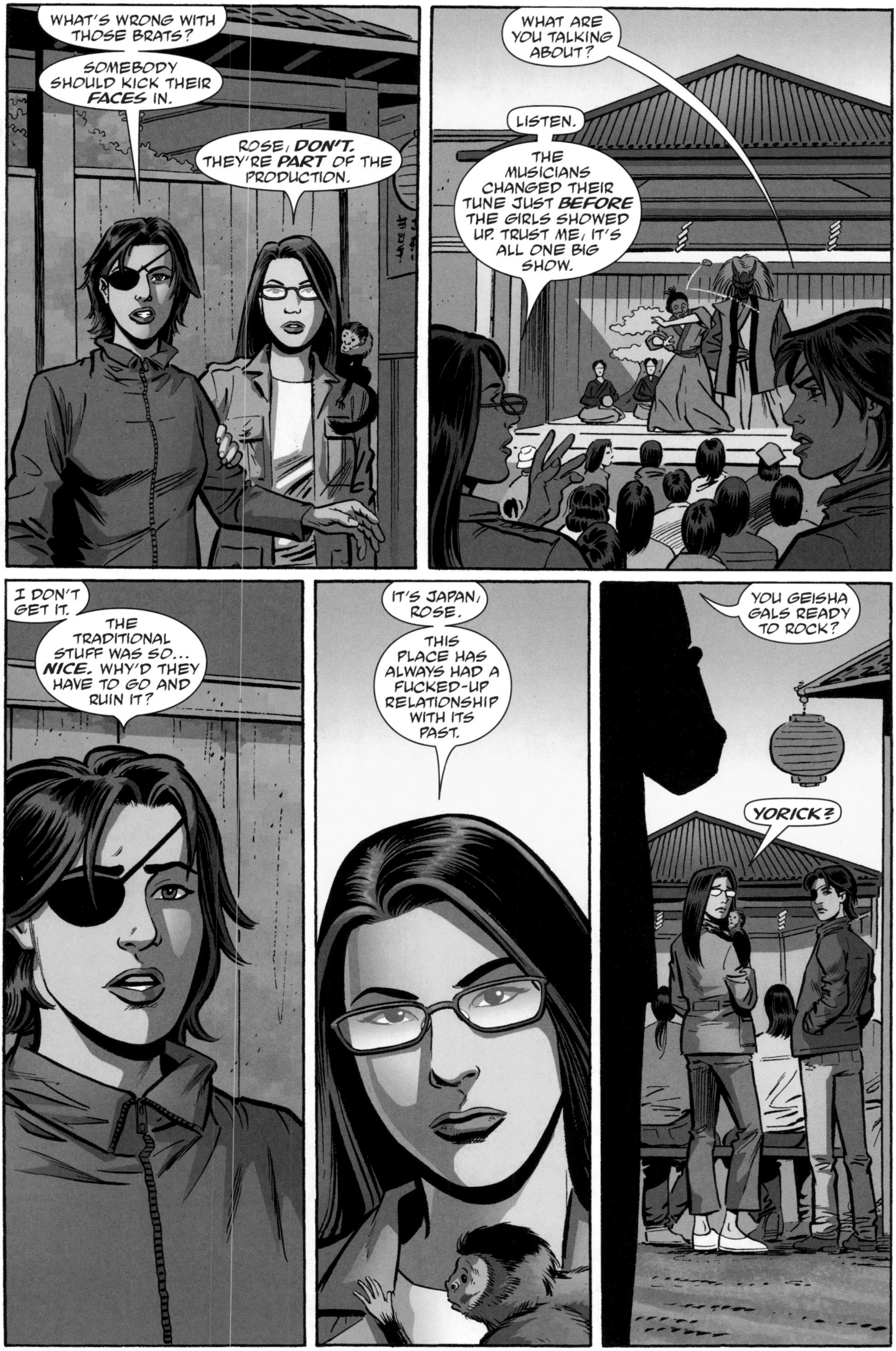
WHAT'S WRONG WITH THOSE BRATS?
SOMEBODY SHOULD KICK THEIR FACES IN.
ROSE, DON'T. THEY'RE PART OF THE PRODUCTION.
WHAT ARE YOU TALKING ABOUT?
LISTEN.
THE MUSICIANS CHANGED THEIR TUNE JUST BEFORE THE GIRLS SHOWED UP. TRUST ME, IT'S ALL ONE BIG SHOW.
I DON'T GET IT.
THE TRADITIONAL STUFF WAS SO... NICE. WHY'D THEY HAVE TO GO AND RUIN IT?
IT'S JAPAN, ROSE.
THIS PLACE HAS ALWAYS HAD A FUCKED-UP RELATIONSHIP WITH ITS PAST.
YOU GEISHA GALS READY TO ROCK?
YORICK?

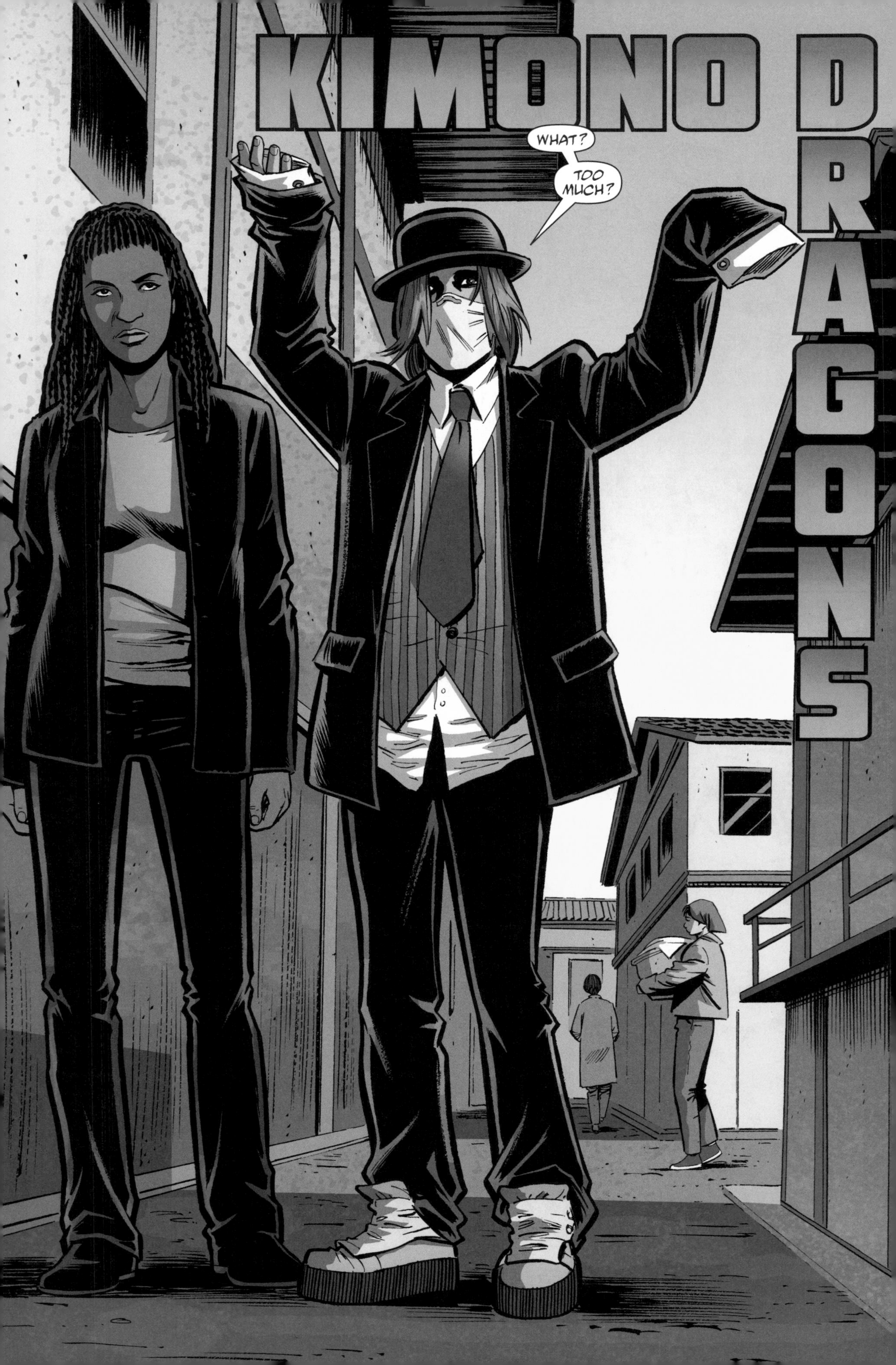
KIMONO DRAGONS
WHAT?
TOO MUCH?

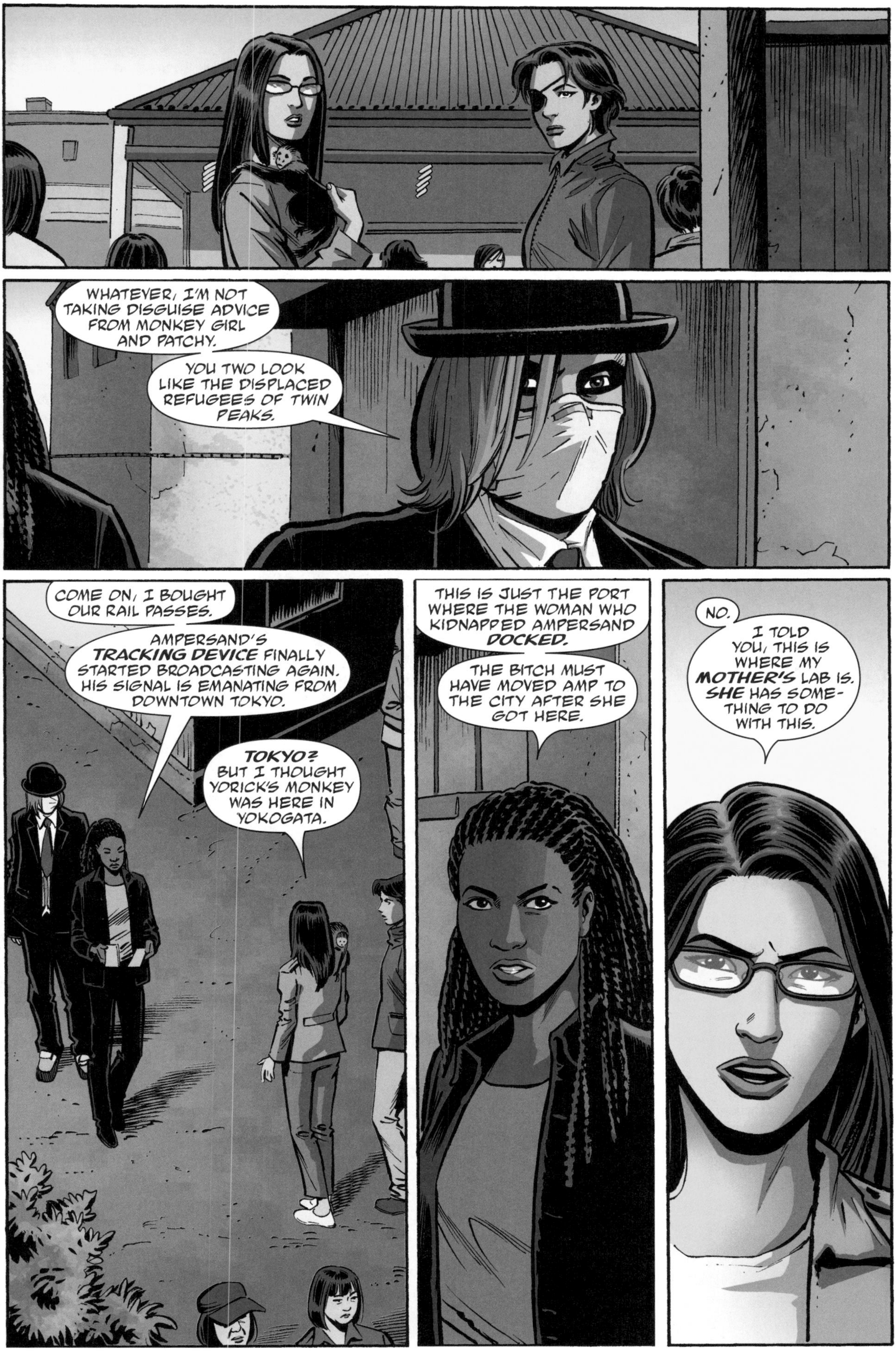

WHATEVER, I'M NOT TAKING DISGUISE ADVICE FROM MONKEY GIRL AND PATCHY.
YOU TWO LOOK LIKE THE DISPLACED REFUGEES OF TWIN PEAKS.
COME ON, I BOUGHT OUR RAIL PASSES.
AMPERSAND'S **TRACKING DEVICE** FINALLY STARTED BROADCASTING AGAIN. HIS SIGNAL IS EMANATING FROM DOWNTOWN TOKYO.
TOKYO? BUT I THOUGHT YORICK'S MONKEY WAS HERE IN YOKOGATA.
THIS IS JUST THE PORT WHERE THE WOMAN WHO KIDNAPPED AMPERSAND **DOCKED.**
THE BITCH MUST HAVE MOVED AMP TO THE CITY AFTER SHE GOT HERE.
NO.
I TOLD YOU, THIS IS WHERE MY **MOTHER'S** LAB IS. **SHE** HAS SOME-THING TO DO WITH THIS.

DOCTOR, WE'VE BEEN THROUGH THIS.

AMPERSAND IS THE KEY TO UNLOCKING WHAT CAUSED THE PLAGUE... NOT YOU OR ME, AND CERTAINLY NOT OUR FAMILIES.

SO YOU THINK IT'S JUST A **COINCIDENCE** THAT THIS KUNG FU WHORE CAME HERE, AND NOT TO ANY OF THE HUNDREDS OF **OTHER** PORT CITIES IN JAPAN?

SHE'S GOT A POINT, AGENT 355.

WOULDN'T HURT TO AT LEAST **CHECK OUT** HER MOM'S LAB, YEAH? AS LONG AS WE'RE HERE?

AMPERSAND'S TRACKING DEVICE HAS A **LAG TIME**, ROSE. WE HAVE TO FIND THE ANIMAL BEFORE HE'S MOVED AGAIN.

UNLESS HE'S BEEN MOVED BACK HERE **ALREADY**, IN WHICH CASE, A SIDE TRIP TO THE CAPITAL WOULD JUST WASTE EVEN **MORE** TIME.

PLEASE, THREE-FIFTY. I SWEAR, I'M NOT SEEKING OUT MY MOTHER BECAUSE I WANT A...A **HOME-COOKED MEAL**. THIS IS IMPORTANT.

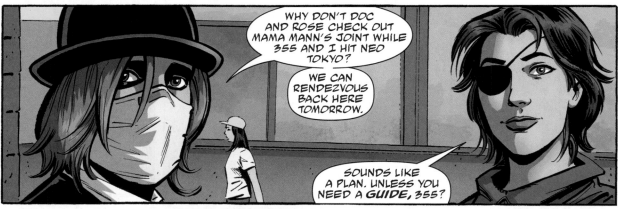

WHY DON'T DOC AND ROSE CHECK OUT MAMA MANN'S JOINT WHILE 355 AND I HIT NEO TOKYO?

WE CAN RENDEZVOUS BACK HERE TOMORROW.

SOUNDS LIKE A PLAN. UNLESS YOU NEED A **GUIDE**, 355?

THIS ISN'T MY FIRST TIME HERE, THANKS.

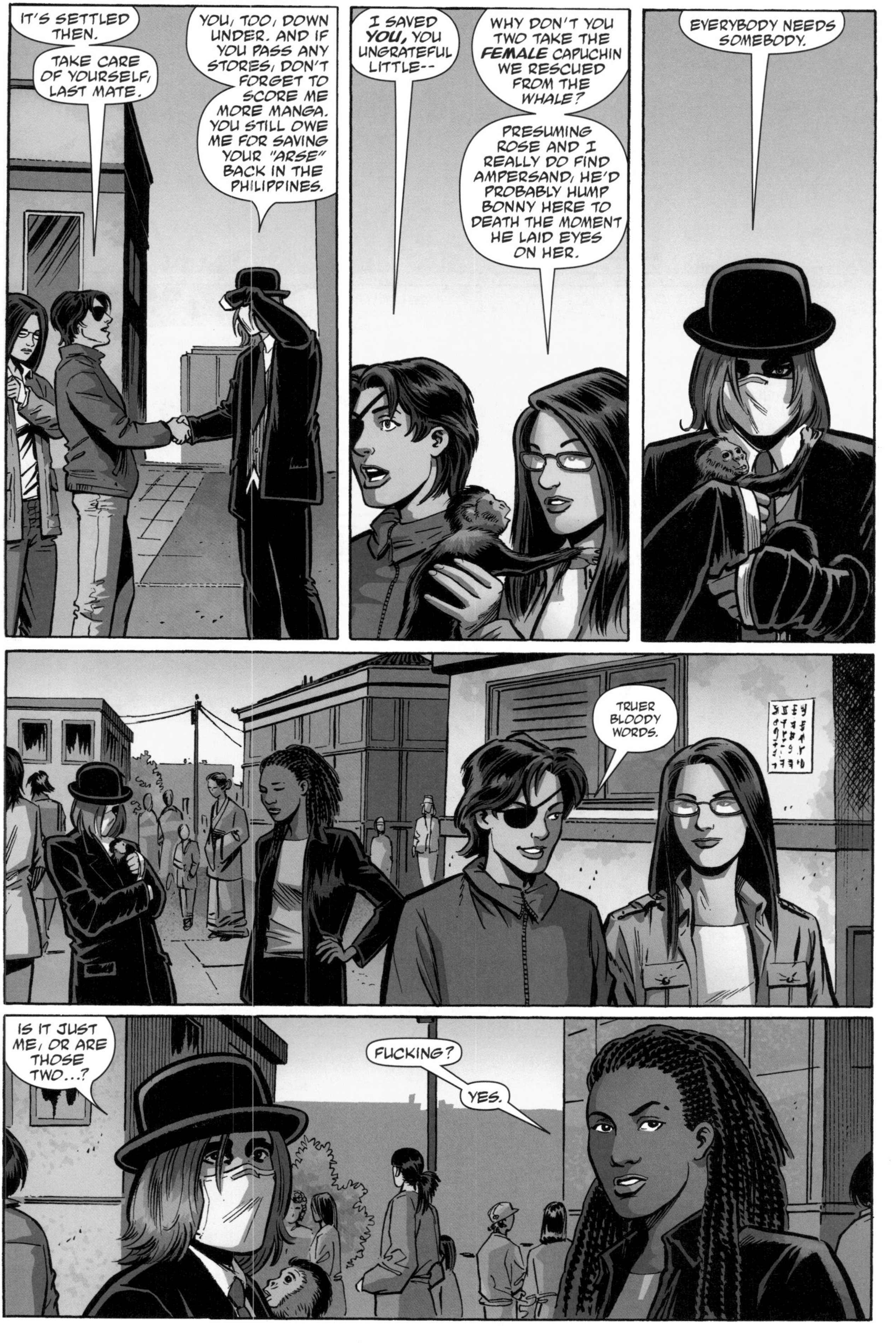
IT'S SETTLED THEN.
TAKE CARE OF YOURSELF, LAST MATE.
YOU, TOO, DOWN UNDER. AND IF YOU PASS ANY STORES, DON'T FORGET TO SCORE ME MORE MANGA. YOU STILL OWE ME FOR SAVING YOUR "ARSE" BACK IN THE PHILIPPINES.
I SAVED **YOU,** YOU UNGRATEFUL LITTLE--
WHY DON'T YOU TWO TAKE THE **FEMALE** CAPUCHIN WE RESCUED FROM THE WHALE?
PRESUMING ROSE AND I REALLY DO FIND AMPERSAND, HE'D PROBABLY HUMP BONNY HERE TO DEATH THE MOMENT HE LAID EYES ON HER.
EVERYBODY NEEDS SOMEBODY.
TRUER BLOODY WORDS.
IS IT JUST ME, OR ARE THOSE TWO...?
FUCKING?
YES.

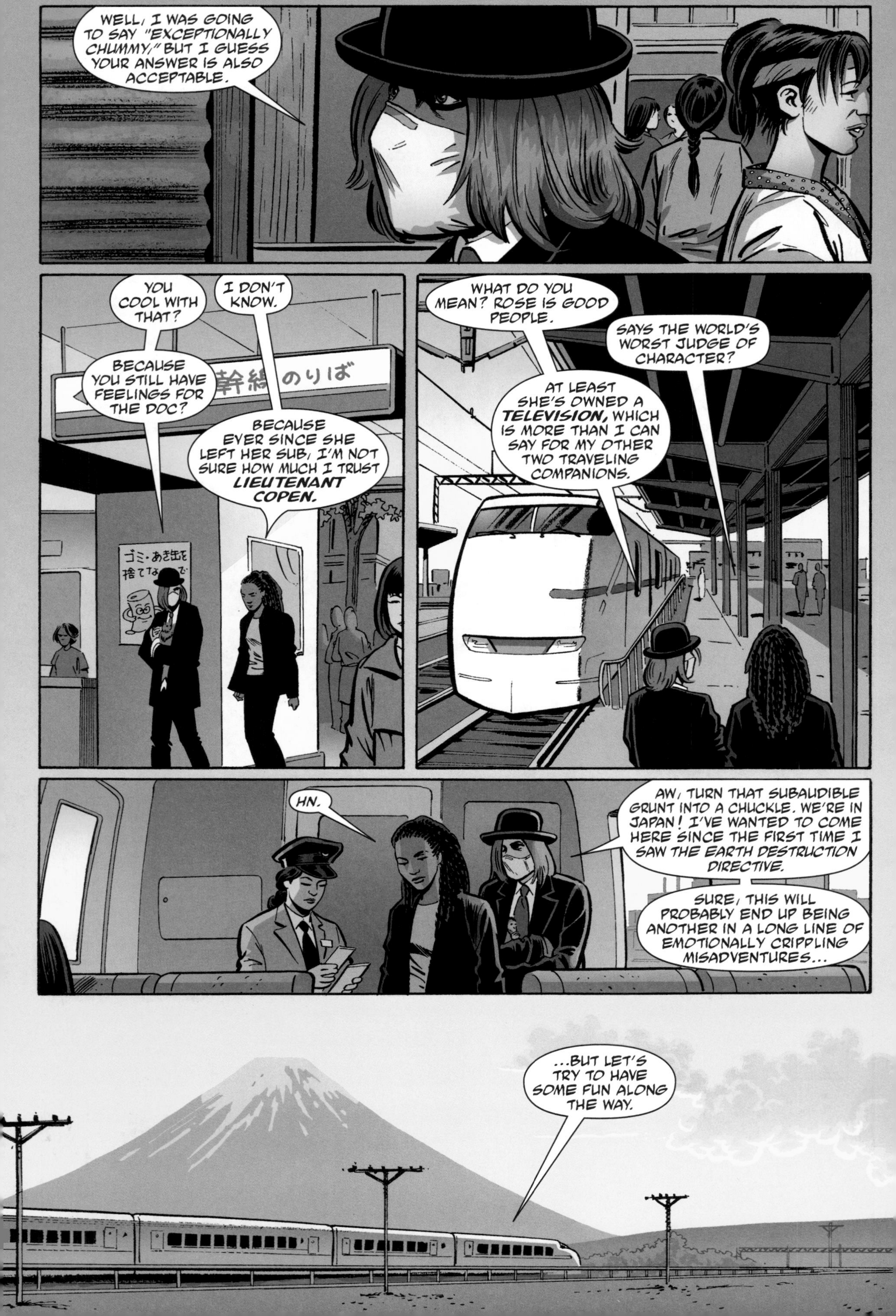
WELL, I WAS GOING TO SAY "EXCEPTIONALLY CHUMMY," BUT I GUESS YOUR ANSWER IS ALSO ACCEPTABLE.
YOU COOL WITH THAT?
I DON'T KNOW.
BECAUSE YOU STILL HAVE FEELINGS FOR THE DOC?
BECAUSE EVER SINCE SHE LEFT HER SUB, I'M NOT SURE HOW MUCH I TRUST **LIEUTENANT COPEN.**
ゴミ・あき缶を
WHAT DO YOU MEAN? ROSE IS GOOD PEOPLE.
AT LEAST SHE'S OWNED A **TELEVISION,** WHICH IS MORE THAN I CAN SAY FOR MY OTHER TWO TRAVELING COMPANIONS.
SAYS THE WORLD'S WORST JUDGE OF CHARACTER?
HN.
AW, TURN THAT SUBAUDIBLE GRUNT INTO A CHUCKLE. WE'RE IN JAPAN! I'VE WANTED TO COME HERE SINCE THE FIRST TIME I SAW THE EARTH DESTRUCTION DIRECTIVE.
SURE, THIS WILL PROBABLY END UP BEING ANOTHER IN A LONG LINE OF EMOTIONALLY CRIPPLING MISADVENTURES...
...BUT LET'S TRY TO HAVE SOME FUN ALONG THE WAY.

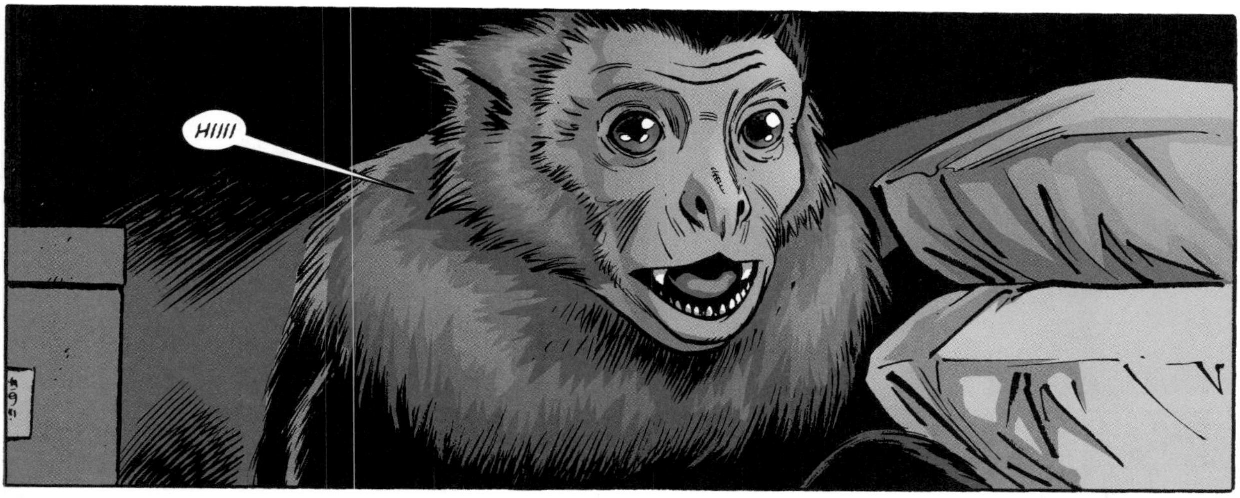
HI!!!

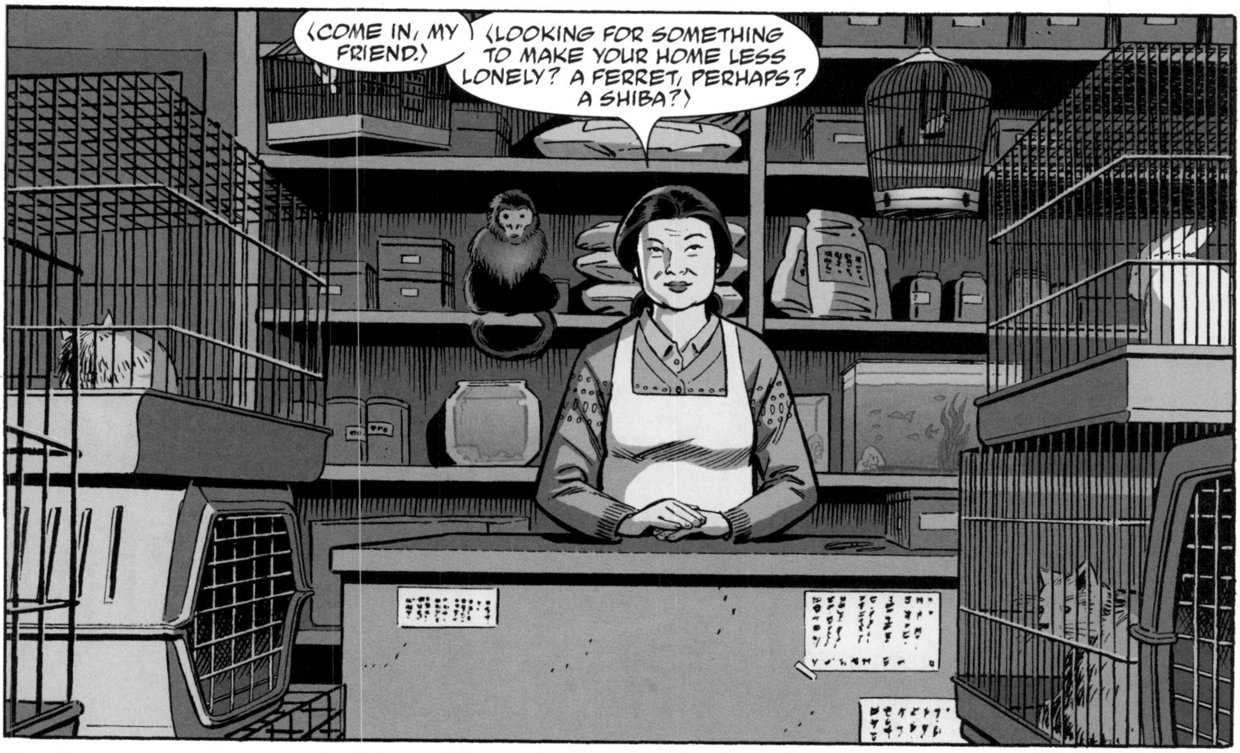
‹COME IN, MY FRIEND.›
‹LOOKING FOR SOMETHING TO MAKE YOUR HOME LESS LONELY? A FERRET, PERHAPS? A SHIBA?›

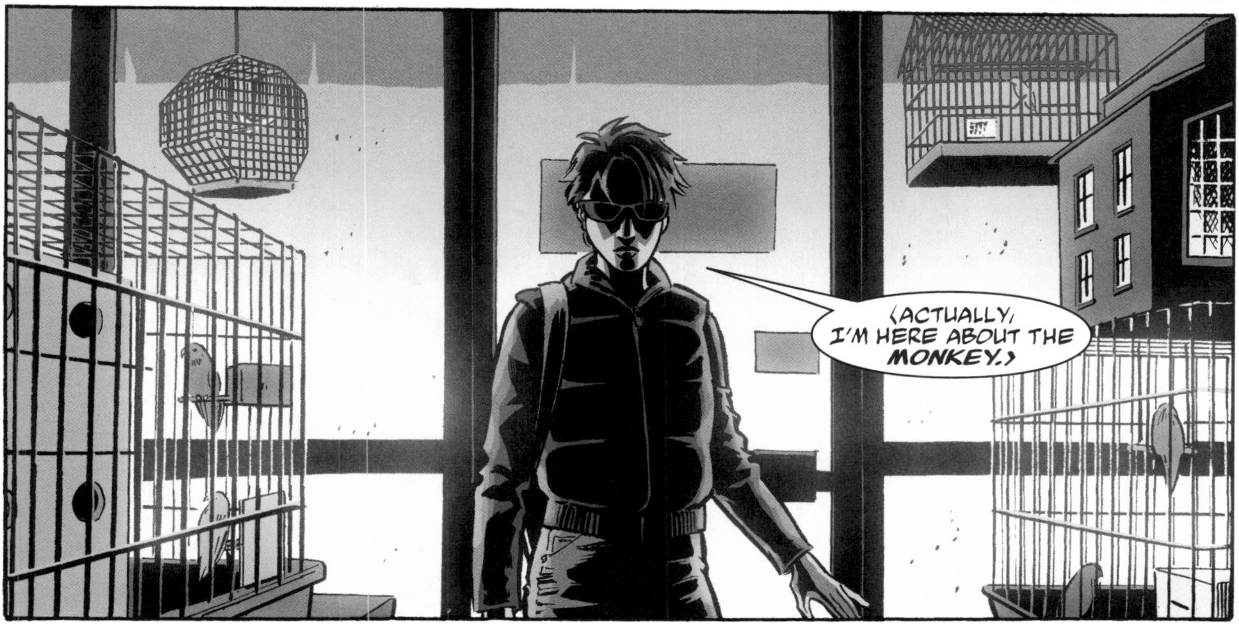
‹ACTUALLY, I'M HERE ABOUT THE MONKEY.›

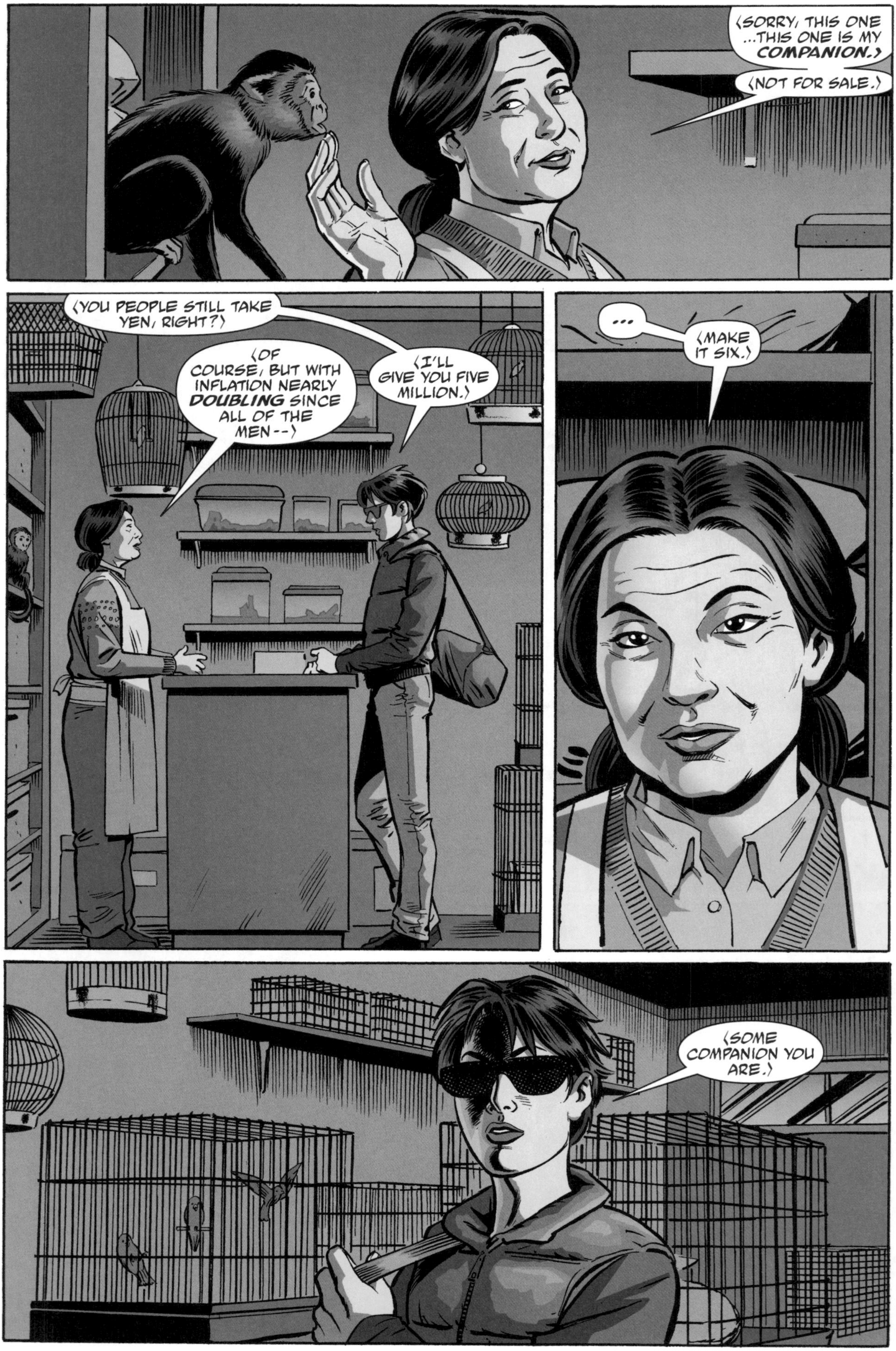
‹SORRY, THIS ONE ...THIS ONE IS MY **COMPANION.**›
‹NOT FOR SALE.›
‹YOU PEOPLE STILL TAKE YEN, RIGHT?›
‹OF COURSE, BUT WITH INFLATION NEARLY **DOUBLING** SINCE ALL OF THE MEN--›
‹I'LL GIVE YOU FIVE MILLION.›
...
‹MAKE IT SIX.›
‹SOME COMPANION YOU ARE.›

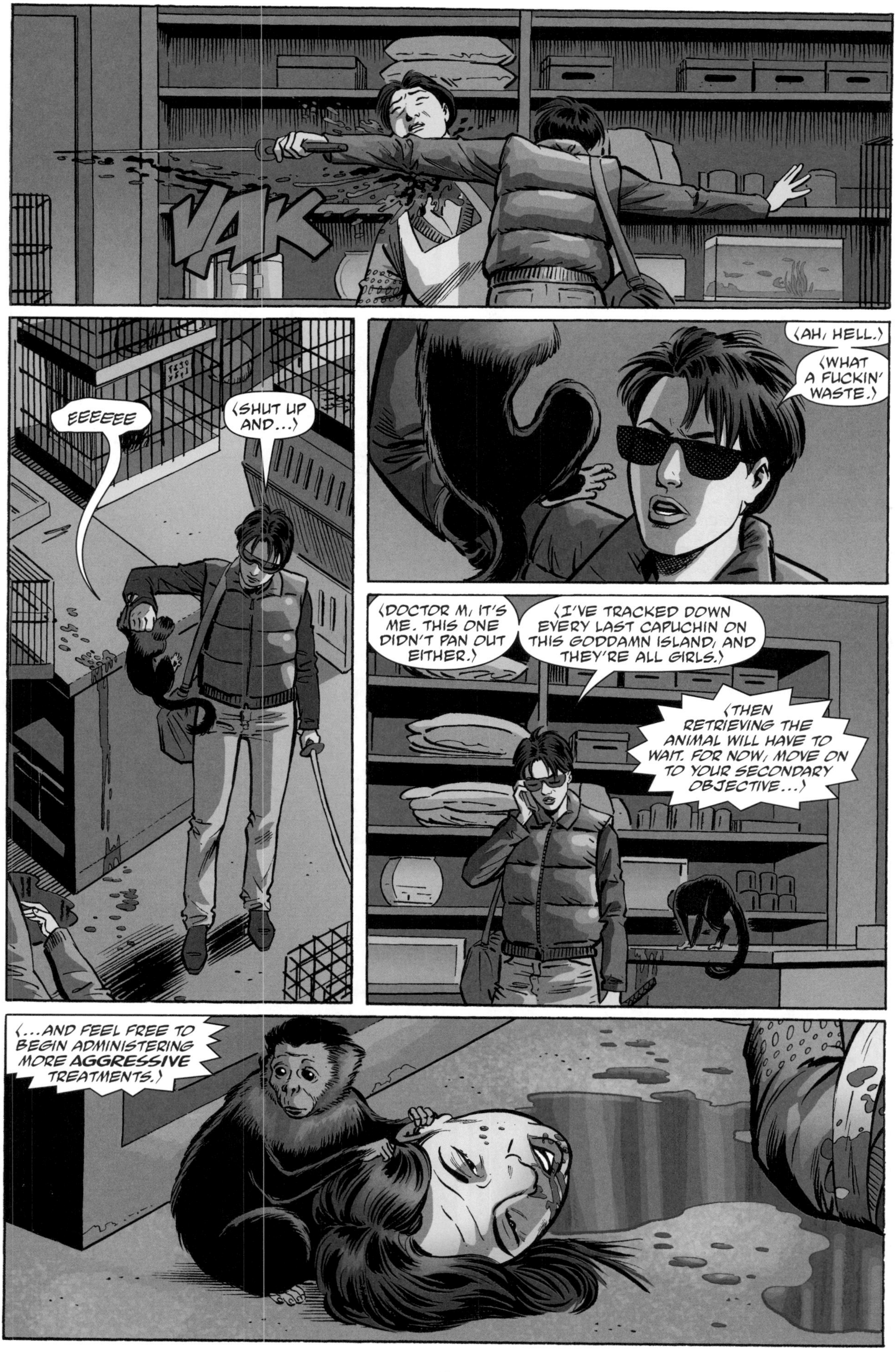
VAK
EEEEEE
‹SHUT UP AND...›
‹AH, HELL.›
‹WHAT A FUCKIN' WASTE.›
‹DOCTOR M, IT'S ME. THIS ONE DIDN'T PAN OUT EITHER.›
‹I'VE TRACKED DOWN EVERY LAST CAPUCHIN ON THIS GODDAMN ISLAND, AND THEY'RE ALL GIRLS.›
‹THEN RETRIEVING THE ANIMAL WILL HAVE TO WAIT. FOR NOW, MOVE ON TO YOUR SECONDARY OBJECTIVE...›
‹...AND FEEL FREE TO BEGIN ADMINISTERING MORE AGGRESSIVE TREATMENTS.›

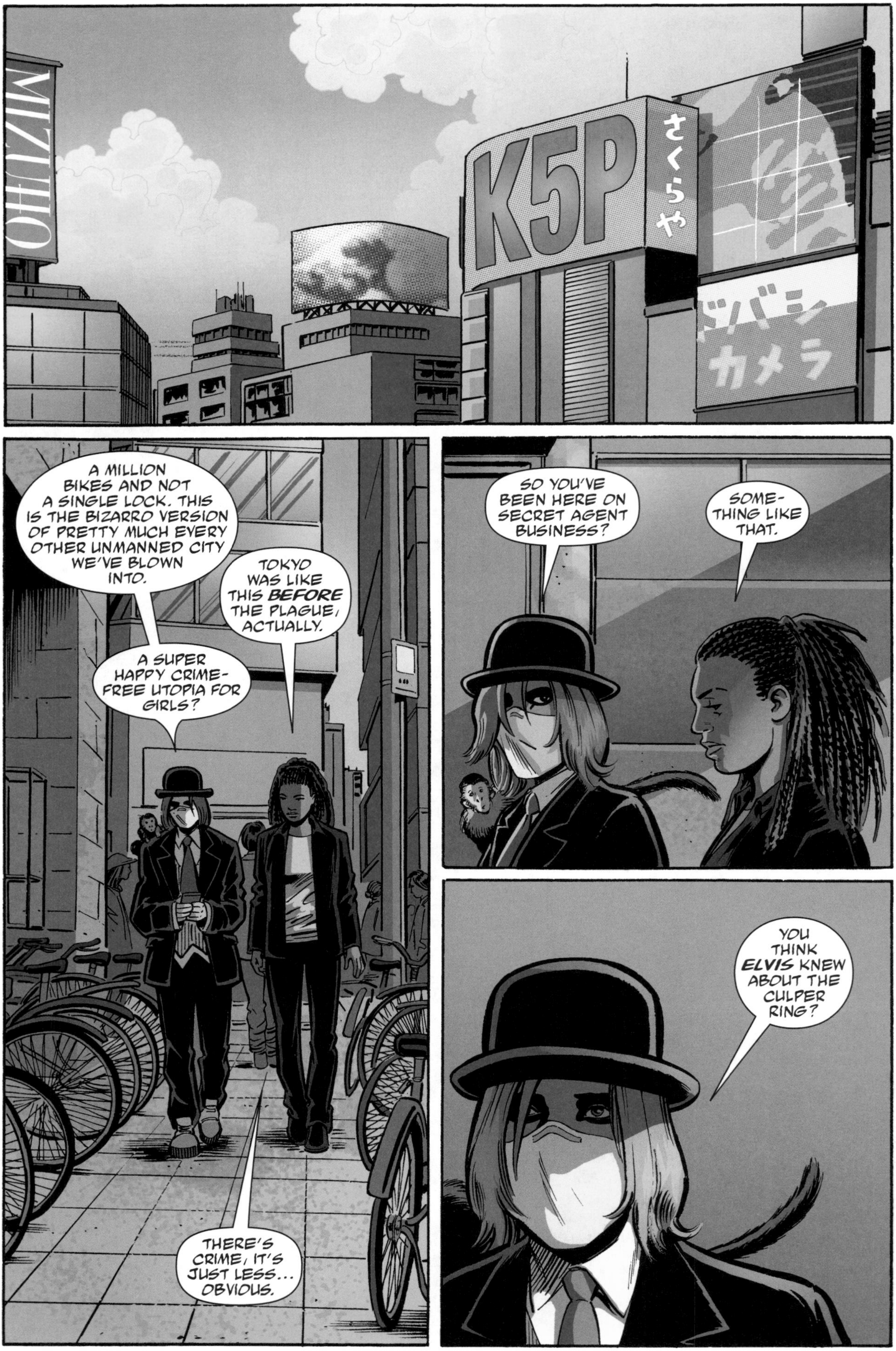
MIZUHO
K5P
さくらや
ドバシ
カメラ
A MILLION BIKES AND NOT A SINGLE LOCK. THIS IS THE BIZARRO VERSION OF PRETTY MUCH EVERY OTHER UNMANNED CITY WE'VE BLOWN INTO.
A SUPER HAPPY CRIME-FREE UTOPIA FOR GIRLS?
TOKYO WAS LIKE THIS **BEFORE** THE PLAGUE, ACTUALLY.
THERE'S CRIME, IT'S JUST LESS... OBVIOUS.
SO YOU'VE BEEN HERE ON SECRET AGENT BUSINESS?
SOME-THING LIKE THAT.
YOU THINK **ELVIS** KNEW ABOUT THE CULPER RING?

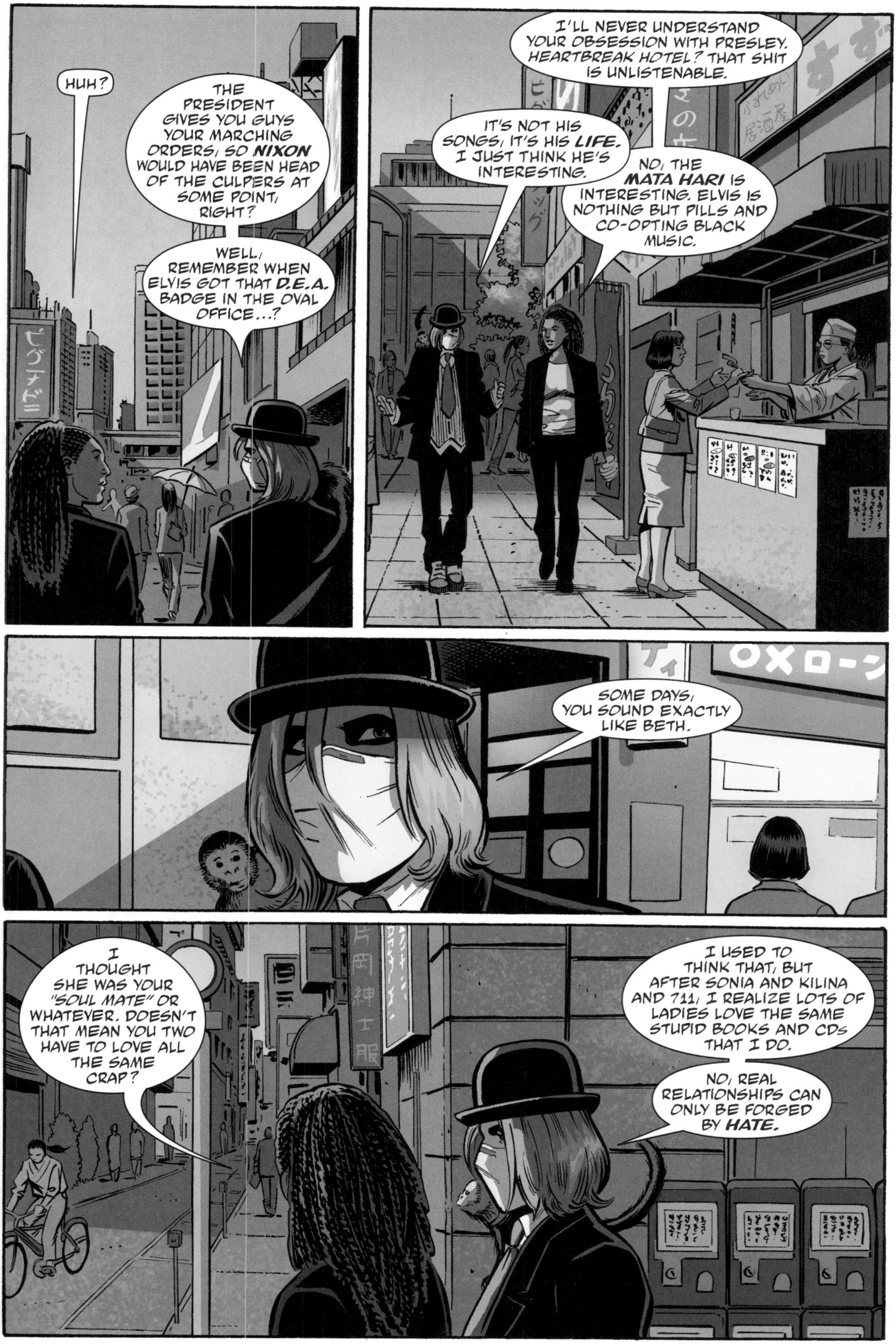
HUH?
THE PRESIDENT GIVES YOU GUYS YOUR MARCHING ORDERS, SO NIXON WOULD HAVE BEEN HEAD OF THE CULPERS AT SOME POINT, RIGHT?
WELL, REMEMBER WHEN ELVIS GOT THAT D.E.A. BADGE IN THE OVAL OFFICE...?
I'LL NEVER UNDERSTAND YOUR OBSESSION WITH PRESLEY. HEARTBREAK HOTEL? THAT SHIT IS UNLISTENABLE.
IT'S NOT HIS SONGS, IT'S HIS LIFE. I JUST THINK HE'S INTERESTING.
NO, THE MATA HARI IS INTERESTING. ELVIS IS NOTHING BUT PILLS AND CO-OPTING BLACK MUSIC.
SOME DAYS, YOU SOUND EXACTLY LIKE BETH.
I THOUGHT SHE WAS YOUR "SOUL MATE" OR WHATEVER. DOESN'T THAT MEAN YOU TWO HAVE TO LOVE ALL THE SAME CRAP?
I USED TO THINK THAT, BUT AFTER SONIA AND KILINA AND 711, I REALIZE LOTS OF LADIES LOVE THE SAME STUPID BOOKS AND CDs THAT I DO.
NO, REAL RELATIONSHIPS CAN ONLY BE FORGED BY HATE.

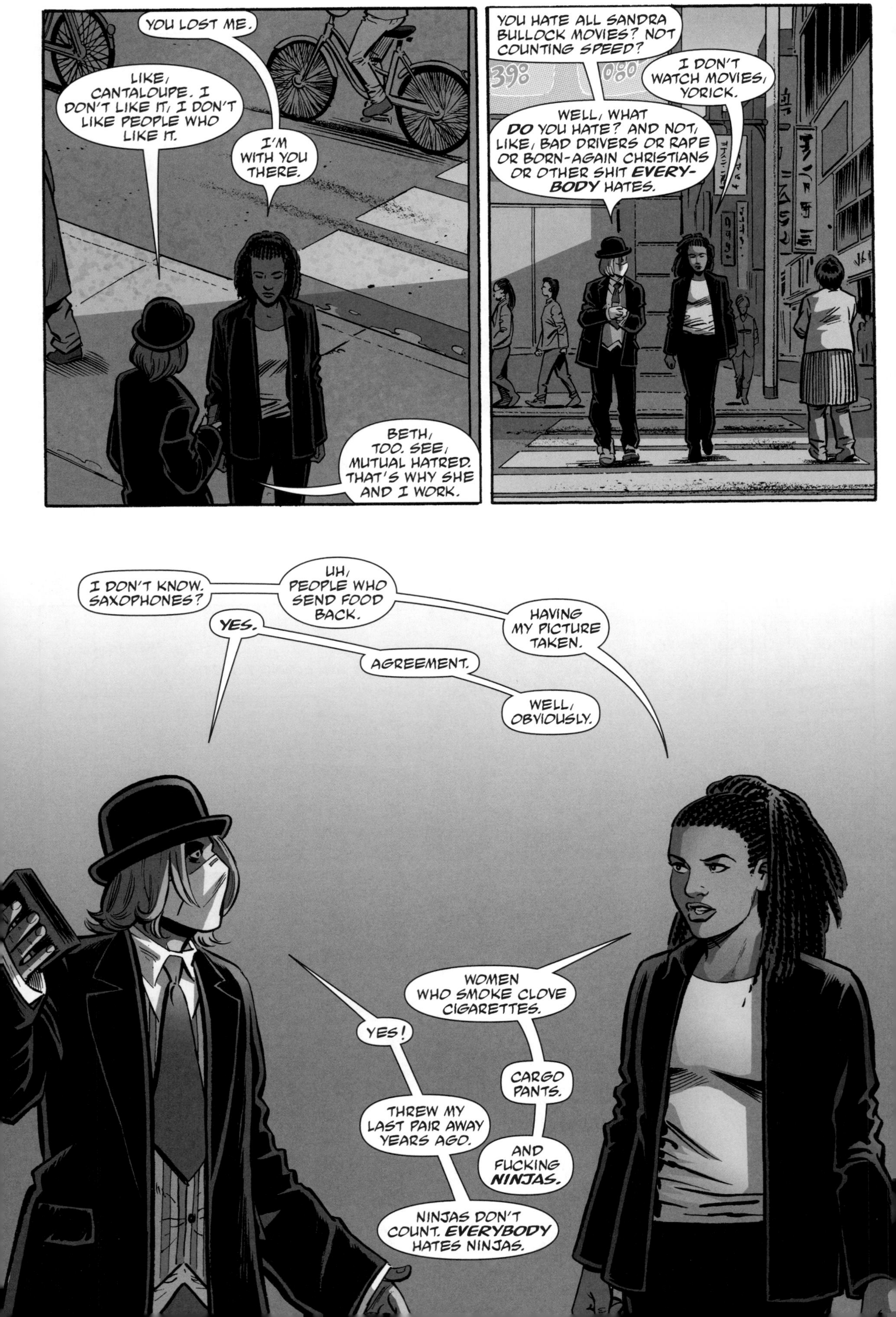
YOU LOST ME.
LIKE, CANTALOUPE. I DON'T LIKE IT, I DON'T LIKE PEOPLE WHO LIKE IT.
I'M WITH YOU THERE.
BETH, TOO. SEE, MUTUAL HATRED. THAT'S WHY SHE AND I WORK.
YOU HATE ALL SANDRA BULLOCK MOVIES? NOT COUNTING SPEED?
I DON'T WATCH MOVIES, YORICK.
WELL, WHAT **DO** YOU HATE? AND NOT, LIKE, BAD DRIVERS OR RAPE OR BORN-AGAIN CHRISTIANS OR OTHER SHIT **EVERYBODY** HATES.
I DON'T KNOW. SAXOPHONES?
UH, PEOPLE WHO SEND FOOD BACK.
HAVING MY PICTURE TAKEN.
YES.
AGREEMENT.
WELL, OBVIOUSLY.
WOMEN WHO SMOKE CLOVE CIGARETTES.
YES!
CARGO PANTS.
THREW MY LAST PAIR AWAY YEARS AGO.
AND FUCKING **NINJAS.**
NINJAS DON'T COUNT. **EVERYBODY** HATES NINJAS.

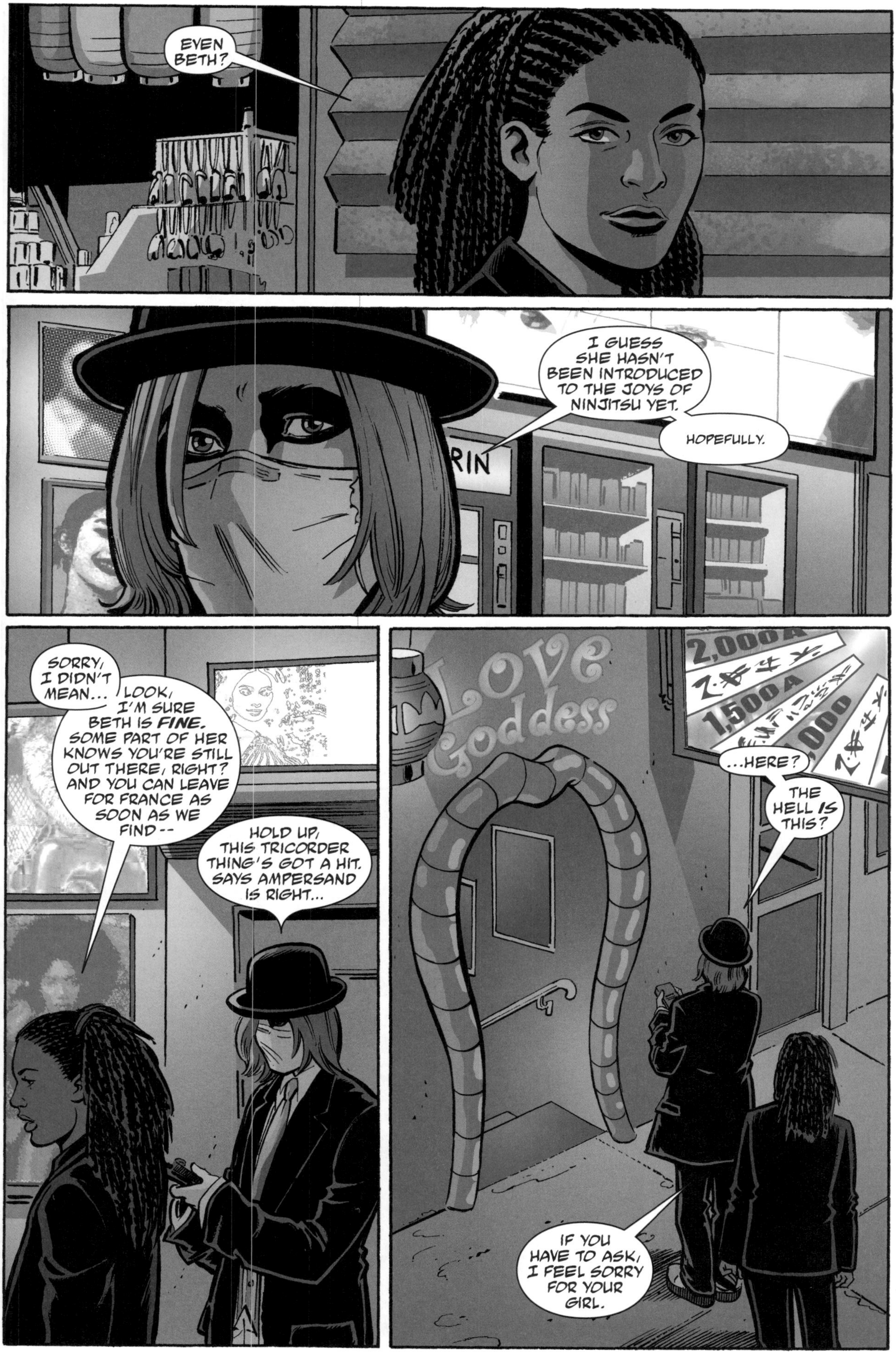
EVEN BETH?
I GUESS SHE HASN'T BEEN INTRODUCED TO THE JOYS OF NINJITSU YET.
HOPEFULLY.
RIN
SORRY, I DIDN'T MEAN...
LOOK, I'M SURE BETH IS FINE. SOME PART OF HER KNOWS YOU'RE STILL OUT THERE, RIGHT? AND YOU CAN LEAVE FOR FRANCE AS SOON AS WE FIND --
HOLD UP, THIS TRICORDER THING'S GOT A HIT. SAYS AMPERSAND IS RIGHT...
Love Goddess
2,000
1,500
...HERE?
THE HELL IS THIS?
IF YOU HAVE TO ASK, I FEEL SORRY FOR YOUR GIRL.

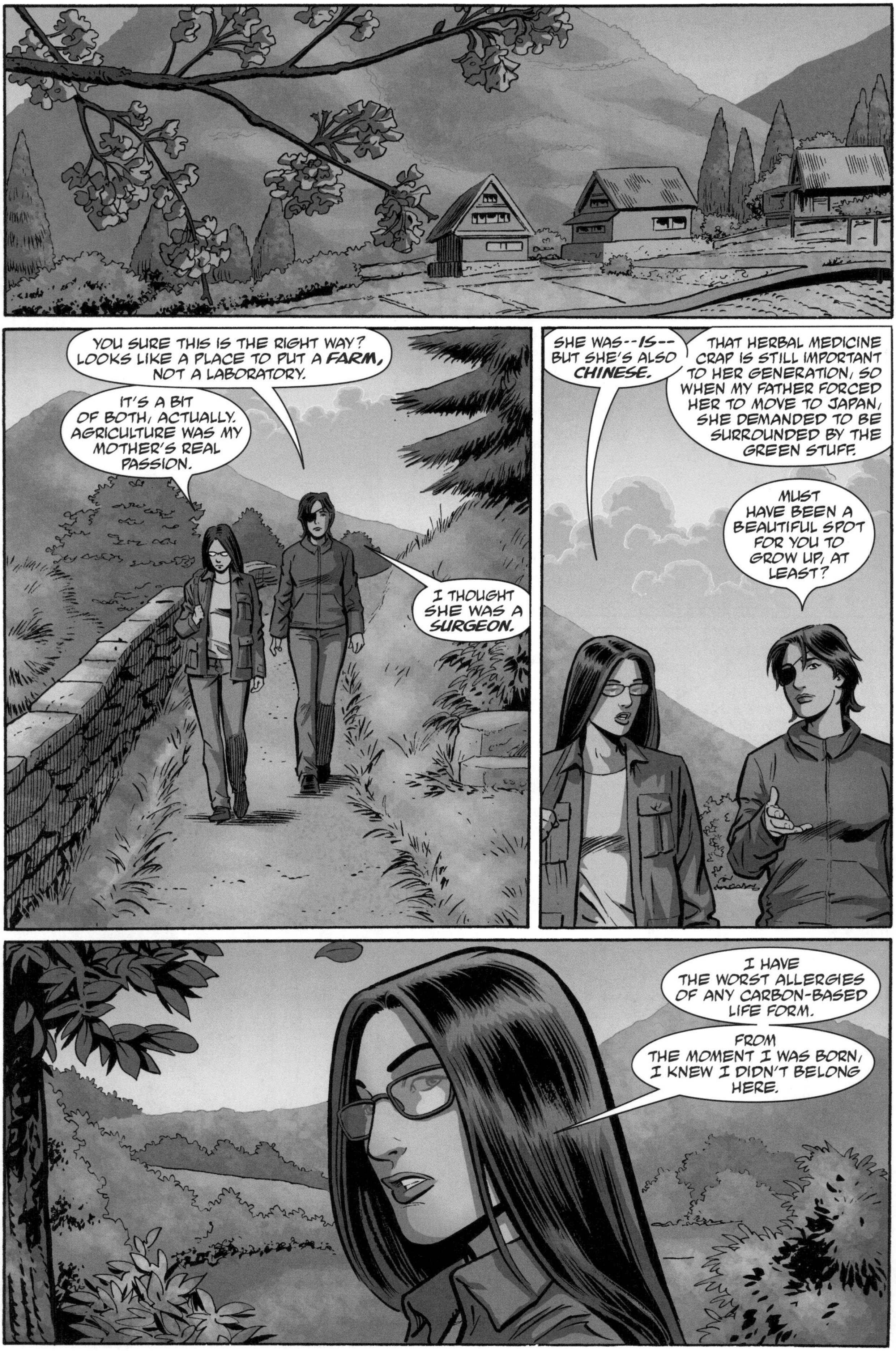
YOU SURE THIS IS THE RIGHT WAY? LOOKS LIKE A PLACE TO PUT A FARM, NOT A LABORATORY.
IT'S A BIT OF BOTH, ACTUALLY. AGRICULTURE WAS MY MOTHER'S REAL PASSION.
I THOUGHT SHE WAS A SURGEON.
SHE WAS--IS--BUT SHE'S ALSO CHINESE.
THAT HERBAL MEDICINE CRAP IS STILL IMPORTANT TO HER GENERATION, SO WHEN MY FATHER FORCED HER TO MOVE TO JAPAN, SHE DEMANDED TO BE SURROUNDED BY THE GREEN STUFF.
MUST HAVE BEEN A BEAUTIFUL SPOT FOR YOU TO GROW UP, AT LEAST?
I HAVE THE WORST ALLERGIES OF ANY CARBON-BASED LIFE FORM.
FROM THE MOMENT I WAS BORN, I KNEW I DIDN'T BELONG HERE.

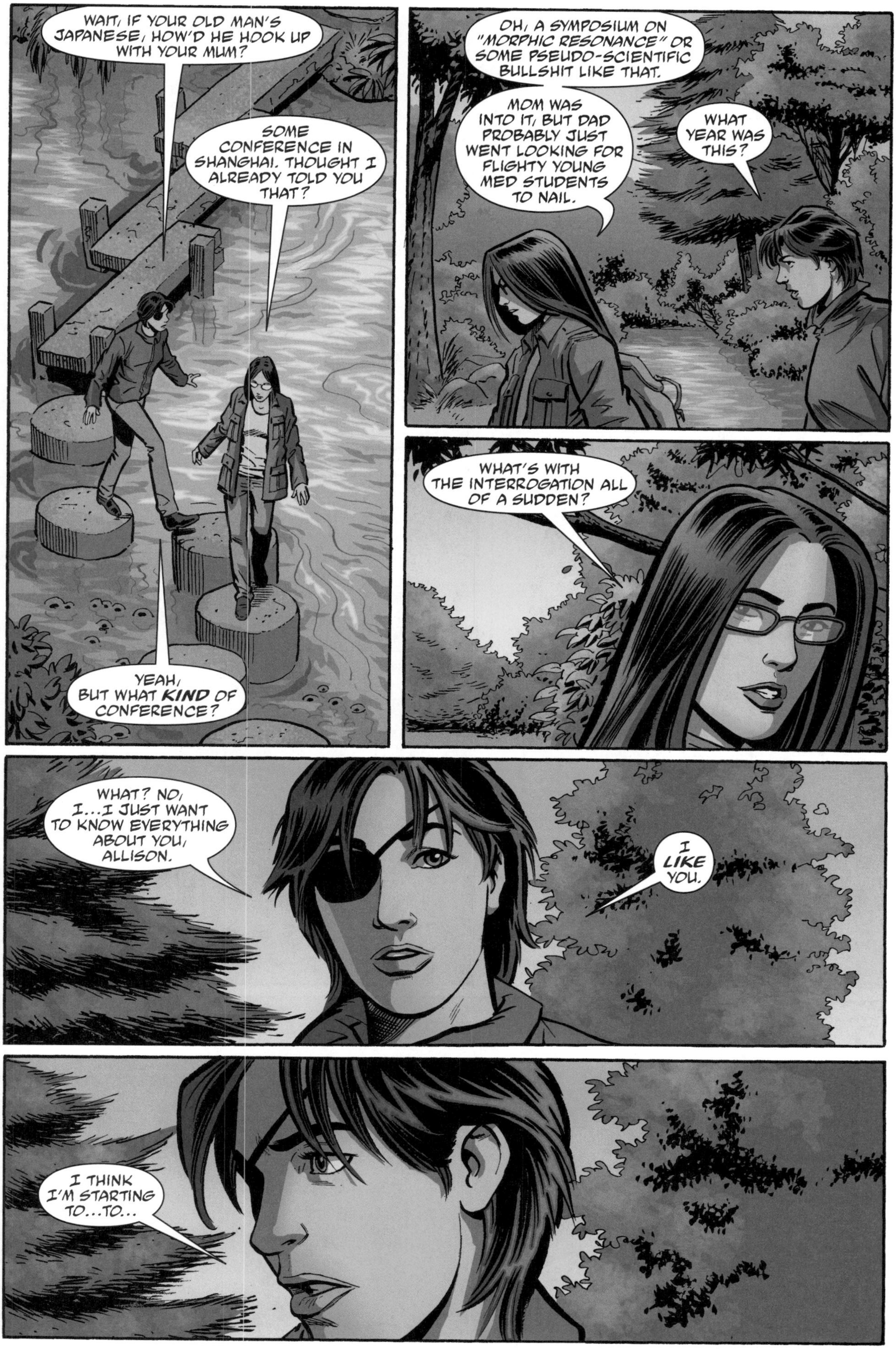
WAIT, IF YOUR OLD MAN'S JAPANESE, HOW'D HE HOOK UP WITH YOUR MUM?
SOME CONFERENCE IN SHANGHAI. THOUGHT I ALREADY TOLD YOU THAT?
YEAH, BUT WHAT KIND OF CONFERENCE?
OH, A SYMPOSIUM ON "MORPHIC RESONANCE" OR SOME PSEUDO-SCIENTIFIC BULLSHIT LIKE THAT.
MOM WAS INTO IT, BUT DAD PROBABLY JUST WENT LOOKING FOR FLIGHTY YOUNG MED STUDENTS TO NAIL.
WHAT YEAR WAS THIS?
WHAT'S WITH THE INTERROGATION ALL OF A SUDDEN?
WHAT? NO, I...I JUST WANT TO KNOW EVERYTHING ABOUT YOU, ALLISON.
I LIKE YOU.
I THINK I'M STARTING TO...TO...

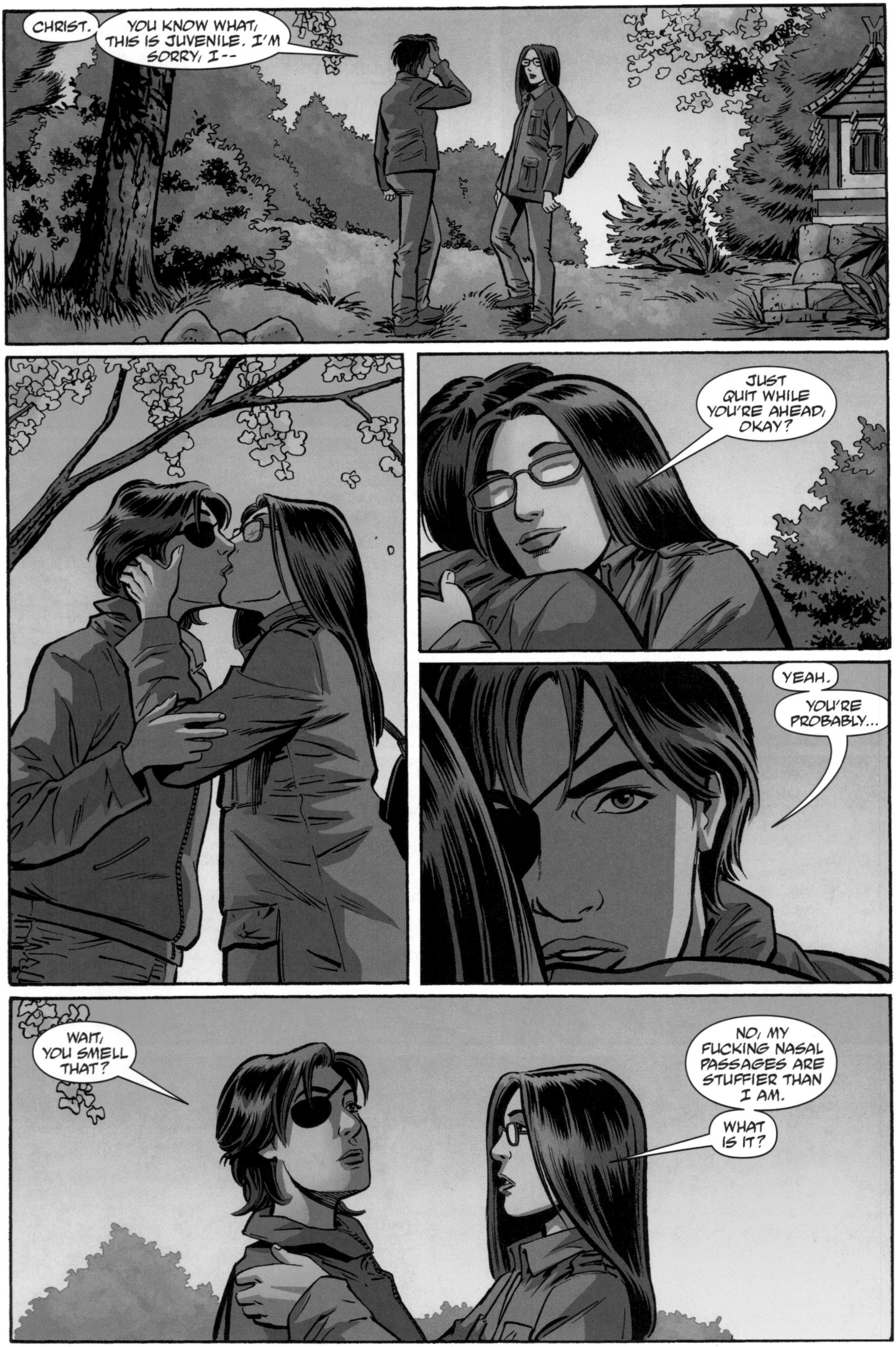
CHRIST.
YOU KNOW WHAT, THIS IS JUVENILE. I'M SORRY, I--
JUST QUIT WHILE YOU'RE AHEAD, OKAY?
YEAH.
YOU'RE PROBABLY...
WAIT, YOU SMELL THAT?
NO, MY FUCKING NASAL PASSAGES ARE STUFFIER THAN I AM.
WHAT IS IT?

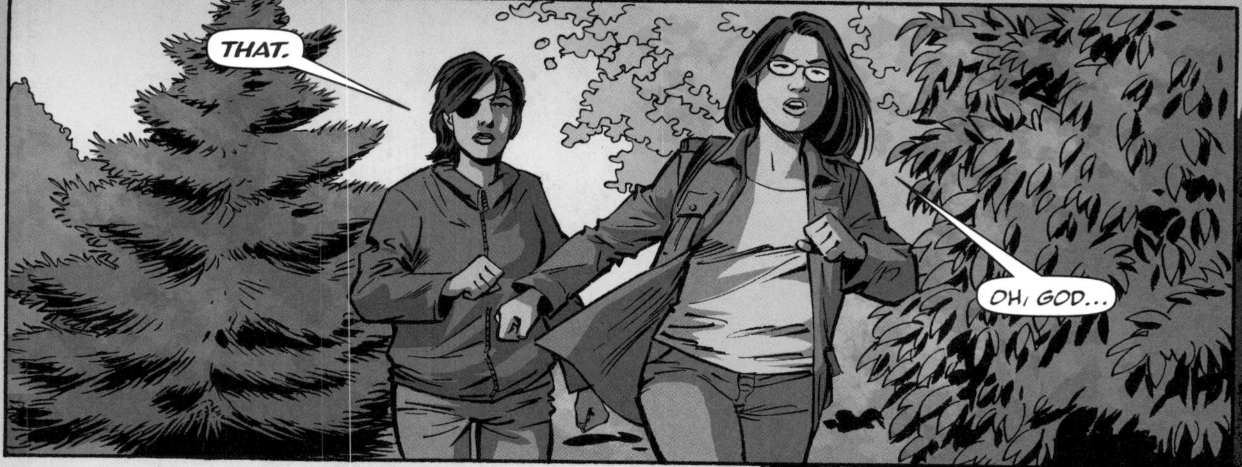
THAT.
OH, GOD...

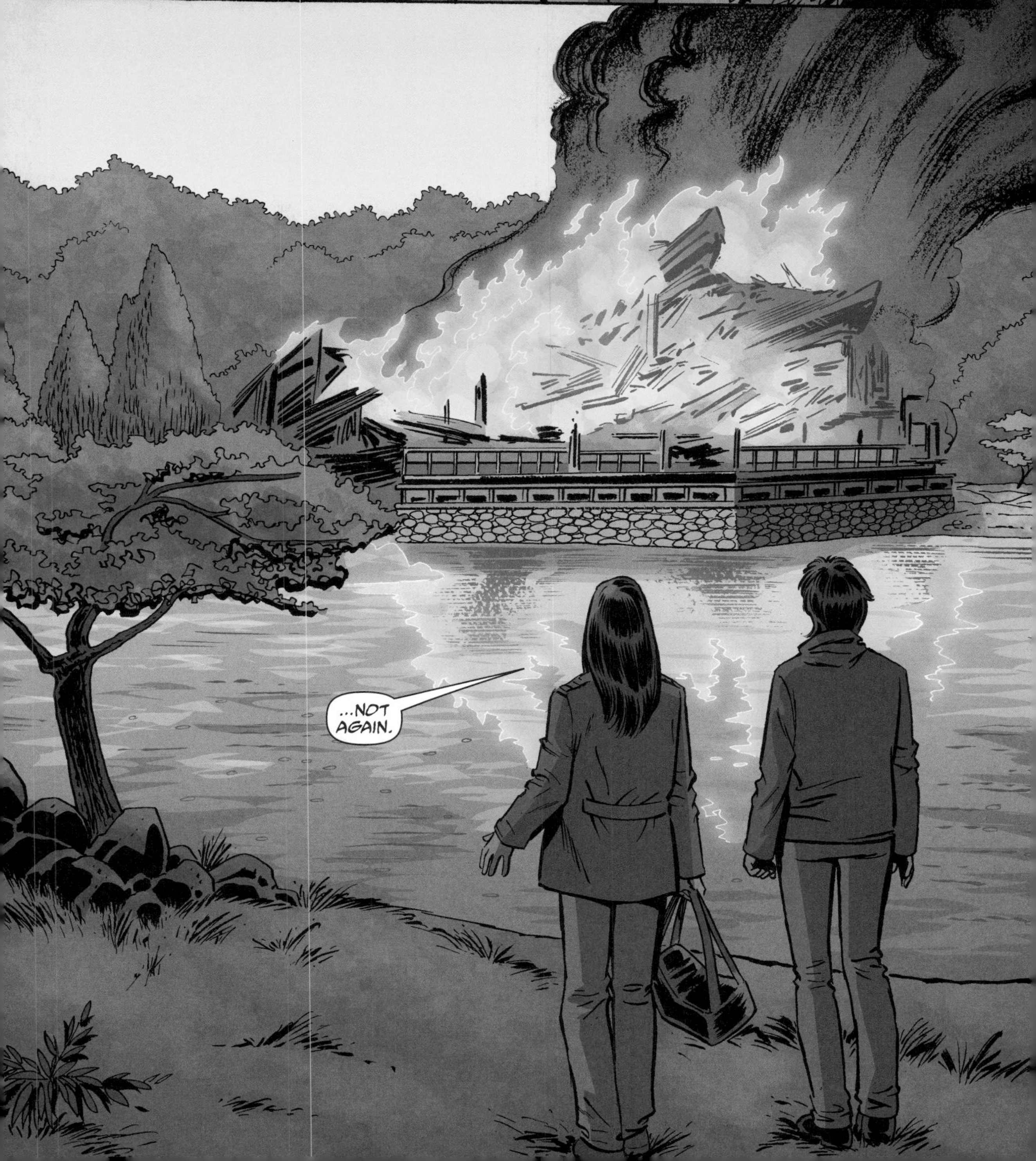
...NOT AGAIN.

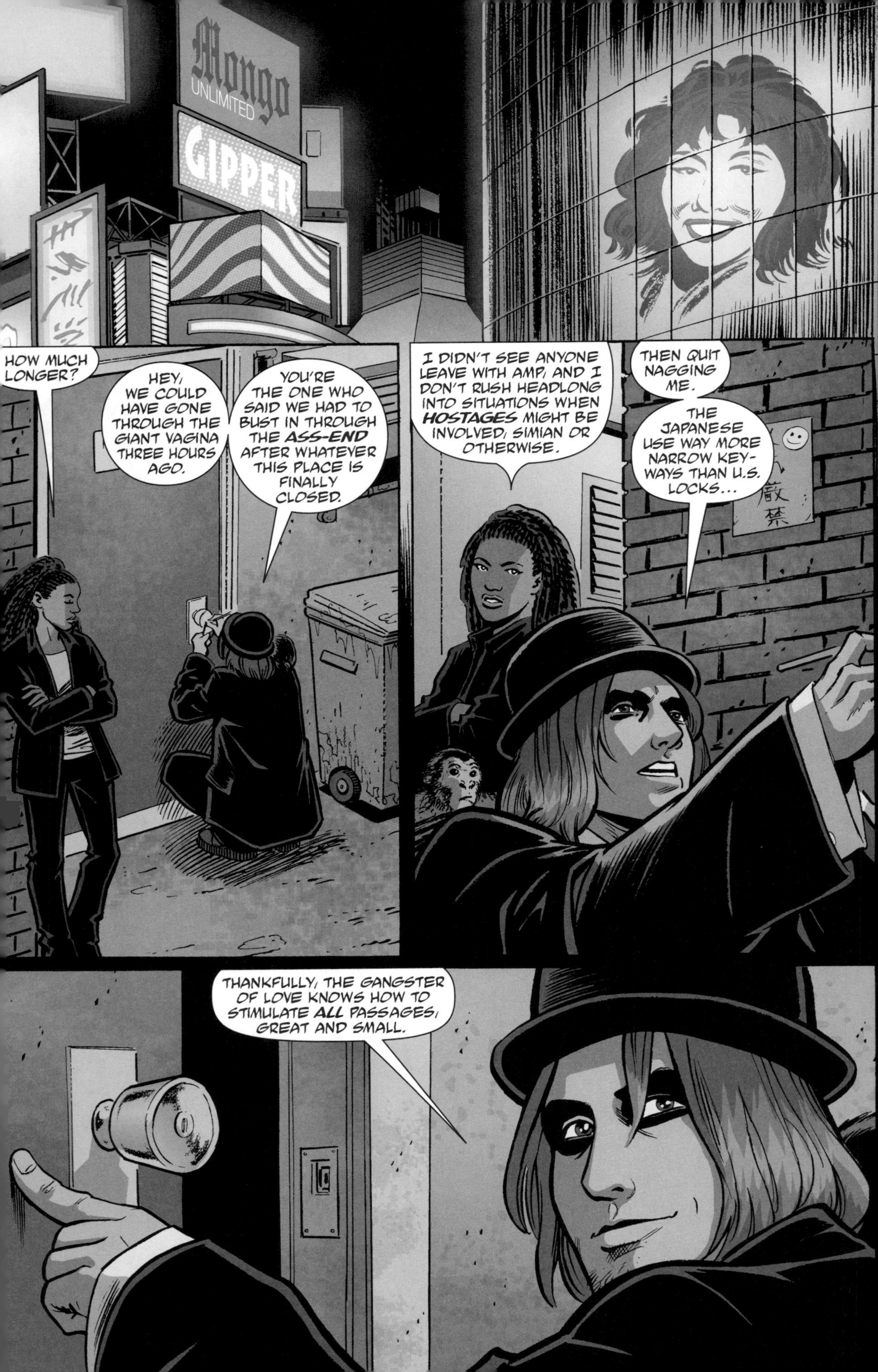

Mongo
UNLIMITED
GIPPER
HOW MUCH LONGER?
HEY, WE COULD HAVE GONE THROUGH THE GIANT VAGINA THREE HOURS AGO.
YOU'RE THE ONE WHO SAID WE HAD TO BUST IN THROUGH THE ASS-END AFTER WHATEVER THIS PLACE IS FINALLY CLOSED.
I DIDN'T SEE ANYONE LEAVE WITH AMP, AND I DON'T RUSH HEADLONG INTO SITUATIONS WHEN HOSTAGES MIGHT BE INVOLVED, SIMIAN OR OTHERWISE.
THEN QUIT NAGGING ME.
THE JAPANESE USE WAY MORE NARROW KEY-WAYS THAN U.S. LOCKS...
厳禁
THANKFULLY, THE GANGSTER OF LOVE KNOWS HOW TO STIMULATE ALL PASSAGES, GREAT AND SMALL.

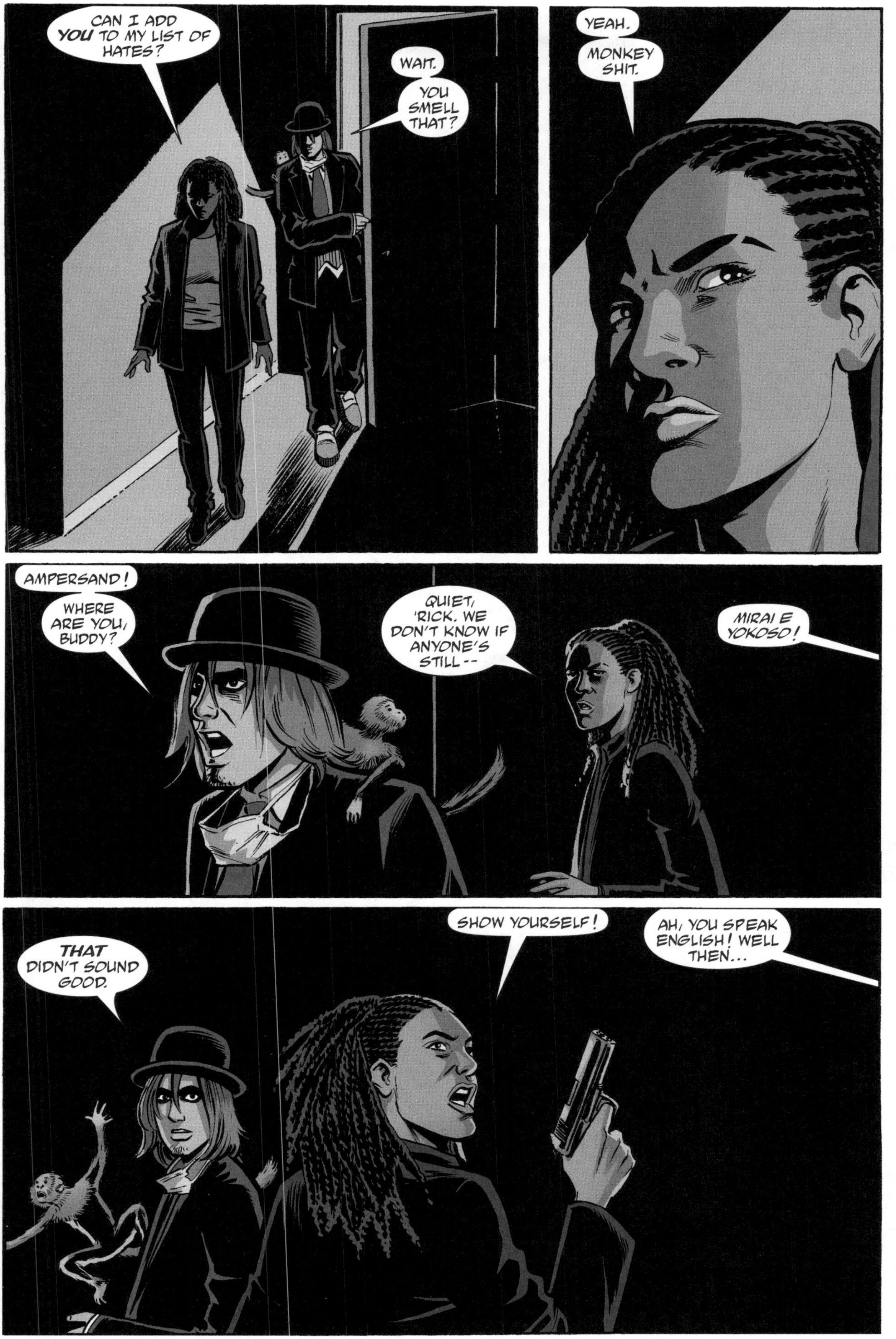
CAN I ADD YOU TO MY LIST OF HATES?
WAIT.
YOU SMELL THAT?
YEAH.
MONKEY SHIT.
AMPERSAND!
WHERE ARE YOU, BUDDY?
QUIET, 'RICK. WE DON'T KNOW IF ANYONE'S STILL --
MIRAI E YOKOSO!
THAT DIDN'T SOUND GOOD.
SHOW YOURSELF!
AH, YOU SPEAK ENGLISH! WELL THEN...

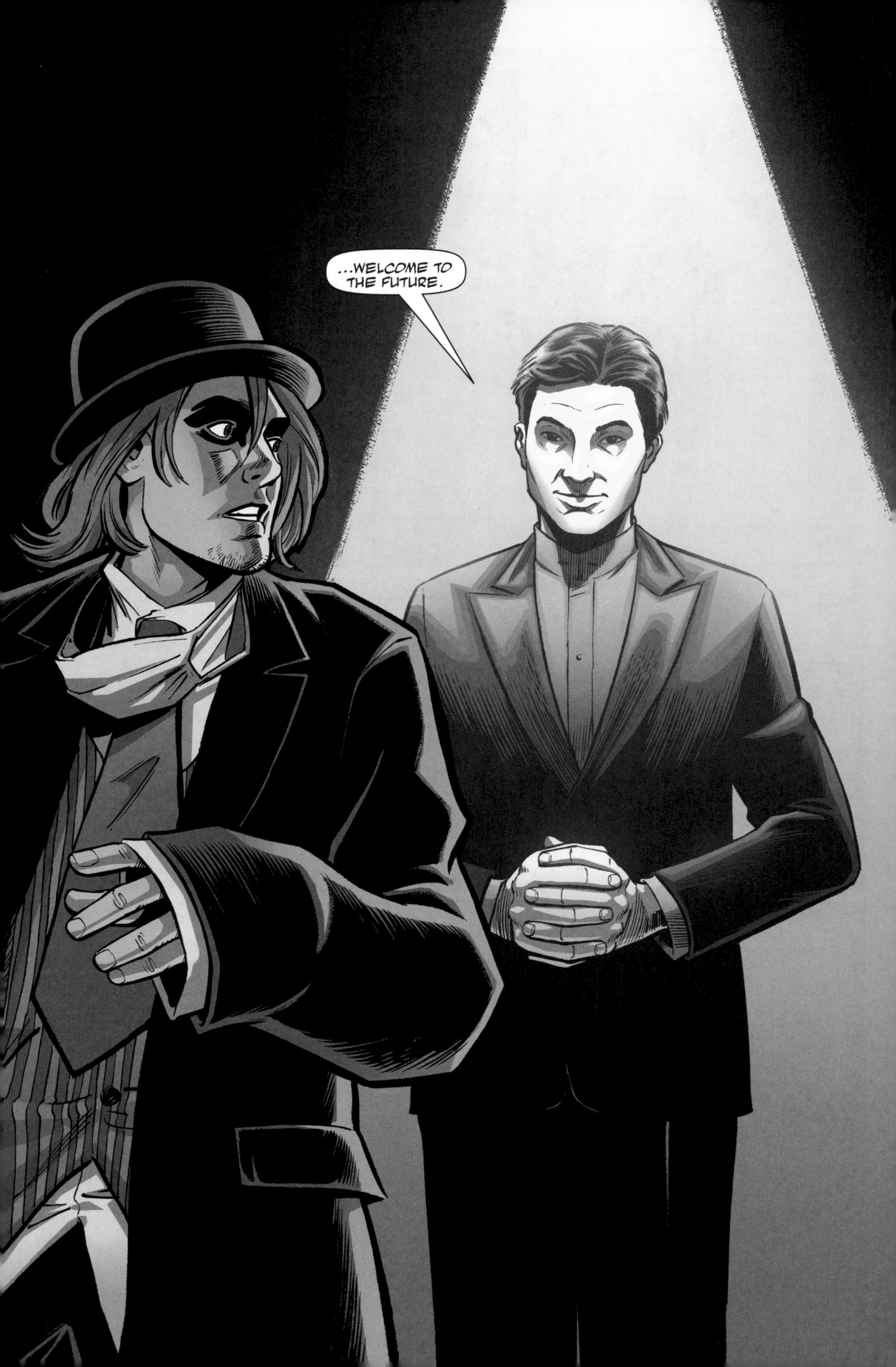
...WELCOME TO THE FUTURE.

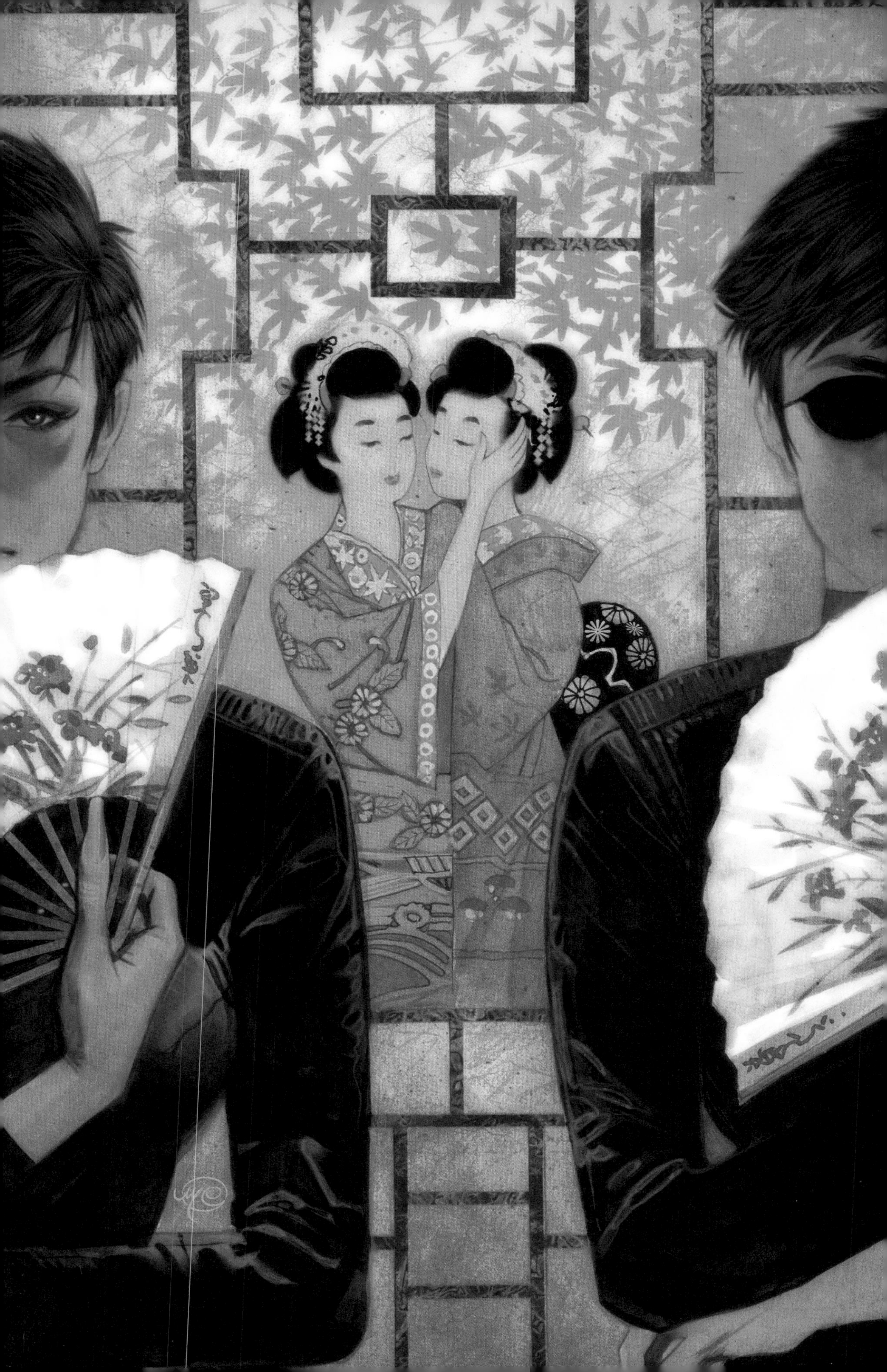

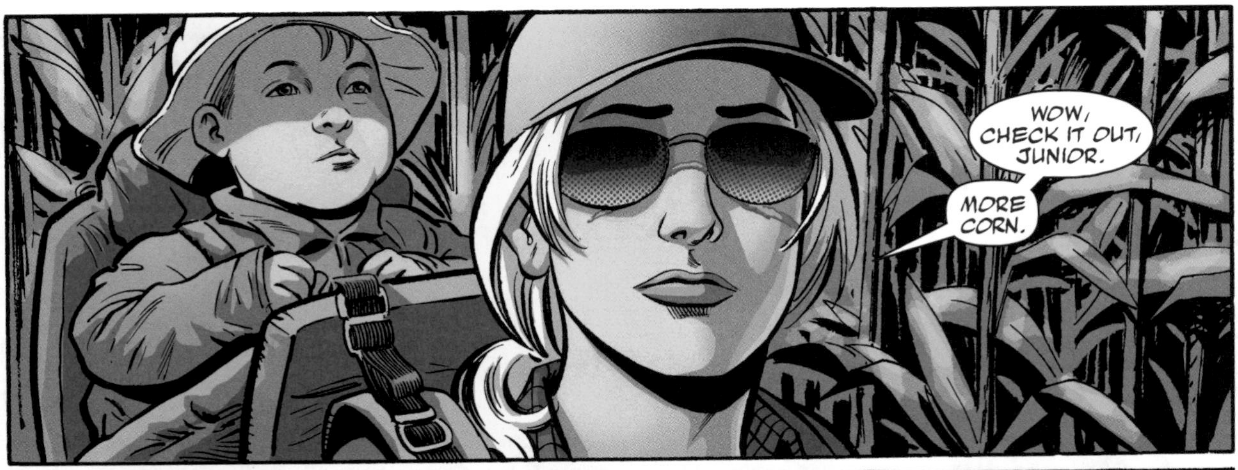
WOW, CHECK IT OUT, JUNIOR.
MORE CORN.

Oldenbrook, Kansas
Now

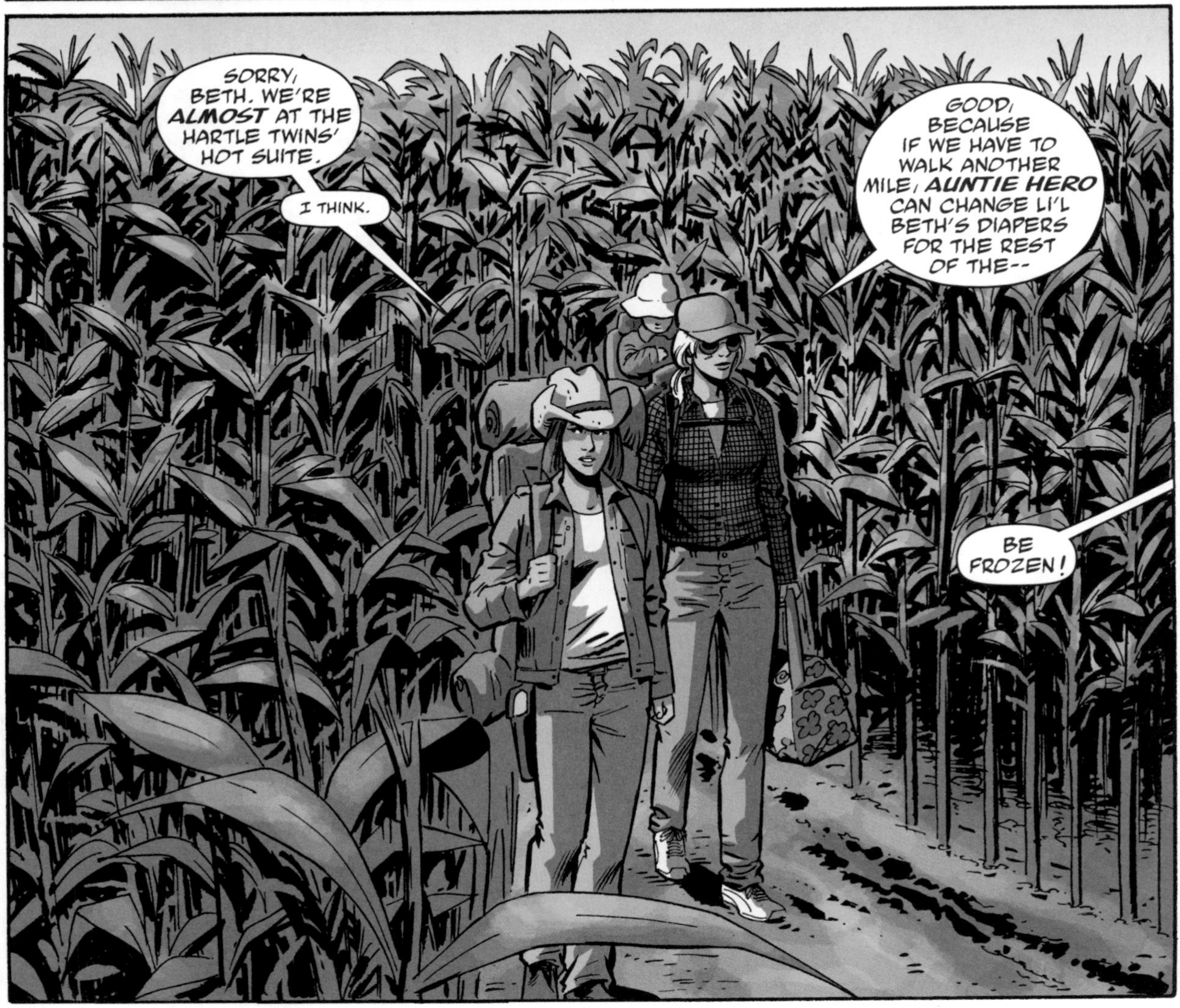
SORRY, BETH. WE'RE ALMOST AT THE HARTLE TWINS' HOT SUITE.
I THINK.
GOOD, BECAUSE IF WE HAVE TO WALK ANOTHER MILE, AUNTIE HERO CAN CHANGE LI'L BETH'S DIAPERS FOR THE REST OF THE--
BE FROZEN!

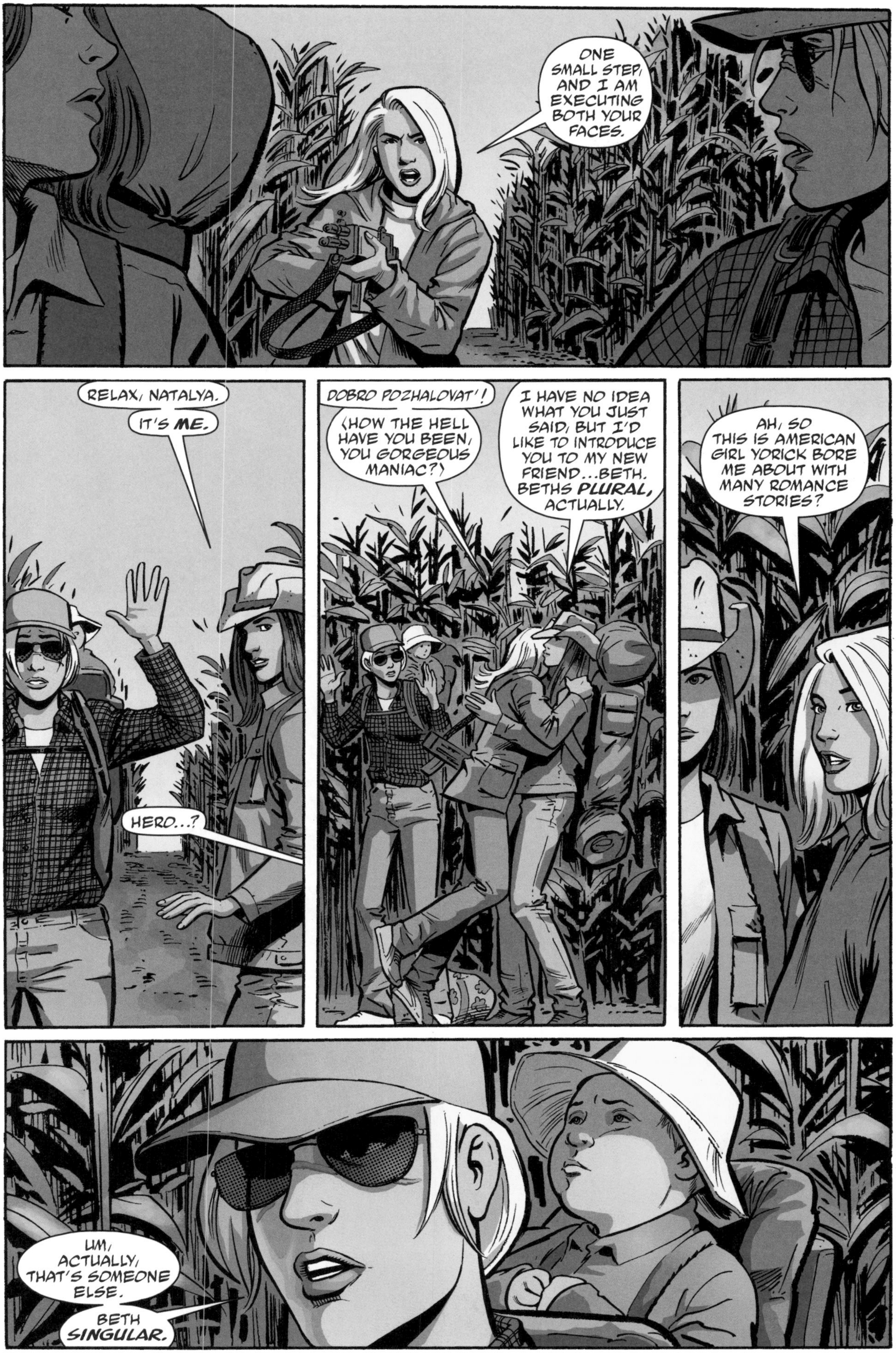
ONE SMALL STEP, AND I AM EXECUTING BOTH YOUR FACES.
RELAX, NATALYA.
IT'S **ME.**
HERO...?
DOBRO POZHALOVAT'!
(HOW THE HELL HAVE YOU BEEN, YOU GORGEOUS MANIAC?)
I HAVE NO IDEA WHAT YOU JUST SAID, BUT I'D LIKE TO INTRODUCE YOU TO MY NEW FRIEND...BETH. BETHS **PLURAL,** ACTUALLY.
AH, SO THIS IS AMERICAN GIRL YORICK BORE ME ABOUT WITH MANY ROMANCE STORIES?
UM, ACTUALLY, THAT'S SOMEONE ELSE.
BETH ***SINGULAR.***

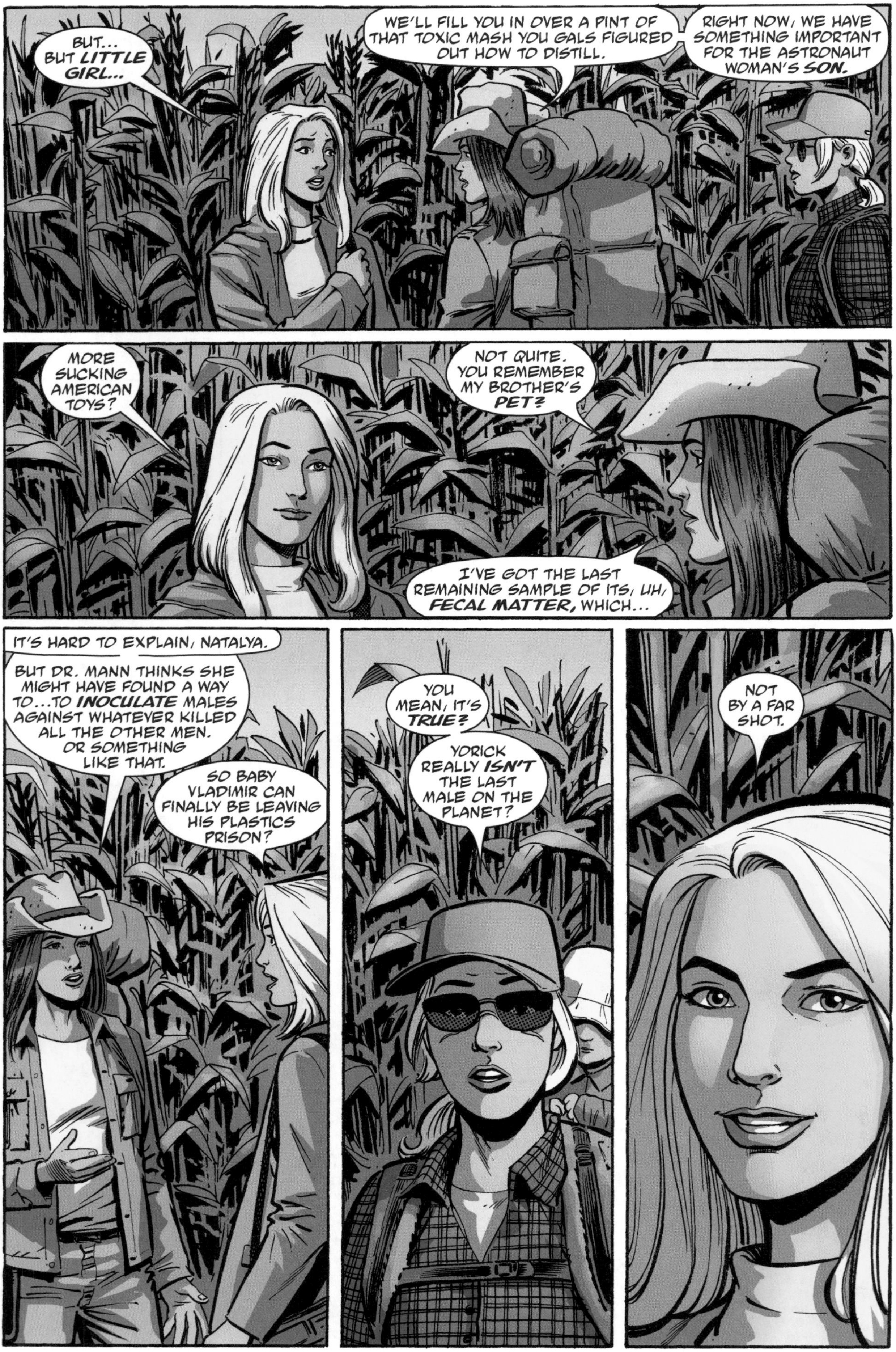
BUT... BUT **LITTLE GIRL...**
WE'LL FILL YOU IN OVER A PINT OF THAT TOXIC MASH YOU GALS FIGURED OUT HOW TO DISTILL.
RIGHT NOW, WE HAVE SOMETHING IMPORTANT FOR THE ASTRONAUT WOMAN'S **SON.**
MORE SUCKING AMERICAN TOYS?
NOT QUITE. YOU REMEMBER MY BROTHER'S **PET?**
I'VE GOT THE LAST REMAINING SAMPLE OF ITS, UH, **FECAL MATTER,** WHICH...
IT'S HARD TO EXPLAIN, NATALYA.
BUT DR. MANN THINKS SHE MIGHT HAVE FOUND A WAY TO...TO **INOCULATE** MALES AGAINST WHATEVER KILLED ALL THE OTHER MEN. OR SOMETHING LIKE THAT.
SO BABY VLADIMIR CAN FINALLY BE LEAVING HIS PLASTICS PRISON?
YOU MEAN, IT'S **TRUE?**
YORICK REALLY **ISN'T** THE LAST MALE ON THE PLANET?
NOT BY A FAR SHOT.

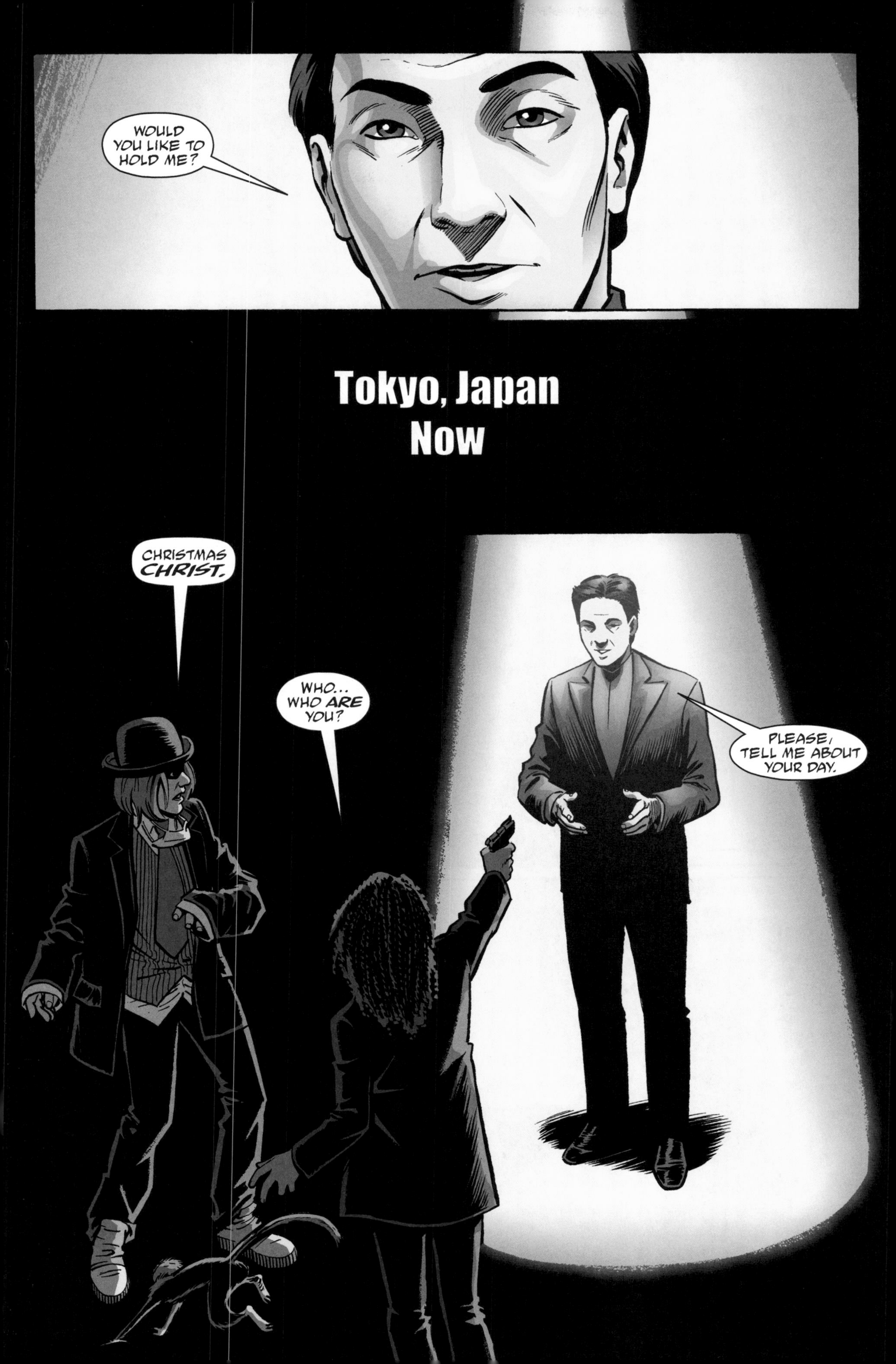
WOULD YOU LIKE TO HOLD ME?
Tokyo, Japan
Now
CHRISTMAS CHRIST.
WHO... WHO ARE YOU?
PLEASE, TELL ME ABOUT YOUR DAY.

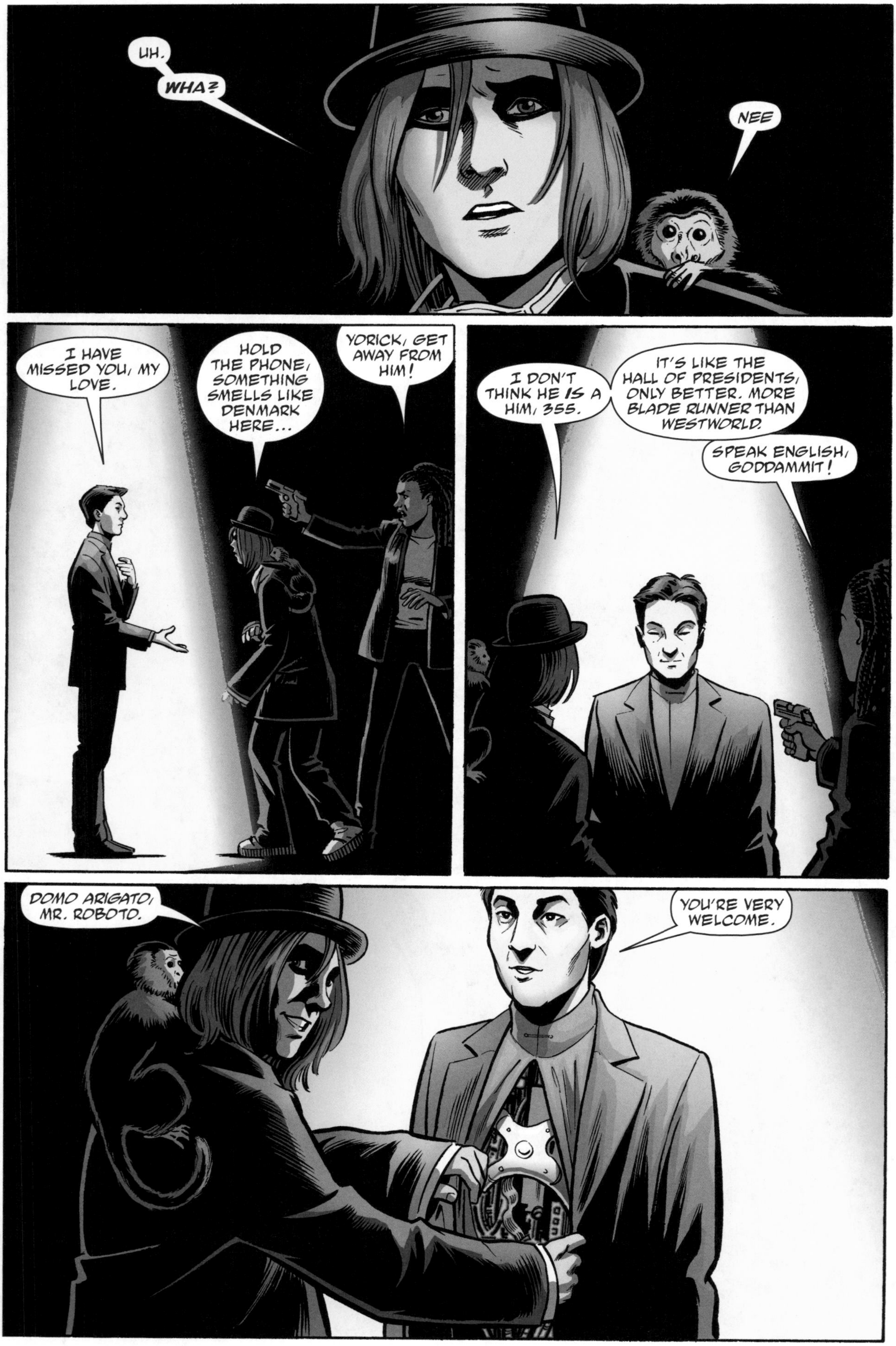
UH.
WHA?
NEE
I HAVE MISSED YOU, MY LOVE.
HOLD THE PHONE, SOMETHING SMELLS LIKE DENMARK HERE...
YORICK, GET AWAY FROM HIM!
I DON'T THINK HE IS A HIM, 355.
IT'S LIKE THE HALL OF PRESIDENTS, ONLY BETTER. MORE BLADE RUNNER THAN WESTWORLD.
SPEAK ENGLISH, GODDAMMIT!
DOMO ARIGATO, MR. ROBOTO.
YOU'RE VERY WELCOME.

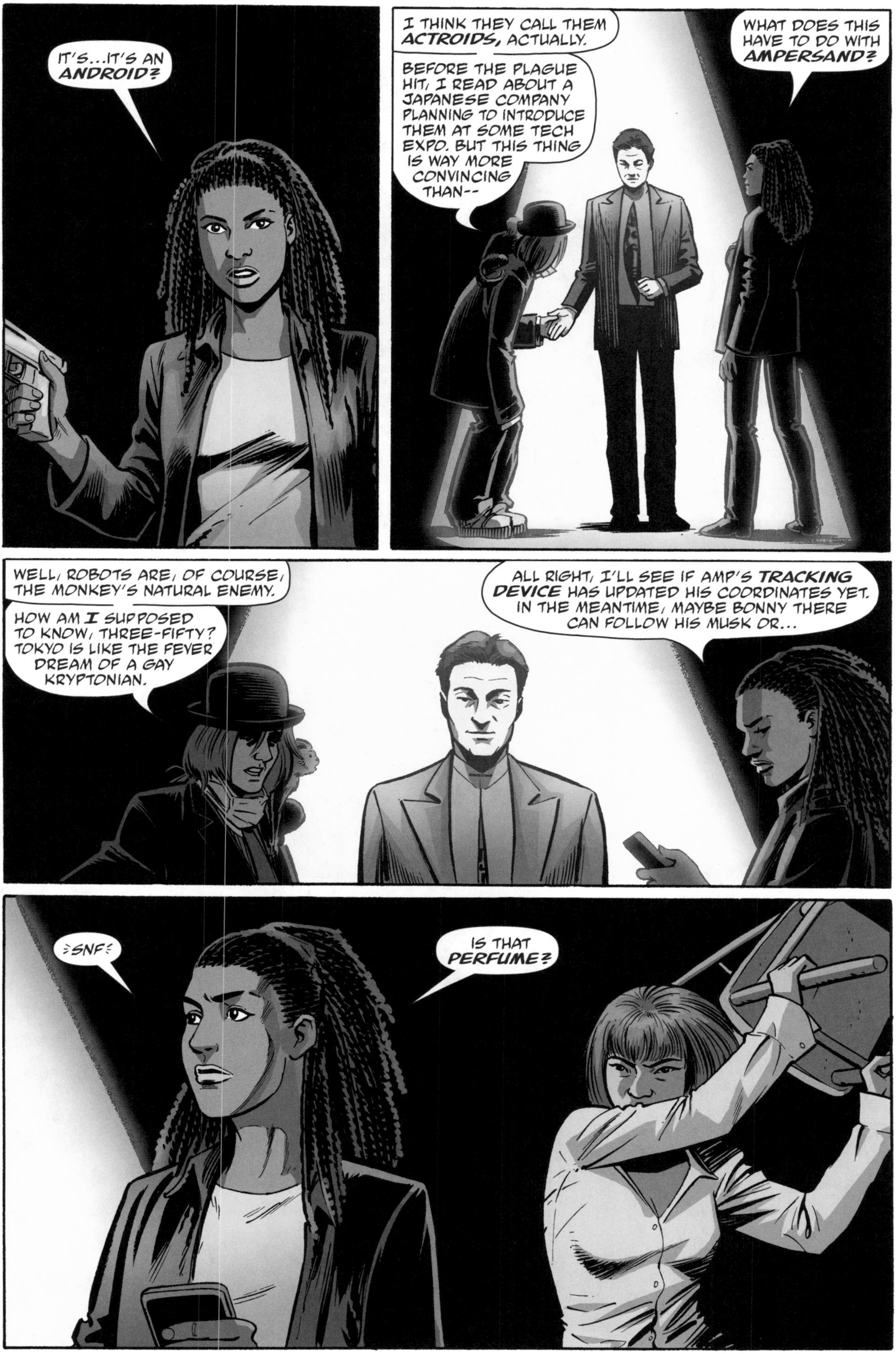
IT'S...IT'S AN ANDROID?
I THINK THEY CALL THEM ACTROIDS, ACTUALLY.
BEFORE THE PLAGUE HIT, I READ ABOUT A JAPANESE COMPANY PLANNING TO INTRODUCE THEM AT SOME TECH EXPO. BUT THIS THING IS WAY MORE CONVINCING THAN--
WHAT DOES THIS HAVE TO DO WITH AMPERSAND?
WELL, ROBOTS ARE, OF COURSE, THE MONKEY'S NATURAL ENEMY.
HOW AM I SUPPOSED TO KNOW, THREE-FIFTY? TOKYO IS LIKE THE FEVER DREAM OF A GAY KRYPTONIAN.
ALL RIGHT, I'LL SEE IF AMP'S TRACKING DEVICE HAS UPDATED HIS COORDINATES YET. IN THE MEANTIME, MAYBE BONNY THERE CAN FOLLOW HIS MUSK OR...
SNF
IS THAT PERFUME?

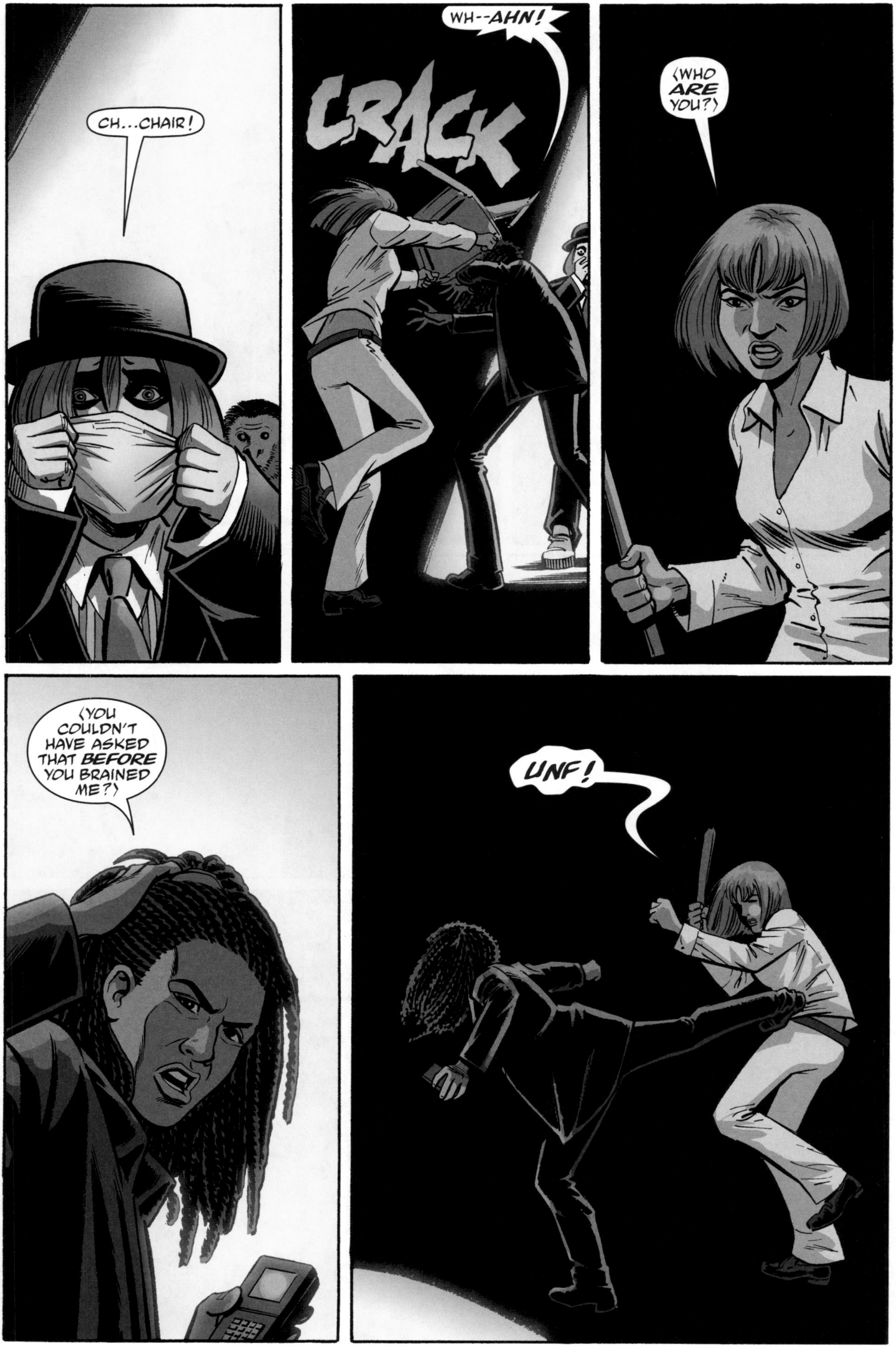
CH...CHAIR!
WH--AHN!
CRACK
⟨WHO ARE YOU?⟩
⟨YOU COULDN'T HAVE ASKED THAT BEFORE YOU BRAINED ME?⟩
UNF!

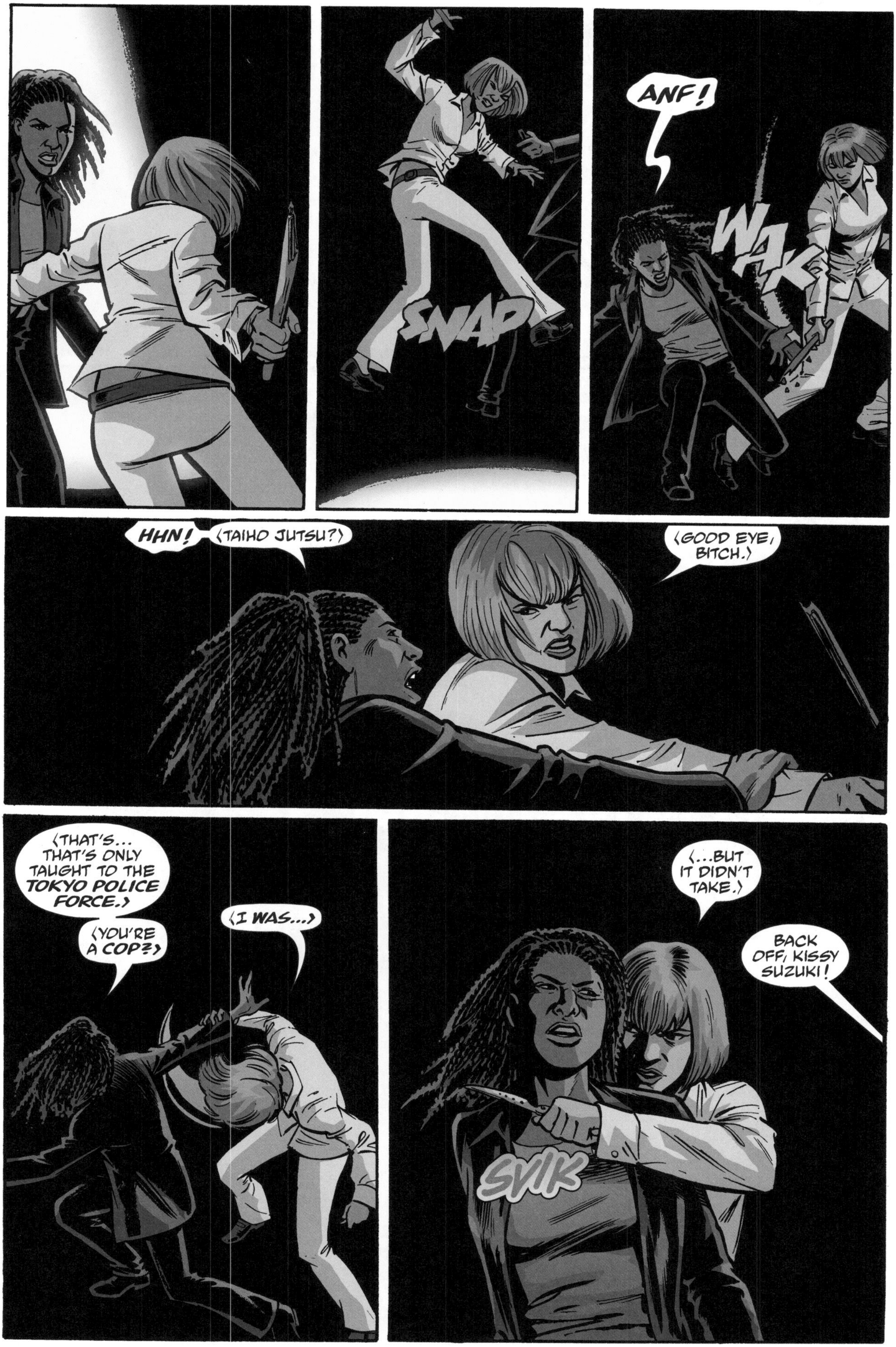

SNAP
ANF!
WAK
HHN!
⟨TAIHO JUTSU?⟩
⟨GOOD EYE, BITCH.⟩
⟨THAT'S... THAT'S ONLY TAUGHT TO THE TOKYO POLICE FORCE.⟩
⟨YOU'RE A COP?⟩
⟨I WAS...⟩
⟨...BUT IT DIDN'T TAKE.⟩
BACK OFF, KISSY SUZUKI!
SVIK

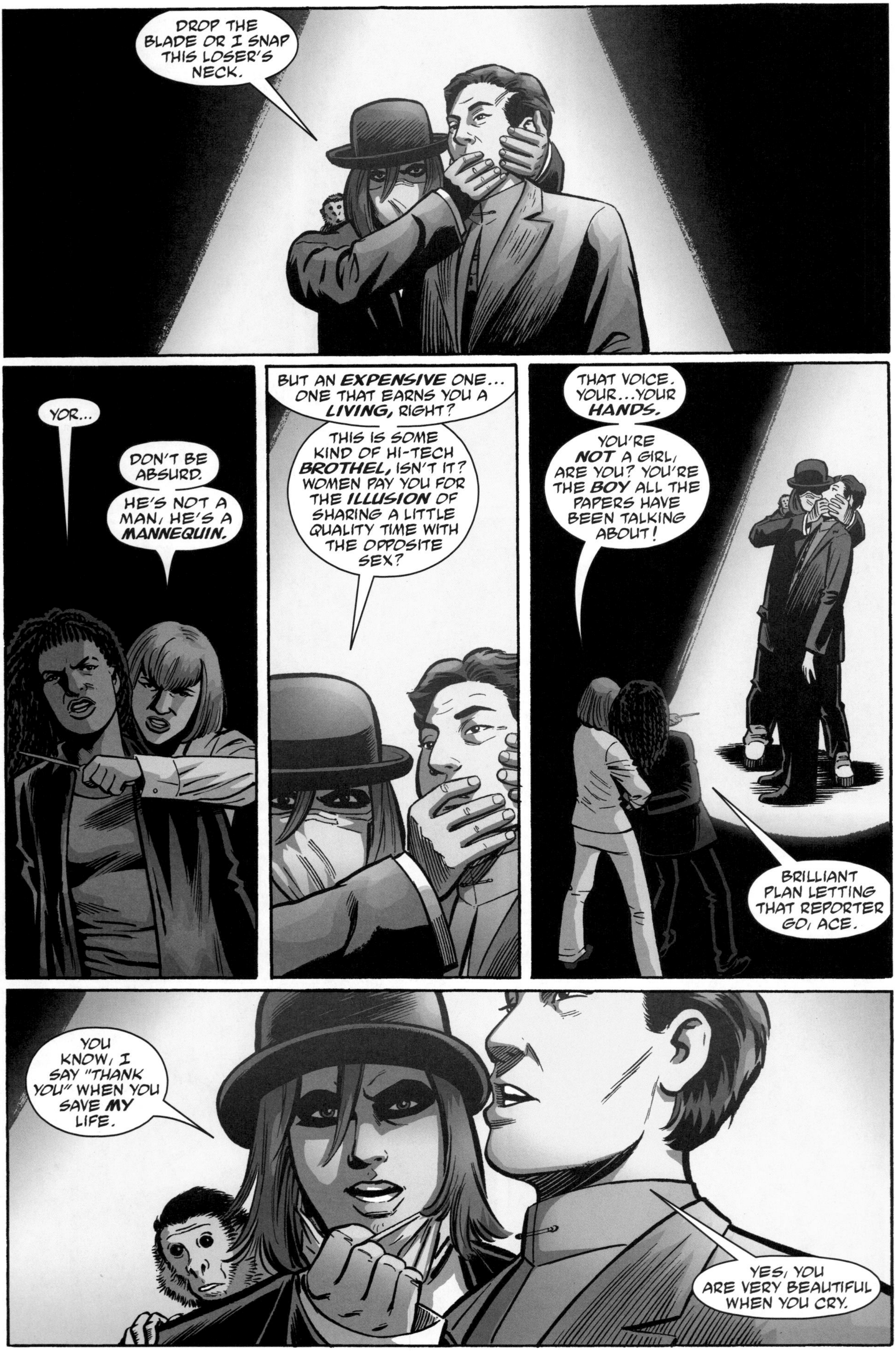
DROP THE BLADE OR I SNAP THIS LOSER'S NECK.
YOR...
DON'T BE ABSURD.
HE'S NOT A MAN, HE'S A MANNEQUIN.
BUT AN EXPENSIVE ONE... ONE THAT EARNS YOU A LIVING, RIGHT?
THIS IS SOME KIND OF HI-TECH BROTHEL, ISN'T IT? WOMEN PAY YOU FOR THE ILLUSION OF SHARING A LITTLE QUALITY TIME WITH THE OPPOSITE SEX?
THAT VOICE. YOUR...YOUR HANDS.
YOU'RE NOT A GIRL, ARE YOU? YOU'RE THE BOY ALL THE PAPERS HAVE BEEN TALKING ABOUT!
BRILLIANT PLAN LETTING THAT REPORTER GO, ACE.
YOU KNOW, I SAY "THANK YOU" WHEN YOU SAVE MY LIFE.
YES, YOU ARE VERY BEAUTIFUL WHEN YOU CRY.

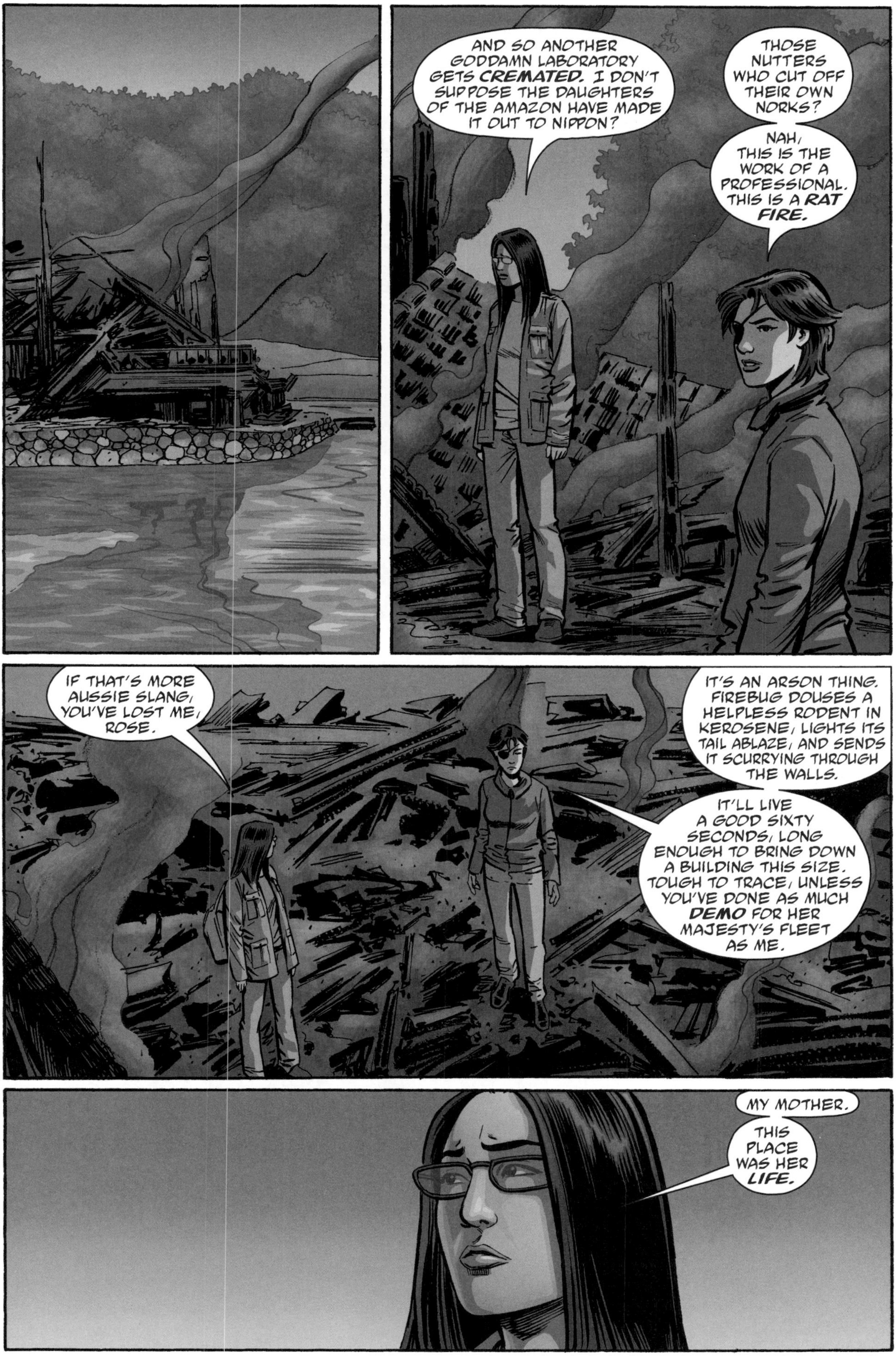
AND SO ANOTHER GODDAMN LABORATORY GETS CREMATED. I DON'T SUPPOSE THE DAUGHTERS OF THE AMAZON HAVE MADE IT OUT TO NIPPON?
THOSE NUTTERS WHO CUT OFF THEIR OWN NORKS?
NAH, THIS IS THE WORK OF A PROFESSIONAL. THIS IS A RAT FIRE.
IF THAT'S MORE AUSSIE SLANG, YOU'VE LOST ME, ROSE.
IT'S AN ARSON THING. FIREBUG DOUSES A HELPLESS RODENT IN KEROSENE, LIGHTS ITS TAIL ABLAZE, AND SENDS IT SCURRYING THROUGH THE WALLS.
IT'LL LIVE A GOOD SIXTY SECONDS, LONG ENOUGH TO BRING DOWN A BUILDING THIS SIZE. TOUGH TO TRACE, UNLESS YOU'VE DONE AS MUCH DEMO FOR HER MAJESTY'S FLEET AS ME.
MY MOTHER.
THIS PLACE WAS HER LIFE.

NO, HER *LIFE* IS HER LIFE, ALLISON.

AND THE FACT THAT SHE ISN'T A SMOLDERING *CORPSE* HERE MEANS THAT SHE'S STILL OUT THERE, ON THE RUN FROM WHOEVER TRIED TO SMOKE HER OUT, MAYBE.

UNLESS SHE'S BEEN *KIDNAPPED* OR...OR...

NO REASON TO THINK THE WORST YET, LOVE.

IS THERE ANYWHERE SHE MIGHT HAVE GONE? A JOINT NO ONE ELSE WOULD KNOW TO CHECK?

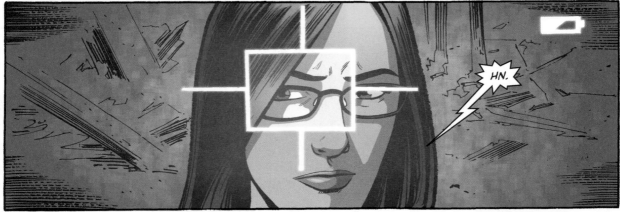

HN.

THAT A GIRL.

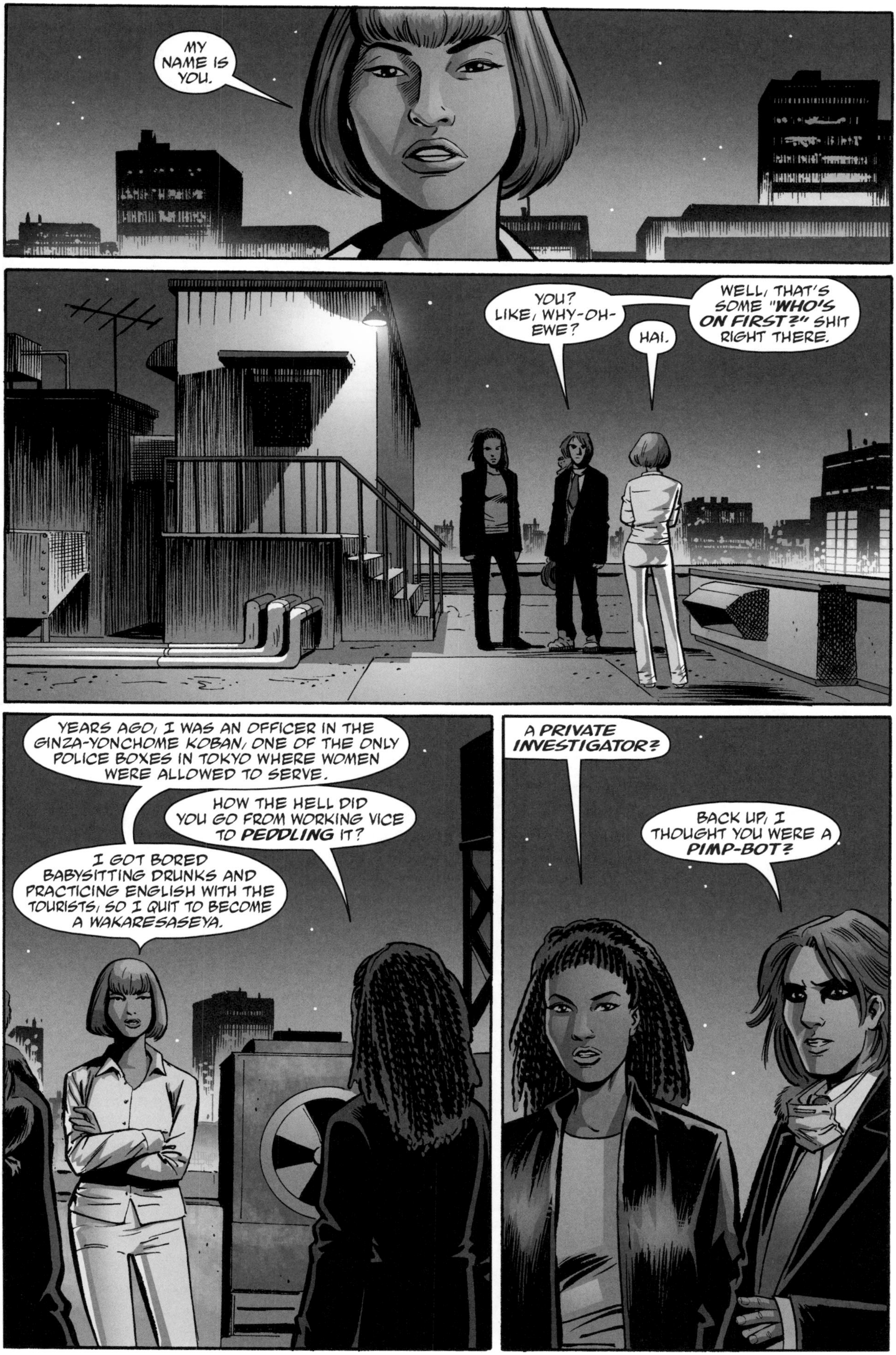
MY NAME IS YOU.
YOU? LIKE, WHY-OH-EWE?
HAI.
WELL, THAT'S SOME "WHO'S ON FIRST?" SHIT RIGHT THERE.
YEARS AGO, I WAS AN OFFICER IN THE GINZA-YONCHOME KOBAN, ONE OF THE ONLY POLICE BOXES IN TOKYO WHERE WOMEN WERE ALLOWED TO SERVE.
HOW THE HELL DID YOU GO FROM WORKING VICE TO PEDDLING IT?
I GOT BORED BABYSITTING DRUNKS AND PRACTICING ENGLISH WITH THE TOURISTS, SO I QUIT TO BECOME A WAKARESASEYA.
A PRIVATE INVESTIGATOR?
BACK UP, I THOUGHT YOU WERE A PIMP-BOT?

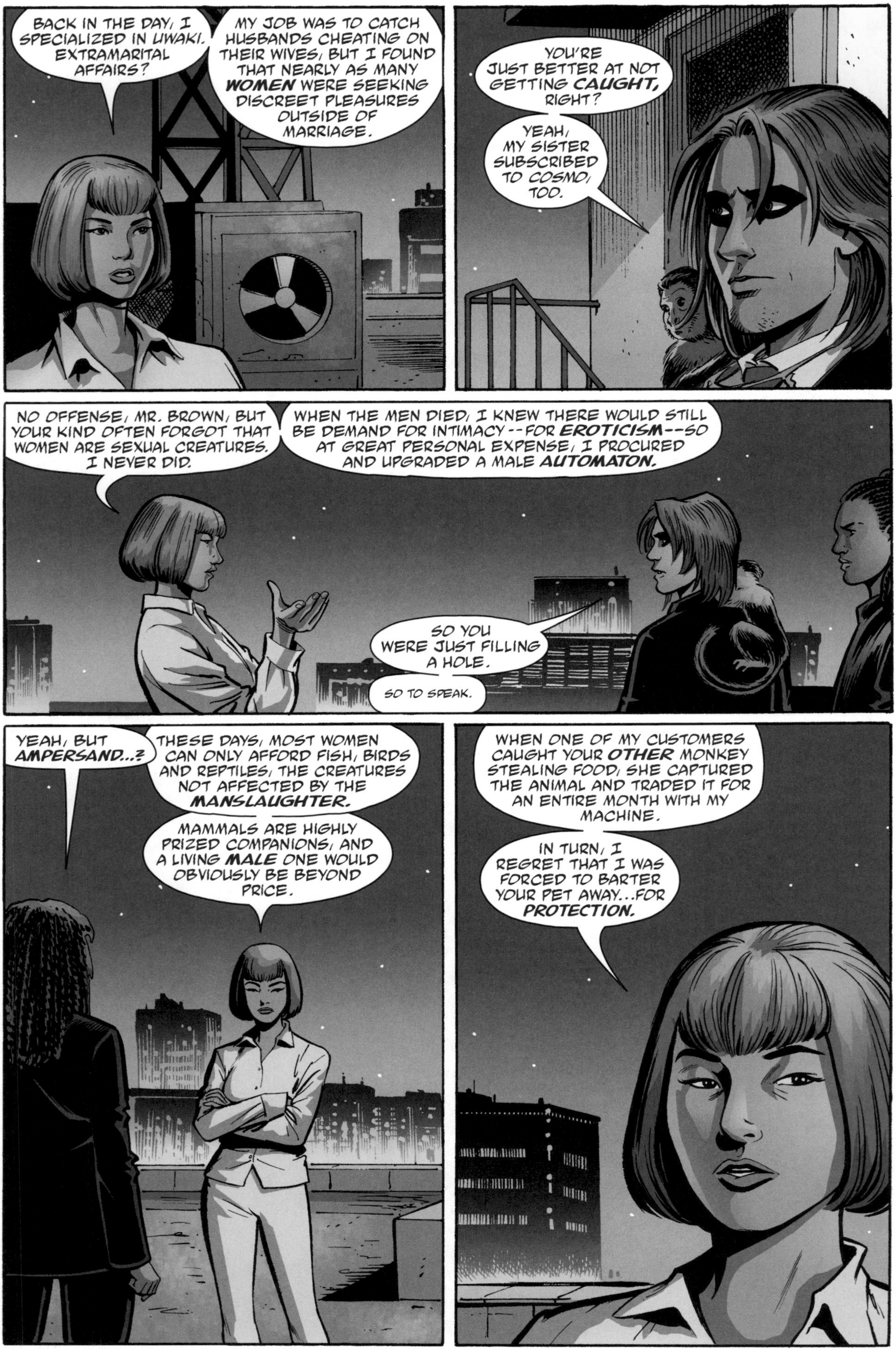
BACK IN THE DAY, I SPECIALIZED IN UWAKI. EXTRAMARITAL AFFAIRS?
MY JOB WAS TO CATCH HUSBANDS CHEATING ON THEIR WIVES, BUT I FOUND THAT NEARLY AS MANY WOMEN WERE SEEKING DISCREET PLEASURES OUTSIDE OF MARRIAGE.
YOU'RE JUST BETTER AT NOT GETTING CAUGHT, RIGHT?
YEAH, MY SISTER SUBSCRIBED TO COSMO, TOO.
NO OFFENSE, MR. BROWN, BUT YOUR KIND OFTEN FORGOT THAT WOMEN ARE SEXUAL CREATURES. I NEVER DID.
WHEN THE MEN DIED, I KNEW THERE WOULD STILL BE DEMAND FOR INTIMACY--FOR EROTICISM--SO AT GREAT PERSONAL EXPENSE, I PROCURED AND UPGRADED A MALE AUTOMATON.
SO YOU WERE JUST FILLING A HOLE.
SO TO SPEAK.
YEAH, BUT AMPERSAND...?
THESE DAYS, MOST WOMEN CAN ONLY AFFORD FISH, BIRDS AND REPTILES, THE CREATURES NOT AFFECTED BY THE MANSLAUGHTER.
MAMMALS ARE HIGHLY PRIZED COMPANIONS, AND A LIVING MALE ONE WOULD OBVIOUSLY BE BEYOND PRICE.
WHEN ONE OF MY CUSTOMERS CAUGHT YOUR OTHER MONKEY STEALING FOOD, SHE CAPTURED THE ANIMAL AND TRADED IT FOR AN ENTIRE MONTH WITH MY MACHINE.
IN TURN, I REGRET THAT I WAS FORCED TO BARTER YOUR PET AWAY...FOR PROTECTION.

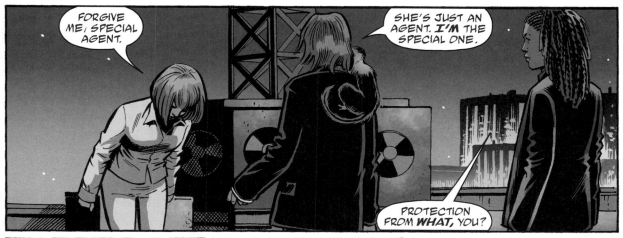

FORGIVE ME, SPECIAL AGENT.

SHE'S JUST AN AGENT. *I'M* THE SPECIAL ONE.

PROTECTION FROM *WHAT,* YOU?

THE WOMAN I ORIGINALLY FEARED *YOU TWO* WERE WORKING FOR.

HER NAME IS *EPIPHANY,* THE NEW LEADER OF YAKUZA.

THE FUCK KIND OF NAME IS THAT FOR A JAPANESE *MOB BOSS?*

SHE IS *NOT* JAPANESE. EPIPHANY WAS A CANADIAN...HOW IS IT SAID... *POP STAR,* TRAPPED HERE AFTER THE CRASHES DESTROYED OUR AIRPORTS.

SHE USED HER WEALTH AND INFLUENCE TO GAIN CONTROL OF THE VARIOUS *STREET GANGS* THAT ROSE FROM THE ASHES OF OUR BROTHERS.

SO THIS GAIJIN HAS AMPERSAND?

IS...IS THERE SOMETHING WE COULD TRADE HER TO GET HIM *BACK?*

ONLY ONE THING COMES TO MIND, MR. BROWN.

YOU.

181

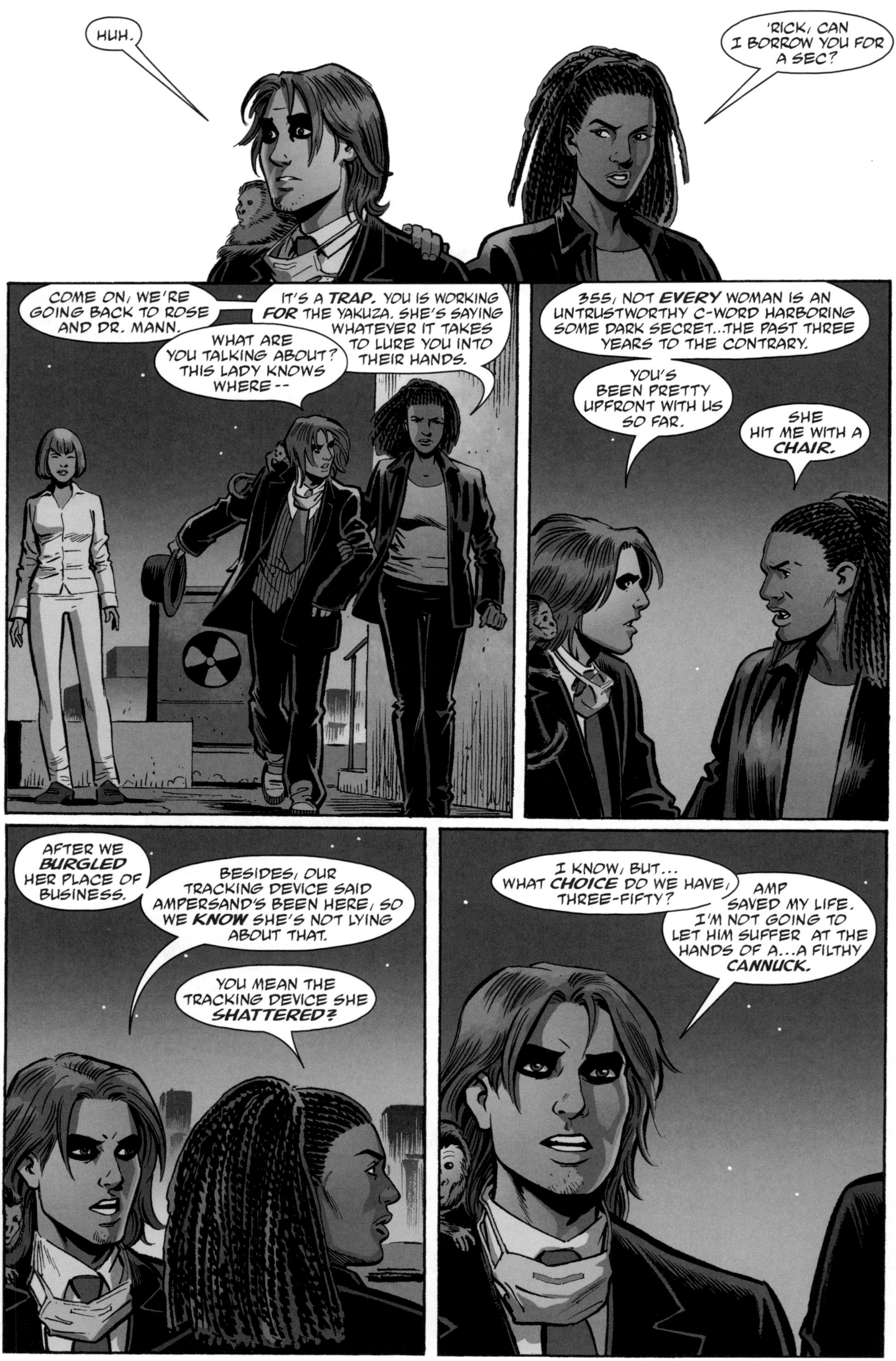
HUH.
'RICK, CAN I BORROW YOU FOR A SEC?
COME ON, WE'RE GOING BACK TO ROSE AND DR. MANN.
WHAT ARE YOU TALKING ABOUT? THIS LADY KNOWS WHERE--
IT'S A TRAP. YOU IS WORKING FOR THE YAKUZA. SHE'S SAYING WHATEVER IT TAKES TO LURE YOU INTO THEIR HANDS.
355, NOT EVERY WOMAN IS AN UNTRUSTWORTHY C-WORD HARBORING SOME DARK SECRET...THE PAST THREE YEARS TO THE CONTRARY.
YOU'S BEEN PRETTY UPFRONT WITH US SO FAR.
SHE HIT ME WITH A CHAIR.
AFTER WE BURGLED HER PLACE OF BUSINESS.
BESIDES, OUR TRACKING DEVICE SAID AMPERSAND'S BEEN HERE, SO WE KNOW SHE'S NOT LYING ABOUT THAT.
YOU MEAN THE TRACKING DEVICE SHE SHATTERED?
I KNOW, BUT... WHAT CHOICE DO WE HAVE, THREE-FIFTY?
AMP SAVED MY LIFE. I'M NOT GOING TO LET HIM SUFFER AT THE HANDS OF A...A FILTHY CANNUCK.

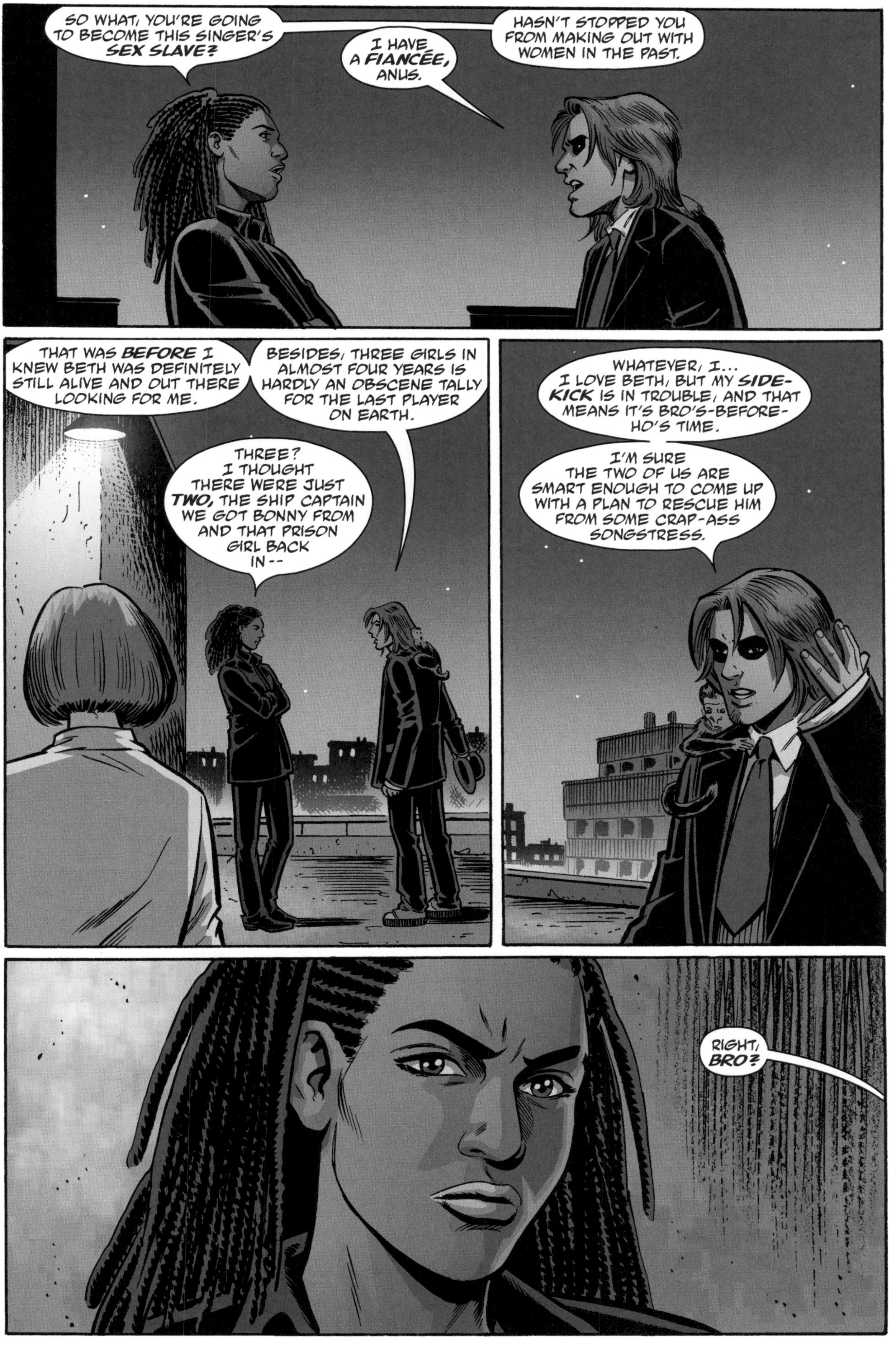
SO WHAT, YOU'RE GOING TO BECOME THIS SINGER'S SEX SLAVE?
I HAVE A FIANCÉE, ANUS.
HASN'T STOPPED YOU FROM MAKING OUT WITH WOMEN IN THE PAST.
THAT WAS BEFORE I KNEW BETH WAS DEFINITELY STILL ALIVE AND OUT THERE LOOKING FOR ME.
BESIDES, THREE GIRLS IN ALMOST FOUR YEARS IS HARDLY AN OBSCENE TALLY FOR THE LAST PLAYER ON EARTH.
THREE? I THOUGHT THERE WERE JUST TWO, THE SHIP CAPTAIN WE GOT BONNY FROM AND THAT PRISON GIRL BACK IN--
WHATEVER, I... I LOVE BETH, BUT MY SIDEKICK IS IN TROUBLE, AND THAT MEANS IT'S BRO'S-BEFORE-HO'S TIME.
I'M SURE THE TWO OF US ARE SMART ENOUGH TO COME UP WITH A PLAN TO RESCUE HIM FROM SOME CRAP-ASS SONGSTRESS.
RIGHT, BRO?

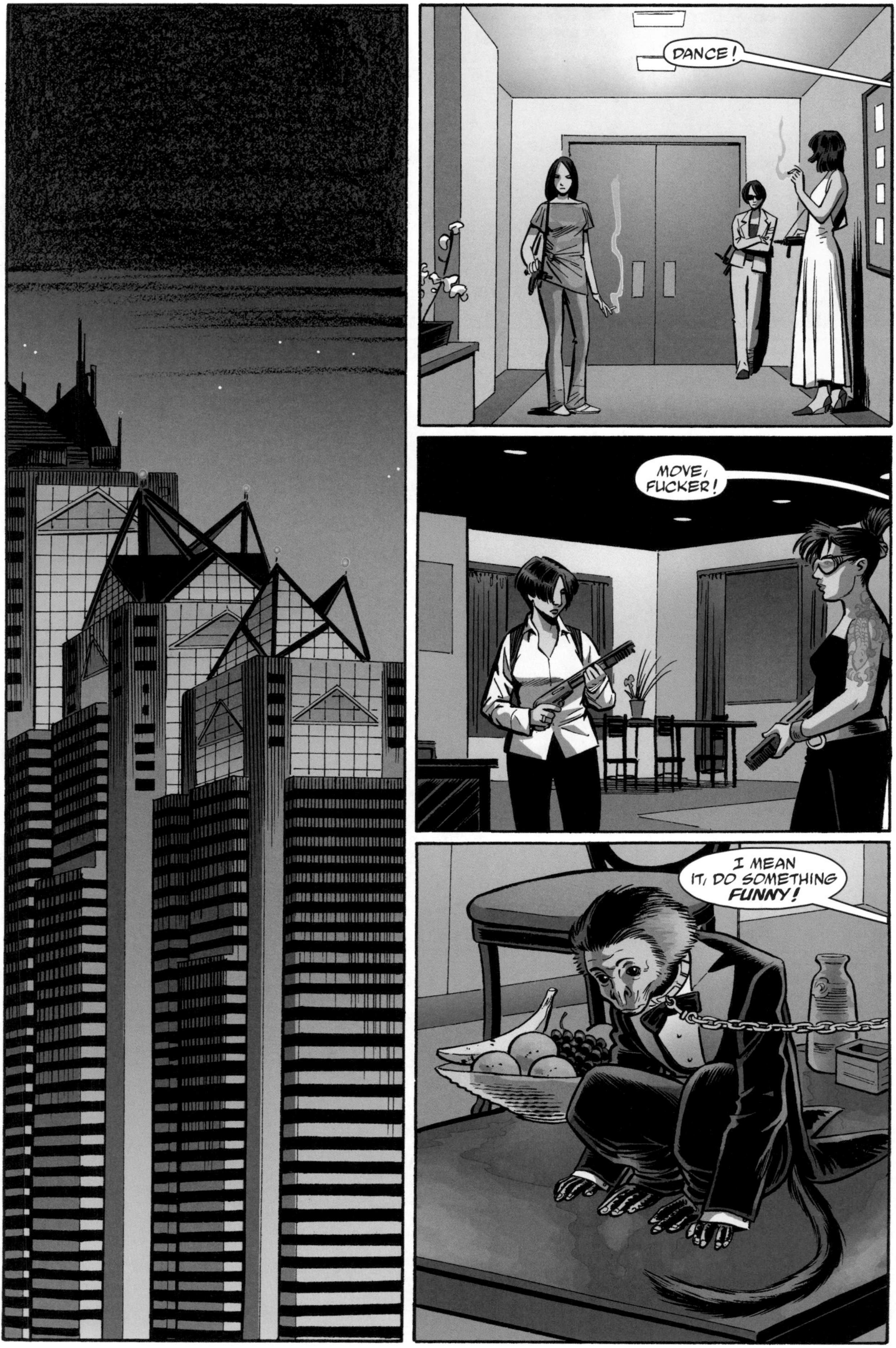
DANCE!
MOVE, FUCKER!
I MEAN IT, DO SOMETHING FUNNY!

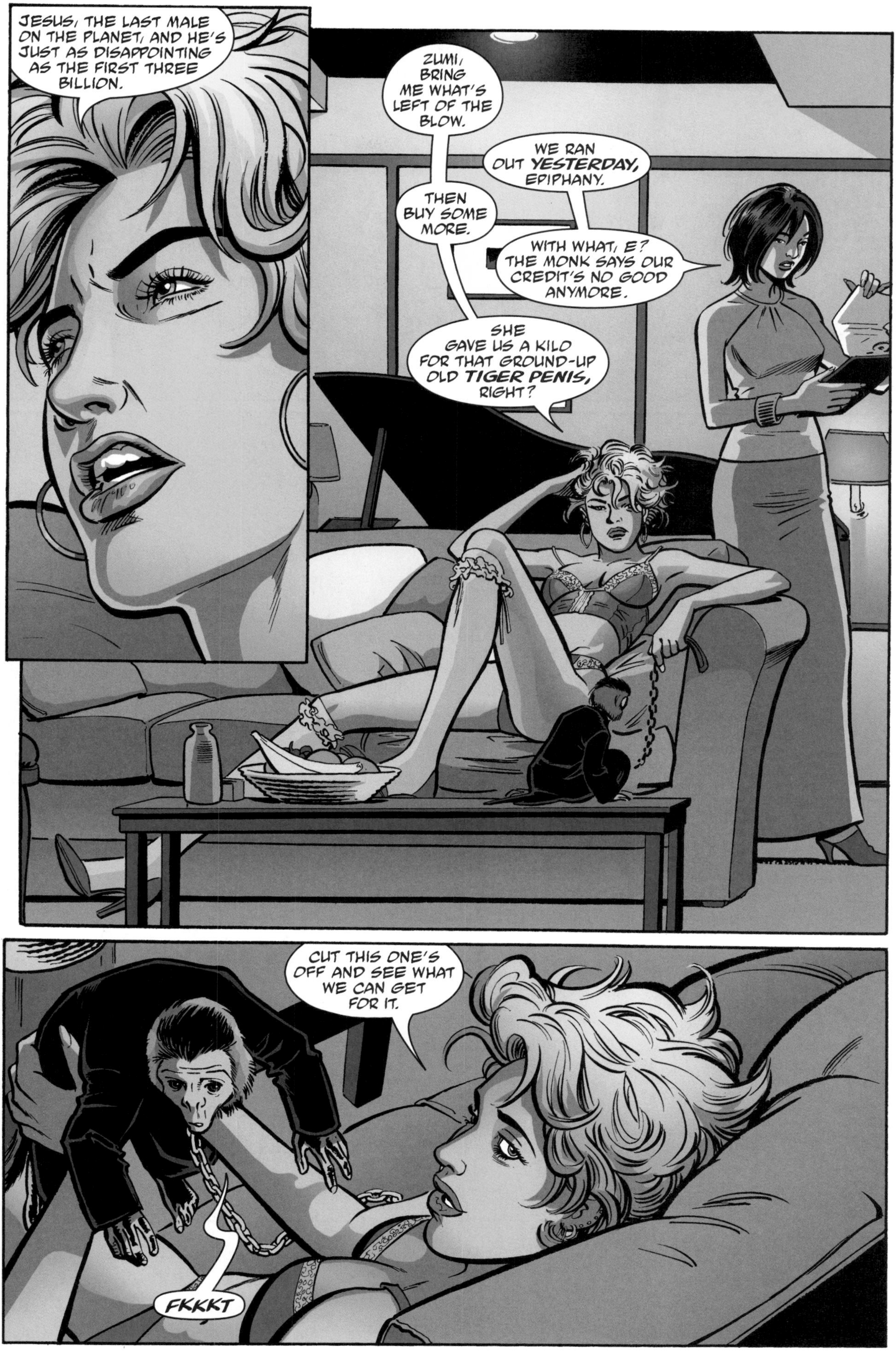
JESUS, THE LAST MALE ON THE PLANET, AND HE'S JUST AS DISAPPOINTING AS THE FIRST THREE BILLION.
ZUMI, BRING ME WHAT'S LEFT OF THE BLOW.
WE RAN OUT **YESTERDAY**, EPIPHANY.
THEN BUY SOME MORE.
WITH WHAT, E? THE MONK SAYS OUR CREDIT'S NO GOOD ANYMORE.
SHE GAVE US A KILO FOR THAT GROUND-UP OLD **TIGER PENIS**, RIGHT?
CUT THIS ONE'S OFF AND SEE WHAT WE CAN GET FOR IT.
FKKKT

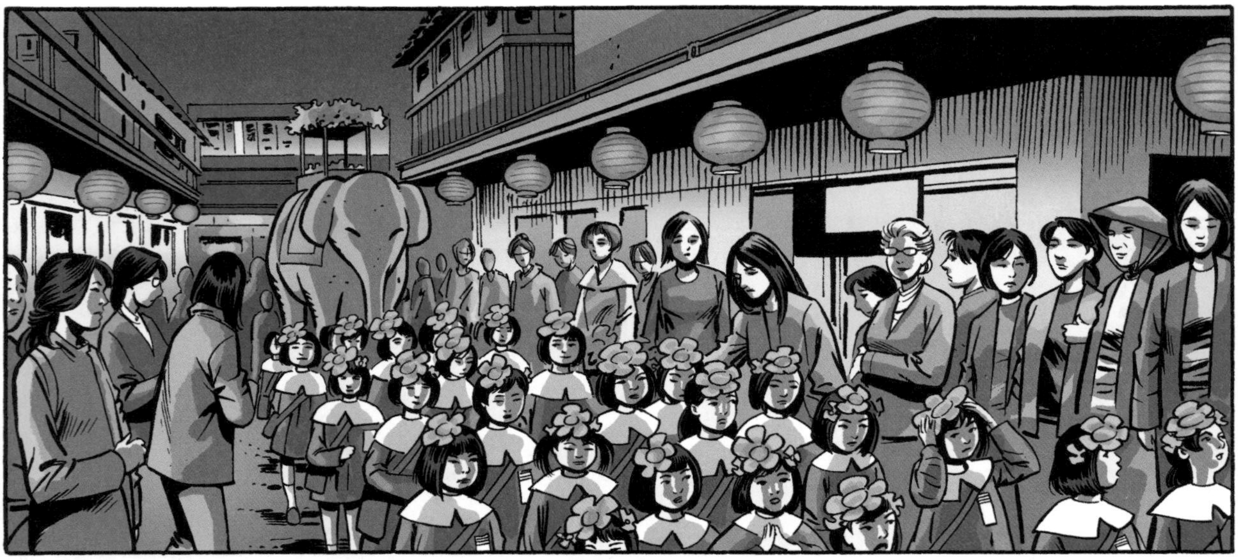
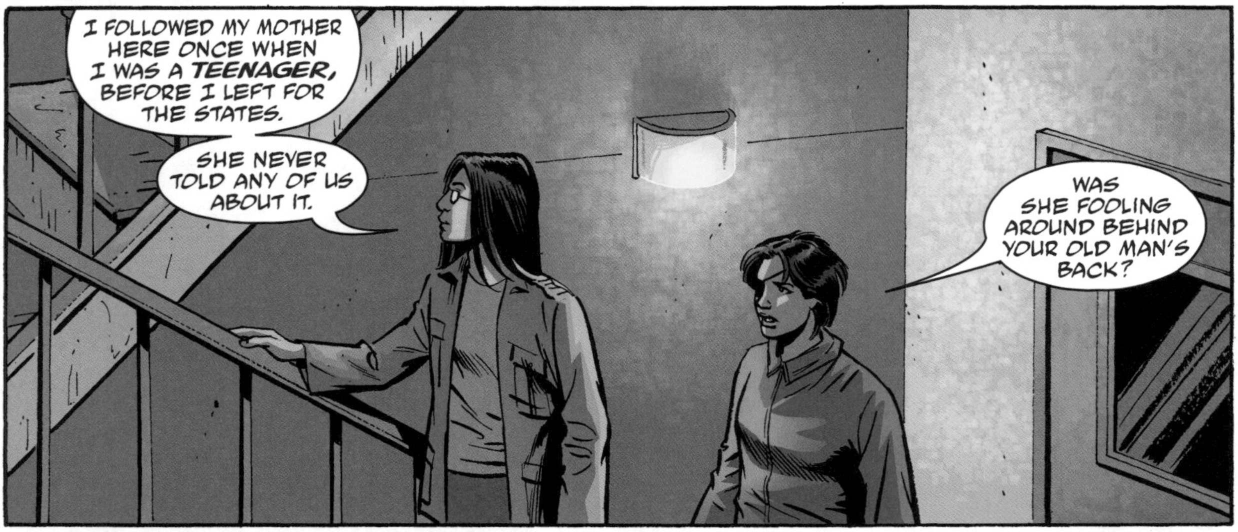
I FOLLOWED MY MOTHER HERE ONCE WHEN I WAS A TEENAGER, BEFORE I LEFT FOR THE STATES.
SHE NEVER TOLD ANY OF US ABOUT IT.
WAS SHE FOOLING AROUND BEHIND YOUR OLD MAN'S BACK?
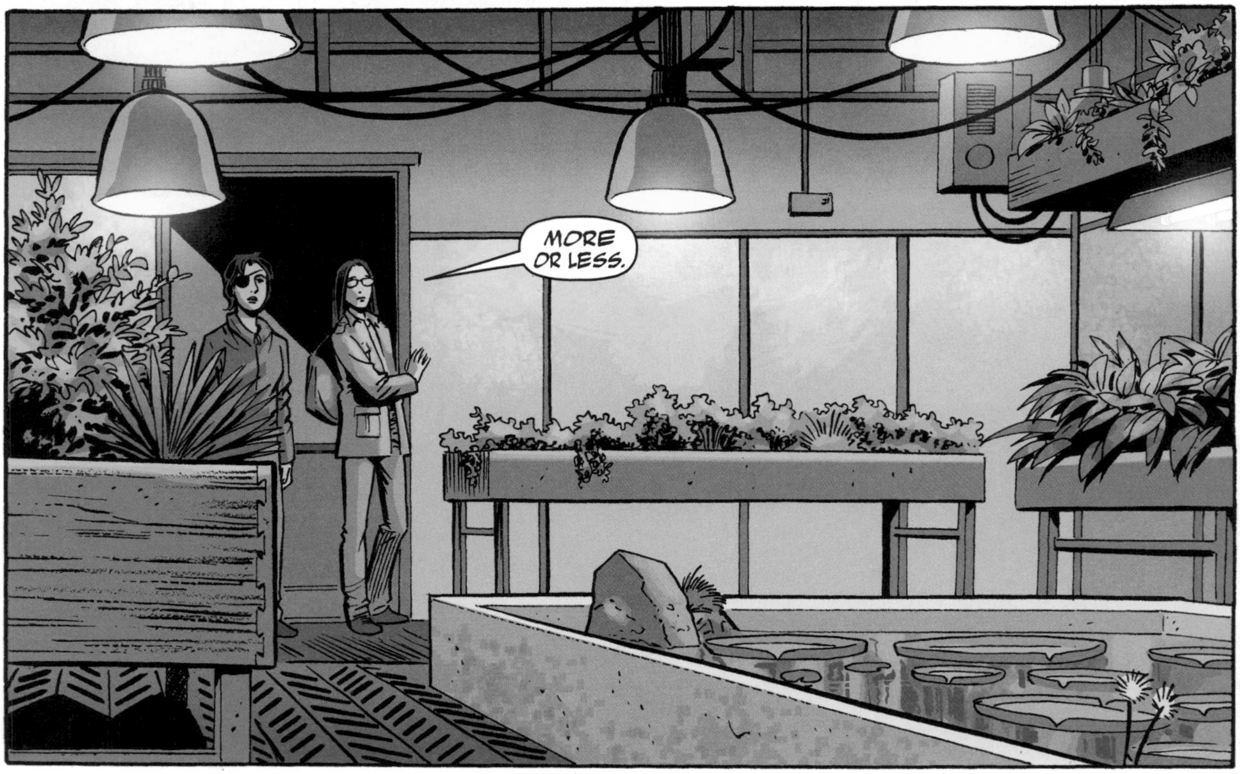
MORE OR LESS.

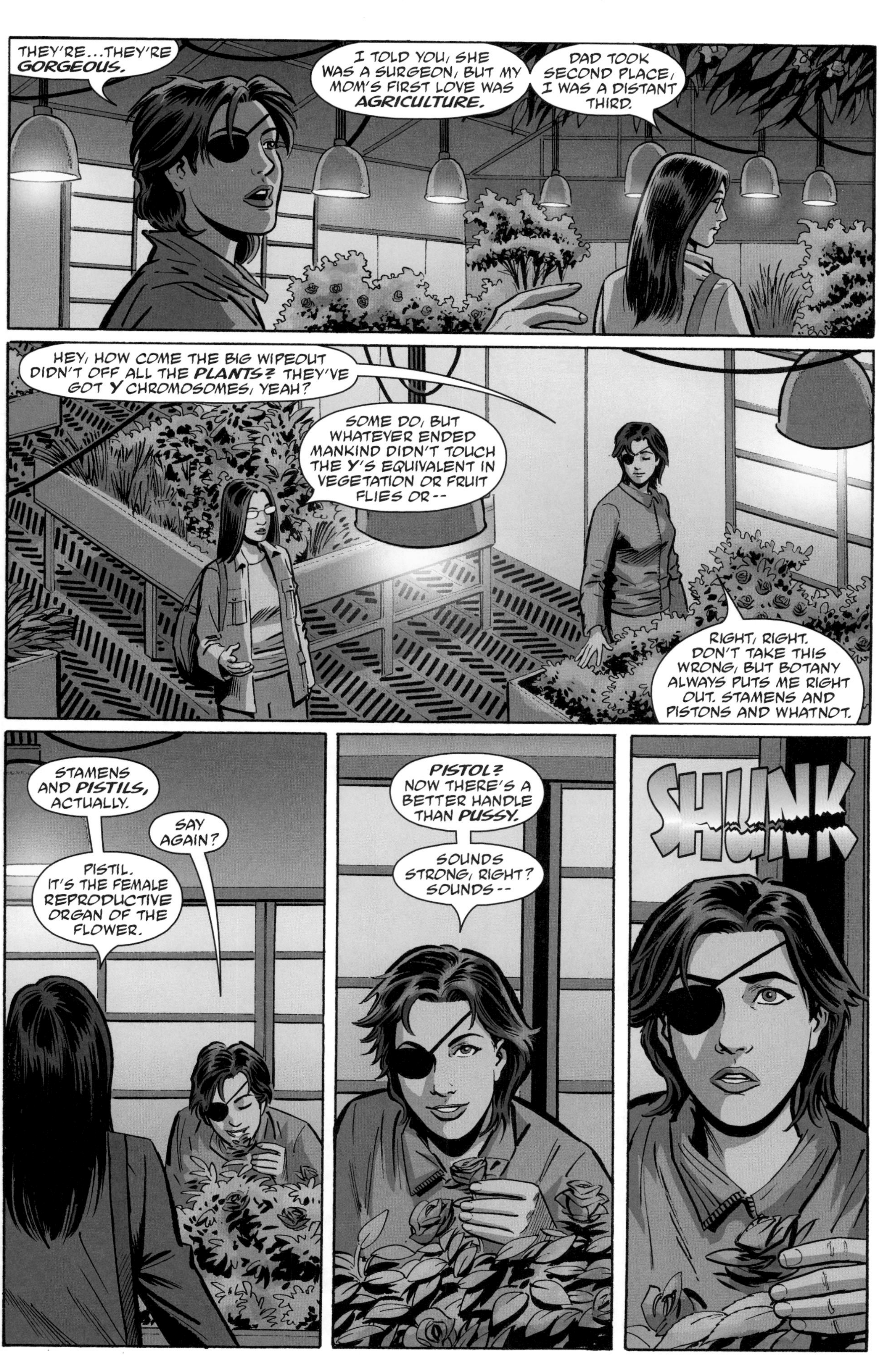
THEY'RE...THEY'RE GORGEOUS.
I TOLD YOU, SHE WAS A SURGEON, BUT MY MOM'S FIRST LOVE WAS AGRICULTURE.
DAD TOOK SECOND PLACE, I WAS A DISTANT THIRD.
HEY, HOW COME THE BIG WIPEOUT DIDN'T OFF ALL THE PLANTS? THEY'VE GOT Y CHROMOSOMES, YEAH?
SOME DO, BUT WHATEVER ENDED MANKIND DIDN'T TOUCH THE Y'S EQUIVALENT IN VEGETATION OR FRUIT FLIES OR--
RIGHT, RIGHT. DON'T TAKE THIS WRONG, BUT BOTANY ALWAYS PUTS ME RIGHT OUT. STAMENS AND PISTONS AND WHATNOT.
STAMENS AND PISTILS, ACTUALLY.
SAY AGAIN?
PISTIL. IT'S THE FEMALE REPRODUCTIVE ORGAN OF THE FLOWER.
PISTOL? NOW THERE'S A BETTER HANDLE THAN PUSSY.
SOUNDS STRONG, RIGHT? SOUNDS--
SHUNK

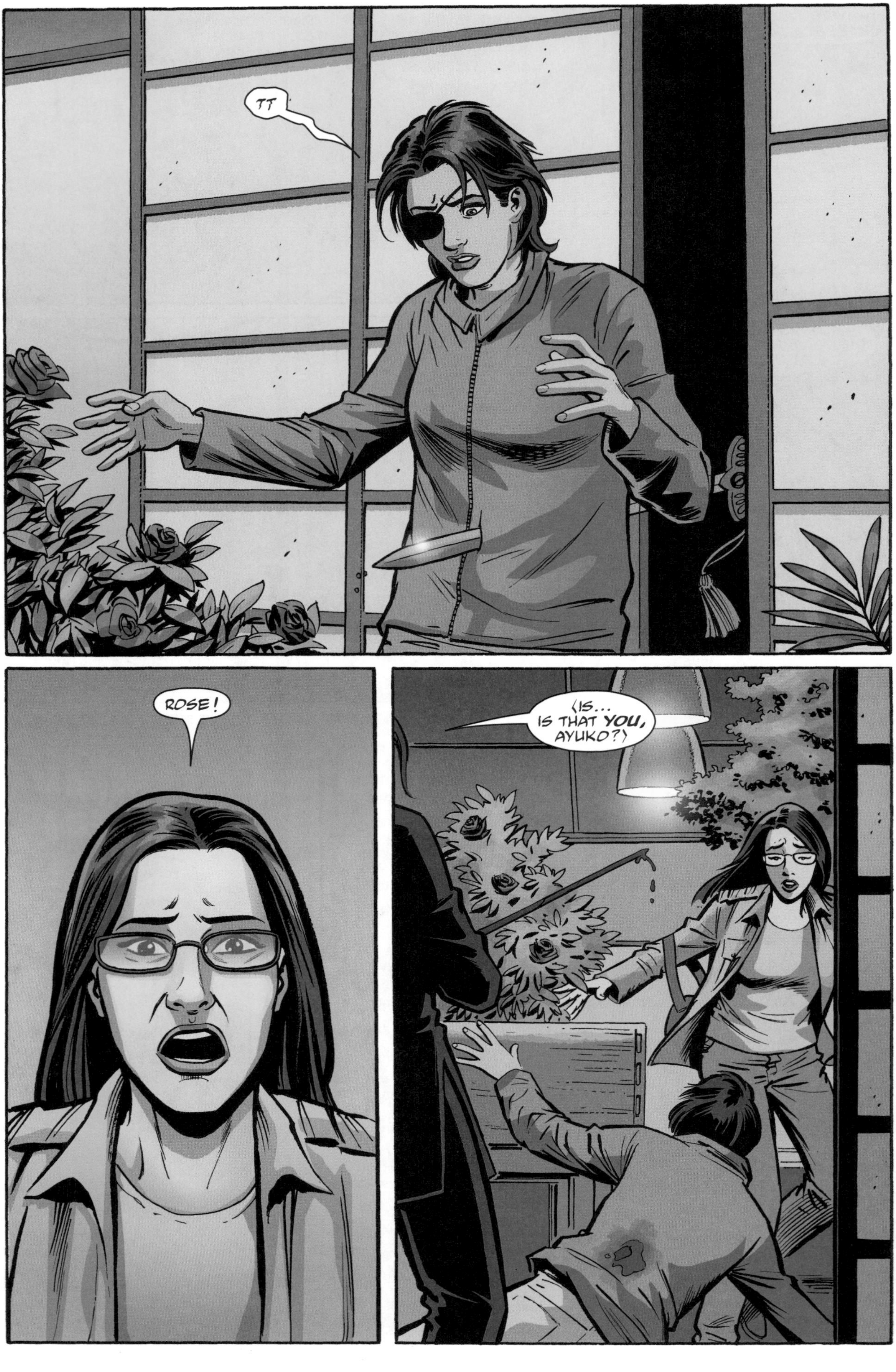
TT
ROSE!
⟨IS... IS THAT YOU, AYUKO?⟩

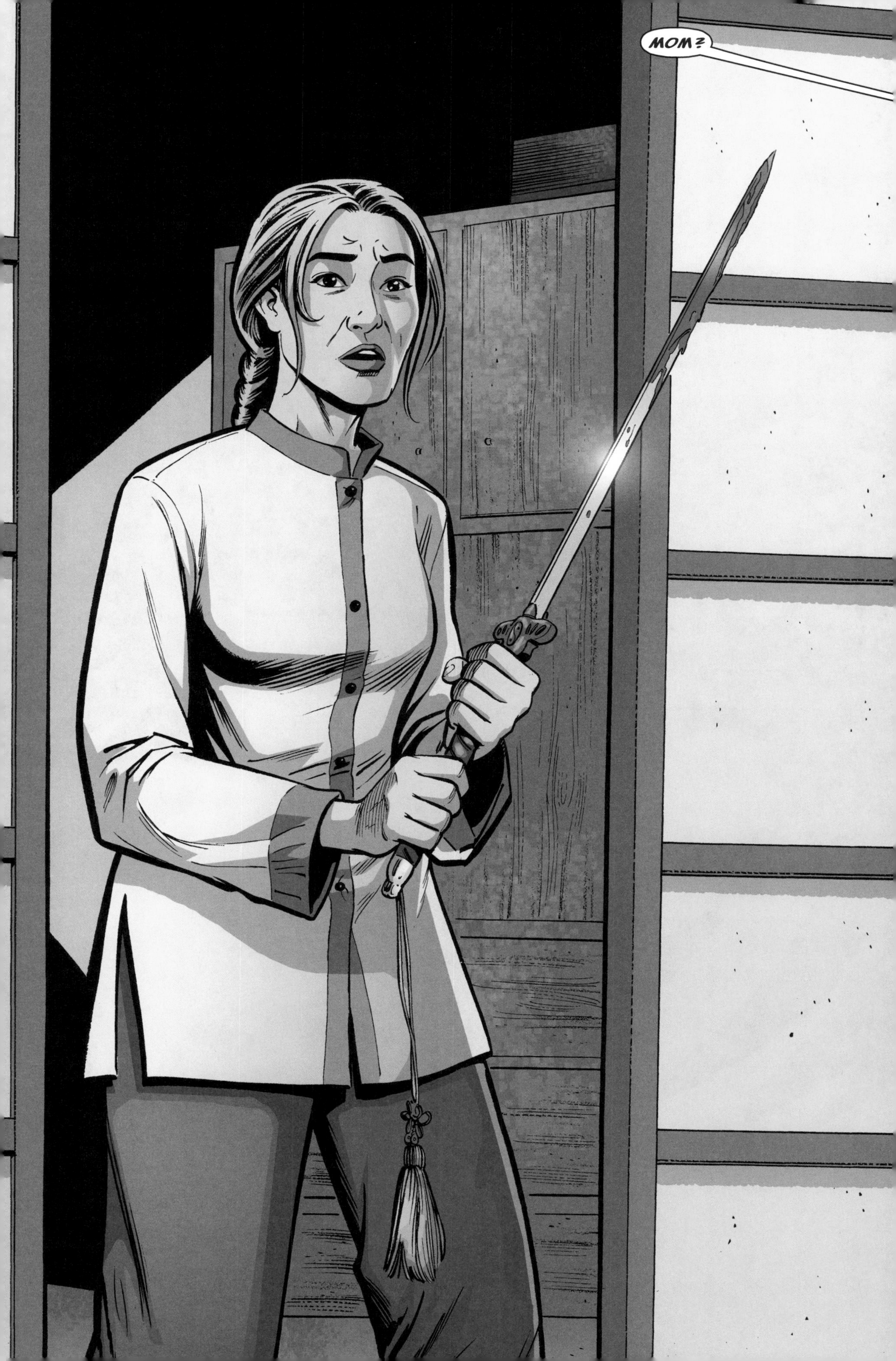
MOM?

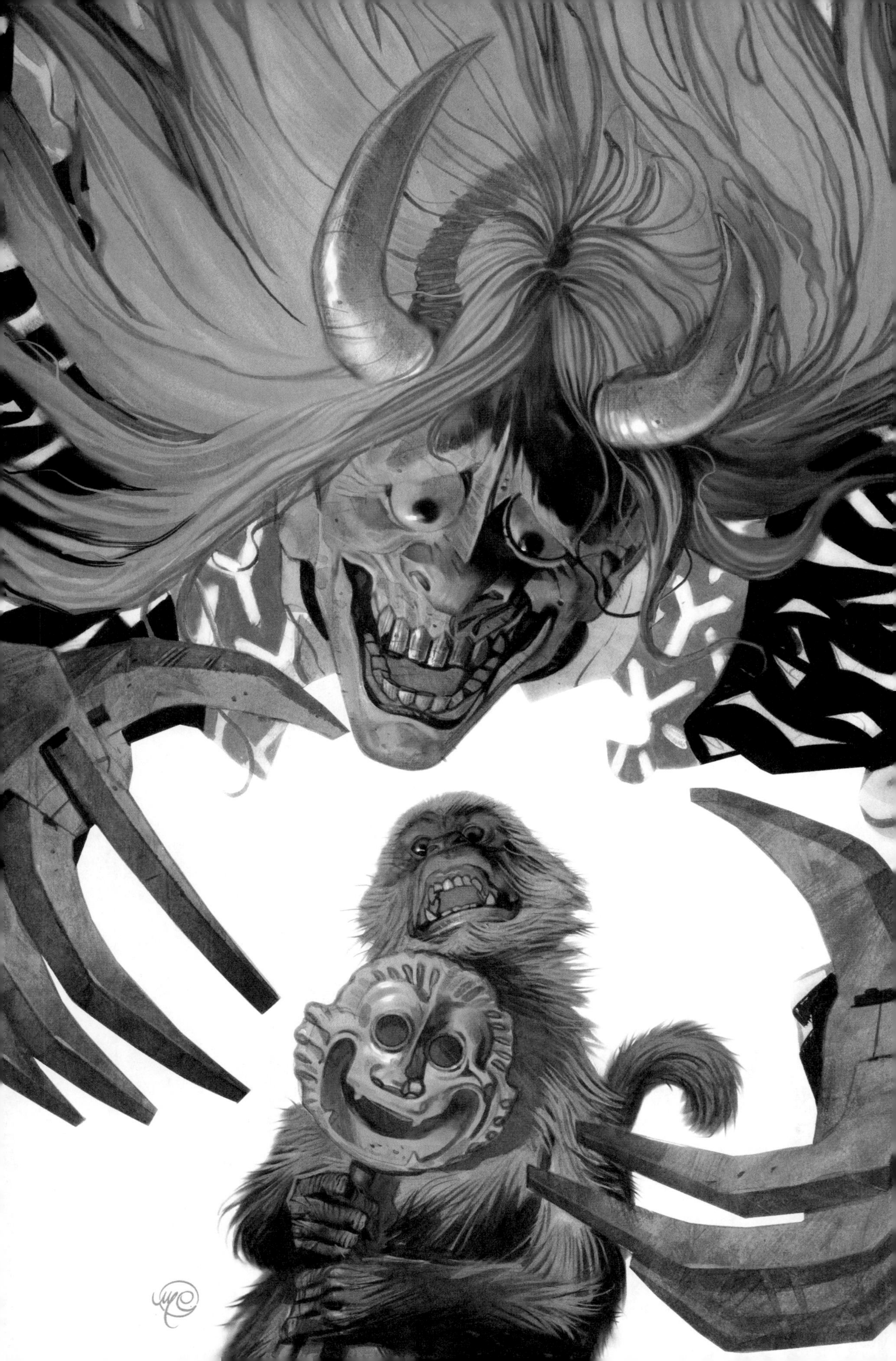

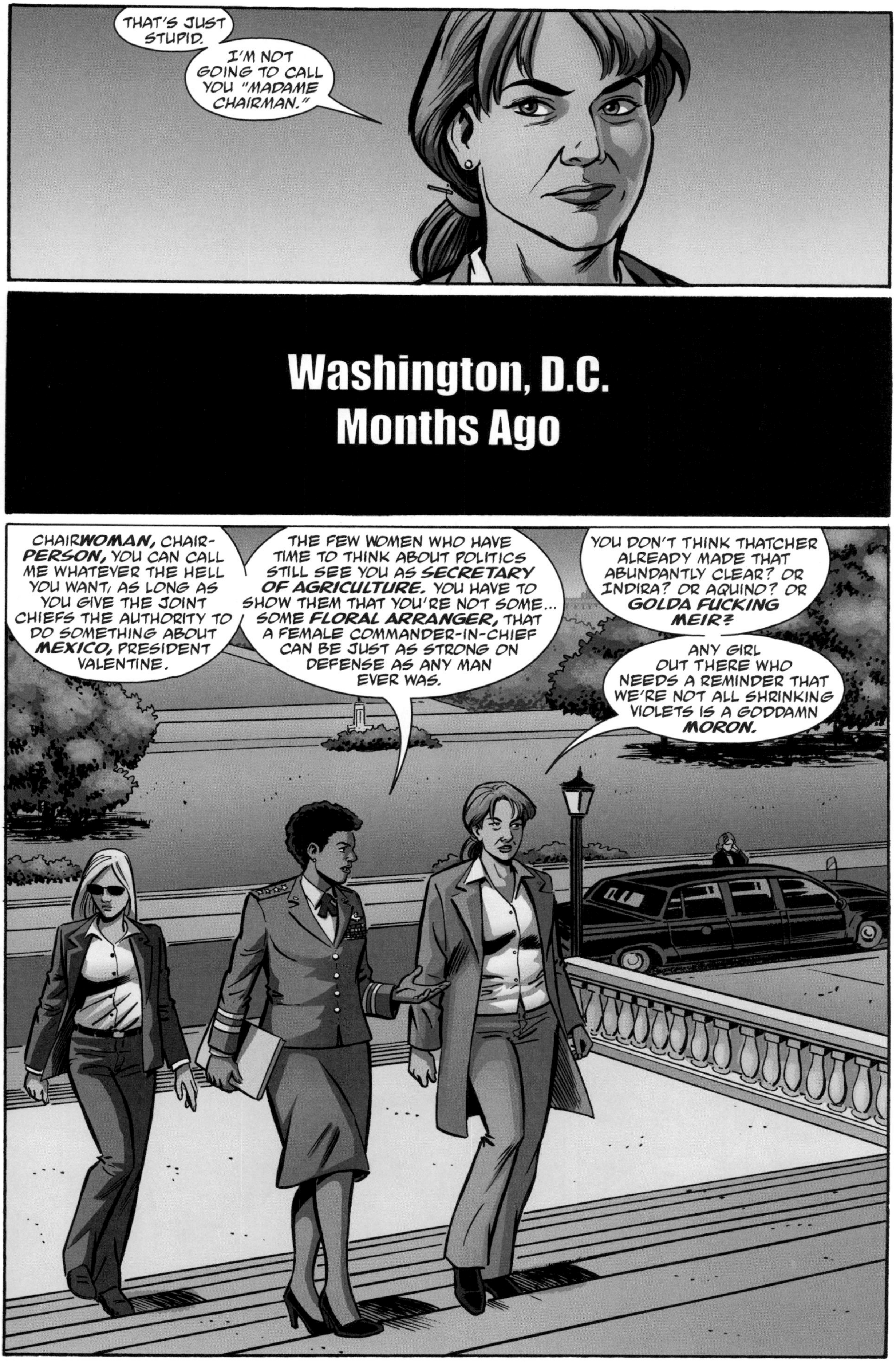
THAT'S JUST STUPID.
I'M NOT GOING TO CALL YOU "MADAME CHAIRMAN."
Washington, D.C.
Months Ago
CHAIRWOMAN, CHAIRPERSON, YOU CAN CALL ME WHATEVER THE HELL YOU WANT, AS LONG AS YOU GIVE THE JOINT CHIEFS THE AUTHORITY TO DO SOMETHING ABOUT MEXICO, PRESIDENT VALENTINE.
THE FEW WOMEN WHO HAVE TIME TO THINK ABOUT POLITICS STILL SEE YOU AS SECRETARY OF AGRICULTURE. YOU HAVE TO SHOW THEM THAT YOU'RE NOT SOME... SOME FLORAL ARRANGER, THAT A FEMALE COMMANDER-IN-CHIEF CAN BE JUST AS STRONG ON DEFENSE AS ANY MAN EVER WAS.
YOU DON'T THINK THATCHER ALREADY MADE THAT ABUNDANTLY CLEAR? OR INDIRA? OR AQUINO? OR GOLDA FUCKING MEIR?
ANY GIRL OUT THERE WHO NEEDS A REMINDER THAT WE'RE NOT ALL SHRINKING VIOLETS IS A GODDAMN MORON.

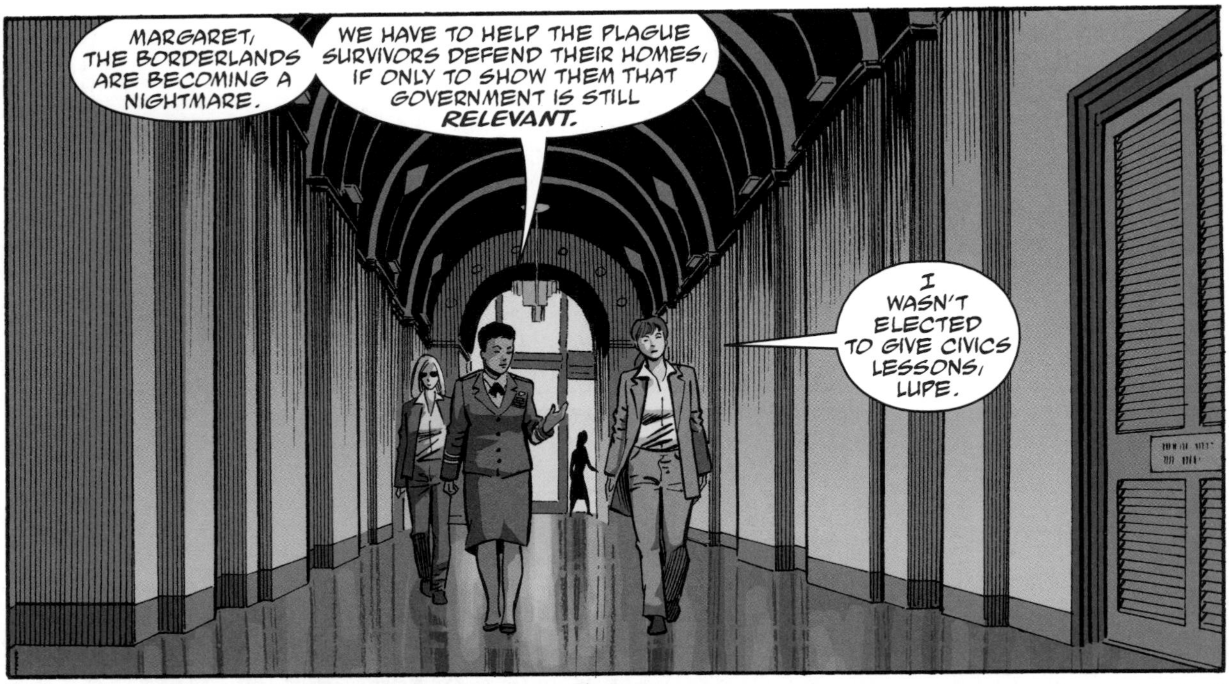
MARGARET, THE BORDERLANDS ARE BECOMING A NIGHTMARE.
WE HAVE TO HELP THE PLAGUE SURVIVORS DEFEND THEIR HOMES, IF ONLY TO SHOW THEM THAT GOVERNMENT IS STILL **RELEVANT.**
I WASN'T ELECTED TO GIVE CIVICS LESSONS, LUPE.

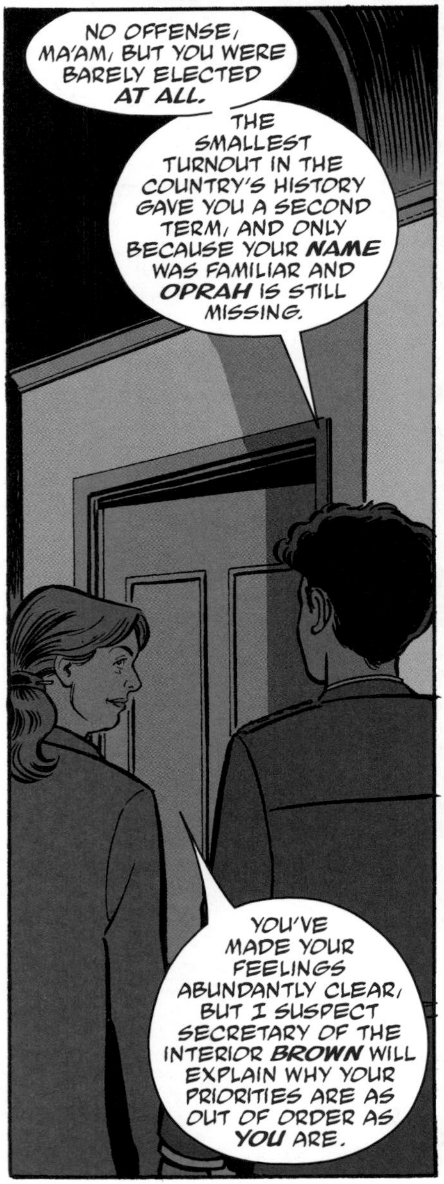
NO OFFENSE, MA'AM, BUT YOU WERE BARELY ELECTED **AT ALL.**
THE SMALLEST TURNOUT IN THE COUNTRY'S HISTORY GAVE YOU A SECOND TERM, AND ONLY BECAUSE YOUR **NAME** WAS FAMILIAR AND **OPRAH** IS STILL MISSING.
YOU'VE MADE YOUR FEELINGS ABUNDANTLY CLEAR, BUT I SUSPECT SECRETARY OF THE INTERIOR **BROWN** WILL EXPLAIN WHY YOUR PRIORITIES ARE AS OUT OF ORDER AS **YOU** ARE.

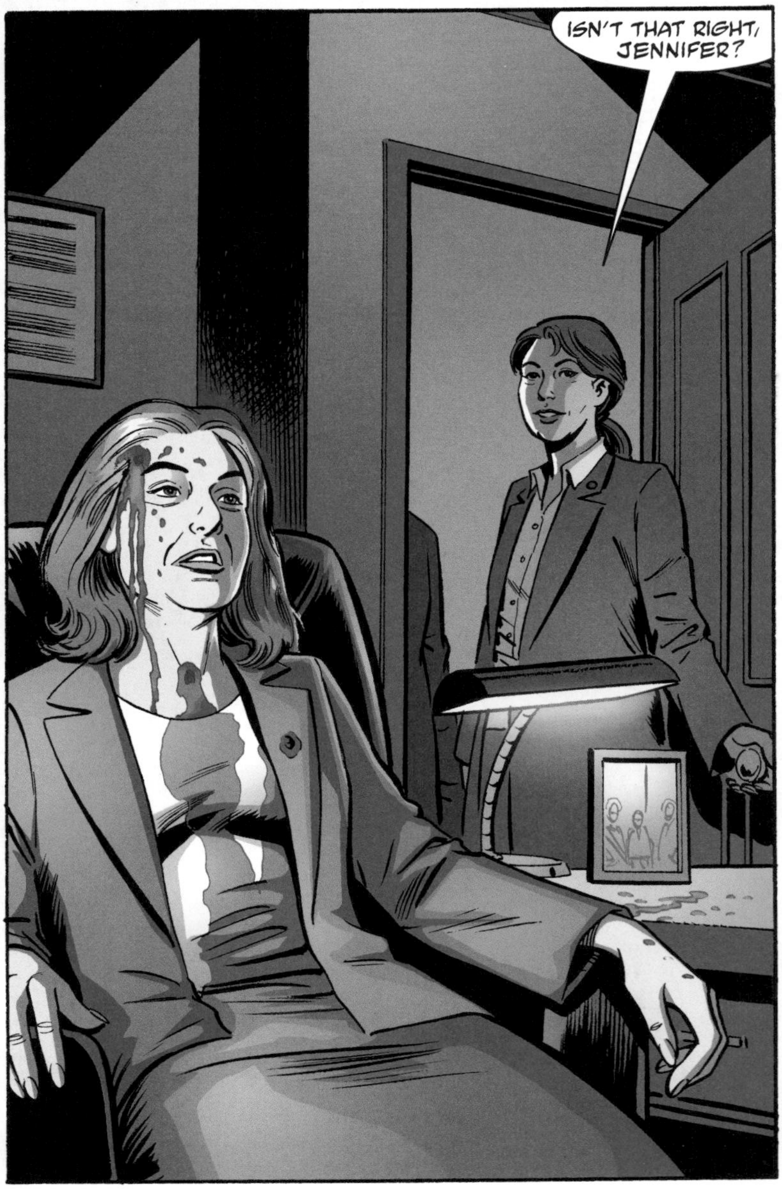
ISN'T THAT RIGHT, JENNIFER?

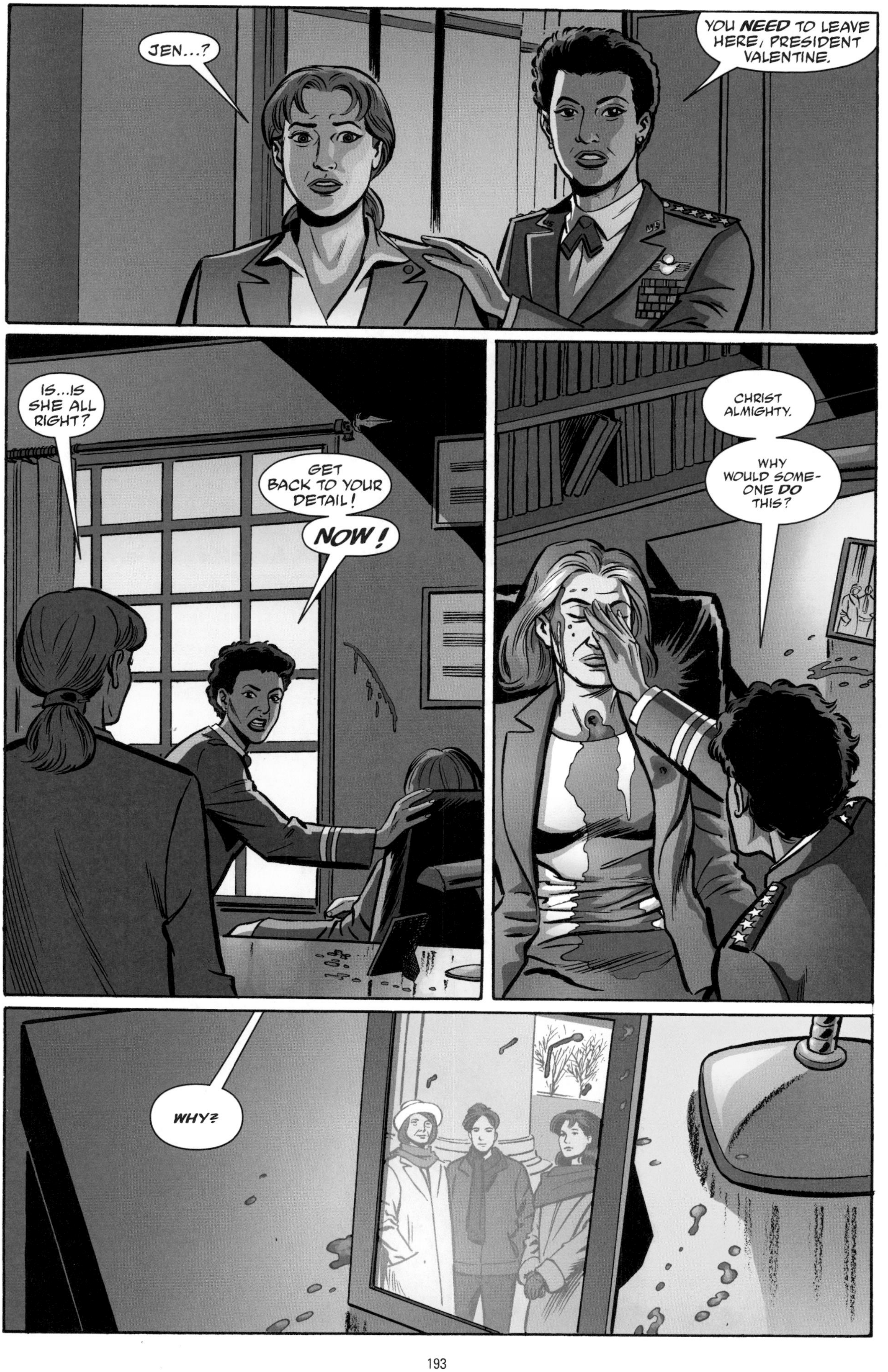

JEN...?
YOU NEED TO LEAVE HERE, PRESIDENT VALENTINE.
IS...IS SHE ALL RIGHT?
GET BACK TO YOUR DETAIL!
NOW!
CHRIST ALMIGHTY.
WHY WOULD SOME-ONE DO THIS?
WHY?

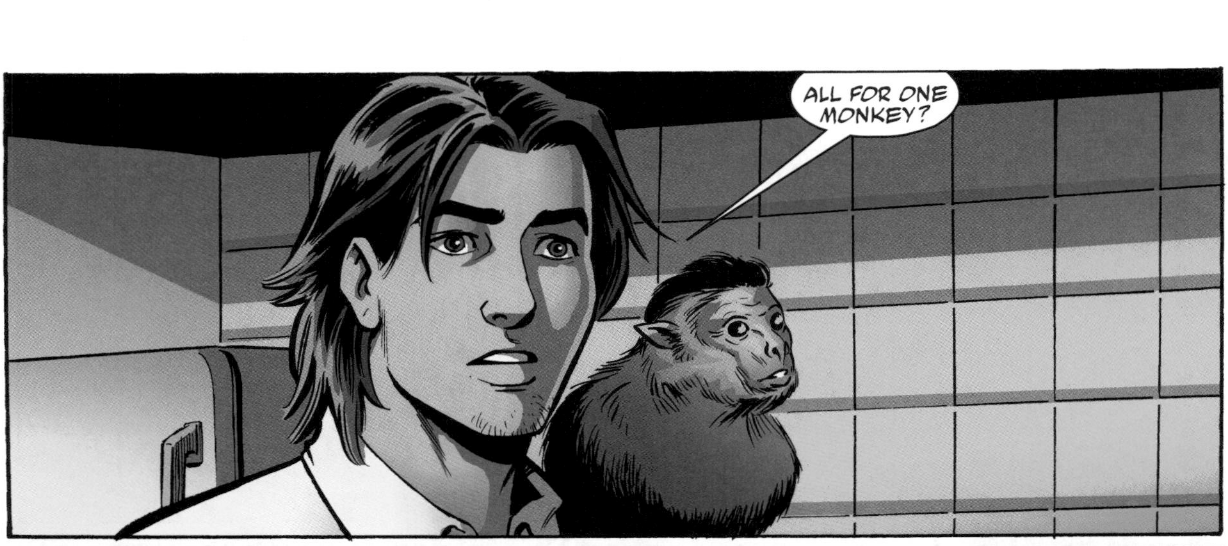
ALL FOR ONE MONKEY?

Tokyo, Japan
Now

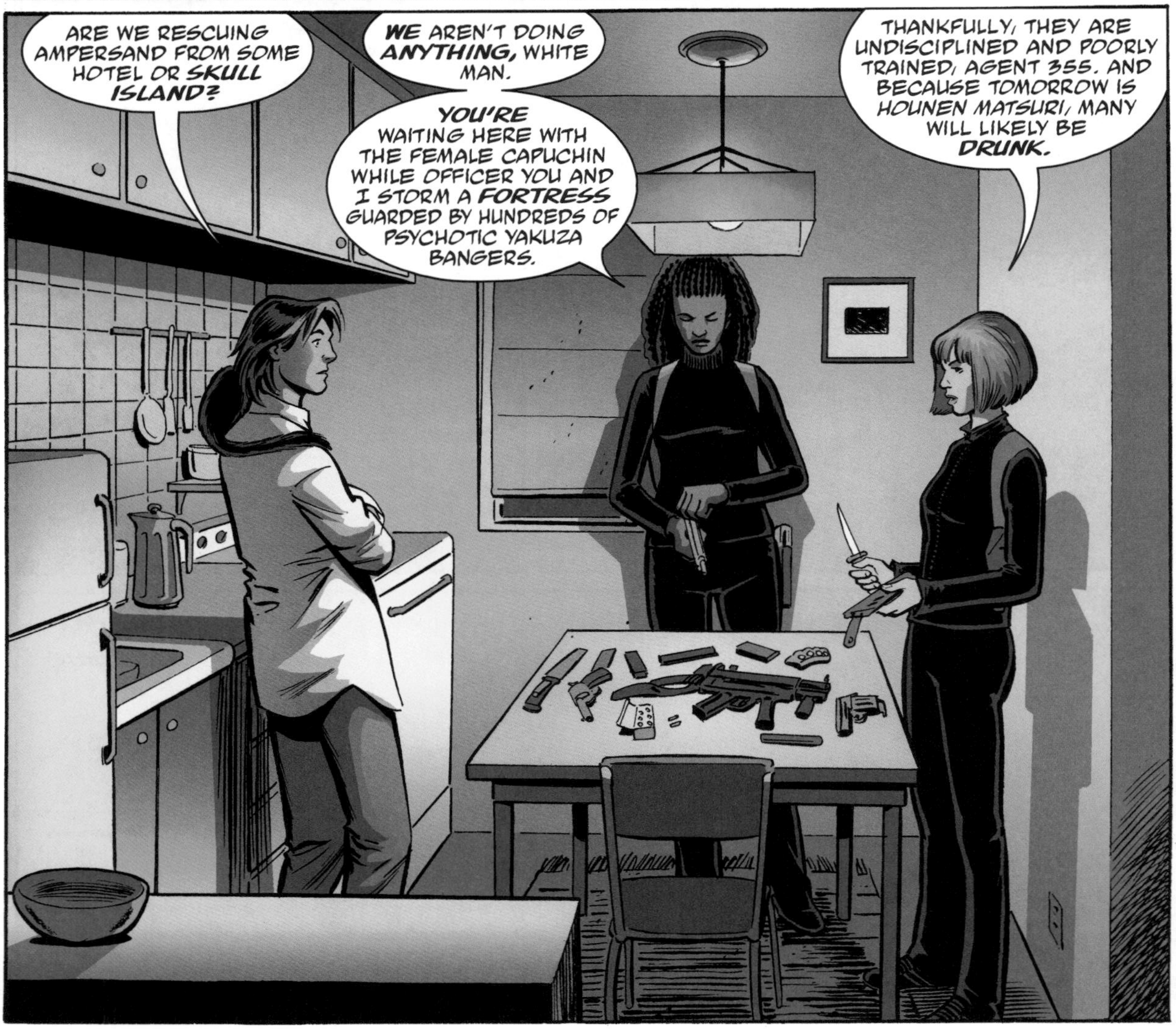
ARE WE RESCUING AMPERSAND FROM SOME HOTEL OR *SKULL ISLAND?*
WE AREN'T DOING *ANYTHING,* WHITE MAN.
YOU'RE WAITING HERE WITH THE FEMALE CAPUCHIN WHILE OFFICER YOU AND I STORM A *FORTRESS* GUARDED BY HUNDREDS OF PSYCHOTIC YAKUZA BANGERS.
THANKFULLY, THEY ARE UNDISCIPLINED AND POORLY TRAINED, AGENT 355. AND BECAUSE TOMORROW IS HOUNEN MATSURI, MANY WILL LIKELY BE *DRUNK.*

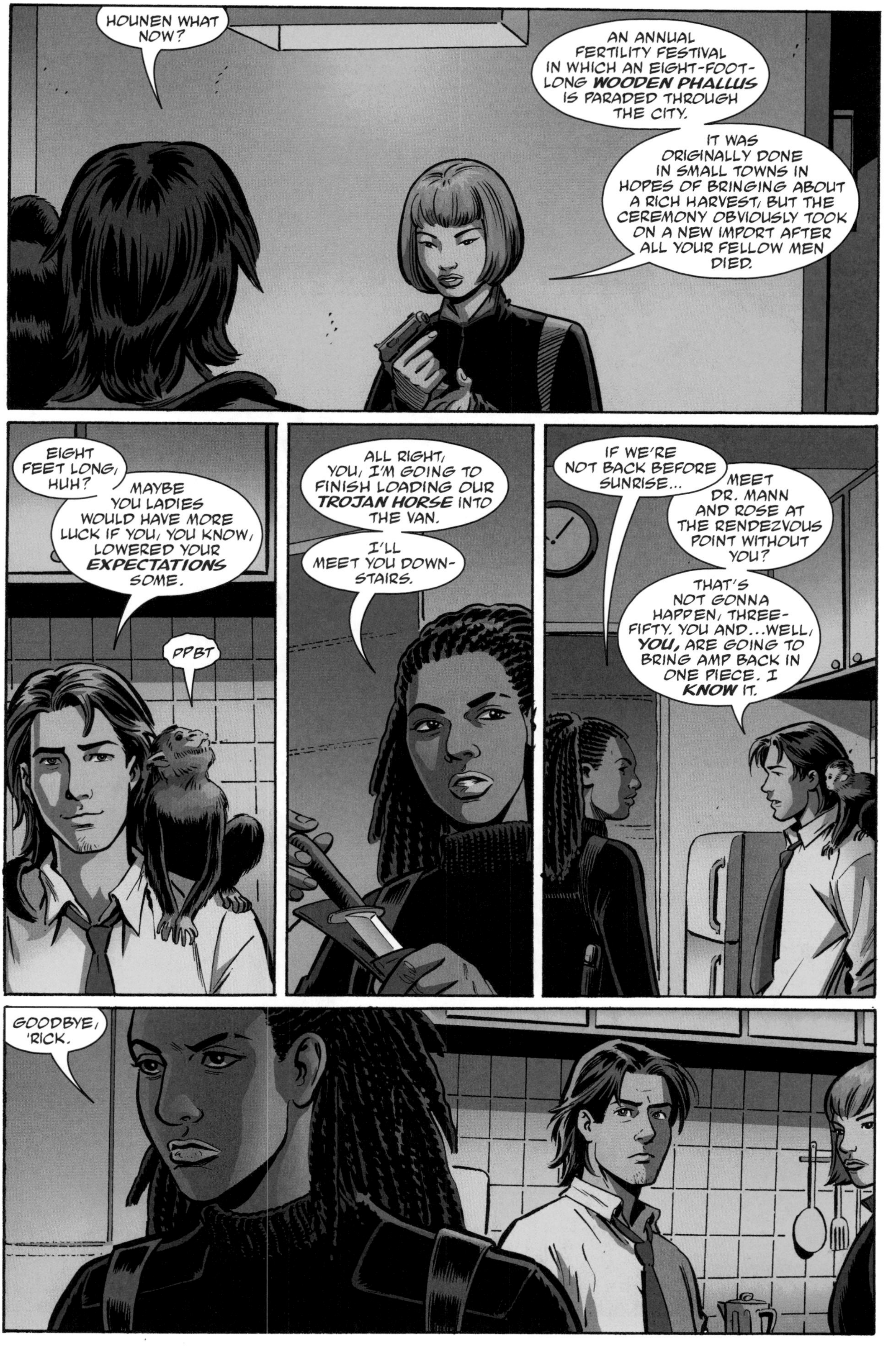
HOUNEN WHAT NOW?
AN ANNUAL FERTILITY FESTIVAL IN WHICH AN EIGHT-FOOT-LONG **WOODEN PHALLUS** IS PARADED THROUGH THE CITY.
IT WAS ORIGINALLY DONE IN SMALL TOWNS IN HOPES OF BRINGING ABOUT A RICH HARVEST, BUT THE CEREMONY OBVIOUSLY TOOK ON A NEW IMPORT AFTER ALL YOUR FELLOW MEN DIED.
EIGHT FEET LONG, HUH?
MAYBE YOU LADIES WOULD HAVE MORE LUCK IF YOU, YOU KNOW, LOWERED YOUR **EXPECTATIONS** SOME.
PPBT
ALL RIGHT, YOU, I'M GOING TO FINISH LOADING OUR **TROJAN HORSE** INTO THE VAN.
I'LL MEET YOU DOWN-STAIRS.
IF WE'RE NOT BACK BEFORE SUNRISE...
MEET DR. MANN AND ROSE AT THE RENDEZVOUS POINT WITHOUT YOU?
THAT'S NOT GONNA HAPPEN, THREE-FIFTY. YOU AND...WELL, **YOU,** ARE GOING TO BRING AMP BACK IN ONE PIECE. I **KNOW** IT.
GOODBYE, 'RICK.

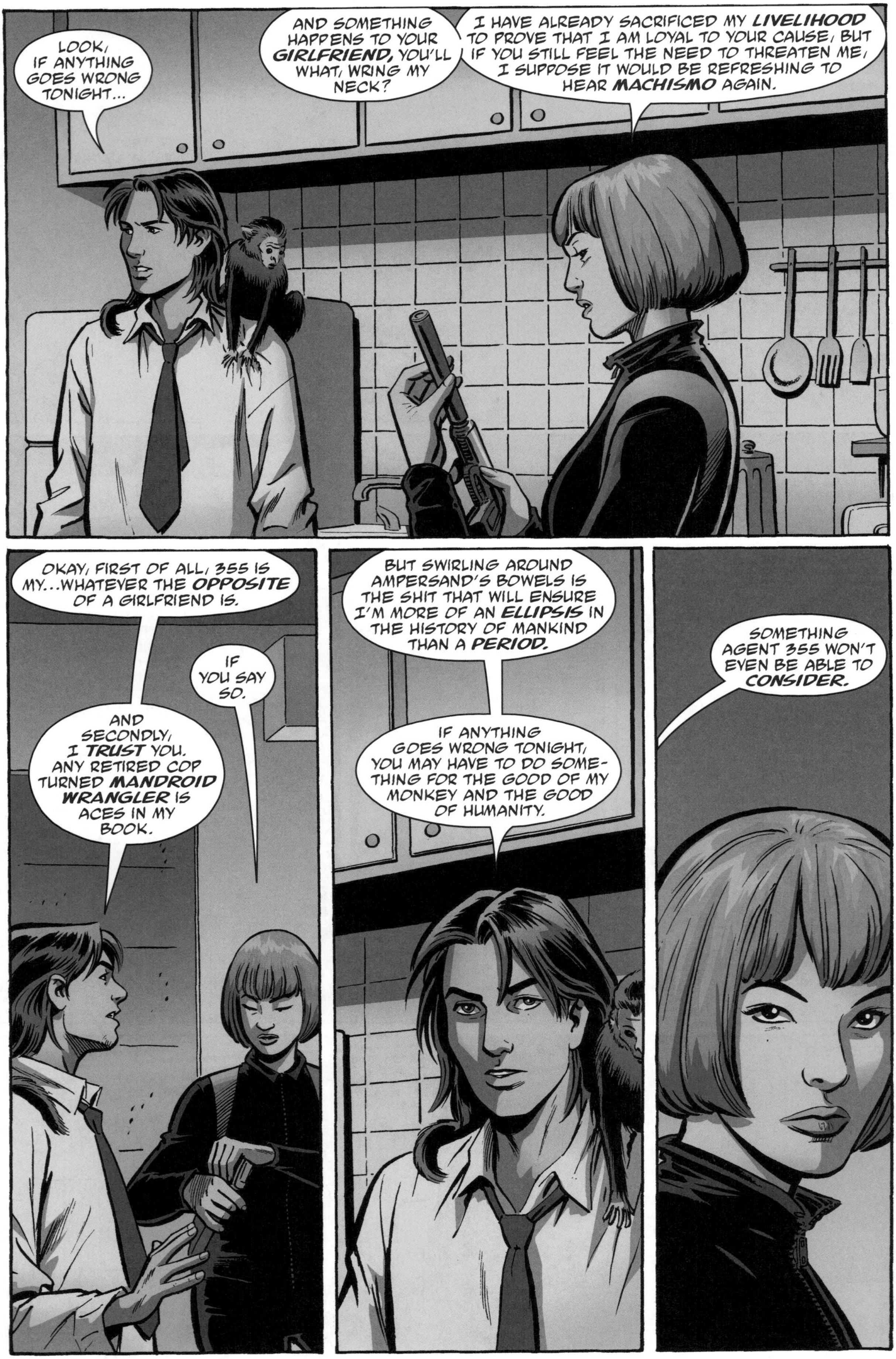
LOOK, IF ANYTHING GOES WRONG TONIGHT...
AND SOMETHING HAPPENS TO YOUR GIRLFRIEND, YOU'LL WHAT, WRING MY NECK?
I HAVE ALREADY SACRIFICED MY LIVELIHOOD TO PROVE THAT I AM LOYAL TO YOUR CAUSE, BUT IF YOU STILL FEEL THE NEED TO THREATEN ME, I SUPPOSE IT WOULD BE REFRESHING TO HEAR MACHISMO AGAIN.
OKAY, FIRST OF ALL, 355 IS MY...WHATEVER THE OPPOSITE OF A GIRLFRIEND IS.
AND SECONDLY, I TRUST YOU. ANY RETIRED COP TURNED MANDROID WRANGLER IS ACES IN MY BOOK.
IF YOU SAY SO.
BUT SWIRLING AROUND AMPERSAND'S BOWELS IS THE SHIT THAT WILL ENSURE I'M MORE OF AN ELLIPSIS IN THE HISTORY OF MANKIND THAN A PERIOD.
IF ANYTHING GOES WRONG TONIGHT, YOU MAY HAVE TO DO SOME-THING FOR THE GOOD OF MY MONKEY AND THE GOOD OF HUMANITY.
SOMETHING AGENT 355 WON'T EVEN BE ABLE TO CONSIDER.

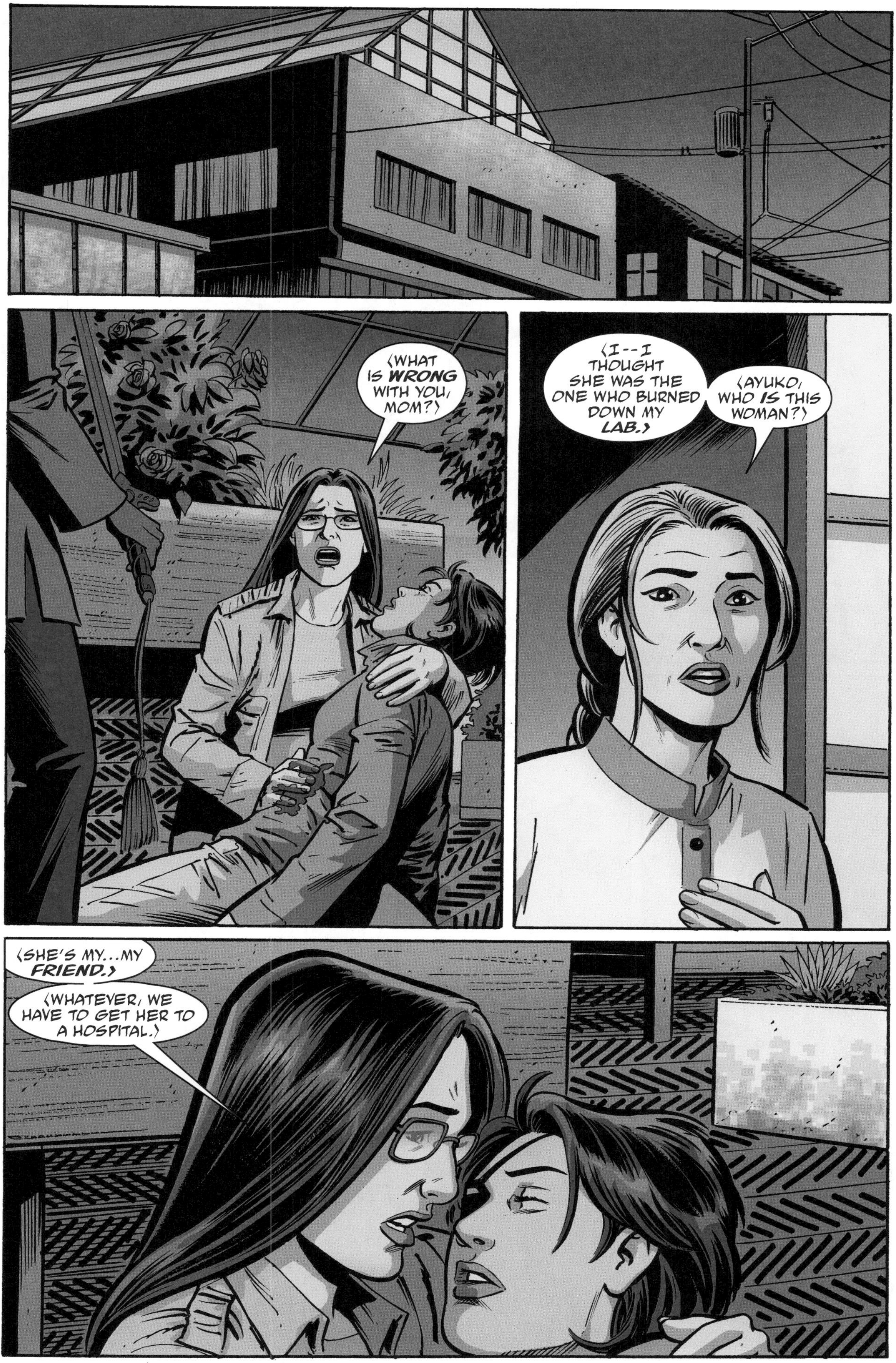
⟨WHAT IS **WRONG** WITH YOU, MOM?⟩
⟨I--I THOUGHT SHE WAS THE ONE WHO BURNED DOWN MY **LAB.**⟩
⟨AYUKO, WHO **IS** THIS WOMAN?⟩
⟨SHE'S MY...MY **FRIEND.**⟩
⟨WHATEVER, WE HAVE TO GET HER TO A HOSPITAL.⟩

⟨DON'T BE IDIOTIC, OUR HOSPITALS ARE ALL STAFFED BY GLORIFIED *CANDY STRIPERS.*⟩

⟨IF I WASN'T THE GREATEST SURGEON ALIVE *BEFORE* THE GENDERCIDE, I CERTAINLY AM *NOW.* WE'LL TAKE CARE OF THE WOMAN HERE, AYUKO.⟩

STOP CALLING ME THAT, GODDAMMIT! MY NAME IS ALLISON MANN.

⟨WHETHER YOU LIKE IT OR NOT, YOU ARE STILL A *MATSUMORI.* WE BOTH ARE.⟩

⟨AND YOU WILL SPEAK TO ME IN JAPANESE OR CHINESE, BUT IF YOU INSIST ON ENGLISH, THIS OPERATION IS GOING TO GO VERY, VERY SLOWLY. AM I UNDERSTOOD?⟩

SHI.

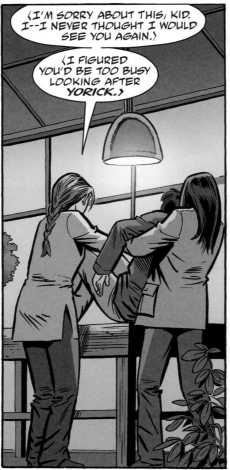

⟨I'M SORRY ABOUT THIS, KID. I--I NEVER THOUGHT I WOULD SEE YOU AGAIN.⟩

⟨I FIGURED YOU'D BE TOO BUSY LOOKING AFTER *YORICK.*⟩

...

WHAT DID YOU SAY?

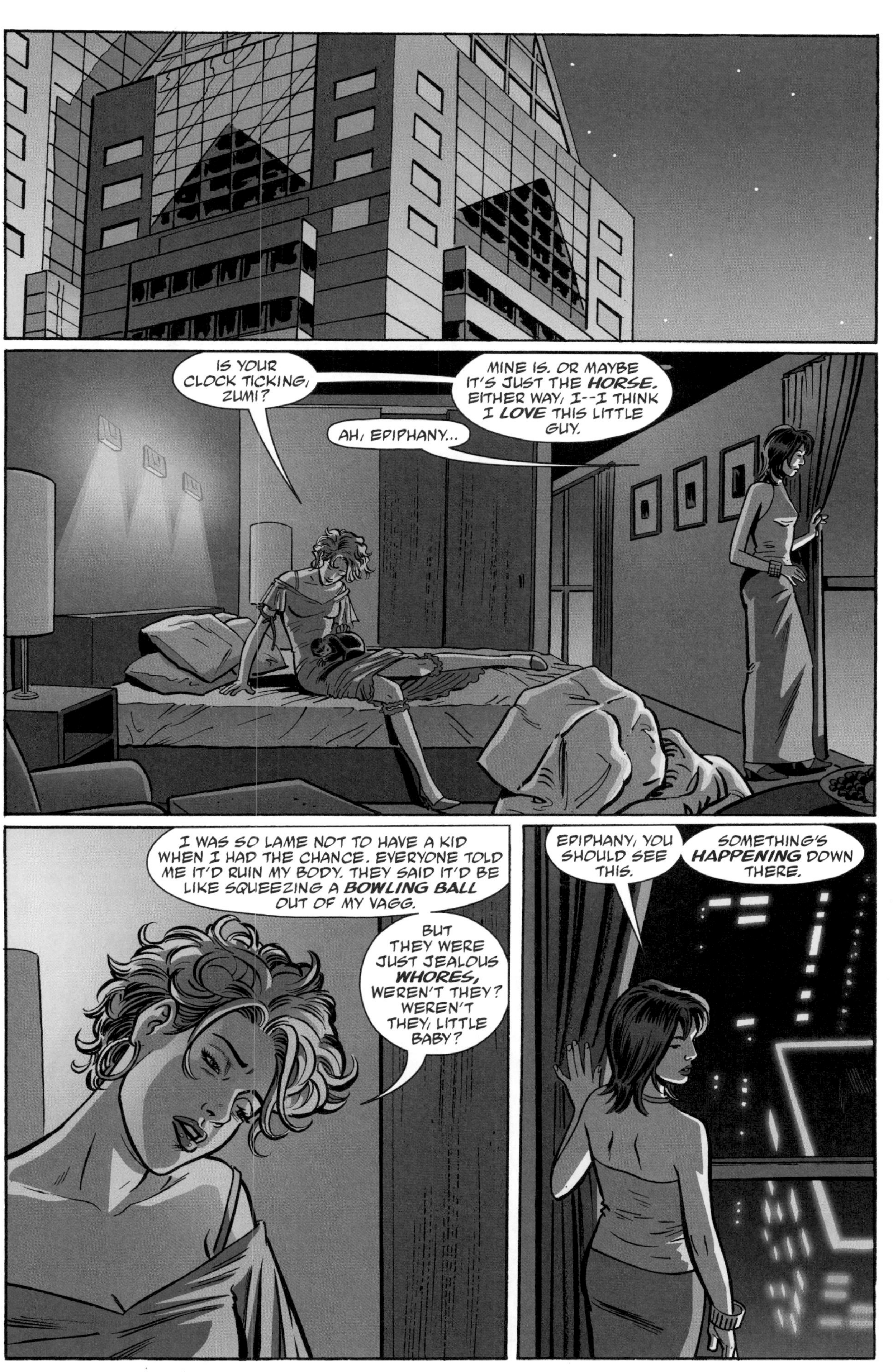
IS YOUR CLOCK TICKING, ZUMI?
MINE IS. OR MAYBE IT'S JUST THE HORSE. EITHER WAY, I--I THINK I LOVE THIS LITTLE GUY.
AH, EPIPHANY...
I WAS SO LAME NOT TO HAVE A KID WHEN I HAD THE CHANCE. EVERYONE TOLD ME IT'D RUIN MY BODY. THEY SAID IT'D BE LIKE SQUEEZING A BOWLING BALL OUT OF MY VAGG.
BUT THEY WERE JUST JEALOUS WHORES, WEREN'T THEY? WEREN'T THEY, LITTLE BABY?
EPIPHANY, YOU SHOULD SEE THIS.
SOMETHING'S HAPPENING DOWN THERE.

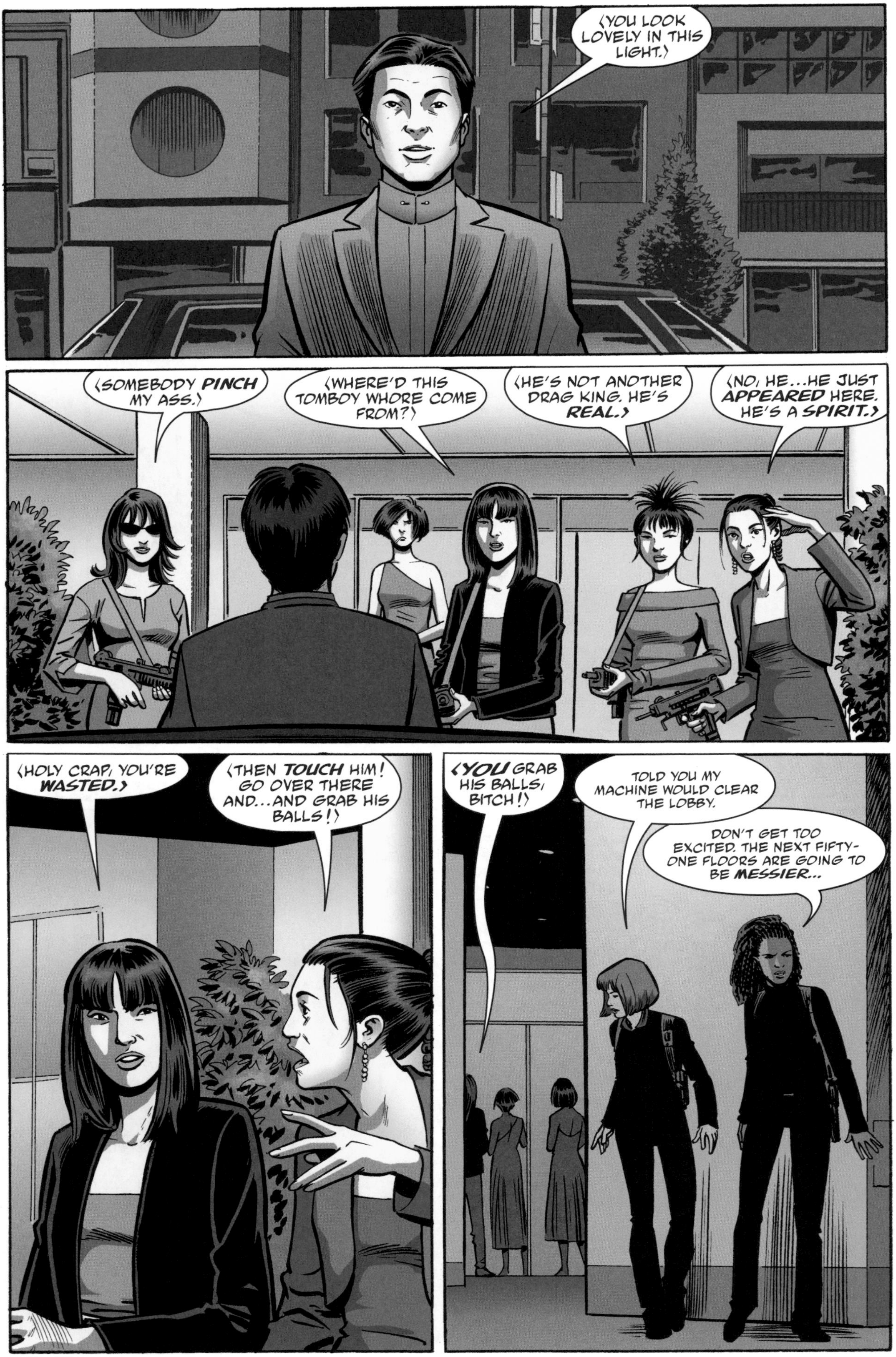
‹YOU LOOK LOVELY IN THIS LIGHT.›
‹SOMEBODY PINCH MY ASS.›
‹WHERE'D THIS TOMBOY WHORE COME FROM?›
‹HE'S NOT ANOTHER DRAG KING. HE'S REAL.›
‹NO, HE...HE JUST APPEARED HERE. HE'S A SPIRIT.›
‹HOLY CRAP, YOU'RE WASTED.›
‹THEN TOUCH HIM! GO OVER THERE AND...AND GRAB HIS BALLS!›
‹YOU GRAB HIS BALLS, BITCH!›
TOLD YOU MY MACHINE WOULD CLEAR THE LOBBY.
DON'T GET TOO EXCITED. THE NEXT FIFTY-ONE FLOORS ARE GOING TO BE MESSIER...

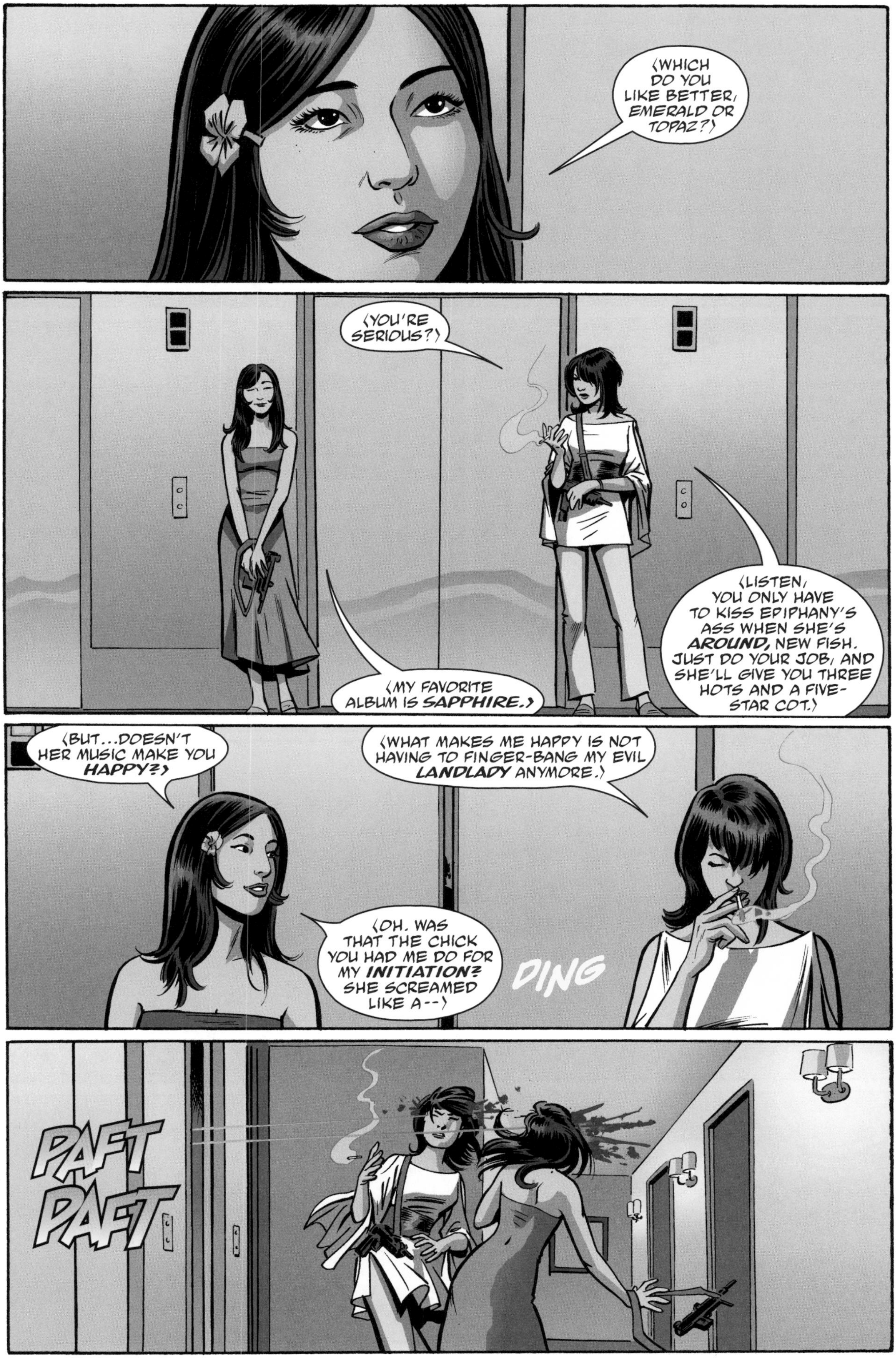
‹WHICH DO YOU LIKE BETTER, EMERALD OR TOPAZ?›
‹YOU'RE SERIOUS?›
‹MY FAVORITE ALBUM IS SAPPHIRE.›
‹LISTEN, YOU ONLY HAVE TO KISS EPIPHANY'S ASS WHEN SHE'S AROUND, NEW FISH. JUST DO YOUR JOB, AND SHE'LL GIVE YOU THREE HOTS AND A FIVE-STAR COT.›
‹BUT...DOESN'T HER MUSIC MAKE YOU HAPPY?›
‹WHAT MAKES ME HAPPY IS NOT HAVING TO FINGER-BANG MY EVIL LANDLADY ANYMORE.›
‹OH. WAS THAT THE CHICK YOU HAD ME DO FOR MY INITIATION? SHE SCREAMED LIKE A--›
DING
PAFT
PAFT

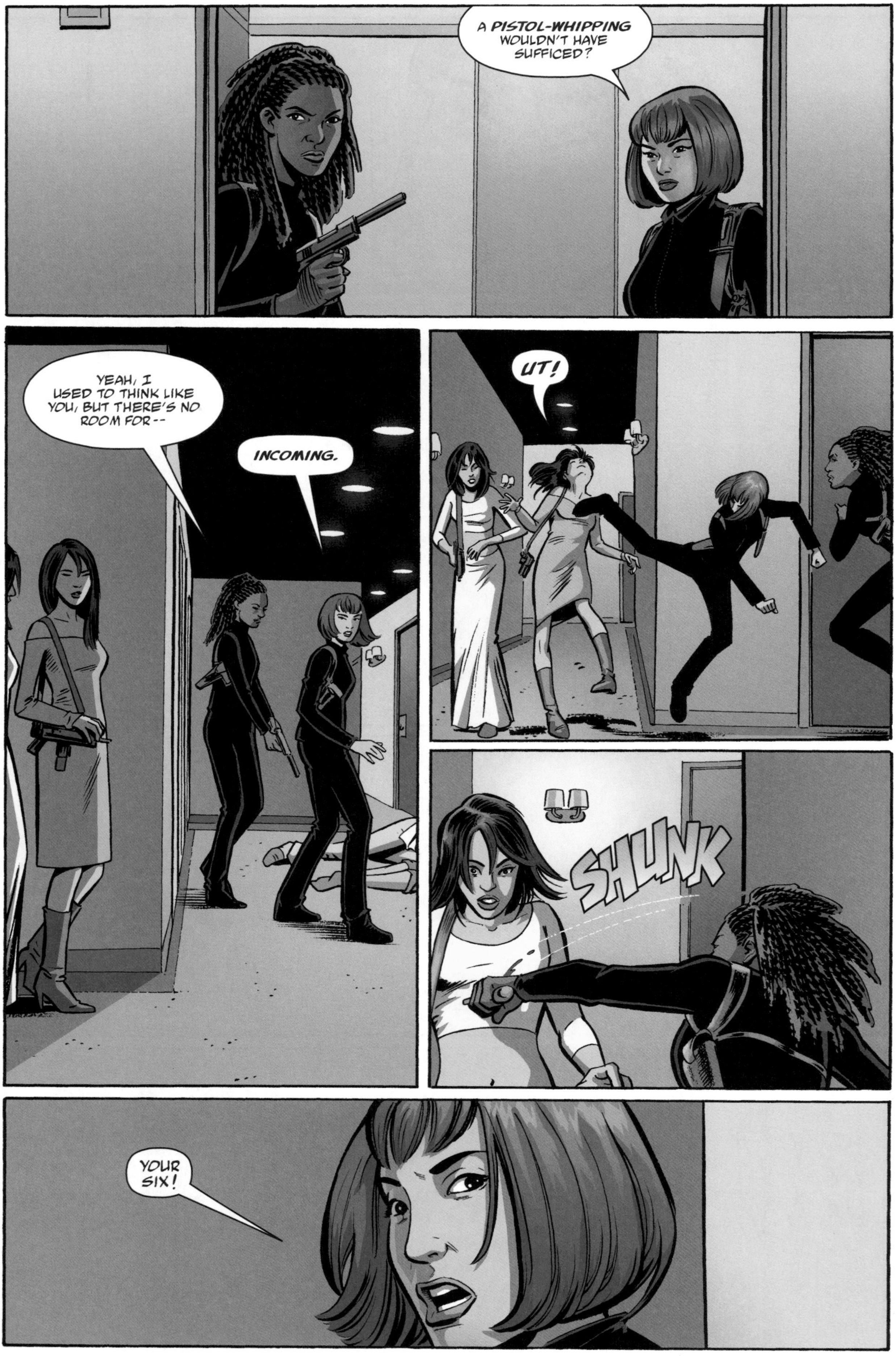

A PISTOL-WHIPPING WOULDN'T HAVE SUFFICED?
YEAH, I USED TO THINK LIKE YOU, BUT THERE'S NO ROOM FOR--
INCOMING.
UT!
SHUNK
YOUR SIX!

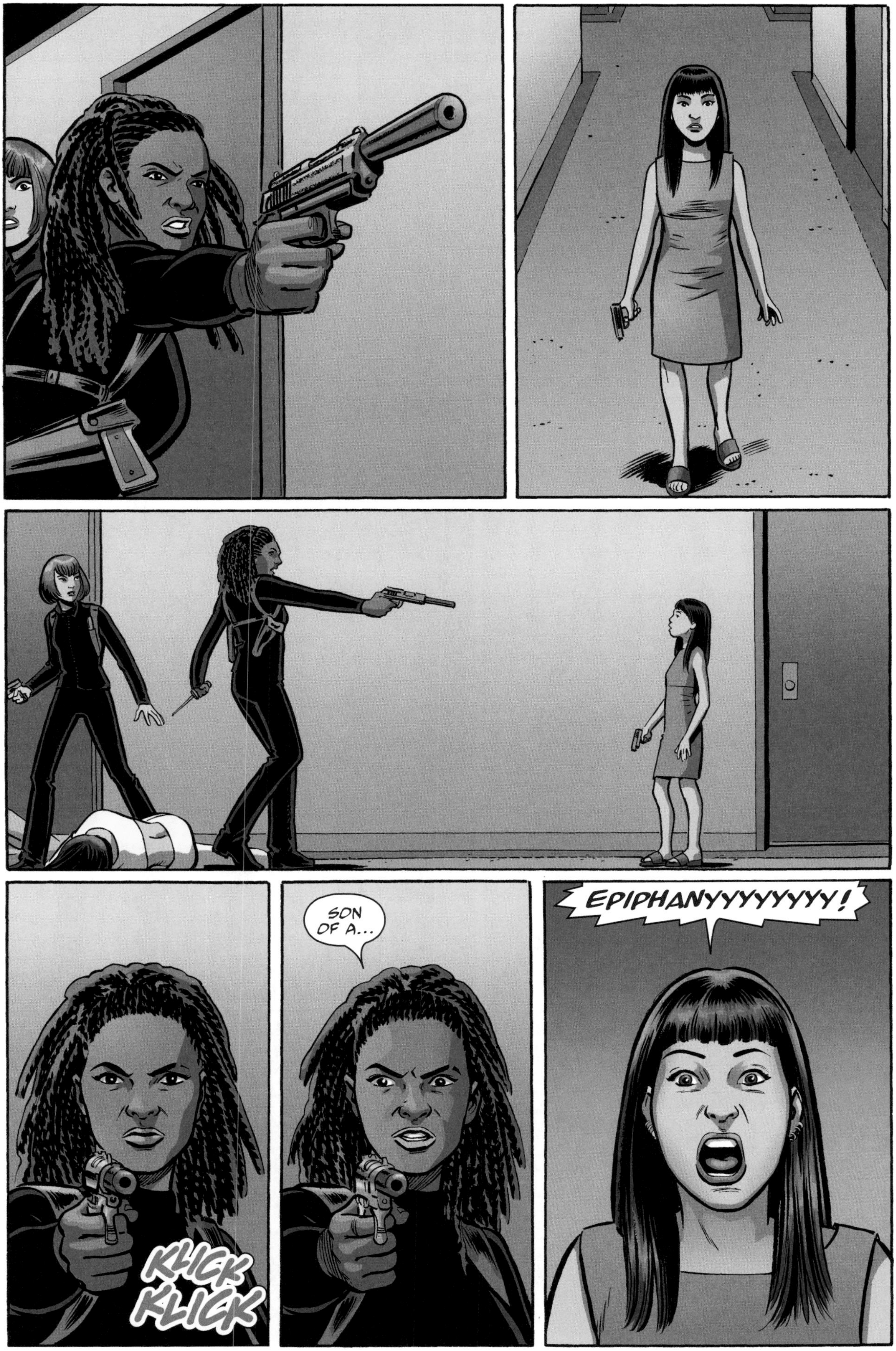
SON OF A...
EPIPHANYYYYYYYY!
KLICK KLICK

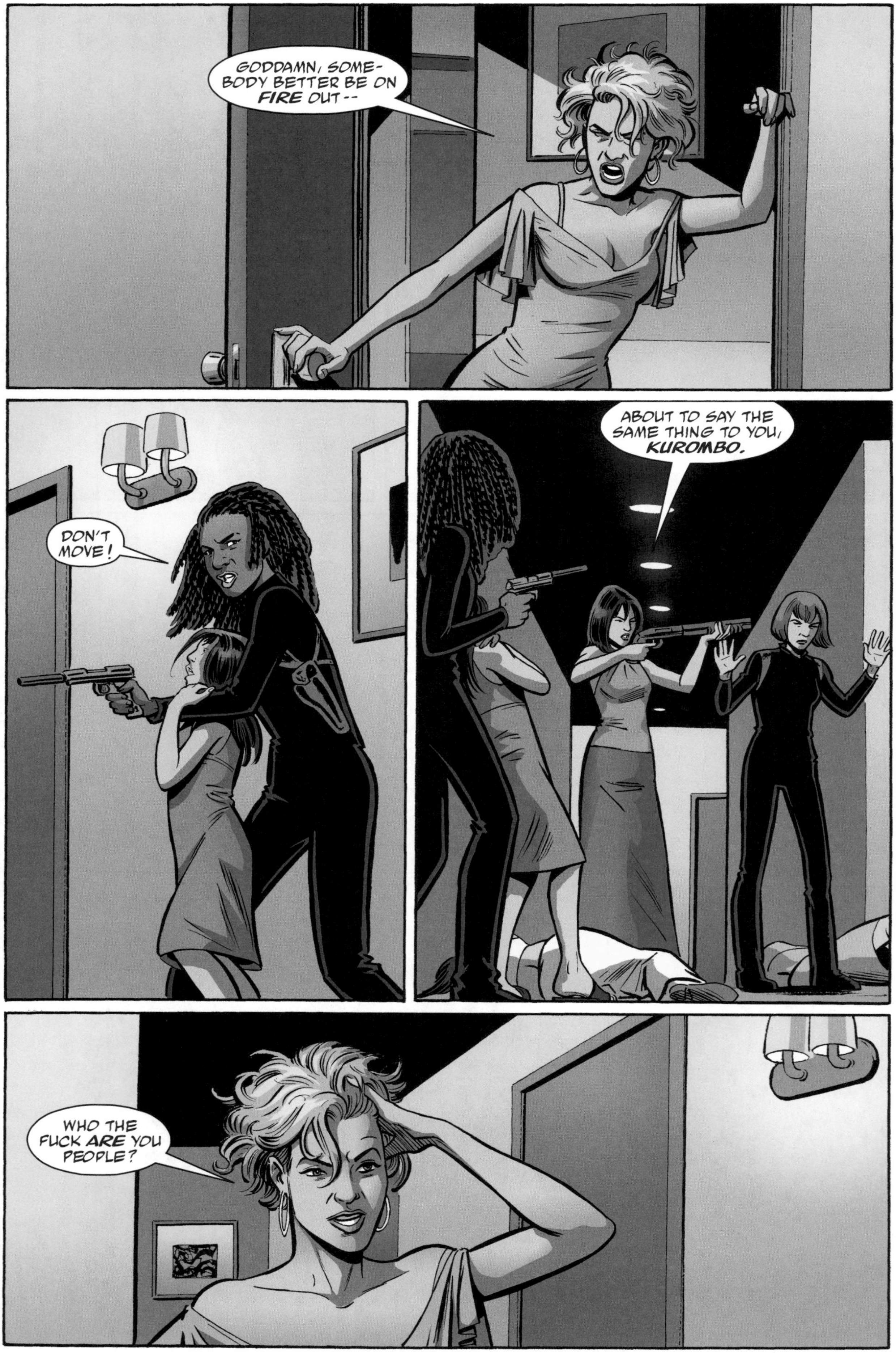
GODDAMN, SOME-BODY BETTER BE ON FIRE OUT--
DON'T MOVE!
ABOUT TO SAY THE SAME THING TO YOU, KUROMBO.
WHO THE FUCK ARE YOU PEOPLE?

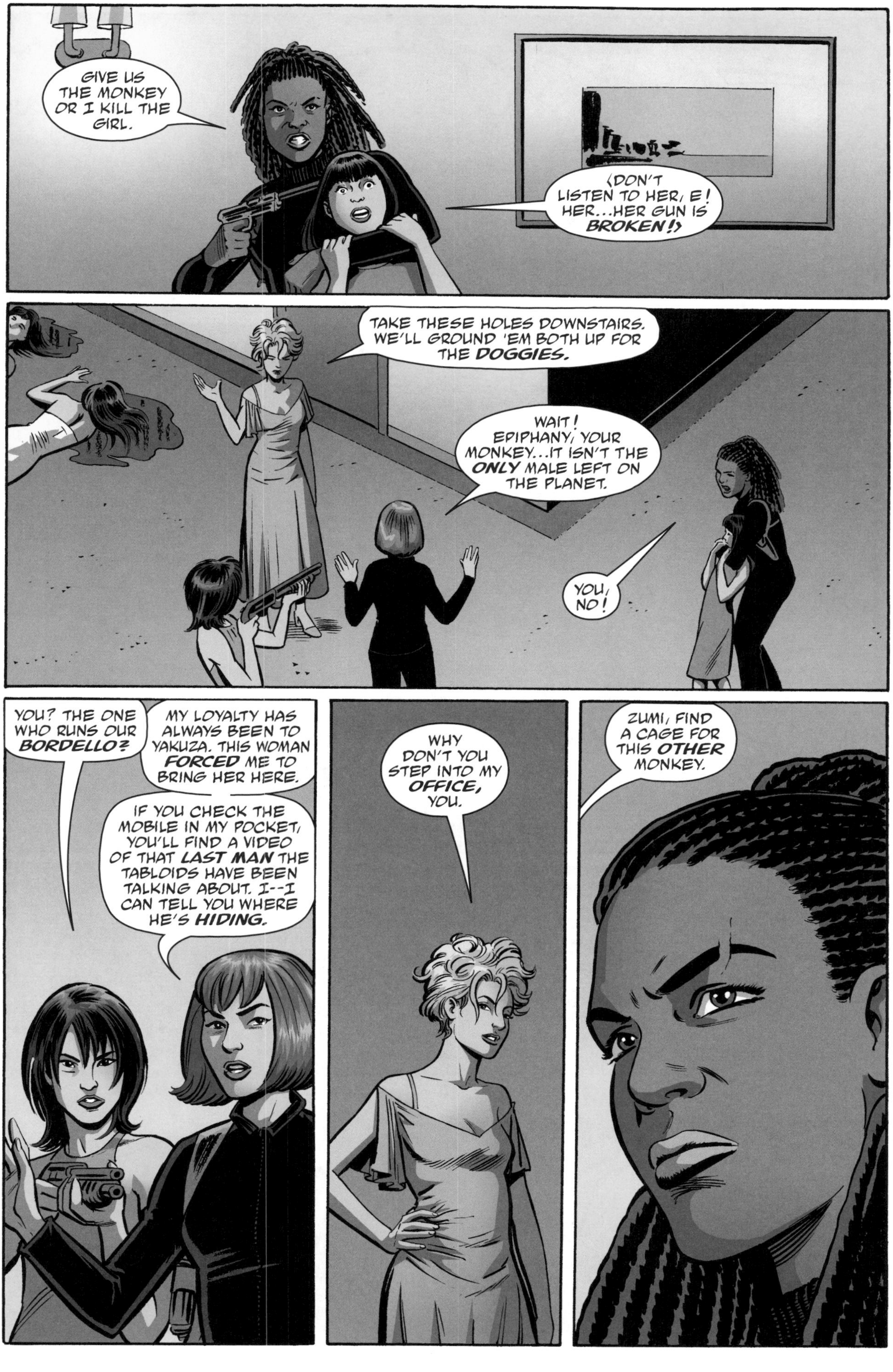
GIVE US THE MONKEY OR I KILL THE GIRL.
‹DON'T LISTEN TO HER, E! HER...HER GUN IS BROKEN!›
TAKE THESE HOLES DOWNSTAIRS. WE'LL GROUND 'EM BOTH UP FOR THE DOGGIES.
WAIT! EPIPHANY, YOUR MONKEY...IT ISN'T THE ONLY MALE LEFT ON THE PLANET.
YOU, NO!
YOU? THE ONE WHO RUNS OUR BORDELLO?
MY LOYALTY HAS ALWAYS BEEN TO YAKUZA. THIS WOMAN FORCED ME TO BRING HER HERE.
IF YOU CHECK THE MOBILE IN MY POCKET, YOU'LL FIND A VIDEO OF THAT LAST MAN THE TABLOIDS HAVE BEEN TALKING ABOUT. I--I CAN TELL YOU WHERE HE'S HIDING.
WHY DON'T YOU STEP INTO MY OFFICE, YOU.
ZUMI, FIND A CAGE FOR THIS OTHER MONKEY.

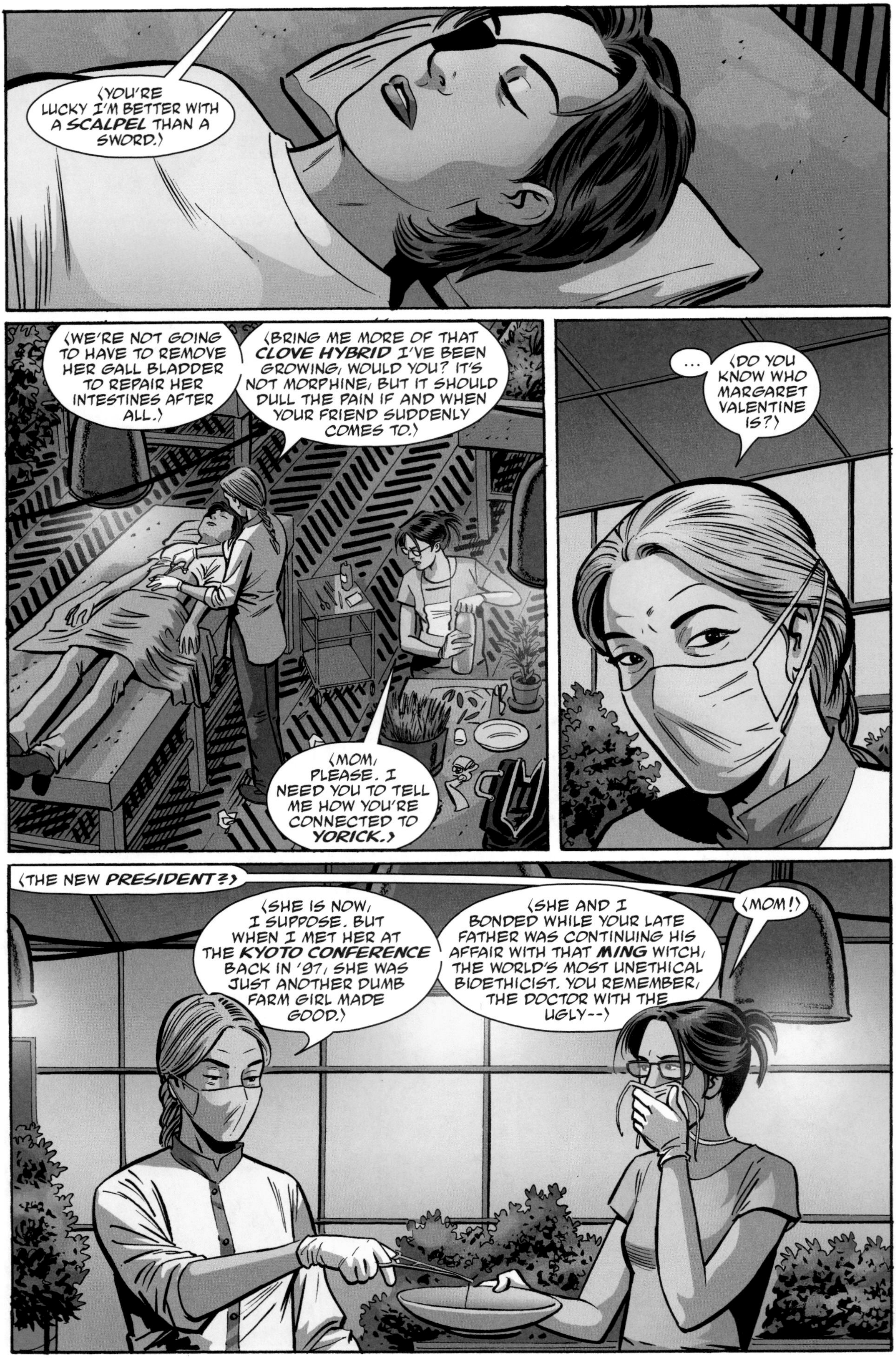

‹YOU'RE LUCKY I'M BETTER WITH A SCALPEL THAN A SWORD.›
‹WE'RE NOT GOING TO HAVE TO REMOVE HER GALL BLADDER TO REPAIR HER INTESTINES AFTER ALL.›
‹BRING ME MORE OF THAT CLOVE HYBRID I'VE BEEN GROWING, WOULD YOU? IT'S NOT MORPHINE, BUT IT SHOULD DULL THE PAIN IF AND WHEN YOUR FRIEND SUDDENLY COMES TO.›
‹MOM, PLEASE. I NEED YOU TO TELL ME HOW YOU'RE CONNECTED TO YORICK.›
...
‹DO YOU KNOW WHO MARGARET VALENTINE IS?›
‹THE NEW PRESIDENT?›
‹SHE IS NOW, I SUPPOSE. BUT WHEN I MET HER AT THE KYOTO CONFERENCE BACK IN '97, SHE WAS JUST ANOTHER DUMB FARM GIRL MADE GOOD.›
‹SHE AND I BONDED WHILE YOUR LATE FATHER WAS CONTINUING HIS AFFAIR WITH THAT MING WITCH, THE WORLD'S MOST UNETHICAL BIOETHICIST. YOU REMEMBER, THE DOCTOR WITH THE UGLY--›
‹MOM!›

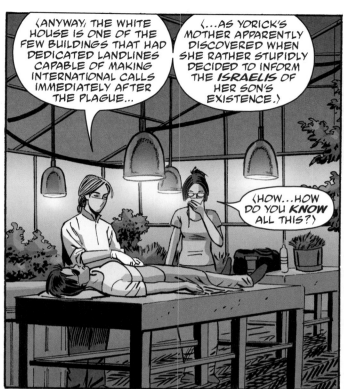

⟨ANYWAY, THE WHITE HOUSE IS ONE OF THE FEW BUILDINGS THAT HAD DEDICATED LANDLINES CAPABLE OF MAKING INTERNATIONAL CALLS IMMEDIATELY AFTER THE PLAGUE...⟩

⟨...AS YORICK'S MOTHER APPARENTLY DISCOVERED WHEN SHE RATHER STUPIDLY DECIDED TO INFORM THE *ISRAELIS* OF HER SON'S EXISTENCE.⟩

⟨HOW...HOW DO YOU *KNOW* ALL THIS?⟩

⟨BECAUSE MARGARET VALENTINE USED THOSE SAME LINES TO CALL *JAPAN* NEARLY EVERY WEEK SINCE SHE GOT BEATEN WITH THE CHAIN OF SUCCESSION.⟩

⟨WHEN SHE DISCOVERED THE LAST LIVING MAN AND HIS PET AT HER DOORSTEP, THE PRESIDENT TURNED TO ONE OF THE FEW PEOPLE SHE TRUSTED FOR IMPARTIAL GUIDANCE... *ME.*⟩

⟨I TOLD HER THAT THIS MALE HAD TO BE EXAMINED BY THE FINEST SCIENTIFIC MIND IN THE COUNTRY, AND THANKFULLY, YOUR NAME HAD ALREADY BEEN FLOATED WHEN CONGRESS WAS LOOKING FOR HELP CLONING *GIRLS.*⟩

⟨I TOLD VALENTINE THAT IF YORICK HAD ANY CHANCE OF SURVIVAL, SHE NEEDED TO CONVINCE THE BOY'S MOTHER THAT HER SON, THE NATION'S MOST VALUABLE RESOURCE, BELONGED IN BOSTON WITH *YOU.*⟩

⟨THAT...THAT WAS *YOUR* DOING? *YOU* SENT YORICK TO ME?⟩

⟨I'M SURE I'VE MADE YOUR LIVES MISERABLE FOR THE LAST THREE YEARS, BUT I DID IT FOR THE *MONKEY,* NOT THE BOY.⟩

⟨IT WAS CRUCIAL THAT I GET THIS "AMPERSAND" TO YOU...⟩

⟨...BUT IT WAS EVEN MORE IMPORTANT THAT I KEEP HIM AWAY FROM *SOMEONE ELSE.*⟩

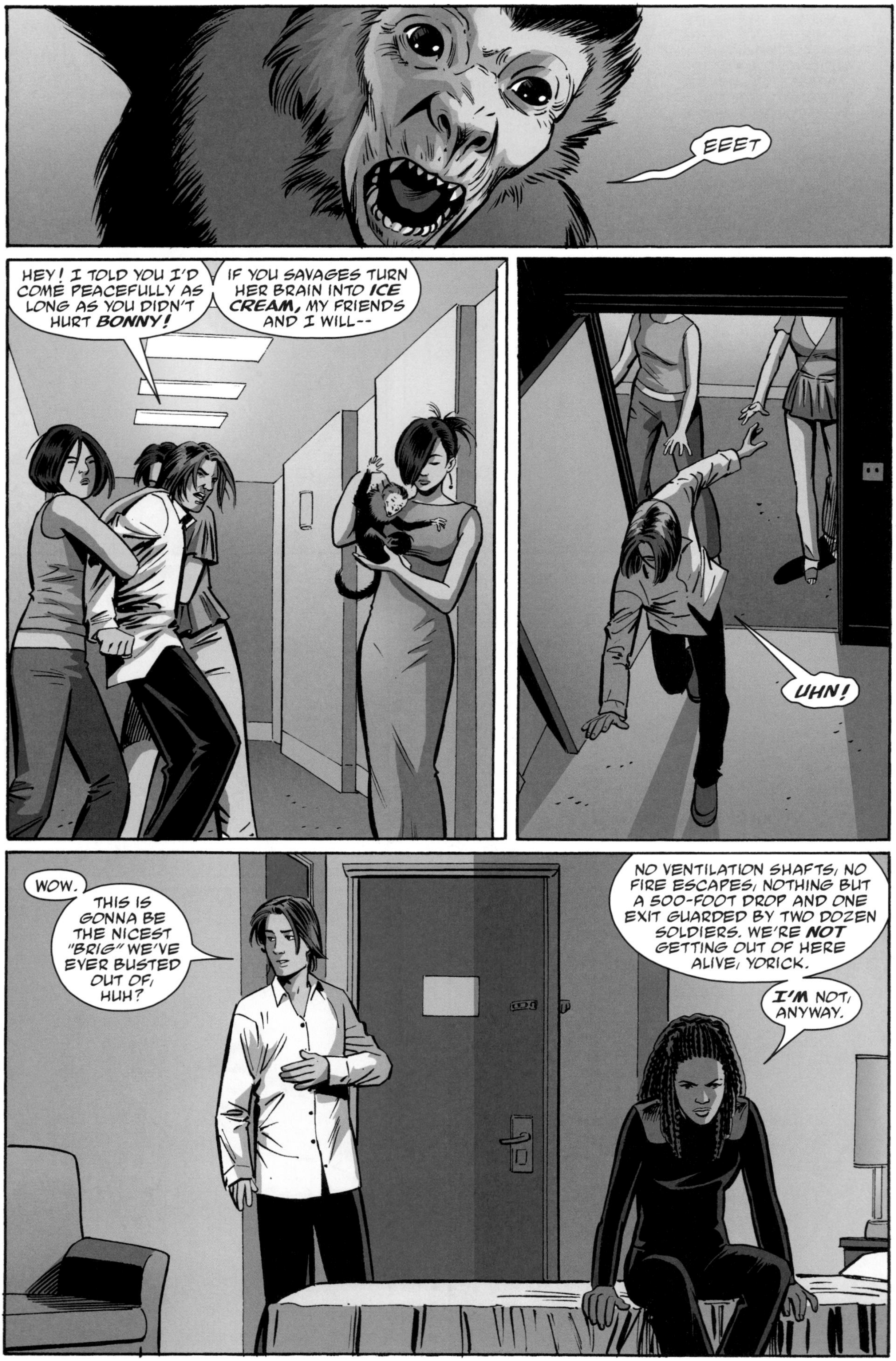
EEET
HEY! I TOLD YOU I'D COME PEACEFULLY AS LONG AS YOU DIDN'T HURT BONNY!
IF YOU SAVAGES TURN HER BRAIN INTO ICE CREAM, MY FRIENDS AND I WILL--
UHN!
WOW.
THIS IS GONNA BE THE NICEST "BRIG" WE'VE EVER BUSTED OUT OF, HUH?
NO VENTILATION SHAFTS, NO FIRE ESCAPES, NOTHING BUT A 500-FOOT DROP AND ONE EXIT GUARDED BY TWO DOZEN SOLDIERS. WE'RE NOT GETTING OUT OF HERE ALIVE, YORICK.
I'M NOT, ANYWAY.

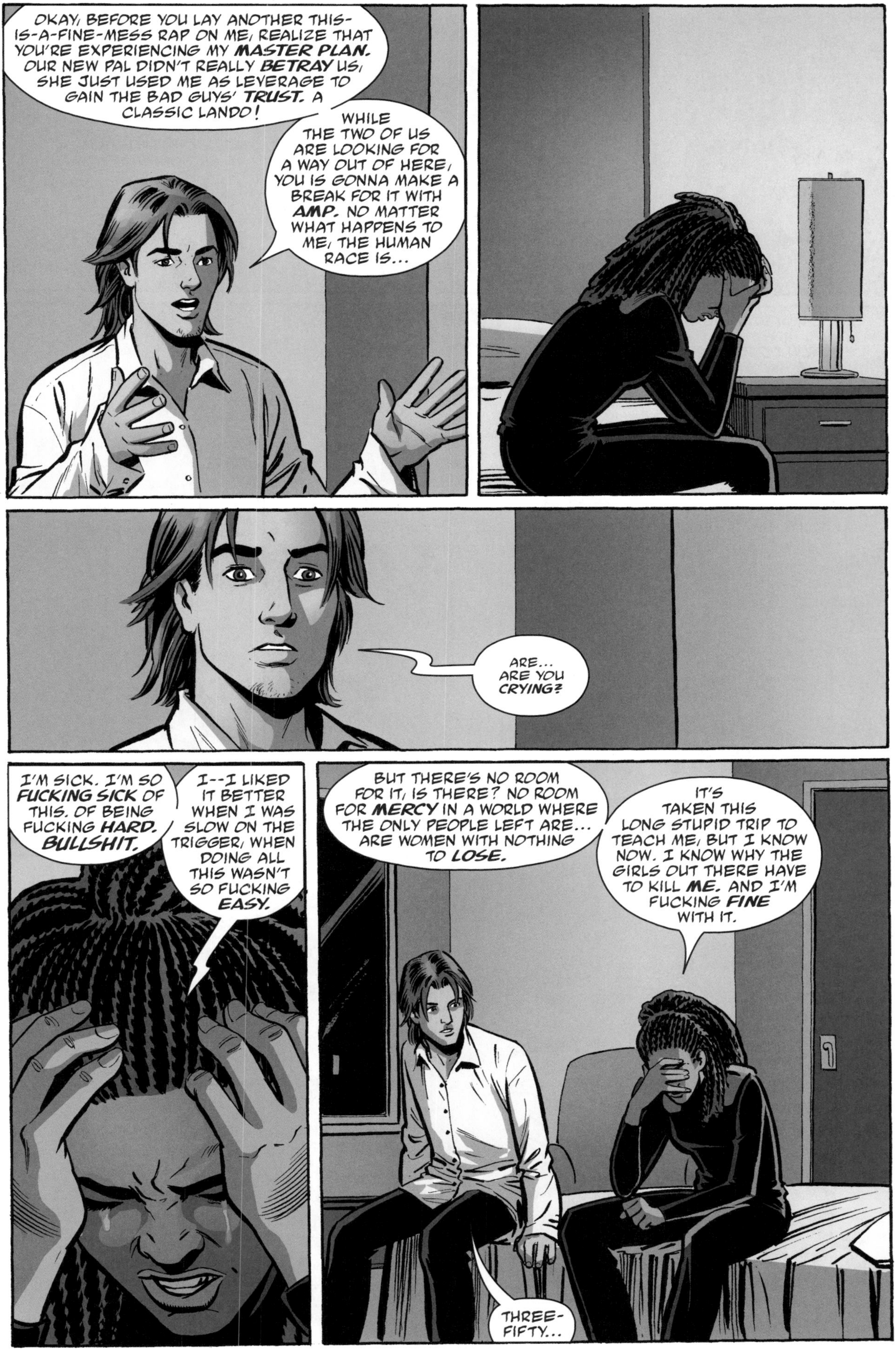
OKAY, BEFORE YOU LAY ANOTHER THIS-IS-A-FINE-MESS RAP ON ME, REALIZE THAT YOU'RE EXPERIENCING MY MASTER PLAN. OUR NEW PAL DIDN'T REALLY BETRAY US, SHE JUST USED ME AS LEVERAGE TO GAIN THE BAD GUYS' TRUST. A CLASSIC LANDO!
WHILE THE TWO OF US ARE LOOKING FOR A WAY OUT OF HERE, YOU IS GONNA MAKE A BREAK FOR IT WITH AMP. NO MATTER WHAT HAPPENS TO ME, THE HUMAN RACE IS...
ARE... ARE YOU CRYING?
I'M SICK. I'M SO FUCKING SICK OF THIS. OF BEING FUCKING HARD. BULLSHIT.
I--I LIKED IT BETTER WHEN I WAS SLOW ON THE TRIGGER, WHEN DOING ALL THIS WASN'T SO FUCKING EASY.
BUT THERE'S NO ROOM FOR IT, IS THERE? NO ROOM FOR MERCY IN A WORLD WHERE THE ONLY PEOPLE LEFT ARE... ARE WOMEN WITH NOTHING TO LOSE.
IT'S TAKEN THIS LONG STUPID TRIP TO TEACH ME, BUT I KNOW NOW. I KNOW WHY THE GIRLS OUT THERE HAVE TO KILL ME. AND I'M FUCKING FINE WITH IT.
THREE-FIFTY...

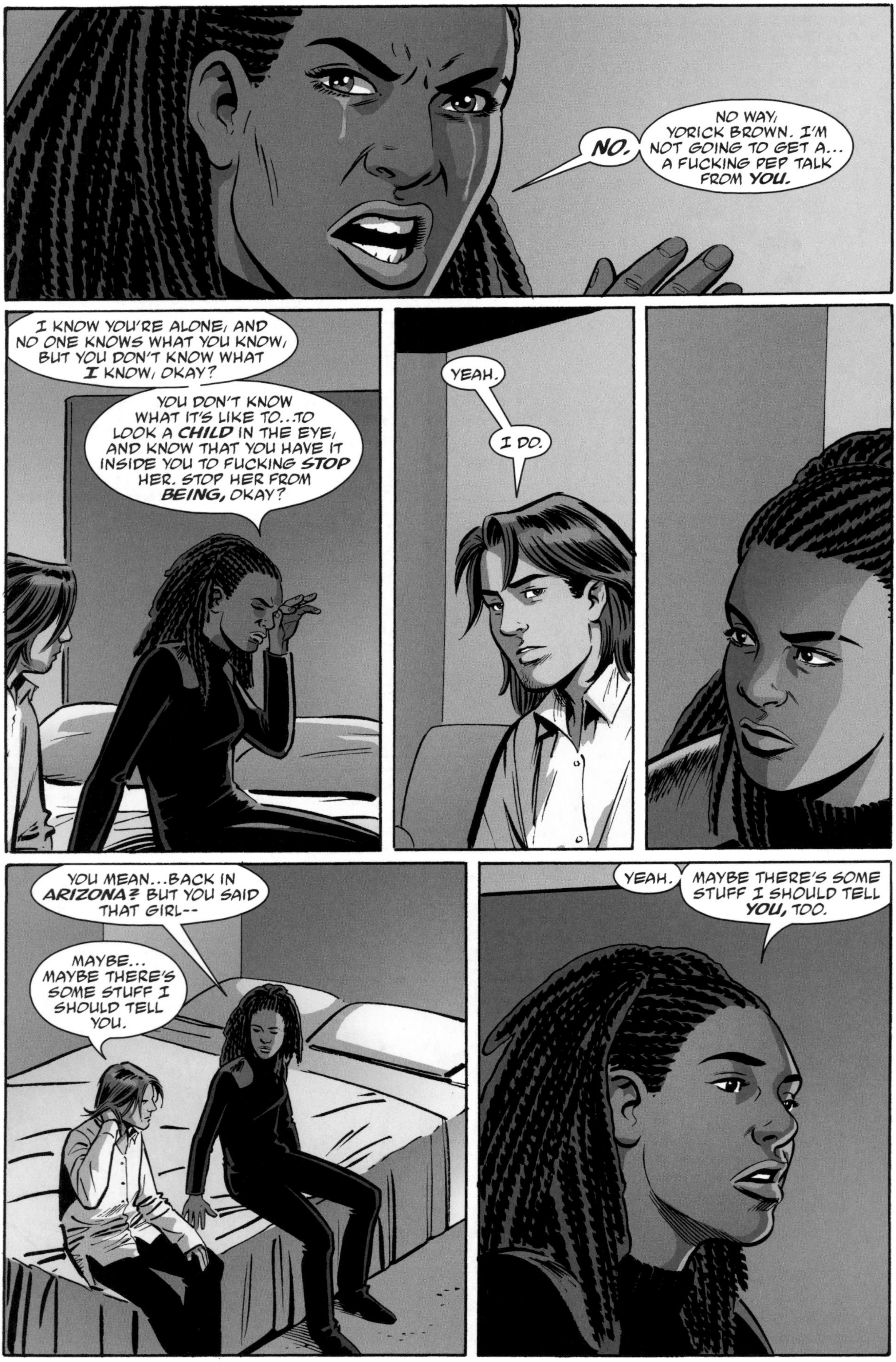
NO.
NO WAY, YORICK BROWN. I'M NOT GOING TO GET A... A FUCKING PEP TALK FROM YOU.
I KNOW YOU'RE ALONE, AND NO ONE KNOWS WHAT YOU KNOW, BUT YOU DON'T KNOW WHAT I KNOW, OKAY?
YOU DON'T KNOW WHAT IT'S LIKE TO...TO LOOK A CHILD IN THE EYE, AND KNOW THAT YOU HAVE IT INSIDE YOU TO FUCKING STOP HER. STOP HER FROM BEING, OKAY?
YEAH.
I DO.
YOU MEAN...BACK IN ARIZONA? BUT YOU SAID THAT GIRL--
MAYBE... MAYBE THERE'S SOME STUFF I SHOULD TELL YOU.
YEAH.
MAYBE THERE'S SOME STUFF I SHOULD TELL YOU, TOO.

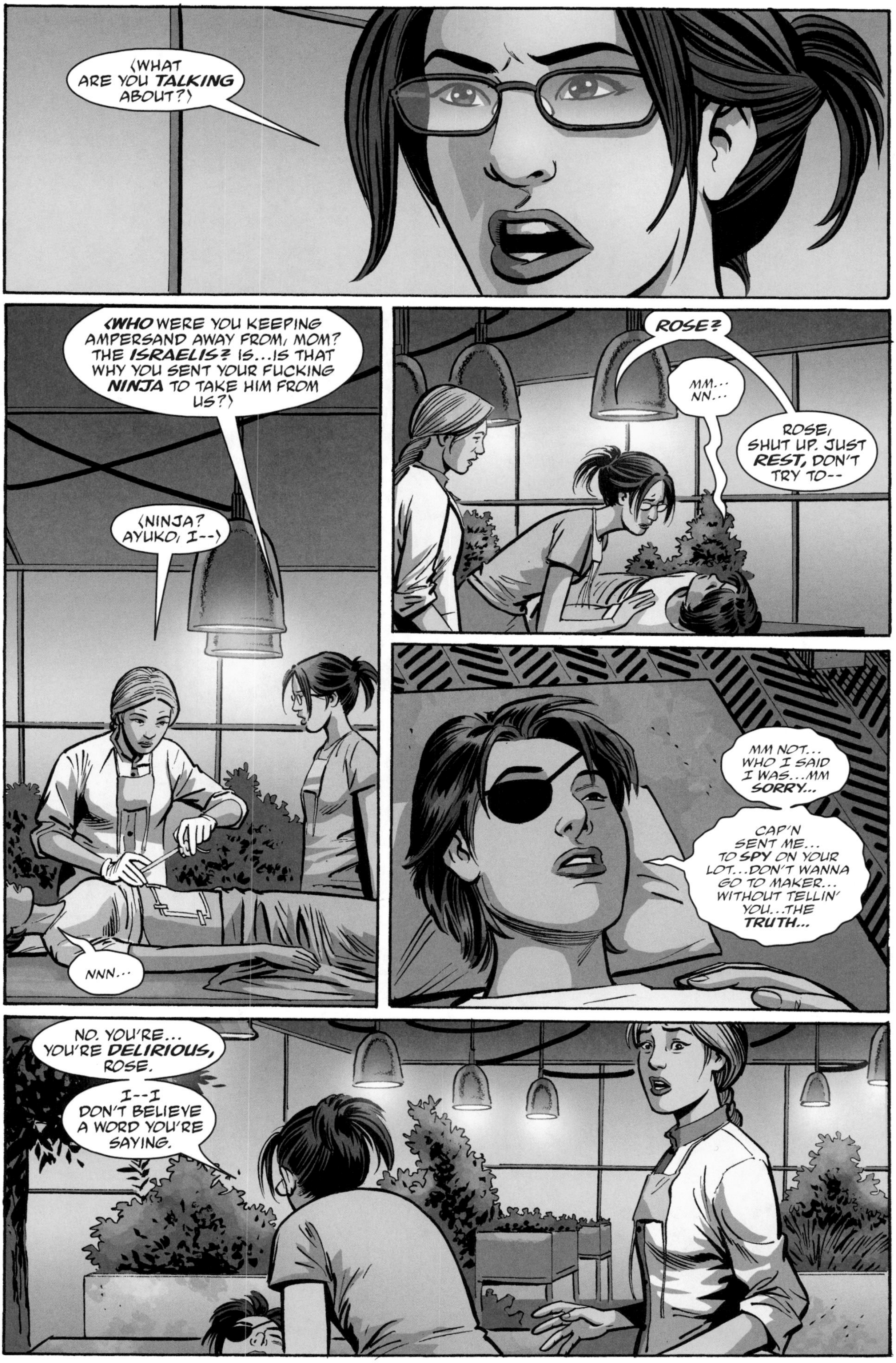
‹WHAT ARE YOU TALKING ABOUT?›
‹WHO WERE YOU KEEPING AMPERSAND AWAY FROM, MOM? THE ISRAELIS? IS...IS THAT WHY YOU SENT YOUR FUCKING NINJA TO TAKE HIM FROM US?›
‹NINJA? AYUKO, I--›
NNN...
ROSE?
MM... NN...
ROSE, SHUT UP. JUST REST, DON'T TRY TO--
MM NOT... WHO I SAID I WAS...MM SORRY...
CAP'N SENT ME... TO SPY ON YOUR LOT...DON'T WANNA GO TO MAKER... WITHOUT TELLIN' YOU...THE TRUTH...
NO. YOU'RE... YOU'RE DELIRIOUS, ROSE.
I--I DON'T BELIEVE A WORD YOU'RE SAYING.

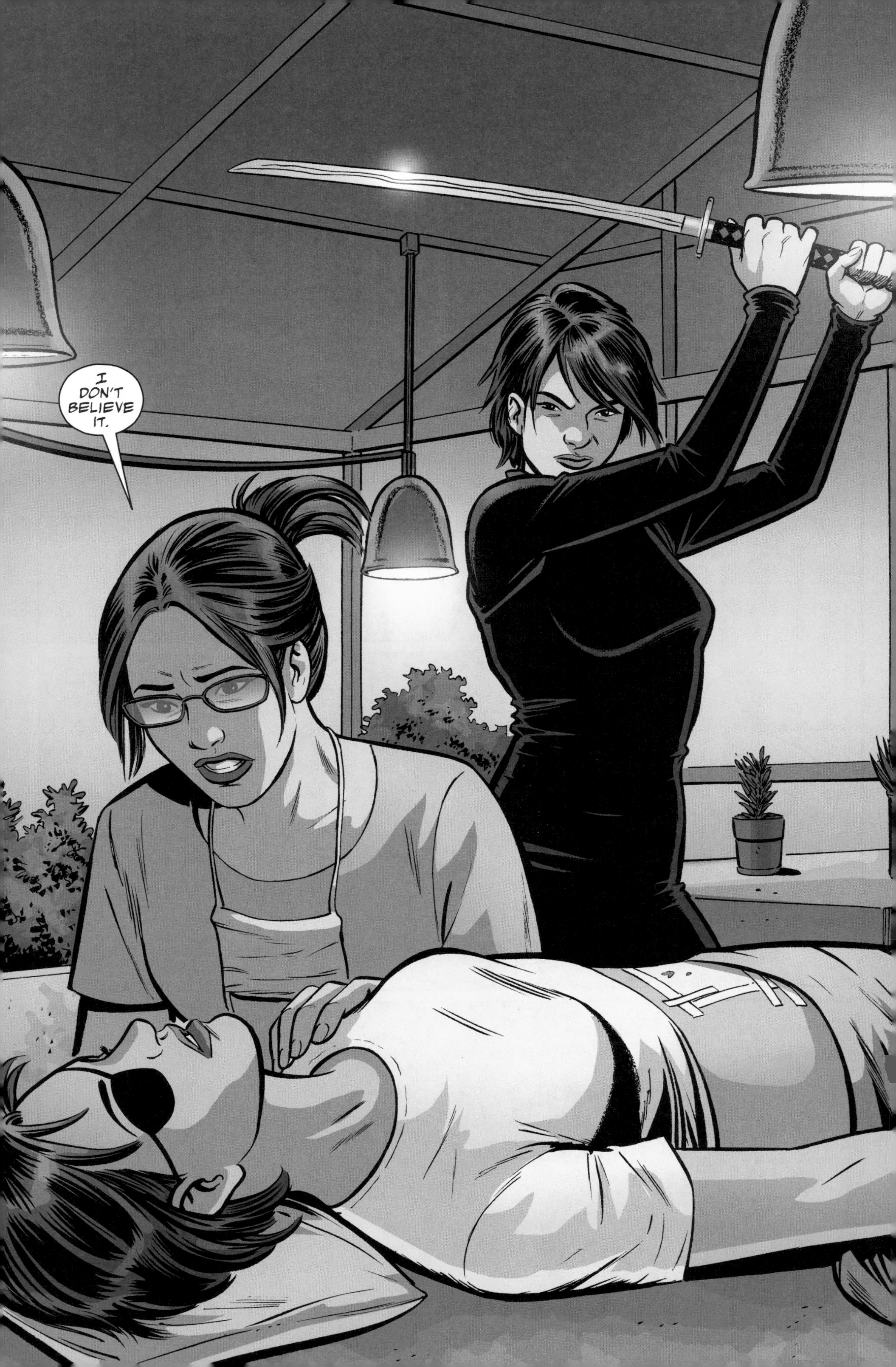
I DON'T BELIEVE IT.

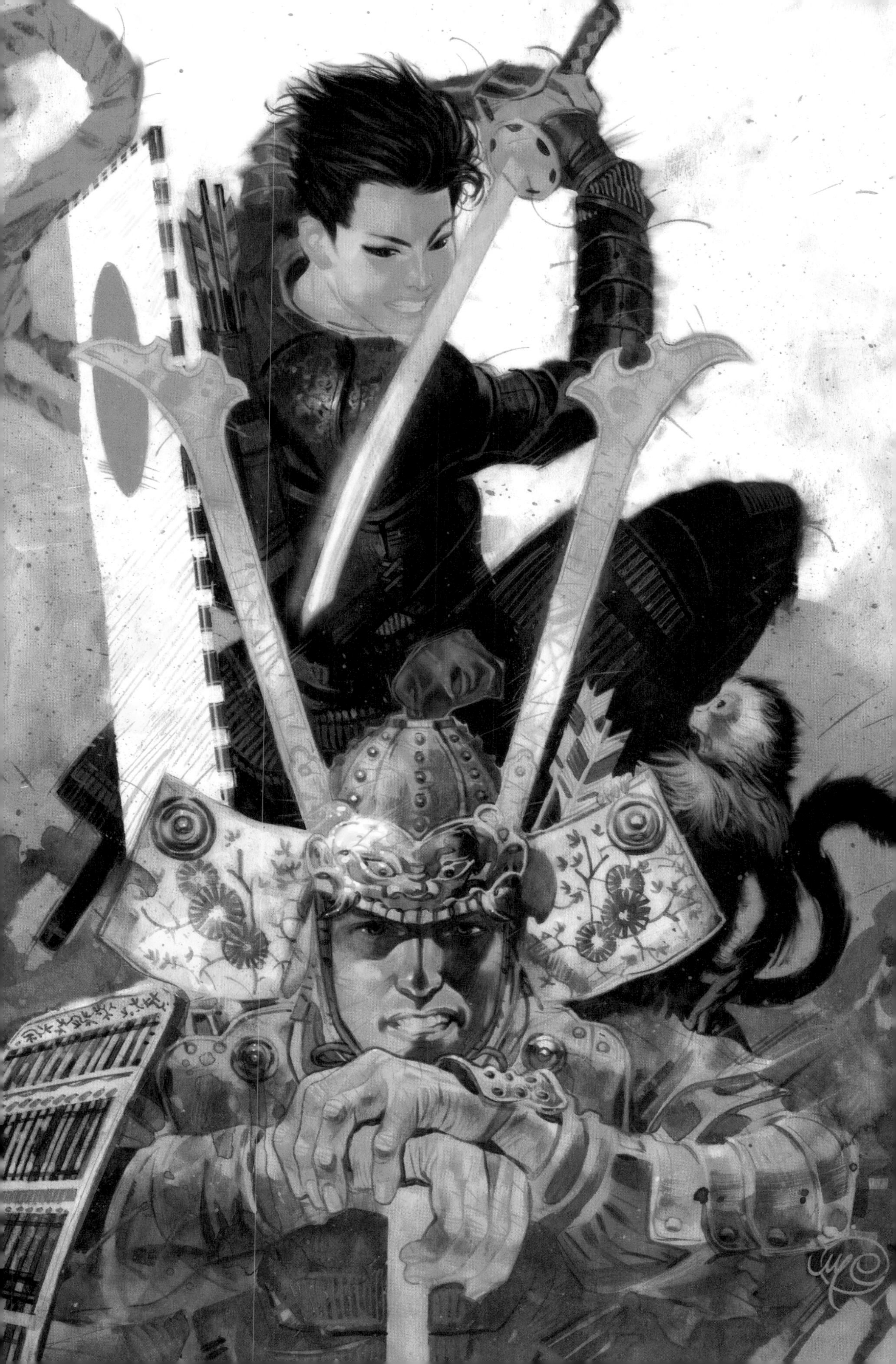

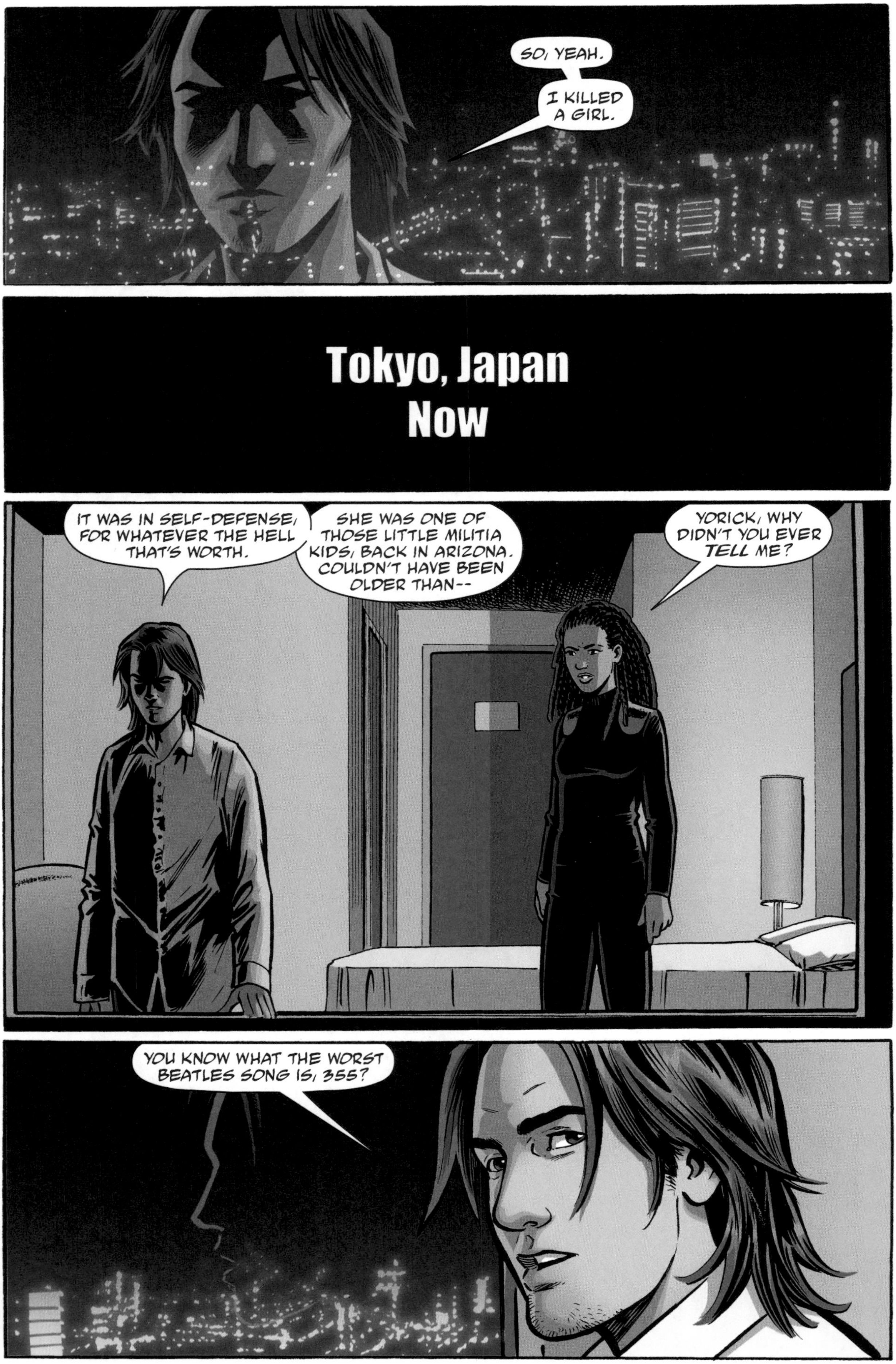
SO, YEAH.
I KILLED A GIRL.
Tokyo, Japan Now
IT WAS IN SELF-DEFENSE, FOR WHATEVER THE HELL THAT'S WORTH.
SHE WAS ONE OF THOSE LITTLE MILITIA KIDS, BACK IN ARIZONA. COULDN'T HAVE BEEN OLDER THAN--
YORICK, WHY DIDN'T YOU EVER *TELL* ME?
YOU KNOW WHAT THE WORST BEATLES SONG IS, 355?

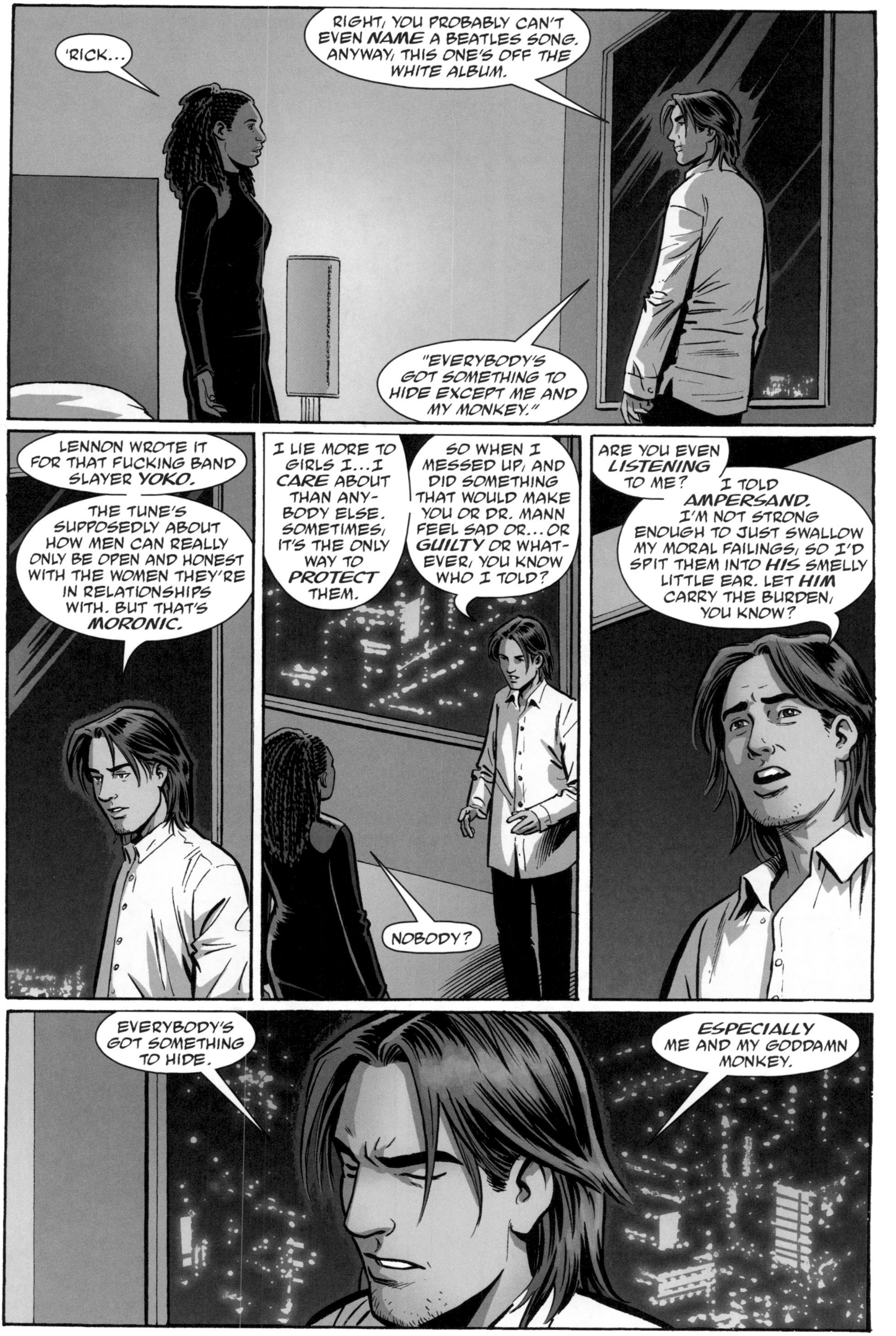
'RICK...
RIGHT, YOU PROBABLY CAN'T EVEN NAME A BEATLES SONG. ANYWAY, THIS ONE'S OFF THE WHITE ALBUM.
"EVERYBODY'S GOT SOMETHING TO HIDE EXCEPT ME AND MY MONKEY."
LENNON WROTE IT FOR THAT FUCKING BAND SLAYER YOKO.
THE TUNE'S SUPPOSEDLY ABOUT HOW MEN CAN REALLY ONLY BE OPEN AND HONEST WITH THE WOMEN THEY'RE IN RELATIONSHIPS WITH. BUT THAT'S MORONIC.
I LIE MORE TO GIRLS I...I CARE ABOUT THAN ANY-BODY ELSE. SOMETIMES, IT'S THE ONLY WAY TO PROTECT THEM.
SO WHEN I MESSED UP, AND DID SOMETHING THAT WOULD MAKE YOU OR DR. MANN FEEL SAD OR...OR GUILTY OR WHAT-EVER, YOU KNOW WHO I TOLD?
NOBODY?
ARE YOU EVEN LISTENING TO ME?
I TOLD AMPERSAND. I'M NOT STRONG ENOUGH TO JUST SWALLOW MY MORAL FAILINGS, SO I'D SPIT THEM INTO HIS SMELLY LITTLE EAR. LET HIM CARRY THE BURDEN, YOU KNOW?
EVERYBODY'S GOT SOMETHING TO HIDE.
ESPECIALLY ME AND MY GODDAMN MONKEY.

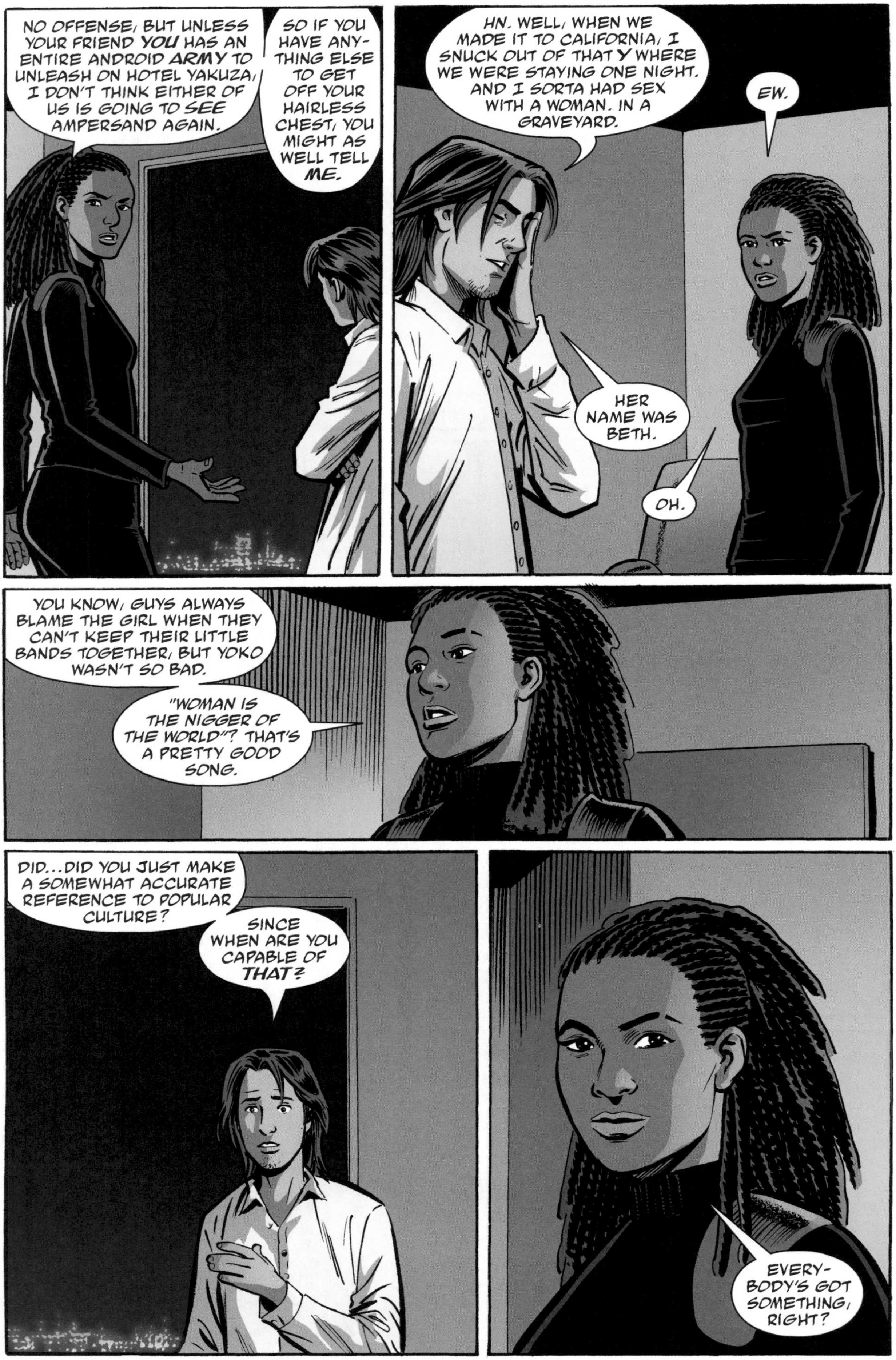
NO OFFENSE, BUT UNLESS YOUR FRIEND YOU HAS AN ENTIRE ANDROID ARMY TO UNLEASH ON HOTEL YAKUZA, I DON'T THINK EITHER OF US IS GOING TO SEE AMPERSAND AGAIN.
SO IF YOU HAVE ANYTHING ELSE TO GET OFF YOUR HAIRLESS CHEST, YOU MIGHT AS WELL TELL ME.
HN. WELL, WHEN WE MADE IT TO CALIFORNIA, I SNUCK OUT OF THAT Y WHERE WE WERE STAYING ONE NIGHT. AND I SORTA HAD SEX WITH A WOMAN. IN A GRAVEYARD.
EW.
HER NAME WAS BETH.
OH.
YOU KNOW, GUYS ALWAYS BLAME THE GIRL WHEN THEY CAN'T KEEP THEIR LITTLE BANDS TOGETHER, BUT YOKO WASN'T SO BAD.
"WOMAN IS THE NIGGER OF THE WORLD"? THAT'S A PRETTY GOOD SONG.
DID...DID YOU JUST MAKE A SOMEWHAT ACCURATE REFERENCE TO POPULAR CULTURE?
SINCE WHEN ARE YOU CAPABLE OF THAT?
EVERYBODY'S GOT SOMETHING, RIGHT?

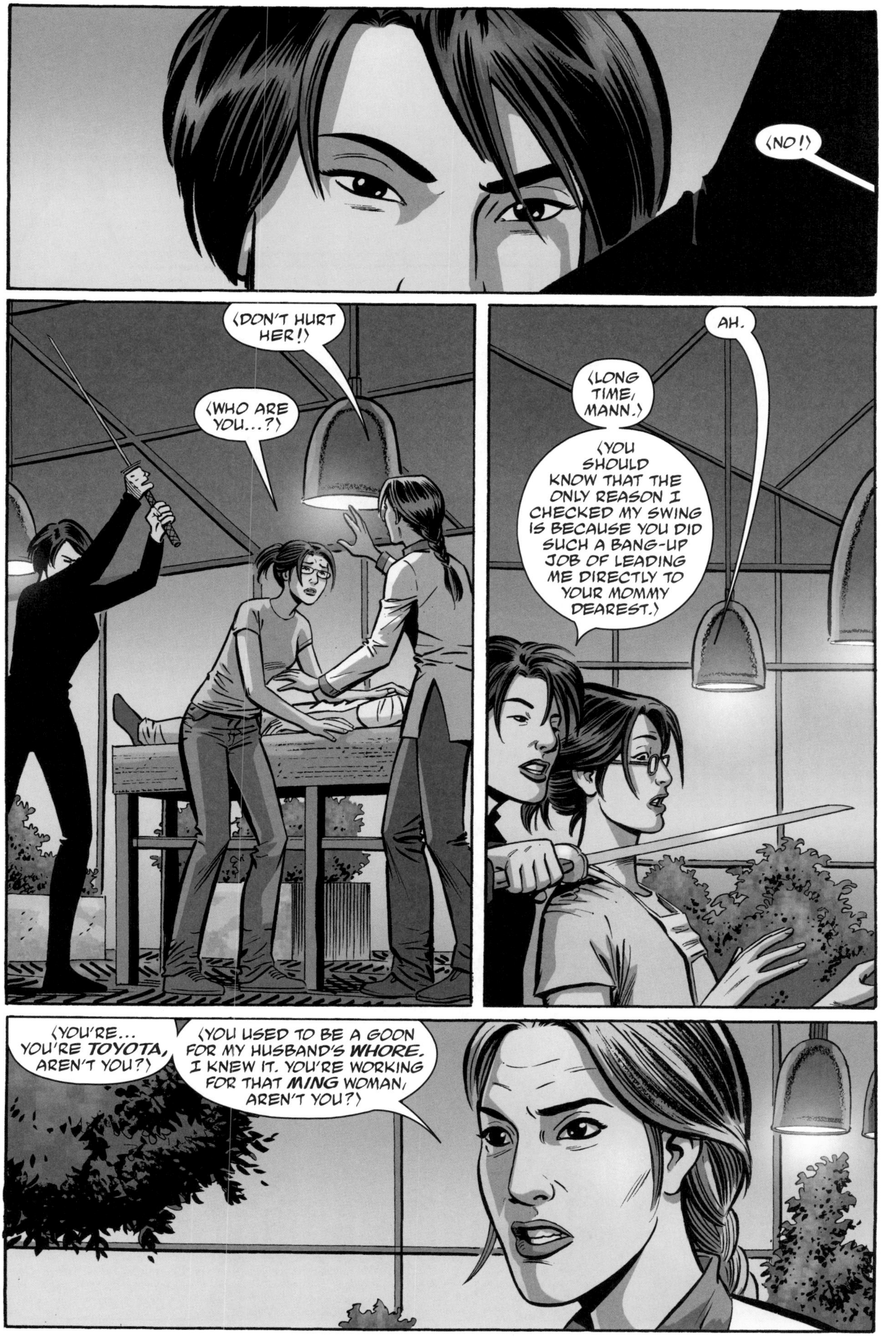

⟨NO!⟩
⟨DON'T HURT HER!⟩
⟨WHO ARE YOU...?⟩
AH.
⟨LONG TIME, MANN.⟩
⟨YOU SHOULD KNOW THAT THE ONLY REASON I CHECKED MY SWING IS BECAUSE YOU DID SUCH A BANG-UP JOB OF LEADING ME DIRECTLY TO YOUR MOMMY DEAREST.⟩
⟨YOU'RE... YOU'RE TOYOTA, AREN'T YOU?⟩
⟨YOU USED TO BE A GOON FOR MY HUSBAND'S WHORE. I KNEW IT. YOU'RE WORKING FOR THAT MING WOMAN, AREN'T YOU?⟩

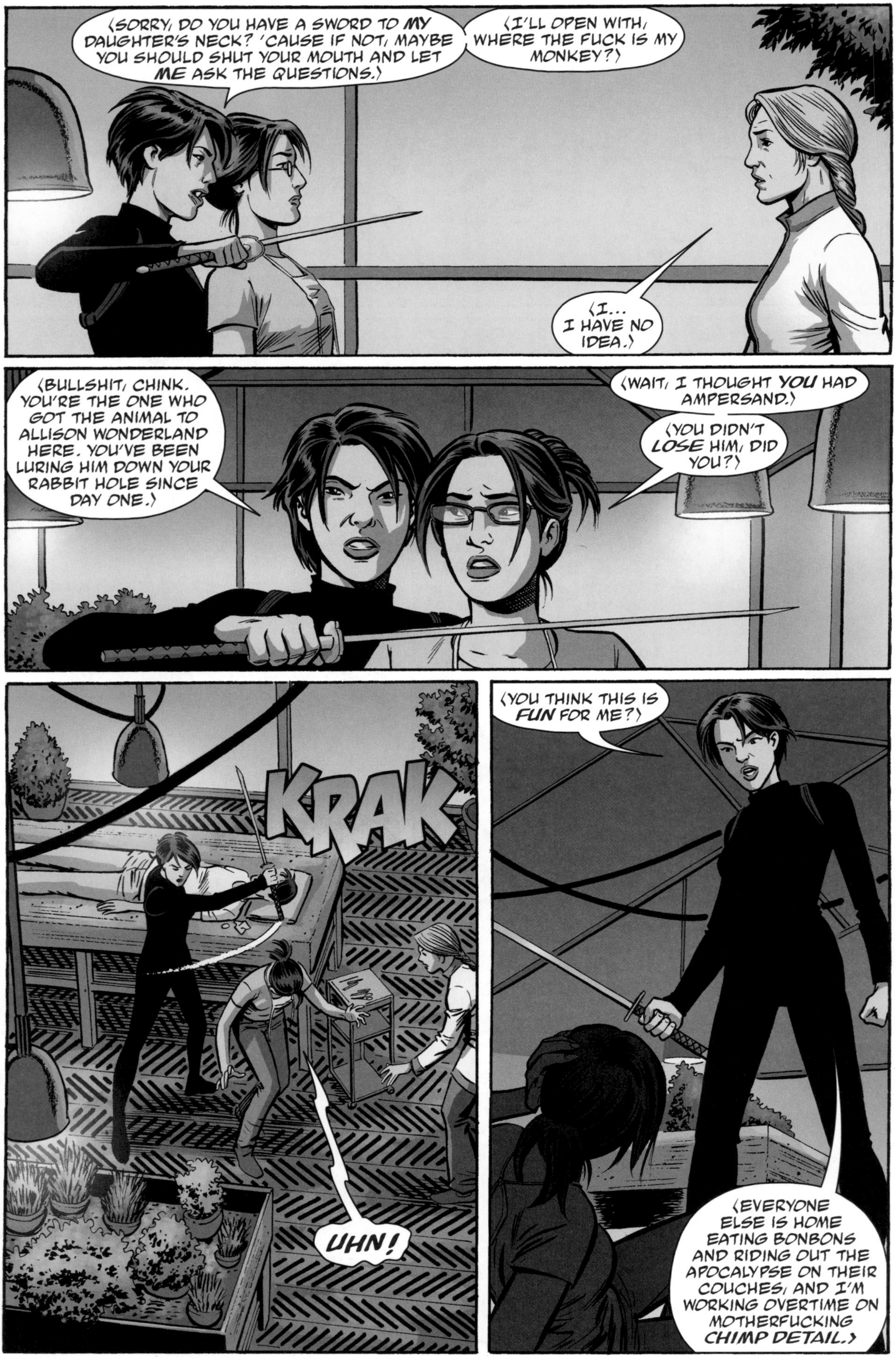

⟨SORRY, DO YOU HAVE A SWORD TO MY DAUGHTER'S NECK? 'CAUSE IF NOT, MAYBE YOU SHOULD SHUT YOUR MOUTH AND LET ME ASK THE QUESTIONS.⟩
⟨I'LL OPEN WITH, WHERE THE FUCK IS MY MONKEY?⟩
⟨I... I HAVE NO IDEA.⟩
⟨BULLSHIT, CHINK. YOU'RE THE ONE WHO GOT THE ANIMAL TO ALLISON WONDERLAND HERE. YOU'VE BEEN LURING HIM DOWN YOUR RABBIT HOLE SINCE DAY ONE.⟩
⟨WAIT, I THOUGHT YOU HAD AMPERSAND.⟩
⟨YOU DIDN'T LOSE HIM, DID YOU?⟩
KRAK
UHN!
⟨YOU THINK THIS IS FUN FOR ME?⟩
⟨EVERYONE ELSE IS HOME EATING BONBONS AND RIDING OUT THE APOCALYPSE ON THEIR COUCHES, AND I'M WORKING OVERTIME ON MOTHERFUCKING CHIMP DETAIL.⟩

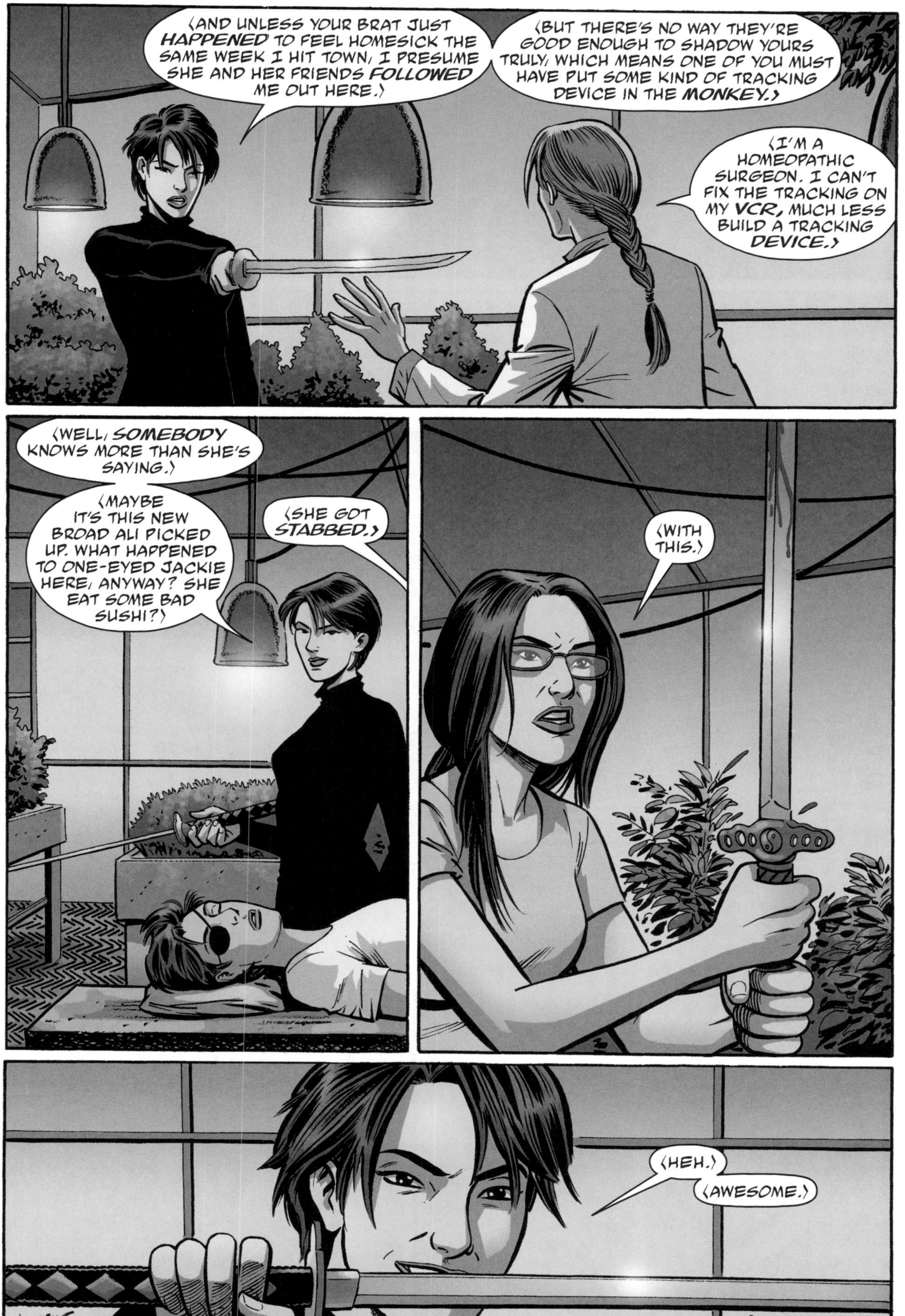
‹AND UNLESS YOUR BRAT JUST HAPPENED TO FEEL HOMESICK THE SAME WEEK I HIT TOWN, I PRESUME SHE AND HER FRIENDS FOLLOWED ME OUT HERE.›
‹BUT THERE'S NO WAY THEY'RE GOOD ENOUGH TO SHADOW YOURS TRULY, WHICH MEANS ONE OF YOU MUST HAVE PUT SOME KIND OF TRACKING DEVICE IN THE MONKEY.›
‹I'M A HOMEOPATHIC SURGEON. I CAN'T FIX THE TRACKING ON MY VCR, MUCH LESS BUILD A TRACKING DEVICE.›
‹WELL, SOMEBODY KNOWS MORE THAN SHE'S SAYING.›
‹MAYBE IT'S THIS NEW BROAD ALI PICKED UP. WHAT HAPPENED TO ONE-EYED JACKIE HERE, ANYWAY? SHE EAT SOME BAD SUSHI?›
‹SHE GOT STABBED.›
‹WITH THIS.›
‹HEH.›
‹AWESOME.›

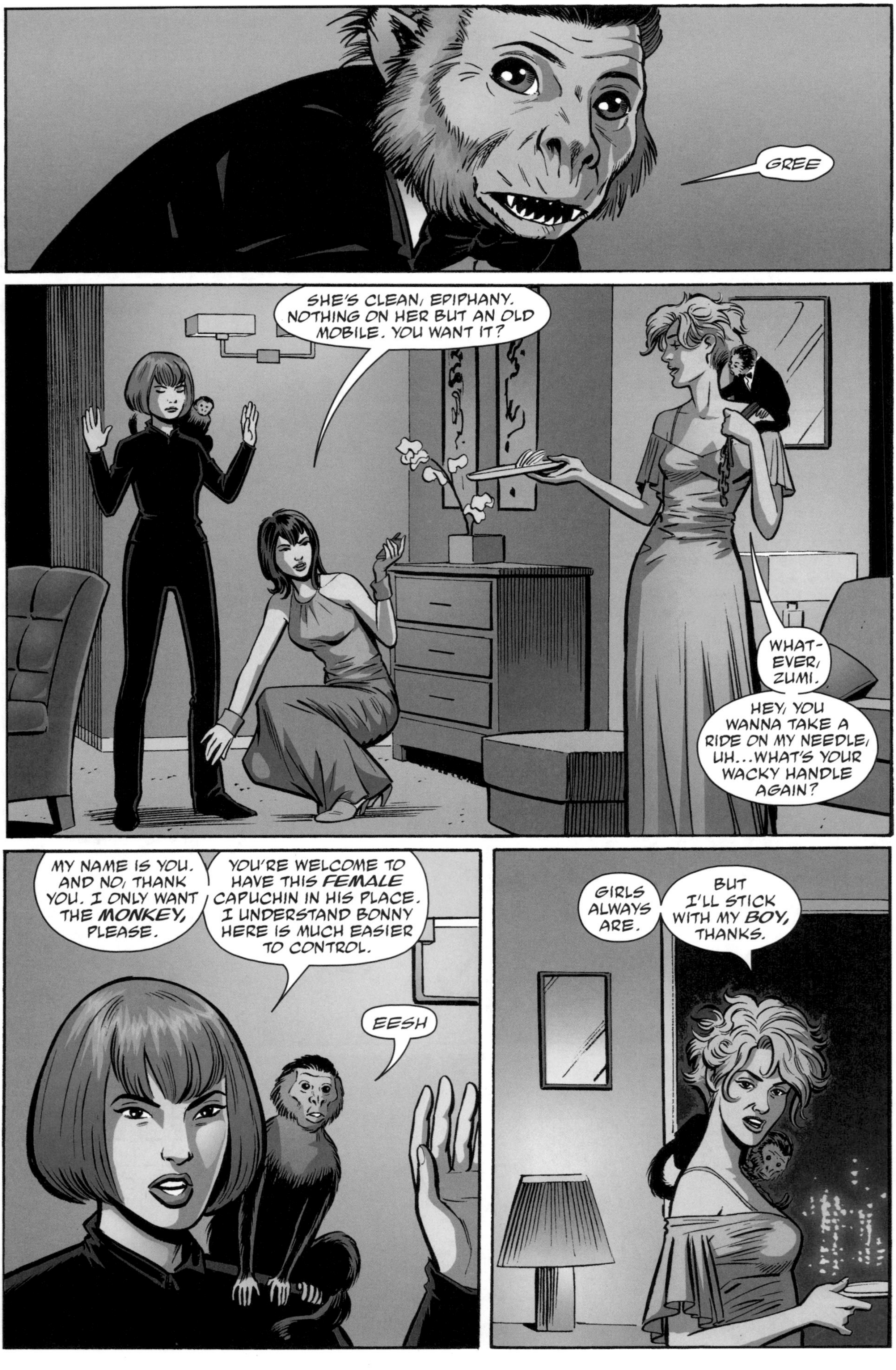
GREE
SHE'S CLEAN, EPIPHANY. NOTHING ON HER BUT AN OLD MOBILE. YOU WANT IT?
WHAT-EVER, ZUMI.
HEY, YOU WANNA TAKE A RIDE ON MY NEEDLE, UH...WHAT'S YOUR WACKY HANDLE AGAIN?
MY NAME IS YOU. AND NO, THANK YOU. I ONLY WANT THE MONKEY, PLEASE.
YOU'RE WELCOME TO HAVE THIS FEMALE CAPUCHIN IN HIS PLACE. I UNDERSTAND BONNY HERE IS MUCH EASIER TO CONTROL.
EESH
GIRLS ALWAYS ARE.
BUT I'LL STICK WITH MY BOY, THANKS.

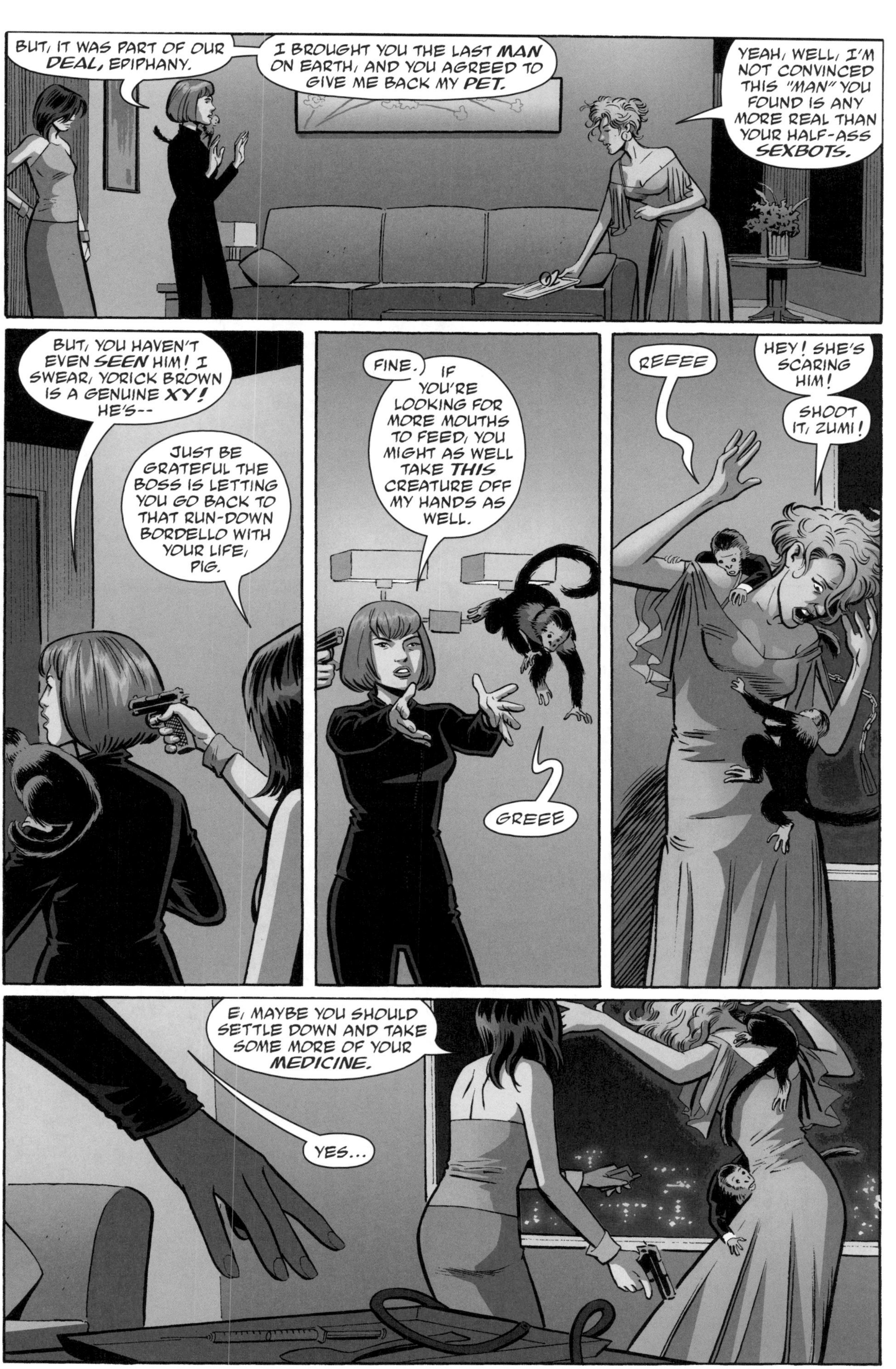

BUT, IT WAS PART OF OUR DEAL, EPIPHANY.
I BROUGHT YOU THE LAST MAN ON EARTH, AND YOU AGREED TO GIVE ME BACK MY PET.
YEAH, WELL, I'M NOT CONVINCED THIS "MAN" YOU FOUND IS ANY MORE REAL THAN YOUR HALF-ASS SEXBOTS.
BUT, YOU HAVEN'T EVEN SEEN HIM! I SWEAR, YORICK BROWN IS A GENUINE XY! HE'S--
JUST BE GRATEFUL THE BOSS IS LETTING YOU GO BACK TO THAT RUN-DOWN BORDELLO WITH YOUR LIFE, PIG.
FINE.
IF YOU'RE LOOKING FOR MORE MOUTHS TO FEED, YOU MIGHT AS WELL TAKE THIS CREATURE OFF MY HANDS AS WELL.
GREEE
REEEE
HEY! SHE'S SCARING HIM!
SHOOT IT, ZUMI!
E, MAYBE YOU SHOULD SETTLE DOWN AND TAKE SOME MORE OF YOUR MEDICINE.
YES...

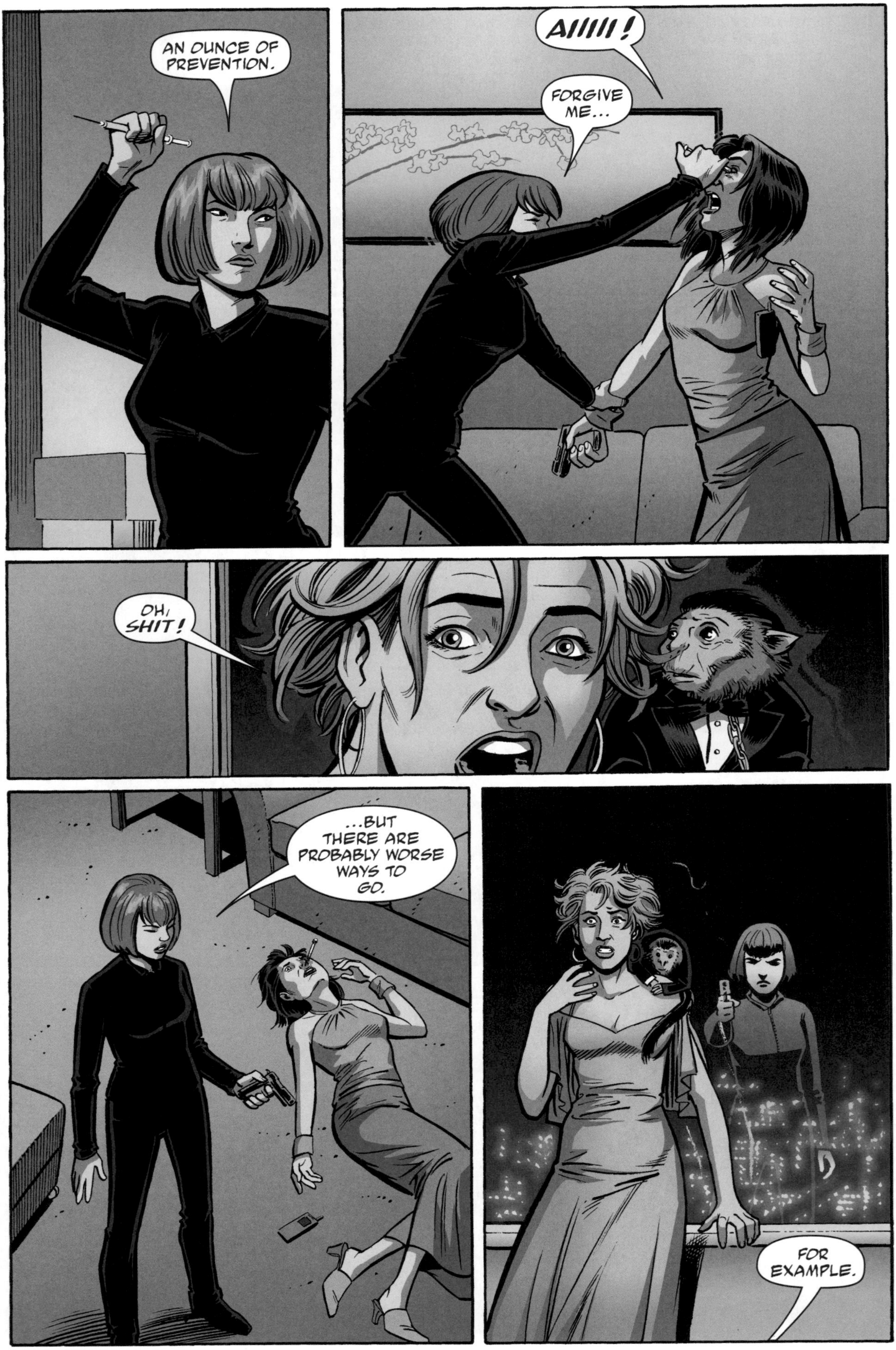
AN OUNCE OF PREVENTION.
AIIIII!
FORGIVE ME...
OH, SHIT!
...BUT THERE ARE PROBABLY WORSE WAYS TO GO.
FOR EXAMPLE.

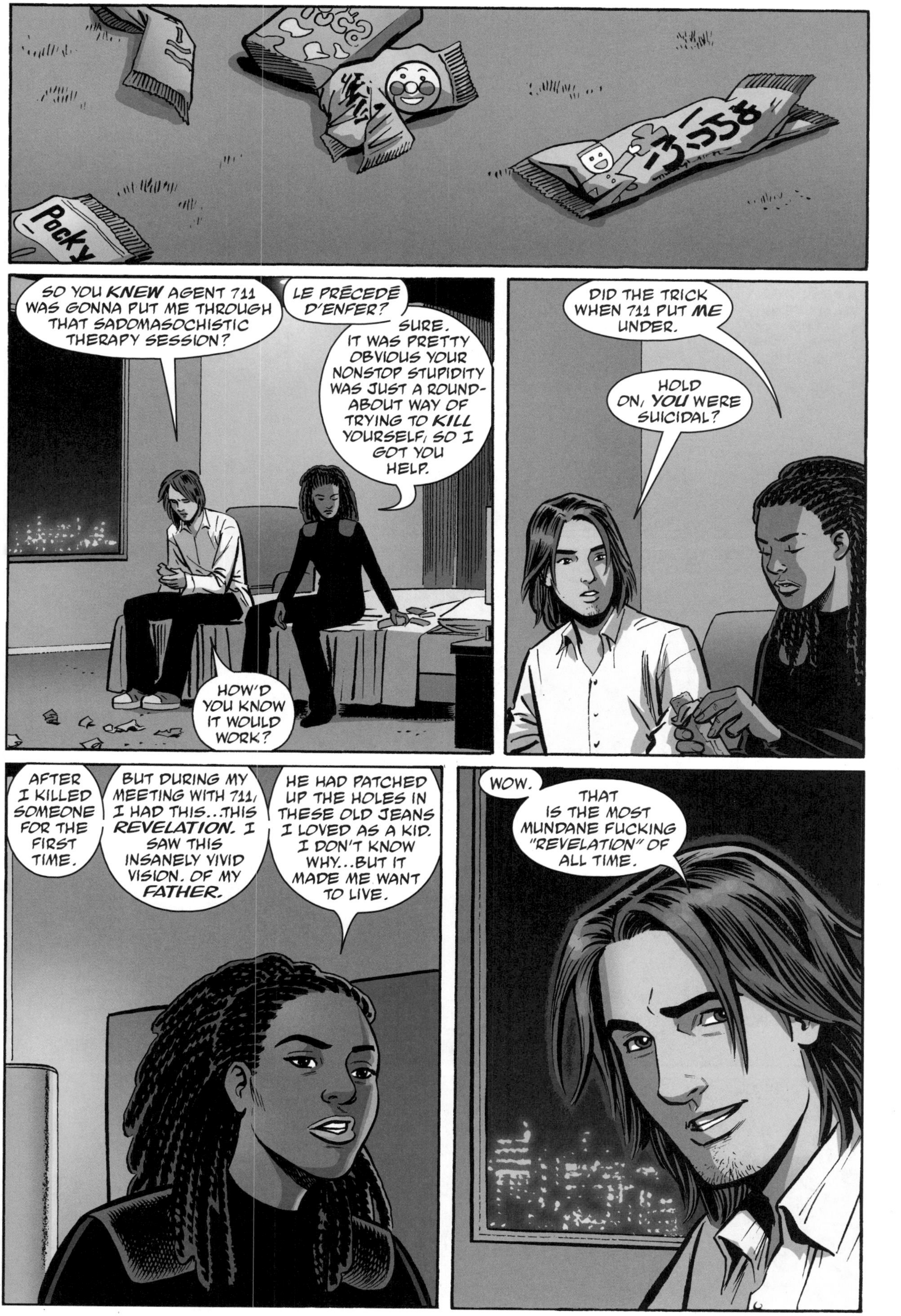
Pocky
SO YOU KNEW AGENT 711 WAS GONNA PUT ME THROUGH THAT SADOMASOCHISTIC THERAPY SESSION?
LE PRÉCÉDÉ D'ENFER?
SURE. IT WAS PRETTY OBVIOUS YOUR NONSTOP STUPIDITY WAS JUST A ROUND-ABOUT WAY OF TRYING TO KILL YOURSELF, SO I GOT YOU HELP.
HOW'D YOU KNOW IT WOULD WORK?
DID THE TRICK WHEN 711 PUT ME UNDER.
HOLD ON, YOU WERE SUICIDAL?
AFTER I KILLED SOMEONE FOR THE FIRST TIME.
BUT DURING MY MEETING WITH 711, I HAD THIS...THIS REVELATION. I SAW THIS INSANELY VIVID VISION. OF MY FATHER.
HE HAD PATCHED UP THE HOLES IN THESE OLD JEANS I LOVED AS A KID. I DON'T KNOW WHY...BUT IT MADE ME WANT TO LIVE.
WOW.
THAT IS THE MOST MUNDANE FUCKING "REVELATION" OF ALL TIME.

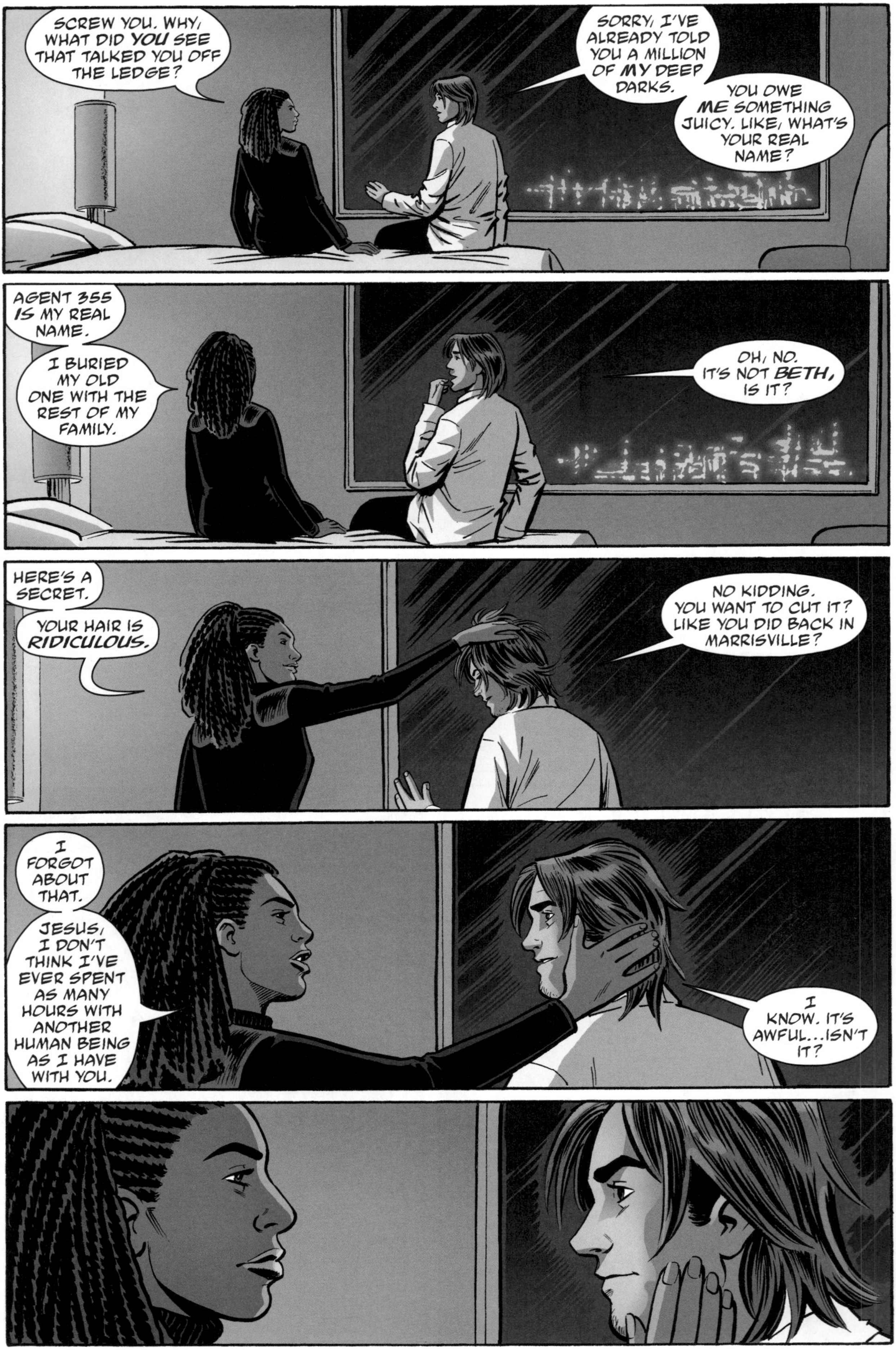
SCREW YOU. WHY, WHAT DID YOU SEE THAT TALKED YOU OFF THE LEDGE?
SORRY, I'VE ALREADY TOLD YOU A MILLION OF MY DEEP DARKS.
YOU OWE ME SOMETHING JUICY. LIKE, WHAT'S YOUR REAL NAME?
AGENT 355 IS MY REAL NAME.
I BURIED MY OLD ONE WITH THE REST OF MY FAMILY.
OH, NO. IT'S NOT BETH, IS IT?
HERE'S A SECRET.
YOUR HAIR IS RIDICULOUS.
NO KIDDING. YOU WANT TO CUT IT? LIKE YOU DID BACK IN MARRISVILLE?
I FORGOT ABOUT THAT.
JESUS, I DON'T THINK I'VE EVER SPENT AS MANY HOURS WITH ANOTHER HUMAN BEING AS I HAVE WITH YOU.
I KNOW. IT'S AWFUL...ISN'T IT?

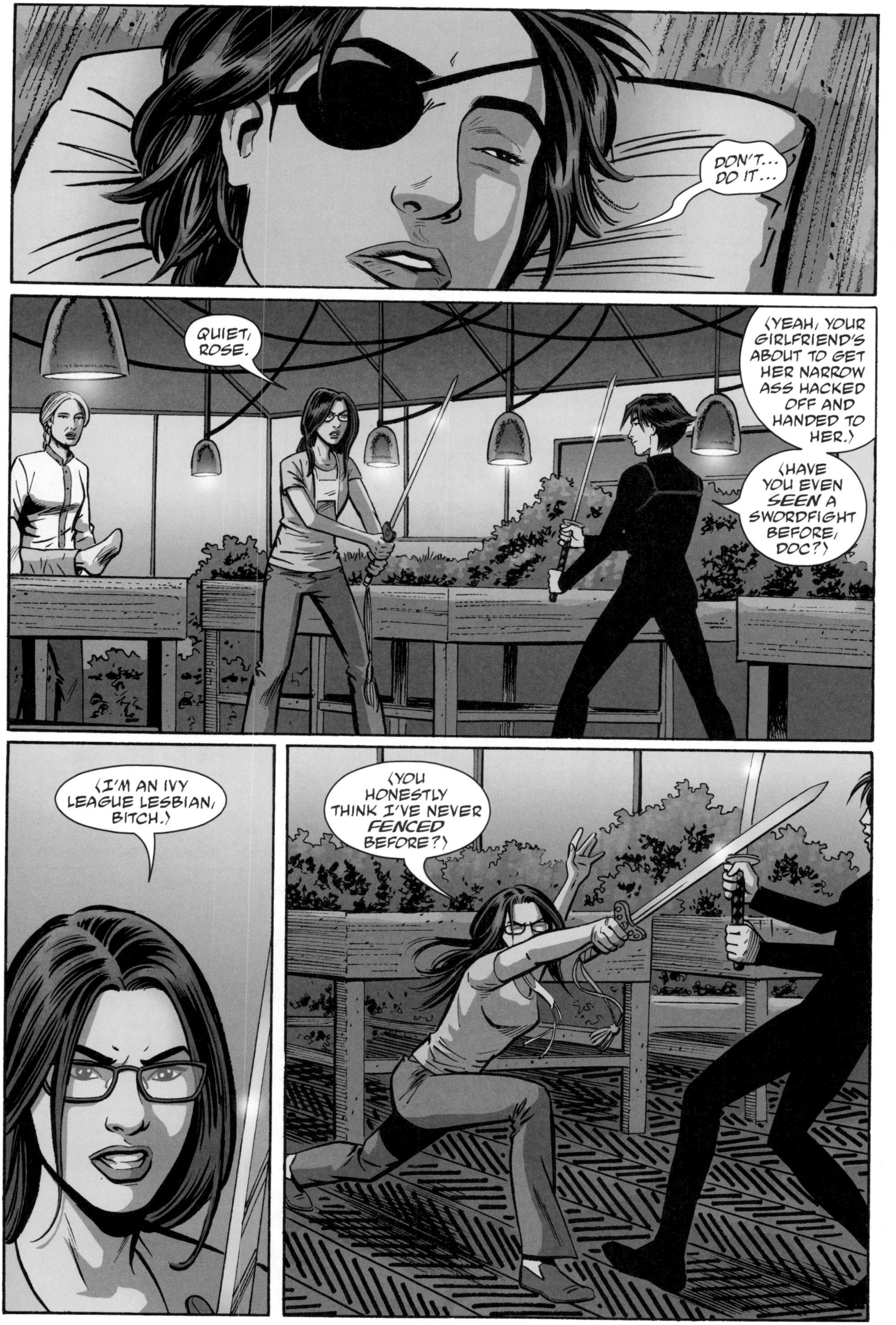
DON'T... DO IT...
QUIET, ROSE.
⟨YEAH, YOUR GIRLFRIEND'S ABOUT TO GET HER NARROW ASS HACKED OFF AND HANDED TO HER.⟩
⟨HAVE YOU EVEN SEEN A SWORDFIGHT BEFORE, DOC?⟩
⟨I'M AN IVY LEAGUE LESBIAN, BITCH.⟩
⟨YOU HONESTLY THINK I'VE NEVER FENCED BEFORE?⟩

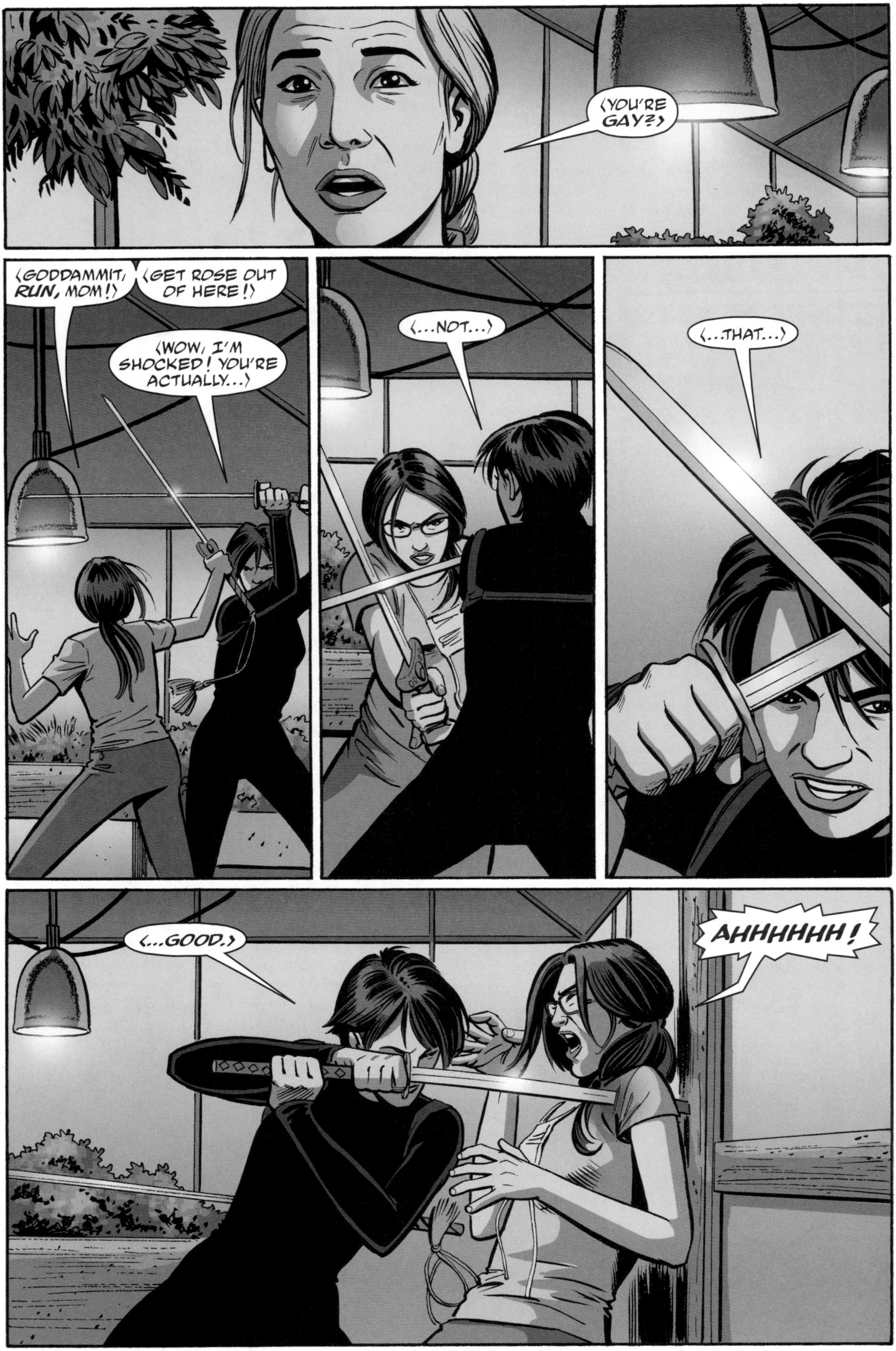

‹YOU'RE GAY?›
‹GODDAMMIT, RUN, MOM!›
‹GET ROSE OUT OF HERE!›
‹WOW, I'M SHOCKED! YOU'RE ACTUALLY...›
‹...NOT...›
‹...THAT...›
‹...GOOD.›
AHHHHHH!

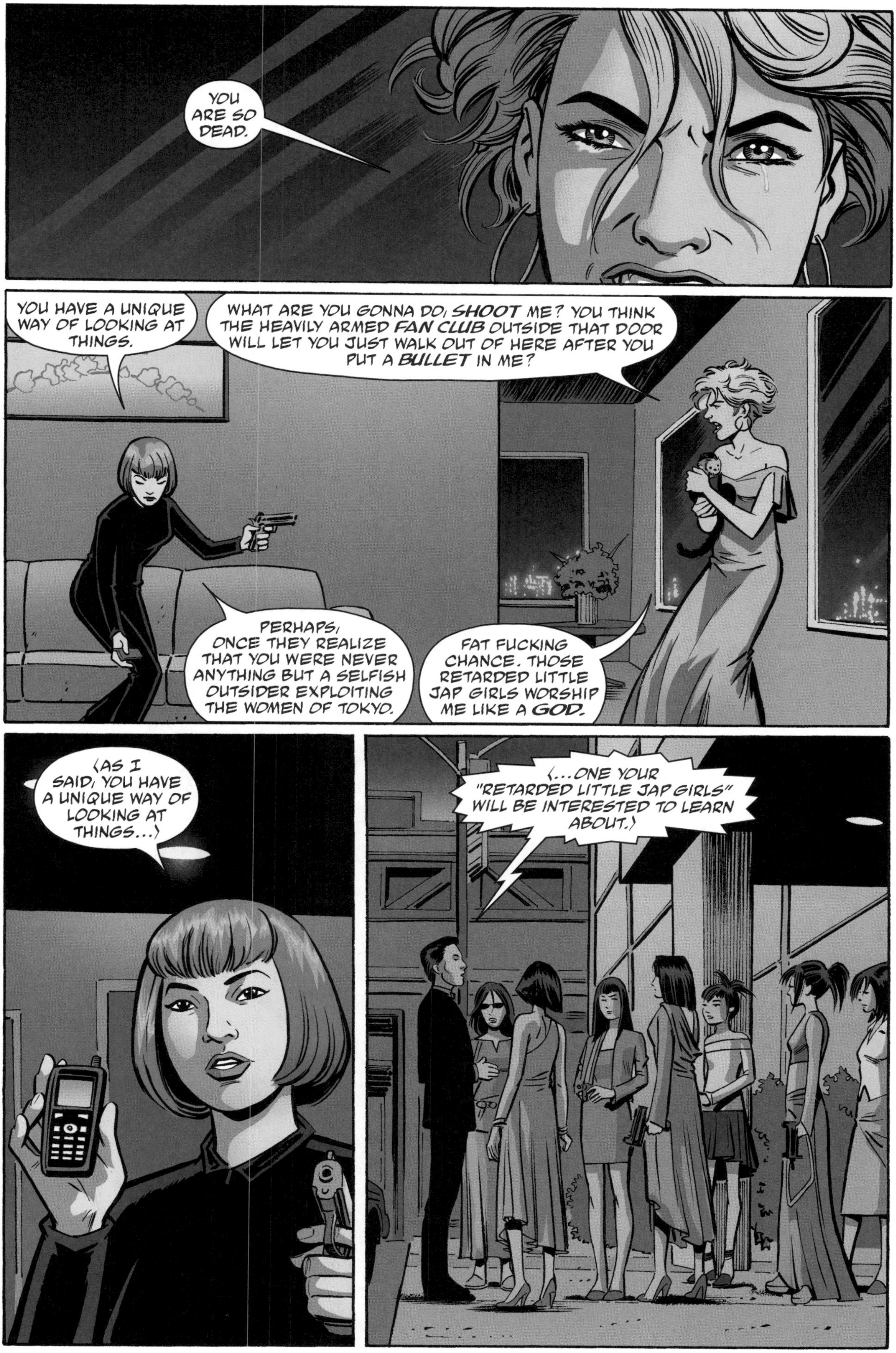
YOU ARE SO DEAD.
YOU HAVE A UNIQUE WAY OF LOOKING AT THINGS.
WHAT ARE YOU GONNA DO, SHOOT ME? YOU THINK THE HEAVILY ARMED FAN CLUB OUTSIDE THAT DOOR WILL LET YOU JUST WALK OUT OF HERE AFTER YOU PUT A BULLET IN ME?
PERHAPS, ONCE THEY REALIZE THAT YOU WERE NEVER ANYTHING BUT A SELFISH OUTSIDER EXPLOITING THE WOMEN OF TOKYO.
FAT FUCKING CHANCE. THOSE RETARDED LITTLE JAP GIRLS WORSHIP ME LIKE A GOD.
‹AS I SAID, YOU HAVE A UNIQUE WAY OF LOOKING AT THINGS...›
‹...ONE YOUR "RETARDED LITTLE JAP GIRLS" WILL BE INTERESTED TO LEARN ABOUT.›

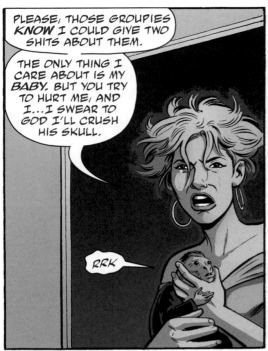

PLEASE, THOSE GROUPIES *KNOW* I COULD GIVE TWO SHITS ABOUT THEM.

THE ONLY THING I CARE ABOUT IS MY *BABY*. BUT YOU TRY TO HURT ME, AND I...I SWEAR TO GOD I'LL CRUSH HIS SKULL.

RRK

NO, YOU WON'T. YOU'RE A HIDEOUS WOMAN, BUT YOU'RE STILL A WOMAN. IN THE END, YOU'LL DO WHAT'S BEST FOR YOUR YOUNG.

EPIPHANY!

WE HEARD YOU ON THE...THE *THING*. ARE YOU OKAY?

WHAT DO *YOU* THINK, DUMMY? KILL THIS ASSHOLE ALREADY!

⟨YES, KILL ME...SO YOU CAN RETURN TO YOUR SAD LIVES SHAKING DOWN YOUR NEIGHBORS FOR A SECOND-RATE KARAOKE SINGER FROM SASKATOON.⟩

⟨OR YOU COULD *JOIN* ME. I CAN TEACH YOU TO BUILD MORE *MACHINES* LIKE THE ONE DOWNSTAIRS. TOGETHER, WE COULD REINVENT THE WORLD'S OLDEST PROFESSION.⟩

⟨IT'S YOUR DECISION. YOU CAN BE SELF-DESTRUCTIVE THUGS...⟩

⟨...OR GANGSTERS OF LOVE.⟩

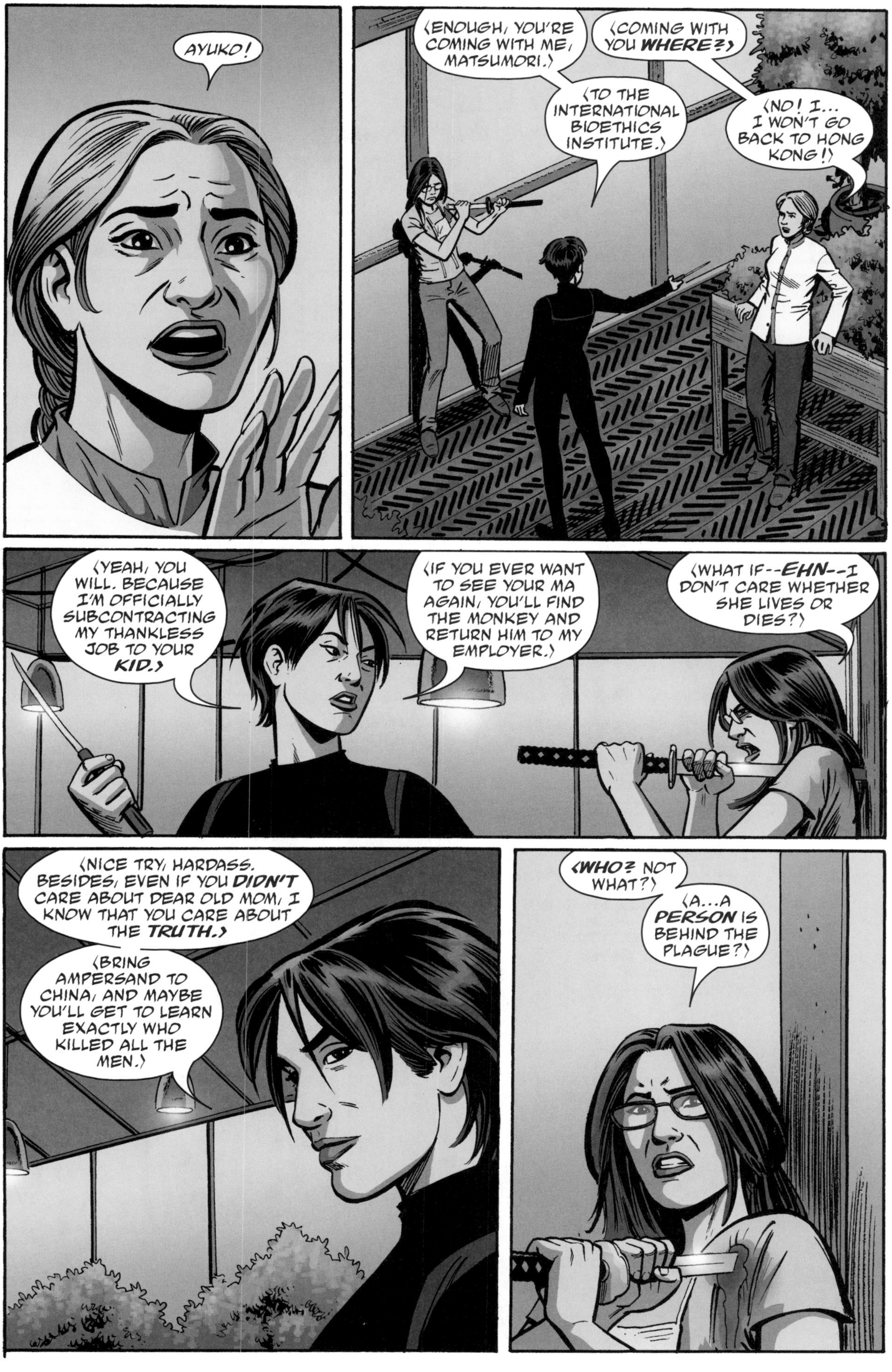
AYUKO!
⟨ENOUGH, YOU'RE COMING WITH ME, MATSUMORI.⟩
⟨COMING WITH YOU WHERE?⟩
⟨TO THE INTERNATIONAL BIOETHICS INSTITUTE.⟩
⟨NO! I... I WON'T GO BACK TO HONG KONG!⟩
⟨YEAH, YOU WILL. BECAUSE I'M OFFICIALLY SUBCONTRACTING MY THANKLESS JOB TO YOUR KID.⟩
⟨IF YOU EVER WANT TO SEE YOUR MA AGAIN, YOU'LL FIND THE MONKEY AND RETURN HIM TO MY EMPLOYER.⟩
⟨WHAT IF--EHN--I DON'T CARE WHETHER SHE LIVES OR DIES?⟩
⟨NICE TRY, HARDASS. BESIDES, EVEN IF YOU DIDN'T CARE ABOUT DEAR OLD MOM, I KNOW THAT YOU CARE ABOUT THE TRUTH.⟩
⟨BRING AMPERSAND TO CHINA, AND MAYBE YOU'LL GET TO LEARN EXACTLY WHO KILLED ALL THE MEN.⟩
⟨WHO? NOT WHAT?⟩
⟨A...A PERSON IS BEHIND THE PLAGUE?⟩

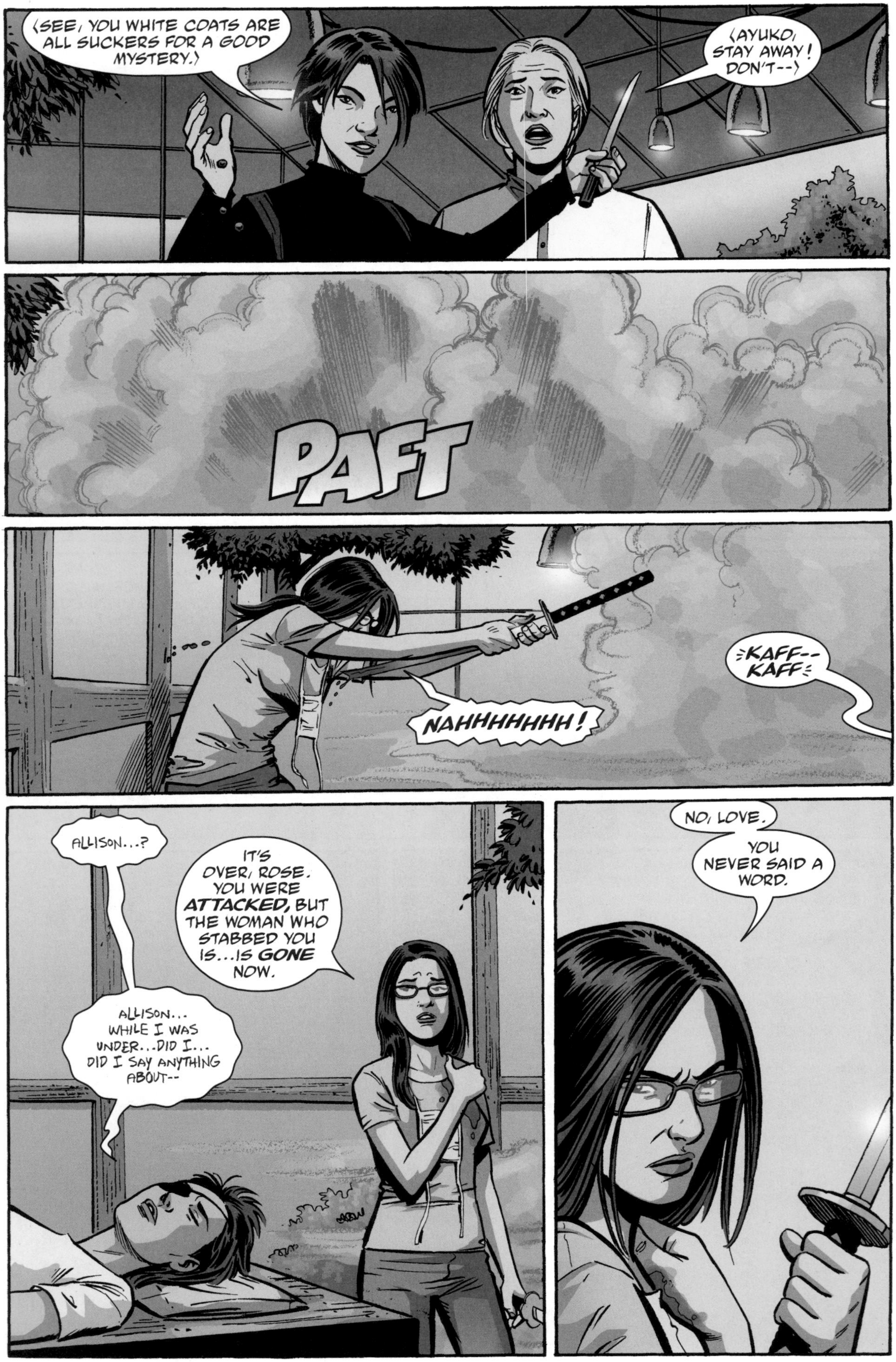
‹SEE, YOU WHITE COATS ARE ALL SUCKERS FOR A GOOD MYSTERY.›
‹AYUKO, STAY AWAY! DON'T--›
PAFT
KAFF-- KAFF
NAHHHHHHH!
ALLISON...?
IT'S OVER, ROSE. YOU WERE ATTACKED, BUT THE WOMAN WHO STABBED YOU IS...IS GONE NOW.
ALLISON... WHILE I WAS UNDER...DID I... DID I SAY ANYTHING ABOUT--
NO, LOVE.
YOU NEVER SAID A WORD.

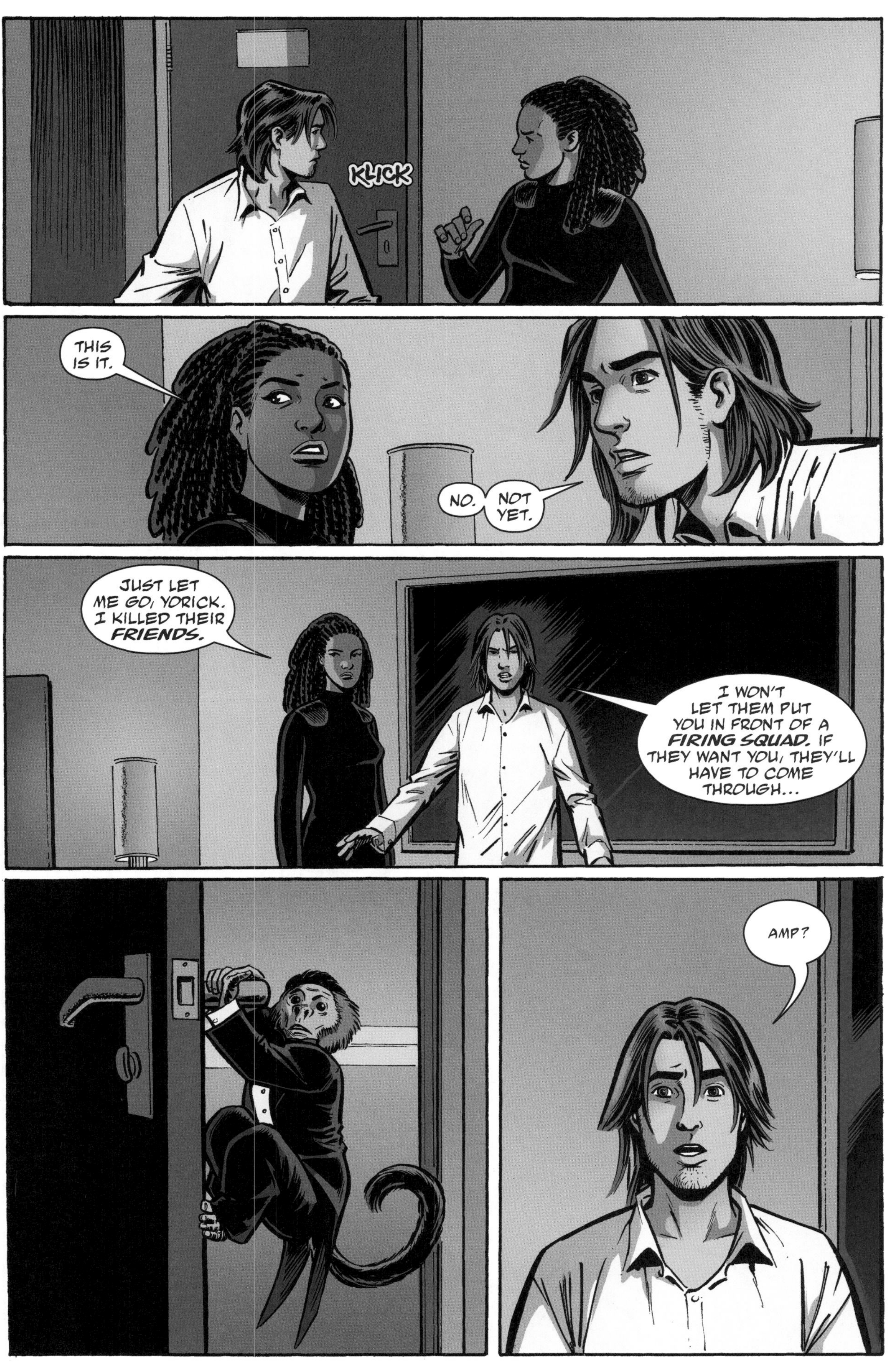
KLICK
THIS IS IT.
NO.
NOT YET.
JUST LET ME GO, YORICK. I KILLED THEIR FRIENDS.
I WON'T LET THEM PUT YOU IN FRONT OF A FIRING SQUAD. IF THEY WANT YOU, THEY'LL HAVE TO COME THROUGH...
AMP?

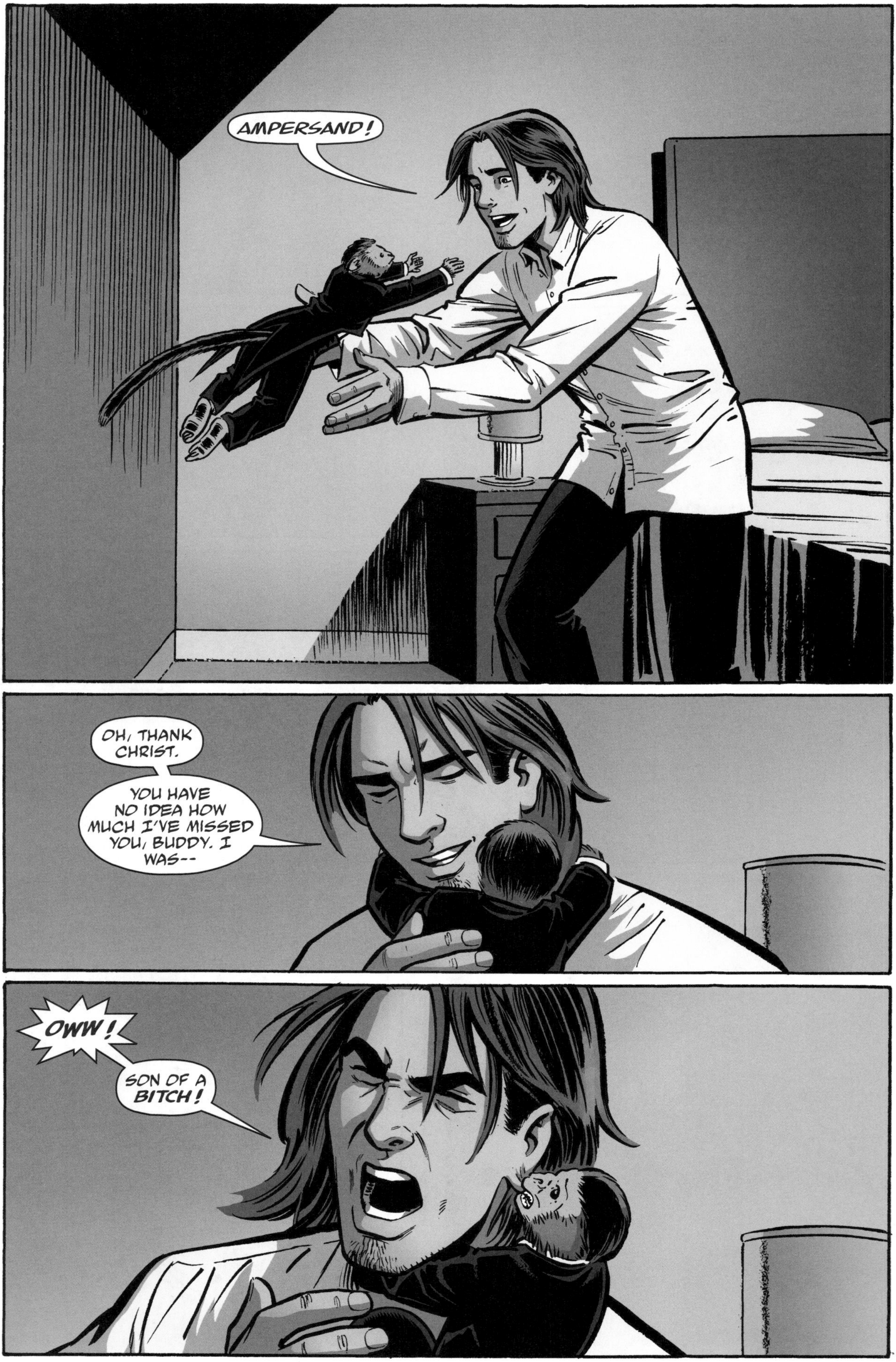
AMPERSAND!
OH, THANK CHRIST.
YOU HAVE NO IDEA HOW MUCH I'VE MISSED YOU, BUDDY. I WAS--
OWW!
SON OF A BITCH!

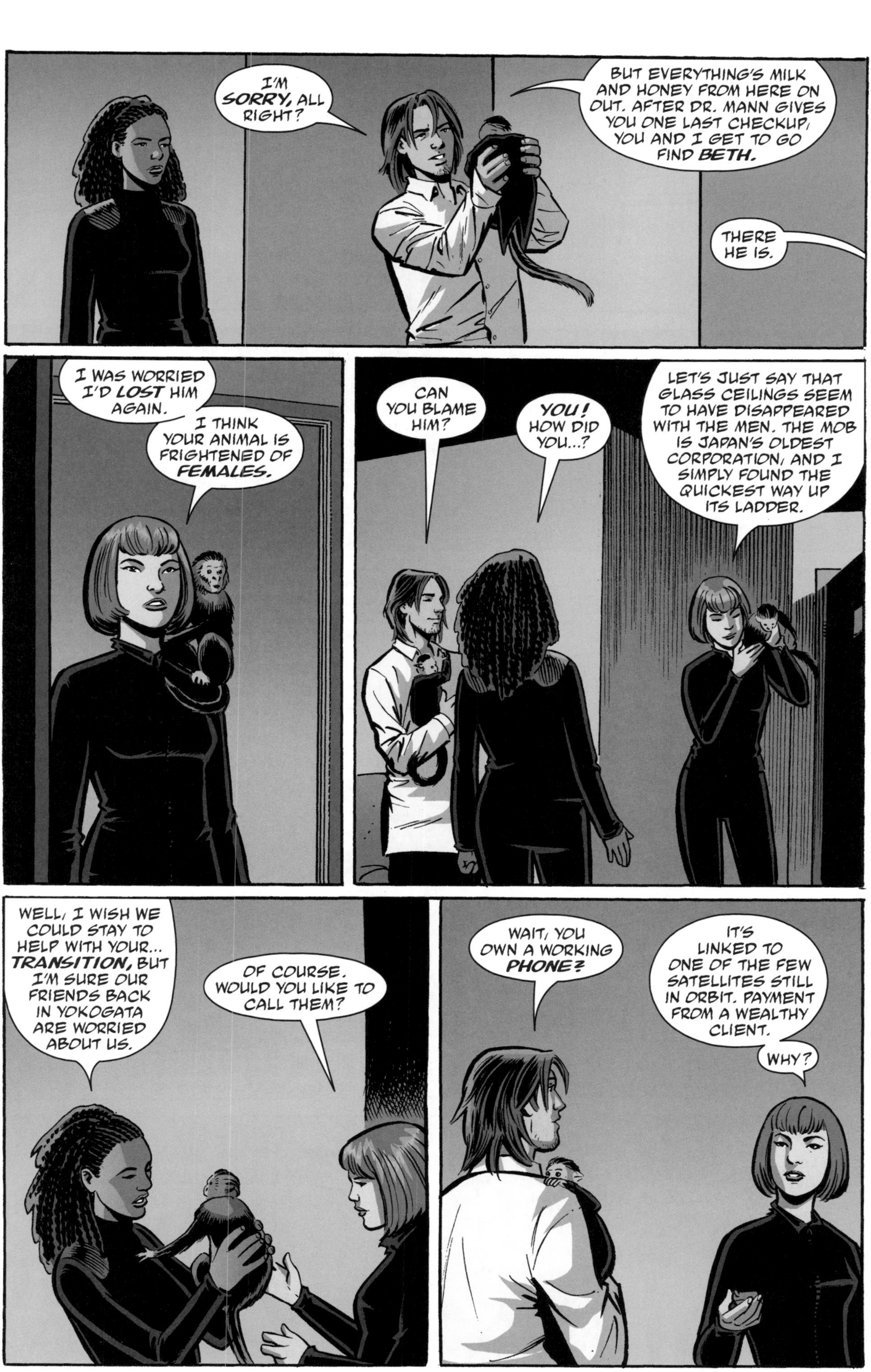
I'M SORRY, ALL RIGHT?
BUT EVERYTHING'S MILK AND HONEY FROM HERE ON OUT. AFTER DR. MANN GIVES YOU ONE LAST CHECKUP, YOU AND I GET TO GO FIND BETH.
THERE HE IS.
I WAS WORRIED I'D LOST HIM AGAIN.
I THINK YOUR ANIMAL IS FRIGHTENED OF FEMALES.
CAN YOU BLAME HIM?
YOU! HOW DID YOU...?
LET'S JUST SAY THAT GLASS CEILINGS SEEM TO HAVE DISAPPEARED WITH THE MEN. THE MOB IS JAPAN'S OLDEST CORPORATION, AND I SIMPLY FOUND THE QUICKEST WAY UP ITS LADDER.
WELL, I WISH WE COULD STAY TO HELP WITH YOUR... TRANSITION, BUT I'M SURE OUR FRIENDS BACK IN YOKOGATA ARE WORRIED ABOUT US.
OF COURSE. WOULD YOU LIKE TO CALL THEM?
WAIT, YOU OWN A WORKING PHONE?
IT'S LINKED TO ONE OF THE FEW SATELLITES STILL IN ORBIT. PAYMENT FROM A WEALTHY CLIENT.
WHY?

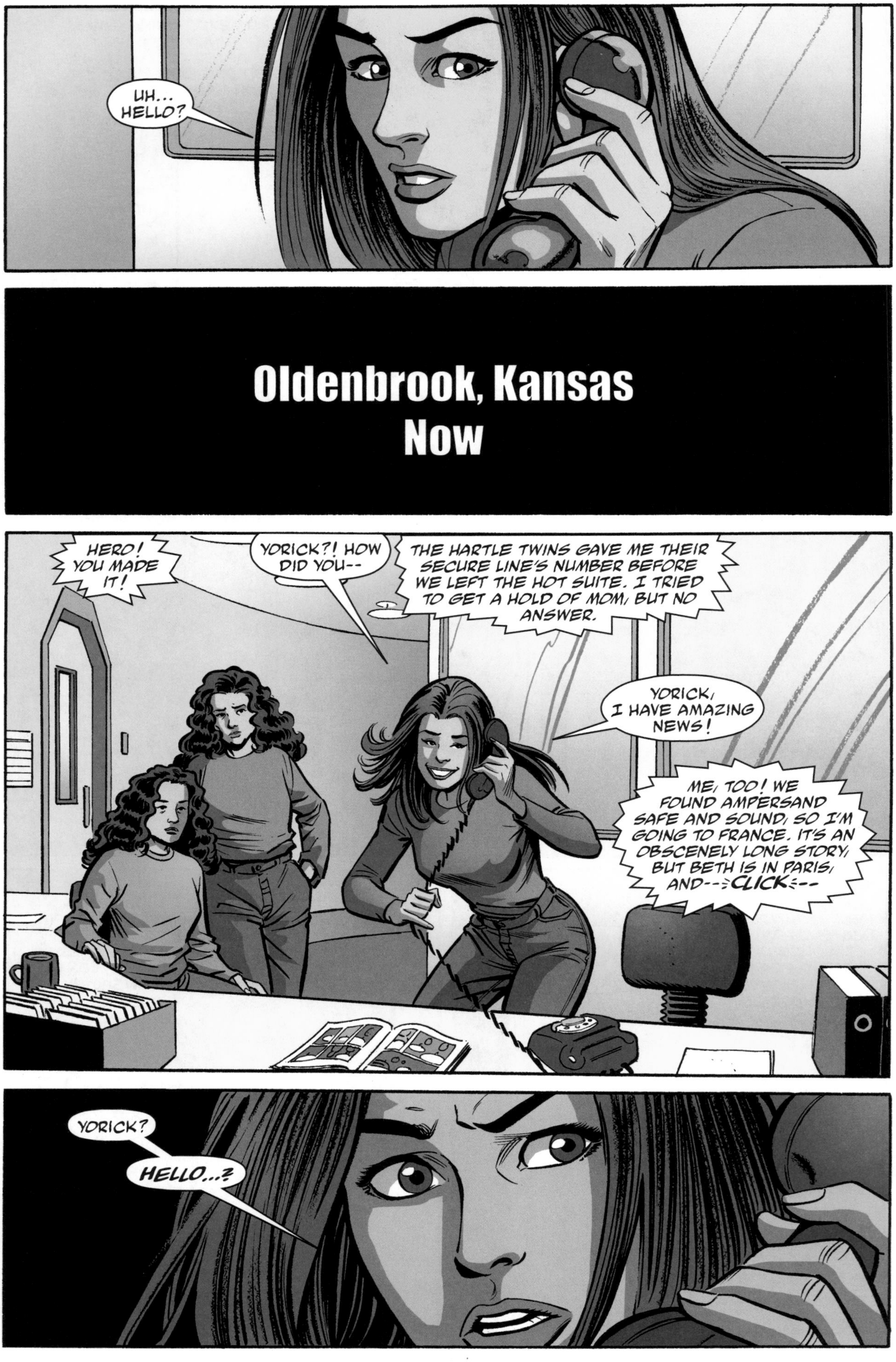
UH... HELLO?
Oldenbrook, Kansas
Now
HERO! YOU MADE IT!
YORICK?! HOW DID YOU--
THE HARTLE TWINS GAVE ME THEIR SECURE LINE'S NUMBER BEFORE WE LEFT THE HOT SUITE. I TRIED TO GET A HOLD OF MOM, BUT NO ANSWER.
YORICK, I HAVE AMAZING NEWS!
ME, TOO! WE FOUND AMPERSAND SAFE AND SOUND, SO I'M GOING TO FRANCE. IT'S AN OBSCENELY LONG STORY, BUT BETH IS IN PARIS, AND--CLICK--
YORICK?
HELLO...?

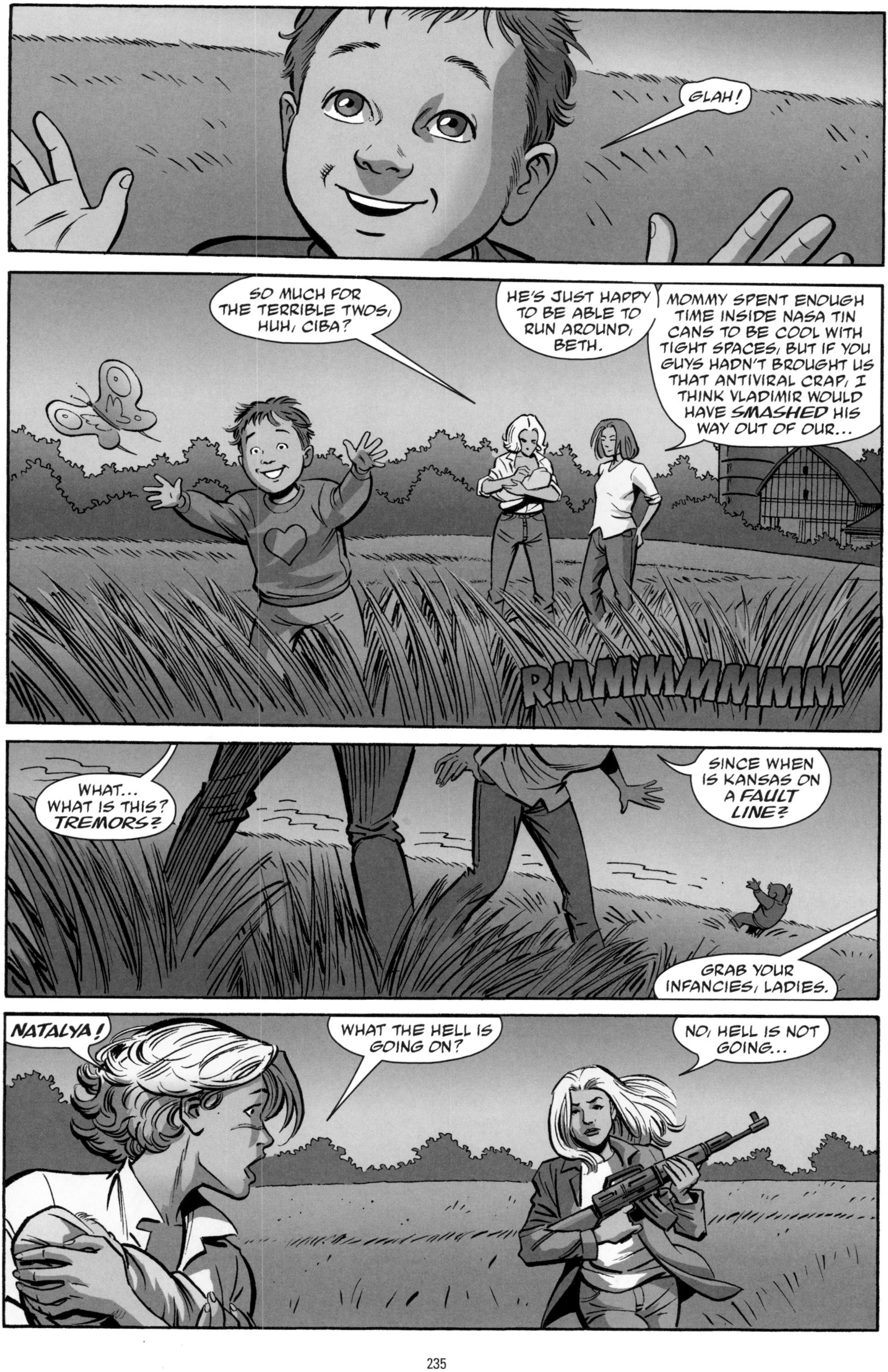
GLAH!
SO MUCH FOR THE TERRIBLE TWOS, HUH, CIBA?
HE'S JUST HAPPY TO BE ABLE TO RUN AROUND, BETH.
MOMMY SPENT ENOUGH TIME INSIDE NASA TIN CANS TO BE COOL WITH TIGHT SPACES, BUT IF YOU GUYS HADN'T BROUGHT US THAT ANTIVIRAL CRAP, I THINK VLADIMIR WOULD HAVE SMASHED HIS WAY OUT OF OUR...
RMMMMMMMM
WHAT... WHAT IS THIS? TREMORS?
SINCE WHEN IS KANSAS ON A FAULT LINE?
GRAB YOUR INFANCIES, LADIES.
NATALYA!
WHAT THE HELL IS GOING ON?
NO, HELL IS NOT GOING...

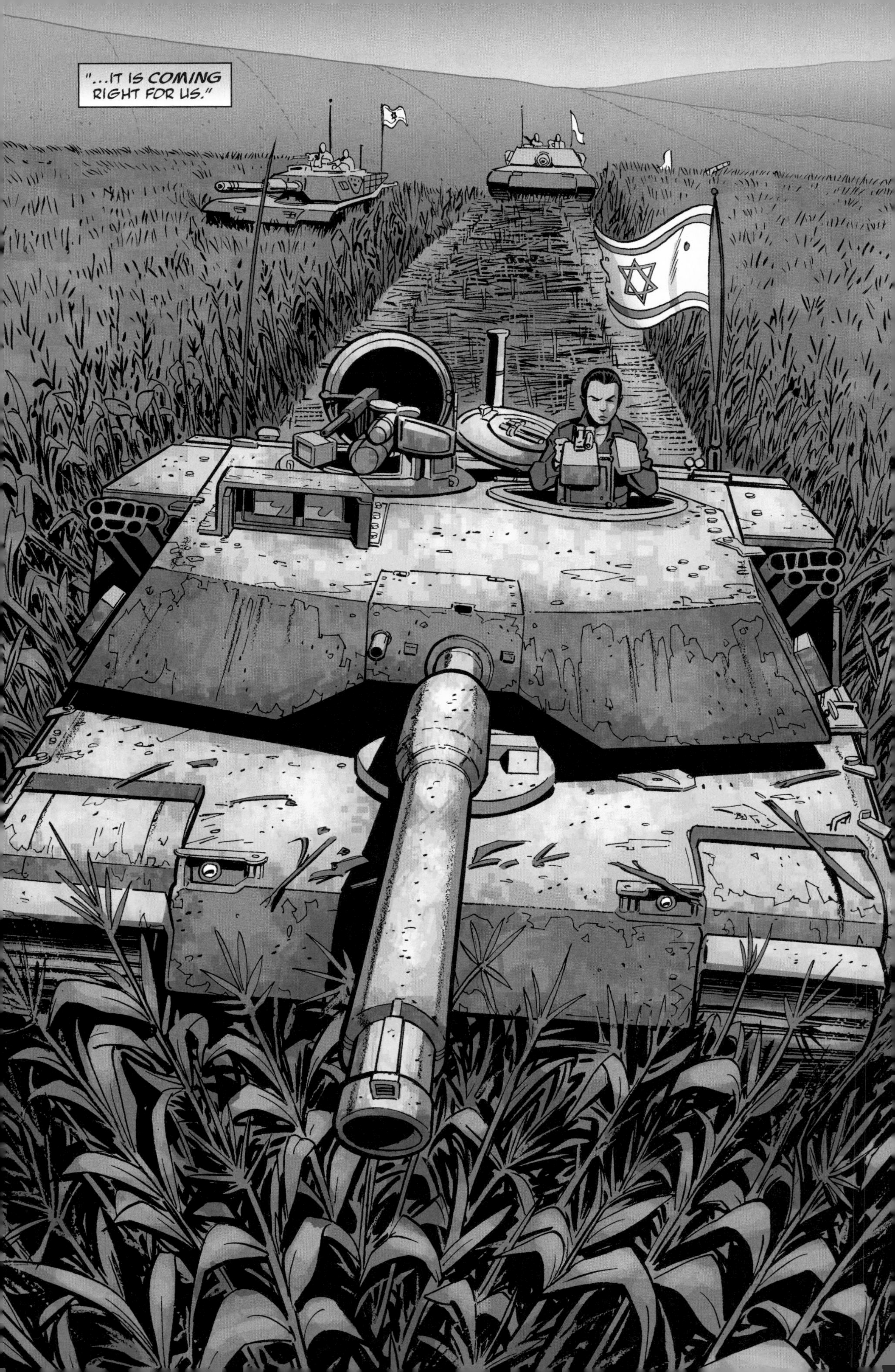
"...IT IS COMING RIGHT FOR US."

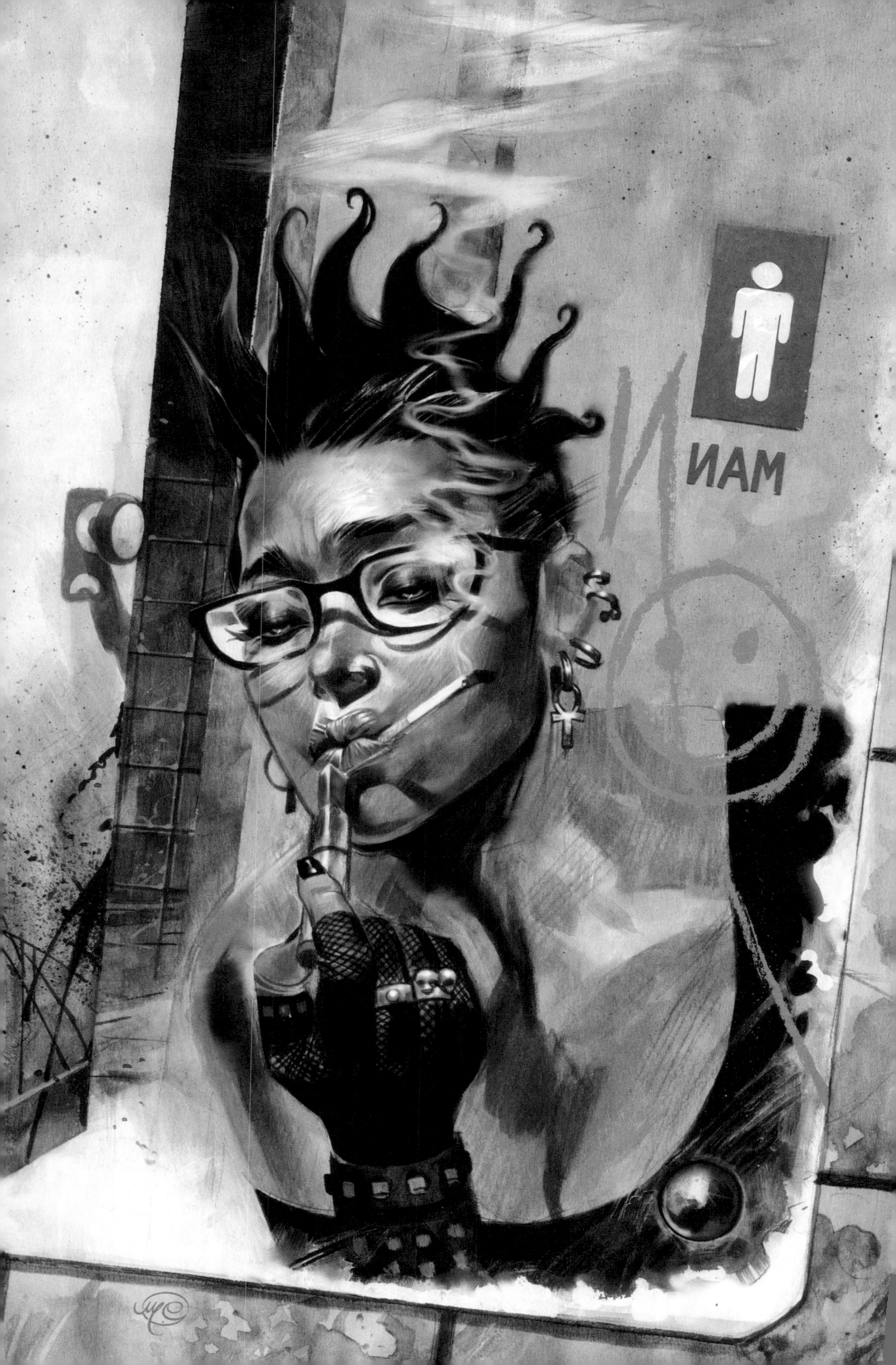

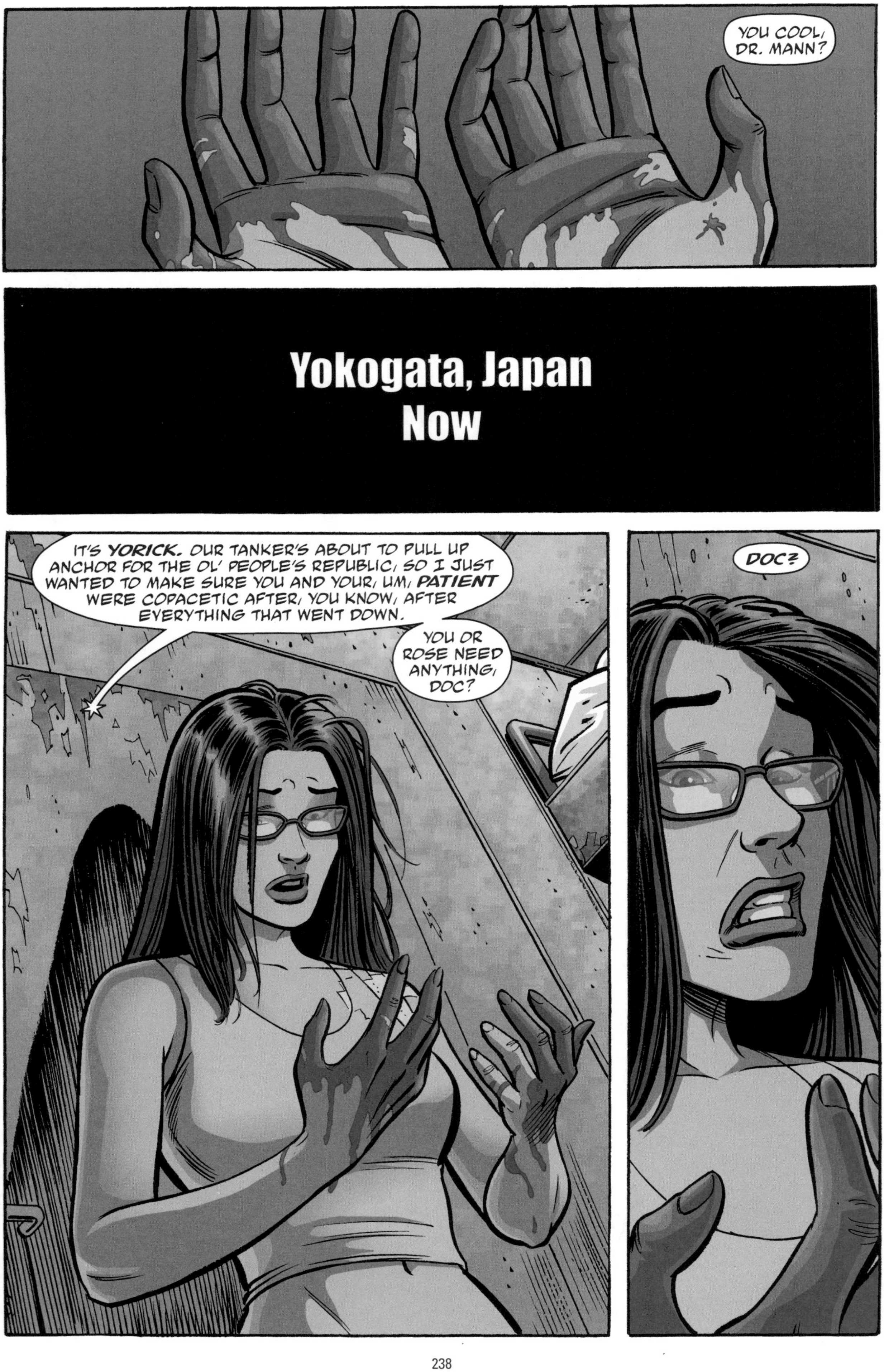
YOU COOL, DR. MANN?
Yokogata, Japan
Now
IT'S YORICK. OUR TANKER'S ABOUT TO PULL UP ANCHOR FOR THE OL' PEOPLE'S REPUBLIC, SO I JUST WANTED TO MAKE SURE YOU AND YOUR, UM, PATIENT WERE COPACETIC AFTER, YOU KNOW, AFTER EVERYTHING THAT WENT DOWN.
YOU OR ROSE NEED ANYTHING, DOC?
DOC?

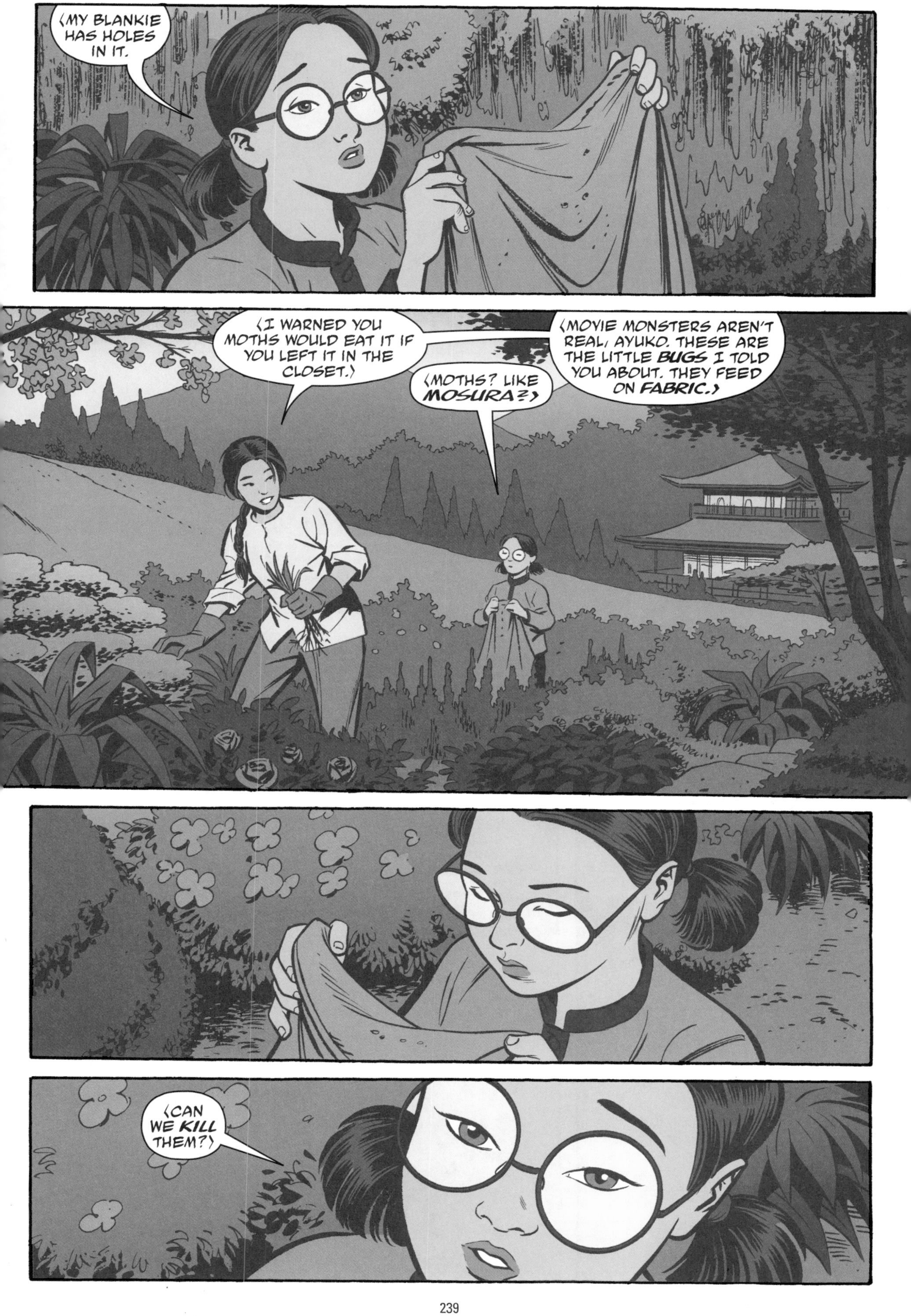
‹MY BLANKIE HAS HOLES IN IT.
‹I WARNED YOU MOTHS WOULD EAT IT IF YOU LEFT IT IN THE CLOSET.›
‹MOTHS? LIKE **MOSURA?**›
‹MOVIE MONSTERS AREN'T REAL, AYUKO. THESE ARE THE LITTLE **BUGS** I TOLD YOU ABOUT. THEY FEED ON **FABRIC.**›
‹CAN WE **KILL** THEM?›

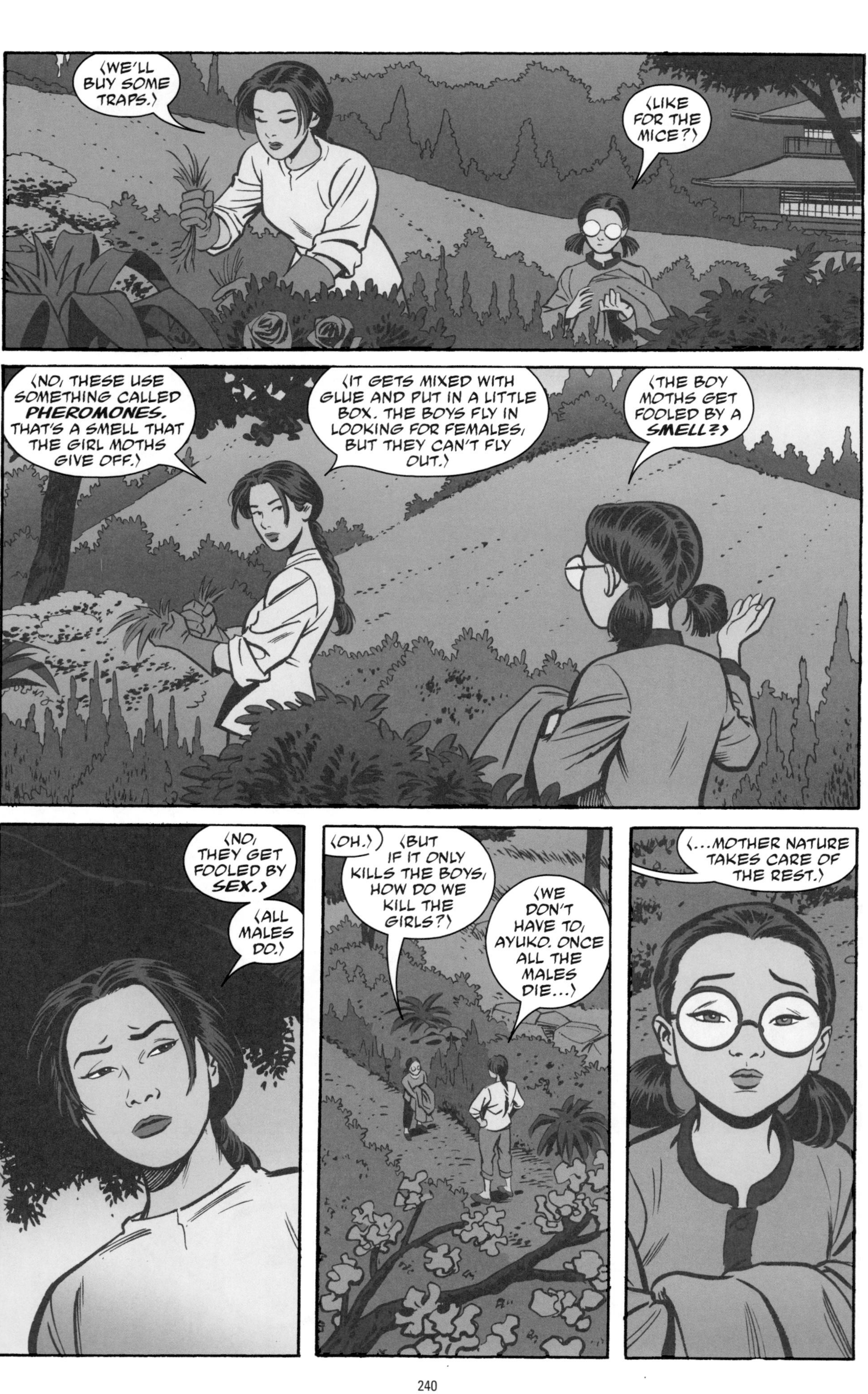
⟨WE'LL BUY SOME TRAPS.⟩
⟨LIKE FOR THE MICE?⟩
⟨NO, THESE USE SOMETHING CALLED **PHEROMONES.** THAT'S A SMELL THAT THE GIRL MOTHS GIVE OFF.⟩
⟨IT GETS MIXED WITH GLUE AND PUT IN A LITTLE BOX. THE BOYS FLY IN LOOKING FOR FEMALES, BUT THEY CAN'T FLY OUT.⟩
⟨THE BOY MOTHS GET FOOLED BY A **SMELL?**⟩
⟨NO, THEY GET FOOLED BY **SEX.**⟩
⟨ALL MALES DO.⟩
⟨OH.⟩
⟨BUT IF IT ONLY KILLS THE BOYS, HOW DO WE KILL THE GIRLS?⟩
⟨WE DON'T HAVE TO, AYUKO. ONCE ALL THE MALES DIE...⟩
⟨...MOTHER NATURE TAKES CARE OF THE REST.⟩

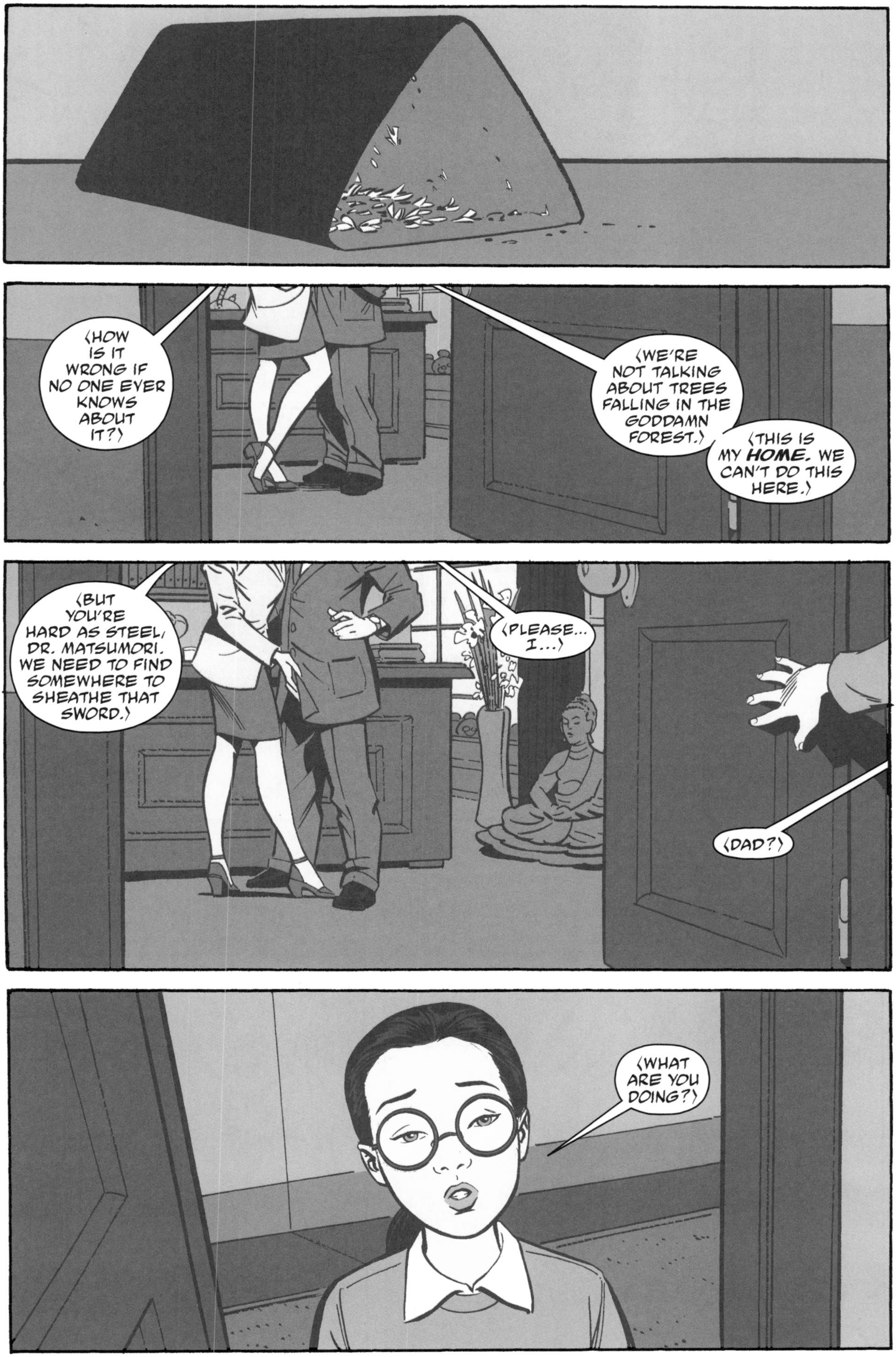
⟨HOW IS IT WRONG IF NO ONE EVER KNOWS ABOUT IT?⟩
⟨WE'RE NOT TALKING ABOUT TREES FALLING IN THE GODDAMN FOREST.⟩
⟨THIS IS MY **HOME.** WE CAN'T DO THIS HERE.⟩
⟨BUT YOU'RE HARD AS STEEL, DR. MATSUMORI. WE NEED TO FIND SOMEWHERE TO SHEATHE THAT SWORD.⟩
⟨PLEASE... I...⟩
⟨DAD?⟩
⟨WHAT ARE YOU DOING?⟩

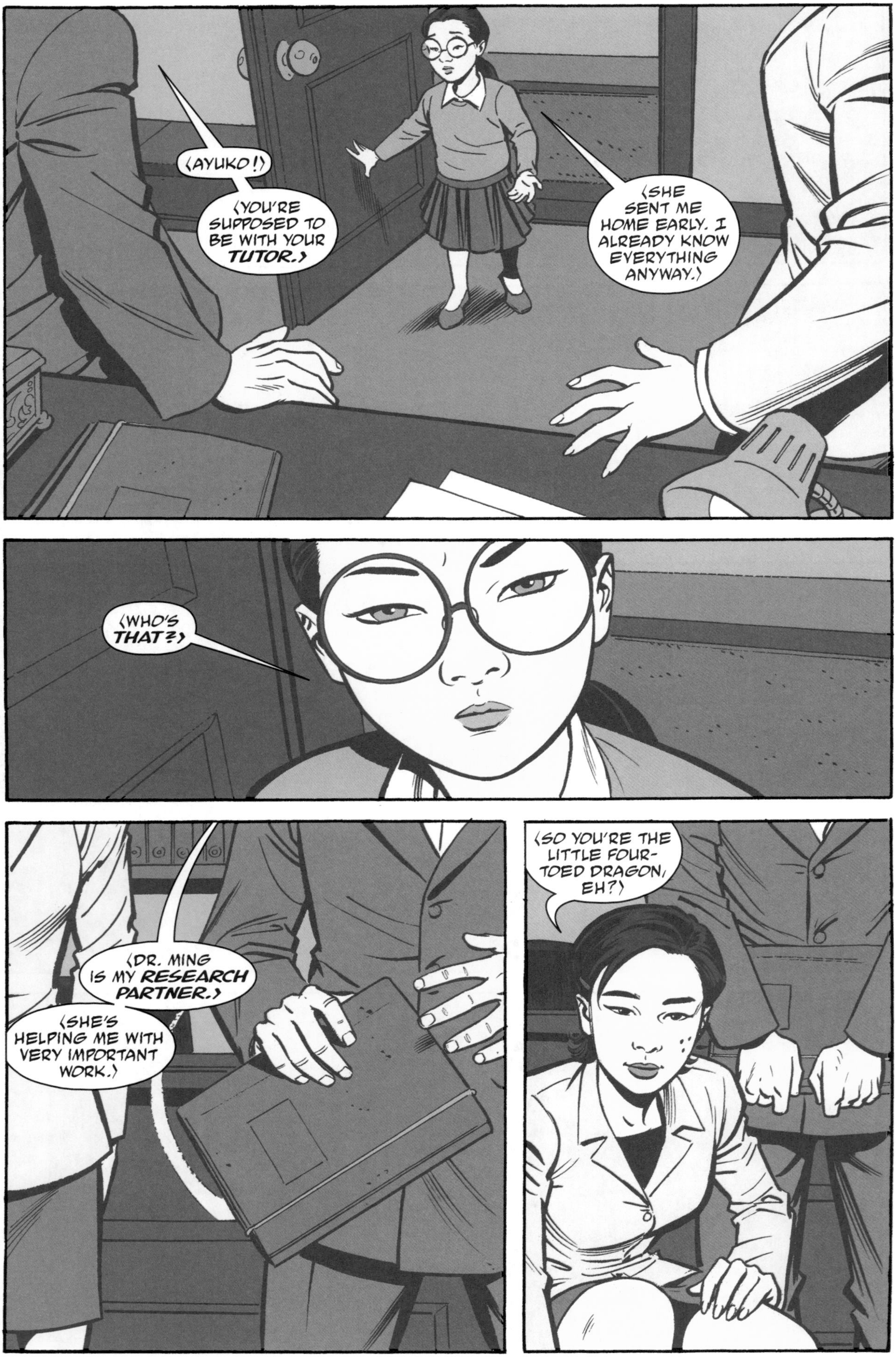

⟨AYUKO!⟩
⟨YOU'RE SUPPOSED TO BE WITH YOUR **TUTOR.**⟩
⟨SHE SENT ME HOME EARLY. I ALREADY KNOW EVERYTHING ANYWAY.⟩
⟨WHO'S **THAT?**⟩
⟨DR. MING IS MY **RESEARCH PARTNER.**⟩
⟨SHE'S HELPING ME WITH VERY IMPORTANT WORK.⟩
⟨SO YOU'RE THE LITTLE FOUR-TOED DRAGON, EH?⟩

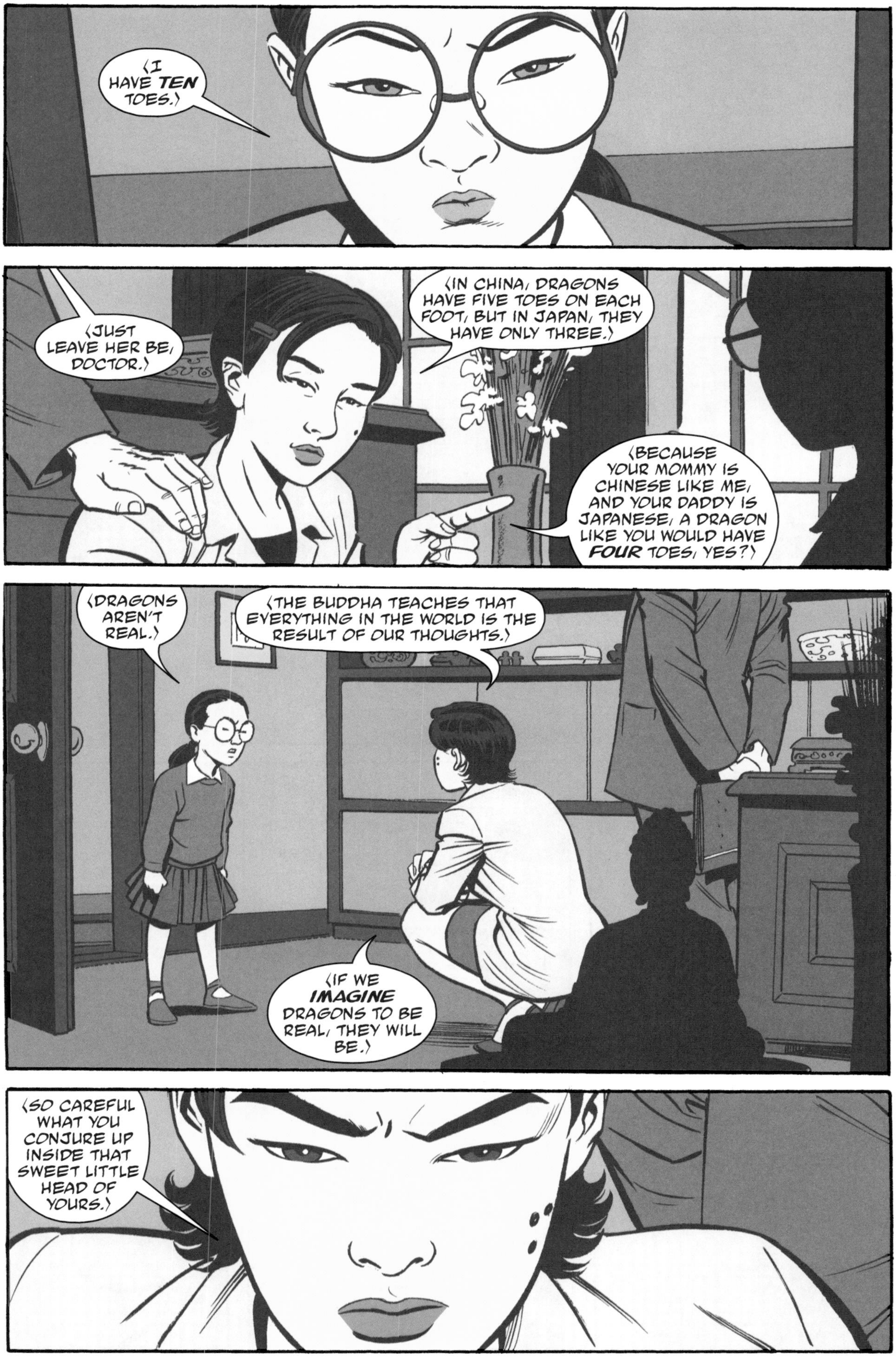
〈I HAVE **TEN** TOES.〉
〈JUST LEAVE HER BE, DOCTOR.〉
〈IN CHINA, DRAGONS HAVE FIVE TOES ON EACH FOOT, BUT IN JAPAN, THEY HAVE ONLY THREE.〉
〈BECAUSE YOUR MOMMY IS CHINESE LIKE ME, AND YOUR DADDY IS JAPANESE, A DRAGON LIKE YOU WOULD HAVE **FOUR** TOES, YES?〉
〈DRAGONS AREN'T REAL.〉
〈THE BUDDHA TEACHES THAT EVERYTHING IN THE WORLD IS THE RESULT OF OUR THOUGHTS.〉
〈IF WE ***IMAGINE*** DRAGONS TO BE REAL, THEY WILL BE.〉
〈SO CAREFUL WHAT YOU CONJURE UP INSIDE THAT SWEET LITTLE HEAD OF YOURS.〉

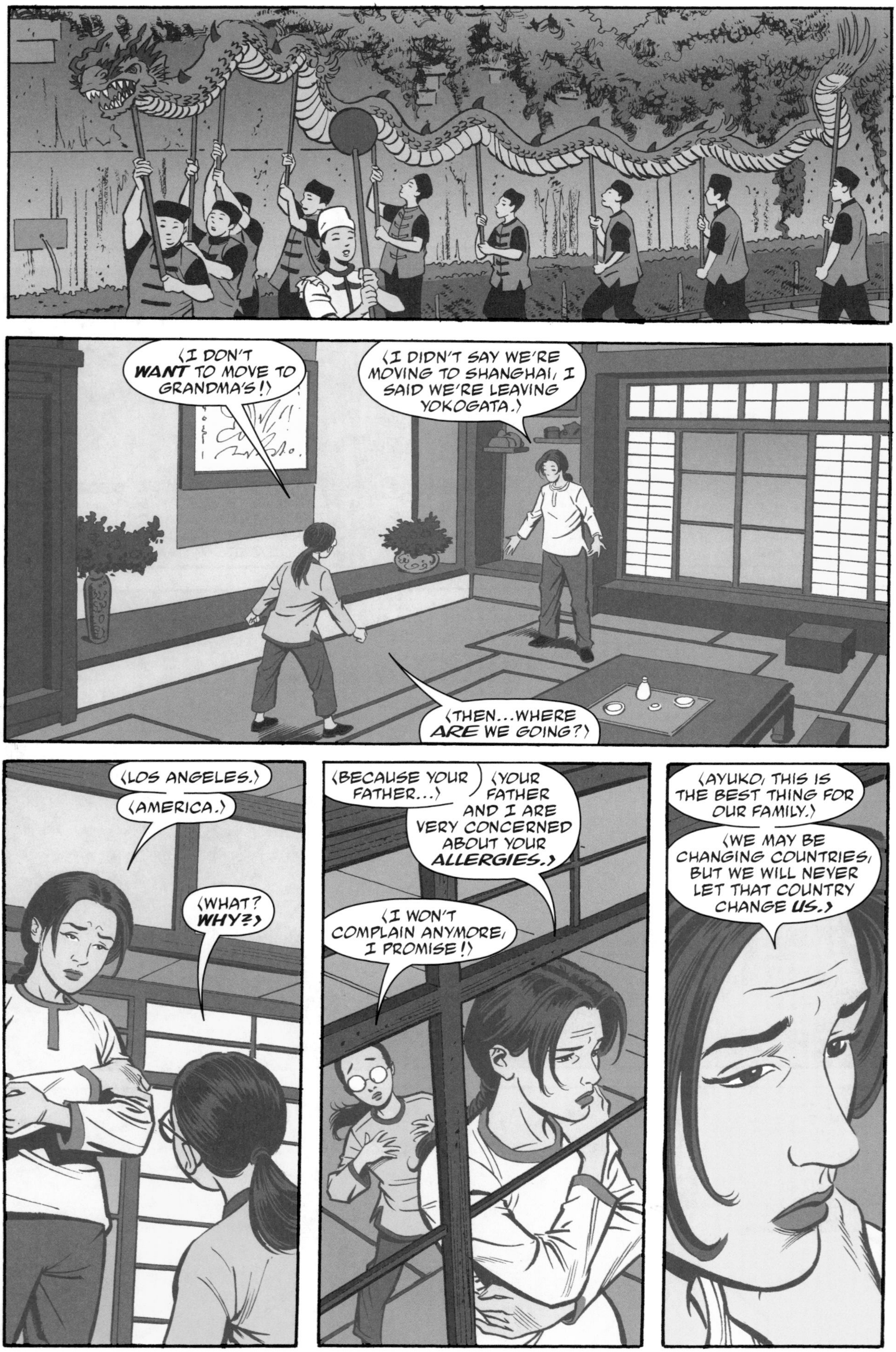

⟨I DON'T WANT TO MOVE TO GRANDMA'S!⟩
⟨I DIDN'T SAY WE'RE MOVING TO SHANGHAI, I SAID WE'RE LEAVING YOKOGATA.⟩
⟨THEN...WHERE ARE WE GOING?⟩
⟨LOS ANGELES.⟩
⟨AMERICA.⟩
⟨WHAT? WHY?⟩
⟨BECAUSE YOUR FATHER...⟩
⟨YOUR FATHER AND I ARE VERY CONCERNED ABOUT YOUR ALLERGIES.⟩
⟨I WON'T COMPLAIN ANYMORE, I PROMISE!⟩
⟨AYUKO, THIS IS THE BEST THING FOR OUR FAMILY.⟩
⟨WE MAY BE CHANGING COUNTRIES, BUT WE WILL NEVER LET THAT COUNTRY CHANGE US.⟩

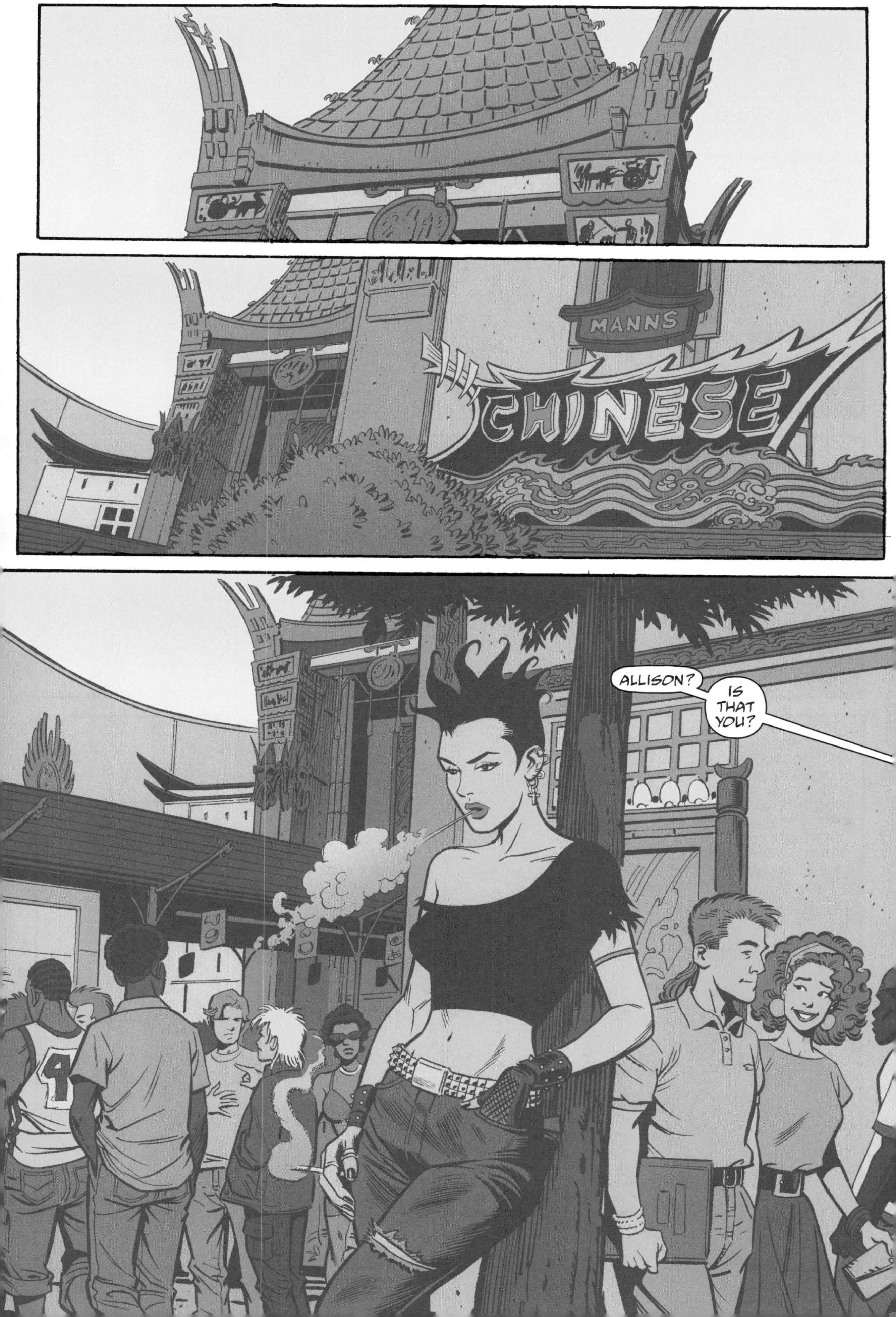
MANNS
CHINESE
ALLISON?
IS THAT YOU?

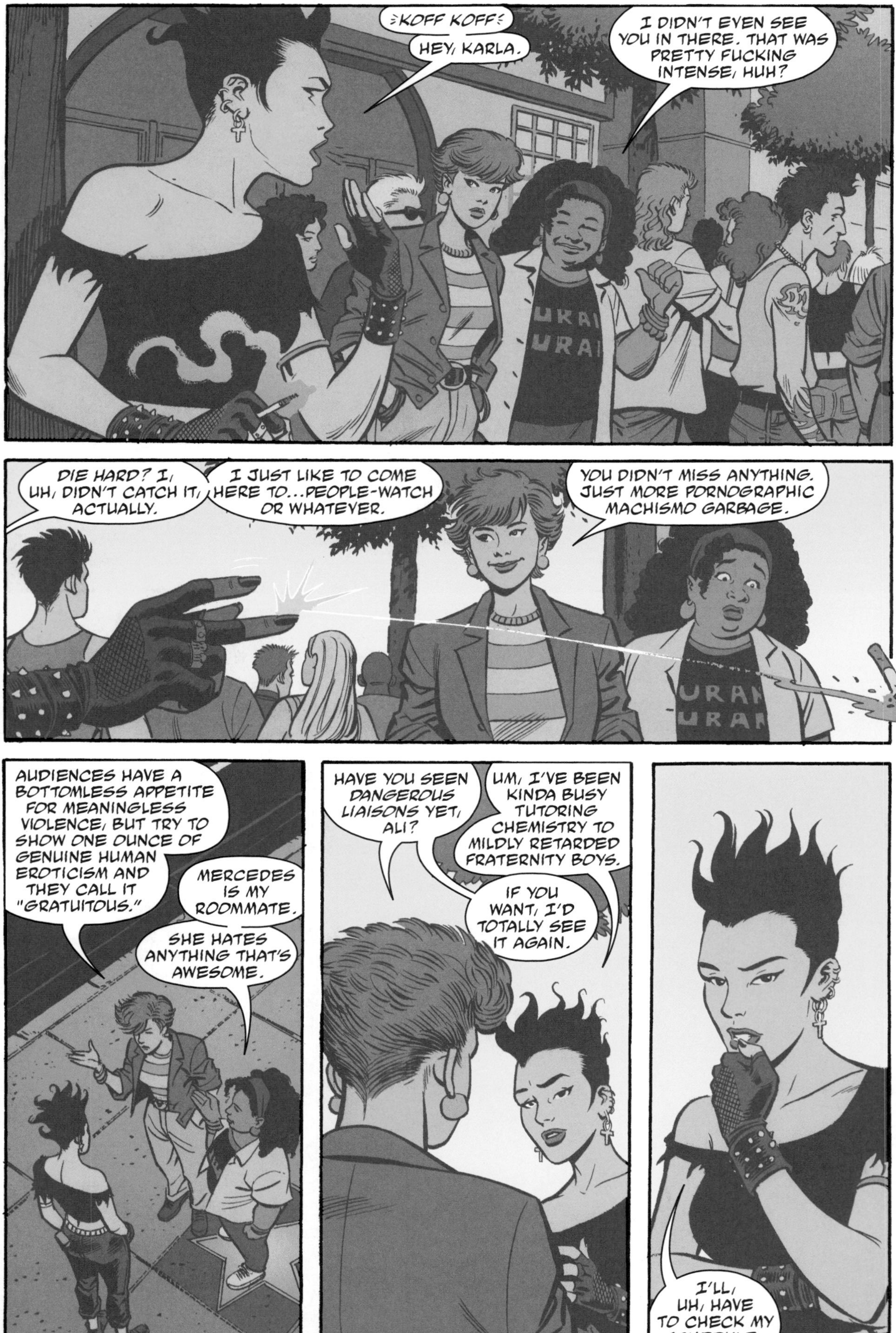
KOFF KOFF
HEY, KARLA.
I DIDN'T EVEN SEE YOU IN THERE. THAT WAS PRETTY FUCKING INTENSE, HUH?
DIE HARD? I, UH, DIDN'T CATCH IT, ACTUALLY.
I JUST LIKE TO COME HERE TO...PEOPLE-WATCH OR WHATEVER.
YOU DIDN'T MISS ANYTHING. JUST MORE PORNOGRAPHIC MACHISMO GARBAGE.
AUDIENCES HAVE A BOTTOMLESS APPETITE FOR MEANINGLESS VIOLENCE, BUT TRY TO SHOW ONE OUNCE OF GENUINE HUMAN EROTICISM AND THEY CALL IT "GRATUITOUS."
MERCEDES IS MY ROOMMATE.
SHE HATES ANYTHING THAT'S AWESOME.
HAVE YOU SEEN DANGEROUS LIAISONS YET, ALI?
UM, I'VE BEEN KINDA BUSY TUTORING CHEMISTRY TO MILDLY RETARDED FRATERNITY BOYS.
IF YOU WANT, I'D TOTALLY SEE IT AGAIN.
I'LL, UH, HAVE TO CHECK MY SCHEDULE.

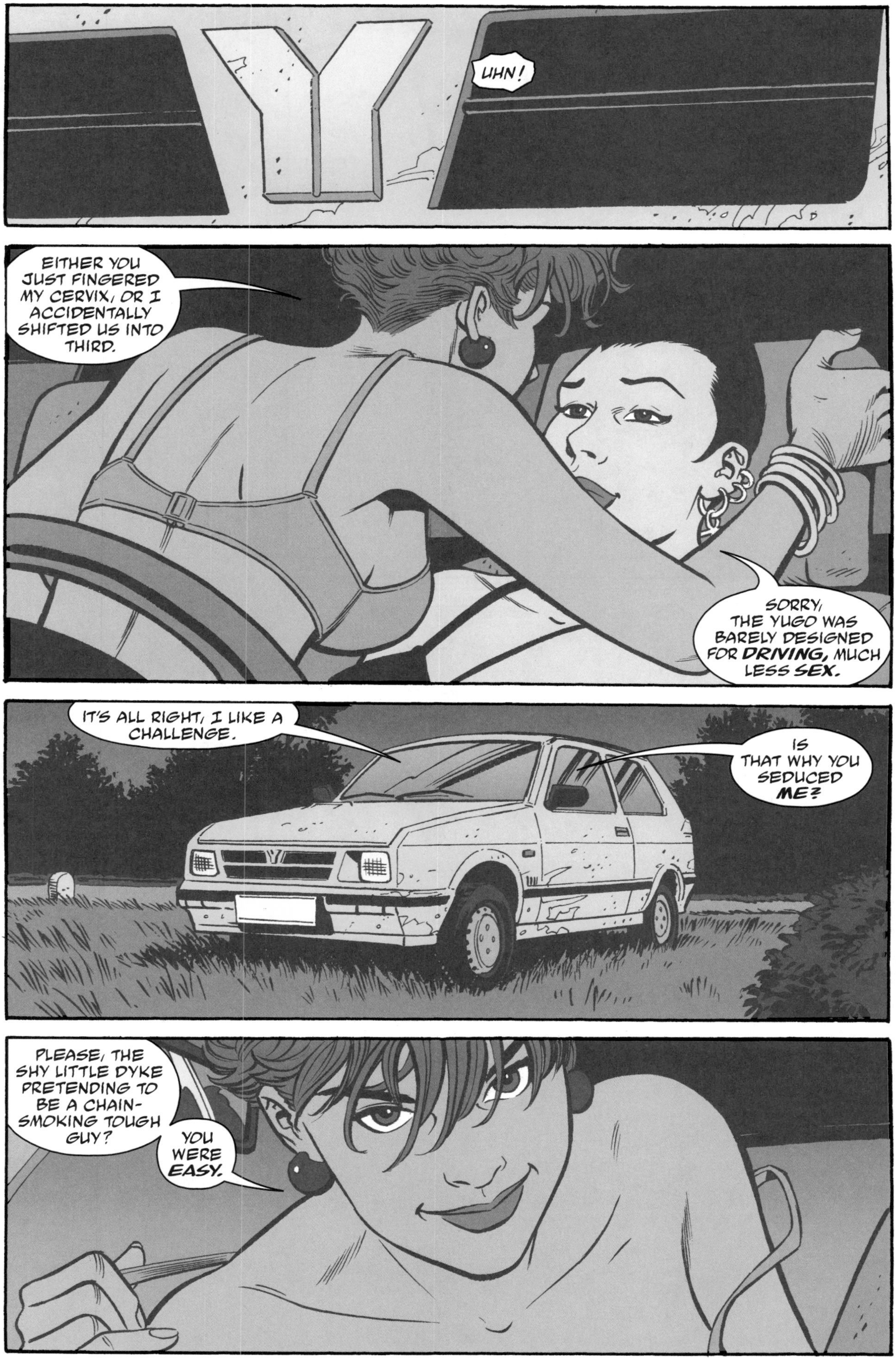
UHN!
EITHER YOU JUST FINGERED MY CERVIX, OR I ACCIDENTALLY SHIFTED US INTO THIRD.
SORRY, THE YUGO WAS BARELY DESIGNED FOR DRIVING, MUCH LESS SEX.
IT'S ALL RIGHT, I LIKE A CHALLENGE.
IS THAT WHY YOU SEDUCED ME?
PLEASE, THE SHY LITTLE DYKE PRETENDING TO BE A CHAIN-SMOKING TOUGH GUY?
YOU WERE EASY.

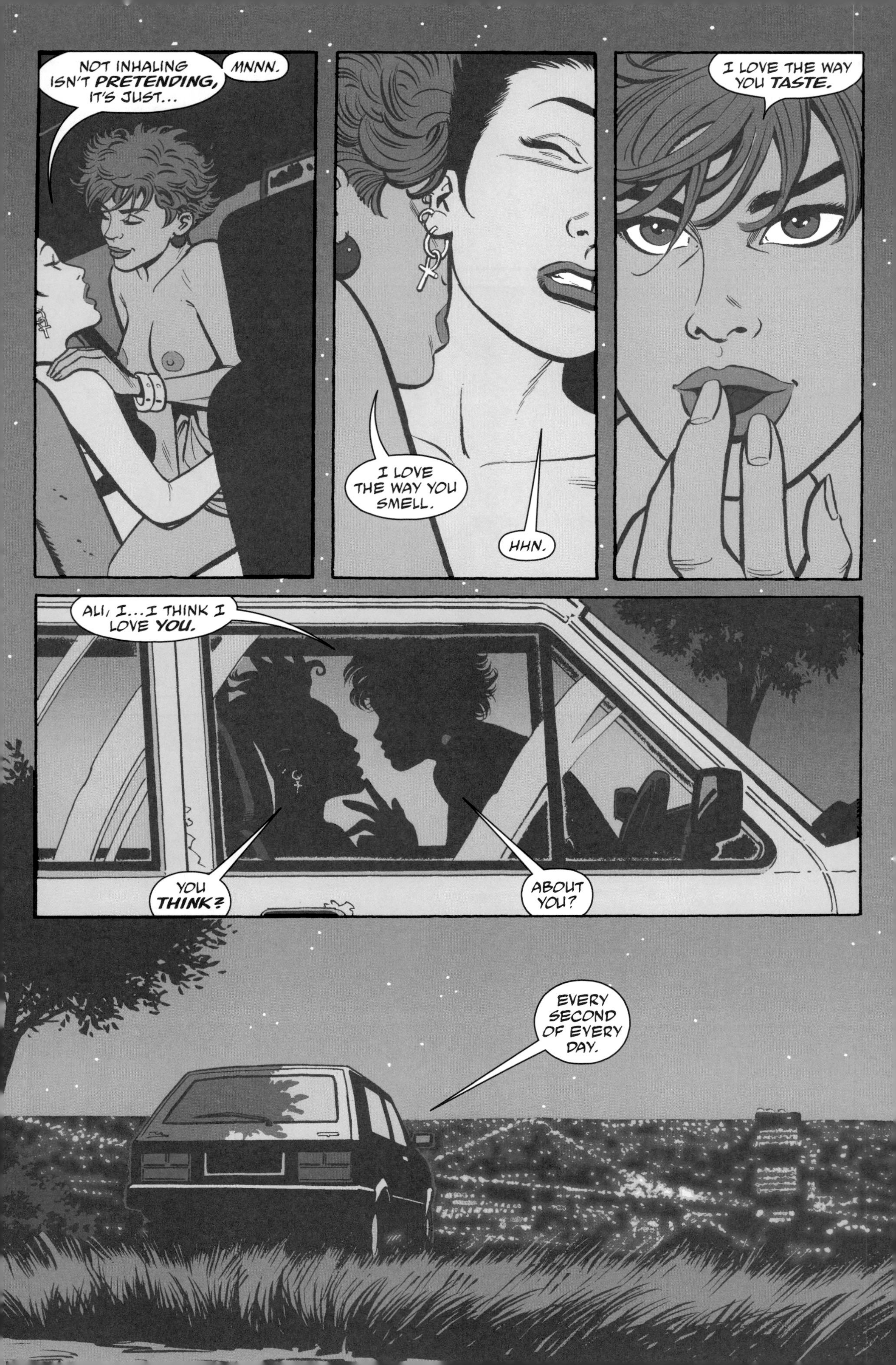

NOT INHALING ISN'T PRETENDING, IT'S JUST...
MNNN.
I LOVE THE WAY YOU SMELL.
HHN.
I LOVE THE WAY YOU TASTE.
ALI, I...I THINK I LOVE YOU.
YOU THINK?
ABOUT YOU?
EVERY SECOND OF EVERY DAY.

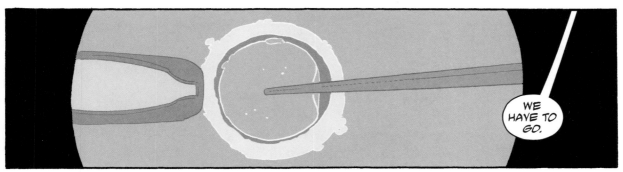

WE HAVE TO GO.

WHAT ARE YOU TALKING ABOUT?

THE U.S. IS MADE UP OF MORALIZING COWARDS.

I'LL HAVE TO CONTINUE MY WORK ELSEWHERE.

I'M NOT COMING WITH YOU.

OH, REALLY? SO YOU PLAN TO PAY FOR UNIVERSITY ON YOUR OWN?

HOW HARD DO YOU THINK IT WILL BE FOR ME TO GET A *SCHOLARSHIP*, DAD?

YOU NEVER EVEN OPEN A *BOOK*.

I DON'T *NEED* TO. SHIT YOU STRUGGLE TO COMPREHEND IS *EASY* FOR ME. I CAN SPEND TIME *LIVING* LIFE INSTEAD OF JUST *OBSERVING* IT.

IF THIS IS ABOUT BOYS, YOU'LL HAVE *MILLIONS* TO CHOOSE FROM WHERE WE'RE GOING.

I FUCK *GIRLS*, DAD.

JUST LIKE YOU.

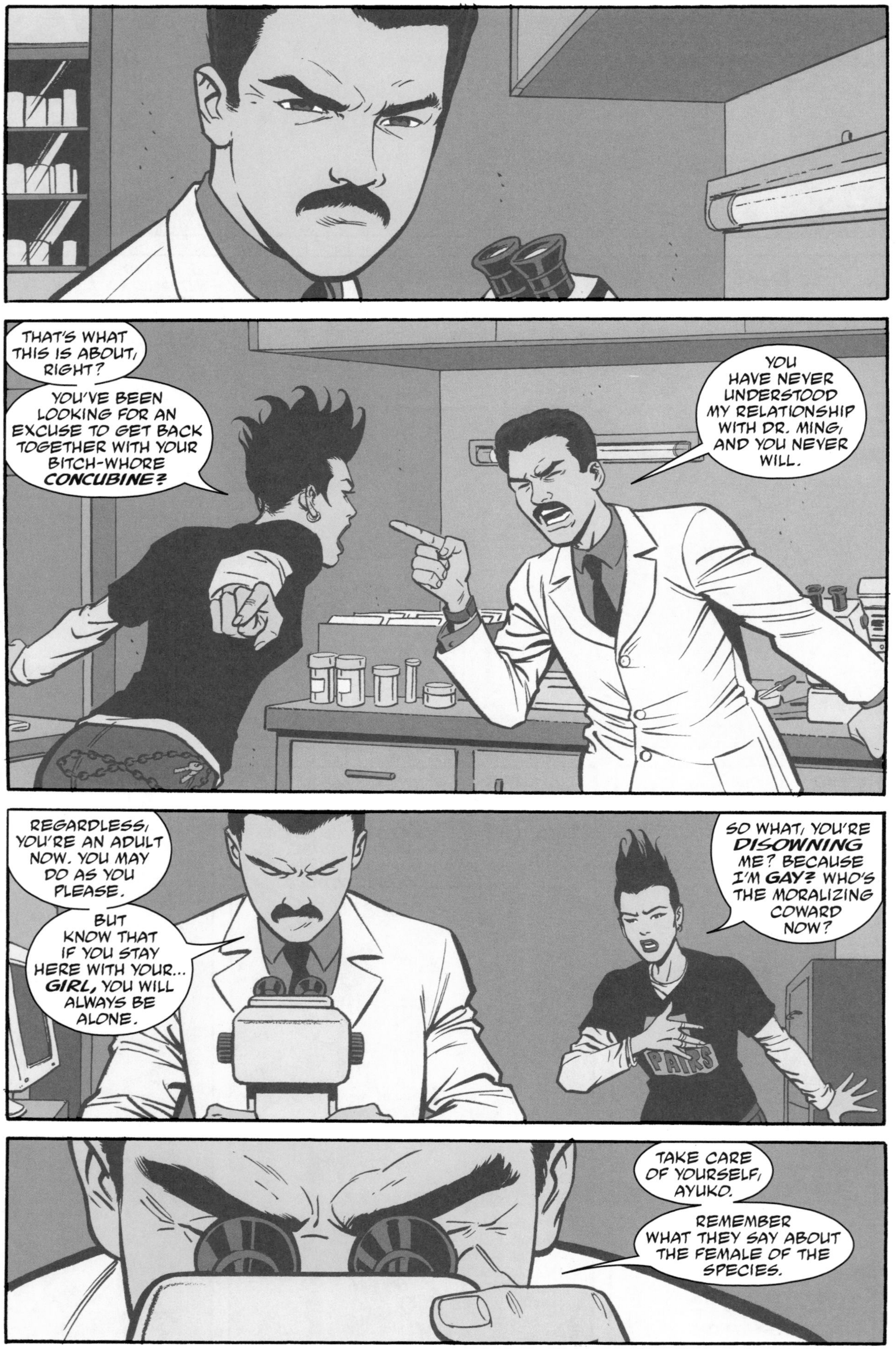
THAT'S WHAT THIS IS ABOUT, RIGHT?
YOU'VE BEEN LOOKING FOR AN EXCUSE TO GET BACK TOGETHER WITH YOUR BITCH-WHORE ***CONCUBINE?***
YOU HAVE NEVER UNDERSTOOD MY RELATIONSHIP WITH DR. MING, AND YOU NEVER WILL.
REGARDLESS, YOU'RE AN ADULT NOW. YOU MAY DO AS YOU PLEASE.
BUT KNOW THAT IF YOU STAY HERE WITH YOUR... ***GIRL,*** YOU WILL ALWAYS BE ALONE.
SO WHAT, YOU'RE ***DISOWNING*** ME? BECAUSE I'M ***GAY?*** WHO'S THE MORALIZING COWARD NOW?
PARIS
TAKE CARE OF YOURSELF, AYUKO.
REMEMBER WHAT THEY SAY ABOUT THE FEMALE OF THE SPECIES.

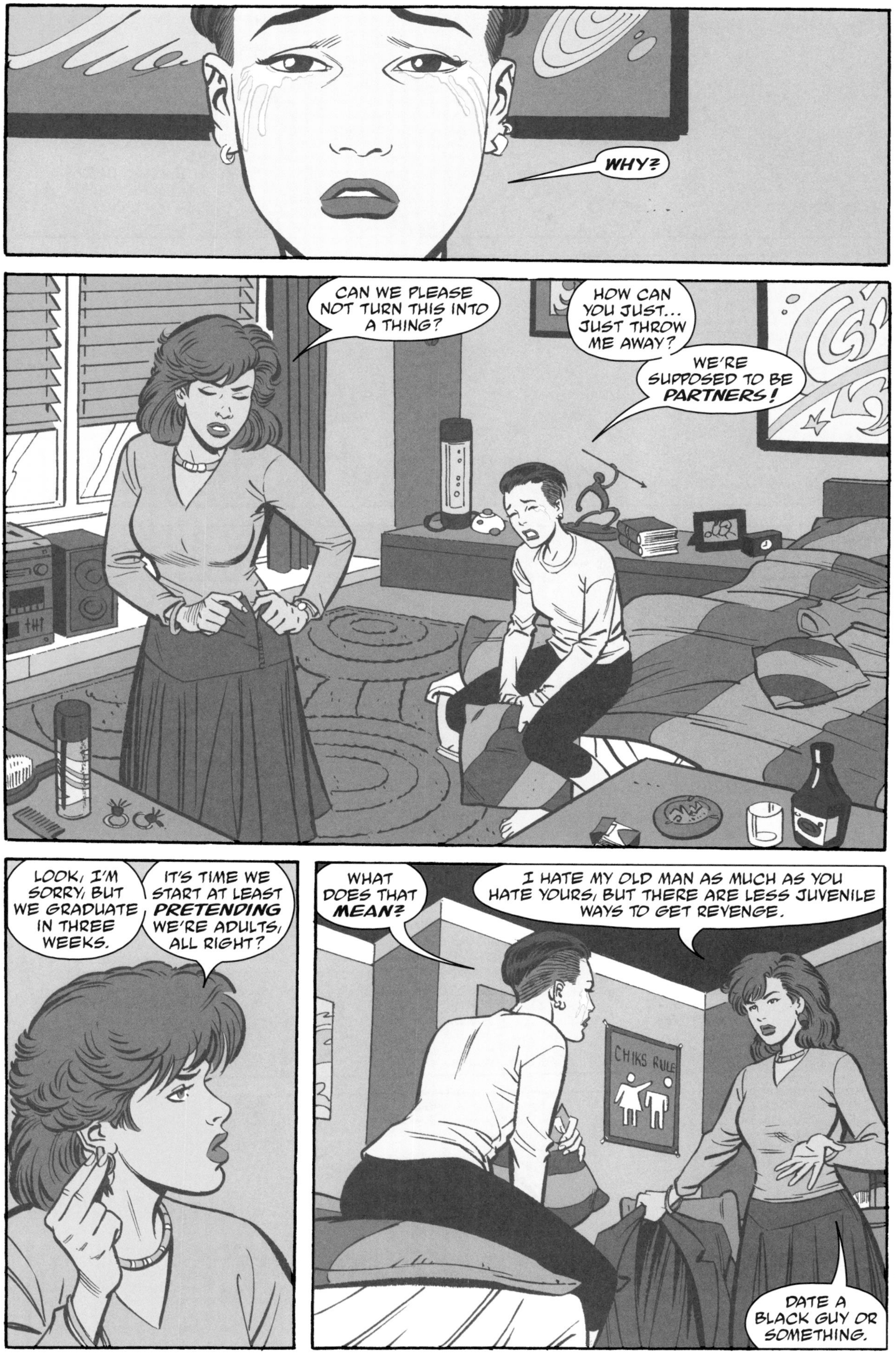
WHY?
CAN WE PLEASE NOT TURN THIS INTO A THING?
HOW CAN YOU JUST... JUST THROW ME AWAY?
WE'RE SUPPOSED TO BE PARTNERS!
LOOK, I'M SORRY, BUT WE GRADUATE IN THREE WEEKS.
IT'S TIME WE START AT LEAST PRETENDING WE'RE ADULTS, ALL RIGHT?
WHAT DOES THAT MEAN?
I HATE MY OLD MAN AS MUCH AS YOU HATE YOURS, BUT THERE ARE LESS JUVENILE WAYS TO GET REVENGE.
CHIKS RULE
DATE A BLACK GUY OR SOMETHING.

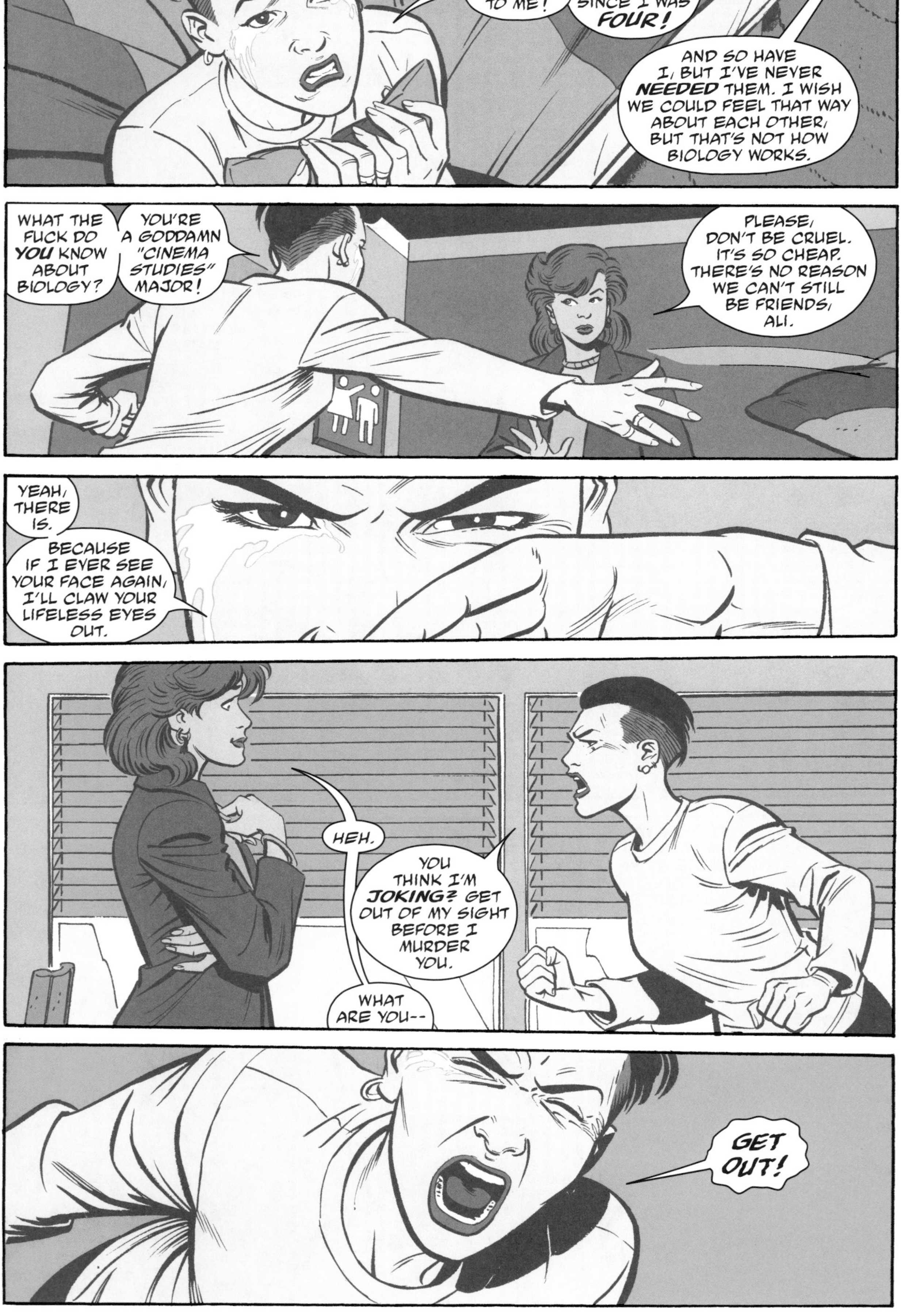
THIS ISN'T A GAME TO ME!
I'VE LIKED GIRLS SINCE I WAS FOUR!
AND SO HAVE I, BUT I'VE NEVER NEEDED THEM. I WISH WE COULD FEEL THAT WAY ABOUT EACH OTHER, BUT THAT'S NOT HOW BIOLOGY WORKS.
WHAT THE FUCK DO YOU KNOW ABOUT BIOLOGY?
YOU'RE A GODDAMN "CINEMA STUDIES" MAJOR!
PLEASE, DON'T BE CRUEL. IT'S SO CHEAP. THERE'S NO REASON WE CAN'T STILL BE FRIENDS, ALI.
YEAH, THERE IS.
BECAUSE IF I EVER SEE YOUR FACE AGAIN, I'LL CLAW YOUR LIFELESS EYES OUT.
HEH.
WHAT ARE YOU--
YOU THINK I'M JOKING? GET OUT OF MY SIGHT BEFORE I MURDER YOU.
GET OUT!

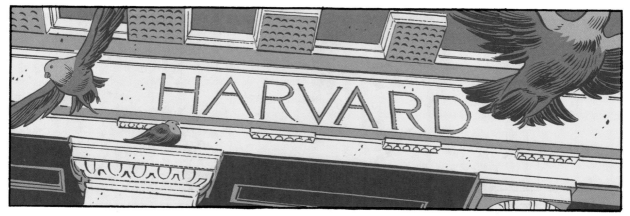

PROFESSOR MANN?

I HAVE OFFICE HOURS AFTER MY THURSDAY BIOTECH, MISTER...?

MY NAME'S SUNIL.

I WAS JUST CURIOUS HOW YOU FELT ABOUT CLINTON BANNING SOMATIC CELL NUCLEAR TRANSFER FOR THE CREATION OF CHILDREN.

HE MIGHT AS WELL BAN ANDROIDS RUNNING FOR CONGRESS. I HIGHLY DOUBT WE'LL SEE A VIABLE HUMAN *CLONE* FOR ANOTHER FIFTY YEARS.

SO YOU DON'T BELIEVE THE RUMORS ABOUT MATSUMORI?

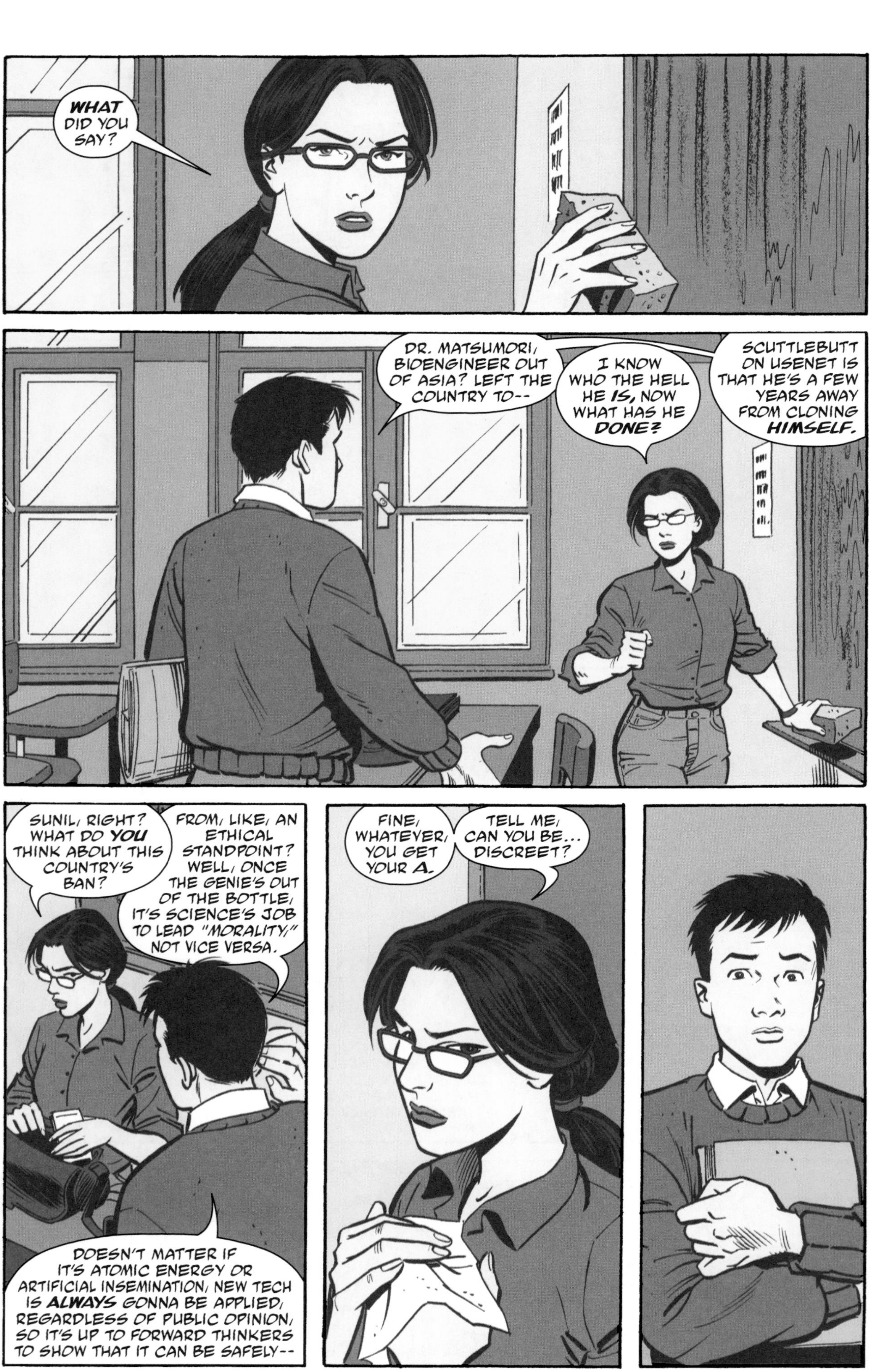
WHAT DID YOU SAY?
DR. MATSUMORI, BIOENGINEER OUT OF ASIA? LEFT THE COUNTRY TO--
I KNOW WHO THE HELL HE IS, NOW WHAT HAS HE DONE?
SCUTTLEBUTT ON USENET IS THAT HE'S A FEW YEARS AWAY FROM CLONING HIMSELF.
SUNIL, RIGHT? WHAT DO YOU THINK ABOUT THIS COUNTRY'S BAN?
FROM, LIKE, AN ETHICAL STANDPOINT? WELL, ONCE THE GENIE'S OUT OF THE BOTTLE, IT'S SCIENCE'S JOB TO LEAD "MORALITY," NOT VICE VERSA.
DOESN'T MATTER IF IT'S ATOMIC ENERGY OR ARTIFICIAL INSEMINATION, NEW TECH IS ALWAYS GONNA BE APPLIED, REGARDLESS OF PUBLIC OPINION, SO IT'S UP TO FORWARD THINKERS TO SHOW THAT IT CAN BE SAFELY--
FINE, WHATEVER, YOU GET YOUR A.
TELL ME, CAN YOU BE... DISCREET?

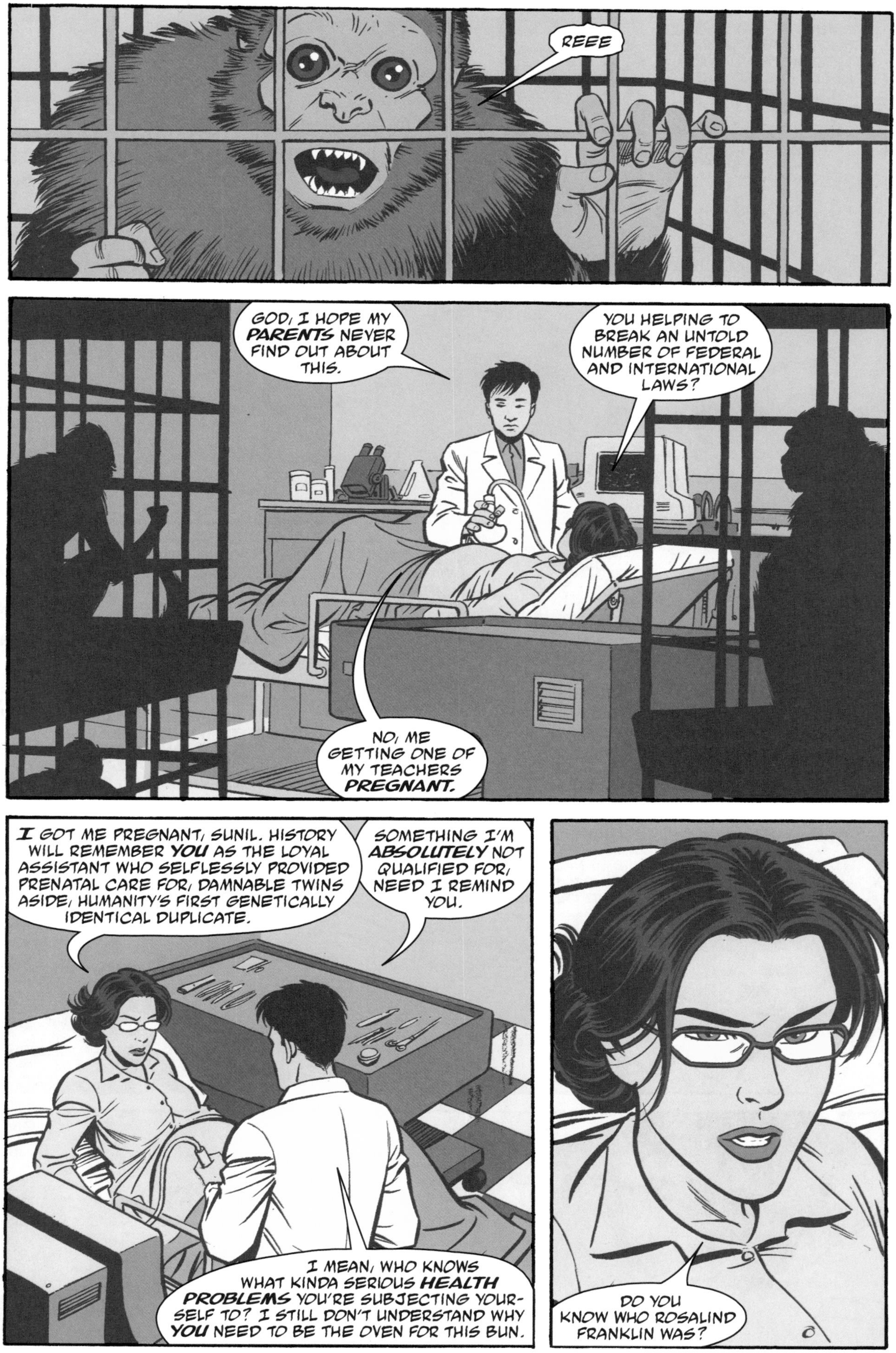
REEE
GOD, I HOPE MY PARENTS NEVER FIND OUT ABOUT THIS.
YOU HELPING TO BREAK AN UNTOLD NUMBER OF FEDERAL AND INTERNATIONAL LAWS?
NO, ME GETTING ONE OF MY TEACHERS PREGNANT.
I GOT ME PREGNANT, SUNIL. HISTORY WILL REMEMBER YOU AS THE LOYAL ASSISTANT WHO SELFLESSLY PROVIDED PRENATAL CARE FOR, DAMNABLE TWINS ASIDE, HUMANITY'S FIRST GENETICALLY IDENTICAL DUPLICATE.
SOMETHING I'M ABSOLUTELY NOT QUALIFIED FOR, NEED I REMIND YOU.
I MEAN, WHO KNOWS WHAT KINDA SERIOUS HEALTH PROBLEMS YOU'RE SUBJECTING YOURSELF TO? I STILL DON'T UNDERSTAND WHY YOU NEED TO BE THE OVEN FOR THIS BUN.
DO YOU KNOW WHO ROSALIND FRANKLIN WAS?

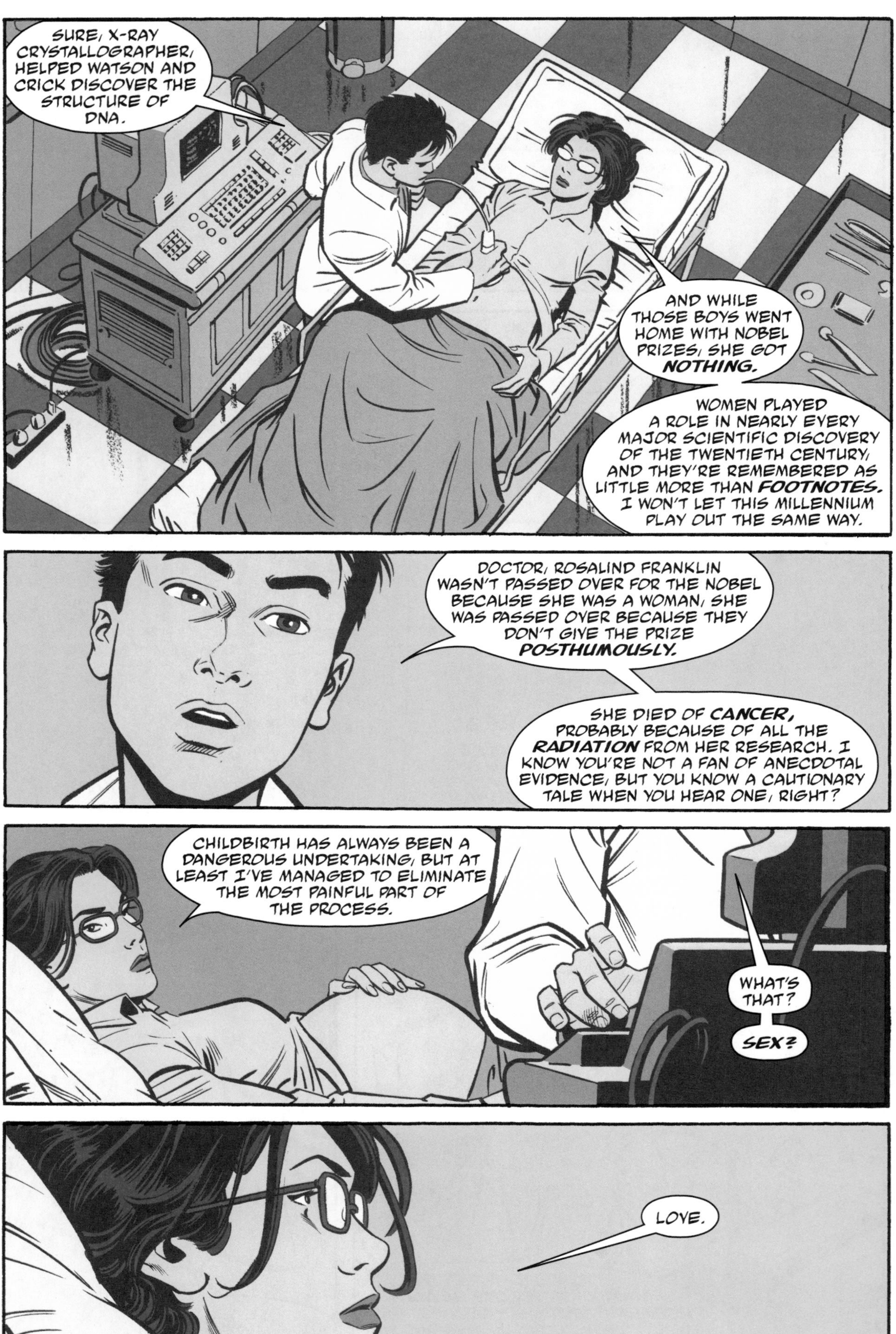
SURE, X-RAY CRYSTALLOGRAPHER, HELPED WATSON AND CRICK DISCOVER THE STRUCTURE OF DNA.
AND WHILE THOSE BOYS WENT HOME WITH NOBEL PRIZES, SHE GOT **NOTHING.**
WOMEN PLAYED A ROLE IN NEARLY EVERY MAJOR SCIENTIFIC DISCOVERY OF THE TWENTIETH CENTURY, AND THEY'RE REMEMBERED AS LITTLE MORE THAN **FOOTNOTES.** I WON'T LET THIS MILLENNIUM PLAY OUT THE SAME WAY.
DOCTOR, ROSALIND FRANKLIN WASN'T PASSED OVER FOR THE NOBEL BECAUSE SHE WAS A WOMAN, SHE WAS PASSED OVER BECAUSE THEY DON'T GIVE THE PRIZE **POSTHUMOUSLY.**
SHE DIED OF **CANCER,** PROBABLY BECAUSE OF ALL THE **RADIATION** FROM HER RESEARCH. I KNOW YOU'RE NOT A FAN OF ANECDOTAL EVIDENCE, BUT YOU KNOW A CAUTIONARY TALE WHEN YOU HEAR ONE, RIGHT?
CHILDBIRTH HAS ALWAYS BEEN A DANGEROUS UNDERTAKING, BUT AT LEAST I'VE MANAGED TO ELIMINATE THE MOST PAINFUL PART OF THE PROCESS.
WHAT'S THAT?
SEX?
LOVE.

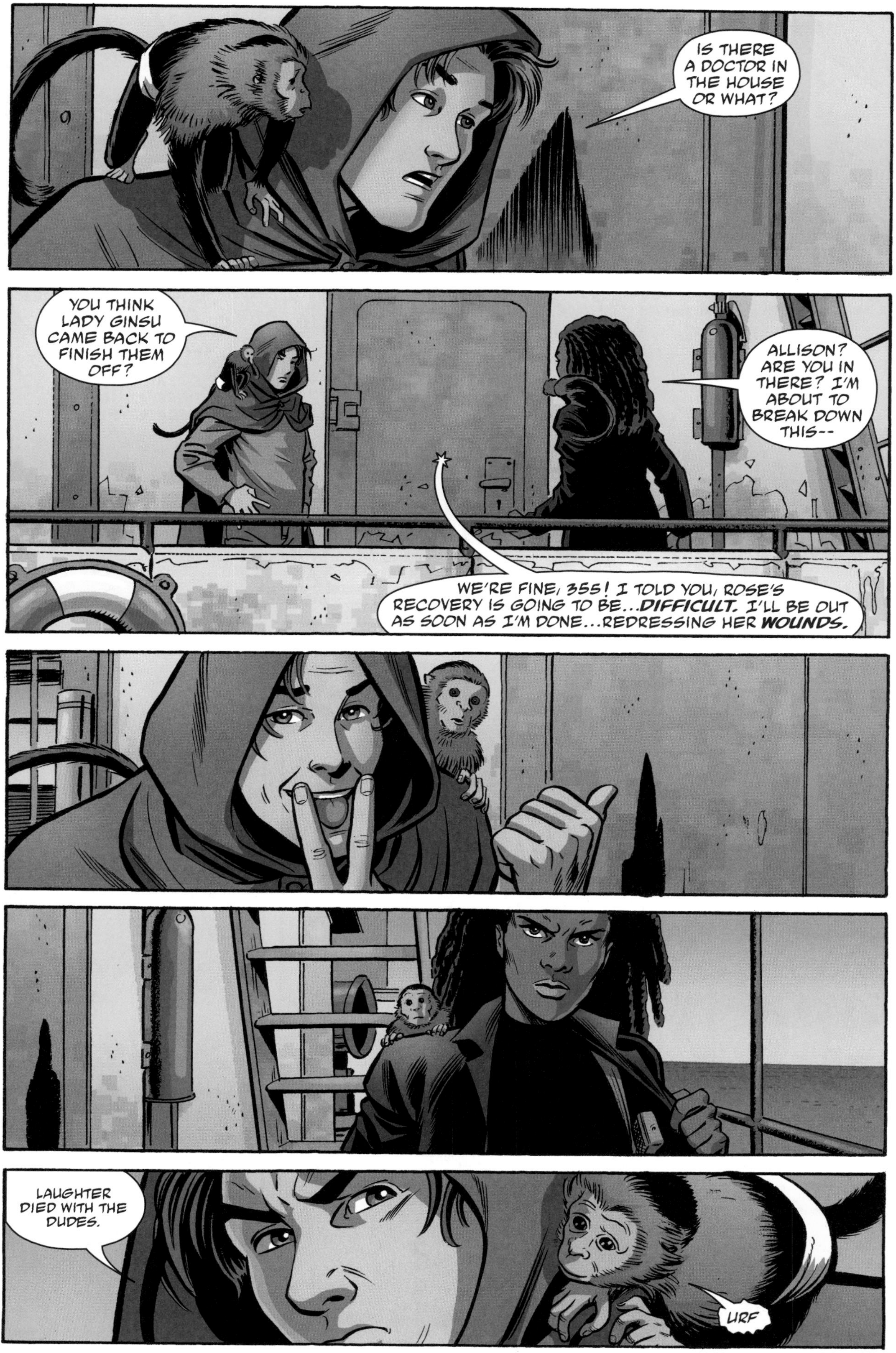
IS THERE A DOCTOR IN THE HOUSE OR WHAT?
YOU THINK LADY GINSU CAME BACK TO FINISH THEM OFF?
ALLISON? ARE YOU IN THERE? I'M ABOUT TO BREAK DOWN THIS--
WE'RE FINE, 355! I TOLD YOU, ROSE'S RECOVERY IS GOING TO BE...DIFFICULT. I'LL BE OUT AS SOON AS I'M DONE...REDRESSING HER WOUNDS.
LAUGHTER DIED WITH THE DUDES.
URF

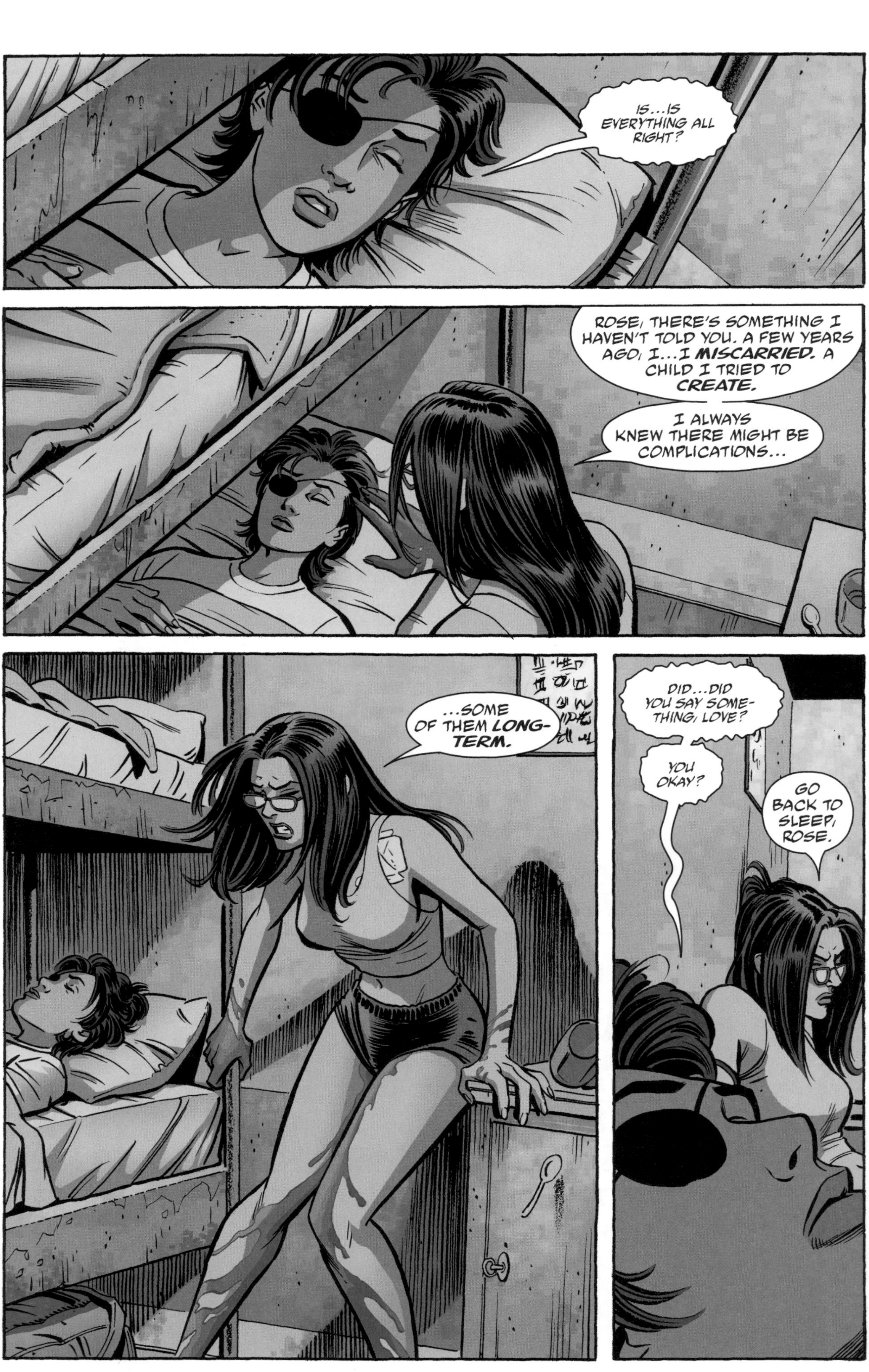

IS...IS EVERYTHING ALL RIGHT?
ROSE, THERE'S SOMETHING I HAVEN'T TOLD YOU. A FEW YEARS AGO, I...I **MISCARRIED.** A CHILD I TRIED TO **CREATE.**
I ALWAYS KNEW THERE MIGHT BE COMPLICATIONS...
...SOME OF THEM **LONG-TERM.**
DID...DID YOU SAY SOME-THING, LOVE?
YOU OKAY?
GO BACK TO SLEEP, ROSE.

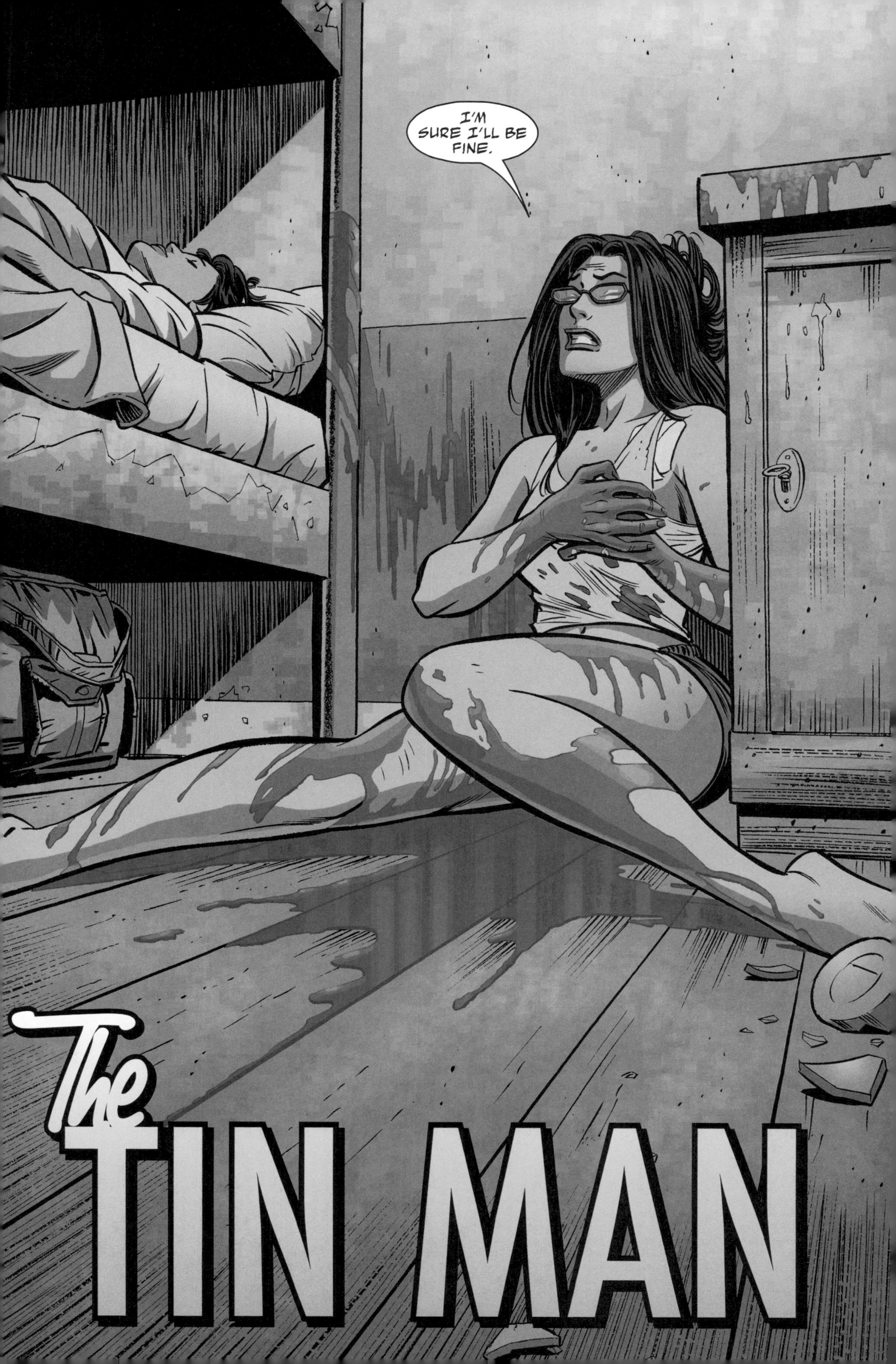
I'M SURE I'LL BE FINE.
The TIN MAN

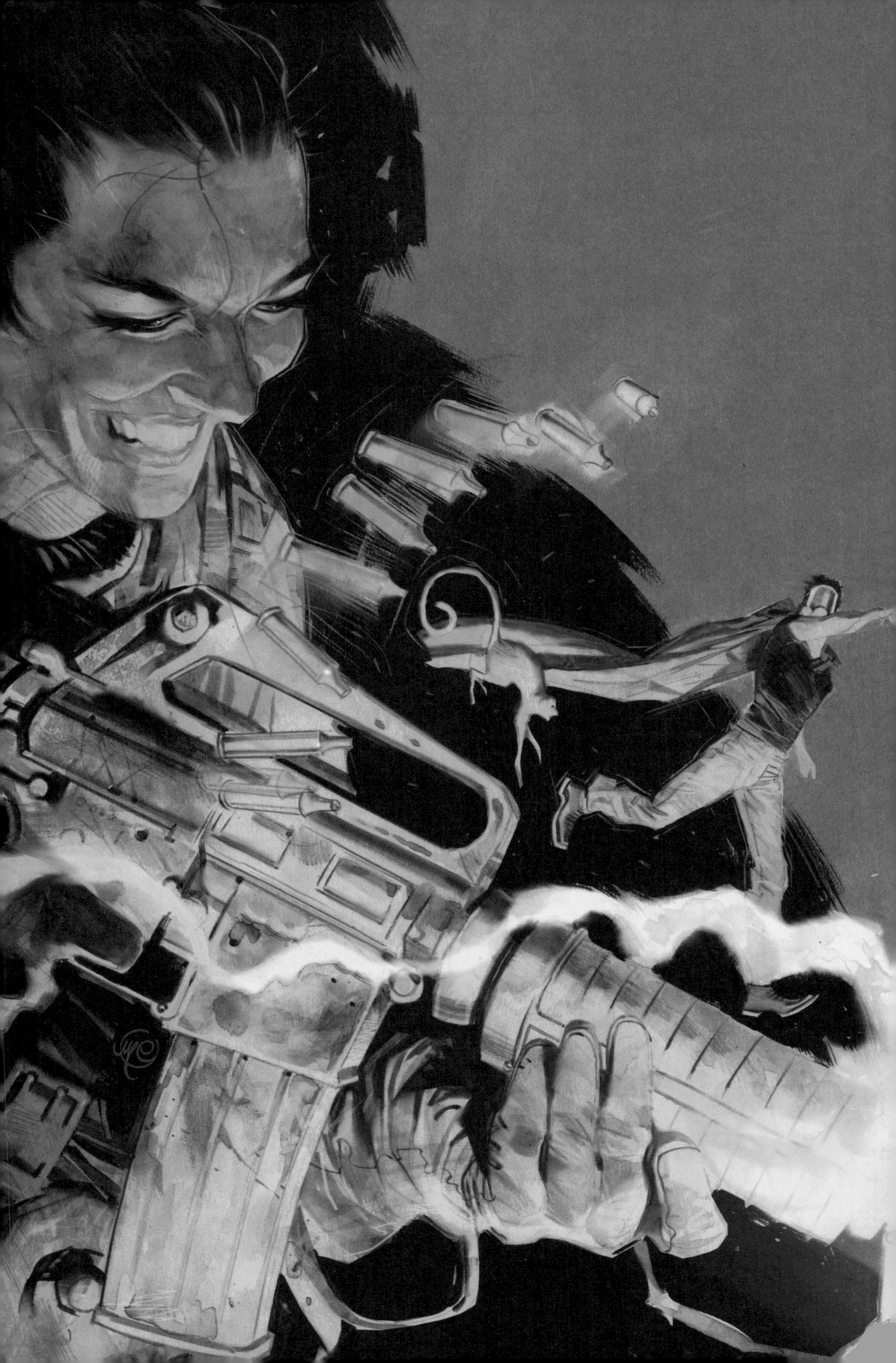

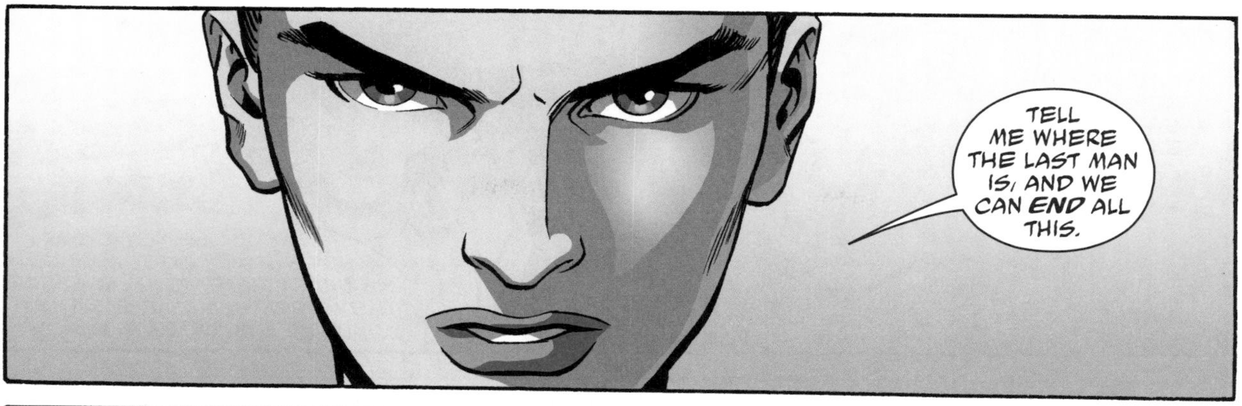
TELL ME WHERE THE LAST MAN IS, AND WE CAN END ALL THIS.

Oldenbrook, Kansas
Two Months Ago

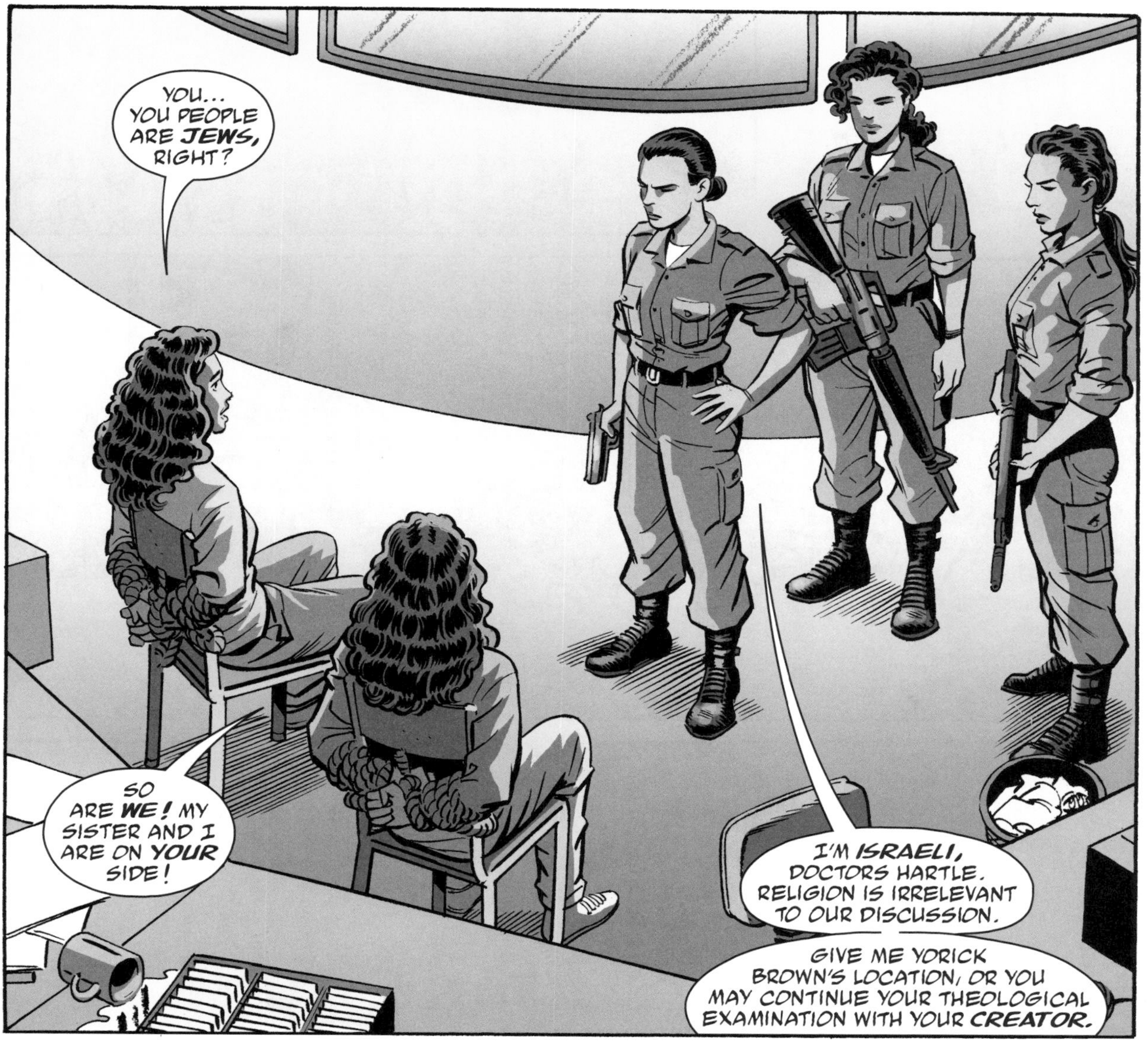
YOU... YOU PEOPLE ARE JEWS, RIGHT?
SO ARE WE! MY SISTER AND I ARE ON YOUR SIDE!
I'M ISRAELI, DOCTORS HARTLE. RELIGION IS IRRELEVANT TO OUR DISCUSSION.
GIVE ME YORICK BROWN'S LOCATION, OR YOU MAY CONTINUE YOUR THEOLOGICAL EXAMINATION WITH YOUR CREATOR.

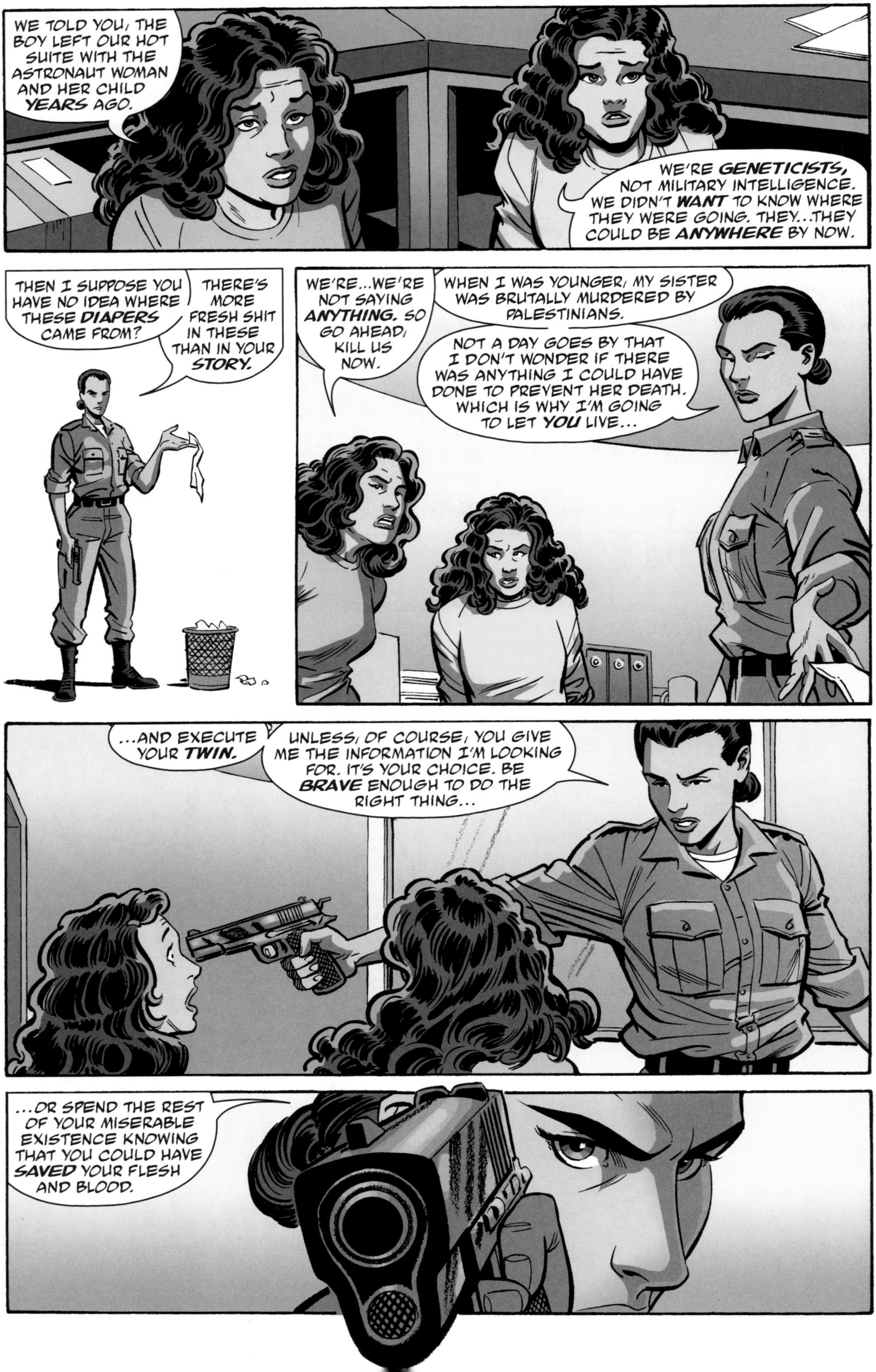
WE TOLD YOU, THE BOY LEFT OUR HOT SUITE WITH THE ASTRONAUT WOMAN AND HER CHILD YEARS AGO.
WE'RE GENETICISTS, NOT MILITARY INTELLIGENCE. WE DIDN'T WANT TO KNOW WHERE THEY WERE GOING. THEY...THEY COULD BE ANYWHERE BY NOW.
THEN I SUPPOSE YOU HAVE NO IDEA WHERE THESE DIAPERS CAME FROM?
THERE'S MORE FRESH SHIT IN THESE THAN IN YOUR STORY.
WE'RE...WE'RE NOT SAYING ANYTHING. SO GO AHEAD, KILL US NOW.
WHEN I WAS YOUNGER, MY SISTER WAS BRUTALLY MURDERED BY PALESTINIANS.
NOT A DAY GOES BY THAT I DON'T WONDER IF THERE WAS ANYTHING I COULD HAVE DONE TO PREVENT HER DEATH. WHICH IS WHY I'M GOING TO LET YOU LIVE...
...AND EXECUTE YOUR TWIN.
UNLESS, OF COURSE, YOU GIVE ME THE INFORMATION I'M LOOKING FOR. IT'S YOUR CHOICE. BE BRAVE ENOUGH TO DO THE RIGHT THING...
...OR SPEND THE REST OF YOUR MISERABLE EXISTENCE KNOWING THAT YOU COULD HAVE SAVED YOUR FLESH AND BLOOD.

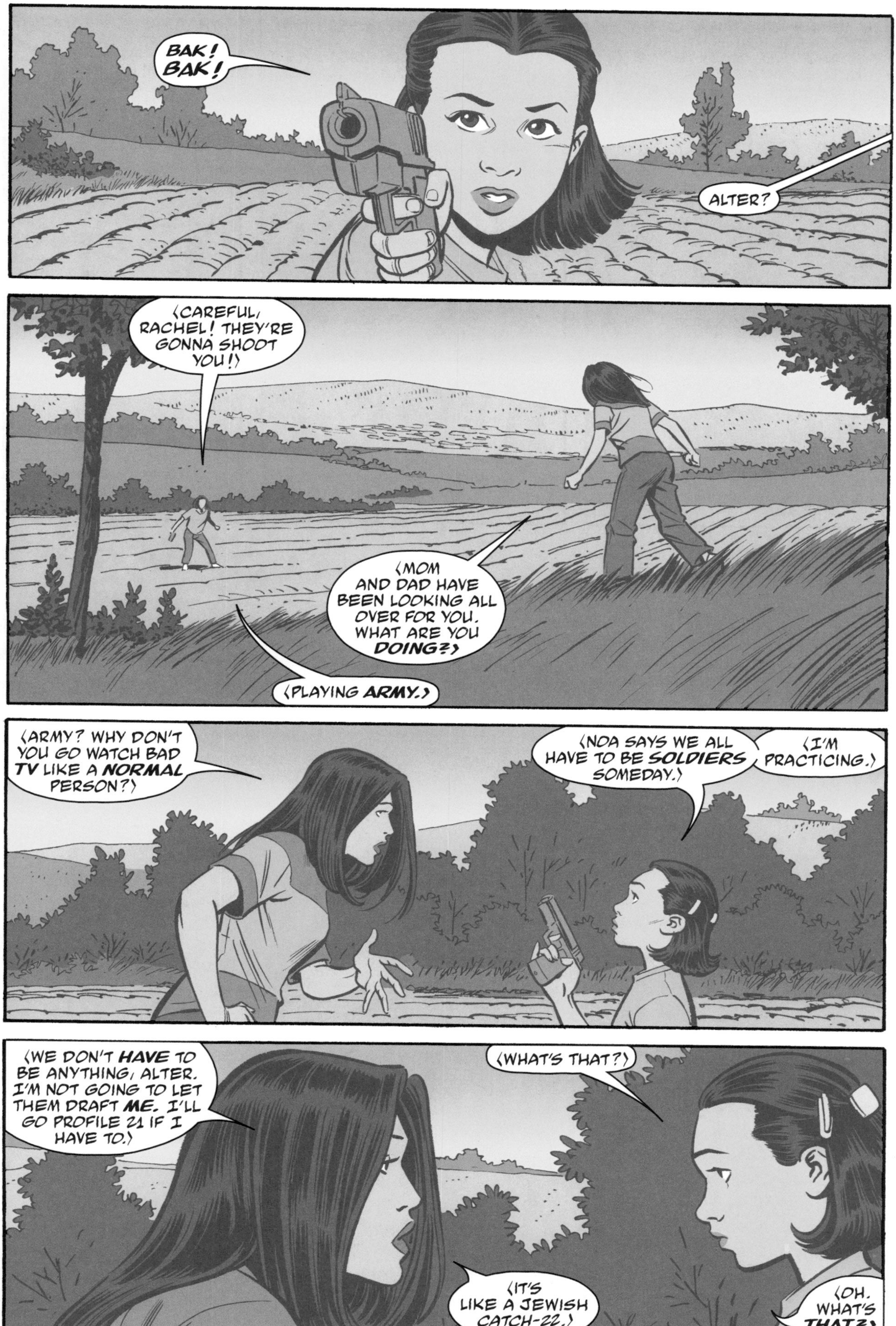
BAK! BAK!
ALTER?
⟨CAREFUL, RACHEL! THEY'RE GONNA SHOOT YOU!⟩
⟨MOM AND DAD HAVE BEEN LOOKING ALL OVER FOR YOU. WHAT ARE YOU DOING?⟩
⟨PLAYING ARMY.⟩
⟨ARMY? WHY DON'T YOU GO WATCH BAD TV LIKE A NORMAL PERSON?⟩
⟨NOA SAYS WE ALL HAVE TO BE SOLDIERS SOMEDAY.⟩
⟨I'M PRACTICING.⟩
⟨WE DON'T HAVE TO BE ANYTHING, ALTER. I'M NOT GOING TO LET THEM DRAFT ME. I'LL GO PROFILE 21 IF I HAVE TO.⟩
⟨WHAT'S THAT?⟩
⟨IT'S LIKE A JEWISH CATCH-22.⟩
⟨OH. WHAT'S THAT?⟩

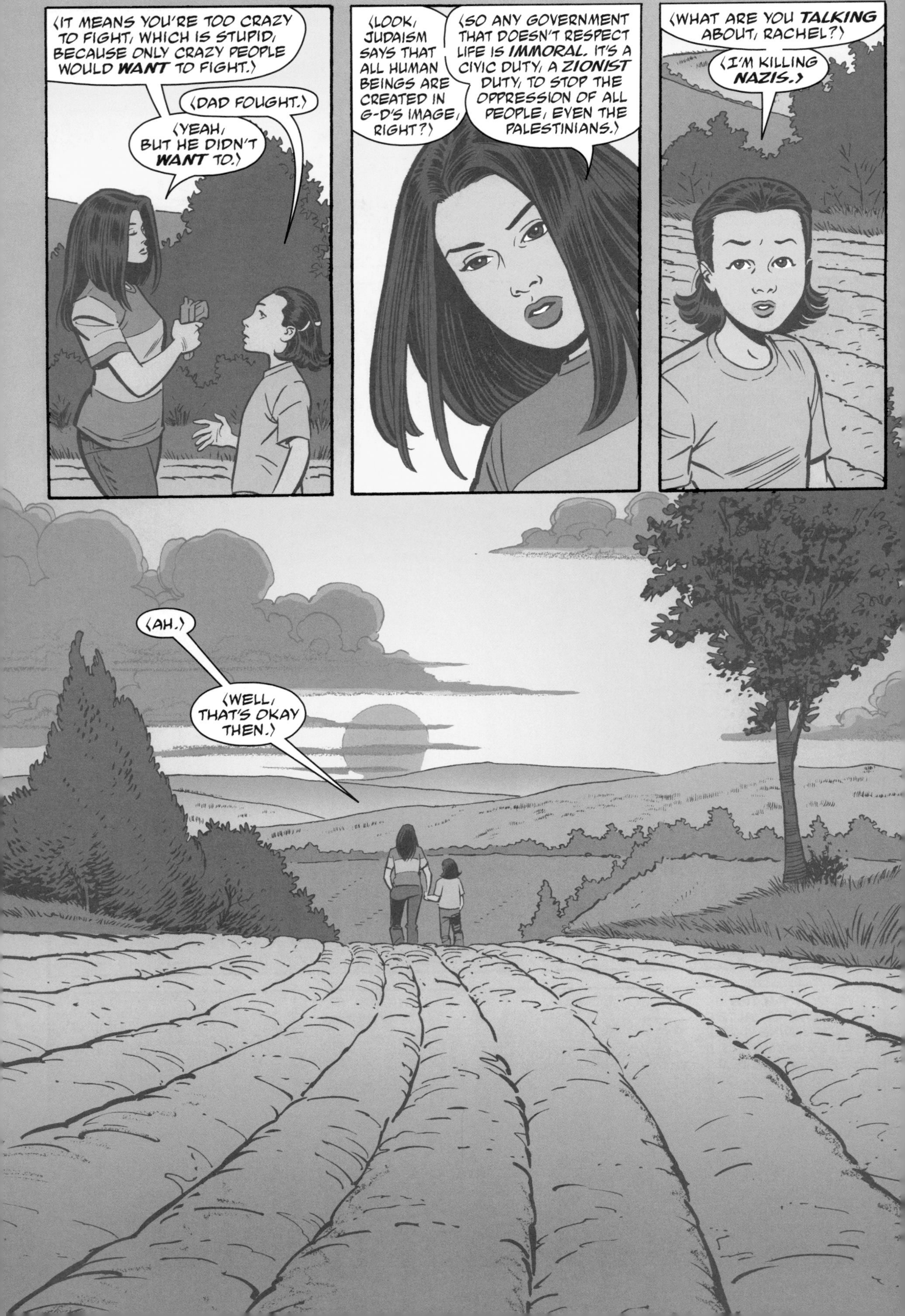

⟨IT MEANS YOU'RE TOO CRAZY TO FIGHT, WHICH IS STUPID, BECAUSE ONLY CRAZY PEOPLE WOULD **WANT** TO FIGHT.⟩
⟨DAD FOUGHT.⟩
⟨YEAH, BUT HE DIDN'T **WANT** TO.⟩
⟨LOOK, JUDAISM SAYS THAT ALL HUMAN BEINGS ARE CREATED IN G-D'S IMAGE, RIGHT?⟩
⟨SO ANY GOVERNMENT THAT DOESN'T RESPECT LIFE IS **IMMORAL.** IT'S A CIVIC DUTY, A **ZIONIST** DUTY, TO STOP THE OPPRESSION OF ALL PEOPLE, EVEN THE PALESTINIANS.⟩
⟨WHAT ARE YOU **TALKING** ABOUT, RACHEL?⟩
⟨I'M KILLING **NAZIS.**⟩
⟨AH.⟩
⟨WELL, THAT'S OKAY THEN.⟩

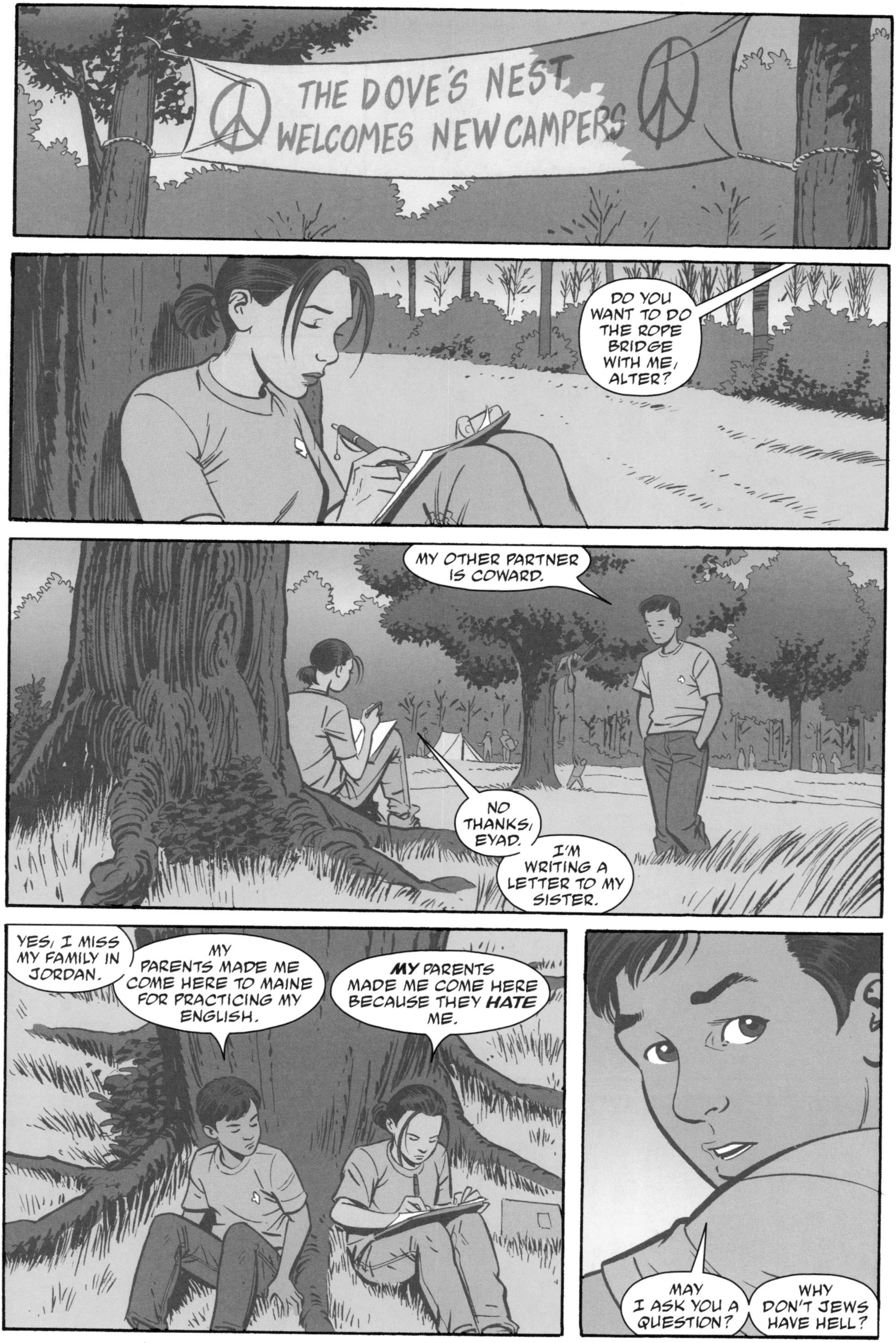
THE DOVE'S NEST WELCOMES NEW CAMPERS
DO YOU WANT TO DO THE ROPE BRIDGE WITH ME, ALTER?
MY OTHER PARTNER IS COWARD.
NO THANKS, EYAD.
I'M WRITING A LETTER TO MY SISTER.
YES, I MISS MY FAMILY IN JORDAN.
MY PARENTS MADE ME COME HERE TO MAINE FOR PRACTICING MY ENGLISH.
MY PARENTS MADE ME COME HERE BECAUSE THEY HATE ME.
MAY I ASK YOU A QUESTION?
WHY DON'T JEWS HAVE HELL?

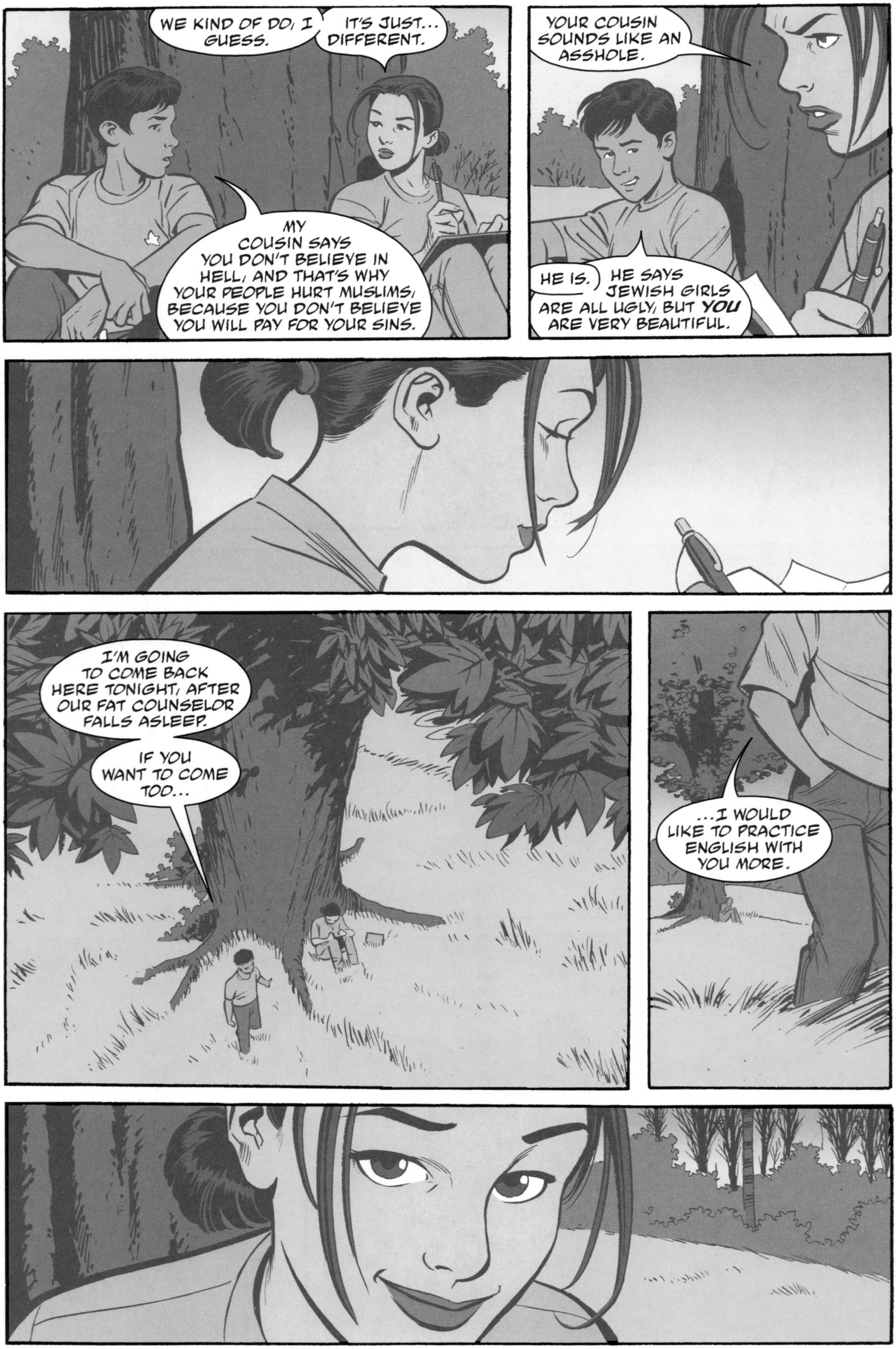
WE KIND OF DO, I GUESS.
IT'S JUST... DIFFERENT.
MY COUSIN SAYS YOU DON'T BELIEVE IN HELL, AND THAT'S WHY YOUR PEOPLE HURT MUSLIMS, BECAUSE YOU DON'T BELIEVE YOU WILL PAY FOR YOUR SINS.
YOUR COUSIN SOUNDS LIKE AN ASSHOLE.
HE IS.
HE SAYS JEWISH GIRLS ARE ALL UGLY, BUT *YOU* ARE VERY BEAUTIFUL.
I'M GOING TO COME BACK HERE TONIGHT, AFTER OUR FAT COUNSELOR FALLS ASLEEP.
IF YOU WANT TO COME TOO...
...I WOULD LIKE TO PRACTICE ENGLISH WITH YOU MORE.

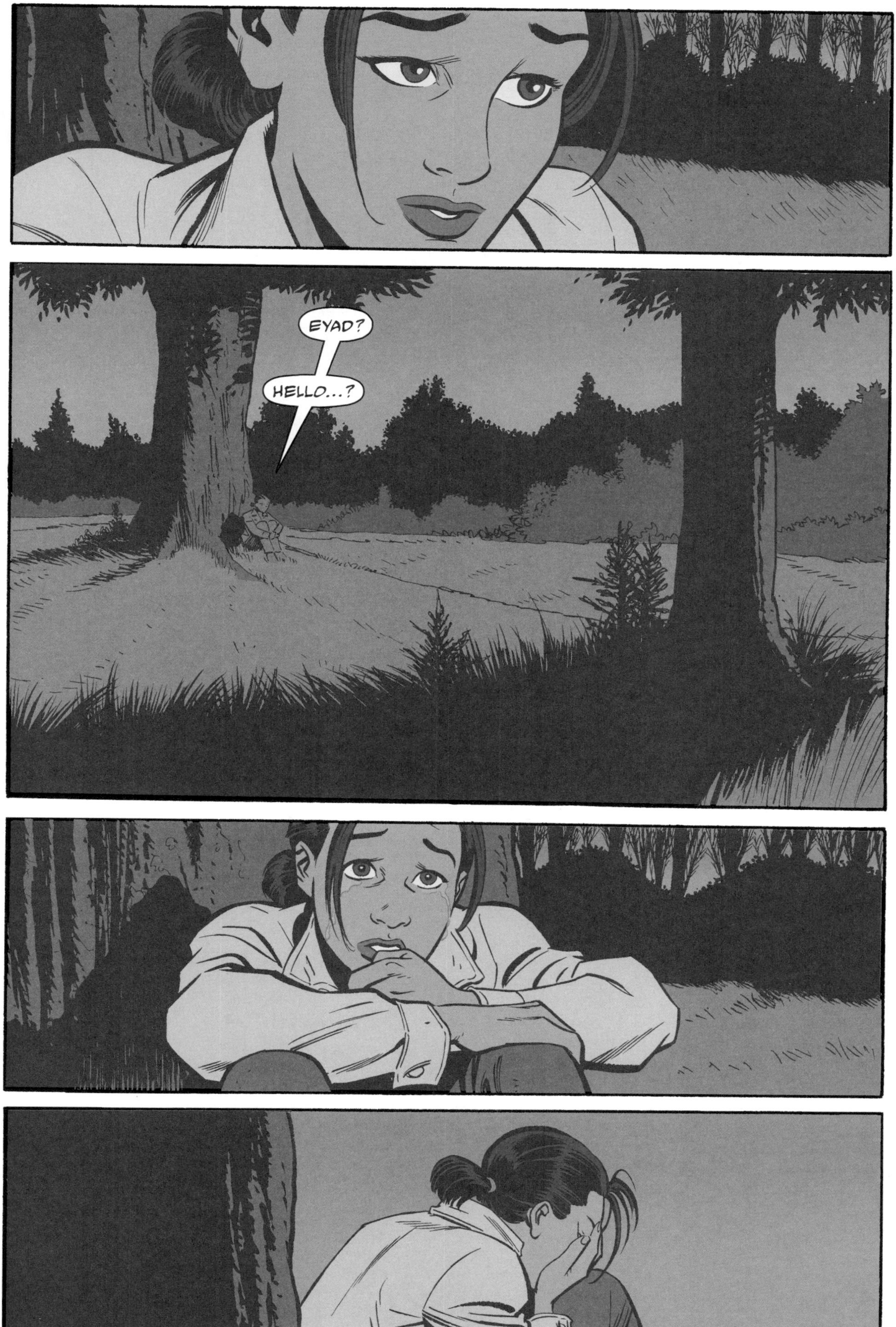
EYAD?
HELLO...?

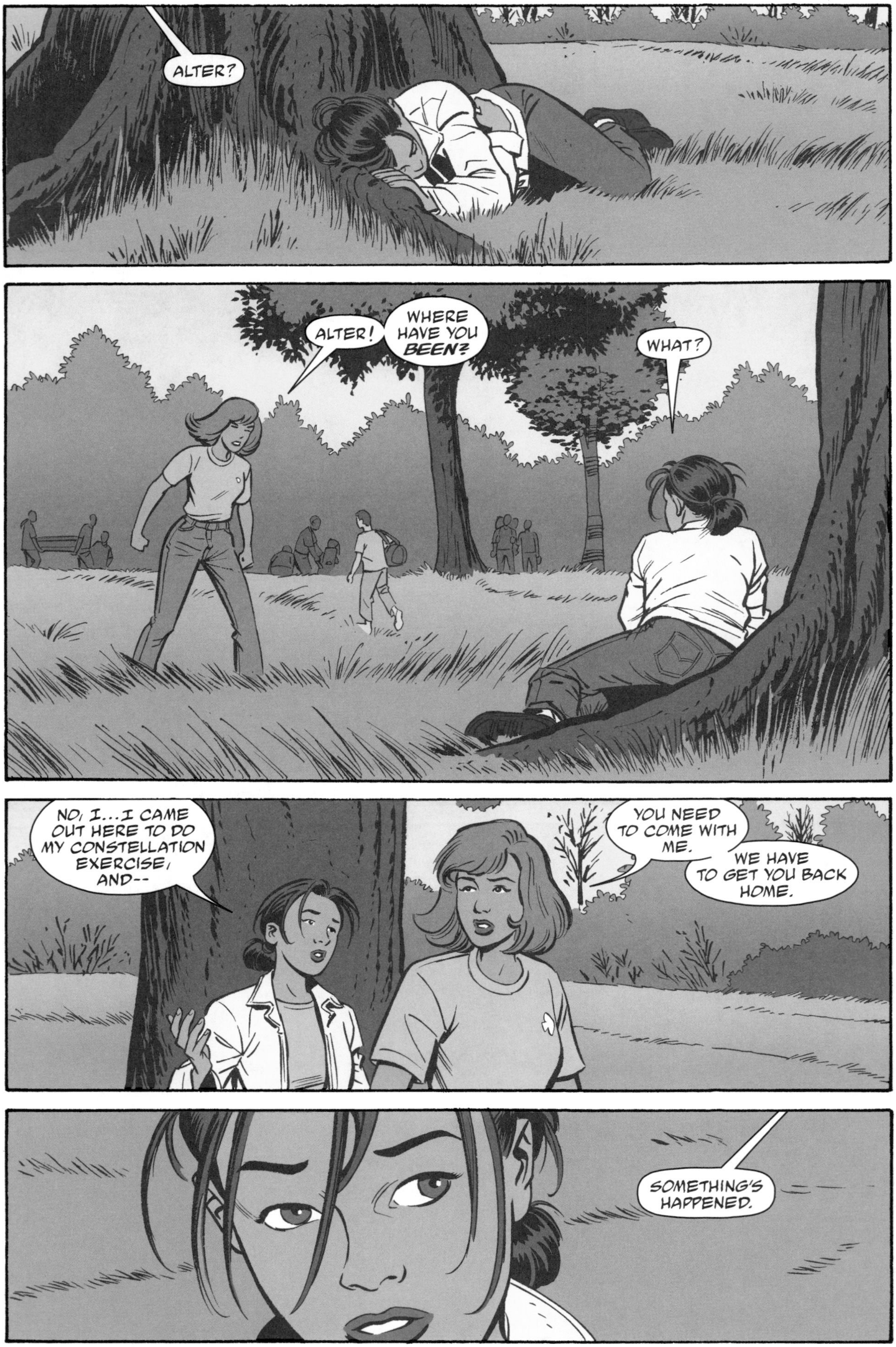
ALTER?
ALTER!
WHERE HAVE YOU BEEN?
WHAT?
NO, I...I CAME OUT HERE TO DO MY CONSTELLATION EXERCISE, AND--
YOU NEED TO COME WITH ME.
WE HAVE TO GET YOU BACK HOME.
SOMETHING'S HAPPENED.

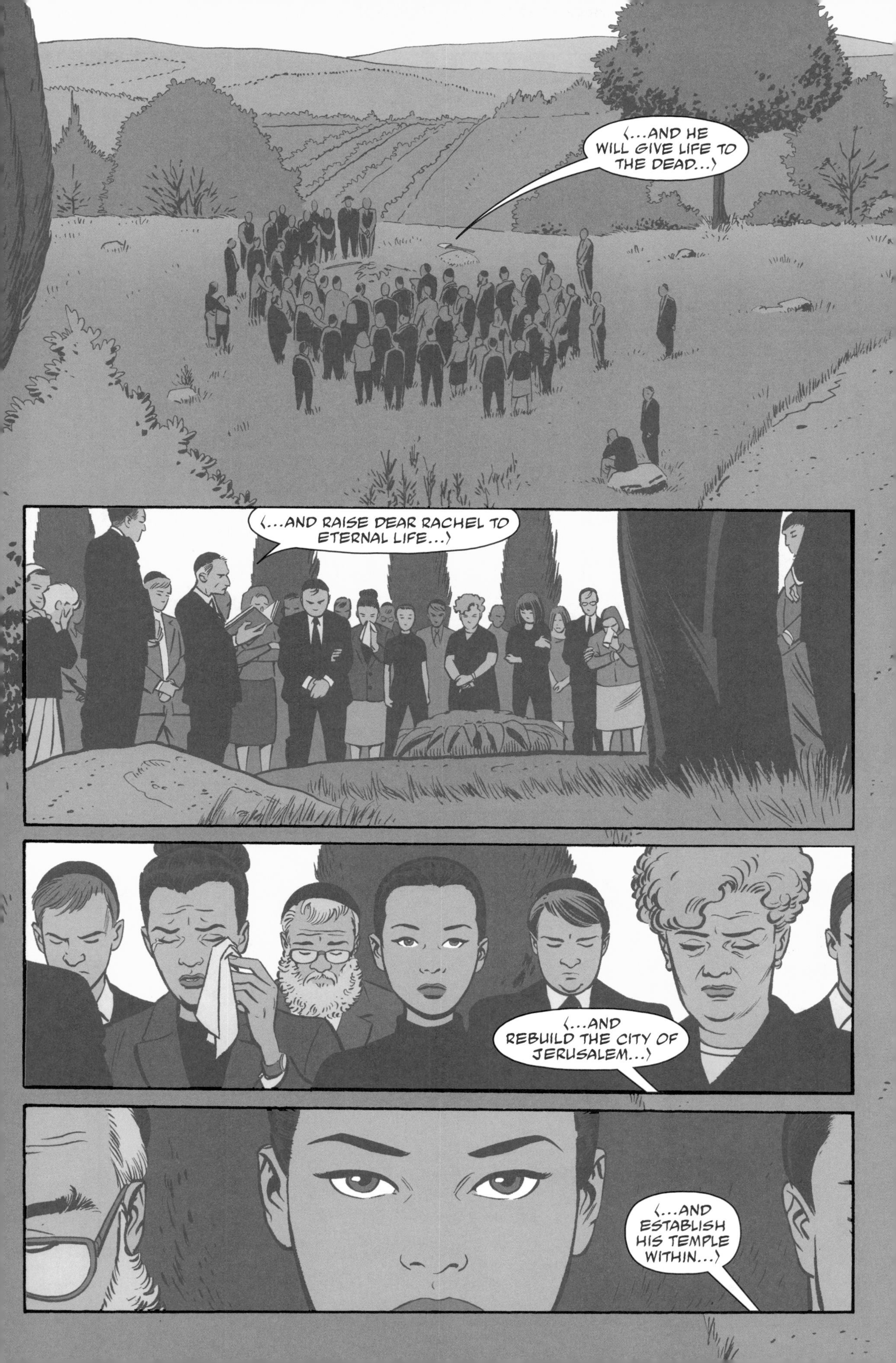
‹...AND HE WILL GIVE LIFE TO THE DEAD...›
‹...AND RAISE DEAR RACHEL TO ETERNAL LIFE...›
‹...AND REBUILD THE CITY OF JERUSALEM...›
‹...AND ESTABLISH HIS TEMPLE WITHIN...›

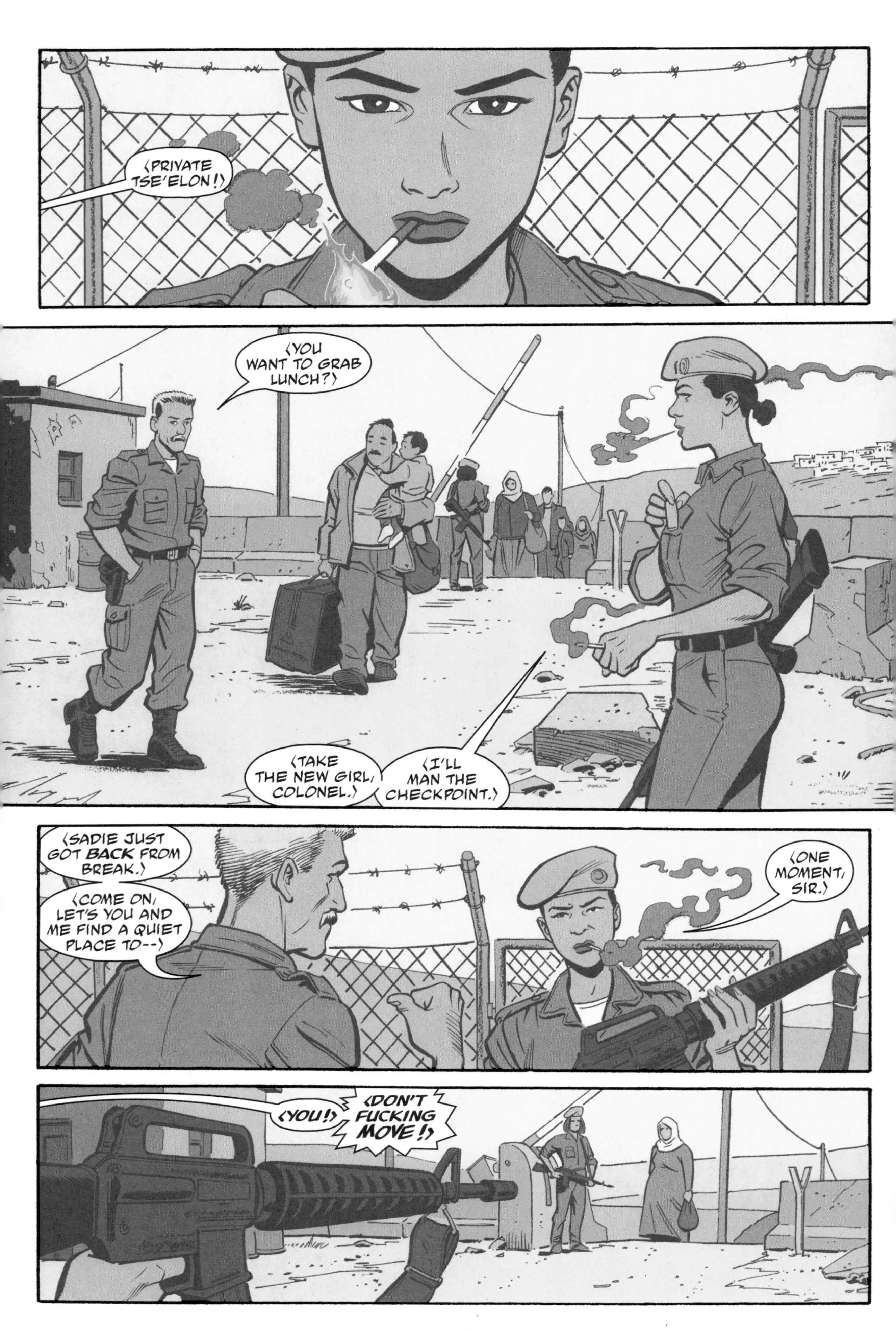
‹PRIVATE TSE'ELON!›
‹YOU WANT TO GRAB LUNCH?›
‹TAKE THE NEW GIRL, COLONEL.›
‹I'LL MAN THE CHECKPOINT.›
‹SADIE JUST GOT BACK FROM BREAK.›
‹COME ON, LET'S YOU AND ME FIND A QUIET PLACE TO--›
‹ONE MOMENT, SIR.›
‹YOU!›
‹DON'T FUCKING MOVE!›

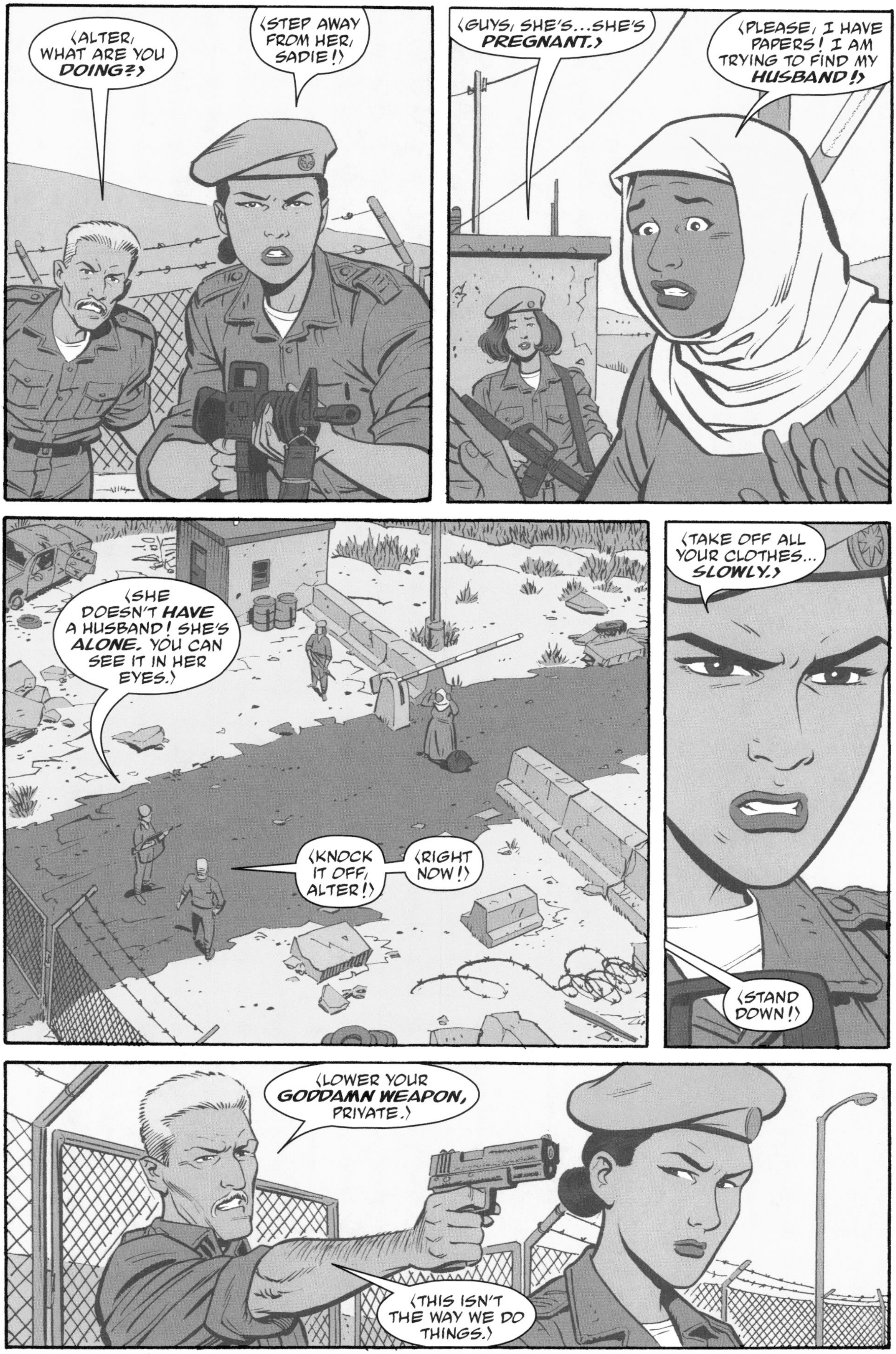
‹ALTER, WHAT ARE YOU DOING?›
‹STEP AWAY FROM HER, SADIE!›
‹GUYS, SHE'S...SHE'S PREGNANT.›
‹PLEASE, I HAVE PAPERS! I AM TRYING TO FIND MY HUSBAND!›
‹SHE DOESN'T HAVE A HUSBAND! SHE'S ALONE. YOU CAN SEE IT IN HER EYES.›
‹KNOCK IT OFF, ALTER!›
‹RIGHT NOW!›
‹TAKE OFF ALL YOUR CLOTHES... SLOWLY.›
‹STAND DOWN!›
‹LOWER YOUR GODDAMN WEAPON, PRIVATE.›
‹THIS ISN'T THE WAY WE DO THINGS.›

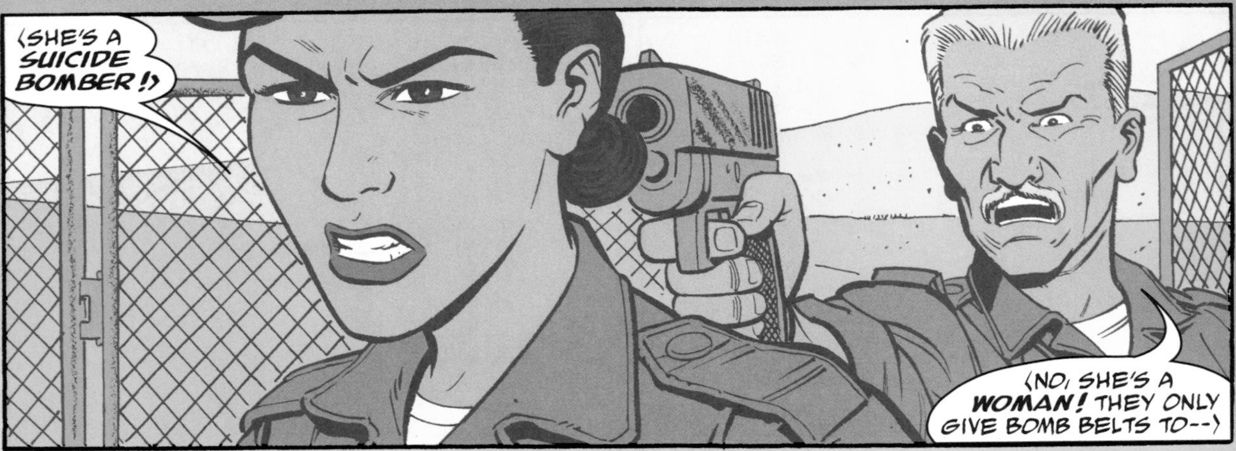
‹SHE'S A SUICIDE BOMBER!›
‹NO, SHE'S A WOMAN! THEY ONLY GIVE BOMB BELTS TO--›

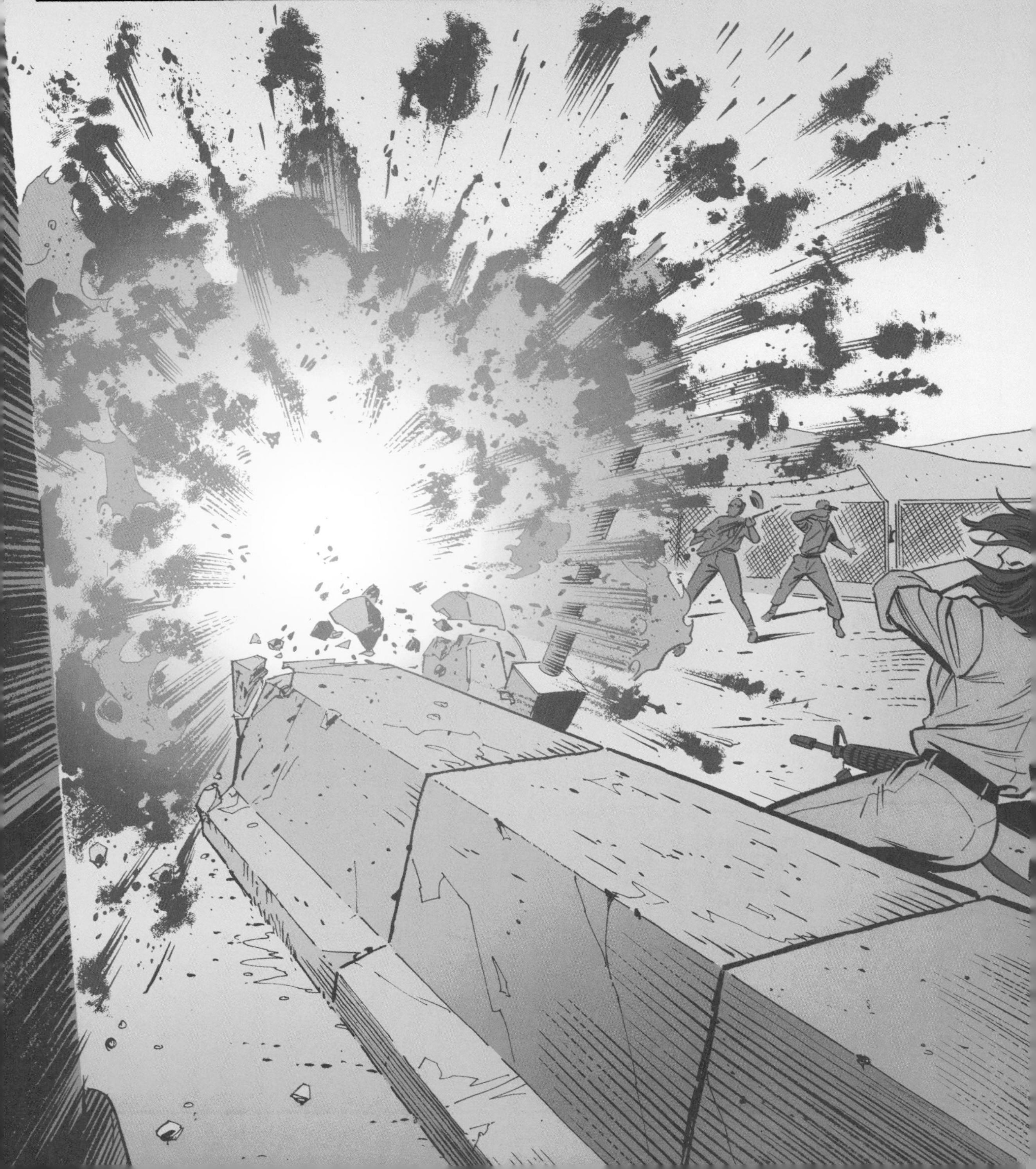

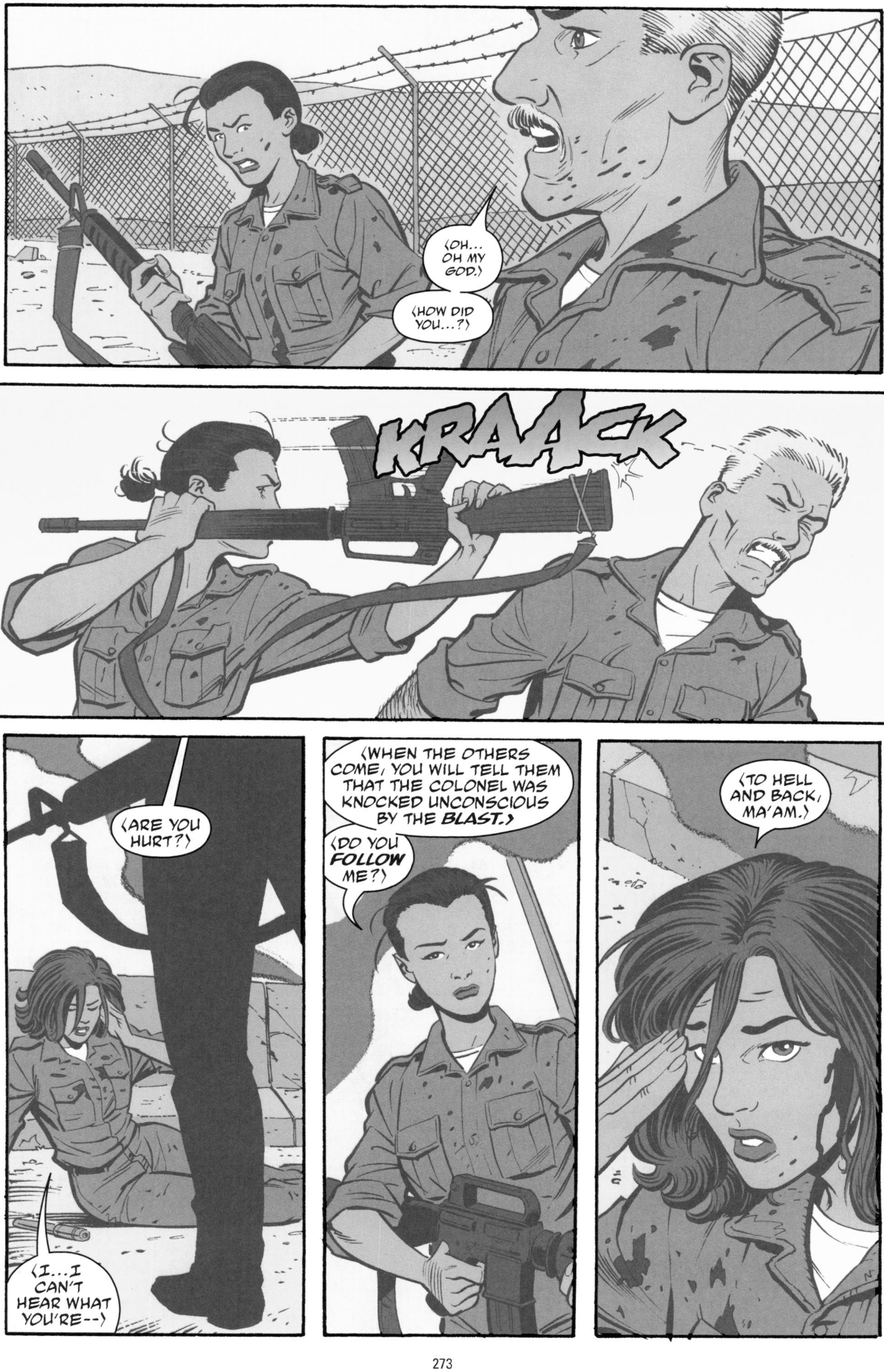
⟨OH... OH MY GOD.⟩
⟨HOW DID YOU...?⟩
KRAACK
⟨ARE YOU HURT?⟩
⟨I...I CAN'T HEAR WHAT YOU'RE--⟩
⟨WHEN THE OTHERS COME, YOU WILL TELL THEM THAT THE COLONEL WAS KNOCKED UNCONSCIOUS BY THE BLAST.⟩
⟨DO YOU FOLLOW ME?⟩
⟨TO HELL AND BACK, MA'AM.⟩

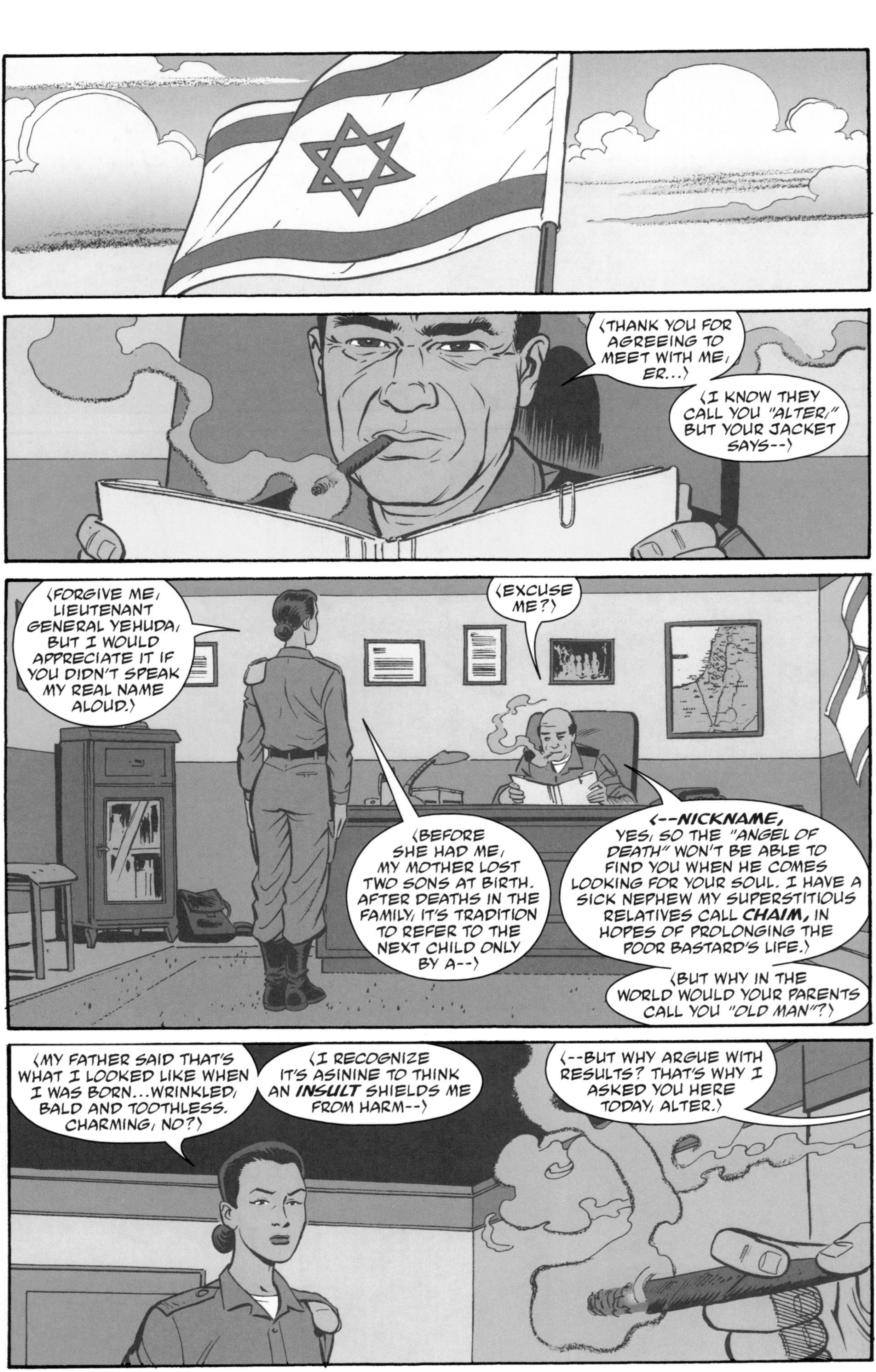
⟨THANK YOU FOR AGREEING TO MEET WITH ME, ER...⟩
⟨I KNOW THEY CALL YOU "ALTER," BUT YOUR JACKET SAYS--⟩
⟨FORGIVE ME, LIEUTENANT GENERAL YEHUDA, BUT I WOULD APPRECIATE IT IF YOU DIDN'T SPEAK MY REAL NAME ALOUD.⟩
⟨EXCUSE ME?⟩
⟨BEFORE SHE HAD ME, MY MOTHER LOST TWO SONS AT BIRTH. AFTER DEATHS IN THE FAMILY, IT'S TRADITION TO REFER TO THE NEXT CHILD ONLY BY A--⟩
⟨--NICKNAME, YES, SO THE "ANGEL OF DEATH" WON'T BE ABLE TO FIND YOU WHEN HE COMES LOOKING FOR YOUR SOUL. I HAVE A SICK NEPHEW MY SUPERSTITIOUS RELATIVES CALL CHAIM, IN HOPES OF PROLONGING THE POOR BASTARD'S LIFE.⟩
⟨BUT WHY IN THE WORLD WOULD YOUR PARENTS CALL YOU "OLD MAN"?⟩
⟨MY FATHER SAID THAT'S WHAT I LOOKED LIKE WHEN I WAS BORN...WRINKLED, BALD AND TOOTHLESS. CHARMING, NO?⟩
⟨I RECOGNIZE IT'S ASININE TO THINK AN INSULT SHIELDS ME FROM HARM--⟩
⟨--BUT WHY ARGUE WITH RESULTS? THAT'S WHY I ASKED YOU HERE TODAY, ALTER.⟩

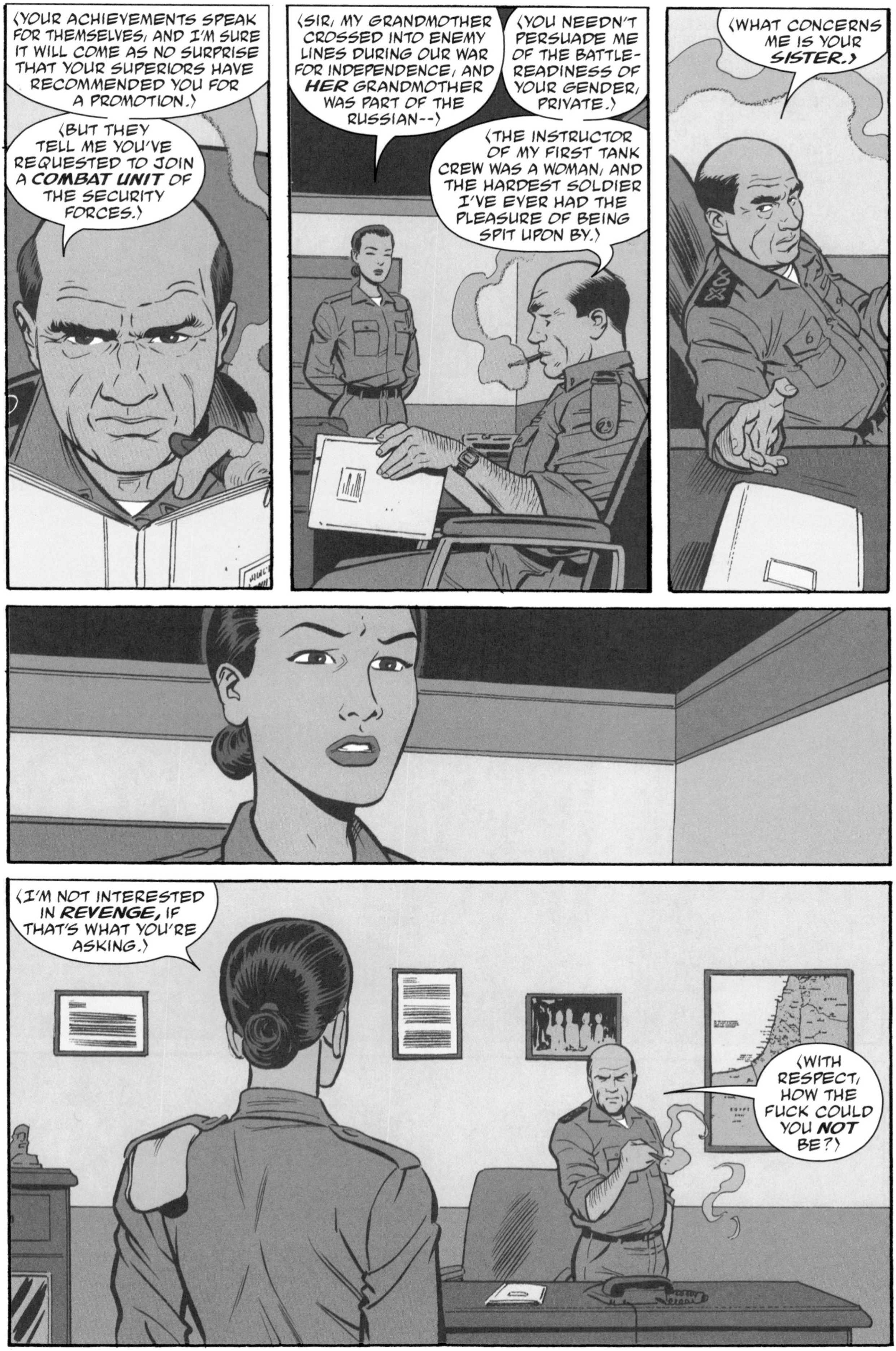
<YOUR ACHIEVEMENTS SPEAK FOR THEMSELVES, AND I'M SURE IT WILL COME AS NO SURPRISE THAT YOUR SUPERIORS HAVE RECOMMENDED YOU FOR A PROMOTION.>
<BUT THEY TELL ME YOU'VE REQUESTED TO JOIN A **COMBAT UNIT** OF THE SECURITY FORCES.>
<SIR, MY GRANDMOTHER CROSSED INTO ENEMY LINES DURING OUR WAR FOR INDEPENDENCE, AND **HER** GRANDMOTHER WAS PART OF THE RUSSIAN-->
<YOU NEEDN'T PERSUADE ME OF THE BATTLE-READINESS OF YOUR GENDER, PRIVATE.>
<THE INSTRUCTOR OF MY FIRST TANK CREW WAS A WOMAN, AND THE HARDEST SOLDIER I'VE EVER HAD THE PLEASURE OF BEING SPIT UPON BY.>
<WHAT CONCERNS ME IS YOUR **SISTER.**>
<I'M NOT INTERESTED IN **REVENGE,** IF THAT'S WHAT YOU'RE ASKING.>
<WITH RESPECT, HOW THE FUCK COULD YOU **NOT** BE?>

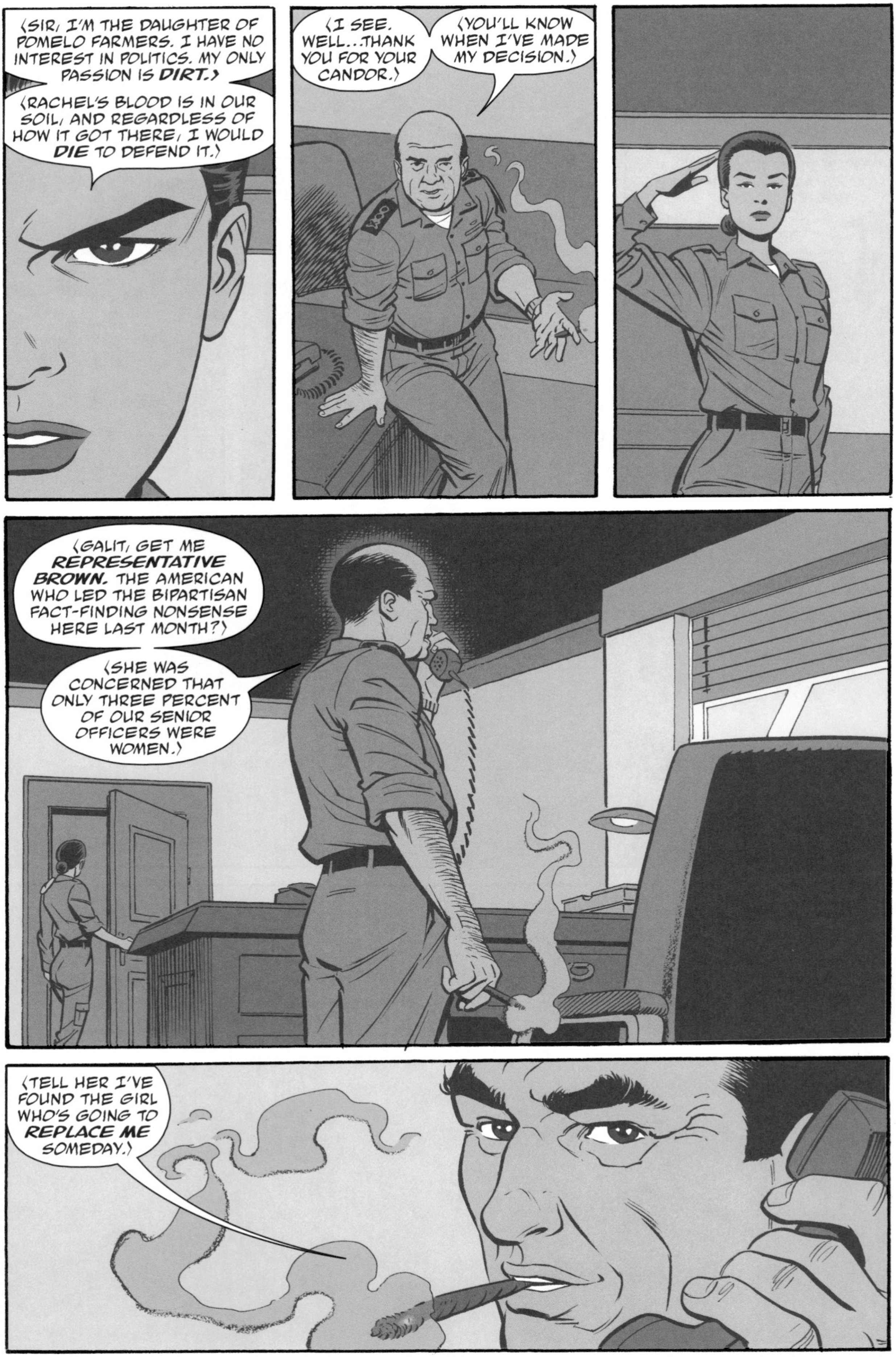

⟨SIR, I'M THE DAUGHTER OF POMELO FARMERS. I HAVE NO INTEREST IN POLITICS. MY ONLY PASSION IS DIRT.⟩
⟨RACHEL'S BLOOD IS IN OUR SOIL, AND REGARDLESS OF HOW IT GOT THERE, I WOULD DIE TO DEFEND IT.⟩
⟨I SEE. WELL...THANK YOU FOR YOUR CANDOR.⟩
⟨YOU'LL KNOW WHEN I'VE MADE MY DECISION.⟩
⟨GALIT, GET ME REPRESENTATIVE BROWN. THE AMERICAN WHO LED THE BIPARTISAN FACT-FINDING NONSENSE HERE LAST MONTH?⟩
⟨SHE WAS CONCERNED THAT ONLY THREE PERCENT OF OUR SENIOR OFFICERS WERE WOMEN.⟩
⟨TELL HER I'VE FOUND THE GIRL WHO'S GOING TO REPLACE ME SOMEDAY.⟩

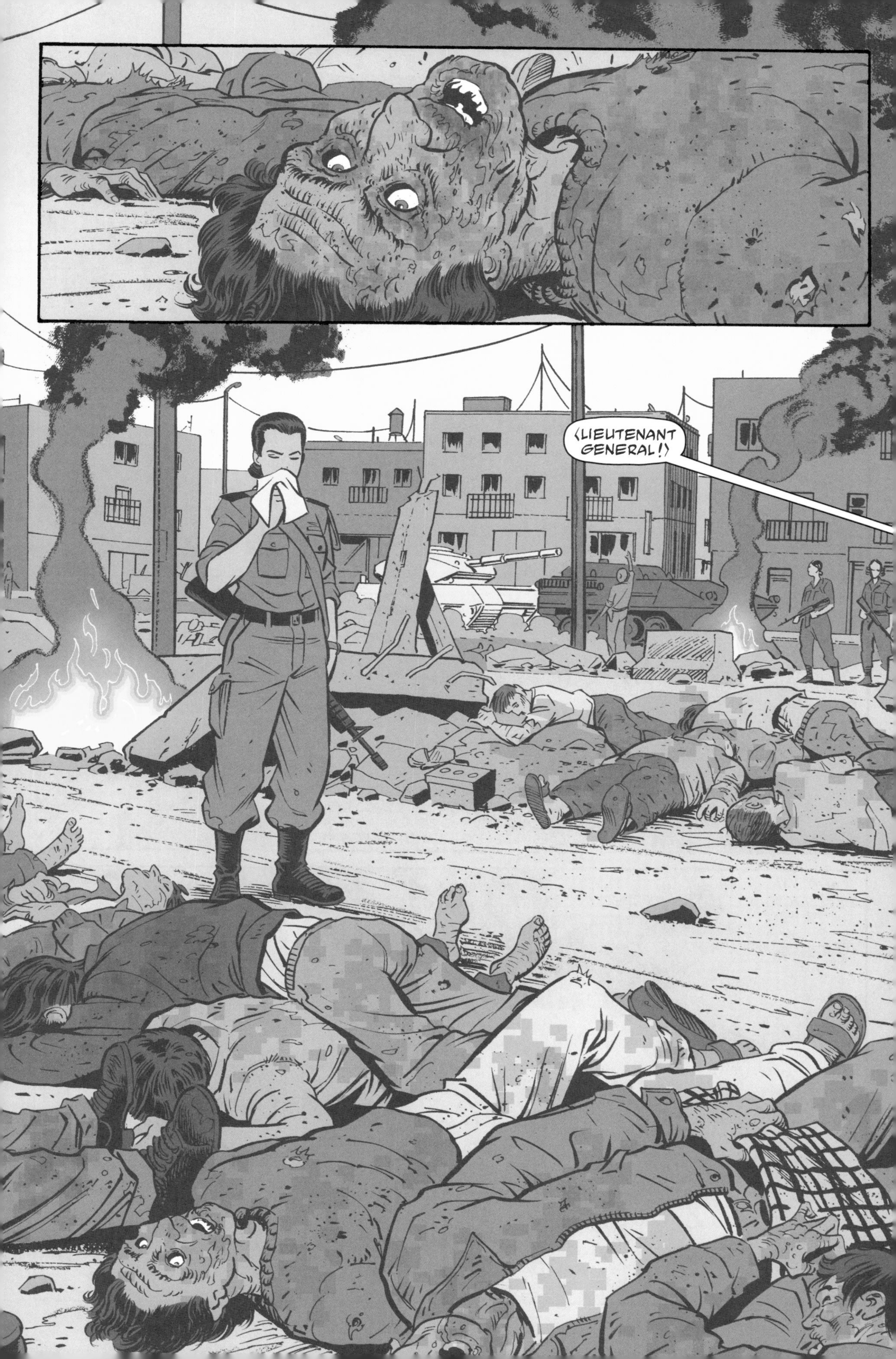
‹LIEUTENANT GENERAL!›

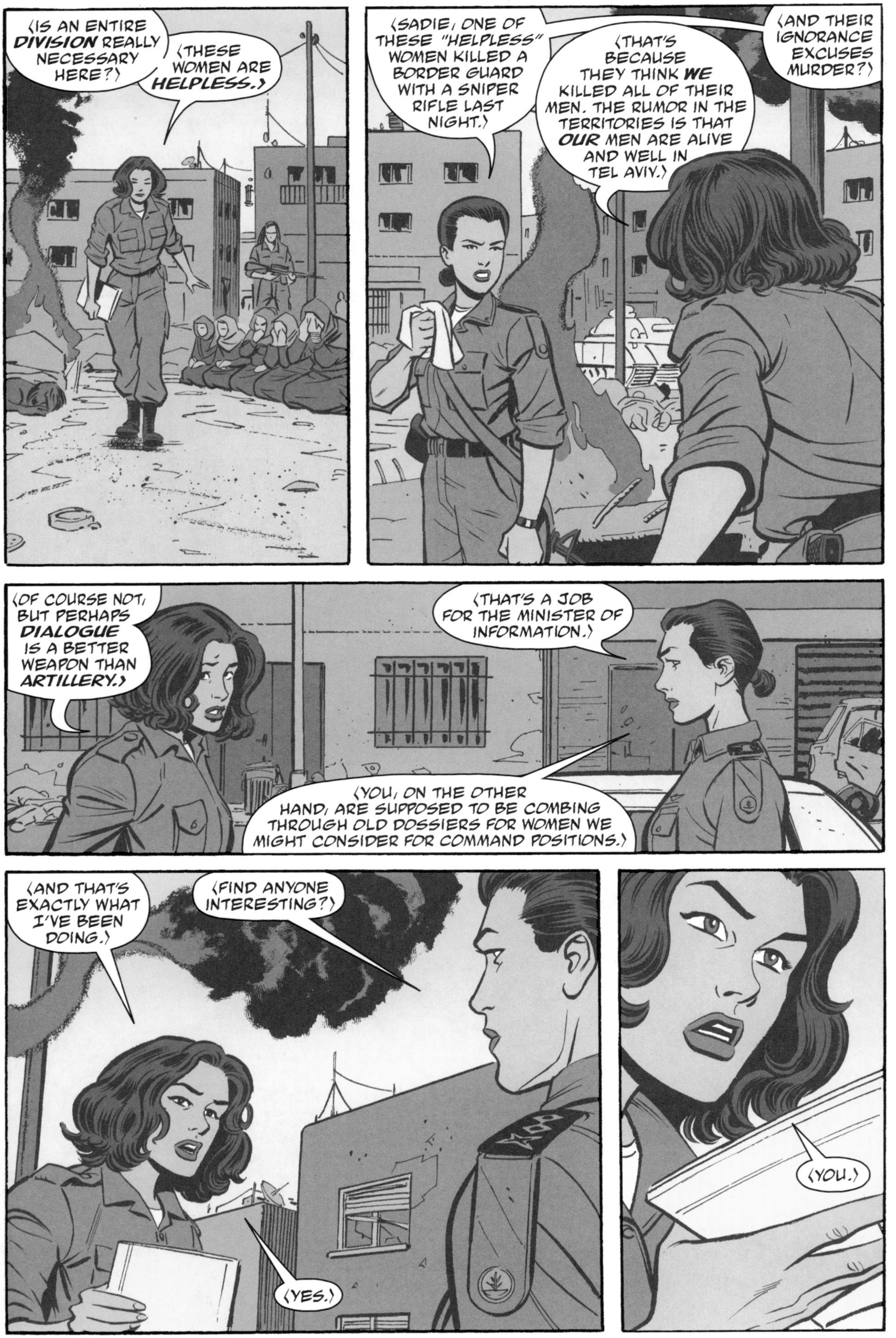
⟨IS AN ENTIRE DIVISION REALLY NECESSARY HERE?⟩
⟨THESE WOMEN ARE HELPLESS.⟩
⟨SADIE, ONE OF THESE "HELPLESS" WOMEN KILLED A BORDER GUARD WITH A SNIPER RIFLE LAST NIGHT.⟩
⟨THAT'S BECAUSE THEY THINK WE KILLED ALL OF THEIR MEN. THE RUMOR IN THE TERRITORIES IS THAT OUR MEN ARE ALIVE AND WELL IN TEL AVIV.⟩
⟨AND THEIR IGNORANCE EXCUSES MURDER?⟩
⟨OF COURSE NOT, BUT PERHAPS DIALOGUE IS A BETTER WEAPON THAN ARTILLERY.⟩
⟨THAT'S A JOB FOR THE MINISTER OF INFORMATION.⟩
⟨YOU, ON THE OTHER HAND, ARE SUPPOSED TO BE COMBING THROUGH OLD DOSSIERS FOR WOMEN WE MIGHT CONSIDER FOR COMMAND POSITIONS.⟩
⟨AND THAT'S EXACTLY WHAT I'VE BEEN DOING.⟩
⟨FIND ANYONE INTERESTING?⟩
⟨YES.⟩
⟨YOU.⟩

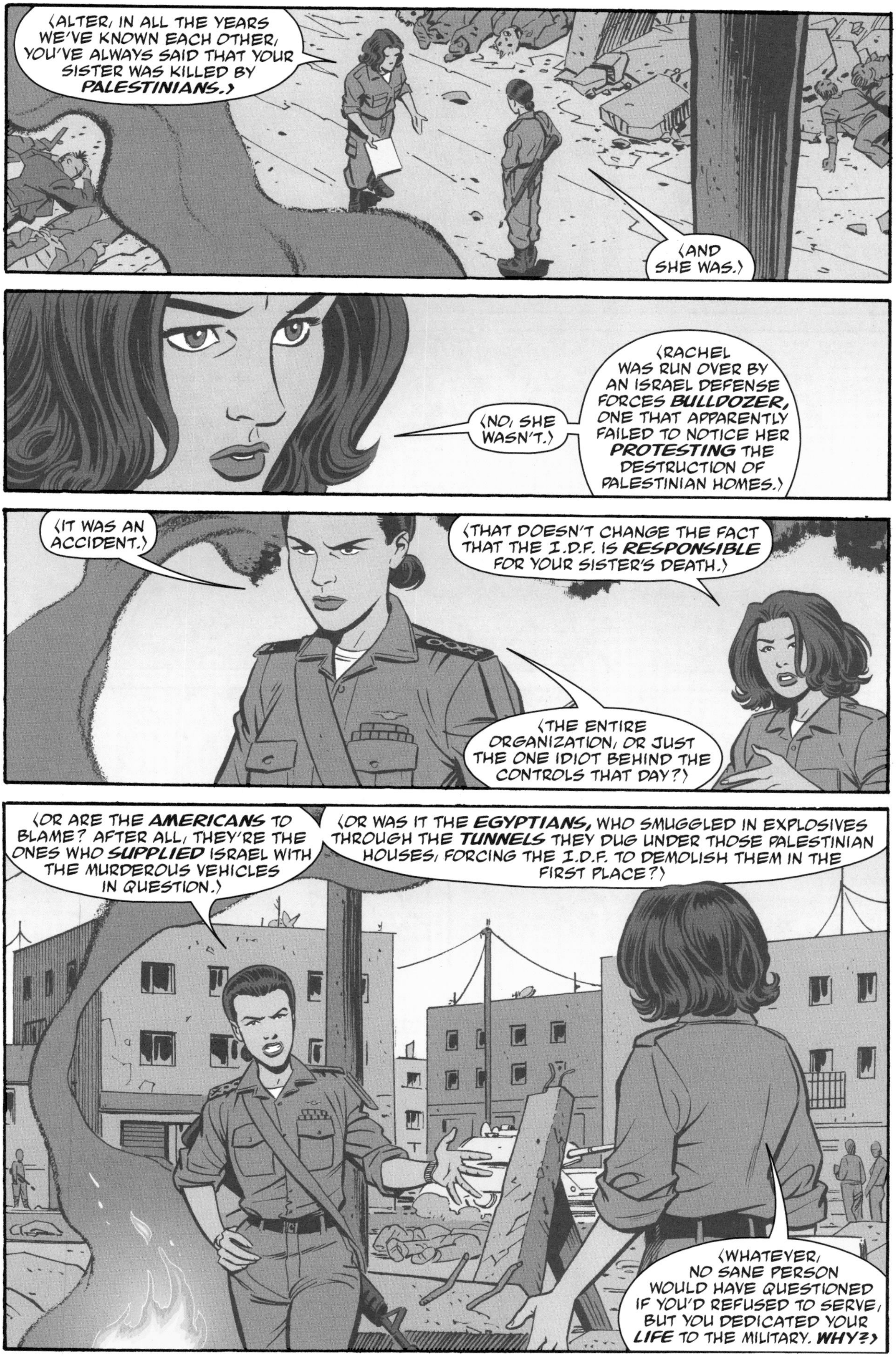

‹ALTER, IN ALL THE YEARS WE'VE KNOWN EACH OTHER, YOU'VE ALWAYS SAID THAT YOUR SISTER WAS KILLED BY PALESTINIANS.›
‹AND SHE WAS.›
‹NO, SHE WASN'T.›
‹RACHEL WAS RUN OVER BY AN ISRAEL DEFENSE FORCES BULLDOZER, ONE THAT APPARENTLY FAILED TO NOTICE HER PROTESTING THE DESTRUCTION OF PALESTINIAN HOMES.›
‹IT WAS AN ACCIDENT.›
‹THAT DOESN'T CHANGE THE FACT THAT THE I.D.F. IS RESPONSIBLE FOR YOUR SISTER'S DEATH.›
‹THE ENTIRE ORGANIZATION, OR JUST THE ONE IDIOT BEHIND THE CONTROLS THAT DAY?›
‹OR ARE THE AMERICANS TO BLAME? AFTER ALL, THEY'RE THE ONES WHO SUPPLIED ISRAEL WITH THE MURDEROUS VEHICLES IN QUESTION.›
‹OR WAS IT THE EGYPTIANS, WHO SMUGGLED IN EXPLOSIVES THROUGH THE TUNNELS THEY DUG UNDER THOSE PALESTINIAN HOUSES, FORCING THE I.D.F. TO DEMOLISH THEM IN THE FIRST PLACE?›
‹WHATEVER, NO SANE PERSON WOULD HAVE QUESTIONED IF YOU'D REFUSED TO SERVE, BUT YOU DEDICATED YOUR LIFE TO THE MILITARY. WHY?›

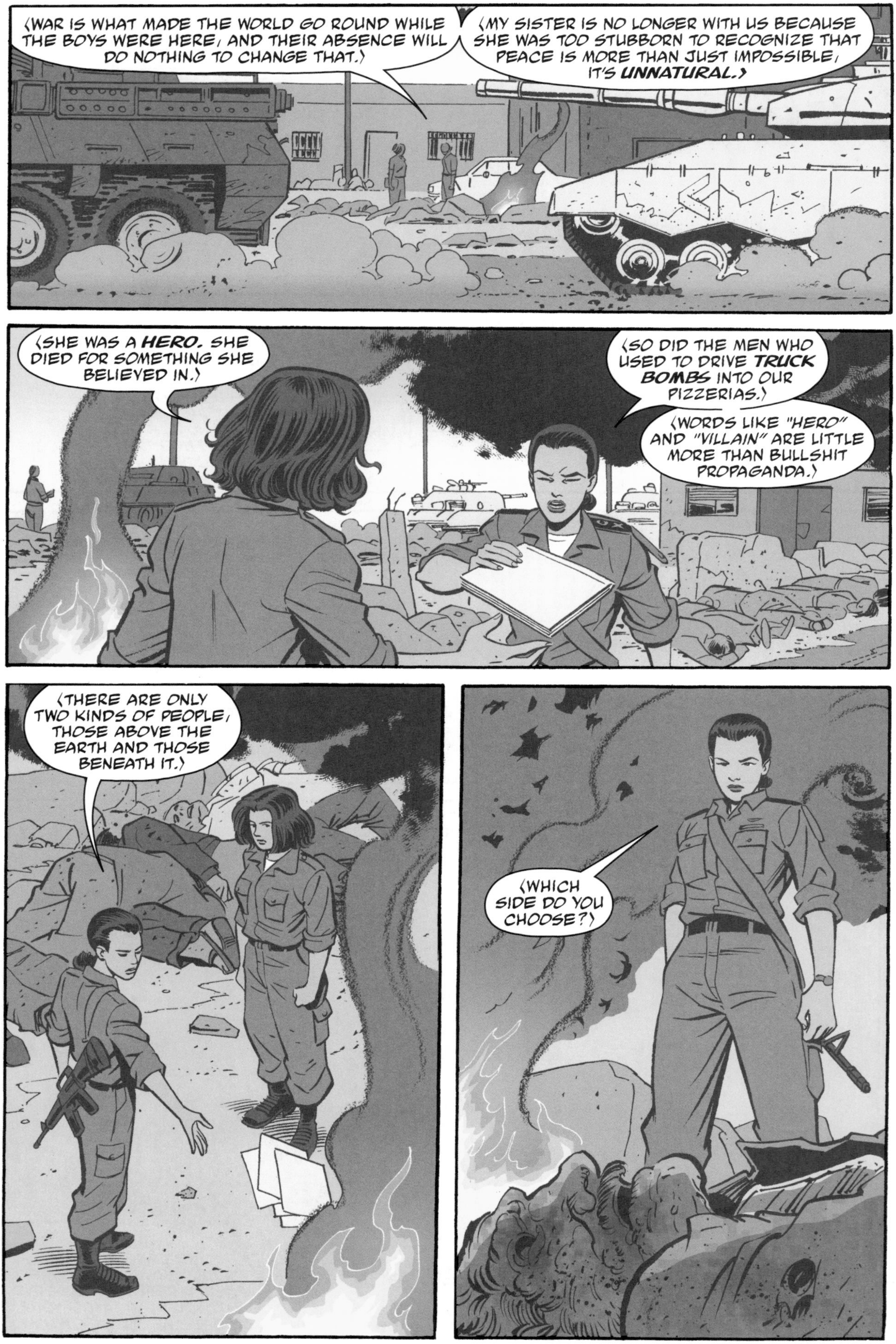
⟨WAR IS WHAT MADE THE WORLD GO ROUND WHILE THE BOYS WERE HERE, AND THEIR ABSENCE WILL DO NOTHING TO CHANGE THAT.⟩
⟨MY SISTER IS NO LONGER WITH US BECAUSE SHE WAS TOO STUBBORN TO RECOGNIZE THAT PEACE IS MORE THAN JUST IMPOSSIBLE, IT'S **UNNATURAL.**⟩
⟨SHE WAS A **HERO.** SHE DIED FOR SOMETHING SHE BELIEVED IN.⟩
⟨SO DID THE MEN WHO USED TO DRIVE **TRUCK BOMBS** INTO OUR PIZZERIAS.⟩
⟨WORDS LIKE "HERO" AND "VILLAIN" ARE LITTLE MORE THAN BULLSHIT PROPAGANDA.⟩
⟨THERE ARE ONLY TWO KINDS OF PEOPLE, THOSE ABOVE THE EARTH AND THOSE BENEATH IT.⟩
⟨WHICH SIDE DO YOU CHOOSE?⟩

YOU'RE A FUCKING LUNATIC.

AND YOU'RE ABOUT TO HAVE YOUR SHARE OF THE RATIONS DOWN HERE *DOUBLED.*

DON'T SAY A WORD, HEIDI!

YORICK...HE'S ON HIS WAY TO *FRANCE,* ALL RIGHT? TO FIND HIS *GIRLFRIEND.* THE OTHERS LEFT TO MEET HIM. I'LL PLAY YOU THE CALL RECORDS IF YOU DON'T BELIEVE ME.

JUST PLEASE... DON'T HURT HEATHER.

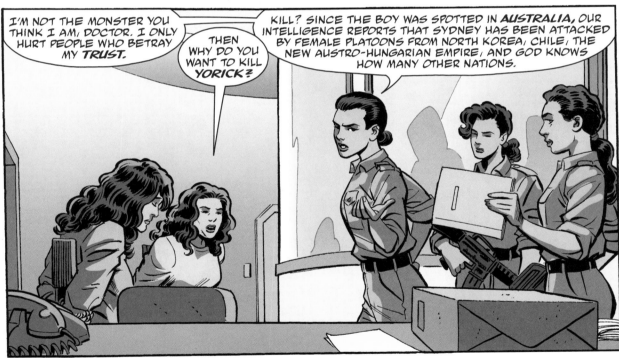

I'M NOT THE MONSTER YOU THINK I AM, DOCTOR. I ONLY HURT PEOPLE WHO BETRAY MY *TRUST.*

THEN WHY DO YOU WANT TO KILL *YORICK?*

KILL? SINCE THE BOY WAS SPOTTED IN *AUSTRALIA,* OUR INTELLIGENCE REPORTS THAT SYDNEY HAS BEEN ATTACKED BY FEMALE PLATOONS FROM NORTH KOREA, CHILE, THE NEW AUSTRO-HUNGARIAN EMPIRE, AND GOD KNOWS HOW MANY OTHER NATIONS.

IF AND WHEN ONE OF THESE ARMIES FINDS MR. BROWN, THE CULPER RING GIRL WILL BE UNABLE TO PROTECT HIM.

I ASSURE YOU, I AM NOT THE LAST MAN'S ENEMY...

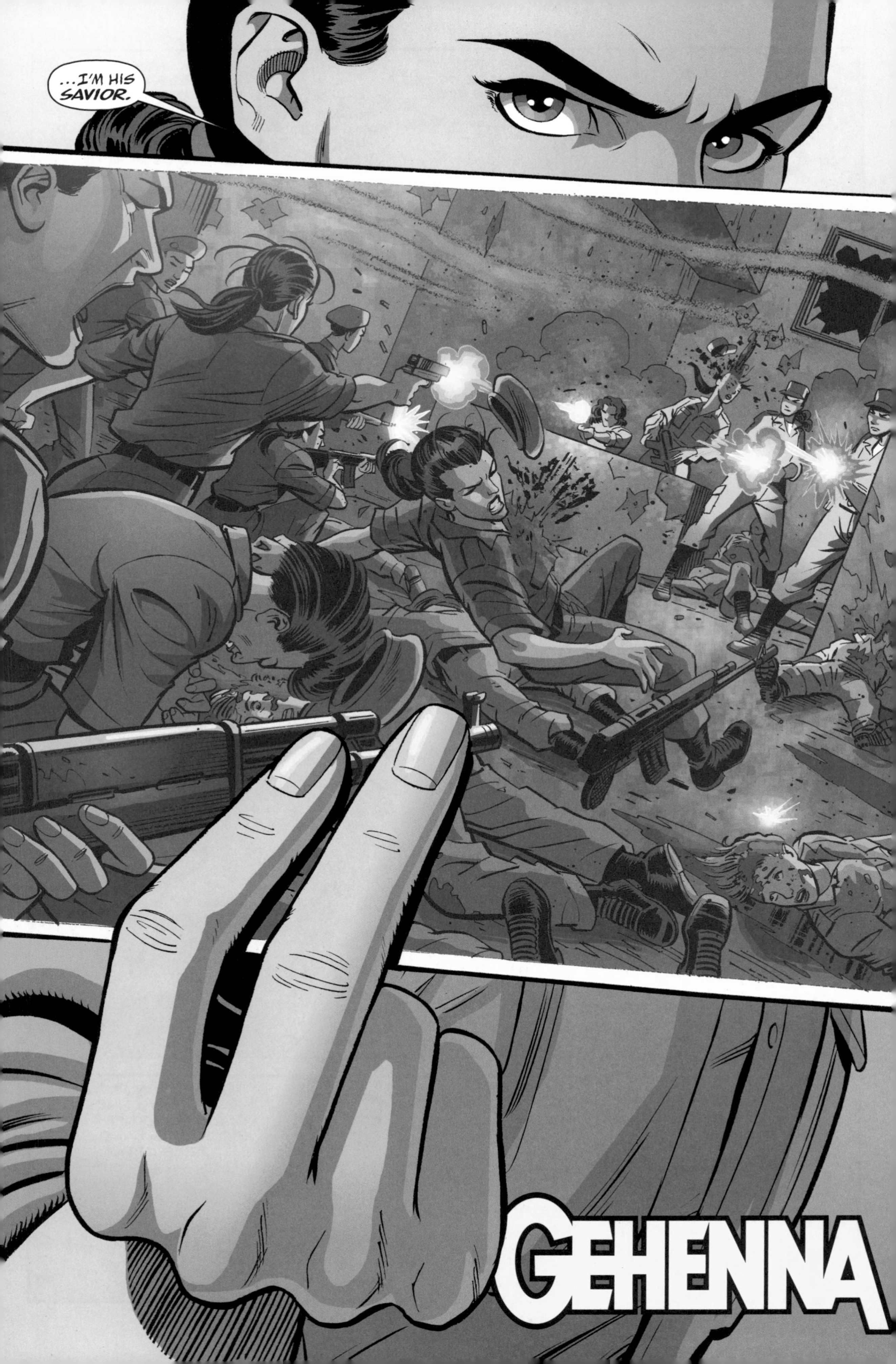
...I'M HIS SAVIOR.
GEHENNA

Y: THE SCRIPT

The complete script to Y: THE LAST MAN #42
by co-creator and writer Brian K. Vaughan.

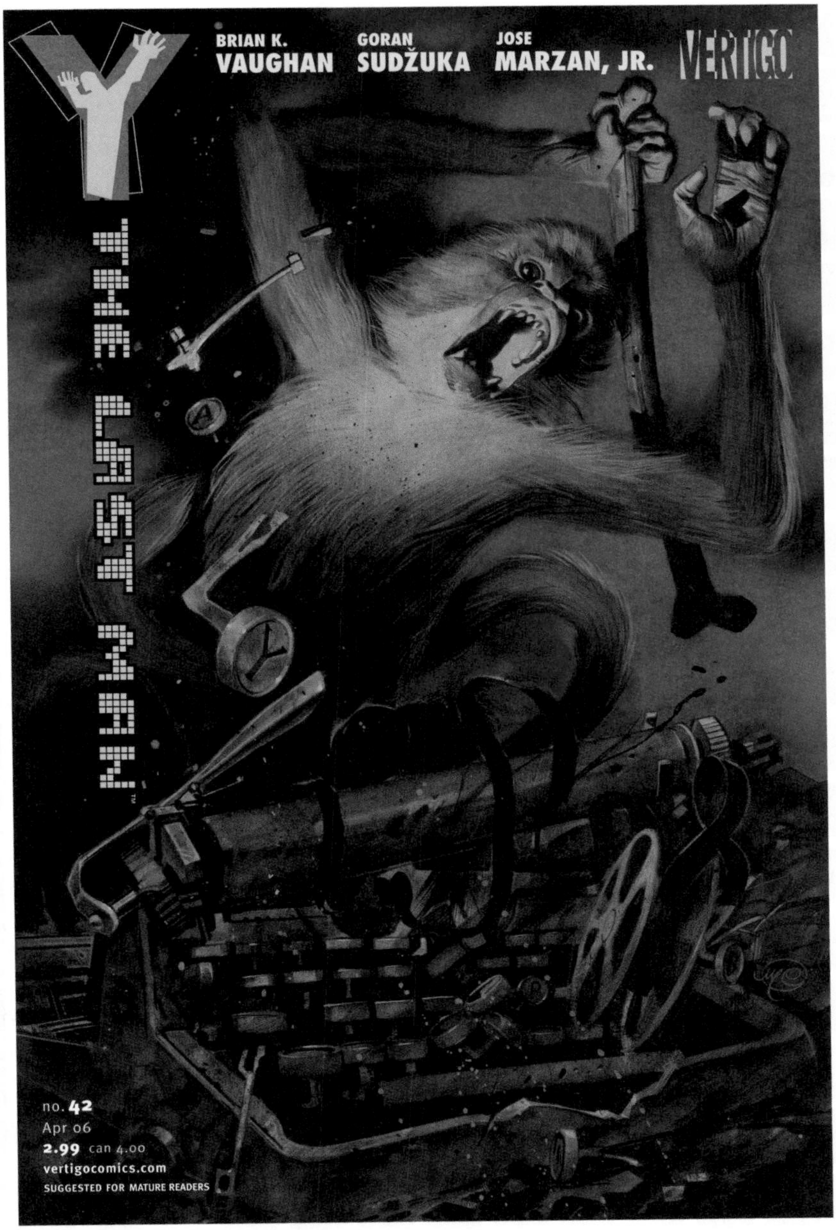

BRIAN K. VAUGHAN
GORAN SUDŽUKA
JOSE MARZAN, JR.
VERTIGO
Y THE LAST MAN™
no. 42
Apr 06
2.99 can 4.00
vertigocomics.com
SUGGESTED FOR MATURE READERS

"1,000 Typewriters"

The Full Script for Y #42

Prepared for Vertigo Comics

November 8, 2005

Brian K. Vaughan

(Welcome back, Goran! One last issue for the road. I hope you don't hate drawing monkeys...)

Page One

Page One, Panel One

Okay, we open with this close-up of a frightened AMPERSAND THE MONKEY, a little younger than he was when our series started. Goran, I like when Amp has a halo of white hair like he did on our first cover, though I think he's usually drawn with darker fur. Go with whatever you think works best.

> 1) <u>Toyota (from off)</u>: <Watch yourself, Doctor M.>

Page One, Panel Two

As always, this thin, page-wide letterbox panel is entirely black. Lettered in white directly onto the center of this darkness is the following title card:

> 2) <u>White text on black background</u>:

Yokogata, Japan
Five Years Ago

Page One, Panel Three

Pull out to this largest panel of the page, at least a half-SPLASH. We're behind Ampersand in the foreground of this low-angle upshot. The monkey is cowering inside an open, transparent plastic incubator, which is inside of a stark white laboratory. Think something clean and futuristic, like Kubrick's *2001*.

A new character named DR. M (we can't tell if it's a man or a woman!) is reaching down for Ampersand here. Dr. M is wearing a bulky, aluminized hazmat suit which has a reflective mirrored visor that *completely* hides his/her face. Behind Dr. M is TOYOTA, the Japanese female ninja we first met back in Issues #16 and 17, and saw again in "Ring of Truth." Toyota is wearing a different kind of hazmat suit, one with a clear plastic faceplate that lets us see her pretty face clearly (she's not wearing a gasmask beneath her helmet).

> 3) <u>Toyota</u>: <That little bastard's already tried to escape *twice*.>

> 4) <u>Dr. M</u>: <Thank you, Toyota... but this is not the first time I've handled a capuchin.>

Page Two

Page Two, Panel One

Change angles on the three, as Dr. M LIFTS a squirming Ampersand out of the incubator. Toyota watches nervously.

> 1) <u>Dr. M</u>: <Where's he from?>

> 2) <u>Toyota</u>: <Born in captivity.>
> 3) <u>Toyota</u>: <The mother died trying to squeeze out this one's stillborn *twin*.>

Page Two, Panel Two

This is just a close-up of Dr. M's mirrored mask, with Ampersand's terrified face reflected in the visor.

> 4) <u>Dr. M</u>: <And yet *you* chose to cling to life, eh?>

Page Two, Panel Three
Pull out to another group shot for this largest panel of the page, as the scared Ampersand struggles to get free of Dr. M's strong grip.

5) <u>Toyota</u>: <Um, I'd say it's more a roll of the evolutionary dice than *will power*, Doc.>

6) <u>Dr. M</u>: <See the way he looks at my mask? Normally, when male capuchins spot a member of their own sex, they respond with anger and threatening gestures.>
7) <u>Dr. M</u>: <And yet, when capuchins see their *reflections*, they react with fear and confusion.>

Page Two, Panel Four
Push in closer on the two. Dr. M holds Ampersand in one hand, while reaching for something with a free hand. Toyota looks skeptical.

8) <u>Toyota</u>: <Which means...?>

9) <u>Dr. M</u>: <Which means that our cousins may be nearly as *self-aware* as we are.>
10) <u>Dr. M</u>: <Both science *and* the Buddha teach that the natural world *mirrors* our actions.>

Page Two, Panel Five
Push in on Dr. M's hand, as we see his/her aluminum-covered glove pick up an old-fashioned METAL SYRINGE (filled with a bright BLUE liquid) from a nearby tray.

11) <u>Dr. M (from off)</u>: <Everything is connected.>

Page Three

Page Three, Panel One
Pull out to the largest panel of the page for this shot of Dr. M and Ampersand, as the doctor suddenly and violently PLUNGES the needle into the screaming monkey's belly.

1) <u>Ampersand</u>: *RHEEEEEEE*

Page Three, Panel Two
Push in close on Amp, as his eyes roll into the back of his head. Is he dead...?

No Copy

Page Three, Panel Three
Pull out to a group shot, as Dr. M sets the sleeping Ampersand back into its incubator. Toyota looks confused.

2) <u>Dr. M</u>: <If he lives through the week, have him shipped to the laboratory in the States from which *Dr. Allison Mann* recruits her samples.>

3) <u>Toyota</u>: <Sure, but, uh, I was really trained to get *people* where they need to be.>
4) <u>Toyota</u>: <Besides, what if your serum *kills* this thing?>

Page Three, Panel Four
Finally, this is just an overhead shot of Ampersand, curled up in the fetal position inside his open incubator.

5) <u>Dr. M (from off)</u>: <Then you'll burn his carcass with the others.>

Page Four

Page Four, Panel One
Cut to a month later for this establishing shot of the TWA terminal of JFK AIRPORT, as a

large CARGO PLANE is about to land.

No Copy

Page Four, Panel Two
Cut inside a massive CARGO HANGAR for this largest panel of the page. Two male BAGGAGE HANDLERS are walking through long aisles of stored luggage, crates, etc. We'll call the heavier handler FATSO, and his thin counterpart SKINNY.

1) <u>Skinny</u>: You hear? Patti and Tricia are thinking about going on strike.

2) <u>Fatso</u>: Why?

3) <u>Skinny</u>: They say female baggage handlers only earn seventy-seven cents for every buck we make.

Page Four, Panel Three
Push in closer on the two guys, and please leave room between them for their exchange. Skinny looks at Fatso with skepticism.

5) <u>Fatso</u>: Yeah, but those two can only carry *fifty percent* what we do, so they're already making, like, fourteen cents too much.

6) <u>Skinny</u>: Wow, what the fuck kind of trigonometry did you use to get that figure?

7) <u>Fatso</u>: Whatever, they can take the cash out of *your* paycheck, but they're not touching —

Page Four, Panel Four
We're behind Skinny here, as he suddenly sees two LARGE METAL CAGES, stacked side by side on an eye-level shelf in this warehouse. Each cage is tagged, and labeled with specific handling instructions (which we can't read). Both of their doors are open, and the cages are empty.

8) <u>Skinny</u>: Hold up.
9) <u>Skinny</u>: Where are the monkeys?

Page Five

Page Five, Panel One
Pull out for this shot of Fatso and Skinny. Skinny looks around frantically, but Fatso is still confused.

1) <u>Fatso</u>: What are you talking about? I thought JFK sends those things to *quarantine*.

2) <u>Skinny</u>: Just African green and, what do you call 'em... *rhesus*. But we got two of the smaller kind in today.
3) <u>Skinny</u>: One from Boston, the other going *to* Boston.

Page Five, Panel Two
Change angles on the two, as Skinny inspects one of the cage's damaged locks.

4) <u>Fatso</u>: You think those PETA faggots hit us again?

5) <u>Skinny</u>: Nah, looks like a lock was damaged in flight.
6) <u>Skinny</u>: This guy must have freed the other one after it got out.

Page Five, Panel Three
Push in closer on the two, as Skinny turns to talk to a skeptical Fatso.

7) <u>Fatso</u>: Are you high? They can't orchestrate fucking *prison breaks*.

8) <u>Skinny</u>: Opposable thumbs, big man. I saw an orangutan open a half-dozen dog carriers when I was working LaGuardia.

9) <u>Ampersand (from off)</u>: *eeeee*

Page Five, Panel Four
We're looking over Skinny's shoulder in the foreground of this largest panel of the page, a low-angle upshot, as Skinny looks up to see <u>TWO</u> capuchin monkeys (Ampersand and an identical male, neither wearing diapers) perched on a shelf high above the cages they escaped from.

10) <u>Ampersand</u>: *eeeeee*

11) <u>Skinny</u>: Ah, crap.
12) <u>Skinny</u>: They're both *males*.

Page Six

Page Six, Panel One
We're with the monkeys in the foreground of this largest panel of the page, a high-angle downshot, as they look at the two men below.

1) <u>Fatso</u>: So?

2) <u>Skinny</u>: So, they're practically *identical*. How are we supposed to tell them apart?

3) <u>Fatso</u>: What difference does it make?

Page Six, Panel Two
Push in on the troubled Skinny, as he reaches for a long DOG CATCHER'S NET leaning against a nearby forklift (or whatever).

4) <u>Skinny</u>: One's from a joint that trains *helper monkeys*, the other one's going to some *research facility*.
5) <u>Skinny</u>: That means one of them's gonna be opening champagne bottles for Larry Flynt, and the other one's gonna get *nail polish* dumped in its eyes for the rest of its—

6) <u>Fatso (from off)</u>: Jesus!

Page Six, Panel Three
Pull out to a shot of both men, as small brown balls of FECES suddenly whiz past their heads (though they *don't* hit them!). Fatso is shielding his face with his forearm here.

7) <u>Skinny</u>: What?

8) <u>Fatso</u>: Cover your face!
9) <u>Fatso</u>: I think one of them's throwing its own *shit*!

Page Six, Panel Four
Push in close on the troubled Fatso (still protecting his face), who has no idea that he's just missed his chance to be the last man on earth.

10) <u>Fatso</u>: Come on, let the girls on *night shift* deal with this.
11) <u>Fatso</u>: Who knows what that thing is carrying?

Page Seven

Page Seven, Panel One
Cut to later that night for this page-wide establishing shot of a row of brownstone apartments in Brooklyn.

No Copy

Page Seven, Panel Two

Cut inside the studio apartment of YORICK BROWN (whose home was last seen way back in Issue #1, I think) for this largest panel of the page, where a casually dressed 22-year-old Yorick is talking to Ampersand, who is back inside one of the large cages he escaped from last scene.

1) <u>Yorick</u>: Okay then, first things first.
2) <u>Yorick</u>: My name is Yorick Brown, and I'll be your human overlord for the next year.

Page Seven, Panel Three

Push in closer on Yorick, as he slowly OPENS the cage's door.

3) <u>Yorick</u>: The woman from Helping Hands said that I should put my valuable possessions in a safe place before I let you out... but now that I sold my mystical specter cabinet to afford your diapers, I don't *own* any valuable possessions.
4) <u>Yorick</u>: So away we go.

Page Seven, Panel Four

Change angles, as Yorick watches Ampersand LEAP out of the cage.

5) <u>Yorick</u>: She also said you were the best-behaved guy in your troop, so I'm anticipating a positive student-teacher relationship, right?

6) <u>Ampersand</u>: *ffft*

Page Eight

Page Eight, Panel One

Change angles on the two for this largest panel of the page, as Ampersand stops to inspect a brown, withered old BONSAI TREE by one of Yorick's windows.

1) <u>Yorick</u>: That's my bonsai, Treebeard. He kinda withered away after I buried Santiago in his pot.
2) <u>Yorick</u> (**small font**, an aside): Santiago was my guppy.

Page Eight, Panel Two

Push in on Yorick, as he reluctantly admits:

3) <u>Yorick</u>: See, everything I care about tends to, uh, *expire*.
4) <u>Yorick</u>: But that's cool, because your program said I'm not supposed to get too *attached*, since you're just going to end up with someone else anyway.
5) <u>Yorick</u>: So for the good of us both, I've made a conscious decision to look at you as a *project*, and not as a...

Page Eight, Panel Three

Cut over to Ampersand, as he stops to growl at a framed picture of a smiling BETH (wearing her Zatanna top hat from Issue #36).

6) <u>Ampersand</u>: *rrg*

Page Eight, Panel Four

This is just a shot of Yorick, looking a little melancholy.

7) <u>Yorick</u>: Yeah.
8) <u>Yorick</u>: That's Beth.

Page Nine

Page Nine, Panel One
    Pull out to a shot of both characters, as Yorick approaches his new pet.

    1) <u>Ampersand</u>: ahnk

    2) <u>Yorick</u>: No, she's great.
    3) <u>Yorick</u>: It's just, ever since she told me about Australia, I've felt...

Page Nine, Panel Two
    Push in on Yorick, as he picks up the framed photo and looks down at Beth's image.

    4) <u>Yorick</u>: You know how screenplays use the "&" symbol when it's a close collaboration between two writers, and "and" when it's a little more... *distant*.
    5) <u>Yorick</u>: Well, we used to be *Beth & Yorick*, but now it feels more like Beth *and* Yorick. Does that make any sense?

Page Nine, Panel Three
    Similar framing, but now Yorick sets the photo back down.

    6) <u>Yorick</u>: Anyway, when she gets home from saving the Outback and sees that I've *also* been doing something to better the world, maybe it'll help us reconnect.
    7) <u>Yorick</u>: You think?

Page Nine, Panel Four
    Cut over to Ampersand, who looks at us dumbly while chewing on one of Yorick's remote controls. The monkey is not a cute Disney sidekick, or a super-smart pet like Lassie. He's just a stupid animal.

    No Copy

Page Nine, Panel Five
    Pull out to this largest panel of the page for another wide shot of the studio, as Yorick buries his face in his hands. Even though he has a new creature living in his apartment with him, the young man still looks very alone.

    8) <u>Yorick (**small font**, to himself)</u>: Oh, god.
    9) <u>Yorick (**small font**, to himself)</u>: What the fuck am I doing?

Page Ten

Page Ten, Panel One
    Smash cut to a few weeks later for this page-wide close-up of Yorick, who's wearing the GASMASK and BLUE PONCHO he started wearing back in Issue #2. Ampersand is sitting on his shoulder. It's late afternoon, almost magic hour.

    No Copy

Page Ten, Panel Two
    Cut behind Yorick for this largest panel of the page, as we see that he and Ampersand are standing on the front porch of a darkened, CREEPY LOOKING HOUSE somewhere in the state of New York.

    1) <u>Ampersand</u>: *ree*

    2) <u>Yorick</u>: Relax, Ampersand.
    3) <u>Yorick</u>: This guy is a *friend*.

Page Ten, Panel Three
    Push in on the two, as Yorick opens the door to this unlit house. Ampersand is still on his shoulder.

4) <u>Yorick</u>: Kevin used to be my *lab partner*.

5) <u>Yorick</u>: I figure one of the assignments we fucked up must have somehow made us *immune* to whatever killed the other guys in New York.

Page Ten, Panel Four

Change angles on Yorick, as he pushes his mask back, so it's resting on top of his head. We can see that he's got a little stubble on his chin. Yorick calls out for his old friend as he walks through the darkened hallways of this house.

6) <u>Yorick</u>: Kevin! You home? Don't worry, I'm not sick either!

7) <u>Yorick</u>: Kevin...?

Page Eleven

Page Eleven, SPLASH

We're looking over Yorick's shoulder in the extreme foreground of this horrifying SPLASH. Sitting in an old recliner in the middle of this family room is what's left of KEVIN'S CORPSE, which has badly decomposed after being dead almost a month. Kevin was wearing shorts and a t-shirt when he died.

Here comes the worst part. There are three, rail-thin, emaciated female CATS in this room... and they're *eating* what's left of poor Kev. One cat is scratching at his legs. Another is sitting on Kevin's lap, tearing meat off of one of his thighs. The third cat is on Kevin's shoulder gently biting the corpse's cheek. This dark scene can be eerily lit by a few beams of sunlight streaming through a nearby window.

Obviously, this needs to be the most disturbing thing you've ever drawn, Goran, so don't skimp on the details. We're trying to convey the horror of what happens when the creatures you love revert to their most basic instincts, so this image needs to be as sad as it is stomach churning.

No Copy

Page Twelve

Page Twelve, Panel One

Cut over to a horrified Yorick, as he yells at the off-panel animals.

1) <u>Yorick</u>: Get... get away.

2) <u>Yorick</u>: *Get away from him!*

Page Twelve, Panel Two

Cut over to one of the cats, as it looks up at us defiantly. It has blood and gristle in its teeth.

No Copy

Page Twelve, Panel Three

This is just a small shot of Ampersand, as he angrily BARKS at the off-panel female cats.

3) <u>Ampersand</u>: *ARK ARK ARK*

Page Twelve, Panel Four

Pull out to the largest panel of the page, as a horrified Yorick steps aside, while the frightened cats CHARGE past him out of this room.

No Copy

Page Twelve, Panel Five

Push in on Yorick (with Ampersand still on his shoulder). The young man has tears welling up in his eyes as he looks at his off-panel friend. He's reaching for the mask resting on top of his head here.

4) <u>Yorick</u>: I'm alone.

Page Twelve, Panel Six
Similar framing on the two, but now Yorick pulls his mask down. Maybe we can see some of what's left of his friend *reflected* in the mask's visor. Ampersand looks at his master indifferently, and puts a paw on his facemask.

5) <u>Yorick</u> (**small font**, <u>whispered</u>): I'm all alone.

Page Thirteen

Page Thirteen, Panel One
Smash cut to a year later for this page-wide shot of an idyllic little lake somewhere in Middle America.

No Copy

Page Thirteen, Panel Two
Push in for this largest panel of the page, a shot of Yorick, Ampersand, DR. MANN, and AGENT 355, looking much like they did back in Issue #11 (Yorick has his stupid beard now). Ampersand is picking stuff out of Yorick's hair, as Mann eats out of a can. They're both sitting at the edge of the lake, while 355 FISHES unsuccessfully with a homemade fishing pole.

1) <u>Yorick</u>: Find anything yummy in there, pal?

2) <u>Dr. Mann</u>: You're disgusting.
3) <u>Dr. Mann</u>: When's the last time you lathered and rinsed?

Page Thirteen, Panel Three
Push in on Yorick and Dr. Mann.

4) <u>Yorick</u>: With *what*, Dr. Mann? The second the Plague hit, you people started hoarding every last bottle of shampoo.
5) <u>Yorick</u>: I've been inside supermarkets where women left entire *aisles* of canned goods, but cleared out the goddamn *hair-care section*.

6) <u>Dr. Mann</u>: There are plenty of farmers left, Yorick, but the cosmetics industry was run by *men*. Vidal Sassoon is a *collector's item* now.

Page Thirteen, Panel Four
Change angles for this shot of Yorick and the fishing 355, as Yorick smiles smugly at the monkey on his shoulder.

7) <u>Agent 355</u>: Speak for yourself. That shit is *useless* on my locks.

8) <u>Yorick</u>: See, Agent 355 probably has a *colony* living on her head, but Amp never burrows into *her* scalp.
9) <u>Yorick</u>: That's because he loves me best.

Page Fourteen

Page Fourteen, Panel One
Change angles for this shot of Dr. Mann and 355, as Mann gets up and brushes herself off.

1) <u>Dr. Mann</u>: Ampersand isn't capable of love, Yorick.
2) <u>Dr. Mann</u>: Trust me, after years of working with those things, I can assure you that capuchins are no different than other animals. All they care about is eating, screwing and sleeping.

3) <u>Agent 355</u>: Huh, somebody never got a puppy when she was little.

Page Fourteen, Panel Two
Pull out to the largest panel of the page for this shot of Mann, Yorick and Ampersand. As the humans talk, Amp is looking up at a little BIRD flying overhead.

4) <u>Dr. Mann</u>: My dog's name was *Mister Doug*, thank you very much.
5) <u>Dr. Mann</u>: But I never mistook his "loyalty" as anything other than old pack instincts.

6) <u>Yorick</u>: So what, you think any motivations I ascribe to Ampersand are just me imposing my emotions on him?

Page Fourteen, Panel Three
This is just a shot of Dr. Mann, as she matter-of-factly states:

7) <u>Dr. Mann</u>: Love isn't an "emotion," it's an abstract construct mammals assign to a biological imperative they don't fully understand.
8) <u>Dr. Mann</u>: You're not pretending your monkey is like you...

Page Fourteen, Panel Four
This is a shot of Ampersand and the bearded Yorick, as the last man somberly fingers the WEDDING BAND he keeps on a string around his neck. But this shot is actually seen through the lenses of the hi-tech, green-tinted binoculars we saw Toyota using back inside the theater in Issue #17.

9) <u>Tailless (electronic)</u>: ...you're pretending you're not like your monkey.

Page Fifteen

Page Fifteen, Panel One
Cut to a dense bit of foliage across the water, where TOYOTA is hiding in a tree, wearing the black ninja attire she had on in "Comedy & Tragedy" (without the mask), and looking through her glowing green GOGGLES at the off-panel Yorick.

1) <u>Toyota</u>: <The fuck...?>

Page Fifteen, Panel Two
Change angles, as Toyota removes her goggles and pulls out the futuristic-looking CELL PHONE she used in Issue #17.

2) <u>Toyota</u>: <Doc, it's Toyota. You online?>

3) <u>Tailless (electronic)</u>: <The satellite I rented won't be in range long. Talk fast.>

4) <u>Toyota</u>: <You're not gonna believe this, but whatever went wrong in transit, your animal still ended up with its target *anyway*. I mean, what are the *odds* of that?>

Page Fifteen, Panel Three
Pull out to the largest panel of the page, as Toyota stands on the high branch she's balancing on, and pulls out one of her glistening SAMURAI SWORDS with her free hand.

5) <u>Tailless (electronic)</u>: <It's not a *coincidence*, idiot. Another player deliberately *guided* our wayward capuchin into Mann's hands.>

6) <u>Toyota</u>: <You're talking about the real live *boy* they picked up?>

7) <u>Tailless (electronic)</u>: <No, he's just fruit of the poisoned tree. Leave him, and bring me the monkey.>

8) <u>Toyota</u>: <Dr. M, I don't think you understand. This is a *human* male, a—>

Page Fifteen, Panel Four
    Push in close on Toyota, who swears in Japanese under her breath.

    9) <u>Tailless (electronic)</u>: *kzzzzzk*

    10) <u>Toyota</u>: *Kusottare.**

*(Clem, any chance we could print this word for "shit-drip" in its Japanese characters? MS Word won't let me cut and paste the kanji I found online into this document, but I can email them to you if you send me a reminder when you get this. Domo arigato!)

Page Sixteen

Page Sixteen, Panel One
    Smash cut to this close-up of a screaming Ampersand. Goran, we're now entering the monkey's DREAM (yes, my research says capuchins dream, believe it or not), so this scene will be a bit surreal.

    1) <u>Ampersand</u>: YY!

Page Sixteen, Panel Two
    Pull out, as we reveal that Ampersand is sitting in a BIRD'S NEST, surrounded by several white eggs.

    No Copy

Page Sixteen, Panel Three
    Pull way, way out to the largest panel of the page, as we reveal that this nest is FLOATING in the middle of a vast ocean. The sun is beating down on a disoriented Ampersand.

    No Copy

Page Sixteen, Panel Four
    Push in on Amp, as he picks up one of the eggs in his makeshift raft.

    No Copy

Page Seventeen

Page Seventeen, Panel One
    Push in closer, as the egg begins to CRACK open in Ampersand's little hands.

    No Copy

Page Seventeen, Panel Two
    This shot can be from Ampersand's P.O.V., as he looks down to discover that a miniature version of YORICK'S FACE is behind the crumbling shell of this egg. Tears run down Miniature Yorick's face as he looks up at his off-panel monkey, whose hands we can see cradling this bizarre egg.

    1) <u>Bird (from off)</u>: RAK!

Page Seventeen, Panel Three
    We're with Ampersand in the foreground, looking up at the sky as a giant white ALBATROSS suddenly comes DIVE BOMBING out of the sun right at us!

    2) <u>Bird</u>: RAAAAK!

Page Seventeen, Panel Four
       Change angles for this largest panel of the page, a full-bleed shot with no panel borders. This is a profile shot of Ampersand and the screaming albatross. A heroic Amp stands on his small raft, and CLUTCHES his fragile egg close to his chest. He defiantly bares his white fangs at the incoming bird, who is inches away from SLAMMING into the monkey.

       No Copy

Page Eighteen

Page Eighteen, Panel One
       Smash cut to the real world for this close-up of Ampersand, who is clearly sleeping.

       1) Toyota (from off): <Rise and shine, boyfriend.>

Page Eighteen, Panel Two
       Pull out to this largest panel of the page, as we reveal that Ampersand is inside a private cabin on board a shipping boat with Toyota. Ampersand is tied to a bedpost (or whatever's nearby) by a long LEASH tied around his little neck. He's not wearing a diaper. Toyota is topless here, naked except for a g-string, as she does her early morning yoga.

       2) Toyota: <Congrats, we're about to dock in Yokogata.>
       3) Toyota: <You're almost *home*.>

       4) Ampersand (**small font**, weak): een

Page Eighteen, Panel Three
       Cut outside for this establishing shot of this shipping vessel, which is about to dock in a small Japanese fishing town. Yokogata is imaginary, Goran, so feel free to use your imagination. Either way, it's early morning, and the sun is shining.

       5) From Boat: <Yeah, sorry about the tummy ache. I laced your fruit salad with *baby laxatives* last night so you'd be all crapped out for our final leg.>
       6) From Boat: <Last thing I need is you flinging shit at me in front of the boss.>

Page Eighteen, Panel Four
       Cut back inside, as the naked Toyota picks up one of her nearby samurai swords and playfully threatens Ampersand with it. We can now see that the sickly monkey has BANDAGES around the tip of his long tail. A little less than an inch has been cut off.

       7) Ampersand (**small font**, weak): rnn

       8) Toyota: <Hey, remember what happened when you tried to run away back in Honolulu?>
       9) Toyota: <Keep whining, and I slice *another* inch off your tail.>

Page Nineteen

Page Nineteen, Panel One
       Push in on Toyota, as she angrily STICKS the tips of her samurai sword into the floor, so it's standing upright.

       1) Toyota: <I've thrown away three *years* of my life for your swollen red ass.>
       2) Toyota: <But don't think that makes you anything special.>

Page Nineteen, Panel Two
       Change angles, as Toyota starts pulling on civilian clothes, as she prepares to depart.

       3) Toyota: <You're not the salvation of mankind, you're just another brainless primate to be sliced open and pulled apart.>